T0305344

"This book offers a comprehensive overview of the main derivative pricing models used in practice across various asset classes. Many numerical examples are provided, and precious implementation details are revealed to the financial community. If the devil is in the details, this is one hell of a book!"
  Fabio Mercurio, Bloomberg

"This book is a dream come true, a must have, a must read and a must use. High-tech financial engineering and numerics are now becoming accessible to the broad quant community."
  Wim Schoutens, Research Professor, University of Leuven

"This is a book I wish I'd owned ten years ago to prepare for the exotic derivatives models hype in equity and rates of the first decade. It saves identifying, finding, screening and reading dozens of papers and treats the full life cycle of the models from theory to implementation. The reader can get quickly familiar with the pre-LSV modelling age. With any luck, the Matlab code will also run on octave."
  Uwe Wystup, Professor of Quantitative Finance/ Founder & CEO, MathFinance

"This book is a nice exposition for those Quants in Financial Engineering who are interested in an overview of modern pricing and calibration techniques in the field of Financial Derivatives. For those who have a strong mathematical background and are interested in implementation issues, this book is a severe choice."
  Dr. Ingo Schneider, Financial Engineering,
  DekaBank

"This handbook is a compendium of useful formulae for computational finance. This – and the fact that the authors provide full Matlab code in all cases – makes this work unique. You can test the code as well as looking at the formulae! This book brings many results in one place. It saves much time. The book will certainly be useful as a reference for practitioners, developers and MFE students. In particular, I also see it as a handbook of algorithms that quants can use as input to their favourite production languages C++, C# and Java."
  Daniel J. Duffy, Founder, Datasim

"In the application of mathematical finance the popularity of a model or theoretical result strongly depends on the ability to provide it with an efficient and robust implementation. Thus, a theory and modelling should naturally be combined with a discussion of its implementation. Being practitioners with a strong academic background, Kienitz and Wetterau provide this complete package in this excellent book; adding a lot of valuable insights."
  Christian P. Fries, Head of Model Development, Group Risk Control, DZ BANK AG
  Frankfurt/ Professor for Quantitative Finance, Department of Mathematics,
  LMU Munich

About the authors

JÖRG KIENITZ is the head of Quantitative Analytics at Deutsche Postbank AG. He is primarily involved in developing and implementing models for pricing complex derivatives structures and for asset allocation. He also lectures at university level on advanced financial modelling and implementation including the University of Oxford's part-time Masters of Finance course. Jörg works as an independent consultant for model development and validation as well as giving seminars for finance professionals. He is a speaker at the major financial conferences including Global Derivatives, WBS Fixed Income and RISK. Jörg is a member of the editorial board of International Review of Applied Financial Issues and Economics and holds a Ph.D. in stochastic analysis from the University of Bielefeld.

DANIEL WETTERAU is a specialist in the Quantitative Analytics team of Deutsche Postbank AG. He is responsible for the implementation of term structure models, advanced numerical methods, optimization algorithms and methods for advanced quantitative asset allocation. Further to his work he teaches finance courses for market professionals. Daniel received a Masters in financial mathematics from the University of Wuppertal and was awarded the Barmenia mathematics award for his thesis.

Financial Modelling

For other titles in the Wiley Finance series
please see www.wiley.com/finance

Financial Modelling

Theory, Implementation and Practice
(with Matlab source)

Jörg Kienitz
Daniel Wetterau

A John Wiley & Sons, Ltd., Publication

Copyright © 2012 John Wiley & Sons Ltd

Cover image: cover images reproduced by permission of Shutterstock.com

Registered office
John Wiley & Sons Ltd, The Atrium, Southern Gate, Chichester, West Sussex, PO19 8SQ, United Kingdom For
details of our global editorial offices, for customer services and for information about how to apply for permission to
reuse the copyright material in this book please see our website at www.wiley.com

All rights reserved. No part of this publication may be reproduced, stored in a retrieval system, or transmitted, in any
form or by any means, electronic, mechanical, photocopying, recording or otherwise, except as permitted by the UK
Copyright, Designs and Patents Act 1988, without the prior permission of the publisher.

Wiley publishes in a variety of print and electronic formats and by print-on-demand. Some material included with
standard print versions of this book may not be included in e-books or in print-on-demand. If this book refers to
media such as a CD or DVD that is not included in the version you purchased, you may download this material at
http://booksupport.wiley.com. For more information about Wiley products, visit www.wiley.com.

Designations used by companies to distinguish their products are often claimed as trademarks. All brand names and
product names used in this book are trade names, service marks, trademarks or registered trademarks of their
respective owners. The publisher is not associated with any product or vendor mentioned in this book. This
publication is designed to provide accurate and authoritative information in regard to the subject matter covered. It is
sold on the understanding that the publisher is not engaged in rendering professional services. If professional advice
or other expert assistance is required, the services of a competent professional should be sought.

Library of Congress Cataloging-in-Publication Data

Kienitz, Joerg.
 Financial modelling : theory, implementation and practice (with Matlab source) / Joerg Kienitz, Daniel Wetterau.
   p. cm.
 Includes bibliographical references and index.
  ISBN 978-0-470-74489-5 (cloth) – ISBN 978-1-118-41331-9 (ebk) – ISBN 978-1-118-41330-2 (ebk) –
ISBN 978-1-118-41329-6 (ebk) 1. MATLAB. 2. Finance–Mathematical models. 3. Numerical analysis.
4. Finance–Mathematical models–Computer programs. 5. Numerical analysis–Computer programs. I. Wetterau,
Daniel, 1981– II. Title.
 HG106.K53 2012
 332.0285′53–dc23

                                                                                            2012029238

A catalogue record for this book is available from the British Library.

To Amberley, Beatrice and Benoît

Jörg

To Sabine

Daniel

Contents

Introduction

1 INTRODUCTION AND MANAGEMENT SUMMARY

The goal of the book is to fill a gap in the literature on financial modelling. Many books and research articles in the field are incomplete – a new model is introduced, an existing model is extended or a certain model topic is analysed but often there is not a hint on implementation or on the practical application of the model. Robustness of implementation, special purpose algorithms, performance analysis of the algorithms or the stability in terms of the model's parameters are all left out. In some cases either the mathematical theory is detailed or a fully flexible software design is suggested where the algorithms for implementing sophisticated models are not presented. In this book we aim to link all the steps of model development. To this end we describe many well-known financial models and provide algorithms as Matlab based software (we use this software as the basis for applying the models in terms of calibration, pricing and simulation). We show the design of an application and provide a source code for all the methods and models discussed. The source code can be used with the software package Matlab, but it is also possible to translate the code into other programming languages such as C#, C++ or Java.

Our aim is a clear separation of concerns. Thus, we separate the analysis of models and their properties from the numerical techniques, and the numerical techniques from the source code of the algorithms written in Matlab. We believe that this is necessary in order to clearly present the material and that, furthermore, this illustrates the life-cycle – model choice, model implementation, model application.

A quantitative analyst, trader or risk manager has to select a model appropriate to the problem under consideration and with respect to its likely progression. Therefore, a qualitative understanding – model properties and applicability – and a quantitative understanding – numerics and implementation – of the model and how given market data are applied to parameterize the model are necessary. Once a model is chosen it has to be implemented, tested and applied to the problem under consideration. To this end fast and reliable pricing methods for simple options have to be implemented. This is necessary since we wish to apply these methods to match market prices with model prices by adjusting the model parameters. This is in fact equivalent to solving a backward problem. Despite the fact that this method is frowned upon by academics and practitioners it is market practice. Finally, exotic payoffs including path-dependency or early exercise features often have to be considered and hedge sensitivities calculated.

For each step of the process a practitioner can, of course, consult different books or research articles that outline every single step in detail. We, however, want to show the whole life-cycle of financial modelling and provide an overview of widely applied models in finance in a single volume. In what follows we wish to outline their features and point to the applications of a particular model. Then, we show how to implement the pricing of simple products which are then used to calibrate model parameters. The fitted parameters of the models can then be applied to the pricing of exotic options. The numerics for each model are separated from the 'recipe' for the implementation using Matlab. As far as we know, ours is the first book to deal with financial modelling in this way.

We think that the book is special because we link the mathematical theory with numerical examples and source code which can be readily used. The results obtained in this book can be checked immediately by the reader applying the source code. The reader is of course free to extend and modify the code to further explore the numerical methods and gain more insights into advanced financial modelling and the underlying mathematical theory. We provide source code for

- Advanced models including stochastic volatility or jumps.
- Fourier transform based modern pricing methods.
- Direct integration with efficient numerical schemes.
- Monte Carlo simulation including special purpose schemes.
- Optimization and calibration using local and global optimizers.
- Calculating Greeks and applying early exercise rights.
- Hedge strategies and model risk.

For example, we price European options using several versions of the fast Fourier transform (FFT). We use this exceptionally fast method for calibrating a wide range of complex models to given market data. Using the derived model parameters we price exotic payoffs applying Monte Carlo simulation techniques with innovative methods such as bridge sampling or quasi random numbers.

Furthermore, we show how to optimize the code in terms of robustness and efficiency and how to extend it to suit your own needs. To this end we show how to incorporate methods from object oriented programming and design patterns in software engineering.

2   WHY WE HAVE WRITTEN THIS BOOK

We wrote this book in order to show how to apply advanced probabilistic and analytic models to financial problems. We also show that it is possible to design and implement flexible and efficient software for pricing and hedging a range of financial instruments. Furthermore, it is possible to obtain model parameters from market data for advanced models. Finally, we have attempted to create an understandable and seamless process, starting with a given financial model, designing its implementation using Matlab and then applying it to real-world situations. To this end we cover the modelling process by describing the characteristics of well-known modelling approaches. We implement each model and finally apply it efficiently to solve financial modelling problems. The mathematical theory is covered but we have placed it in the final chapter since there are many textbooks that review the mathematical fundamentals as well as special issues of advanced numerics and mathematical techniques more rigorously. The interested reader can therefore work through the theoretical aspects but a more practically oriented reader can start right away studying financial models and use the code to work with the models. We believe that this is a feature which makes the book unique; dealing with financial modelling in this way makes it unnecessary to reinvent the wheel since the stony path of implementation has been transformed into a well-paved road by providing all the source code.

3 WHY YOU SHOULD READ THIS BOOK

Advanced probabilistic models such as Lévy processes, stochastic volatility models and numerical procedures to solve financial problems using such models are becoming increasingly popular. They will soon become vital for risk management purposes and pricing applications. To be prepared for this era finance professionals should have studied the most popular models and should have dealt with the numerical methods appropriate to master such models. The numerical methods in this case are Fourier analysis, direct integration and Monte Carlo simulation. The models are able to capture many market phenomena, such as smiles or fat tails, that are often observed in financial markets data and further highlight the risks involved.

4 THE AUDIENCE

For whom is this book intended? We have written this book for those finance professionals who design, develop and apply advanced financial models. Especially we have in mind those people who wish to go beyond the Gaussian model paradigm. We apply modern mathematical tools and discuss their implementation to price and risk manage a wide range of financial instruments. We assume that the reader has a working knowledge of financial modelling, for example as discussed in Wilmott, P. (2007) or Hull, J. (2011), as well as some hands-on experience with Matlab or some other object oriented programming language, for instance C++, as discussed in Duffy, D. (2004 and 2006). Using this book, you can define financial models and integrate them into the Matlab software framework.

Using another programming language such as C++, C# or Java it is possible to translate the code into this language. At the time of writing there are many specialized libraries available that can replace Matlab functions, such as optimizers or fast Fourier transform algorithms.

This book is also aimed at students in financial engineering and related disciplines. It can serve as a basis to extend financial models or it can be used directly to apply models to financial market data for quantitative studies in economics or risk management courses. Furthermore, the material can be used for preparing reports and thesis projects in all quantitative finance disciplines. Finally, the book can function as a bridge between IT and quantitative finance because it demonstrates how Matlab code is produced from financial and mathematical models. Working with other programming languages such as C++ or VBA the methods are also applicable using available mathematical libraries or the Matlab runtime kernel via packaging functions using *dll*, *xll* or *COM* components.

Therefore, the primary target audience are people working in the financial industry and those studying for a degree in finance, or doing research or lecturing in that area. The book provides a wealth of examples and starting points for developing customized solutions. It can act as a guide for those starting out in the world of financial modelling and it can also serve as the basis for setting up complex and advanced models for finance professionals. Hence we recommend this book to financial engineers, quantitative researches, traders, risk managers, risk controllers as well as to students and academics in this field and those engaged in research towards a masters or doctoral thesis. Lecturers will find plenty of illustrated examples in the book, which are very useful for the application of theoretical topics in finance. Furthermore, it will be of use to students on programming courses on quantitative finance and numerics for financial applications.

We believe our text forms the ideal complement to earlier books by Duffy, D. (2004 and 2006) and Duffy, D. and Kienitz, J. (2009), where the focus is on developing software architectures in C++.

This book should be of interest to anyone who would benefit from understanding and using (advanced) financial models and to those who learn how to implement such models.

Since we provide ready to use code for the whole work-flow (model choice, implementation and calibration to market data), the reader can apply each model when studying this book. Tables and figures can be reproduced and certain modelling aspects can be further explored immediately.

Finally, we must alert our readers to the fact that we do not give any warranty for completeness, nor do we guarantee that the code is error free. Any damage or loss incurred in the application of the software and the concepts suggested in the book are entirely the reader's responsibility.

5 THE STRUCTURE OF THIS BOOK

The book has three parts. Each part consists of a number of chapters which, taken together, deal with a specific aspect of the problem of modelling financial problems. The contents of the parts can be summarized as follows:

- Part I – Financial Markets and Popular Models
  In the first part of the book we summarize financial markets facts and argue that fat tails, volatility smiles and other observed phenomena are not in line with the usual modelling approach using *Geometric Brownian Motion* or VaR models based on the *Normal Distribution*. To this end we give an overview of well-known financial models and their properties. For instance, we analyse the impact of parameter changes on implied volatility surfaces, risk neutral densities or typical sample paths and returns.
- Part II – Numerical Methods and Recipes
  In this part of the book we consider the numerical methods necessary for implementing and using the models introduced in Part I. We describe fundamental techniques such as fast Fourier transform, Quadrature methods, optimization or Monte Carlo simulation. To this end we provide the source code for all techniques discussed. This covers advanced numerical schemes for applying the Fourier transform such as the COS- or the CONV method or special purpose simulation schemes for stochastic volatility models.

  The code is not restricted to simple applications. We deal with the application of Fourier transforms and Monte Carlo methods to handle early exercises and the stable calculation of Greeks for discontinuous payoffs. In particular we apply the *Adjoint Method* and *Proxy Simulation* techniques. Moreover, we give an overview of different approaches to optimization and guide the reader through several techniques including *Differential Evolution* or *Sequential Quadratic Programming*. Of course, we provide the implementation for the methods discussed. This is the first time that such methods are both considered and their implementation described in a single book.
- Part III – Implementation, Software Design and Mathematics
  The basic and efficient application of Matlab is discussed in the last part of the book. We start with an introduction to the Matlab package and show the basics that a financial engineer

should know. Then, we discuss the object oriented approach and illustrate it by developing a calibration engine. In doing so, we discuss design patterns and class hierarchies to achieve our goal.

The parts are divided into 13 chapters. The structure of the book is as follows:

Part I Financial Markets and Popular Models
Introduction
Chapter 1 – Financial Markets – Data, Basics, Derivatives
Chapter 2 – Diffusion Models
Chapter 3 – Models with Jumps
Chapter 4 – Multi-Dimensional Models
Part II – Numerical Methods and Recipes
Chapter 5 – Option Pricing by Transform Techniques and Direct Integration
Chapter 6 – Advanced Topics using Transform Techniques
Chapter 7 – Monte Carlo Simulation and Applications
Chapter 8 – Monte Carlo Simulation – Advanced Issues
Chapter 9 – Calibration and Optimization
Chapter 10 – Model Risk – Calibration, Pricing and Hedging
Part III – Implementation, Software Design and Mathematics
Chapter 11 – Matlab – Basics
Chapter 12 – Matlab – Object Oriented Development
Chapter 13 – Math Fundamentals

6   WHAT THIS BOOK DOES NOT COVER

This book assumes some knowledge of finance and we do not aim to discuss the whole theory in this book. Thus, for instance, we do not cover in detail such important techniques as change of numeraire, arbitrage or the fundamental theorem of option pricing. We assume that the reader knows what options and financial instruments are and wishes to apply numerical techniques to such problems and, in doing so, to gain some practical understanding of the mathematics involved. We also assume that the reader has a working knowledge of Matlab. In particular, you should be familiar with the following topics:

• Handling matrices and vectors.
• Fundamental Matlab syntax.
• Functions and function handles.

We do think, however, that it is possible to learn the Matlab prerequisites in a very short time. For instance, the reader can start with Chapter 11 and work through the given material and experiment with the source code.

Finally, we hope that you enjoy this book as much as we have enjoyed working on it. For feedback, updates and questions concerning the book and its content please feel free to contact kienitzwetterau_FinModelling@gmx.de.

Good luck with applying the numerical methods to your problem under consideration!

Jörg Kienitz and Daniel Wetterau

7 CREDITS

At this stage it is time to thank many collaborators and especially students prepraing their thesis during internships within the Quantitative Analytics group of Deutsche Postbank AG. We thank Philipp Beyer for analysing Forward Start options in Lévy process based models, Beyer, P. and Kienitz, J. (2009), Holger Kammeyer for working on the Heston–Hull–White model, Kammeyer, H. and Kienitz, J. (2012a), Kammeyer, H. and Kienitz, J. (2012b), Kammeyer, H. and Kienitz, J. (2012c), Ines Weber for exploring Monte Carlo methods for options with early exercise opportunities, Sven Glaser for working on CMS Spread option pricing and finally Nikolai Nowaczyk for researching into the application of adjoint methods for calculating Greeks, Nowakcyk, N. and Kienitz, J. (2011).

Furthermore, we thank our colleague Manuel Wittke for fruitful discussions and research, Kienitz, J., Wetterau, D. and Wittke, M. (2011), Kienitz, J. and Wittke, M. (2010) and many suggestions on early stages of the manuscript as well as collaborating on the issues presented in Chapter 10. Further joint work is in preparation, Kienitz, J., Wetterau, D. and Wittke, M. (2013).

Christian Fries has to be mentioned for stimulating discussions on mathematical and financial topics.

Daniel J. Duffy is greatly acknowledged for suggestions on early versions of the manuscript.

Special thanks to Dr. Ingo Schneider and Wojciech Slusarski for carefully reading versions of the manuscript and for their many helpful remarks and comments.

Finally, Graeme West has to be mentioned. He started to read the manuscript but sadly died. Joerg Kienitz wishes to thank Graeme for stimulating discussions and for the invitation to lecture at AIMS Summer School in Cape Town, 2011.

8 CODE

We have to stress that the code used for implementing the models and the numerical methods presented in this book is not static. We work on the code by improving it in terms of speed, accuracy or by just fixing *bugs*. To this end the code available from the download section or directly from the authors' web-site is updated, improved or extended from time to time. We keep the reader informed on the web-site, www.jkienitz.de.

Furthermore, if you spot any errors or you wish to submit some new numerical method as a Matlab function, a new model or some improvement of the method illustrated in this book you are very welcome. Please send any feedback to kienitzwetterau_FinModelling@gmx.de.

For the current book the code can be obtained by download. Thus, there is no CD included in this book. A dedicated website for the code is http://www.mathworks.de/matlabcentral/fileexchange/authors/246981.

Part I

FINANCIAL MARKETS AND POPULAR MODELS

1

Financial Markets – Data, Basics and Derivatives

1.1 INTRODUCTION AND OBJECTIVES

The first chapter is to introduce the models that appear in subsequent chapters and, in so doing, to highlight the necessity of applying advanced numerical techniques. Since we wish to apply mathematical models to financial problems, we first have to analyse the markets under consideration. We have to check the available data upon which we build our models. Then, we have to investigate which models are appropriate and, finally, we need to decide on numerical methods to solve the modelling problem.

We motivate using market data; we highlight the nature of risk and the problems which arise with inappropriate modelling. The final conclusion is that the observed market structures need sophisticated models, numerically challenging implementation and deeply involved special purpose algorithms. Furthermore, we provide answers and suggestions to the following questions:

- What kind of objects do we have to model?
- What kind of distributions are necessary? Do we need anything other than the Gaussian distribution?
- What kind of patterns do we observe and which model is capable of reproducing such patterns?
- How complex should a model be?
- Which mathematical methods do we need? PDE? SDE? Numerical Mathematics?

We do not rate the models, but we do give advice on the numerical methods which can be applied to implement the different models and on what kind of market observation is covered by a certain model. We work out several methods which can be applied. The reader can try the different solutions and – very important – check the implementation, the stability and the robustness. Furthermore, the code provided can be modified to fit the special modelling issues.

Since financial models have to be implemented as computer programs, or they have to be integrated into a pricing library, numerical methods are required. The most fundamental risk of a model is, of course, its inapplicability in a certain setting. To this end we have to analyse which risk factors can be modelled using a certain class of models and we have to be aware of the risk factors that have not been taken into account. But once we have decided to apply a particular model, and we think that we are applying it appropriately, we face the following challenges:

- Appropriate numerical techniques.
- Approximations used should be robust, efficient and accurate.
- Black box solutions should be avoided.
- The implementation should be stable and reliable.

1.2 FINANCIAL TIME-SERIES, STATISTICAL PROPERTIES OF MARKET DATA AND INVARIANTS

To use a mathematical model for gaining insights and applying it to financial market data we need to choose some quantities or risk factors which we model. To this end we consider the notion of a *market invariant*. Fix a starting point t_{start} in time and an estimation interval τ. The interval τ could be one day or one month, for instance. Suppose from a market data provider we can get the data for an index $X(t)$, $t \in \mathcal{T}$, with

$$\mathcal{T} := \{t_{\text{start}}, t_{\text{start}} + \tau, \ldots, t_{\text{start}} + n \cdot \tau\}, \quad n \in \mathbb{N}.$$

We regard $X(t)$ as a random variable. A random variable X is called a market invariant for t_{start} and estimation interval τ if the realizations

- are *independent*
- are *identically distributed.*

A simple but effective method to test if a random variable qualifies as an invariant is the following:

- Take a time series X_s, $s = t, t + \tau, \ldots, t + n \cdots \tau = T$ of the possible invariant.
- Split the time series into two parts

$$X_t^1 = x_t^1, \quad t \in \{t_{\text{start}}, \ldots, [T - t_{\text{start}}/2\tau] \cdot \tau\}$$
$$X_t^2 = x_t^2, \quad t \in \{([T - t_{\text{start}}/2\tau] + 1) \cdot \tau, \ldots, T\}.$$

- Plot histograms corresponding to X^1 and X^2.
- Plot lagged time series $\tilde{X}_t := X_{t-\tau}$ against X_t.

Let us illustrate this test on time series for index and swap data. Before we actually start let us illustrate the dependence structure corresponding to independent, positively and negatively dependent random variables. To this end we take as an example the normal distribution with zero mean and a given covariance matrix, Σ. For our examples we choose three different covariance matrices, namely,

$$\Sigma_0 = \begin{pmatrix} 1 & 0 \\ 0 & 1 \end{pmatrix}, \quad \Sigma_1 = \begin{pmatrix} 1 & 0.99 \\ 0.99 & 1 \end{pmatrix}, \quad \Sigma_2 = \begin{pmatrix} 1 & -0.99 \\ -0.99 & 1 \end{pmatrix}.$$

The dependence structure is displayed in Figure 1.1.

We call a market invariant X *time homogeneous* if the distribution of X does not depend on the chosen time point t_{start}. In the sequel we consider Equity, Index, Interest Rate and Option markets. First, we consider index time series for the *S&P 500*, the *Nikkei*, the *FTSE* and the *DAX*. We argue that the prices of the indices do not obey the properties necessary to be an invariant.

The first observation regarding the data is that if we plot the lagged time series directly we get Figure 1.2. This clearly shows that the plain data are not independent and therefore not an invariant.

Furthermore, when we plot histograms with respect to the observed data we cannot find a suitable distributional description. Figure 1.3 shows the corresponding histograms.

Now, we consider the logarithmic returns computed from the time series. We see a very different picture. Figures 1.4 and 1.5 suggest that these quantities are invariants.

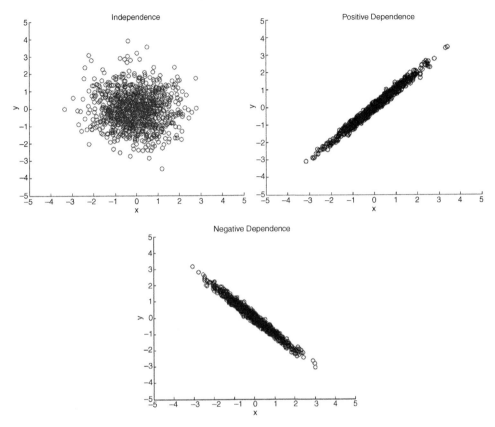

Figure 1.1 Time series generated from a normal distribution with covariance given by Σ_0 (top left), Σ_1 (top right) and Σ_2 (bottom) reflecting independence, positive and negative dependence

Thus, without further discussion we take as a suitable choice for a market invariant in the equity market the *logarithmic returns*, given by

$$H(t, \tau) := \log\left(\frac{S(t + \tau)}{S(t)}\right). \tag{1.1}$$

In fact, let $g : \mathbb{R} \to \mathbb{R}$ be a function, then $g(H)$ is a market invariant.

Taking realized prices of an index it is difficult to assign probabilistic concepts. It is not clear how to obtain relevant statistical information using such prices. On the contrary, the logarithmic returns introduced in Equation (1.1) show that the observed time series are independent and some parametric probability distribution can be assigned.

Other market invariants can also be derived. For a general and formal treatment see Meucci, A. (2007). We consider the case of the interest rate market. The zero coupon bonds, $DF(t, T)$ and the ratio $\frac{DF(t,T)}{DF(t-\tau,T)}$ might be considered as invariants. But since they tend to 1, respectively its redemption at expiry, zero coupon bonds are not time-homogeneous and therefore not market invariants. For further illustration let us take non-overlapping total returns, R^v, with

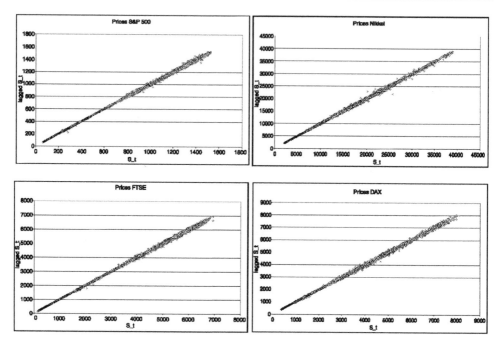

Figure 1.2   Lagged Time Series data of daily index closing prices for S&P 500 (top left), Nikkei (top right), FTSE (bottom left) and DAX (bottom right) calculated from daily index closing prices

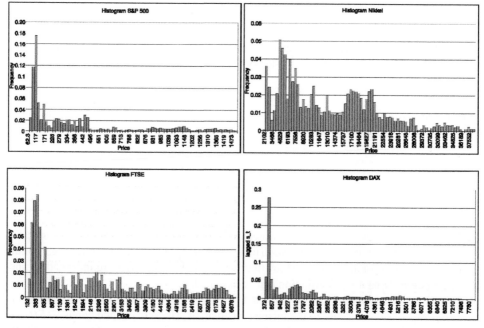

Figure 1.3   Histograms of daily index closing prices for S&P 500 (top left), Nikkei (top right), FTSE (bottom left) and DAX (bottom right)

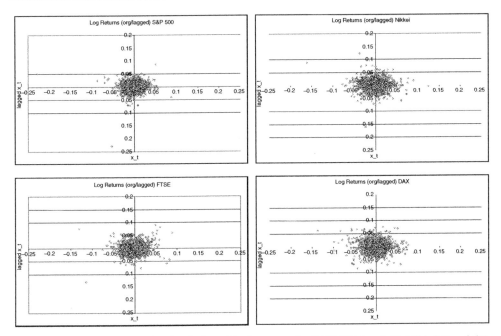

Figure 1.4 Lagged time series for the logarithmic returns for S&P 500 (top left), Nikkei (top right), FTSE (bottom left) and DAX (bottom right) calculated from time series of the daily closing prices

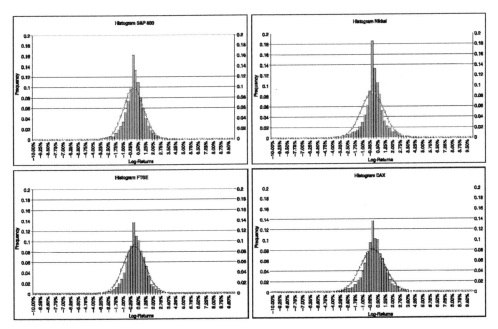

Figure 1.5 Histogram for logarithmic returns for S&P 500 (top left), Nikkei (top right), FTSE (bottom left) and DAX (bottom right) calculated from time series for daily closing prices. Furthermore, the figure shows a moment matched normal distribution

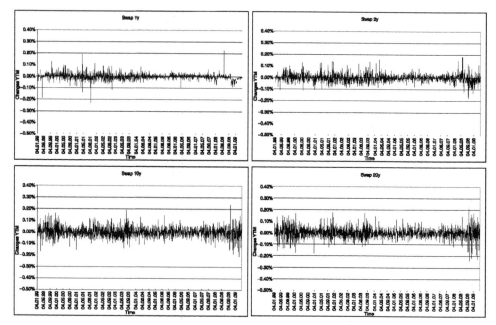

Figure 1.6 Time Series for Changes in Yield to Maturity for 1Y swap rate (top left), 2Y swap rate (top right), 10Y swap rate (bottom left) and 20y swap rate (bottom right)

maturity v. Thus,

$$R^v(t) = \frac{DF(t, t+v)}{DF(t-\tau, t-\tau+v)},$$

and therefore $g(R^v(t))$ are market invariants since they are time homogeneous, independent and identically distributed. A convenient invariant is the change in *yield to maturity* (Y_{2m}) and the changes in Y_{2m} denoted by Y:

$$Y_{2m}(t, v) := -\frac{1}{v} \log(DF(t, t+v))$$
$$Y(t, v, \tau) := Y_{2m}(t, v) - Y_{2m}(t-\tau, v).$$

As in the equity market we observe that the time series generated by the changes of the yield to maturity shows the desired properties. The time series of the changes in the yield to maturity derived from different quoted swap rates are plotted in Figure 1.6.

The corresponding historical distributions are plotted in Figure 1.7 and we again see that the assignment of some parametric probability distribution can be achieved.

Another method is to measure the logarithmic returns generated by investing a certain amount of currency using the current quoted rate for a pre-specified period.

Finally, let us consider the option market. For example, for a plain Vanilla Call option, the time value depends on the price of the underlying, on the yield and on the volatility. Therefore, we write the price of a European Call option, C, as

$$C(T-t, K, S(t), r(t), \sigma(t, S(t), K^{\text{ATM}}(t)).$$

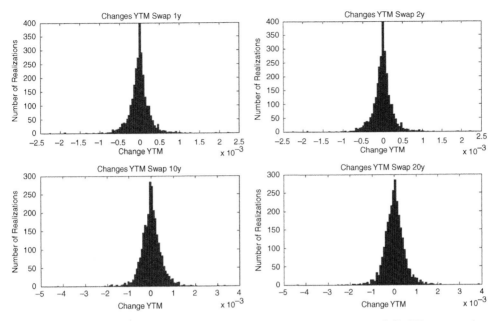

Figure 1.7   Histograms for Changes in Yield to Maturity for 1Y swap rate (top left), 2Y swap rate (top right), 10Y swap rate (bottom left) and 20Y swap rate (bottom right)

For reasons of liquidity we only consider ATM forward volatility. This means that the strike price is equal to the forward $S(T)$. Since we have already identified the invariants for $S(t)$ and $r(t)$ we are left with the problem of determining the invariants for σ. For time homogeneity reasons we consider a fixed time period v and the corresponding maturity $K(t)$

$$\sigma(t, K(t), t + v).$$

The option price fluctuates if the underlying does, but this is not the case for volatility since

$$\sigma \approx \sqrt{\frac{2\pi}{v} \frac{C(T + v)}{S(T)}}.$$

If we take differences in rolling ATM forward volatility:

$$\sigma(t, K^{\text{ATM}}(t), t + v) - \sigma(t - \tau, K^{\text{ATM}}(t - \tau), t - \tau + v).$$

This choice fulfils the constraints on invariants.

1.2.1   Real World Distribution

Suppose we have identified a market invariant such as the logarithmic returns of an index. We are now interested in the historical distribution of the invariant since this can be used as an input to some financial model. This could, for instance, be an asset allocation algorithm.

Figure 1.8 illustrates the difference of the real world distribution of the German DAX index from realized data. Furthermore, we determined the first and the second moment, which are the expectation and the standard deviation. For comparison to the real world distribution we used a moment matched Gaussian distribution. We see that this distribution is not capable of

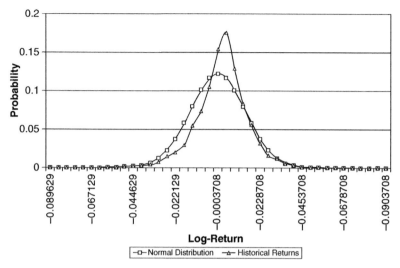

Figure 1.8 DAX index distribution of logarithmic returns and normal density with matched mean and variance

matching the shape of the historical distribution. In what follows we show that calculating risk figures using the Gaussian distribution or using it for asset allocation purposes causes some severe problems.

Applying the Gaussian distribution does not lead to a reasonable description of the risks involved in financial markets. Methods based on calculating risk rely on the computation of *quantiles* of a cumulative distribution. The quantile function is the functional inverse of the cumulative distribution. If $\mathbb{P}$ is the cumulative distribution taking values in $[0, 1]$, we fix a number $\alpha \in [0, 1]$ and determine the value of x for which $\mathbb{P}(x) = \alpha$. Then, x is referred to as the α-quantile. Methods based on the computation of quantiles include Value-at-Risk (VaR), Conditional-Value-at-Risk (CVaR), (1.2), or time series analysis for asset allocation.

We base our consideration on Shaw, W.T. (2011). We define *CVaR* which is also known as *expected shortfall*. This risk figure can be related to VaR by

$$\alpha - \text{CVaR} := \alpha - \frac{\int_{-\infty}^{\alpha} F(x)dx}{F(\alpha)} \geq \alpha - \text{VaR}. \tag{1.2}$$

Let us briefly discuss the inadequacy of using the Gaussian distribution for modelling real world distributions and applying it to identify risk. The real world or statistical distribution is the distribution obtained by time series analysis. Recently, the credit crisis of 2008 showed that the Gaussian assumption for modelling gave rise to many errors.

Often statements of the type "We have seen a sequence of 25 standard deviation events" or "several 10 standard deviation events occurred several days in a row" could be heard in interviews or appeared in the financial press. This illustrates the inadequacy of the Gaussian hypothesis in financial modelling. Statistically, for a 25 standard deviation event to happen it would need longer than the lifetime of the universe. But reality shows that extreme events occur much more often than is suggested by models based on the Gaussian assumption. This

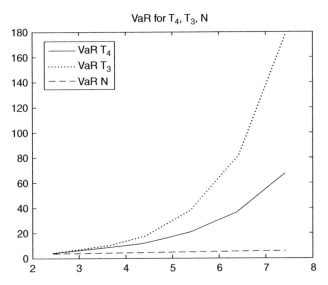

Figure 1.9 Risk Measure VaR for the Student distribution with 3 degrees of freedom, 4 degrees of freedom and the Gaussian distribution

makes us very aware that Non-Gaussian modelling is necessary and we therefore provide the numerical tools to handle this modelling approach.

Figure 1.9 plots the VaR for different probability distributions, namely the Student distributions with 3 and 4 degrees of freedom as well as the normal distribution. We see the very low values for the VaR with respect to the normal distribution. Choosing the Gaussian distribution suggests that the tail risk is very small. Tail events, thus, cannot be neglected. But by choosing another distribution, such as the Student distribution with a small degree of freedom, we observe that the tail risk is significant.

Other risk measures have been suggested, for instance the expected shortfall (CVaR). Figure 1.10 illustrates that for the Gaussian distribution switching from VaR to CVaR has no effect. Both risk measures lead to similar results. However, changing the distribution to a Non-Gaussian distribution shows that switching from VaR to CVaR leads to different risk figures.

The Matlab functions StuCVaR, Stunorm and FMinusOne, illustrated in Figures 1.11 and 1.12, are used to compute the CVaR for the Student distribution. The code displayed in Figure 1.13 is used to compute the VaR.

Another method that may be used here is to identify the key drivers of risk by applying *principal component analysis*, PCA. These key drivers are simulated in stress tests or in some likely scenario. However, when applying PCA care has to be taken since there are several pitfalls. We refer to West, G. (2005) for illustrations and an analysis of the risks involved in PCA.

1.3 IMPLIED VOLATILITY SURFACES AND VOLATILITY DYNAMICS

Time series are not the only source of information for modelling the financial market. There are many liquid instruments for which prices are quoted on information systems or prices

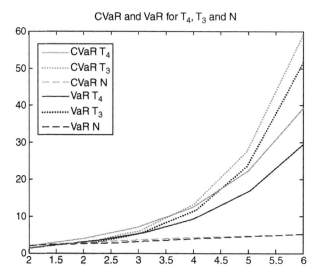

Figure 1.10   Risk Measures CVaR and VaR for the Student distribution with 3 degrees of freedom, 4 degrees of freedom and the Gaussian distribution. Only for the Student distributions do we see that the risk figures are distinct

```
function y = StuCVaR(x,n)
% General method to compute CVaR for Student distribution with n
% degrees of freedom
    f = @(t,n) -(n^(n-2)*(n+t.^2).^(.5-.5*n)*gamma(.5*(n-1)) ...
        /(2*sqrt(pi)*gamma(.5*n)));
    arg = FMinusOne(x,n);
    y = sqrt((n-2) / n) * f(arg,n)./x;
end
```

Figure 1.11   Matlab code for computing the CVaR for a general Student distribution. $x \in [0, 1]$ and n gives the degrees of freedom

```
function y = FMinusOne(x,n)
    if(x < .5)
        arg = 2 * x;
    else
        arg = 2*(1-x);
    end

    y = sign(x-.5) .* sqrt(n*(1./betaincinv(arg,n/2,.5)-1));
end
```

Figure 1.12   Matlab code for computing the inverse distribution function for a general Student distribution. $x \in [0, 1]$ and n gives the degrees of freedom

```
function y = Stunorm(u,n)
    y = sqrt((n-2)/n)*FMinusOne(u,n);
end
```

Figure 1.13   Matlab code for computing the norm using a general Student distribution. $u \in [0, 1]$ and n gives the degrees of freedom

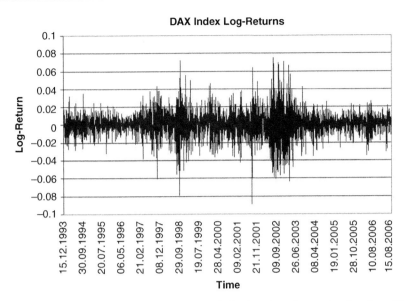

Figure 1.14   Daily logarithmic returns for the DAX index based on time series data from 15.12.1993 until 15.08.2006

can be obtained from brokers. Such quotes are a valuable source of information. Quants try to beg out model parameters from such quotes. This well-known practice is termed the *procedure of calibration*. While we do not discuss the pros and cons of calibration in this book, we do assess the process of calibration for determining some model parameters from given market quotes for a particular model. We wish to find model parameters which most closely match the observed prices. However, using this method completely ignores stability and other modelling issues. For instance, the market quotes can be weighted to assign more weight to liquid options and thus lead to a higher impact when determining the parameters. But the reader may well ask if the calibration makes sense at all, since every day, or even in shorter periods, model parameters change. Despite the criticism of calibration, this is market practice and we do provide the numerical methods and tools to perform calibration. We emphasize that calibrating models needs great care and that all aspects, such as parameter stability or robustness, have to be taken into account.

In this section we consider implied volatility surfaces. Implied volatility is a convenient way to quote option prices.

1.3.1   Is There More than just a Volatility?

Here we show that there is evidence that there are more notions and meanings to the word volatility. The classical meaning of volatility is the one suggested by the Black–Scholes formula.

We can also base the considerations on observed time series data. For example, let us consider Figure 1.14. The figure shows the logarithmic returns of the DAX index based on a time series of daily data from 15.12.1993 to 15.08.2006. We see that there are periods showing very low activity but other regimes where the daily logarithmic returns change very fast. The

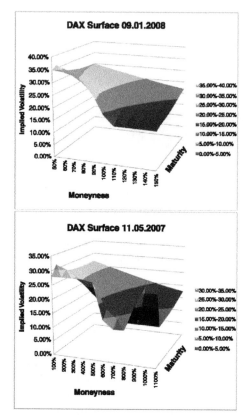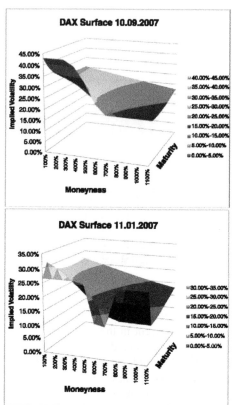

Figure 1.15   DAX Implied Volatility Surfaces for 09.01.2008 (upper left), 10.09.2007 (upper right), 11.05.2007 (lower left) and 11.01.2007 (lower right)

returns also exhibit large absolute values. In fact, it seems that it is impossible to relate a single positive number to the dynamic of the DAX. The dynamic seems to be at least time dependent or even stochastic as in Figure 1.14. Some periods of small moves are followed by small moves, and large moves are followed by large moves. This observation is called *volatility clustering*.

If we consider the implied volatility observed at a given time point, we note that with respect to strike and maturity the implied volatilities do change considerably. Figure 1.15 shows the implied volatility surface for the German DAX index at four different dates, namely 09.01.2008, 10.09.2007, 11.05.2007 and 11.01.2007. We see that not only the height of the surface differs significantly. Comparing the given dates the shapes are also very different. One can see that either a *skew*, high volatility for low strikes and low volatility for high strikes, or a *smile*, high volatility for low and high strikes and low volatilities around the current forward, which is the *ATM strike*, is possible.

This does not fit in terms of aggregating the risk into one single number. In fact, there are many financial products that are very sensitive to changes in the shape of the volatility surface. But, even worse, there are instruments that are sensitive to the movement of the implied volatility surface. We consider such options when we introduce the numerical methods for pricing.

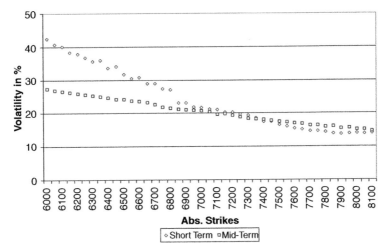

Figure 1.16 A typical shape of the implied volatility structure for DAX options. Plotted are implied volatilities quoted for short-term and mid-term options. The shape suggests that the skew flattens out for large times to maturity

The skew inherent in the implied volatility surface for equity or index options has many causes. We have observed a flat implied volatility surface since the crash in October 1987. A firm's value of equity can be seen as the present value of all its future income plus its assets minus its debt. Assets may have very different relative volatilities than debt, which can give rise to a leverage related skew. Furthermore, supply and demand might be another reason for the skew. Equivalently, downward risk insurance is more desired due to the intrinsic asymmetry of positions in equity. Due to their financial rationale, it is more natural for equity or indices to be held for a long period than for a short one. This makes protection against downward moves more important. Finally, declining stock or index prices are more likely to give rise to massive portfolio re-balancing. Therefore volatility rises if stock or index prices increase. This asymmetry occurs naturally from the existence of thresholds below which positions must be cut unconditionally for regulatory reasons.

The interest rate market smile is caused by the many different market activities of central banks, pension funds or governments. Trading, speculation, hedging or simply investment strategies cause supply and demand for protection against low as well as high interest rate levels. A typical smile shape is the hockey stick.

Foreign exchange rates are quoted in terms of an exchange rate for one currency against another. The smile is caused by anticipating government policies, trade policies and/or hedging activity caused by firms and banks. Foreign investors seek protection against FX rates. Due to the strength of one currency against another the smile can be asymmetric.

Two figures illustrate this phenomenon. First, Figure 1.16 once more illustrates that options having different strikes and different times to maturity are priced using different volatilities.

There is an index that measures realized volatilities. This index is the *VDAX*. Figure 1.17 shows data from the VDAX time series.

Traditionally, smile models have been assessed according to how well they fit market option prices across strikes and maturities. However, the pricing of most recent exotic structures, such as reverse cliquets or Napoleons, is more dependent on the assumptions made for the

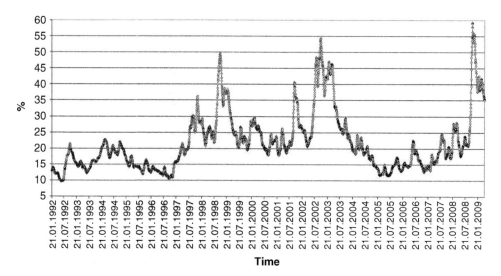

Figure 1.17 Time series for the German Volatility Index VDAX from 21.01.1992 till 21.01.2009. Indicated is the assumption of a time-dependent and even a stochastic volatility

future dynamics of implied volatilities than on today's Vanilla Option prices. We have different assumptions on the smile dynamics, for instance:

- Constant (Black–Scholes).
- Spot smile and spot term structure (Local-Volatility, Merton).
- Moving smile (height, smiling, skewness, . . .) (Stochastic Volatility).
- Floating smile property (Lévy).

After gathering information from financial markets we consider different notions for volatility which later lead to financial models based on different stochastic processes. For the different notions of volatility and their connection we refer the reader to Gatheral, J. (2006) and Lee, R. (2002).

1.3.2 Implied Volatility

Let us assume that some financial asset $S(t)$ is modelled by the SDE

$$dS(t) = rS(t)dt + \sigma S(t)dW(t).$$

The parameter σ is the implied volatility. Using σ it is possible to value European Calls and Puts by the Black–Scholes formula. The price of a European Call option, respectively European Put option, is linked by a one-to-one relation to the implied volatility. Thus, option prices can be quoted by just one number regardless of the current spot price.

1.3.3 Time-Dependent Volatility

If we assume that volatility of the underlying price is a deterministic function of time, the process can be defined by the SDE

$$dS(t) = rS(t)dt + \sigma(t)S(t)dW(t),$$

with $\sigma : \mathbb{R} \to \mathbb{R}^+$ being a positive real-valued function. We define the average volatility, σ_{Av}, by

$$\sigma_{\text{Av}} := \sqrt{\frac{1}{T} \int_0^T \sigma^2(t)dt}.$$

It is well known that $\log(S(t))$ is normal with mean $(r - \frac{\sigma_{\text{Av}}^2}{2})T$ and variance $\sigma_{\text{Av}}T$. A European Call option can be priced using the average volatility. But hence the average volatility is given as an integral expression, the function $\sigma(\cdot)$ cannot be derived from a finite set of European Call option prices. Thus, to restrict the degrees of freedom in a time-dependent volatility model the modeller can use a parametric form of the volatility function $\sigma(\cdot)$.

A further generalization is the time-dependent and spot-dependent volatility.

1.3.4 Stochastic Volatility

Further generalization of the concept of volatility leads to a consideration of *stochastic volatility*. In contrast to the other models volatility by itself is a stochastic process and driven by another Brownian motion.

$$dS(t) = r S(t)dt + f(\sigma(t))dW(t)$$
$$d\sigma(t) = \mu(\sigma, t)dt + \alpha(\sigma, t)V(t)dW_2(t)$$
$$\langle dW_1(t), dW_2(t) \rangle = \rho dt.$$

As in the case of time-dependent volatility it is possible to define an average volatility depending on the realization ω:

$$\sigma_{\text{SAv}}(\omega) = \sqrt{\frac{1}{T} \int_0^T \sigma^2(\omega, t)dt}.$$

In contrast to the time-dependent volatility, the expected value of the average volatility is not equal to the implied volatility. If $C(T, K)$ denotes the European Call option price, we have

$$dC(K, T) = e^{-rT} \mathbb{E} \left[-rK H(S(T) - K) + \frac{1}{2}\sigma^2(T)S^2(T)\delta(S(T) - K) \right] dT,$$

with H and δ denoting the *Heavyside* function and the δ distribution.

1.3.5 Volatility from Jumps

There is yet another way for a process to move. Let us take a diffusion process to which we add another stochastic process, which is called the *jump part*. This process does not continuously contribute to the movement but instead there are rare events called *jump times*. In the case of a jump, the jump height is drawn from some probability distribution. The corresponding value is added to the current value. This procedure finally leads to the sample path.

Despite the fact that a process can consist of a diffusion and a jump part, another class of processes has been researched. This class only move by jumps. Jumps are then no longer rare events, but the jumps stochastically vary in size and small jumps contribute to the movement. *Pure jump processes*, as such processes are called, become increasingly important for modelling.

1.3.6   Traders' Rule of Thumb

There are some rules of thumb for modelling volatility. Three of these rules are called the *sticky-strike*, *sticky-moneyness* and the *sticky-delta* rule. Some traders used to adhere strictly to these rules. Therefore, we shall explain them briefly here.

Let us consider a given implied volatility surface V at time t_0. For each time to maturity T, each strike K and level of the underlying S, the function V assigns a value called the *implied volatility*. Mathematically, we can view V as a function

$$IV : \mathbb{R}^+ \times \mathbb{R}^+ \times \mathbb{R}^+ \to \mathbb{R}^+$$
$$(K, T, S) \mapsto V(K, T, S).$$

Often we do not consider the current value of the underlying and regard IV as a function of maturity and strike only. Given IV, the sticky-strike rule postulates that for a given time to maturity T the skew varies linearly. Let $v(T)$ denote the slope of the skew that is $v(t) := \frac{\partial C}{\partial K}\big|_{K=S(0)}$. For some function $v_1 : \mathbb{R}^+ \to \mathbb{R}$ the value of the implied volatility is then given

$$IV(K, T) = IV(S(t_0), T) + v_1(t)(S(t_0) - K).$$

First of all, we observe that there is no level dependence of the implied volatility. However, the formula is appealing for equity markets and not too far out of the money strikes. Since we have no level dependence on the spot when modelling the skew we exactly recover the standard Black–Scholes Delta for the options.

Let us now consider the quantity K/S and look at another parametrization of IV. The quantity K/S is called *moneyness*; we will come across this concept and that of log-moneyness, $\log(K/S)$ again later in the book. We wish to introduce some level dependence to V. The rule we now consider is called the *sticky-moneyness rule* and is a little bit more involved. Given IV, the sticky-moneyness rule postulates that if time passes from t_0 to $t_0 + \Delta$ and the asset moves, the volatility of an option for a given strike K sticks to the moneyness. We therefore look at another function $v_2 : \mathbb{R}^+ \to \mathbb{R}$ and consider

$$IV(K, T) = V(S(t_0), T) + v_2(t)(1 - K/S(T))S(t_0).$$

The sticky-delta rule is now an approximation to the sticky–moneyness rule. For strikes not too far away from the current spot level the volatility is approximated by

$$IV(K, T) = V(S(t_0), T) + v_2(t)(S(T) - K).$$

1.3.7   The Risk Neutral Density

The risk neutral density is closely linked to the notion of volatility since European Call or Put options determine (in principle) the *risk neutral density*. For a European Call option we have

$$C(K, T) = e^{-r(T-t)}\mathbb{E}[\max(S(T) - K, 0)|S(t)]$$
$$= e^{-r(T-t)} \int_0^\infty \max(S(T) - K, 0)q(S(T)|S(t))dS(T),$$

with some probability density q. The probability density that prices all European Call options is called the risk neutral density. With respect to this formula, Breeden, D. and Litzenberger, R. (1978) show that q can be obtained from the continuum of all European Call option prices by differentiation

$$\frac{\partial^2 C}{\partial K^2} = e^{-r(T-t)} q(S(T)). \tag{1.3}$$

We use variants of the risk neutral density. Often it is convenient to consider the risk neutral density not with the forward but with the logarithmic moneyness. To this end, let p denote the density and q the density of $\log(S(T)/S(0))$, then, p and q are related by

$$p(x) = q(\log(x/S(0)))/x$$
$$q(x) = p(S(0)\exp(x))S(0)\exp(x).$$

In reality there are only quotes available for a discrete set $\mathcal{K} := \{K_1, \ldots, K_N\}$. Thus, further assumptions on strike values $K < K_1$ and $K > K_N$ as well as for strikes K which do not belong to $\mathcal{K}$ but $K_1 < K < K_N$ have to be made. This is directly linked to the issue of using extrapolation and interpolation methods. Some standard interpolation techniques such as linear interpolation are not sufficient for discovering the risk neutral density.

The interpolation method has to be *arbitrage free*. This means that using the interpolated option prices should not lead to arbitrage possibilities as this would lead to unusable volatility structures for the traders and for risk management.

However, having specified extrapolation and interpolation schemes and applying (1.3), one may observe that risk neutral distributions are in general not symmetric and differ significantly from the Gaussian distribution. We discuss several different distributions which we apply for modelling in this book.

A cumulative distribution $F_X(x) := \mathbb{P}(X \leq x)$ is said to obey a fat tail of order α if

$$1 - F_X(x) \sim x^{-\alpha} \text{ as } x \to \infty.$$

This property is linked to the *kurtosis* of the distribution which we consider in the sequel. Let μ be the mean of the distribution. If for the density function

$$f(\mu - x) = f(\mu + x)$$

holds, we say the distribution is symmetric. If this is not the case, the distribution is asymmetric or skewed.

To this end, higher moments become important for analysing time series for financial models. The moments encode properties of the distribution.

The Gaussian distribution, for instance, is completely determined by two parameters. Knowing the mean and the standard deviation or, equivalently, the variance is sufficient to determine the probability distribution. Other distributions with a richer structure can therefore be more realistically applied to financial data showing fat tails, asymmetry and other shapes. For such distributions these features are related to the higher moments. Knowing only the first two moments is not enough information in this case. Below we consider the first four moments and their sampled counterparts, also called *empirical moments*.

The first moment, the *expectation*, is given by

$$\mu = \mathbb{E}[X] \tag{1.4}$$

$$\hat{\mu} = \frac{1}{N} \sum_{j=1}^{N} x_j \tag{1.5}$$

and the second moment, the *variance* or its square root, the *volatility*

$$\sigma = \sqrt{\mathbb{E}[(X - \mu)^2]} \tag{1.6}$$

$$\hat{\sigma} = \frac{1}{\sqrt{N}} \sqrt{\sum_{j=1}^{N} (x_j - \hat{\mu})^2}. \tag{1.7}$$

Financial time series in general show significant skewness

$$\text{sk} = \frac{\mathbb{E}[(X - \mathbb{E}[X])^3]}{\mathbb{V}[S]^3} \tag{1.8}$$

$$\hat{\text{sk}} = \frac{1}{N} \sum_{j=1}^{N} \frac{(x_j - \hat{\mu})^3}{\hat{\sigma}^3} \tag{1.9}$$

and, finally, kurtosis

$$\text{ku} = \frac{\mathbb{E}[(X - \mathbb{E}[X])^4]}{\mathbb{V}[S]^2} \tag{1.10}$$

$$\hat{\text{ku}} = \frac{1}{N} \sum_{j=1}^{N} \frac{(x_j - \hat{\mu})^4}{\hat{\sigma}^4} \tag{1.11}$$

and therefore are heavily tailed and peaked.

A symmetric distribution, for instance the normal distribution, has skewness 0. If a distribution has fatter tails to the left (right) the skewness is negative (positive).

The normal distribution has kurtosis equal to 3. If the distribution is flatter (higher peaked) than the normal distribution, it has kurtosis smaller (bigger) than 3.

We have reviewed the real world probability density and the risk neutral density. We observed that symmetric, non-fat-tailed distributions often fail to model observed market structures and therefore the risks. To this end we have to apply other distributions and other stochastic processes for modelling apart from the Gaussian model. In the next section we show some financial applications where we wish to apply the more general concepts. To that efficient and robust techniques have to be considered. This is the main topic of the current book.

1.4 APPLICATIONS

Finally, we address the applications we are considering in this book. We wish to use advanced mathematical models for

- Asset Allocation.
- Pricing, Hedging and Risk Management.

Therefore, we discuss these topics in what follows.

1.4.1 Asset Allocation

Suppose a trading desk or a fund manager wishes to create a certain yield. To structure the portfolio several financial assets can be used. Each asset may create a certain yield. But there are also risks, the volatilities, and, furthermore, it may become important how the different assets and asset classes interact with each other. To this end we ask ourselves the question: Is there a way to earn a certain yield and at the same time minimize the risk?

If it is possible to buy and sell securities, options and structured products of different types we have to take into account the distribution of the risk factors. This distribution determines the future value of the portfolio. To obtain the distribution we have to not only estimate parameters describing the movement of a single risk factor but also, moreover, determine the dependencies of the risk factors.

Now, suppose we know the probability distribution but we are faced with another problem: the investment is restricted to certain portfolios. For instance, the fund manager is only allowed to restructure 10% of the portfolio and it must contain 15% equity but not more than 25%. Here we have to solve an optimization with constraints.

In the book we provide measures for the risk and tools to set up the problem as well as applying the optimization.

1.4.2   Pricing, Hedging and Risk Management

Suppose we have a given portfolio consisting of financial products. The portfolio may, for instance, include options, swaps, equities or structured products. This portfolio is exposed to several risk factors. We consider market risk, credit risk and liquidity risk. Then, we have to identify the key risk factors. A *hedge* is an immunization of the portfolio with respect to a given risk factor. For instance, we consider a portfolio consisting only of a European Call option. The standard risk factor which is considered is the spot price of an underlying asset. Thus, a change of the spot price causes a move in the option value.

Let us now consider a hedge against small moves of the underlying. To this end a trader buys or sells a certain amount of the underlying to account for this move. In general we consider two methods for hedging a single option or even a whole trading book:

- Dynamic Hedging.
  Dynamic hedging refers to a trading strategy we eventually apply to adjust a given portfolio to reduce or even cancel out the risk. If we have identified risk factors, we are interested in the sensitivity of the portfolio to a change in this factor. Having some pricing model at hand we can calculate model sensitivities. These sensitivities are also called the *Greeks*. We adjust the portfolio by buying or selling an amount of an instrument corresponding to the risk factor. Thus, when risk factors move, the hedging portfolio has to be changed. Since restructuring the hedge portfolio costs money, we have to decide when and how often we have to re-balance it to reduce the risk.
- Static Hedging.
  Another approach to hedging is the concept of static hedging. A static hedge is a portfolio of financial instruments that approximately or even exactly replicates the payoff of some exotic option or structured product. The static replication does not depend on a certain model but on the structure of the derivatives contracts. But when it comes to pricing the replicating portfolio a model dependence comes in. When we apply static hedging the portfolio is only set up at the beginning and then never altered. Sometimes we decide to hedge only a portion of the risk. The corresponding strategy is a sub-hedge. The opposite of a sub-hedge is a super hedge.

Let us briefly consider static hedging. To illustrate the concept we consider a function

$$f : I \to \mathbb{R}$$
$$S \mapsto f(S)$$

such that f is monotonically increasing and for some number K_0 we have $f(K_0) = 0$. Then we can find an approximate replication in terms of Call option payoffs by

$$f(S) \approx \sum_{i=1}^{N} \omega(K_i)(S - K_i)^+.$$

The weights ω_i, $i = 1, \ldots, N$ can be determined and they are given by

$$\omega_0 = f'(K_0); \omega_1 = f''(K_1 - K_0); \ldots; \omega_i = f''(K_i)(K_{i+1} - K_i),$$

which in the limit leads to a full replication

$$f(S) = f'(K_0)(S - K_0)^+ + \int_{K_0}^{\infty} f''(K)(S - K)^+ dK.$$

If the function f is monotonically decreasing and $f(K_0) = 0$ we have

$$f(S) \approx \sum_{i=1}^{N} \tilde{\omega}_i(K_i)(K_i - S)^+,$$

with weights

$$\tilde{\omega}_0 = -f'(K_0); \tilde{\omega}_1 = -f''(K_0 - K_1); \ldots; \tilde{\omega}_N = -f''(K_N)(K_{N-1} - K_N),$$

which than leads to a replication formula applicable for Put payoffs and we find for the limit

$$f(S) = -f'(K_0)(K_0 - S)^+ + \int_0^{K_0} f''(K)(K - S)^+ dK.$$

We consider the approach for two different instruments and explain its application. First, we remark that for $f(S) := ((S - K)^+)^2$ we have $2((S - K)^+)^2 \int_K^{\infty}(S - x)^+ dx$ and $\mathbb{E}[((S - K)^+)^2] = 2 \int_K^{\infty} \mathbb{E}[(S - x)^+] dx$.

Now, we are in a position to consider some well-known derivatives which can be statically hedged.

- Constant Maturity Swaps.
  We consider the set of time points $T_a, T_{a+1}, \ldots, T_b$ and the swap rate

$$S_{a,b} := \frac{P(t, T_a) - P(t, T_b)}{A_a(t)}; A_a(t) := \sum_{j=a+1}^{b} \tau_j P(t, T_j).$$

The expectation of the swap rate with respect to the T_i forward measure is

$$\mathbb{E}^{T_i}[S_{a,b}(T_a)] = \frac{A_a(0)}{P(0, T_a + \delta)} \mathbb{E}^A \left[S_{a,b}(T_a)^2 \frac{P(T_A, T_a + \delta)}{A_a(T_a)} \right].$$

In the final equation the second factor can be approximated and differentiated with respect to the swap rate and, then, replication is applied. This leads to the notion of convexity adjustment for constant maturity swaps.

- Variance Swaps.

We consider the payoff of a log contract

$$\int_0^T \sigma(t)dt = 2\int_0^T \frac{1}{S(t)}dS(t) - 2\log\left(\frac{S(T)}{S(0)}\right)$$

and using the fact that the quadratic variation is $\left\langle \frac{\int_0^T \sigma^2(t)dt}{T} \right\rangle = \frac{2}{T}\left\langle \log\left(\frac{F}{S(T)}\right)\right\rangle$ we have

$$\frac{2}{T}\left(\int_0^{S(T)} \frac{\langle(K-S(T))^+\rangle}{K^2}dK + \int_F^\infty \frac{\langle(S(T)-K)^+\rangle}{K^2}dK\right)$$

and therefore a method to statically hedge the Variance Swap.

In fact, we cheated when stating the replication formula for CMS. It is market standard to use cash settled swaptions instead of physically delivered swaptions. To this end the replication formula should involve a change of numeraire.

To this end let M and N be two different numeraires with associated measures Q_M and Q_N. The numeraires represent the ones associated with cash settled and physically settled swaptions. Furthermore, let f_r denote the quotient M/N and $Y(t) = f(S(t))$ for some twice differentiable function f. Now, let us consider another twice differentiable function g and we are interested in the values of options with payoffs:

$$g(S(T))(S(T)-k)^+ \text{ and } g(S(T))(k-S(T))^+.$$

Let C_0 and P_0 denote the corresponding values of the options. Then, if we set $h(x) := f/g$ and $\omega := \partial^2/\partial x^2 h f_r$

$$V_0(Y(T)) = f' f_r(K) + C_0(K) - P_0(K)$$
$$+ \int_0^K \omega(x)P_0(x)dx + \int_K^\infty \omega(x)C_0(x)dx$$

provided that $K \geq 0$ such that $f(K) = 0$, $g'(K) \neq 0$.

We can now take for f and g the physically settled and the cash settled annuity. The above formula, then, leads to the replication formula for CMS using cash settled swaptions.

Wittke, M. (2011) considers the convexity correction computed via a replication portfolio for CMS. Let us consider the implementation in Matlab. We take, for instance, the SABR model to determine the smile. First, we give the code for computing the weights.

The function weights (Figure 1.18) uses the function annuity, as illustrated in Figure 1.19.

The weights are multiplied by the payer, respectively receiver swaption prices of the replication portfolio. The corresponding swaptions are valued using a Black formula. The volatility we use for pricing is determined by the SABR model. This model is used to incorporate the observed swaption smile in the market. However, some of the shortcomings of the SABR model and the rule of thumb formula are also considered below.

Now, having the weights and the swaption prices of the replication portfolio, we can use the current forward as the strikes to determine the convexity adjustment. Using the above algorithms, especially the code from Figure 1.20, we have evaluated our first static hedge using Matlab. The above mentioned shortcomings of the SABR model lead to unstable convexity adjustments so we need more advanced methods to robustly and effectively price CMS and CMS options.

```
function [value] = weights(strikes,tenor,yearfrac)

    NStrikes = length(strikes);
    value = zeros(1,NStrikes-1);

    for i = 1:1:NStrikes-1
    wSum = 0;
        for j = 1:1:i
            tmp = (strikes(i+1)-strikes(j))/(strikes(i+1)-strikes(i));
            wSum = wSum + value(1,j)*tmp;
        end
    value(1,i) = (strikes(i+1)-strikes(1)) ...
        /(annuity(strikes(i+1),tenor,yearfrac)* ...
            (strikes(i+1)-strikes(i)))-wSum;
    end

end
```

Figure 1.18 Matlab implementation for the weights used for replicating CMS caplets and floorlets

1.5 GENERAL REMARKS ON NOTATION

Let us consider a stochastic process $S(t)$ as well as the logarithm of S. The process $X(t) := \log(S(t))$ is given by:

$$S(t) = S(0)\exp(\mu(t, S(t))t - \omega(t) + \sigma_L(t, S(t))W(t)) \tag{1.12}$$

$$X(t) = X(0) + (r - d)t - \omega(t) + L(t) \tag{1.13}$$

or equivalently in terms of the corresponding *Stochastic Differential Equations*:

$$dS(t) = \mu(t, S(t))dt + \sigma_L(t, S(t))dW(t) \tag{1.14}$$

$$dX(t) = \tilde{\mu}(t, S(t))dt + \tilde{\sigma}_L(t, S(t))dW(t). \tag{1.15}$$

The process ω is called the *martingale adjustment*. We consider several methods for making an exponential model into a martingale. For the examples we always stick to the subtraction of the mean value to assure the martingale property.

For specific markets either prices or volatilities are quoted. To this end the modeller has to account for the given quotes. For example, we may wish to set up a calibration procedure. If the market quotes implied volatilities but not option prices, it would be reasonable to use an approximation formula or a closed form solution for the quoted volatility instead of a pricing formula. This is reasonable since the price has to be transformed into a volatility, which can be very time consuming. The appendix of this chapter, Section 1.7, gives several market quotes including swaption volatilities, CMS and CMS Spread options. Such quotes can be used for calibration purposes or to verify prices. In general, the modeller has to decide which kinds of market data to choose. There are several types of information available:

```
function value = annuity(x,tenor,yearfrac)
    value = 1./x.*(1-(1./(1+x.*yearfrac).^(tenor./yearfrac)));
end
```

Figure 1.19 Calculating the annuity for determining the weights for CMS caplet and floorlet replication

```
function [value] = Caplet_Rep_SABR(fs, strike, ...
        maturity, tenor, yearfrac, ...
        alpha, beta, nu, rho)
    w = weights(strike,tenor,yearfrac);         % calc weights
    swaptions = payerSwaptionSABR(fs, strike, ...
        maturity, tenor, yearfrac, ...
        alpha, beta, nu, rho);                  % swaption prices
    value = w*swaptions(1:end-1)';              % caplet
end

function [value] = Floorlet_Rep_SABR(fs, strike, ...
        maturity, tenor, yearfrac, ...
        alpha, beta, nu, rho)
    w = weights(strike,tenor,yearfrac);
% replication weights
    swaptions = receiverSwaptionSABR(fs, strike, ...
        maturity, tenor, yearfrac, ...
        alpha, beta, nu, rho);                  % swaption prices
    value = w*swaptions(1:end-1)';              % floorlet
end
```

Figure 1.20   Code for implementing the replication method for CMS caplets and floorlets. The functions payerSwaptionSABR and receiverSwaptionSABR are implemented by using the SABR model

- Historical Data (time series).
- Quoted Option Prices.
- Liquid Options / Illiquid Options.
- Broker Prices for Exotics.

Often there is not a particularly good choice of quotes. Thus, the modeller has to rely on the data that are available. For things which can go wrong by choosing raw market data the reader is referred to Kienitz, J., Wetterau, D. and Wittke, M. (2011).

1.6 SUMMARY AND CONCLUSIONS

In this chapter we have reviewed market observable data from the financial markets. We identified several notions of volatility and we observed that the Gaussian modelling assumption, which is ubiquitous in modelling, is not adequate. Finally, we identified several applications such as asset allocation, pricing and hedging where the application of sophisticated models is needed. We argued that the following steps are crucial for correct modelling:

- Market Data.
- Model Choice.
- Calibration.
- Pricing.
- Hedging / Risk Management.

Assessing the market data and undertaking a statistical analysis on which the model choice is based is crucial. To be able to use complex mathematical models with confidence, appropriate numerical algorithms are necessary. We have written this book to cover such algorithms for a wide range of models. We provide well-known and widely applied models that are capable of modelling the market observable structures. The models can be efficiently and effectively implemented. Our choice here is Matlab, for which we provide source code for all the examples discussed in this book. In this way it is possible to extend the classical applications to much more complex models. We show the impact of parameters for each model and describe all the numerical techniques in detail. Using the source code the reader can try out the models and test if the implementation is efficient and stable enough for proprietary applications.

1.7 APPENDIX – QUOTES

Tables 1.1, 1.2, 1.3 and 1.4 give examples for market quotes for interest rate options, equity options or foreign exchange options. Such market quotes can be applied to infer model parameters, test models and numerical methods.

Table 1.1 Market quotes for the spread over 3M-Euribor for constant maturity swaps (CMS). This spread reflects the convexity adjustment

Swap	2Y Index	5Y Index	10Y Index	20Y Index	30Y Index
5Y	51.7/57.7	100.7/109.7	147.9/157.9	154.6/174.6	139.1/164.1
10Y	45.5/51.5	81.6/90.6	117.0/127.0	107.2/127.2	97.8/122.8
15Y	40.5/46.5	66.2/75.2	91.1/101.1	82.6/102.6	79.2/104.2
20Y	35.6/41.6	56.7/65.7	71.1/91.1	79.8/99.8	77.7/107.7

Table 1.2 Market quotes for CMS spread options quoted as caps (Cap) or floors (Flr)

	FWD	ATM	Flr −0.25	Flr −0.10	Flr 0.00	Cap 0.25	Cap 0.50	Cap 0.75	Cap 1.00	Cap 1.50
1y	1.33	27.4	0.7	0.8	0.9	82.8	64.7	47.1	30.8	8.1
2y	1.28	82.1	5.0	5.8	6.4	188.1	147.4	108.5	73.0	24.1
3y	1.17	150.3	11.3	13.3	14.8	269.7	209.1	152.8	103.0	36.6
4y	1.05	228.6	21.6	25.3	28.3	333.9	256.3	185.8	125.5	46.9
5y	0.96	311.9	35.8	41.9	46.7	389.7	297.3	215.0	145.9	57.3
7y	0.83	490.1	74.9	86.7	95.9	497.3	378.7	275.4	190.6	82.5
10y	0.71	777.4	157.7	178.7	194.9	650.0	498.4	369.0	264.5	131.4
15y	0.50	1293.8	351.7	394.8	427.6	826.4	643.7	490.2	367.2	208.4
20y	0.39	1743.8	533.4	596.6	643.6	995.8	785.4	608.3	465.3	275.8

Table 1.3 Market quotes for implied volatility for the German DAX index. The implied volatilities are quoted for different levels of moneyness K/S and maturity T. We use a model which is calibrated to bid/ask prices of quoted option prices and then calculate an implied volatility surface for pricing

T/M	0.5	1.0	1.5	2.0	2.5	3.0	3.5	4.0	4.5	5.0
50%	39.29%	36.44%	34.64%	33.52%	32.50%	31.93%	31.57%	31.35%	31.15%	31.05%
60%	37.37%	34.31%	32.68%	31.79%	30.99%	30.59%	30.37%	30.28%	30.17%	30.16%
70%	34.61%	31.90%	30.59%	30.01%	29.46%	29.26%	29.18%	29.21%	29.20%	29.28%
80%	31.13%	29.27%	28.42%	28.20%	27.94%	27.93%	28.00%	28.15%	28.25%	28.42%
90%	27.15%	26.50%	26.22%	26.41%	26.43%	26.62%	26.84%	27.11%	27.31%	27.56%
100%	22.97%	23.70%	24.03%	24.64%	24.97%	25.34%	25.70%	26.10%	26.39%	26.73%
110%	19.06%	20.97%	21.90%	22.94%	23.55%	24.10%	24.60%	25.12%	25.50%	25.91%
120%	17.00%	18.75%	19.98%	21.33%	22.19%	22.91%	23.54%	24.16%	24.63%	25.12%
130%	16.75%	17.50%	18.54%	19.97%	20.97%	21.79%	22.52%	23.25%	23.79%	24.35%
140%	16.75%	17.13%	17.68%	18.93%	19.94%	20.80%	21.60%	22.39%	22.99%	23.60%
150%	16.75%	17.12%	17.31%	18.23%	19.13%	19.97%	20.78%	21.61%	22.25%	22.90%

Table 1.4   Market quotes of the swaption smile

	Receivers −150	−100	−50	−25	ATM	Payers +25	+50	+100	+150
1m2y	41.42	15.27	5.20	2.23	47.94	−0.71	−0.91	−0.43	0.58
1m5y	32.22	17.48	7.54	3.52	40.64	−2.24	−3.84	−5.44	−5.60
1m10y	21.95	12.80	5.74	2.68	32.34	−1.82	−3.15	−4.45	−4.47
1m20y	22.24	13.68	6.48	3.11	30.90	−2.47	−4.57	−7.45	−8.52
1m30y	31.54	20.48	10.92	5.83	34.12	−3.19	−6.05	−10.4	−12.4
3m2y	39.58	15.43	5.74	2.51	48.12	−1.31	−2.17	−2.98	−3.06
3m5y	20.16	9.94	3.77	1.61	38.64	−0.77	−1.16	−1.15	−0.57
3m10y	16.66	9.35	3.91	1.77	30.21	−1.40	−2.44	−3.57	−3.75
3m20y	17.44	10.38	4.66	2.22	28.32	−1.95	−3.59	−5.83	−6.74
3m30y	20.12	12.17	5.51	2.50	30.90	−2.21	−4.12	−6.92	−8.32
6m2y	32.83	13.90	5.13	2.21	48.13	−1.50	−2.63	−4.05	−4.72
6m5y	21.18	11.10	4.43	1.97	37.33	−1.52	−2.65	−3.92	−4.28
6m10y	14.89	8.32	3.45	1.55	29.18	−1.21	−2.10	−3.04	−3.16
6m20y	14.65	8.60	3.80	1.80	27.23	−1.59	−2.91	−4.72	−5.51
6m30y	15.41	9.17	4.10	1.92	29.75	−1.64	−3.03	−5.07	−6.14
9m2y	28.13	12.23	4.53	1.98	47.18	−1.49	−2.64	−4.18	−5.03
9m5y	16.61	8.75	3.55	1.60	35.62	−1.29	−2.32	−3.71	−4.41
9m10y	13.31	7.45	3.11	1.41	28.58	−1.12	−1.98	−2.98	−3.26
9m20y	12.58	7.38	3.29	1.56	26.61	−1.36	−2.50	−4.17	−5.07
9m30y	13.49	7.94	3.53	1.66	28.67	−1.46	−2.71	−4.62	−5.74
1y2y	24.66	11.11	4.13	1.80	45.97	−1.46	−2.59	−4.12	−4.96
1y5y	14.98	7.97	3.25	1.47	34.41	−1.19	−2.14	−3.43	−4.11
1y10y	12.13	6.85	2.86	1.28	27.89	−1.05	−1.88	−2.94	−3.39
1y20y	11.92	6.96	3.03	1.40	26.05	−1.20	−2.19	−3.47	−4.07
1y30y	12.89	7.54	3.32	1.55	27.90	−1.35	−2.50	−4.22	−5.19
2y2y	14.15	7.16	2.80	1.24	37.32	−1.11	−1.99	−3.21	−3.84
2y5y	11.08	6.11	2.52	1.14	29.49	−0.94	−1.68	−2.71	−3.24
2y10y	9.23	5.27	2.24	1.02	25.35	−0.85	−1.54	−2.58	−3.30
2y20y	9.25	5.37	2.31	1.06	24.32	−0.90	−1.66	−2.75	−3.29
2y30y	10.24	5.94	2.63	1.23	25.74	−1.05	−1.92	−3.25	−4.00
5y2y	7.69	4.28	1.80	0.80	24.38	−0.61	−1.06	−1.52	−1.58
5y5y	7.33	4.14	1.74	0.79	21.97	−0.62	−1.09	−1.71	−1.91
5y10y	6.83	3.93	1.69	0.78	20.71	−0.64	−1.14	−1.77	−2.02
5y20y	8.04	4.57	1.91	0.86	20.90	−0.66	−1.16	−1.71	−1.79
5y30y	8.27	4.70	1.99	0.91	22.19	−0.78	−1.39	−2.13	−2.38
10y2y	4.99	2.89	1.28	0.58	18.15	−0.46	−0.82	−1.24	−1.36
10y5y	5.28	3.02	1.28	0.58	17.92	−0.47	−0.83	−1.28	−1.44
10y10y	6.54	3.71	1.52	0.65	18.81	−0.49	−0.87	−1.33	−1.46
10y20y	7.30	4.09	1.68	0.75	19.44	−0.58	−1.01	−1.50	−1.62
10y30y	7.70	4.31	1.78	0.80	19.65	−0.63	−1.10	−1.63	−1.75

2

Diffusion Models

2.1 INTRODUCTION AND OBJECTIVES

This chapter deals with financial models based on diffusion processes. Such models are represented by a stochastic differential equation driven by a Brownian motion. Many well-known financial models are based on the assumption of a diffusion process. We consider three classes of models: *Local Volatility Models (LVM)*, *Stochastic Volatility Models (SVM)* and *Stochastic Rates, Stochastic Volatility Models (SRSVM)*.

After describing the three main classes we have selected some well-known representatives of each class. Our choice is motivated by what we believe are widely applied models or are those especially suitable for illustrating certain modelling facts. We consider the following models in detail:

- Bachelier and Black–Scholes Model (Normal / Geometric Brownian Motion).
- Hull–White Model (Ornstein–Uhlenbeck Process).
- Displaced Diffusion Model (DD Model).
- Constant Elasticity of Variance Model (CEV Model).
- Heston Model (HSV Model).
- Stochastic-α, β, ρ Model (SABR Model).
- Heston–Hull–White Model (HHW Model).

Our approach is to describe each model in terms of the model parameters and their impact on modelling the market. To do this we consider the risk neutral density, the implied volatility (skew/smile), typical paths and modelled returns. We also consider the pricing of simple options which are used for calibrating a model. By calibration we mean a method to retrieve model parameters from quoted market prices. We either give analytic formulae, approximation formulae or the characteristic function which can be used to compute the price numerically.

The code to produce all the figures is provided in the supporting material for this book.

2.2 LOCAL VOLATILITY MODELS

In this subsection we consider the class of *Local Volatility Models (LVM)*. Let us take an interval $I \subset \mathbb{R}^+$ and a function $\sigma_L : I \times \mathbb{R} \to \mathbb{R}^+$. A local volatility model is represented by the following stochastic differential equation:

$$dS(t) = \sigma_L(t, S(t))dW(t) \qquad (2.1)$$

$$S(0) = S_0.$$

Success in applying LVM can be traced back to the work of Dupire, B. (1994) and Derman, E. and Kani, I. (1994). They realized that under the assumption of risk neutrality a unique state-dependent diffusion process can be constructed which is consistent with all market prices for European options where these are quoted. The diffusion coefficient σ_L of the process is a function of state and time.

- Local Volatility does not represent a model of how volatilities actually evolve.
- Local volatilities should be thought of as representing some kind of average over all possible instantaneous volatilities in a stochastic volatility environment.
- Local Volatility models are the simplest models that permit pricing of exotic options consistent with the known vanilla prices.
- Since only a finite number of options is quoted inter- and extrapolation are necessary and therefore the method depends on the applied numerical methods.

We briefly review the approach of Dupire, B. (1994) since it clarifies the concept of (local) volatility. Let us fix a maturity T and the current spot price S_0. Further, we assume, albeit wrongly, that there is a collection of European Call option prices $\{C(K, t)\}$ for all possible strike levels $K \in (0, +\infty)$ and time points $t \in (0, T)$ available. Then, from these prices by using (1.3) it is possible to recover the risk neutral density.

We summarize the main formulae illustrating the relationship between local volatilities, implied volatilities and European Call option prices. The results with further discussions and proofs can be found, for example, in Gatheral, J. (2006), Rebonato, R. (2004) or Andersen, L. and Piterbarg, V. (2010a, b and c). For a fixed spot price $S(0) = S_0$ and by denoting the price of a European Call option with strike K and maturity T by $C(K, T)$, we have the following relationship between prices, $C(K, T)$, and the local volatility, $\sigma(K, T)$:

$$\sigma_L^2(K, T) = \frac{2}{K^2} \frac{\frac{\partial C(K,T)}{\partial T}}{\frac{\partial C(K,T)}{\partial K^2}}. \tag{2.2}$$

Equation (2.2) serves as a definition of local volatility for any asset price model. Since the right hand side of the equation only takes Call prices as the input, we can relate implied Black volatilities, denoted by $\sigma_{BS}(K, T)$ to the local volatility diffusion coefficient $\sigma_L(K, T)$ by:

$$\sigma_L^2(K, T) = \frac{\frac{\partial V}{\partial T}}{1 - \frac{y}{V} \frac{\partial V}{\partial y} + \frac{1}{4}\left(-\frac{1}{4} - \frac{1}{V} + \frac{y^2}{V^2}\right)\left(\frac{\partial V}{\partial y}\right)^2 + \frac{1}{2}\frac{\partial^2 V}{\partial y}}, \tag{2.3}$$

where we used $V = \sigma_{BS}^2(K, T)T$ and $y = \log(K/S(T))$. Equation (2.3) is a reformulation of Equation (2.2).

Another relationship for the implied volatility is remarkable. The Call prices, $C(K, T)$, and the implied variance which is the squared implied volatility, $\sigma_{BS}^2(K, T)$, are related by

$$C(K, T) = S - \frac{\sqrt{SK}}{\pi} \int_0^\infty \mathcal{R}\left(e^{iuk}e^{-\frac{1}{2}(u^2+\frac{1}{4})\sigma_{BS}^2 T}\right) \frac{1}{u^2 + \frac{1}{4}} du. \tag{2.4}$$

We have seen that in principle it would be possible to recover the local volatility surface from market quotes. However, this requires a continuum of option prices but in practice only a small number of prices around the current forward price, known as the ATM price, are quoted and can be used to set up the local volatility surface. Thus, this concept relies on the interpolation and extrapolation method applied by the modeller. To this end practitioners tend to use parametric models. We consider the following parametric version of the LVM, called the *separable approach*:

$$dS(t) = (r - d)dt + \lambda(t)f(S(t))dW(t) \tag{2.5}$$

$$S(0) = S_0.$$

In Equation (2.5) the diffusion coefficient σ_L from Equation (2.1) is replaced by a function f depending only on the current price of the asset. Typical choices are $f(x) = x^\beta$, $f(x) = (x + a)$ or $f(x) = (x + a)^\beta$.

These choices lead to tractable models. While for both modelling approaches closed form valuation formulae are available, the displaced diffusion version is also easy to sample. The latter is a nice feature if we wish to apply Monte Carlo simulation for pricing exotic options or to use scenario-based risk analysis.

Often the separable approach given in Equation (2.5) is too restrictive and fitting market observable data needs more flexibility. To this end we apply a functional form for σ_L. A flexible choice is $\sigma_L(t, x) := (x + a(t))^{\beta(t)}$. The local volatility in this case depends on time since the $a : \mathbb{R}^+ \rightarrow \mathbb{R}$ and $\beta : \mathbb{R}^+ \rightarrow \mathbb{R}$ are functions of time and space. This approach reflects the timely change of parameters and allows for greater flexibility. The price to pay is that the valuation formulae are more involved. We cover the valuation in Section 4.5, when we deal with *Markovian Projection* and *Parameter Averaging*.

2.2.1 The Bachelier and the Black–Scholes Model

In this section we consider two simple choices for $\sigma_L(t, S)$, namely $\sigma_L(t, S) := \sigma_B$ and $\sigma_L(t, S) := \sigma_{BS}S(t)$. The choices lead to the *Bachelier* and to the *Black–Scholes* models. The Bachelier model can be characterized in terms of its stochastic differential equation. It is given by

$$dS(t) = \mu S(t)dt + \sigma_B dW(t) \tag{2.6}$$

$$S(0) = S_0.$$

In Black, F. and Scholes, M. (1973) the authors consider the following model for an asset price dynamic:

$$dS(t) = \mu S(t)dt + \sigma_{BS}S(t)dW(t) \tag{2.7}$$

$$S(0) = S_0.$$

The numbers σ_B and σ_{BS} are positive real numbers, $\mu := r - d$ is the drift coefficient, r is the riskless rate and d is the dividend yield. The Bachelier and the Black–Scholes models can be seen as simple local volatility models.

There is a one-to-one relationship between the model parameters called volatility, σ_B, respectively σ_{BS}, and Call option prices. The volatility does not depend on the current value of the spot price or on any other market variable. Therefore, it is common practice to quote option prices in terms of implied normal volatility or implied log-normal volatility.

Pricing Formulae

For European Call and Put option prices there are analytic pricing formulae available. In the case of the Bachelier model denoting the spot price by $S(0)$:

$$C(K,T) = \left(S(0)e^{-dT} - e^{-rT}K\right)\mathcal{N}(d_1) + \sigma_B\sqrt{T}n(d_1) \tag{2.8}$$

$$P(K,T) = \left(S(0)e^{-dT} - e^{-rT}K\right)\mathcal{N}(-d_1) + \sigma_B\sqrt{T}n(d_1), \tag{2.9}$$

with the abbreviation

$$d_1 = \frac{S(0)\exp((r-d)T) - K}{\sigma\sqrt{T}}$$

and $\mathcal{N}(\cdot)$ denotes the cumulative normal distribution and $n(\cdot)$ the corresponding probability density. For the Black–Scholes model we have:

$$C(K,T) = S(0)e^{-dT}\mathcal{N}(d_1) - e^{-rT}K\mathcal{N}(d_2) \tag{2.10}$$

$$P(K,T) = S(0)e^{-dT}\mathcal{N}(-d_1) - e^{-rT}K\mathcal{N}(-d_2), \tag{2.11}$$

where we used

$$d_1 = \frac{\log\left(\frac{S(0)}{K}\right) + (r - d + \frac{\sigma^2}{2})T}{\sigma\sqrt{T}}; \quad d_2 = d_1 - \frac{\sigma^2}{2}T.$$

Pricing in the Bachelier Model   The price of a European Call option in the Bachelier model can also be computed by

$$C(K,T) = \begin{cases} (S-K)^+ + \frac{|S-K|}{4\sqrt{\pi}}\tilde{\gamma}\left(-\frac{1}{2}, \frac{(S-K)^2}{2\sigma_B^2 T}\right) & \text{if } S \neq K \\ (S-K)^+ + \frac{\sigma_B\sqrt{T}}{\sqrt{2\pi}} & \text{otherwise} \end{cases}.$$

In the pricing formula $\tilde{\gamma}(a, b)$ denotes the upper incomplete Γ-function which corresponds to the Matlab function 1-gammainc(a,b) with gammainc being the incomplete Γ-function. For the function gammainc there is also an inverse called gammaincinv.

Thus, it is also possible to analytically determine the implied normal volatility from prices using the Matlab function gammaincinv.

Risk Neutral Density

The risk neutral densities corresponding to the Bachelier and Black–Scholes models respectively are the Gaussian (or Normal) and the logarithmic Normal density with volatility σ_B and σ_{BS} respectively. Figure 2.1 shows the effect of changing the volatility parameter on the risk neutral density. Here, we consider the parameter set $T = 5$, $r = d = 0$, $S(0) = 100$ and $\sigma_B = 0.02$ for the Bachelier model and $T = 3$, $r = d = 0$, $S(0) = 100$ and $\sigma_{BS} = 0.2$ for the Black–Scholes model. These parameters serve as the base scenario.

For both models the effect of increasing the volatility is that the probability density becomes more widespread on the state space. Decreasing the volatility leads to concentration around the mean and therefore the distribution becomes more peaked.

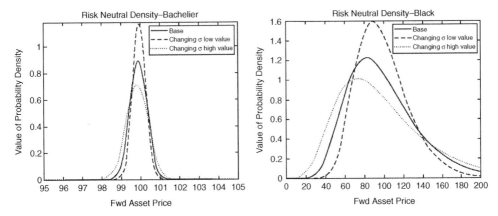

Figure 2.1 Density for the Bachelier (left) model with $T = 5$, $r = d = 0$ and different values of $\sigma_B = 0.015, 0.02, 0.025$ and the Black–Scholes model (right) with $T = 3$, $r = d = 0$ and different values of $\sigma_{BS} = 0.15, 0.2, 0.25$

Typical Paths and Returns

The paths generated by the Bachelier and the Black–Scholes models are almost surely continuous. In what follows we consider the effect of changing the volatility. To this end we fix the random numbers used to generate a particular sample path for the model. Then, we change the volatility parameter. Figure 2.2 shows that the random shocks used to generate the paths are leveraged by the volatility parameter. The higher the value of the volatility the noisier the generated paths appear. This is easy to see when we suppose the random shock generated by considering a Gaussian variate is of size z. Then, for two values $\sigma_1 < \sigma_2$ we have $\sigma_1|z| < \sigma_2|z|$. Thus, the effect of the random movement is scaled by the size of the volatility parameter. This effect not only explains the behaviour of the paths shown in Figure 2.2 but, moreover, that for the logarithmic returns shown in Figure 2.3.

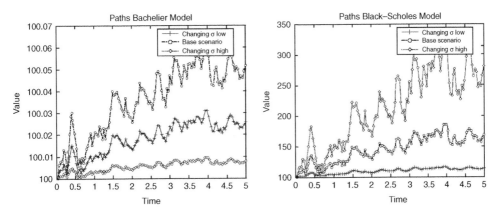

Figure 2.2 Generated paths – Bachelier model (left) for different values of $\sigma_B = 0.01, 0.02, 0.03$ and the Black–Scholes model (right) for different values of $\sigma_{BS} = 0.05, 0.2, 0.4$

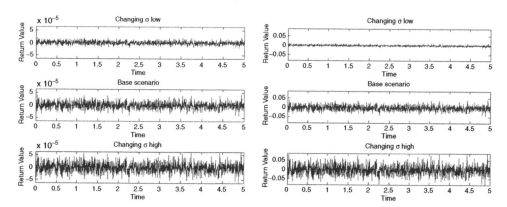

Figure 2.3 Generated Return Time Series – Bachelier model (left) for different values of $\sigma_B = 0.01, 0.02, 0.03$ and Black–Scholes model (right) for different values of $\sigma_{BS} = 0.05, 0.2, 0.4$

Skew and Smile

There is only one degree of freedom for both the Bachelier and the Black–Scholes models, (2.6) and (2.7). But we observe that there is no skew in the Black–model but only for the Bachelier model. Figure 2.4 shows the implied volatility surface generate by the Black–Scholes model.

2.2.2   The Hull–White Model

In Chapter 1 we reviewed several market data which led us to consider models other than the simple Bachelier and Black–Scholes models. In particular, practitioners have used mean reverting models to reflect the long-time convergence observed in certain markets, for example volatility and interest rates. This leads to consideration of multi-dimensional models with random drivers for the interest rate, the equity and the volatility. We consider a mean reverting

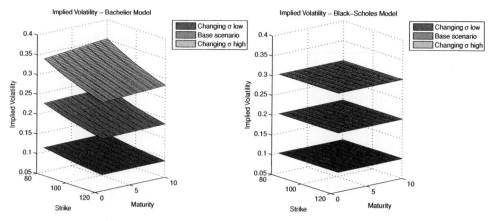

Figure 2.4 The implied volatility surface for the Bachelier model (left) and the Black–Scholes model (right). We have taken $T = 1, \ldots, 10$, $K = 80, \ldots, 120$ and $\sigma_B = 10, 20, 30$, respectively $\sigma_B = 0.1, 0.2, 0.3$

process for modelling interest rates. To this end we consider the Hull–White model for the *short rate* and show how to price some interest rate options.

Stochastic Differential Equation

We start with a model often applied for modelling the short rate dynamic. Suppose we consider the evolution of a bank account B over time starting at $B(0) = 1$. Usually, it is assumed that the bank account evolves due to

$$dB(t) = r(t)B(t)dt.$$

This ordinary differential equation has the solution

$$B(t) = \exp\left(\int_0^t r(s)ds\right). \tag{2.12}$$

Thus, investing one unit of currency at time 0 is worth $B(t)$ at time t. The stochastic variable $r(t)$ describes the instantaneous yield on the bank account. The process r is called the short rate.

The model we consider now is the Hull–White model and it is given by the following SDE:

$$dr(t) = \lambda(\theta(t) - r(t))dt + \eta dW(t) \tag{2.13}$$

$$r(0) = r_0. \tag{2.14}$$

The parameter λ is the mean reversion speed and determines how fast a diverging behaviour from θ of the process r is penalized and pulled back towards θ. The function θ is used to recover the initial term structure of interest rates at time 0. The volatility parameter is given by the positive number η. In fact, the short rate r can become negative with positive probability given by

$$\mathcal{N}\left(-\frac{f^M(0,t) + \frac{\eta^2}{2\lambda^2}\left(1 - e^{-\lambda t}\right)^2}{\sqrt{\frac{\eta^2}{2\lambda}\left[1 - e^{-2\lambda t}\right]}}\right).$$

The function $f^M(\cdot)$ will be introduced later. It is related to the current quoted market prices for interest bearing instruments. The model can be analysed by considering *Ornstein–Uhlenbeck Processes*.

We follow the description in Brigo, D. and Mercurio, F. (2006). Applying Itô's formula to the exponential function we get

$$d(\exp(\lambda t)r(t)) = \lambda \exp(\lambda t)r(t)dt + \exp(\lambda t)dr(t)$$
$$= \lambda \exp(\lambda t)r(t)dt + \exp(\lambda t)(\lambda(\theta(t) - r(t))dt + \exp(\lambda t)\eta dW(t))$$
$$= \exp(\lambda t)(\lambda\theta(t)dt + \eta dW(t)).$$

Integrating, we have

$$r(t) = \exp^{-\lambda(t-s)} r(s) + \lambda \int_s^t \exp^{-\lambda(t-u)} \theta(u)du + \eta \int_s^t \exp^{-\lambda(t-u)} dW_u. \tag{2.15}$$

Since it can be shown that $\lim_{t \to \infty} \mathbb{E}[r(t)|\mathcal{F}_0] = \theta(t)$, the rate r reverts to the initial term structure. It is often convenient to work with the following representation of the short rate r:

$$r(t) = \tilde{r}(t) + \psi(t). \tag{2.16}$$

The *Hull–White decomposition* given by (2.16) is used to represent r in terms of a stochastic part, $\tilde{r}$, and a deterministic one, ψ. We have the following stochastic differential equation for $\tilde{r}$:

$$d\tilde{r}(t) = -\lambda\tilde{r}(t)dt + \eta dW(t); \quad \tilde{r}(0) = 0. \tag{2.17}$$

The latter is a standard mean reverting Ornstein–Uhlenbeck process.

Characteristic Function

Using the representation (2.16) the characteristic function of the model is available in closed form. Denoting $\tau := T - t$ it is given by

$$\varphi_{\text{HW}}(u, t, T) = \exp\left(\int_t^T \psi(s)ds + iu\psi(T)\right)\exp(A(u, \tau) + B(u, \tau)\tilde{r}(t)), \tag{2.18}$$

with functions $A(\cdot, \cdot)$ and $B(\cdot, \cdot)$ given by

$$A(u, \tau) = \frac{\eta^2}{2\lambda^3}\left(\lambda\tau - 2\left(1 - e^{-\lambda\tau}\right) + \frac{1}{2}\left(1 - e^{-2\lambda\tau}\right)\right) - iu\frac{\eta^2}{2\lambda^2}\left(1 - e^{-\lambda\tau}\right)^2$$

$$- \frac{u^2\eta^2}{4\lambda}\left(1 - e^{-2\lambda\tau}\right)$$

$$B(u, \tau) = iue^{-\lambda\tau} - \frac{\left(1 - e^{-\lambda\tau}\right)}{\lambda}.$$

Finally, the function $\psi(\cdot)$ is given by

$$\psi(t) = e^{-\lambda t}r(0) + \lambda\int_0^t e^{-\lambda(t-s)}\theta(s)ds$$

$$\psi(T) = f^M(0, T) + \frac{\eta^2}{2\lambda^2}\left(1 - e^{-\lambda T}\right)^2,$$

where we again used the instantaneous forward rate f^M which can be calculated from market observed zero coupon bonds P^M by the following equation:

$$f^M(0, t) := -\frac{\partial \log(P^M(0, t))}{\partial t}.$$

We have used the superscript f^M to denote that we have calculated the instantaneous forward rate from market quoted rates. But $P(t, T)$ can also be given by some models. In this case we denote the forward rate simply by f.

The forward rate is given as the conditional expectation in the T-forward measure of the short rate $r(t)$. We have

$$\mathbb{E}^T[r(T)|\mathcal{F}_t] = f(t, T).$$

As described above, the function $\theta(t)$ is used to match the initial term structure. To achieve the fit we set

$$\theta(t) = f(0,t) + \frac{1}{\lambda}\frac{\partial}{\partial t}f(0,t) + \frac{\eta^2}{2\lambda^2}\left(1 - e^{-2\lambda t}\right). \tag{2.19}$$

The initial term structure is the spot term structure for zero coupon bonds calculated from market quoted interest rates. Such rates include money market rates such as Euribor, Libor or swap rates, but any interest bearing instrument can be used. FRA rates and futures are popular with market participants. The algorithm for calculating the discount or zero curve is called *stripping the curve*. See Kienitz, J., Wetterau, D. and Wittke, M. (forthcoming) for details.

We have implemented the function in Matlab using the code given in Figure 2.5. We highlight the use of an interest rate curve which is given by the variable `ircurve` which is an input to the characteristic function. This input is necessary to determine the function θ.

Risk Neutral Density

Let $f : \Omega \times [s,t] \longrightarrow \mathbb{R}$ be Itô integrable and deterministic; this means that it does not depend on the variable $\omega \in \Omega$ and is in fact a function $f(\omega, \cdot) : [s,t] \to \mathbb{R}$. Then, we find for the distribution

$$\int_s^t f(u)dW_u \sim \mathcal{N}\left(0, \int_s^t f^2(u)du\right).$$

Thus, we find for the conditional expectation for $R(t)$ given $\mathcal{F}_s$:

$$\mathbb{E}[r(t) \mid \mathcal{F}_s] = \exp^{-\lambda(t-s)} r(s) + \lambda \int_s^t \exp^{-\lambda(t-u)} \theta(u)du \tag{2.20}$$

$$\mathbb{V}[r(t) \mid \mathcal{F}_s] = \frac{\eta^2}{2\lambda}\left(1 - \exp^{-2\lambda(t-s)}\right). \tag{2.21}$$

We are in a position to compute the risk neutral density for the model using the normal distribution. Figure 2.6 summarizes the effect of changing the model parameters η, λ and the yield curve.

Pricing Formulae

Since the Hull–White model is applied to term structure modelling we give the basic formulae for pricing zero coupon bonds and Caps and Floors.

Zero Bond In order to compute zero bond values we have to know the distribution of the integrated short rate process given by $R_{t,T} = \int_t^T r(u)du \mid \mathcal{F}_t$. Here we use the fact that integrated Gaussian processes are Gaussian again. The parameters are

$$\mathbb{E}[R_{t,T} \mid \mathcal{F}_t] = B(t,T)(r(t) - \psi_t) + \log\left(\frac{P^M(0,t)}{P^M(0,T)}\right) + \frac{1}{2}(V(0,T) - V(0,t)) \tag{2.22}$$

```
function phi = cf_hullwhite(u,T,lambda,eta,ircurve)
% Hull White
    %maturity dates
    date_t = add2date(ircurve.Settle,0);
    date_T = add2date(ircurve.Settle,T);

    %time to maturity
    tau_0_T = diag(yearfrac(ircurve.Settle,date_T));
    %CURRENTLY equals zero
    tau_0_t = diag(yearfrac(ircurve.Settle,date_t));
    %CURRENTLY equal tau_0_T
    tau_t_T = diag(yearfrac(date_t,date_T));

    %used for short rate and  instantaneous forward rate calculations
    Delta = 1e-6;
    P0_T = ircurve.getDiscountFactors(date_T);
    %CURRENTLY P(0,t) equals one since t = 0
    P0_t = 1.0;
    P0_t_plus_Delta = interp1([ircurve.Settle;ircurve.Dates],...
        [1.0;ircurve.Data],datenum(date_t+Delta),'linear');

    %short rate
    instR = (1.0/P0_t_plus_Delta-1)...
      /yearfrac(ircurve.Settle,datenum(date_t+Delta));
    %instantaneous forward rate
    instF = -(P0_t_plus_Delta - P0_t)...
      /yearfrac(ircurve.Settle,datenum(date_t+Delta))./P0_t;

    %auxiliary variables
    aux = eta*eta/lambda/lambda;
    sigma2_func = @(t)aux*(t + (exp(-lambda*t)...
        .*(2.0 - 0.5*exp(-lambda*t))-1.5)/lambda);
    B_t_T = (1.0-exp(-lambda*tau_t_T))/lambda;
    %CURRENTLY psi_t = instantaneous forward rate since tau_0_t = 0
    psi_t = instF + .5*aux*(1-exp(-lambda*tau_0_t)).^2;

    %variance of integrated short rate
    sigma2_R = feval(sigma2_func,tau_t_T);

    %mean of integrated short rate
    mu_R = B_t_T.*(instR - psi_t) + diag(log(P0_t./P0_T)) ...
        + 0.5*(feval(sigma2_func,tau_0_T) - feval(sigma2_func,tau_0_t));

    phi = 1i*u*mu_R - 0.5*u.*u*sigma2_R;
end
```

Figure 2.5 The log-characteristic function for the Hull–White model

and with

$$V(t,T) = \mathbb{V}[R_{t,T} \mid \mathcal{F}_t]$$

$$\mathbb{V}[R_{t,T} \mid \mathcal{F}_t] = \frac{\eta^2}{\lambda^2}\left(T - t + \frac{2}{\lambda}e^{-\lambda(T-t)} - \frac{1}{2\lambda}e^{-2\lambda(T-t)} - \frac{3}{2\lambda}\right). \quad (2.23)$$

Then, the zero bond is given by

$$P(t,T) = A(t,T)\exp(-B(t,T)r(t)), \quad (2.24)$$

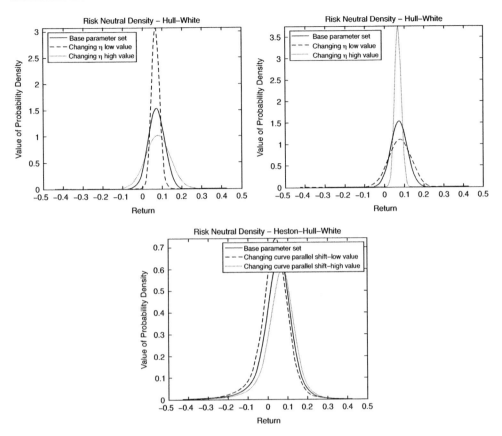

Figure 2.6 Risk neutral density for the returns using $T = 10$, spot value of $S(0) = 100$ and different values for the mean reversion speed $\lambda = 0.05, 0.1, 0.5$ (top left), different values for the volatility of variance $\eta = 0.01, 0.02, 0.03$ (top right) and for the initial term structure by -1bp, 0bp and $+1$bp (bottom)

with functions A and B

$$A(t, T) := \frac{P^M(0, T)}{P^M(0, t)} \exp\left(B(t, T) f^M(0, t) - \frac{\eta^2}{4\lambda}(1 - \exp(-2\lambda t))B(t, T)^2 \right)$$

$$B(t, T) := \frac{1}{\lambda}(1 - \exp(-\lambda(T - t))).$$

This formula can be implemented using the model parameters as well as the necessary computations using a yield curve.

Caps and Floors   It is possible to use the characteristic function (2.18) for pricing, but it is much more convenient to use analytic formulae. Such formulae are available for pricing caps and floors. Thus, let $\mathcal{T} := \{t_0, \ldots, t_N = T\}$ be a discretization of $[0, T]$.

$$Cap(K, T) = \sum_{i=1}^{N} [P(t, t_{i-1})\mathcal{N}(-h_i + \eta_i) - (1 + K\tau_i)P(t, t_i)\mathcal{N}(-h_i)],$$

with the volatility

$$\eta_i = \eta \sqrt{\frac{1 - \exp(-2\lambda(t_{i-1} - t))}{2\lambda}} B(t_i - 1, t_i)$$

$$h_i = \frac{1}{\eta_i} \log \left(\frac{P(t, t_i)(1 + K\tau_i)}{P(t, t_{i-1})} \right) + \frac{\eta_i}{2}.$$

The corresponding value for the floor is

$$Floor(K, T) = \sum_{i=1}^{N} [P(t, t_i)\mathcal{N}(h_i) - (1 + K\tau_i)P(t, t_{i-1})\mathcal{N}(h_i - \eta_i)].$$

Each caplet is a Put option, and each floorlet is a Call option on a zero coupon bond.

Typical Paths and Returns

We omit presentation of the sample paths since the model is driven by a Brownian motion and the model parameters are fixed. Thus, we expect that typical sample paths and returns are very similar to the Bachelier and Black–Scholes models.

2.2.3   The Constant Elasticity of Variance Model

Another popular model is covered in Schroder, M. (1989) and Andersen, L. and Andreasen, J. (2000). This model is known as the *Constant Elasticity of Variance* model, or *CEV* model for short. It is determined by the SDE (2.25).

$$dS(t) = \mu S(t)dt + \sigma_{CEV} S(t)^\beta dW(t) \tag{2.25}$$

$$S(0) = S_0.$$

Comparing this model to the Black–Scholes or the Bachelier model we observe that there is an additional parameter. The exponent β is called the CEV exponent. To further illustrate the properties of the CEV model we consider the transformation (see Schroder, M. (1989)) of the model to a squared Bessel process, given by

$$dZ(t) = 2\sqrt{Z(t)}dW(t) + \delta dt.$$

The latter process has been studied in depth by mathematicians and its properties carry over to the CEV model. The transformation suggested by Schroder, M. (1989) is firstly transform $S(t)$ to $X(t) = S(t)^{1-\beta}/(1 - \beta)$, set $Y(t) = X(t)^2$. This leads to a time-changed squared Bessel process of dimension $\delta = (1 - 2\beta)/(1 - \beta)$. Finally, consider the time change $v(t) = \sigma_{CEV}^2 t$ which leads to $Y(t) = Z(v(t))$. Let us briefly summarize the relationship in terms of the parameter β. The parameter range for β in the CEV model, $-\infty < \beta < \frac{1}{2}$, $\frac{1}{2} \leq \beta < 1$ and $\beta > 1$, corresponds to $0 < \delta < 2$, $-\infty < \delta \leq 0$ and $2 < \delta < \infty$, which is the parameter range for δ in the squared Bessel process.

- The solutions are non-explosive.
- For $\delta < 2$, $Z = 0$ is an attainable boundary.
- For $\delta \geq 2$ it has a unique solution and zero is not attainable.

- For $0 < \delta < 2$ it does not have a unique solution unless a boundary condition has been specified for the solution $Z = 0$.
- For $\delta \leq 0$ there is a unique strong solution and 0 is an absorbing boundary.

Furthermore, for the process Z, the transition density and the cumulative density are known in closed form. We use the fact that

$$S(t) = \left((1 - \beta)\sqrt{Z(v(t))} \right)^{1/(1-\beta)}.$$

Thus, using the transformation $h : s \mapsto ((1 - \beta)\sqrt{s})^{1/(1-\beta)}$ with inverse $h^{-1} = s^{2(1-\beta)}/(1 - \beta)^2$, then $S(t) = h(Z(t))$ and we get for the density, for given spot price $S(0)$.

$$p(S(t)|S(0)) = q^\delta(v(t), Z(0), h^{-1}(s)) \frac{dh^{-1}(s)}{dS}.$$

Further considerations can be found in Chen, B., Oosterlee, C.W. and van der Weide, H. (2010).

Applications The CEV dynamics is often applied to model the skew in Libor Market Models (see Andersen, L. and Andreasen, J. (2000)). Let us consider the dynamics of the forward rate $F_i(t)$ in the *spot measure*:

$$dF_i(t) = F_i(t)^\beta \sigma_{i,\text{CEV}}(t) \sum_{k=0}^{i} \frac{\tau_k F_k(t)^\beta \left(\sigma_k^{\text{CEV}} \right)^T}{1 + \tau_k F_k(t)} dt$$

$$+ F_i(t)^\beta \sigma_{i,\text{CEV}}(t) dW_{\text{Spot}}(t).$$

Pricing Formulae

It is possible to derive a pricing formula for European Calls and Puts. We set $v := \frac{1}{2(1-\beta)}$ and use the results obtained in Lesniewski, A. (2009) or Chen, B., Oosterlee, C.W. and van der Weide, H. (2010). Then, we have the following formulae for a Call and a Put option respectively and absorbing boundary conditions:

$$C_{\text{absorb}}(K, T) = S(0) \left(1 - \chi_{\text{NC}}^2 \left(\frac{4v^2 K^{1/v}}{\sigma_{\text{CEV}}^2 T}; 2v + 2; \frac{4v^2 S(0)^{1/v}}{\sigma_{\text{CEV}}^2 T} \right) \right) \qquad (2.26)$$

$$-K \chi_{\text{NC}}^2 \left(\frac{4v^2 S(0)^{1/v}}{\sigma_{\text{CEV}}^2 T}; 2v; \frac{4v^2 K^{1/v}}{\sigma_{\text{CEV}}^2 T} \right)$$

$$P_{\text{absorb}}(K, T) = S(0) \chi_{\text{NC}}^2 \left(\frac{4v^2 K^{1/v}}{\sigma_{\text{CEV}}^2 T}; 2v + 2; \frac{4v^2 S(0)^{1/v}}{\sigma_{\text{CEV}}^2 T} \right) \qquad (2.27)$$

$$-K \left(1 - \chi_{\text{NC}}^2 \left(\frac{4v^2 S(0)^{1/v}}{\sigma_{\text{CEV}}^2 T}; 2v; \frac{4v^2 K^{1/v}}{\sigma_{\text{CEV}}^2 T} \right) \right).$$

On the other side for non-absorbing boundaries we have:

$$C_{\text{reflect}}(K, T) = S(0) \chi_{\text{NC}}^2 \left(\frac{4v^2 K^{1/v}}{\sigma_{\text{CEV}}^2 T}; -2v; \frac{4v^2 S(0)^{1/v}}{\sigma_{\text{CEV}}^2 T} \right) \qquad (2.28)$$

$$-K \left(1 - \chi_{\text{NC}}^2 \left(\frac{4v^2 S(0)^{1/v}}{\sigma_{\text{CEV}}^2 T}; -2v + 2; \frac{4v^2 K^{1/v}}{\sigma_{\text{CEV}}^2 T} \right) \right)$$

$$P_{\text{reflect}}(K, T) = S(0) \left(1 - \chi^2_{\text{NC}} \left(\frac{4v^2 K^{1/v}}{\sigma^2_{\text{CEV}} T}; -2v; \frac{4v^2 S(0)^{1/v}}{\sigma^2_{\text{CEV}} T} \right) \right) \qquad (2.29)$$

$$- K \chi^2_{\text{NC}} \left(\frac{4v^2 S(0)^{1/v}}{\sigma^2_{\text{CEV}} T}; -2v + 2; \frac{4v^2 K^{1/v}}{\sigma^2_{\text{CEV}} T} \right).$$

For $\beta < \frac{1}{2}$ and reflecting boundary at 0 the density integrates to 1 but the process is a sub-martingale. However, for absorbing boundary at 0 it does not integrate to 1 but the process is a martingale. To this end to prevent arbitrage almost always the absorbing boundary at 0 is assumed. For $\frac{1}{2} \leq \beta \leq 1$ the process is a martingale.

For the reader's convenience we include the formula for a Call option from Schroder, M. (1989). This formula also accounts for a risk-free rate.

$$C(K, T) = S \left(1 - \chi^2_{\text{NC}} \left(2z, \frac{3 - 2\beta}{1 - \beta}, 2x \right) \right) - K e^{-rT} \chi^2_{\text{NC}} \left(2x, \frac{1}{1 - \beta}, 2z \right) \qquad (2.30)$$

$$k = \frac{2r}{2\sigma^2 (1 - \beta)(\exp(2(1 - \beta)rT) - 1)}$$

$$x = kS^{2(1-\beta)} \exp(2(1 - \beta)rT)$$

$$z = kK^{2(1-\beta)}$$

Let us consider the volatility in the CEV model. Taking the Black–Scholes model we have $\sigma_L = \sigma_{\text{BS}} S(t)$ whereas for the CEV we have $\sigma_L =$. Thus, the CEV volatility is related to Black–Scholes implied volatility by

$$\sigma_{\text{CEV}} = \sigma_{\text{BS}} S(0)^{1-\beta} \qquad (2.31)$$

It is common to determine the CEV implied volatility in terms of the Black–Scholes volatility and use Equation (2.31) to convert to CEV volatility.

Risk Neutral Density

The CEV model can be seen as an arithmetic average of a normal and a logarithmic-normal model. We take $v = 1/2(1 - \beta)$, $\tau = T - t$, $x = S(t)$, $X = S(T)$. Then, for the transition density we have

$$p(X, T; x, t) = \frac{\sqrt{x X^{1-4\beta}}}{(1 - \beta)\sigma^2_{\text{CEV}} \tau} \exp \left(-\frac{x^{2(1-\beta)} + X^{2(1-\beta)}}{2(1 - \beta)^2 \sigma^2_{\text{CEV}} \tau} \right)$$

$$I_v \left(\frac{(xX)^{1-\beta}}{(1 - \beta)^2 \sigma^2_{\text{CEV}} \tau} \right).$$

The function I_v is the modified Bessel function of the first kind given by

$$I_v(z) = \left(\frac{z}{2} \right)^v \sum_{k=0}^{\infty} \frac{(z^2/4)^k}{k! \Gamma(v + k + 1)}.$$

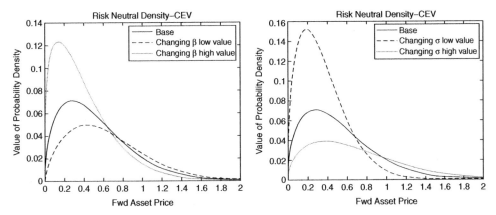

Figure 2.7 Risk neutral density for $T = 10$, spot value of 0.03 and different values of the exponent $\beta = 0.3, 0.5, 0.7$ (left) and different values of the volatility parameter $\sigma_{\text{CEV}} = 0.15, 0.2, 0.25$

Denoting

$$p^* = \frac{1}{2} \left(\frac{x}{\lambda} \right)^{(r-2)/4} \exp\left(-\frac{x + \lambda}{2} \right) I_{(r-2)/2}(\sqrt{\lambda x}),$$

we have in condensed form

$$p(X, T; x, t) = \frac{4\nu x X^{1/\nu - 2}}{\sigma_{\text{CEV}}^2 \tau} p^* \left(\frac{4\nu^2 X^{1/\nu}}{\sigma_{\text{CEV}}^2 \tau}; 2\nu + 2; \frac{4\nu^2 x^{1/\nu}}{\sigma_{\text{CEV}}^2 \tau} \right).$$

In Figure 2.7 we have plotted the different effects of parameter changes on the risk neutral density.

The probability for being absorbed at 0 can be calculated explicitly. For $S(0) > 0$ it is given by

$$\mathbb{P}(S(t) = 0) = \frac{1 - \gamma \left(\frac{1}{2(1-\beta)}, \frac{S(0)^{2(1-\beta)}}{2(1-\beta)^2 \sigma_{\text{CEV}}^2 \tau} \right)}{\Gamma \left(\frac{1}{2(1-\beta)} \right)}, \tag{2.32}$$

where $\gamma(\cdot, \cdot)$ is the incomplete lower gamma function. Finally, it is possible to calculate the cumulative distribution for the model with absorbing, $\mathbb{P}_{\text{absorb}}$, as well as with reflecting boundary, $\mathbb{P}_{\text{reflect}}$, at 0.

$$\mathbb{P}_{\text{absorb}}(S(t) \leq x) = 1 - \chi^2(a, b; c)$$

$$\mathbb{P}_{\text{reflect}}(S(t) \leq x) = \chi^2(c, 2 - b; a).$$

With $a := \frac{S(0)^{1(1-\beta)}}{(1-\beta)^2 \sigma_{\text{CEV}}^2 \tau}$, $b = \frac{1}{1-\beta}$ and $c = \frac{x^{2(1-\beta)}}{(1-\beta)^2 \sigma_{\text{CEV}}^2 \tau}$.

Sample Paths and Returns

The paths are continuous, but sampling from this model is not straightforward when we wish to consider a large time step.

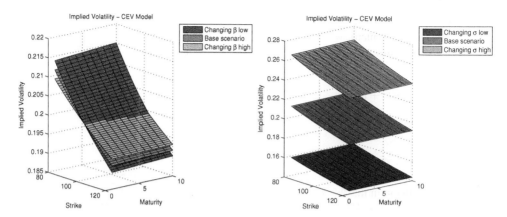

Figure 2.8   The implied volatility surface for different values of the exponent $\beta = 0.4, 0.5, 0.6$ (left) and for the volatility $\sigma_{\text{CEV}} = S(0)^{1-\beta}\sigma_i$, $\sigma_i = 0.15, 0.2, 0.25$ (right)

Skew and Smile

Finally, we analyse the capabilities of generating a skew or smile for the implied volatilities. Figure 2.8 shows that the model is able to generate a descent skew by changing the parameter β and that a change in volatility σ_{CEV} results in a parallel shift of the surface. Generating a convex shape causing a smile of the implied volatility is not possible in this model.

2.2.4   The Displaced Diffusion Model

Displaced Diffusion (DD) models are capable of modelling skewed implied volatility structures. They are frequently applied by interest rate quants. For instance, a displaced diffusion version of the Libor Market Model is used to model the skew inherent in quoted cap and swaption prices. Since simulation is easy by standard numerical schemes, and the ability to fit the skew as good as in the CEV setting, this explains why the DD model is often the first choice among quants.

The Stochastic Differential Equation

The DD model was introduced by Rubinstein, M. (1983) and has been applied in various situations. For applications of this model the reader is referred to Rebonato, R. (2004) or Andersen, L. and Piterbarg, V. (2010a, b and c) among others. Let us consider the following model:

$$dS(t) = \mu(S(t) + a)dt + \sigma_{\text{DD}}(t)(S(t) + a)dW(t) \tag{2.33}$$

$$S(0) = S_0.$$

The only parameter which is different from the standard Black–Scholes model is the parameter $a > 0$. This parameter is called the *displacement parameter*. The model is a particular case of an LVM. We see that it fits into the framework if we set $\lambda(t) = \sigma_{\text{DD}}(t)$ and $f(S(t)) = (S(t) + a)$ in (2.5).

Applications The DD dynamics is widely applied to model the skew in Libor Market Models (see Joshi, M. and Rebonato, R. (2001)). Let us examine the dynamics of the forward rate $F_i(t)$ in the *spot measure*:

$$d(F_i(t) + a) = (F_i(t) + a)\sigma_i^{DD}(t) \sum_{k=0}^{i} \frac{\tau_k(F_k(t) + a)\left(\sigma_k^{DD}\right)^T}{1 + \tau_k F_k(t)} dt$$

$$+ (F_i(t) + a)\sigma_i^{DD}(t) dW_{Spot}(t).$$

In this case we have denoted the corresponding volatility by $\sigma_i^{DD}(t)$ since we have to use a lower index for each Libor. Especially in interest rate models, it has proved convenient to write the displaced diffusion in the following form:

$$dS(t) = \sigma_{DD}(aS(t) + (1-a)L)dW(t).$$

In this parametrization σ_{DD} controls the overall level of the volatility and a controls the slope of the volatility (the skew). Changing σ_{DD} does not affect the slope and changing a does not affect the overall level of volatility. Setting $L \approx S(0)$ allows us to see σ_{DD} as the relative volatility as in the Black–Scholes model in Subsection 2.2.1 since $aS(0) + (1-a)L \approx S(0)$.

The DD model can be seen as an arithmetic average between a normal and a logarithmic-normal model.

Any local volatility model, (2.1), can be approximated by

$$dS(t) \approx \sigma_L(S(0)) + \sigma_L'(S(0))(S(t) - S(0))dW(t),$$

and therefore, setting $\sigma_{DD} := \frac{\sigma_L(S(0))}{S(0)}$, $\beta = \sigma_L'(S(0))\frac{S(0)}{\sigma_L(S(0))}$ and $L = S(0)$, it is approximated to the first order with a displaced diffusion model. For instance taking a CEV model and setting $\sigma_{DD} = \sigma_{CEV}S(0)^{\beta-1}$, $a = \beta$ and $L = S(0)$ shows why the displaced diffusion model can be well approximated by a CEV model.

Pricing Formulae

In the DD model we have the following pricing formulae for European Call and Put options (see, for instance, Rebonato, R. (2002) or Rubinstein, M. (1983)):

$$C(K, T) = e^{-rT}\left((S(0) + a)\mathcal{N}(d_1) - K^*\mathcal{N}(d_2)\right) \tag{2.34}$$

$$P(K, T) = e^{-rT}\left(K^*\mathcal{N}(-d_2) - (S(0) + a)\mathcal{N}(-d_1)\right), \tag{2.35}$$

with $K^* = K + a$ and

$$d_1 = \frac{\log\left(\frac{S(0)+a}{K^*}\right) + \frac{\sigma_{DD}^2}{2}T}{\sigma_{DD}\sqrt{T}}; \quad d_2 = d_1 - \sigma_{DD}^2 T.$$

For time-dependent volatility we replace σ_{DD}^2 by $v_{DD}^2(t_0, t_1) := \int_{t_0}^{t_1} \sigma_{DD}^2(u)du$. We can ask ourselves which value of the volatility would produce the same Call option prices when using the standard Black–Scholes formula. This means we consider the volatility σ_{DD} such that $C_{DD}(K, T) = C_{BS}(K, T)$. Using the pricing formula (2.34) Rebonato, R. (2004) shows that

European Call option ATM prices can be recovered to a reasonable degree of accuracy by setting

$$\sigma_{DD} \approx \frac{S_0}{S_0 + a}\sigma_{BS} \tag{2.36}$$

or the refined approximation

$$\sigma_{DD} \approx \frac{S_0}{S_0 + a}\sigma_{BS}\frac{1 - \frac{1}{24}\sigma_{BS}^2 T}{1 - \frac{1}{24}\left(\frac{S_0}{S_0+a}\sigma_{BS}\right)^2 T}. \tag{2.37}$$

For general strike prices we refer the reader to Marris, D. (1999).

Risk Neutral Distribution

We consider the risk neutral density of the DD model. Since the density is not available in closed form, we use the pricing formula for Call prices and differentiate twice with respect to strike to get the density. Figure 2.9 summarizes the effect of the displacement parameter a and the volatility σ_{DD}.

For the model (2.33) it is possible to calculate the moments of $X(t)$. To do so we fix a natural number k, then we have

$$\mathbb{E}\left[\left(\frac{S(t) + a}{S(0) + a}\right)^k\right] = \exp\left(\frac{k(k-1)}{2}\sigma_{DD}(t)\right).$$

Thus, for instance, computing the second moment leads to

$$\mathbb{E}[(S(t) + a)^2] = (S(0) + a)^2 e^{\sigma_{DD}^2 t}$$

$$\mathbb{E}[S(t)^2] = (S(0) + a)^2 e^{\sigma_{DD}^2 t} - 2a\mathbb{E}[S(t)] - a^2$$

$$= S(0)^2 + (S(0) + a)^2 \left(e^{\sigma_{DD}^2} - 1\right).$$

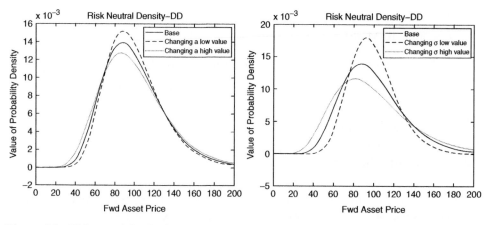

Figure 2.9   Risk neutral density for $T = 3$, spot value of 100 and different values of the displacement parameter $a = 1, 10, 20$ (left) and different values of the volatility parameter $\sigma_{DD} = 0.15, 0.2, 0.25$

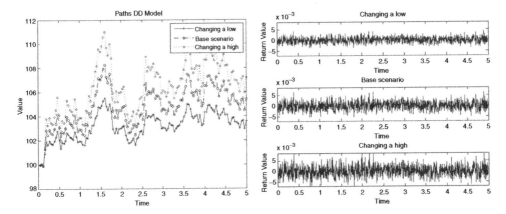

Figure 2.10 Generated paths (left) and returns (right) – DD model for different values of $a =$ 0.0, 50, 100

Sample Paths and Returns

The paths generated by the model are continuous since the stochastic driver is a Brownian motion. However, we have introduced a timely dependence for the volatility given by the displacement. To this end we plotted typical sample paths in Figure 2.10.

Skew and Smile

A new feature is observed when we consider the implied volatility surface generated by the model. We see two effects in this model. The first observation stems from changing the displacement parameter a and the second from changing the volatility σ. While changing the volatility affects the implied volatility surface to move parallel up or down, the displacement is able to generate a curved shape of the surface. Hence, this model is used in financial modelling to incorporate a volatility skew. It is the basic building block of skew in Libor Market Models. We illustrate the skews generated by the models in Figure 2.11.

2.2.5 CEV and DD Models

Now let us see how CEV and DD models are related to one another (see Marris, D. (1999) or Svoboda, S. (2006)). To understand the close connection we take the following model:

$$dS(t) = (\eta S(t) + S(0)(1 - \eta))\sigma^M dW(t). \tag{2.38}$$

The parameters η and σ^M are constants. The DD model fits into this more general model by setting $a = S(0)\frac{1-\eta}{\eta}$ and $\sigma^{DD} = \eta\sigma^M$.

Taking $\sigma^M = S(0)^{\beta-1}\sigma^{CEV}$ we find

$$\left.\frac{\partial(S(t)^\beta(\sigma^{CEV})^2)dt}{\partial S(t)}\right|_{S(t)=S(0)} = \left.\frac{\partial((S(t)+a)(\sigma^{DD})^2)dt}{\partial S(t)}\right|_{S(t)=S(0)}. \tag{2.39}$$

A rule of thumb is that the closer β is to 1, the better the DD model approximates the CEV model.

We have discussed the relationship of CEV to DD models. There is a combination of both models applied by practitioners, which is called the *displaced CEV model*.

$$dS(t) = (S(t) + a)^\beta \, dW(t) \tag{2.40}$$

$$S(0) = S_0.$$

The pricing is still possible in closed form (see, for instance, Andersen, L. and Piterbarg, V. (2010a)).

2.3 STOCHASTIC VOLATILITY MODELS

We would now like to introduce a class of models called *Stochastic Volatility Models (SVM)* which extends the classical Black–Scholes framework or the local volatility framework. The class of models we consider is capable of modelling not only skew but also smile. The class of models is still numerically tractable. We observe that:

- Historical volatility of traded assets displays significant variability. Therefore, it is natural to take into account non-constant volatility for hedging purposes and for evaluating the profit and loss for suggested hedges.
- Many structured products and derivatives are sensitive to the future shape and the level of the implied volatility surface.
- New trading ideas and products on realized volatility such as variance swaps, skew swaps or moment swaps assume that implied volatility is not only an implicit risk factor but also a tradable risky asset.

The concept of an SVM applies the idea of a second source of randomness. Therefore, we are adding another source risk to the modelling. It is a proper assumption that the randomness of volatility is modelled dependent on the asset. This is called *leverage*. Furthermore, ideas and market practice from different kinds of markets make it necessary to consider such models. To this end a general stochastic volatility model is given by the following set of SDEs:

$$dS(t) = \mu S(t)dt + \sigma(V(t), S(t))dW(t) \tag{2.41}$$

$$dV(t) = \mu_V(t, V(t))dt + \sigma_V(t, V(t))dZ(t)$$

$$S(0) = s_0$$

$$V(0) = v_0.$$

Most of the stochastic volatility models incorporate a skew by virtue of allowing correlated Brownian motions W and Z driving the asset and the volatility. This can also be achieved by a local volatility function and two uncorrelated Brownian motions. Often the function $\sigma(V(t), S(t))$ is given in *separable form*, which is $\sigma(V(t), S(t)) := \sigma(t)\sqrt{V(t)}c(S(t))$ for some function c. Well-known financial models include:

- Heston model; Heston, S. (1993).
- SABR model; Hagan, P.S., Kumar, D., Lesniewski, A.S. and Woodward, D.E. (2002).
- Schoebel–Zhu model; Schoebel, R. and Zhu, J. (1999).
- Hull–White model; Hull, J. and White, A. (1987).
- Scott–Chesny model; Chesney, M. and Scott, L. (1989).
- Stein–Stein model; Stein, E.M. and Stein, J.C. (1991).

It is not possible to consider every single proposed stochastic volatility model. Here, we consider the Heston model and the SABR model in detail since, in our experience, these models are widely applied in the financial industry.

2.3.1 Pricing European Options

At this stage it is necessary to briefly introduce other methods for pricing European Call and Put options. Closed form solutions, Equations (2.10), (2.11), (2.26), (2.27), (2.34) and (2.35), determine the price of these options in the LVM model class. We describe a unified approach for a general class of models. Following this approach makes it necessary to consider the characteristic function of a model and not the actual pricing formula.

Pricing using the Characteristic Function

We use the characteristic function of a given financial model to price several options. It is possible to give the price of European Call or Put options in terms of a general Black formula or as an integral formula.

We assume that φ is the characteristic function of the underlying model and that it is analytic and bounded in a strip, $0 \leq \mathcal{I}(z) \leq 1$, meaning that the imaginary part of z is between 0 and 1. We consider $\varphi_1(z) := e^{-\log(S(t)) - (r-d)(T-t)} \varphi(z - i)$ and $\varphi_2(z) := \varphi(z)$. The cumulative distribution functions $\mathcal{D}_j$ of the log-spot price are given by

$$\mathcal{D}_j(y) = \frac{1}{2} + \frac{1}{\pi} \int_0^\infty \mathcal{R}\left(\frac{\varphi_j(z)e^{-izy}}{iz}\right) dz, \quad j = 1, 2,$$

where we denoted $y = \log(K)$. Then, the value of a European Call, Put option $C(K, T)$ with maturity T and strike K at time t is

$$C(K, T) = e^{-dT} S(0)\mathcal{D}_1 - e^{-rT} K \mathcal{D}_2 \tag{2.42}$$

$$P(K, T) = -\left[e^{-dT} S(0)(1 - \mathcal{D}_1) - e^{-rT} K(1 - \mathcal{D}_2)\right]. \tag{2.43}$$

There is another method available called direct integration which and is more efficient than the generalized Black formula since only a single numerical integration is required.

Let us assume that the logarithmic asset price $x(T)$ has an analytic characteristic function φ in the strip $S_z = \{z \in \mathbb{C} | \alpha \leq \mathcal{I}(z) \leq \beta, \alpha, \beta \in \mathbb{R}\}$ and that the function $e^{-cx} f(x)$ is integrable with $c \in S_f$. The set S_f is the strip on which the Fourier transform of the payoff, $\hat{f}$, exists and is analytic. If $S_F = S_f \cap S_z$ is not empty, the time 0 option value $C(K, T)$ is given by

$$C(K, T) = \frac{e^{-rT}}{2\pi} \int_{ic-\infty}^{ic+\infty} \varphi(-z)\hat{f}(z)dz, \tag{2.44}$$

with $z \in S_F$ and $c \in \mathcal{I}(z)$.

For the models under consideration we give the characteristic function of the corresponding model. Hence, we implicitly give the pricing methodology for European Call and Put options.

We give the Matlab code for the characteristic functions here. In later chapters we use a slightly different implementation. We expand on this issue later.

One final remark is in order. If we consider the pricing for a financial asset $S(t)$ of the form

$$S(t) = S(0) \exp((r - d)t + X(t)),$$

we often find different notations of the characteristic function. Some use the characteristic function corresponding to S and others corresponding to X. By Φ we denote the characteristic function with respect to X and by φ that corresponding to S. Both functions are related by

$$\varphi(u) = \exp(iu(\log(S(t)) + (r - d)t))\Phi(u). \tag{2.45}$$

Approximation of Implied Black Volatilities

The success of numerous complex models lies in the fact that the characteristic function of the model is available in closed form. In this case, it is possible to use the results from Subsection 2.3.1. But there are other models where the characteristic function is not known in closed form and no approximation to it has been derived. For such models it might be possible to derive an approximation of the Black implied volatility instead.

For general stochastic volatility models it is possible to find a Taylor series expansion for the implied volatility using results from differential geometry. First, the stochastic volatility model is written in terms of the forward price. The SDE is

$$dF = \sigma_F(F, \Sigma)dW \tag{2.46}$$

$$d\Sigma = \mu_V(\Sigma)dt + \sigma_V(\Sigma)dZ \tag{2.47}$$

$$\langle dW, dZ \rangle = \rho dt. \tag{2.48}$$

From this equation we derive the asymptotic value of the transition probability from starting at initial states S_0, σ_0 at time 0 to S and Σ at maturity T. This can be achieved by using a heat kernel expansion. Determine the expected value of the variance given by

$$\mathbb{E}\left[\sigma_F^2(S, \Sigma)\delta(F - S)\right].$$

This equation is integrated with respect to time. Finally, the same formula is compared to a Black–Scholes model to infer the implied volatility. This implied volatility is then given as a Taylor series expansion. We use such an expansion result when we consider the SABR stochastic volatility model.

Since the actual derivation of the result needs advanced methods from differential geometry, we will not go into greater detail here. The interested reader can consult Henry-Labordere, P (2005) or Hagan, P.S., Kumar, D., Lesniewski, A.S. and Woodward, D.E. (2002).

2.3.2   Risk Neutral Density

The risk neutral density corresponding to a model is not in general known in closed form. Thus, it is only possible to compute the density numerically or to derive approximate solutions.

Let us consider the following methods:

- Risk neutral density from Call prices using the second derivative $\frac{\partial^2 C}{\partial K^2}$.
- Risk neutral density from the characteristic function and application of inversion of Fourier transform.
- Approximate solutions using Riemannian geometry, Perturbation analysis and Forward and Backward Kolmogorov equations.

As we have already outlined, the risk neutral density can be calculated by differentiating the Call option price twice with respect to the strike price. This calculation can be carried out using a finite difference technique.

The calculation method using the characteristic function is a numerical method. To compute the risk neutral density we apply the inversion for Fourier transforms. The integral appearing in this equation is computed by application of the fast Fourier transform.

The approximate solutions are based on different mathematical concepts. A general method based on Riemannian Geometry has been proven useful.

2.3.3 The Heston Model (and Extensions)

In this section we consider the Heston stochastic volatility, model which is given by the following set of stochastic differential equations:

$$dS(t) = \mu S(t)dt + \sqrt{V(t)}S(t)dW_1(t) \tag{2.49}$$

$$dV(t) = \kappa(\Theta - V(t))dt + v\sqrt{V(t)}dW_2(t) \tag{2.50}$$

$$S(0) = S_0$$

$$V(0) = V_0$$

$$\langle dW_1, dW_2 \rangle = \rho dt. \tag{2.51}$$

The parameter κ models the mean reversion speed of the variance, Θ is the long term variance, v is the volatility of variance, ρ is the correlation of the driving Brownian motions W_1 and W_2, S_0 is the spot asset price and V_0 is the spot variance. In the literature two cases are considered. With respect to the parameters κ, Θ and v we have two possibilities, namely,

$$2\kappa\Theta \geq v^2 \tag{2.52}$$

$$2\kappa\Theta < v^2. \tag{2.53}$$

The model fulfils the *Feller property* if Equation (2.52) holds. The meaning of the Feller condition is that if it is fulfilled the process never hits 0, but if it is not fulfilled the process V can reach 0. This is the case when Equation (2.53) holds. To obtain a unique solution to the SDE we have to specify a boundary condition at 0. In quantitative finance the chosen boundary condition is that the process remains in 0. We call this the *absorbing boundary condition*. If the process reaches 0 and is allowed to leave 0 it is called a *reflecting boundary*.

We are able to calculate the moments of the variance $V(t + \Delta)$ at time $t + \Delta$ conditional on the value of the variance $V(t)$ at time t. The (conditional) expectation and the (conditional) variance are given by

$$\mathbb{E}[V(t + \Delta)|V(t)] = \Theta + (V(t) - \Theta)\exp(-\kappa\Delta) \tag{2.54}$$

$$\mathbb{V}[V(t + \Delta)|V(t)] = \frac{V(t)v^2}{\kappa}\exp(-\kappa\Delta)(1 - \exp(-\kappa\Delta)) \tag{2.55}$$

$$+ \frac{\Theta v^2}{2\kappa}(1 - \exp(-\kappa\Delta))^2.$$

This representation is applied to moment-matching techniques for Monte Carlo simulation.

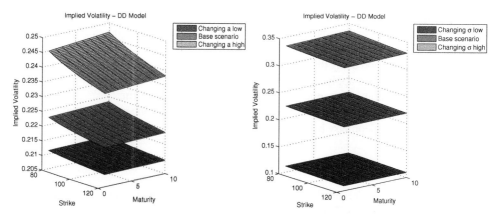

Figure 2.11 The implied volatility smile for different values of parameter $a = 5, 10, 20$ (left) and $\sigma_{\text{DD}} = 0.1, 0.2, 0.3$ (right)

Characteristic Function

The characteristic function, φ_{H}, for the Heston model is available in closed form. It is given by

$$\varphi_{\text{H}}(u, t, T) = \exp(A_H(u, t, T) + B_\sigma(u, t, T)V(t) + iuX(t)),\qquad(2.56)$$

with

$$A_H(u, t, T) = \frac{\kappa \Theta}{v^2}\left((\kappa - \rho vui - D)(T - t) - 2\log\left(\frac{G\exp(-D(T - t))}{G - 1} - 1\right)\right)$$

$$B_\sigma(u, t, T) = \frac{\kappa - \rho vui - D}{\omega^2}\left(\frac{1 - \exp(-D(T - t))}{1 - G\exp(-D(T - t))}\right)$$

$$G = \frac{\kappa - \rho vui - D}{\kappa - \rho vui + D}$$

$$D = \sqrt{(\kappa - \rho vui)^2 + u(i + u)v^2}.$$

The implementation in Matlab is given in Figure 2.12.

In what follows we consider the flexibility of the model to produce market observed shapes of the skew, smile and the risk neutral density. To this end we fix a set of parameters, called the *base scenario*, shift the parameters and observe the effect of the shift. Finally, we consider typical paths generated by the model. The base scenario we fix for the Heston model is given by the following parameter set:

- $V(0) = 0.02$
- $\Theta = 0.02$
- $\kappa = 0.1$
- $\rho = 0$
- $v = 0.2$
- $T = 10$.

```
function y = cf_heston(u,lnS,T,r,d,V0,theta,kappa,omega,rho)

alfa = -.5*(u.*u + u*1i);
beta = kappa - rho*omega*u*1i;
omega2 = omega * omega;
gamma = .5 * omega2;

D = sqrt(beta .* beta - 4.0 * alfa .* gamma);

bD = beta - D;
eDt = exp(- D * T);

G = bD ./ (beta + D);
B = (bD ./ omega2) .* ((1.0 - eDt) ./ (1.0 - G .* eDt));
psi = (G .* eDt - 1.0) ./ (G - 1.0);
A = ((kappa * theta) / (omega2)) * (bD * T - 2.0 * log(psi));

y = A + B*V0 + 1i*u*(lnS+(r-d)*T);

end
```

Figure 2.12   The log-characteristic function of the Heston model

Risk Neutral Density

Figure 2.13 summarizes the results obtained by shifting the parameters from the base scenario. First, we observe that changing the level of the spot variance and the long term variance have the same effect on the risk neutral density. Decreasing these parameters leads to a more peaked distribution whereas increasing the values leads to a more widespread distribution, which is what we would expect. For the other parameters the outcome of shifting might not be so obvious. First, changing the parameter ρ leads to an asymmetric distribution shape. For the base scenario, $\rho = 0$, the distribution is symmetric around 0. Negative values of ρ cause a left-skewed and positive values of ρ cause a right-skewed shape.

The mean reversion level κ leads to a highly peaked distribution when increased and a flat distribution when decreased. It seems that κ kills the skew. In fact, high values of κ very quickly pull the variance to its mean reverting level.

Finally, the volatility of variance ν offers another way to control the overall level of volatility. Examination of Figure 2.13 leads us to expect that the calibration of the Heston model is unstable since there are several parameters which cause similar or opposite effects on the shape of the distribution. Hence, we expect that we will have to reduce the number of parameters to calibrate in order to achieve stability or that we will have to introduce restrictions on the parameters.

Skew and Smile

The Heston model is able to generate skew or smile shaped structures for the implied volatility. Since the risk neutral densities and the implied volatilities are closely related, the explanations given above of the effects of increasing or decreasing the parameters do also apply in this case.

Figure 2.14 summarizes our findings. In contrast to the results obtained for the risk neutral density, it can be seen in the top row of the figure that increasing the initial variance directly

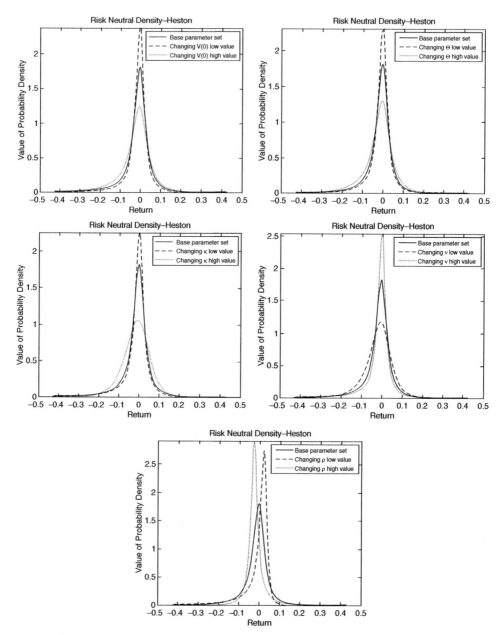

Figure 2.13 Risk neutral density for the returns using $T = 10$, spot value of $S(0) = 100$ and different values for the initial variance $V(0) = 0.01, 0.02, 0.03$ (top left), the long term variance $\Theta = 0.01, 0.02, 0.03$ (top right), different values for the mean reversion speed $\kappa = 0.0001, 0.1$ and 0.5 (mid left), the volatility of variance $\nu = 0.1, 0.2, 0.3$ (mid right), and different values for the correlation $\rho = -0.8, 0, 0.8$ (bottom)

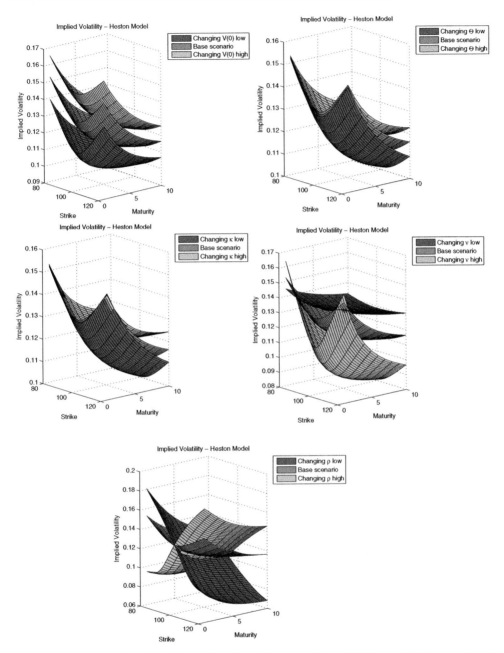

Figure 2.14   We consider $T = 1, \ldots, 10$ and a strike range of $\kappa = 80, 81, \ldots, 120$. For $r = d = 0$ and a spot value of $S(0) = 100$ we consider the following changes of the base scenario: $V(0) = 0.015, 0.02, 0.025$ (top left), $\Theta = 0.015, 0.02, 0.025$ (top right), $\kappa = 0.05, 0.1, 0.2$ (mid left), $v = 0.1, 0.2, 0.4$ (mid right) and finally $\rho = -0.8, 0, 0.8$ (bottom)

Table 2.1 Heston Model. Summary of parameters and instruments that influence the corresponding parameters

Parameter	Instrument
$V(0)$	ATM volatility level
Θ	Long term volatility level
κ	Butterflies
ν	Butterflies
ρ	Risk reversals

leads to a parallel shift where the overall volatility is increased. Decreasing it also leads to a parallel shift but the overall level is decreased. The long term level, Θ, however, only affects the long end with respect to the time to maturity of the volatility surface.

The same effect can be observed when changing the mean reversion speed κ. The shapes of the surfaces are nearly identical. From a trader's point of view, the effect of the parameters is encoded in tradable market structures and is summarized in Table 2.1.

Typical Paths and Returns

For the Heston stochastic volatility model we have to analyse the typical paths for both the asset and the volatility. The base scenario in this case is given by the following parameter set:

- $S(0) = 100$
- $T = 2$
- $V(0) = 0.04$
- $\Theta = 0.04$
- $\kappa = 0.2$
- $\rho = 0$
- $\nu = 0.1$.

We expect to observe the effect already studied when we considered risk neutral densities and implied volatility surfaces. Figure 2.15 summarizes the findings for the asset paths and Figure 2.16 those for the stochastic variance. We describe only the results for increasing the parameters since the opposite effect then holds for the scenario where the parameters are decreased. Starting by increasing $V(0)$ leads to an overall higher volatility, which can be directly observed on the variances. The paths are parallel shifted by a certain amount. This affects the asset price path and can be observed implicitly. The long term variance level Θ impacts the long end of the variance path which is also implicitly given for the asset path. For the asset path, the effect can best be observed near maturity.

Again, the effect of mean reversion is comparable to the effect of changing Θ. Increasing κ is qualitatively the same as decreasing Θ.

Increasing the volatility of variance ν leads to much higher values for realized variance and a more volatile behaviour of the sample path for the asset.

Finally, changing the correlation ρ does not affect the variance path, but clearly it does affect the asset path. We have to admit that we first simulated the variance and then used the representation $\rho W_1 + \sqrt{1 - \rho^2} W_2$ for sampling the asset path. Therefore, clearly, we see the effect only on the asset path!

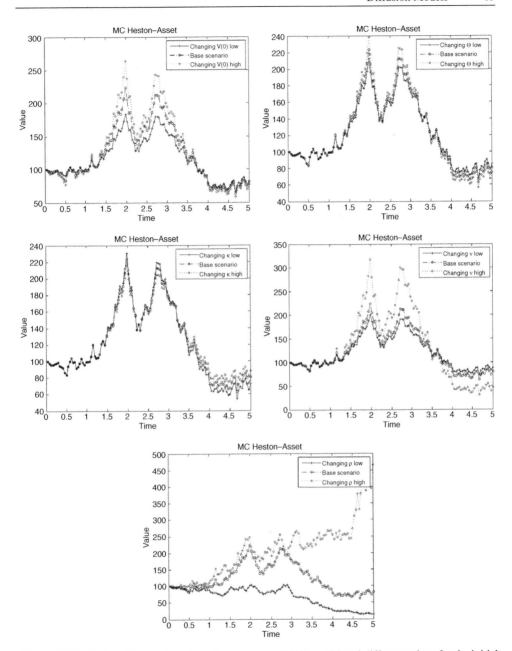

Figure 2.15 Paths of the asset for $T = 2$, spot value of $S(0) = 100$ and different values for the initial variance $V(0) = 0.01, 0.04, 0.08$ (top left), the long term variance $\Theta = 0.01, 0.04, 0.08$ (top right), different values for the mean reversion speed $\kappa = 0.005, 0.2, 0.5$ (mid left), the volatility of variance $v = 0.05, 0.1, 0.3$ (mid right) and different values for correlation $\rho = -0.8, 0, 0.8$ (bottom)

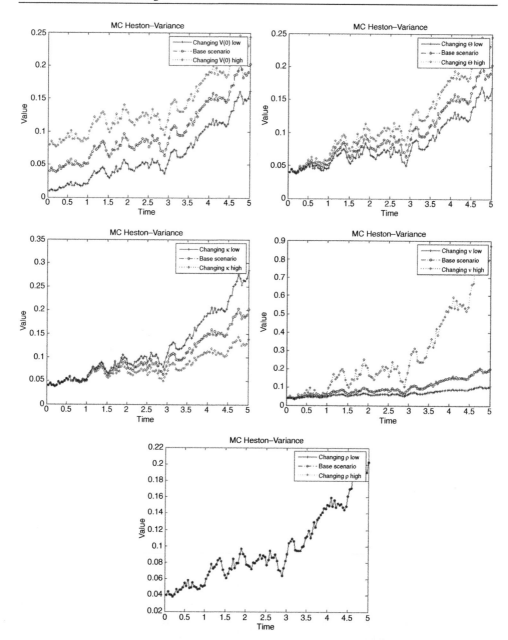

Figure 2.16 Paths of the variance for $T = 2$, spot value of $S(0) = 100$ and different values for the initial variance $V(0) = 0.01, 0.04, 0.08$ (top left), the long term variance $\Theta = 0.01, 0.04, 0.08$ (top right), the mean reversion speed $\kappa = 0.005, 0.2, 0.5$ (mid left), the volatility of variance $v = 0.05, 0.1, 0.3$ (mid right) and correlation $\rho = -0.8, 0, 0.8$ (bottom)

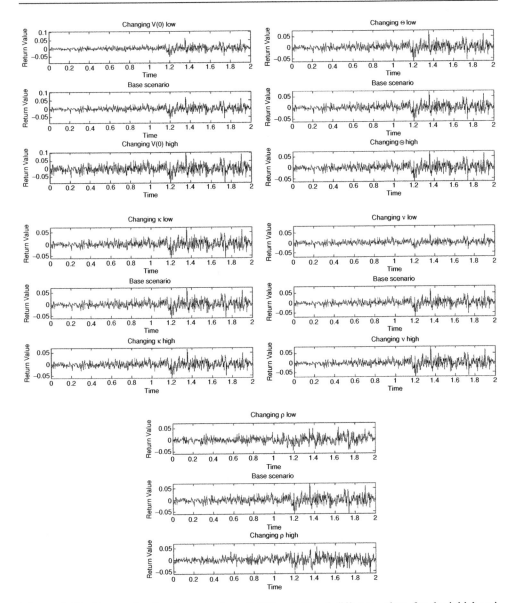

Figure 2.17 Returns for $T = 2$, spot value of $S(0) = 100$ and different values for the initial variance $V(0) = 0.01, 0.04, 0.08$ (top left), the long term variance $\Theta = 0.01, 0.04, 0.08$ (top right), different values for the mean reversion speed $\kappa = 0.005, 0.2, 0.5$ (mid left), the volatility of variance $\nu = 0.05, 0.1, 0.3$ (mid right) and different values for correlation $\rho = -0.8, 0, 0.8$ (bottom)

The same explanations hold true for the logarithmic returns generated by the Heston model. Figure 2.17 gives the results obtained by simulation. However, we observe that the time series considered in Chapter 1, where we looked at market data, shows a different qualitative behaviour. We will come to that point later when we add jumps to the models and when we consider models driven exclusively by jumps.

```
function y = cf_ddheston(u,lnS,T,r,d,V0,theta,kappa,omega,rho,lambda,b)
% Displaced Diffusion Heston
U = 1i*u;
v = 0.5*(lambda*b)^2*U.*(U-1);
theta_star = kappa -rho*omega*lambda*b*U;
gamma = sqrt(theta_star.^2-2*omega^2*v);
Avu = kappa * theta / omega^2 *(2*log(2*gamma./(theta_star ...
    + gamma-exp(-gamma*T).*(theta_star-gamma)))+(theta_star-gamma)*T);
Bvu = 2*v.*(1-exp(-gamma*T))./((theta_star+gamma) ...
    .*(1-exp(-gamma*T))+2*gamma.*exp(-gamma*T));

y = Avu + Bvu*V0 + U *(lnS+(r-d)*T);
end
```

Figure 2.18   The log-characteristic function for the DD Heston model

Further Remarks

In particular, in interest rate modelling a displaced diffusion version of the Heston model is commonly applied (see, for instance, Andersen, L. and Piterbarg, V. (2010a)). The model is governed by the following set of SDEs:

$$dS(t) = \lambda (aS(t) + (1-a)L) \sqrt{V(t)} dW(t) \qquad (2.57)$$

$$dV(t) = \kappa (\Theta - V(t)) dt + v\sqrt{V(t)} dZ(t) \qquad (2.58)$$

$$S(0) = S_0$$

$$V(0) = V_0$$

$$\langle dW(t), dZ(t) \rangle = \rho dt. \qquad (2.59)$$

The effect of a non-zero value of the correlation parameter ρ can already be modelled by choosing the suitable displacement component a. Thus, it is common practice to assume $\rho = 0$. The characteristic function for the model can be implemented in Matlab by the code given in Figure 2.18.

In interest rate modelling a change of numeraire is a very common technique. For instance, switching from the risk neutral to the forward or the annuity measure can simplify a given pricing problem. Using such a change of numeraire affects the drift of the stochastic volatility equation if $\rho \neq 0$.

This property is the main motivation for choosing $\rho = 0$. This is very important for interest rate modellers, especially when implementing a Libor Market Model. Furthermore, it is possible to separate effects of skewness and smile, that is the convexity of the implied volatility. The assumption $\rho = 0$ is discussed further in Chapter 8 of Andersen, L. and Piterbarg, V. (2010a).

For the displaced diffusion Heston model a closed form pricing formula is available.

$$C = \frac{1}{a} \text{Black}(aS + (1-a)L; T, aK + (1-a)L, \lambda a) - \frac{aK + (1-a)L}{2\pi a}$$

$$\cdot \int_{-\infty}^{+\infty} \frac{\exp\left((\frac{1}{2} + iu) \log\left(\frac{aS+(1-a)L}{aK+(1-a)L}\right)\right)}{u^2 + \frac{1}{4}} q\left(\frac{1}{2} + iu\right) du. \qquad (2.60)$$

The function q is given by

$$q(u) = \varphi_H\left(\frac{(\lambda a)^2}{2}u(u-1), u; T\right) - \exp\left(\frac{(\lambda a)^2}{2}V(0)Tu(u-1)\right),$$

with

$$\varphi_H(u, v; T) = A(u, v; T) + B(u, v)V(0)$$

$$A(u, v; T) = \frac{\theta V(0)}{\eta^2}\left[2\log\left(\frac{2\gamma}{\Theta + \gamma - e^{-\gamma T}(\Theta - \gamma)}\right) + (\Theta - \gamma)T\right]$$

$$B(u, v; T) = \frac{2u(1 - e^{-\gamma T})}{(\Theta + \gamma)(1 - e^{-\gamma T}) + 2\gamma e^{-\gamma T}}$$

$$\gamma = \sqrt{\Theta^2 - 2\eta^2 u}$$

$$\Theta = \theta - \rho\eta\lambda av.$$

The latter is the same representation as for the standard Heston model. By way of illustration, let us show the effect of the parameters λ and a on the implied volatility surface. To this end we fix the other parameters of the model, namely $V(0) = \Theta = 0.02$, $\kappa = 0.1$, $v = 0.2$, $\rho = 0$. As in the previous examples we consider the maturities $T = 1, \ldots, 10$ and the strike range $K = 80, \ldots, 120$. As usual we set $S = 100$ and $r = d = 0$.

Thus, we see that using the characteristic function the density or the implied volatility density can be computed. The effects of the additional parameters on the skew are displayed in Figure 2.19.

2.3.4 The SABR Model

Another model that is widely applied, especially for foreign exchange and interest rate markets, is the SABR stochastic volatility model. To appreciate how it works, we review the model in more detail. The SABR (stochastic α, β, ρ) model was introduced in Hagan, P.S., Kumar, D., Lesniewski, A.S. and Woodward, D.E. (2002) to manage the smile risk. The model is given in terms of a set of SDEs:

$$dS(t) = \sigma(t)S(t)^\beta dW(t) \tag{2.61}$$

$$d\sigma(t) = \sigma(t)vdZ(t) \tag{2.62}$$

$$S(0) = S_0$$

$$\sigma(0) = \sigma_0$$

$$\langle dW(t), dZ(t)\rangle = \rho dt. \tag{2.63}$$

Here S_0 is the spot asset price and σ_0 is the spot value of volatility. The other model parameters are the CEV parameter β, the volatility of volatility v and the correlation ρ between the Brownian motions W and Z driving the asset and the volatility dynamics.

The coefficient β determines the local volatility of the SABR model. This is often referred to as the *backbone of implied volatility*.

We explore the meaning of the parameters by considering possible shapes of the risk neutral density as well as implied volatilities generated by the SABR model. The volatility process is a logarithmic normal process and therefore it is not mean reverting but on average increases with respect to time. This causes the second moment in the SABR model to be unbounded, which is known as *volatility explosion*.

Pricing Formulae

Using an approximation formula for implied volatility derived in Hagan, P.S., Kumar, D., Lesniewski A.S. and Woodward, D.E. (2002), it is possible to apply Equations (2.10) and (2.11) to price European Call and Put options. To do this the implied Black volatility σ_{BS} has to be replaced by a function, σ_{SABR}, depending on the strike and the model parameters

$$\sigma_{SABR}(K,T) \approx \frac{\sigma_0}{(SK)^{\frac{1-\beta}{2}}\left(1 + \frac{(1-\beta)^2}{24}\log^2(S/K) + \frac{(1-\beta)^4}{1920}\log^4(F/K) + \dots\right)} \frac{z}{x(z)}$$

$$\left(1 + \left(\frac{(1-\beta)^2\sigma_0^2}{24(SK)^{1-\beta}} + \frac{\rho\beta v\sigma_0}{4(SK)^{\frac{1-\beta}{2}}} + v^2\frac{2-3\rho^2}{24}\right)T + \dots\right),$$

with

$$z = \frac{v}{\sigma_0}(SK)^{\frac{1-\beta}{2}}\log(S/K), \quad x(z) = \log\left(\frac{\sqrt{1-2z\rho+z^2}+z-\rho}{1-\rho}\right).$$

We have reproduced the original formula given in Hagan, P.S., Kumar, D., Lesniewski, A.S. and Woodward, D.E. (2002) here. There are many extensions and improvements to this formula. One improvement has been derived in Obloj, J. (2007). Here the implied volatility is given by an expansion formula:

$$\sigma \approx I^0(x)(1 + I^1(x)\tau) + O(\tau^2), \tag{2.64}$$

with

$$I^0(x) = \begin{cases} \alpha K^{\beta-1} & x = 0 \\ \frac{x\alpha(1-\beta)}{S^{1-\beta}-K^{1-\beta}} & v = 0 \\ vx/\log(\frac{\sqrt{1-\rho z_1+z_1^2}+z_1-\rho}{1-\rho}) & \beta = 1 \\ vx/\log(\frac{\sqrt{1-\rho z+z^2}+z-\rho}{1-\rho}) & \beta < 1 \end{cases}$$

$$I^1(x) = \frac{(\beta-1)^2}{24}\frac{\alpha^2}{(SK)^{1-\beta}} + \frac{1}{4}\frac{\rho v\alpha\beta}{(SK)^{(1-\beta)/2}} + \frac{2-3\rho^2}{24}v^2$$

and

$$z_1 = \frac{vx}{\alpha} \quad z = \frac{v}{\alpha}\frac{S^{1-\beta}-K^{1-\beta}}{1-\beta}.$$

We used the Matlab code given in Figure 2.20 to compute the implied volatility from the SABR model.

The price of European Call and Put options can then be computed using the code given in Figure 2.21.

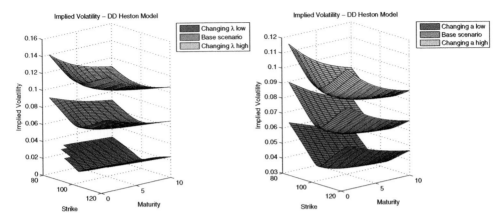

Figure 2.19 Consider the smile in the DD Heston model for $T = 1, \ldots, 10$ and a strike range of $K = 80, 81, \ldots, 120$. For $r = d = 0$ and a spot value of $S(0) = 100$. The following changes apply to the base scenario: $\lambda = 0.5, 1, 1.5$ (left) and $a = 0.2, 0.5, 0.8$ (right)

Below, in Figures 2.24–2.27, we consider the flexibility of the model to produce market observed shapes of the skew, smile and the risk neutral density. To do so, we fix a set of parameters, the base scenario. We shift the parameters and observe the effect of this shift. Finally, we consider typical paths and returns generated by the model.

Risk Neutral Distribution

The probability density for a given maturity T is not available in closed form. There exist approximation formulae for the density (see Hagan, P., Lesniewski, A. and Woodward, D. (2005), Henry-Labordere, P. (2005), Paulot, L. (2009) or Wu, Q. (2010)). Using Equation (1.3) we can infer the density from Call prices. We consider the risk neutral density for the SABR model. We fix a maturity T and consider the change of the distribution by changing the model parameters. The base scenario for the SABR model is determined by setting $S(0) = 0.05$, $\sigma(0) = 0.1$, $\rho = 0$, $\beta = 0.5$, $\nu = 0.2$ and $T = 1$. This scenario represents some interest rate modelling setting.

```
function y = svol_2 (a, b, r, n, f, k, t)
    z = n./a.*(f*k).^((1-b)/2).*log(f./k);
    x = log((sqrt(1 - 2*r*z + z.^2) + z - r)/(1-r));
    Term1 = a ./ (f*k).^((1-b)/2) ./ (1 + (1-b)^2/24*log(f./k).^2 ...
        + (1-b)^4/1920*log(f./k).^4);
    Term2 = z ./ x;
    Term2(abs(x-z) < 1e-10) = 1;
    Term3 = 1 + ((1-b)^2/24*a^2./(f*k).^(1-b) ...
        + r*b*n*a/4./(f*k).^((1-b)/2) + (2-3*r^2)/24*n.^2)*t;
    y = Term1.*Term2.*Term3;
end
```

Figure 2.20 Matlab code for computing the implied volatility for the SABR stochastic volatility model

```
function y = sprice(a, b, r, n, f, k, t,cp)
% calculates the sabr price cp == 1 Call else Put using the standard
% Hagan et al. formula
sigma = svol_2(a,b,r,n,f,k,t);                              % vol
d1= (log(f./k)+(0.5*t*sigma.*sigma))./(sqrt(t)*sigma);% Quant 1
d2= (log(f./k)-(0.5*t*sigma.*sigma))./(sqrt(t)*sigma);% Quant 2

if cp==1
    y = f.*normcdf( d1,0,1)-k.*normcdf( d2,0,1);            % Call price
else
    y = k.*normcdf(-d2,0,1)-f.*normcdf(-d1,0,1);            % Put price
end
end
```

Figure 2.21 Matlab code for computing the price of European Call and Put options using the parameters of the SABR stochastic volatility model

Since we wish to illustrate the impact of each model parameter, we have chosen parameter sets which do not lead to instabilities in the model. The instabilities and the solutions for removing these are covered in Subsection 2.3.5.

For our purposes let us use the expansion of the SABR density derived by Wu, Q. (2010). Paulot, L. (2009) also researched expansions of the density and derived an approximating formula, but we do not cover those results here. For the expansion, Wu, Q. (2010), we need the following parameters:

$$\tau = (T - t)/T,$$

$$u = (f^{1-\beta} - F^{1-\beta})/(\alpha(1 - \beta)\sqrt{T}),$$

$$v = \log(\alpha/A)/(v\sqrt{T}),$$

$$a_{11} = -\beta F^{(\beta-1)} A/v(u - \rho v),$$

$$a_{10} = u^2 v - \rho u v^2,$$

$$a = 2\rho + \beta F^{\beta-1} A/v,$$

$$b = 2 + \beta(1 - \beta)F^{2(\beta-1)} A^2/v^2,$$

$$c = \beta F^{\beta-1} A/v,$$

$$a_{23} = \rho^4(20 - 6b) - 12\rho^3 a + \rho^2(3a^2 - 28 + 12b) + 12a\rho + 8 - 3a^2 - 6b,$$

$$a_{22} = u^2(3a^2 - 12a\rho + 6b(-1 + \rho^2) + 2\rho^2 + 10)$$

$$-2uv(\rho^3(2 + 3b) + \rho^2(-9a + 3c) + \rho(10 + 3a^2 - 3b) - (3a + 3c))$$

$$+v^2((2 + 3(a - 2\rho)^2)\rho^2 + 6c\rho(-1 + \rho^2) - 2),$$

$$a_{21} = u^4 + v^4\rho^2 + u^3 v(8\rho - 6a) + uv^3(8\rho^3 - 6a\rho^2) + u^2 v^2(-14\rho^2 + 12a\rho - 4),$$

$$a_{20} = 3u^4 v^2 - 6u^3 v^3 \rho + 3u^2 v^4 \rho^2.$$

```
function y = psabr31(t,T,f,F,alpha,A,beta,nu,rho)
tau = (T-t)/T;
if beta == 1
    u = (log(f) - log(F))./(alpha * sqrt(T));
else
    u = (f^(1-beta)-F.^(1-beta))/(alpha*(1-beta)*sqrt(T));
end
v = log(alpha./A)./(nu*sqrt(T));

a11 = -beta * F.^(beta-1).*A./nu .*(u-rho*v);
a10 = u.^2*v-rho*u.*v.^2;

y = 1./(nu*T*F.^beta.*A.^2).*(1+nu*sqrt(T)./(2*(-1+rho^2)) ...
    .*(a11+a10/tau))./(2*pi*tau*sqrt(1-rho^2)) ...
    .*exp(-(u.^2-2*rho*u.*v+v.^2)./(2*tau*(1-rho^2)));
end
```

Figure 2.22 Matlab implementation of the approximation formula for the two-dimensional SABR density. First order from Wu, Q. (2010)

With the variables defined above, the density $p(\cdot)$ starting at forward f and spot volatility a is given by

$$p(F, A; f, a) = \frac{1}{vTF^\beta A^2}(1 + \frac{v\sqrt{T}}{2(-1 + \rho^2)}(a_{11} + a_{10}/\tau) \tag{2.65}$$

$$+ \frac{v^2 T}{24(1 - \rho^2)^2}(a_{23}\tau + a_{22} + a_{21}/\tau + a_{20}/\tau^2))/(2\pi\tau\sqrt{1 - \rho^2})$$

$$\times \exp\left(-\frac{u^2 - 2\rho uv + v^2}{2\tau(1 - \rho^2)}\right).$$

Figures 2.22 and 2.23 show two implementations in Matlab. The implementations differ only in the number of summands in the approximation.

If we wish to consider the density of the asset, we have to integrate Equation (2.65) with respect to volatility. Let us consider $p(F; f, a) = \int_0^\infty p(F, A; f, a)dA$. Now, Figure 2.24 summarizes the results. The CEV coefficient determines the backbone. The parameter α determines the overall level of volatility and is directly related to the ATM volatility level. The parameters ρ and v are related to the skewness and the convexity of volatility.

We use results from Islah, O. (2009) and Chen, B., Oosterlee, C.W. and van der Weide, H. (2010). Given the initial volatility, the terminal volatility and the integrated volatility over the considered time interval, it is possible to calculate the cumulative distribution function of S. It is given by

$$\mathbb{P}\left(S(t) \le x | S(0) > 0, \alpha(t) > 0, \int_0^t \alpha(s)^2 ds\right) = 1 - \chi^2(a; b, c). \tag{2.66}$$

```
function y = psabr32(t,T,f,F,alpha,A,beta,nu,rho)
tau = (T−t)/T;
u = (f^(1−beta)−F^(1−beta))/(alpha*(1−beta)*sqrt(T));
v = log(alpha./A)./(nu*sqrt(T));
a11 = −beta * F^(beta−1).*A./nu.*(u−rho*v);
a10 = u^2*v−rho*u*v.^2;

a = 2*rho+beta*F^(beta−1)*A./nu;
b = 2+beta*(1−beta)*F^(2*(beta−1))*A.^2./nu^2;
c = beta*F^(beta−1)*A./nu;

a23 = rho^4*(20−6*b)−12*rho^3*a+rho^2*(3*a.^2−28+12*b)+12*a*rho+8 ...
      −3*a.^2−6*b;
a22 = u^2*(3*a.^2−12*a*rho+6*b*(−1+rho^2)+2*rho^2+10) ...
      − 2*u*v.*(rho^3*(2+3*b)+rho^2*(−9*a+3*c)+rho*(10+3*a.^2−3*b) ...
      −(3*a+3*c)) + v.^2.*((2+3*(a−2*rho).^2)*rho^2 ...
      +6*c*rho*(−1+rho^2)−2);
a21 = u^4+v.^4*rho^2+u^3*v.*(8*rho−6*a)+u*v.^3.*(8*rho^3−6*a*rho^2) ...
      +u^2*v.^2.*(−14*rho^2+12*a*rho−4);
a20 = 3*u^4*v.^2−6*u^3*v.^3*rho+3*u^2*v.^4*rho^2;
y = 1./(nu*T*F^beta*A.^2).*(1+nu*sqrt(T)./(2*(−1+rho^2)) ...
    .*(a11+a10/tau)+(nu^2*T)./(24*(1−rho^2)^2) ...
    .*(a23*tau+a22+a21/tau+a20/tau^2))./(2*pi*tau*sqrt(1−rho^2)) ...
    .*exp(−(u^2−2*rho*u*v+v.^2)./(2*tau*(1−rho^2))));
end
```

Figure 2.23 Matlab implementation of the approximation formula for the two-dimensional SABR density. Second order from Wu, Q. (2010)

where the parameters are

$$a = \frac{1}{v(t)} \left(\frac{S(0)^{1-\beta}}{(1-\beta)} + \frac{\rho}{v}(\alpha(t) - \alpha(0))^2 \right)^2$$

$$b = 2 - \frac{1 - 2\beta - \rho^2(1-\beta)}{(1-\beta)(1-\rho^2)}$$

$$c = \frac{x^{2(1-\beta)}}{(1-\beta)^2 v(t)}$$

$$v(t) = (1-\rho^2) \int_0^t \alpha(s)ds.$$

Skew and Smile

For a given maturity, T, the SABR model is capable of producing a smile shaped implied volatility. Figure 2.25 shows the corresponding implied volatilities generated for the parameter changes. The base scenario we fix for the SABR model is determined by setting $S(0) = 100$, $\sigma(0) = 0.2$, $\rho = 0$, $\beta = 0.5$, $v = 0.2$ and $T = 1$.

This is a scenario representing some equity modelling setting. We are fully aware that the SABR model is often applied to interest rates and FX markets. But since the forwards are very small for interest rates this can lead to instabilities, which we cover in Subsection 2.3.5.

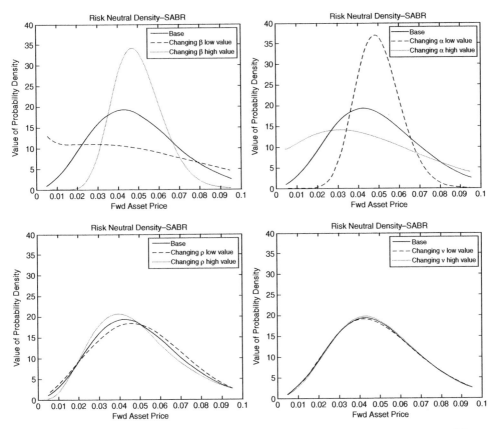

Figure 2.24 Risk neutral density for the returns using $T = 1$, spot value of $S(0) = 0.05$ and different values for the CEV exponent $\beta = 0.3, 0.5, 0.7$ (top left), different values for the spot volatility parameter $\alpha = 0.15, 0.2, 0.25$ (top right), different values for the correlation $\rho = -0.6, 0, 0.6$ (bottom left) and different values for the volatility of volatility $\nu = 0.1, 0.2, 0.3$ (bottom right)

Typical Paths and Returns

We plot typical paths for illustrating realizations of a path following a SABR dynamic. We take the base scenario and change the model parameters. Figures 2.26 and 2.27 show the paths with their respective returns generated using a SABR dynamic.

2.3.5 SABR – Further Remarks

The application of the SABR model is very attractive since there is an approximation formula to the Black implied volatility, for instance, Equation 2.64. For a wide range of market data the application of the formula is feasible. It is most suitable for calibration and pricing since it is fast and can be implemented easily. However, care has to be taken when applying the approximation and it seems that it is only safe to apply it for interpolation purposes. For many complex products we need further values of implied volatilities. These volatilities are often far left or far right from the current forward level. To this end we have to apply extrapolation. Using

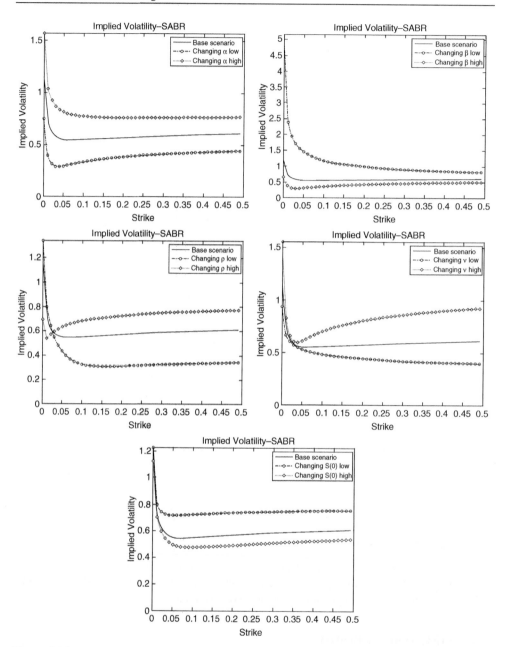

Figure 2.25 Implied volatility smile for SABR. We use $T = 1$ and different values for the spot volatility $\alpha = 0.15, 0.2, 0.25$ (top left), the CEV exponent $\beta = 0.3, 0.5, 0.7$ (top right), the correlation parameter $\rho = 0.15, 0.2, 0.25$ (mid left), the volatility of volatility $v = -0.6, 0, 0.6$ (mid right) and the spot value $S(0) = 0.1, 0.2, 0.3$ (bottom)

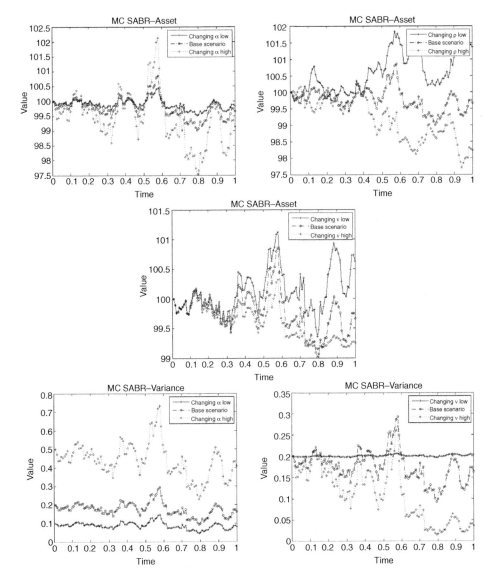

Figure 2.26 Paths of the asset for $T = 1$, spot value of $S(0) = 100$ and different values for the initial variance $\alpha = 0.05, 0.1, 0.2$ (top left), the correlation $\rho = -0.8, 0.8, 0.8$ (top right) and the volatility of volatility $\nu = 0.005, 0.1, 0.2$ (mid). For the volatility paths the corresponding value can be found on the bottom. We have omitted the case for ρ as we have set the simulation and so the effect of changing ρ is only visible for the asset paths

the standard SABR formula we observe that the volatilities for far out of the money calls are too high and for the other wing, that is the far left, could lead to negative values of the risk neutral density.

First we show that the standard approximation cannot be used since the corresponding density can become negative and therefore arbitrage is possible. Furthermore, when evaluating

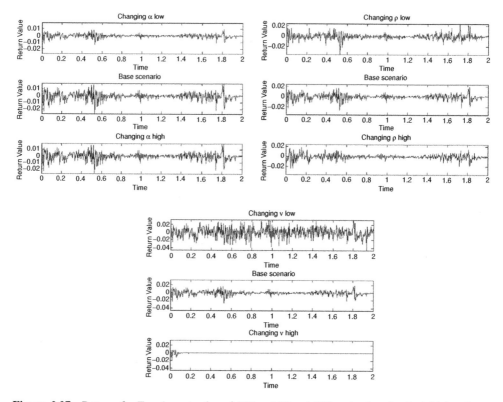

Figure 2.27 Returns for $T = 1$, spot value of $S(0) = 100$ and different values for the initial variance $\alpha = 0.05, 0.1, 0.2$ (top left), the correlation $\rho = -0.8, 0.8, 0.8$ (top right) and the volatility of volatility $\nu = 0.005, 0.1, 0.2$ (bottom) and the same for the volatility paths. We have omitted the case for ρ as we have set the simulation and so the effect of changing ρ is only visible for the asset paths

market instruments called *Constant Maturity Swaps* the volatilities for the strike range $K \in (0, \infty)$ are used. These strike levels are used to determine the so-called *Convexity Adjustment*. Using the standard SABR approximation formula this might lead to a monotone increasing convexity adjustment with respect to the strike. To cover these eventualities several rules of thumb have been proposed.

- **Constant Extrapolation**
  It has been market practice to cut off the smile for low and high values and use constant extrapolation. This method can be formalized as follows. Let us fix strikes k_l and k_u and we assume that the approximation formula is valid for $k \in (k_l \leq k \leq k_u)$.

$$\tilde{\sigma}(k) := \begin{cases} \sigma(k_l), & k < k_l \\ \sigma(k), & k_l \leq k \leq k_u. \\ \sigma(k_u), & k > k_u \end{cases} \tag{2.67}$$

The Matlab code is:

```
function y = svol_flat(a, b, r, n, f, k, t,low,high)
% computes the sabr implied volatility using flat extrapolation
klow = low*f; khigh = high*f;
y = svol_2(a,b,r,n,f,k,t);              % standard SABR
y(k<klow) = svol_2(a,b,r,n,f,klow,t);   % const value at klow
y(k>khigh) = svol_2(a,b,r,n,f,khigh,t); % const value at khigh
end
```

- **Regimes of Volatility**
  Since constant extrapolation is not an appropriate solution other methods have been used by practitioners. One is the choice of general volatility regimes. In the simplest case we choose

$$\tilde{\sigma}(k) := \begin{cases} \sigma(k) \cdot f_1(k), & k < k_l \\ \sigma(k), & k_l \le k \le k_u. \\ \sigma(k) \cdot f_2(k), & k > k_u \end{cases} \qquad (2.68)$$

Possible choices of the functions f_1 and f_2 are

$$f_n(k) = (1 + a|k - k_l|)^{-1}, \quad n = 1, 2$$
$$f_n(k) = (1 + a(k - k_l)^2)^{-1}, \quad n = 1, 2.$$

The constant extrapolation is a special case if we choose $f_1(k) = \sigma(k_l)/\sigma(k)$ and $f_2(k) = \sigma(k_u)/\sigma(k)$. The implementation in Matlab is given by the function svol_regime.

```
function y = svol_regime(a, b, r, n, f, k, t,low,high)
% SABR implied volatility with using regimes
nu = 0 * k;           % allocation
klow = low*f;         % low strike for regime
khigh = high*f;       % high strike for regime
mu1 = 1; mu2 = 3;     % parameters for regime
nu(k<klow) = n * 1 ./ sqrt(1+mu1*(k(k<klow)-klow).^2);
nu(k>khigh) = n * 1 ./ sqrt(1+mu2*(k(k>khigh)-khigh).^2);
nu((klow <= k) & (k <= khigh)) = n;
 y =  svol_2(a,b,r,nu,f,k,t);
end
```

- **Price Extrapolation**

  Extrapolating the price is suggested in Benaim, S., Dodgson, M. and Kainth, D. (2010). Let us consider

  $$\tilde{C}(k, T) := \begin{cases} C_1(k; \alpha), & k < k_l \\ C(k, \sigma(k)), & k_l \leq k \leq k_u. \\ C_2(k; \beta), & k > k_u \end{cases} \quad (2.69)$$

  where $\alpha = \{\alpha_1, \ldots, \alpha_{d_1}\}$ and $\beta = \{\beta_1, \ldots, \beta_{d_2}\}$ are parameter sets and C_1 and C_2 are functions. The parameters can be chosen such that the prices fit smoothly at k_l and k_u and the tails can be controlled.

  However, negative densities can be avoided, but for some parameter sets the admissible range $[k_l, k_{\text{ATM}}]$ is very small.

- **Density Extrapolation – Proposed Solution**

  Let us consider the following approach to extrapolation (see Kienitz, J. (2011)). With respect to the difficulties of the approaches discussed so far we propose to extrapolate the density. This allows for positive densities and – with some numerical effort – let us match the observed prices within the observed bid–ask spread. We consider two functions called the *lower extrapolation* and *upper extrapolation* for the SABR density. The functions are given by

  $$p_l(x) := x^{\mu_l} \exp(a_l + b_l x + c_l x^2) \quad (2.70)$$

  $$p_u(x) := x^{\mu_u} \exp(a_u + b_u x^{-1} + c_u x^{-2}). \quad (2.71)$$

  Moreover, we specify a range $[k_l, k_u]$ where we apply the standard SABR density. Outside this interval we use the proposed extrapolation methods. Using the representation allows a smooth fit for the modified density at the cut off points k_l and k_u. Furthermore, it is possible directly to control the tail behaviour using the constants $\mu_l > 0$ and $\mu_u < 0$.

Let us summarize the density extrapolation approach and some of its consequences:

- The choice of k_l and k_u can be used to more closely fit option prices or other quoted prices such as CMS.
- The parameters μ_l and μ_u can be used to control the tails.
- The parameters a_l, b_l and c_l as well as a_u, b_u and c_u can be applied to smoothly fit the density.
- Option prices have to be computed numerically.
- F_X and F_X^{-1} can be computed numerically and efficiently.
- Can be directly applied for copula pricing.
- The parameters have to be calibrated to match the forward and quoted option prices.

For pricing European Call options we proceed as follows. First, we consider the density

$$p_{\text{MSABR}} = \begin{cases} p_l(x), & x < k_l \\ p_{\text{SABR}}(x), & x \in [k_l, k_u]. \\ p_u(x), & x > k_u \end{cases} \quad (2.72)$$

We have used the function psabr for computing the density in the admissible region. In our case this is the density implied by the SABR approximation formula with the code given in Figures 2.28 and 2.29.

```
function y = psabr_4_2(a, b, r, n, f, k, t,m, mu, nu, l, u)
% sabr prices using an admissible region kl <= k <= ku
% for 0 <= k <= kl we use f(x) = x^mu exp(a + bx + cx^2)
% for ku < k < +infty we use f(x) = x^(-nu) exp(a + bx^(-1) + cx(-2)
% a big range (small kl and big ku) guarantee prices are in line
%
% this is the preferred version of the density for computations
%
eps = 0.0001;                                    % .1 bp

s = @(x) psabr(a, b, r, n, f, x, t);
index = find(s(k)>0,1,'first');

if isempty(index)
   kl = 1 *f;
else
    kl = max(1 * f,k(index)+(f-k(index))/m);% lower strike level
end
s1 = s(kl-eps); s2 = s(kl); s3 = s(kl+eps)% calc of derivatives

V1 = log(s2);                                    % log density
U2 = (s3-s1)/(2*eps);                            % deriv of density
V2 = U2/s2;                                      % deriv of log density
U3 = (s3-2*s2+s1)/eps^2;                         % 2nd deriv of density
V3 = U3/s2 - V2^2;                               % 2nd deriv of log density

% fix mu and solve
%         V1 = mu log kl + a + b kl + c kl^2
%         V2 = mu / kl + b + 2c kl
%         V3 = - mu / kl^2 + 2c

cl = .5*(V3+mu/kl^2);
bl = V2-mu/kl - 2*cl*kl;
al = V1 - mu * log(kl) - bl*kl - cl*kl^2;

% upper strike level
ku = u * f;
s = @(x) psabr(a, b, r, n, f, x, t);             % sabr price for calls
s1 = s(ku-eps); s2 = s(ku);s3 = s(ku+eps);       % for calc derivs

V1 = log(s2);                                    % log Call price

U2 = (s3-s1)/(2*eps);                            % deriv of  density
V2 = U2/s2;                                      % deriv of log density

U3 = (s3-2*s2+s1)/eps^2;                         % 2nd deriv of density
V3 = U3/s2 - (U2/s2)^2;                          % 2nd deriv of density

% fix nu and solve
%         V1 = -nu log ku + a + b/ku + c/ku^2
%         V2 = -nu / ku - b / ku^2 - 2c/ku^3
%         V3 = nu / ku^2 + 2 b / ku^3 - 6 c / ku^4

cu = (-1.5*nu / ku + .5*V3 * ku - V2)*ku^3/5;
bu = -ku^2*(V2 + nu/ku +2*cu/ku^3);
au = V1 + nu * log(ku) - bu / ku - cu / ku^2;

yl = real(k(k<kl).^mu .* exp(al + bl .* k(k<kl) + cl * k(k<kl).^2));
ym = real(psabr(a,b,r,n,f,k((kl<=k)&(k<=ku)),t));
yu = real(k(k>ku).^(-nu) .* exp(au+bu./k(k>ku)+cu./k(k>ku).^2));

y = [yl ym yu];                                  % output
end
```

Figure 2.28   Matlab code for computing the density with stable extrapolation

```
function y = psabr(a,b,r,n,f,k,t)
% sabr risk neutral density using standard Hagan et al. pricing formula
% sprice(...)
    eps = 0.0001;

    y1 = real(sprice(a,b,r,n,f,k+eps,t,1));
    y2 = real(sprice(a,b,r,n,f,k,t,1));
    y3 = real(sprice(a,b,r,n,f,k-eps,t,1));
    y = (y1-2*y2+y3)/eps^2;
end
```

Figure 2.29 Matlab code for computing the SABR density from the implied volatilities indicated by the approximation formula

The price of the Call option is then

$$C(K,T) = \int_{K}^{\infty} p_{\text{MSABR}}(x)dx. \tag{2.73}$$

Since the functions appearing in the integration are smooth, we approximate the integral in (2.73) using Riemann sums. The corresponding code is presented in Figure 2.30.

```
function y = sprice_4_2_fast(a, b, r, n, f, k, t,m, mu, nu, l, u, cp)
% sabr prices using the risk neutral density psabr_4
% and integrating this density with respect to the payoff

eps = 0.001;
nl = length(k);
y = ones(1,nl);

rr = 0:eps:.5;

F1 = @(x) x .* psabr_4_2(a, b, r, n, f, x, t, m, mu, nu, l, u);
F2 = @(x) psabr_4_2(a, b, r, n, f, x, t, m, mu, nu, l, u);

y1 = F1(rr);
y2 = F2(rr);

y1 = cumsum(y1(end:-1:1)); y1 = y1(end:-1:1);
y2 = cumsum(y2(end:-1:1)); y2 = y2(end:-1:1);

    % call
for j = 1:nl;
    index = find(rr>=k(j),1,'first');
    y(j) = eps*(y1(index) - k(j) * y2(index));
end

if (cp ~= 1)
    y = k - f + y;
end

end
```

Figure 2.30 Matlab code for computing the price of a European Call option using the modified SABR density

There are still some outstanding issues. For some parameter sets it is not even possible to derive the stable extrapolation since the shortcomings are already observed around the current forward strike. Then, it is not possible to specify an interval with $f \in [k_l, k_u]$. Hence, we have to reject the use of the SABR model and switch to some other model that will lead to stable results around the current forward. Some methods which might be used in this case are the *Vanna Volga Method* or the *SVI* model (see Gatheral, J. (2006), Wystup, U. (2008) or Castanga, A. and Mercurio, F. (2007) for further information).

Let us give an indication of how the calibration is done. First, we have to take care that the forward is preserved. The piece of code that handles the calibration is provided in Figure 2.31.

We have employed the objective function given in Figure 2.32. Of course, we could only have used Call or Put option prices. Another approach would be to use Call option prices to the right of the forward and Put options for strikes smaller than the forward level.

For the calibration we assumed that we calibrated a SABR model to given market data. From this calibration we retrieve the optimal parameters for the extrapolation by matching Call or Put option prices. As mentioned it would also be possible to use Call options for the right tail and Put options for the left tail. We can furthermore choose the tail decay and only calibrate the bounds of the admissible interval k_l and k_u.

2.4 STOCHASTIC VOLATILITY AND STOCHASTIC RATES MODELS

Let us consider the general SDE of a stochastic volatility model, (2.41). The parameter r is assumed to be a fixed positive real number representing the riskless rate. We wish to extend the basic stochastic volatility model by a stochastic model which allows for the rate being a stochastic process. This modelling framework has been examined by many researchers. Many stochastic volatility models have been extended by short rate processes for the rates or other processes such as the Libor Market Model (see for instance Fries, C. (2006), Grzelak, L.A., Oosterlee, C.W. and van Weeren, S. (2008) or Grzelak, L., Oosterlee, C.W. and van Weeren, S. (2009)).

In the following we consider the *Heston–Hull–White model*. The volatility is modelled as a square root process as given in Subsection 2.3.3 and the rate by a mean reverting Hull–White process as in Subsection 2.2.2.

This model is analysed in Grzelak, L.A., Oosterlee, C.W. and van Weeren, S. (2008), Hout t', K., Bierkens, J., Ploeg Van der, A.P.C. and Panhuis t', J. (2007), Grzelak, L., Oosterlee, C.W. and van Weeren, S. (2011), Grzelak, L., Oosterlee, C.W. and van Weeren, S. (2009), Kammeyer, H. and Kienitz, J. (2012a), Kammeyer, H. and Kienitz, J. (2012b) and Kammeyer, H. and Kienitz, J. (2012c). Using the above approaches it is also possible to consider a square root process to model the short rate.

2.4.1 The Heston–Hull–White Model

The Heston–Hull–White model is presented in this section. In this model the constant r is replaced by a stochastic process which models the short rate. The chosen process is the same as in the Hull–White model. The model is represented by the following set of SDEs:

$$dS(t) = (r(t) - d)S(t)dt + \sqrt{V(t)}S(t)dW_1(t) \tag{2.74}$$

```
f = 0.03; t =1;                              % forward time
a = 0.25; b = 0.5; r = -.5; n = 0.2;         % sabr parameters

k = 0:0.0001:1;                              % strike range

call = sprice(a, b, r, n, f, k, t,1);        % Call prices (standard sabr)
put = sprice(a, b, r, n, f, k, t,0);         % Put prices (standard sabr)
put(1) = 0;
call(1) = f;                                 % assures forward is matched

Nparam = 4;                                  % number of calibrated params

% objective function
of = @(x) of_sabr(a,b,r,n,f,k,t,x(3),x(4),x(1),x(2),call,put);

x0 = [.25*f; 25.5*f; 1.8; 2.4];
% starting values                  %

A = zeros(Nparam,Nparam); bc= zeros(Nparam,1);
Aeq = A; beq = bc;
lb = [.25*f; f; 1; 3];                          % lower bound
ub = [f; 30*f; 1.5; 5];                         % upper bound
y = fmincon(of,x0,A,bc,Aeq,beq,lb,ub);   % optimization

% verification of results
xval = 0:0.001:.25;                          % x-values
[cl, bl, al, cu, bu, au] = psabr_param_3(a, b, r, n, f, t,...
               y(3),y(4),y(1),y(2));
yval = psabr_5(a, b, r, n, f, xval, t, y(1), y(2), ...
          y(3), cl, bl,al, y(4), cu,bu,au);% y-values calculated

plot(xval,yval);                             % plot the results
Factor = 1000000;                            % used for plotting

yval_call = sprice_5(a, b, r, n, f, xval, t, y(1), y(2), ...
      y(3), cl, bl,al, y(4), cu,bu,au, 1);    % SABR Call prices
figure; hold on;
    plot(xval,Factor*yval_call,'r');
    plot(k,Factor*call,'g');
hold off;

yval_put = sprice_5(a, b, r, n, f, xval, t, y(1), y(2), ...
      y(3), cl, bl,al, y(4), cu,bu,au, 0);    % SABR Put prices
figure; hold on;
    plot(xval,Factor*yval_put,'r');
    plot(k,Factor*put,'g');
hold off;

fval = sprice_5(a, b, r, n, f, 0, t, y(1), y(2), ...
      y(3), cl, bl,al, y(4), cu,bu,au, 1);    % calculate forward value
y                                            % calibrated values
f - fval                                     % difference to forward
```

Figure 2.31 Code for calibrating the SABR density using the extrapolation method. Four parameters are calibrated. This is the lower bound and upper bound of the feasible region and the tail decay parameters for the left and right tail

```
function y = of_sabr(a, b, r, n, f, k, t, mu, nu, kl, ku, call, put)
% objective function for SABR calibration
    [kl, cl, bl, al, ku, cu, bu, au] = ...
        psabr_param_2(a, b, r, n, f, k, t,mu,nu, kl, ku);

    callkl = interpl(k,call,kl);        % get value at kl
    putku = interpl(k,put,ku);          % get value at ku

    % using only Call or Put prices is enough
    % can use Put left of atm and calls right!!!
    % that is Put for [kl,f] and calls (f,ku]
    y = (sprice_5(a, b, r, n, f, kl, t, kl, ku, ...
        mu, cl, bl,al, nu, cu,bu,au, 1) ...
        - callkl)^2;            % Call prics
    y = y + (sprice_5(a, b, r, n, f, 0, t, kl, ku, ...
        mu, cl, bl,al, nu, cu,bu,au, 0) ...
        - f)^2;                 % atm price
    y = y + (sprice_5(a, b, r, n, f, ku, t, kl, ku, ...
        mu, cl, bl,al, nu, cu,bu,au, 0) ...
        - putku)^2;             % Put prices
```

Figure 2.32 Objective function for the SABR calibration

$$dV(t) = \kappa(\Theta - V(t))dt + v\sqrt{V(t)}dW_2(t) \tag{2.75}$$

$$dr(t) = \lambda(\Theta_r(t) - r(t))dt + \eta dW_3(t) \tag{2.76}$$

$$S(0) = S_0$$

$$V(0) = V_0$$

$$r(0) = r_0$$

$$\langle dW_i, dW_j \rangle = \rho_{ij}dt \quad i, j = 1, 2, 3.$$

The SDEs (2.74) and (2.75) correspond to those of the Heston stochastic volatility model, Sub-section 2.3.3, while the stochastic evolution of Equation (2.76) corresponds to the Hull–White model, Subsection 2.2.2. Thus, the parameters κ, λ, Θ, v, Θ_r and η have the same interpretation as in the other models.

The correlation matrix – using informal notation – is given by

$$\begin{pmatrix} dt & dW_1 dW_2 & dW_1 dW_3 \\ dW_1 dW_2 & dt & dW_2 dW_3 \\ dW_1 dW_2 & dW_2 dW_3 & dt \end{pmatrix} = \begin{pmatrix} 1 & \rho_{12} & \rho_{13} \\ \rho_{12} & 1 & \rho_{23} \\ \rho_{13} & \rho_{23} & 1 \end{pmatrix} dt \tag{2.77}$$

which models the dependency of the asset price, the variance and the rate processes. From a modelling viewpoint we wish to be able to assign a full correlation structure and therefore choose ρ_{ij} arbitrarily in the admissible range $(-1, 1)$. Furthermore, to actually have a correlation matrix it has to be positive definite. We face a practical drawback in this setting since it is not clear how to infer the dependency of variance and rates. Using a standard calibration procedure gives values which match the market prices used as calibration instruments. We propose to use the model parameters to recover quoted option prices more accurately.

The full correlation setting poses some severe mathematical problems since we wish to have a tractable model. To this end we have to consider the class of *affine models*. We call a model affine if the corresponding characteristic function (or after a suitable transformation – for example to the log price process) is of the form

$$\varphi = \exp\left(E_1(u, t)X_1(0) + E_2(u, t)X_2(0) \ldots + E_d(u, t)X_d(0) + F(u, t)\right), \qquad (2.78)$$

with the processes $E_i, i = 1, \ldots, d$ and F do not depend on $X_i, i = 1, \ldots, d$. This representation corresponds to an affine stochastic process. The general correlation structure, (2.77), does not lead to a model in affine form. There is no known explicit expression for the characteristic function. A simplification is to use correlation matrices which lead to affine models. This is, for instance, the case if the correlation between the rates and the assets and between the rates and the stochastic variance is set to 0. To have more flexibility in modelling the dependency the model can be approximated by an affine model. In what follows we consider both approaches.

Characteristic Function

We wish to apply the general pricing methodology for stochastic volatility models. To this end we rely on an analytic expression for the characteristic function of the model. As mentioned, we have to consider two cases for the Heston–Hull–White model. We call the cases the *simple* and the *full correlation structure*. The implementation of the characteristic function is given in Figure 2.33.

Simple Correlation Structure – $\rho_{1,3} = \rho_{2,3} = 0$ We consider the Cholesky decomposition of (2.77) and transform to the log asset price, $X(t) = \log(S(t))$. We find that the model is affine if $\rho_{1,3} = \rho_{2,3} = 0$. For the log transformation, by Itô's formula we have

$$dX(t) = \frac{1}{S(t)}dS(t) - \frac{1}{2}\frac{1}{S(t)^2}(dS(t))^2$$

$$= r(t)dt - \frac{v(t)}{2}dt + \sqrt{v_t}dW(t)$$

$$= r(t)dt + dX(H_t), \qquad (2.79)$$

X_H is the log price process of the standard Heston model, (2.49) to (2.50), with the short rate $r(t)$ set to 0. Integrating (2.79) from s to T gives

$$X(T) = R_{s,T} + X(H_T), \qquad (2.80)$$

with initial condition $X_s = X_{Hs}$. The additional summand $R_{s,T} = \int_s^T r(t)dt$ can be interpreted as a correction to the term $r(T - s)$ that the pure Heston model would produce assuming a constant short rate r.

Thus, the Heston–Hull–White characteristic function, $\phi_{HHW}(u, t, T)$ is given by

$$\phi_{HHW}(u, t, T) = \phi_H(u, t, T)\exp\left(B_r(u, \tau)r(t) + A_r(u, \tau)\right), \qquad (2.81)$$

where ϕ_H is the Heston characteristic function with zero short rate. The functions A_r and B_r are given in closed form.

$$B_r(u, \tau) = \frac{(1 + iu)(1 - e^{-\lambda \tau})}{\lambda}$$

$$A_r(u, \tau) = -\frac{1}{2}\left(\frac{\eta^2 \tau}{\lambda^2}(1 + iu) - \eta^2 B_r(u, \tau)\right) + \Theta(u, \tau)$$

$$\Theta(u, \tau) = (1 - iu)\left(\log\left(\frac{P(0, t)}{P(0, T)}\right)\right.$$
$$\left. + \frac{\eta^2}{2\lambda^2}\left(\tau + \frac{2(e^{-\lambda T} - e^{-\lambda t})}{\lambda} - \frac{e^{-2\lambda T} - e^{-2\lambda t}}{2\lambda}\right)\right).$$

The function Θ is used to incorporate the market observed term structure of interest rates. We show how this function is derived after discussing more general correlation settings. Next we consider two models allowing for a full correlation structure. These models are introduced in Grzelak, L.A., Oosterlee, C.W. and van Weeren, S. (2008).

Correlation Structure (H1-HW) – $\rho_{1,3} \neq 0$ Now, let us examine the following model considered in Grzelak, L., Oosterlee, C.W. and van Weeren, S. (2011):

$$dS(t) = r(t)S(t)dt + \sqrt{V(t)}S(t)dW_1(t) \tag{2.82}$$
$$+ (\rho_{1,2} - \tilde{\rho}_{1,2})\sqrt{V(t)}S(t)dW_2(t)$$
$$+ \rho_{1,3}\sqrt{V(t)}S(t)dW_3(t)$$

$$dV(t) = \kappa(\Theta - V(t))dt + v\sqrt{V(t)}dW_2(t) \tag{2.83}$$

$$dr(t) = \lambda(\theta(t) - r(t))dt + \eta dW_3(t) \tag{2.84}$$

$$\langle dW_1(t), dW_2(t) \rangle = \tilde{\rho}_{1,2}$$
$$\langle dW_1(t), dW_3(t) \rangle = 0$$
$$\langle dW_2(t), dW_3(t) \rangle = 0.$$

with $\tilde{\rho}_{1,2}^2 = \rho_{1,2}^2 + \rho_{1,3}^2$.

We have used the above model as it does not lead to an affine model. To make it into an affine model, we first use the logarithmic transform of the asset prices and then choose an approximation to $\rho_{1,3}\sqrt{V(t)}$ using a deterministic or some other suitable stochastic function. Appropriate means that the affinity condition holds. We use the following approximation:

$$\rho_{1,3}\sqrt{V(t)} \approx \rho_{1,3}\mathbb{E}[\sqrt{V(t)}]$$

$$\approx \sqrt{\Theta(1 - e^{\kappa t}) + V(0)e^{-\kappa t} - \frac{v^2}{8\kappa}\frac{(-e^{-\kappa t})(\Theta e^{\kappa t} - \Theta + 2V(0))}{\Theta e^{\kappa t} - \Theta + V(0)}}$$

$$=: F(t)$$

$$\approx a + b\exp(-ct).$$

```
function y = cf_hestonhullwhite(u,lnS,T,r,d,V0,theta,kappa,omega,...
    rho,lambda,eta,ircurve)
% Heston Hull White:
% correlation(variance,rate)=correlation(asset,rate)=0
% dr(t)=lambda(curve-r(t))dt + eta dW(t);
% curve is intial term structure
y = cf_heston(u,lnS,T,0,d,V0,theta,kappa,omega,rho) ...
        + cf_hullwhite(u+1i,T,lambda,eta,ircurve);
end
```

Figure 2.33   The log-characteristic function of the Heston–Hull–White model

The final approximation is used to compute the characteristic function in closed form. The parameters a, b and c are determined by

$$a = \sqrt{\Theta - \frac{v^2}{8\kappa}}, \quad b = \sqrt{V(0)} - a \quad c = -\log\left(\frac{F(1)-a}{b}\right).$$

For the model described by the stochastic differential Equations (2.82) to (2.84) the characteristic function is approximately given by

$$\phi_{\text{HHW Full}} \approx \exp\left(A(u,\tau) + B_S(u,\tau)x(0) + B_V(u,\tau)V(0) + B_r(u,\tau)r(0)\right), \tag{2.85}$$

with the functions

$$B_S(u,\tau) = iu \tag{2.86}$$

$$B_r(u,\tau) = \frac{iu-1}{\lambda}(1-e^{-\lambda\tau}) \tag{2.87}$$

$$B_V(u,\tau) = \frac{(1-e^{-d\tau})}{\gamma^2(1-ge^{-d\tau})}(\kappa - \gamma\tilde{\rho}_{12}iu - d) \tag{2.88}$$

$$A(u,\tau,\gamma) = \sum_{i=1}^{4} I_i. \tag{2.89}$$

Setting $d = \sqrt{(v\rho_{1,2} - \kappa)^2 - v^2(iu(iu-1))}$, $g = \frac{\kappa - v\rho_{1,2}iu - d}{\kappa - v\rho_{1,2}iu + d}$. Finally, the values $I_1,\ldots,I_4$ are given by integrals which can be evaluated analytically or approximated. We have

$$I_1 = \Theta_r(iu-1)\left(\tau + \frac{e^{-\lambda\tau}-1}{\lambda}\right)$$

$$I_2 = \frac{\kappa\theta T}{v^2}\left(\kappa - v\rho_{1,2}iu - d\right) - \frac{2}{v^2}\log\left(\frac{1 - g\exp(-dT)}{1-g}\right)$$

$$I_3 = \frac{\eta^2(i+u)^2}{4\lambda^3}(3 + e^{-2\lambda\tau} - 4e^{-\lambda\tau} - 2\lambda\tau)$$

$$I_4 \approx iu\eta\frac{\rho_{1,3}(iu-1)}{c\lambda^2(c+\lambda)}e^{-(c+\lambda)\tau}(b\lambda(c - e^{\lambda\tau}(c+\lambda - \lambda e^{c\tau})) + ac(c+\lambda)e^{c\tau}$$

$$\cdot(1 + e^{\lambda\tau}(\lambda\tau - 1))).$$

We have implemented this in Matlab, as shown in Figure 2.34.

```
function y = cf_h1hw(u,lnS,T,r0,d,V0,theta,kappa,omega,lambda,eta,...
          rho12,rho13,thetar)
% Heston Hull White with % correlation(variance,rate) = 0
% dr(t) = lambda(r-r(t))dt + eta dW(t); r constant


    D1 = sqrt((omega*rho12*1i*u-kappa).^2-omega^2*1i*u.*(1i*u-1));
    g = (kappa-omega*rho12*1i*u-D1)./(kappa-omega*rho12*1i*u+D1);

    a = sqrt(theta - .125 * omega^2/kappa);
    b = sqrt(V0) - a;
    ct=.25*omega^2*(1-exp(-kappa))/kappa;
    lambdat=4*kappa*V0*exp(-kappa)/(omega^2*(1-exp(-kappa)));
    d2=4*kappa*theta/omega^2;
    F1 = sqrt(ct*(lambdat-1)+ct*d2+ct*d2/(2*(d2+lambdat)));
    c = -log((F1-a)/b);

    I1 = thetar * (1i*u-1) * (T+(exp(-lambda * T)-1)/lambda);
    I2 = kappa*theta/omega^2*(T*(kappa-omega*rho12*1i*u-D1)...
        -2*log((1-g.*exp(-D1*T))./(1-g)));
    I3 = eta^2*(1i+u).^2/(4*lambda^3)*(3+exp(-2*lambda*T)...
        -4*exp(-lambda*T)-2*lambda*T);
    I4 = -eta*rho13/lambda *(1i*u+u.^2)*(b/c*(1-exp(-c*T))+a*T...
        +a/lambda*(exp(-lambda*T)-1)+b/(c-lambda)*exp(-c*T)...
        *(1-exp(-T*(lambda-c)))));


    A = I1+I2+I3+I4;
    BV = (1-exp(-D1*T))./(omega^2.*(1-g.*exp(-D1*T)))...
        .*(kappa-omega*rho12*1i*u-D1);
    Br = (1i*u-1)/lambda*(1-exp(-lambda*T));

    y = A + 1i*u * (lnS + (r0-d)*T) + BV * V0  + Br * r0;
end
```

Figure 2.34   The log-characteristic function of the H1-HW model

We used a deterministic approximation to $\sqrt{V(t)}$ to compute the characteristic function by approximating I_4. To further improve the accuracy a stochastic approximation can be applied (see Grzelak, L., Oosterlee, C.W. and van Weeren, S. (2011)), but we do not give the implementation here. Finally, using the stochastic approximation in order to compute the characteristic function we have to apply a numerical integration to compute

$$I_4 = iu \int_0^\tau \mathbb{E}\left[\sqrt{V(T-s)}\right] C(u,s)ds$$

$$= -\frac{1}{\lambda}(iu+u^2) \int_0^\tau \mathbb{E}\left[\sqrt{V(T-s)}\right]\left(1-e^{-\lambda s}\right) ds.$$

This is certainly more time-consuming than following the deterministic approach. For the stochastic approximation it is proposed to use

$$\sqrt{V(t)} = \mathcal{N}\left(C(t)(\lambda(t)-1)+c(t)d+\frac{C(t)d}{2(d+\lambda(t))}, C(t)-\frac{C(t)d}{2(d+\lambda(t))}\right),$$

with

$$C(t) = \frac{v^2}{4\kappa}\left(1 - e^{-\kappa t}\right), \quad d = \frac{4\kappa\Theta}{v^2}, \quad \lambda(t) = \frac{4\kappa V(0)e^{-\kappa t}}{v^2\left(1 - e^{-\kappa t}\right)}.$$

The full derivation including all proofs can be found in Grzelak, L., Oosterlee, C.W. and van Weeren, S. (2011). In principle it is possible to use the extended Heston–Hull–White model for risk management and pricing applications. The market parameters can be derived analogously to the simple model. The only thing we have to change is the characteristic function.

Incorporating an initial term structure   For financial application we wish to use an initial term structure. Thus, we have to provide a method to compute the function $\theta(\cdot)$ such that the current zero bond prices fit the observed discount curve. To do so we adopt the approach outlined in Brigo, D. and Mercurio, F. (2006). The method uses the relationship (2.19) which relates the model parameters to the initial discount curve. This method has already been considered when we reviewed the Hull–White model. For completeness we give the derivation in this more general setting.

$$\theta(0, \tau) = \exp\left(A(u, \tau) + B_X(u, \tau)X(0) + B_V(u, \tau)V(0)\right.$$

$$\left. + B_r(u, \tau)r(0) + \Theta(u, \tau)\right). \tag{2.90}$$

The model zero bond prices are given by the formula

$$P(0, T) = \exp\left(\int_0^T \psi(s)ds + A(0, T)\right),$$

and the function $\psi(\cdot)$ is given in terms of the instantaneous forward rate f

$$\psi(s) = f(0, s) + \frac{\eta^2}{2\lambda^2}(1 - e^{-\lambda s})^2.$$

The other part of the integrand, the function $A(\cdot, \cdot)$, is given by

$$A(0, T) = \frac{\eta^2}{2\lambda^3}\left(-\frac{3}{2} - \frac{1}{2}e^{-2\lambda T} + \lambda T\right).$$

Finally, we obtain for the function Θ

$$\Theta(u, \tau) = (1 - iu)\left(\log(P(0, \tau)) + \frac{\eta^2}{2\lambda^3}\left(\tau\lambda + 2(e^{-\lambda\tau} - 1) - \frac{1}{2}(e^{-2\lambda\tau} - 1)\right)\right).$$

Using this setting we are able to incorporate the initial term structure into the model.

Risk Neutral Distribution

In order to assess the influence of certain model parameters, let us consider the following base scenario:

- Spot variance: $V(0) = 0.02$
- Long term variance: $\Theta = 0.02$
- Mean reversion speed: $\kappa = 0.1$
- Volatility of variance: $v = 0.2$

Table 2.2   The initial term structure given as a discount curve. This is the base input to the analysis for the effect of the model parameters for the Heston–Hull–White model

T	Discount	T	Discount	T	Discount
0,003	0.999884333380315	3	0.882870065420196	17	0.477507905873099
0,08	0.996803132736937	4	0.847186544281939	18	0.456481811728753
0,17	0.993568709230647	5	0.812742515687365	19	0.436385788738282
0,25	0.990285301195274	6	0.779459552415061	20	0.417350253831050
0,33	0.986945903402709	7	0.747152463119429	21	0.399187111819286
0,41	0.983557350486521	8	0.715745016074346	22	0.381865611666566
0,5	0.980185549124449	9	0.685138723808460	23	0.365435617455498
0,58	0.976782934344041	10	0.655753392359115	24	0.349786183601181
0,66	0.973361992614499	11	0.627333845297308	25	0.334806921914717
0,75	0.969976793305220	12	0.599226698198774	26	0.320548897004994
0,83	0.966616749933289	13	0.572763319281569	27	0.306983265264429
0,92	0.962914317958160	14	0.547259133751455	28	0.294081800917050
1	0.959904777446077	15	0.523441996253080	29	0.282443547729164
2	0.920091903961326	16	0.499646068368557	30	0.269929224010243

- Correlation: $\rho = 0$
- Mean reversion speed rate: $\lambda = 0.1$
- Volatility rate: $\eta = 0.02$.

Table 2.2 gives the initial term structure as the discount curve.

Since we have already analysed the implications of changing the parameters for the Heston model, we now change the parameters for the initial term structure, the mean reversion of the spot rate and the volatility of the spot rate. The corresponding densities for the returns can be observed in Figure 2.35. The effect of the volatility is shown in the top left graph. Decreasing the volatility leads to a more peaked distribution since most of the mass is concentrated around the mean. The opposite effect is observed when the volatility is increased. The mean reversion shows the opposite effect on the risk neutral distribution. Increasing the mean reversion speed of the rates causes a more peaked distribution. Finally, the initial term structure leads to a negatively skewed distribution when we decrease it and to a more positively skewed distribution when we increase it.

Skew and Smile

In this section we consider the skew and smile generated by the Heston–Hull–White model. We have already shown the effect for the parameters in the basic Heston model in Subsection 2.3.3. Thus, with the explanations from the section on risk neutral densities in mind, we can observe the same effects for the implied volatility smile.

Decreasing the volatility of the rate, η, leads to negative nearly parallel shift of the whole implied volatility surface. Increasing this volatility parameter increases the overall level of implied volatility. The contrary occurs with the mean reversion parameter. Increasing leads to a lower level of the implied volatility surface and decreasing it leads to a higher level of volatility. Finally, Figure 2.36 also shows the effect both of increasing and decreasing the initial term structure. In this case increasing leads to higher levels of volatility, and vice versa.

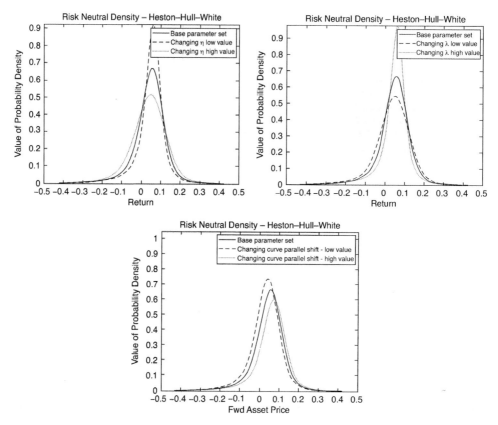

Figure 2.35 Risk neutral density of the Heston–Hull–White model for the returns using $T = 10$, spot value of $S(0) = 100$ and different values for the mean reversion speed $\lambda = 0.05, 0.1, 0.5$ (top left), for the volatility of variance $\eta = 0.01, 0.02, 0.03$ (top right) and for the initial term structure $V(0) = -1\text{bp}, 0\text{bp}$ and $+1\text{bp}$ (bottom)

Typical Paths and Returns

Since plotting the sample paths and the returns does not lead to any new insights, we omit these procedures for the Heston–Hull–White model.

2.5 SUMMARY AND CONCLUSIONS

We have now investigated several financial models based on diffusion processes. The first part of this chapter dealt with local volatility models; the second part introduced additional sources of randomness. We considered stochastic volatility models including the Heston and the SABR models. Applying such models we assume that the volatility is driven by another – possibly correlated – Brownian motion. Finally, we also allowed the rates to be stochastic processes driven by a further, possibly correlated, Brownian motion. To this end we considered the Heston–Hull–White model as our primary example. For all the models considered we have

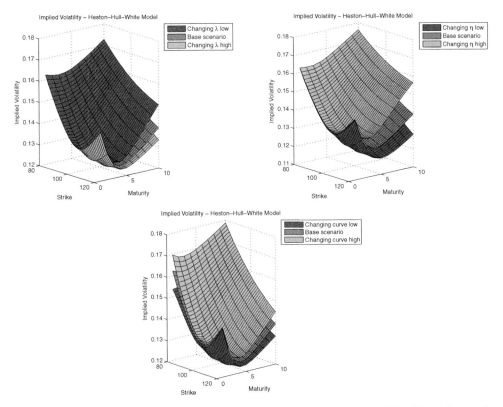

Figure 2.36 The implied volatility smile for the Heston–Hull–White Model for $T = 1, 2, \ldots, 10$ years, spot value of $S(0) = 100$ and different values for the mean reversion speed of the short rate $\lambda = 0.1, 0.2, 0.3$ (top left), different values for the volatility of the short rate $\eta = 0.01, 0.02, 0.03$ (top right) and for the initial term structure $V(0) = -100\text{bp}, 0\text{bp}$ and $+100\text{bp}$ (bottom)

summarized the model properties and the impact of the model parameters to reflect observed structures in financial markets.

For each of the model classes considered we have examined widely applied examples in detail. In particular, we have shown how the model parameters affect the skew/smile, the risk neutral density and a typical sample path. For each of the models we have provided formulae for pricing European Call and Put options.

3

Models with Jumps

3.1 INTRODUCTION AND OBJECTIVES

The aim of this chapter is, first, to extend the class of diffusion models to include jumps representing rare events. Second, it is to consider processes which are exclusively driven by jumps. As observed in Chapter 1, implied volatility surfaces exhibit a term structure of volatility as well as a significant skew/smile along the range of strikes. Furthermore, the risk neutral as well as the real-world distribution exhibit fat tails or they are asymmetric. We aim to introduce classes of models which are capable of modelling the market variables for such cases.

To this end we aim to apply more realistic distribution functions and price processes and we wish to approximate the market implied volatility surface. The first class of models extends the class of diffusion models by modelling rare events such as defaults, credit events, crashes or draw downs by adding an uncorrelated *compound Poisson process* to the diffusion. The second class of models does not necessarily have a diffusion part at all. Such processes are exclusively driven by jumps. The models we consider are based on *Lévy processes*. The current chapter deals with the implications for financial modelling when such processes are applied and we investigate some well-known and widely applied models, for instance the *Variance Gamma model*.

We have split this chapter into two parts. The first part reviews the basics needed for extending the models by allowing jump-diffusion processes for the stochastic driver. As mentioned, this is done by adding a compound Poisson process. We cover three models in detail, namely the *Merton model*, the *Bates model* and the *Bates–Hull–White model*. By combining different jump mechanisms or stochastic volatility drivers we get a variety of tractable models. Other models which are applied in practice such as the Kou model are not covered here. However, the methods for pricing and risk management which we discuss in this book can be applied to all models for which the characteristic function is known in closed form.

The diffusion models which we extend by adding jumps are the Black–Scholes, the Heston and the Heston–Hull–White models. The jump mechanism we apply here relies on the assumption that the jumps are distributed due to a logarithmic normal distribution.

The second part of this chapter introduces models based on Lévy processes. For the simplest model we have taken the exponential of a Brownian motion leading to the well-known Black–Scholes model. Now, we let the stochastic process be some Lévy process. Again, we analyse the properties of the models in terms of the risk neutral densities of the logarithmic returns and the ability to generate different structures of the implied volatility surface and we show typical paths. For general Lévy models the jump structure is encoded in the *Lévy measure*. This measure can be seen as a more general jump mechanism as it is used to model jump-diffusion processes.

Financial models based on Lévy models show very appealing properties for modelling time series and generating skew/smile but not when we consider different maturities at the same time. This is due to the fact that such models impose strong restrictions on the shape of the future volatility surface. In fact, the surface is the same for all forward starting Call options when we view them in terms of logarithmic moneyness, that is we take $\log(S/K)$ as the underlying. This property is called the *floating smile property*. To be more flexible when fitting option prices we introduce stochastic volatility Lévy models. To this end we review the concept of *stochastic clocks* and the modelling of business time.

The basic models we examine are:

- Variance Gamma.
- Normal Inverse Gaussian.
- CGMY/KoBoL.

We extend the basic models by a stochastic clock. The resulting stochastic volatility versions of the models are given in terms of the applied clock. The clocks we are considering are:

- Gamma Ornstein–Uhlenbeck clock.
- Cox–Ingersoll–Ross clock.

3.2 POISSON PROCESSES AND JUMP DIFFUSIONS

We start our considerations by defining the Poisson process and consider basic properties of this process. Besides a diffusion it is one of the basic building blocks of a jump-diffusion model. The jump times are modelled by a Poisson process. Once a jump occurs the jump height is drawn from its jump distribution.

3.2.1 Poisson Processes

We consider the *random times* $(\tau_n)_n$, $n \in \mathbb{N}$. For given n it is a mapping

$$\tau_n : \Omega \to \mathbb{R}^+$$
$$\omega \mapsto \tau_n(\omega).$$

Then, we take the following *counting process*:

$$N(t) = \sum_{n=0}^{\infty} 1_{\tau_n \leq t}. \tag{3.1}$$

For a given random variable $X : \Omega \to \mathbb{R}^+$, the random variable $1_{X \leq t}$ is 1 if $X(\omega) \leq t$ and 0 otherwise. Thus, N counts the number of random times smaller or equal to t.

The process is a Poisson process with *jump intensity* $\lambda \in \mathbb{R}^+$ if

$$\mathbb{P}[N(t) = k] = e^{-\lambda t} \frac{(\lambda t)^k}{k!}, \quad k \in \mathbb{N}. \tag{3.2}$$

In general the process $N(t)$ is not a martingale. To make it into a martingale we subtract its expected value at time t. This leads to the process given by:

$$N_C(t) := N(t) - \mathbb{E}[N(t)]. \tag{3.3}$$

The process $N_C(t)$ is called a *compensated Poisson process*.

Instead of the indicator random variable appearing in Equation (3.1) we could have chosen a random variable Y with distribution, F_Y, independent of the process $N(t)$. Let us fix the counting process $N(t)$ with intensity $\lambda > 0$ and let $Y_n, n = 1, \ldots$ be a sequence of independent identically distributed random variables, such that $Y_n \sim F_Y$. Consider the process given by

$$N_Y(t) := \sum_{n=0}^{N(t)} Y_n. \qquad (3.4)$$

$N_Y(t)$ is called a *compound Poisson process*. For financial modelling several distributions F_Y have been proposed. Two choices are $F_Y = \mathcal{N}(\mu_J, \sigma_J)$ and $F_Y \sim \Gamma(a, b)$.

A *Jump-Diffusion process* is a process consisting of a diffusion process with drift and a compensated Poisson process denoted by J. Such a process is represented by the SDE:

$$dX(t) = \mu dt + \sigma dW(t) + dJ(t)$$
$$X(0) = x_0$$
$$J(0) = 0$$
$$\langle dW, dJ \rangle = 0.$$

The compound Poisson process J can be described as follows:

- We have a Poisson process $N(t)$ with intensity λ.
- Every time the process jumps one draws an independent and identically distributed random variable J.
- (A special case would be $J = \text{const}$).
- The probability distribution of J is $\mathbb{P}(J \in A) = \nu(A)/\lambda$.
- Thus, $\nu(\mathbb{R}) = 1$.

The measure ν determines the jump behaviour. We analyse the measure ν in more detail in the following sections.

3.2.2 The Merton Model

In this section we consider the *Merton model* which was introduced in Merton, R. (1976). The SDE governing the evolution in this model is given by

$$dS(t) = \mu S(t)dt + \sigma S(t)dW(t) + S(t)(Y - 1)dN(t) \qquad (3.5)$$
$$S(0) = S_0$$
$$N(0) = 0, \quad \mu_j = \ln(1 + a) - \frac{b^2}{2}, \sigma_j = b, \quad a > -1, b \geq 0$$
$$\langle dW, Y \rangle = 0, \quad \langle dW, N \rangle = 0.$$

The compound Poisson process has logarithmic normal distributed jumps. If we choose the drift to be $r - d - \sigma^2/2 - \lambda \mathbb{E}[Y]$, we get a martingale. The parameters r, d and σ are as in the Black–Scholes model. They are the risk neutral rate, the dividend yield and the volatility. The process $N(t)$ is a standard Poisson process which models the number of jumps and has intensity $\lambda > 0$. Y is the jump size distribution which in this case is a log-normal distribution. N, Y and W are independent.

With the log-normal assumption for the jumps, Y has the following representation:

$$Y = \mu_J \exp\left(-\frac{1}{2}\sigma_J^2 + \sigma_J Z\right), \quad Z \sim \mathcal{N}(0, 1).$$

```
function phi = cf_merton(u,lnS,T,r,d,sigma,a,b,lambda)
% Merton Jump Diffusion
    phi = cf_bs(u,lnS,T,r,d,sigma) ...
        + cf_jumplognormal(u,a,b,lambda,T);
end
```

Figure 3.1 Matlab code for implementing the logarithmic characteristic function of the Merton model. This consists of two factors. The first factor is the characteristic function from the Black–Scholes model. The second factor corresponds to a logarithmic normal jump part. Both characteristic functions can be multiplied since the jump and the diffusion part are independent

The martingale correction we use is

$$
r - d - \frac{\sigma^2}{2} - \lambda \left(e^{-\frac{\sigma_J^2}{2} - \mu_J} - 1 \right)
$$

Pricing Formulae

Pricing of European Call and Put options can be done either by using the general pricing formula since the characteristic function of the model can be derived in closed form or by using sums of Black-type formulae. The latter lead to fast convergence since the summands of the corresponding formula decay exponentially fast. In the no dividend case we have

$$
C(K,T) = \sum_{k=0}^{\infty} \frac{(\lambda t)^k}{k!} e^{-\lambda t} e^{rt + k\mu_J + \frac{k}{2}\sigma_J} \left(S(0)\mathcal{N}(d_{1,k}) - K\mathcal{N}(d_{2,k}) \right), \tag{3.6}
$$

with

$$
d_{1,k} = \frac{\log\left(\frac{S(0)}{K}\right) + \left(\left(r + \frac{\sigma^2}{2} \right) t + k(\mu_J + \sigma_J^2) \right)}{\sqrt{\sigma^2 t + k\sigma_J^2}}
$$

$$
d_{2,k} = \frac{\log\left(\frac{S(0)}{K}\right) + \left(\left(r - \frac{\sigma^2}{2} \right) t + k(\mu_J + \sigma_J^2) \right)}{\sqrt{\sigma^2 t + k\sigma_J^2}}.
$$

Characteristic Function

To apply the general pricing methods we have to rely on the characteristic function which is known in closed form in the Merton model. Figures 3.1 and 3.2 give the Matlab code for

```
function phiJump = cf_jumplognormal(u,a,b,lambda,T)
% LogNormalJump for Merton and Bates
    phiJump = lambda*T*(-a*u*1i + ...
    (exp(u*1i*log(1.0+a)+0.5*b*b*u*1i.*(u*1i-1.0))-1.0));
end
```

Figure 3.2 Matlab implementation for the characteristic function of a logarithmic normal jump component

implementing the logarithmic characteristic function. The final function can be composed of two factors since the diffusion and the jump part are independent and thus the characteristic function is the product of the characteristic functions for the diffusion and the jump model.

For the logarithmic normal jump distribution it is possible to compute the characteristic function explicitly. The code for implementation is given in Figure 3.2.

The characteristic function for the Merton model is then given as the product of the characteristic functions of the Black–Scholes model and the logarithmic normal jump part. The latter is given by

$$\varphi_{\text{LNJ}} = \exp\left(\lambda T \left(-aiu + \left(\exp\left(iu\log(1+a) + \frac{1}{2}b^2 iu(iu-1)\right) - 1\right)\right)\right) \qquad (3.7)$$

and thus, the characteristic function is

$$\varphi_{\text{Merton}}(u) = \exp\left(i\mu ut - \frac{\sigma^2 u}{2}t + \lambda t\left(e^{i\mu_J u - \frac{1}{2\sigma_J^2 u^2} - 1}\right)\right). \qquad (3.8)$$

The resulting process is a martingale if $\varphi_{\text{Merton}}(-i) = 1$ which is equivalent to

$$\mu + \frac{\sigma^2}{2} + \lambda\left(e^{i\mu_J u - \frac{1}{2\sigma_J^2 u^2} - 1}\right) = 1.$$

Risk Neutral Density

As for the other models we first consider the risk neutral density and its shape dependent on the parameters. Since we have

$$\mathbb{P}(X(t) \in A) = \sum_{k=0}^{\infty} \mathbb{P}(X(t) \in A|N(t) = k)\mathbb{P}(N(t) = k),$$

we can show that the probability density is given by

$$p(X, T; x, t) = \exp(-\lambda(T-t)) \sum_{k=0}^{\infty} \frac{(\lambda(T-t))^k \exp\left(-\frac{((X-x)-(r-d)(T-t)-k\mu_J)}{2(\sigma^2(T-t)+k\sigma_J^2)}\right)}{k!\sqrt{2\pi(\sigma^2(T-t)+k\sigma_J^2)}}. \qquad (3.9)$$

The series in (3.9) converges very fast. From a mathematical point of view, the fast convergence stems from the fact that multiplication with $\exp(-\ldots)$ and division by $k!$ is applied. Both quantities become very small for large values of k. Figure 3.3 displays the results. Changing the average mean of the jumps, μ_J, leads to skewness for the distribution. The jump size volatility, σ_J, controls the peakedness of the density. For small values it is peaked and flat for large values. Finally, the jump intensity also controls the shape of the distribution in terms of peakedness. Decreasing the jump intensity has the effect that the mass is more concentrated around the mean value. We illustrate the effects of changing the model parameters in Figure 3.8.

For the Merton model the moments are known explicitly. We have:

$$c_1 := \mathbb{E}[X(t)] = t(r - d + \lambda\mu_J)$$
$$c_2 := \mathbb{V}[X(t)] = t(\sigma^2 + \lambda\sigma_J^2 + \lambda\mu_J^2)$$
$$c_3 = t\lambda(3\sigma_J^2\mu_J + \mu_J^3)$$
$$c_4 = t\lambda(3\sigma_J^3 + \sigma\mu_J^2\sigma_J^2 + \mu_J^4).$$

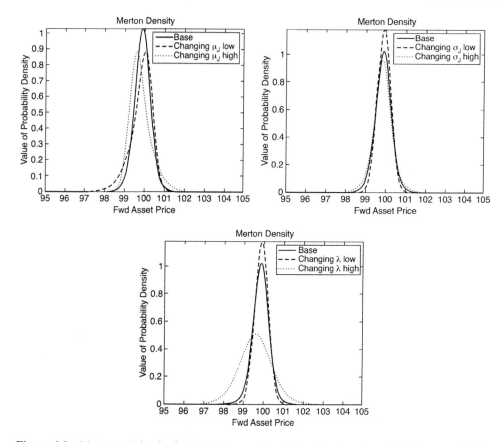

Figure 3.3   Risk neutral density for the Merton model and changing the values of the base scenario for $\mu_J = -0.5, 0, 0.5$ (top left), $\sigma_J = 0, 0.3411, 1$ (top right) and $\lambda = 0, 0.1016, 1$ (bottom)

We have denoted the third and fourth moments respectively by c_3 and c_4. The c is an abbreviation for *cumulant*.

Skew and Smile

In contrast to the Black–Scholes model the implied volatility surface is not constant in the Merton model. The shape of the surface is determined by the model parameters σ, μ_J, σ_J and λ. To this end we consider the following base scenario:

- $S(0) = 100$
- $\sigma = 0.1518$
- $\lambda = 0.1016$, $\mu_J = 0$ and $\sigma_J = 0.3411$.

We shift the parameters one after the other and summarize the results in Figure 3.4. In contrast to local volatility models the jump-diffusion models are able to generate not only a skew but a smile shaped structure for the implied volatility surface. The shape of the smile can be very steep for short dated options. This phenomenon makes jump-diffusion models applicable for modelling short dated options in FX markets where this smile shape can be observed.

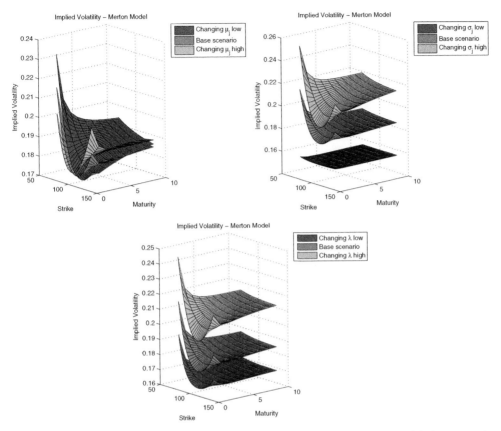

Figure 3.4   Implied volatility surface for the Merton model and changing the values of the base scenario
for $\mu_J = -0.1, 0, 0.1$ (top left), $\sigma_J = 0.1, 0.3411, 0.5$ (top right) and $\lambda = 0.05, 0.1016, 0.2$ (bottom)

Typical Paths and Returns

Finally, we show some typical paths for varying parameters in the Merton model. We plot
the corresponding return series. With respect to the paths and returns we observe another
qualitative behaviour. The paths show some very large movements, the jumps. The jump times
are distributed with respect to a Poisson distribution. Thus, if we increase the jump intensity
we observe that more jumps are likely to happen per time interval. Changing the parameters μ_J
and σ_J we do not observe that the number of jumps increases or decreases but that the average
jump size increases for increasing μ_J and the non-uniformity of the jump sizes increases if
the parameter σ_J is increased. Figures 3.5 and 3.6 summarize our findings.

3.2.3   The Bates Model

The *Bates model* is an extension of the Heston model. Let us consider the SDE:

$$dS(t) = (r - d)S(t)dt + \sqrt{V(t)}S(t)dW_1(t) + (Y - 1)\, S(t)dN(t)$$
$$dV(t) = \kappa(\Theta - V(t))dt + v\sqrt{V(t)}dW_2(t)$$

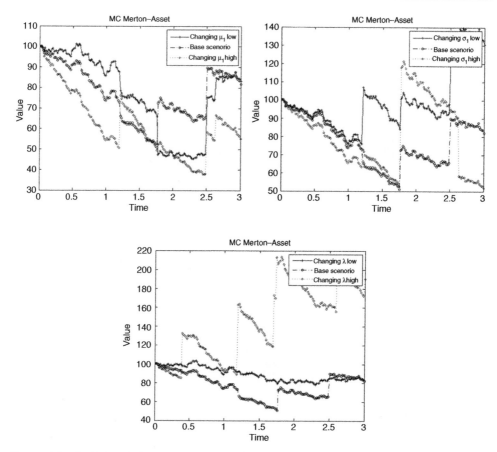

Figure 3.5 Typical paths generated using the Merton model. We consider varying the parameters $\mu_J = 0.05, 0.2, 0.5$ (top left), $\sigma_J = 0.2, 0.25, 2$ (top right) and $\lambda = 0.2, 1, 2$ (bottom)

$$S(0) = S_0$$
$$V(0) = V_0$$
$$N(0) = 0$$
$$\langle dW_1, dW_2 \rangle = \rho dt$$
$$\langle dW_i, N \rangle = \langle dW_i, Y \rangle = 0, \quad i = 1, 2.$$

The parameters r and d of the model are the risk neutral rate r, the dividend yield d. From the Heston stochastic volatility we have the parameters $V(0)$ for the spot variance, Θ for the long term variance, $\kappa > 0$ modelling reversion speed, v for the volatility of variance and $\rho \in [-1, 1]$ representing the correlation of the driving Brownian motions W_1 and W_2. The parameters governing the jump behaviour of the model are $\lambda > 0$ the jump intensity, $\mu_J \in \mathbb{R}$ the average jump size and $\sigma_J > 0$ the jump volatility.

Pricing Formulae and Characteristic Function

The characteristic function is known in closed form. We assume that the diffusion driving the asset as well as the stochastic variance are independent of the compound Poisson process.

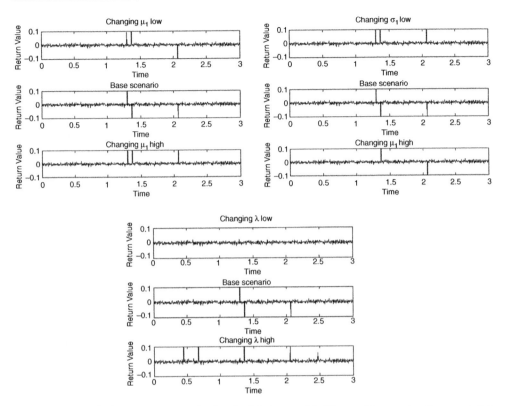

Figure 3.6 Typical returns generated using the Merton model. We consider varying the parameters $\mu_J = 0.05, 0.2, 0.5$ (top left), $\sigma_J = 0.2, 0.25, 2$ (top right) and $\lambda = 0.2, 1, 2$ (bottom)

Thus, it can be calculated by multiplying the corresponding characteristic functions and then adding the corresponding logarithms. The implementation of the logarithmic version is given in Figure 3.7.

Risk Neutral Density

For the first numerical illustration we fix the base scenario.

- $V(0) = \Theta = 0.02$
- $\kappa = 0.1$, $\nu = 0.2$ and $\rho = -0.5$
- $\lambda = 0.2$, $\mu_J = 0.1$ and $\sigma_J = 0.2$.

```
function phi = cf_bates (u, lnS, T, r, d, V0, theta, kappa, omega, rho, ...
                          a, b, lambda)
% Bates
    phi = cf_heston (u, lnS, T, r, d, V0, theta, kappa, omega, rho) ...
    + cf_jumplognormal (u, a, b, lambda, T);
end
```

Figure 3.7 Matlab code for implementing the characteristic function for the Bates model. This consists of two factors, one from a Heston model and the other from a log-normal jump component

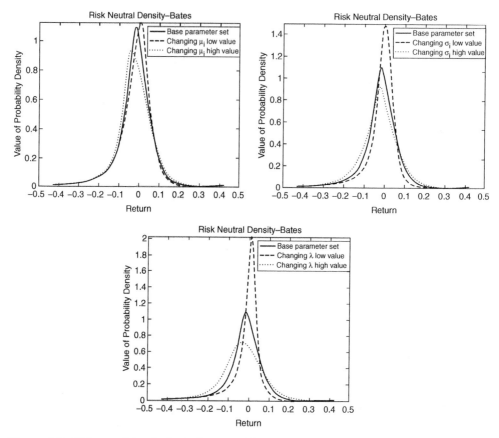

Figure 3.8 Risk neutral density for the Bates model and $\mu_J = 0, 0.1, 0.2$ (top left), $\sigma_J = 0.01, 0.2, 0.3$ (top right) and $\lambda = 0, 0.2, 0.5$ (bottom)

For the analysis we consider the effect of increasing and decreasing the model parameters. We focus our considerations on the parameters governing the jump behaviour of the process since we have already analysed the qualitative behaviour for the parameters governing the stochastic volatility in Chapter 2.

As we have already observed for the Merton model, μ_J affects the location of the mean value, the parameter σ_J determines the width of the distribution and λ determines the peakedness.

Skew and Smile

The Heston stochastic volatility model allows for modelling skew and smile shaped implied volatility surfaces. Introducing jumps allows for a significant smile for short dated options. Thus, combining the Heston model with a jump model of logarithmic normal jumps allows for a more pronounced short dated smile shape of implied volatility. This is illustrated in Figure 3.9. We take as the base scenario $\lambda = 0.15$, $\sigma_J = 0.1$ and $\mu_J = 0$. Both increasing and decreasing μ_J change the skew. Decreasing the value moves the whole skew to the left and increasing it moves it to the right. The volatility, σ_J, shifts the whole implied volatility.

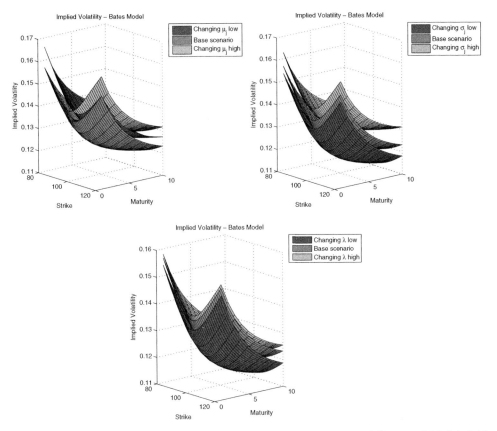

Figure 3.9   Volatility smiles for the Bates model and $\mu_J = -0.1, 0, 0.1$ (top left), $\sigma_J = 0.05, 0.1, 0.15$ (top right) and $\lambda = 0.05, 0.15, 0.2$ (bottom)

Decreasing the value shifts the surface down and increasing it shifts the surface up. Finally, changing λ leads to a nearly parallel shift of the surface.

However, we must warn readers that there is a price to pay for increasing the flexibility, for instance a pronounced smile for short dated options. We now have three additional model parameters. This is important when we focus on the inference of market parameters from option prices. Many model parameters decrease model stability.

Typical Paths and Returns

For the paths and returns we expect to observe the same phenomenon as we saw when considering the Merton model. The higher the jump frequency, the more jumps we expect to see. The parameters μ_J and σ_J then determine how pronounced and in which direction the process jumps. Our finding are summarized in Figures 3.10 and 3.11 which were generated using $T = 3$ years and 750 steps. The parameters are

- $V(0) = \Theta = 0.04$
- $\kappa = 0.2$, $v = 0.1$ and $\rho = 0$
- $\lambda = 0.2$, $\mu_J = 0.2$ and $\sigma_J = 0.25$.

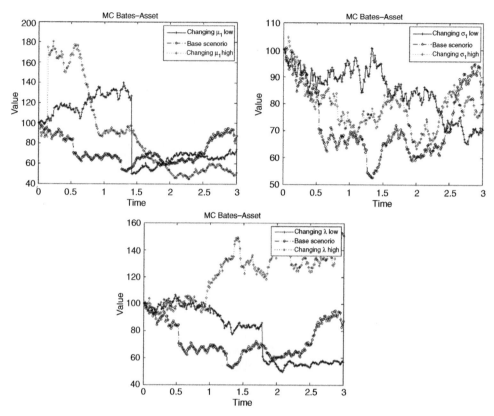

Figure 3.10 Typical paths for the Bates model. We consider risk neutral density for the Bates model and $\mu_J = -0.5, 0, 0.5$ (top left), $\sigma_J = 0.1, 0.25, 0.5$ (top right) and $\lambda = 0, 0.2, 0.5$ (bottom)

Our aim is to compare the paths for the different parameter sets. However, this is not really possible for jump-diffusion models. In order to compare the effect of the parameters for diffusion processes we fixed the random number stream. Thus, we were able to base our simulation on exactly the same random numbers.

This technique is only applicable when considering the effect of μ_J and σ_J. In this case we do not change the jump intensity and thus we can sample the jump times from a Poisson distribution. However, if we change the jump intensity, λ, the number of jumps is no longer the same for the different paths.

Yet we think that the qualitative behaviour is still illustrated well enough. This means that values of μ_J determine the average jump height, σ_J the standard deviation around μ_J and, finally, λ the average number of jumps which leads to a larger number of jumps for larger values of λ. This can be seen by examining Figures 3.10 and 3.11.

3.2.4 The Bates–Hull–White Model

It is straightforward to extend the stochastic volatility model considered in the last section to a model with stochastic rates. Let us take the Heston–Hull–White model and add an independent compound Poisson process. This is in analogy to the Merton and the Bates model.

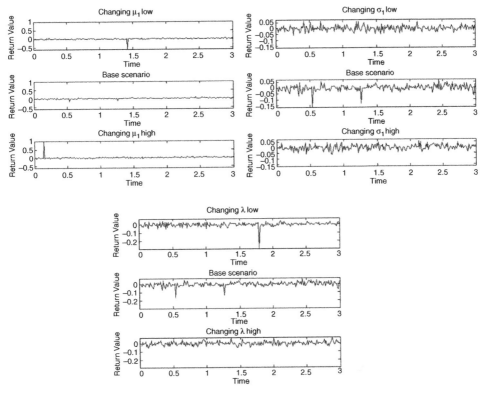

Figure 3.11   Typical returns for the Bates model and $\mu_J = -0.5, 0, 0.2$ (top left), $\sigma_J = 0.01, 0.2, 0.3$ (top right) and $\lambda = 0.05, 0.2, 0.5$ (bottom)

Since we do not expect anything new here, we just give the logarithmic version of the characteristic function. Then, the reader can study the implied volatility surface, the risk neutral density and the paths using the code we provide as additional material for this book. The implementation of the characteristic fuction of the Bates–Hull–White model is given in Figure 3.12.

3.3 EXPONENTIAL LÉVY MODELS

Let us extend our considerations to another class of models and cover financial models based on *Lévy processes*. In contrast to the models considered so far, such models are pure jump models and do not necessarily have a Brownian motion component.

For a Lévy process, $L(t)$, we take the asset price dynamic given by

$$S(t) = S(0) \exp\left((r - d)t + L(t)\right), \tag{3.10}$$

with r being the risk free rate and d being the dividend yield. In order to use the proposed model, Equation (3.10), for pricing, we have to make the discounted asset price into a martingale. To this end we consider two parameterizations:

$$S(t) = S(0) \exp\left((r - d)t + \omega(t) + L(t)\right) \tag{3.11}$$

$$S(t) = S(0) \exp\left((r - d)t + L(t)\right)/\omega(t). \tag{3.12}$$

The quantity $\omega(t)$ is called the *martingale correction* and (3.11) is known as the *additive adjustment*; (3.12) is the *multiplicative adjustment*. Let us consider the issue of choosing the function ω in more detail. For the moment it is enough to know that $\omega(t)$ is chosen such that it makes the discounted process into a martingale by adjusting it to the correct mean.

We do not give any pricing formulae in this section. When we consider a particular model we give the expression and the implementation for the model's characteristic function. This model characteristic is sufficient to apply numerical techniques for pricing options.

As for diffusions and jump-diffusion processes, we give an overview of the model's properties. The model parameters are considered and we show typical shapes of the implied volatility surface, density and typical paths. Furthermore, we consider the *Lévy measure* of the models to illustrate the jump distribution.

For considerations in later chapters we use the Variance Gamma model as our reference model. Algorithms and results are often illustrated in terms of this model despite the fact that the methods can be applied to any model based on Lévy processes.

We specify the models in terms of the characteristic function since we have found this to be the most convenient way. Well-known models covered in this chapter are:

- Variance Gamma model (VG).
- Normal Inverse Gaussian model (NIG).
- CGMY model (CGMY).

Such models are capable of explaining the jumpy behaviour in return time series and can be fitted to the empirical distribution. However, when it comes to fitting the current implied volatility surface the quality can be relatively poor due to the fact that such models have restrictive constraints on the future shape of the volatility surface.

Let us now consider stochastic volatility versions of the above models. This feature can be built into the model by considering stochastic time changes, a concept that corresponds to adding a stochastic volatility component to a Brownian motion. Due to their properties, in this case the time-scaling property, such models can also be interpreted as stochastic time changes.

The class of models obtained in this way shows a good fit to the surface and retains the properties of the class built on Lévy processes. Before we go into the details and describe the models' properties, let us start with the *Floating Smile Property* which illustrates why Lévy models are restrictive for volatility modelling.

Floating Smile Property   Let us consider the risk neutral dynamics for a model based on some Lévy process L:

$$S(t) = S(0) \exp((r - d)t + \omega(t) + L(t)).$$

We denote by $IV_t(K, T)$ the implied volatility surface at time t in terms of the absolute strike and by $IV_t(m, T)$ the surface in terms of moneyness, $m = K/S(t)$. Then, we observe that for all t we have

$$IV_t(m, T) = IV_0(m, T).$$

```
function phi = cf_bateshullwhite(u,lnS,T,r,d,V0,theta,kappa,omega,...
    rho,a,b,lambda,lambda1,eta,ircurve)
% Bates Hull White
    phi = cf_heston(u,lnS,T,r,d,V0,theta,kappa,omega,rho)...
        + cf_jumplognormal(u,a,b,lambda,T)...
        + cf_hullwhite(u+1i,T,lambda1,eta,ircurve);
end
```

Figure 3.12   Matlab code for the logarithmic version of the characteristic function of the Bates–Hull–White model. This is composed of three factors. The first factor is the characteristic function of the Heston model, the second is the logarithmic normal jump and the third the characteristic function of the Hull–White model

This means that the future shape of the implied volatility surface stays the same. In terms of moneyness the forward implied volatility surface is the same as the current surface. The shape of the surface depends only on the moneyness and the time to maturity.

The surface   For the special models and the influence of the parameters on the surface we summarize some general facts here which we can apply when considering a special model.

If the Lévy measure has a negative skewed distribution, this leads to a negatively skewed implied volatility surface. This shape is often observed for option on equities. If the Lévy measure is symmetric, the implied volatility exhibits a smile. Flattening of the implied volatility surface with respect to maturity can be explained at least for square integrable processes S, $\mathbb{V}(S(T)) < \infty$. In this case the central limit theorem in Chapter 13, Subsection 13.2.3, proves that the distribution $(X(T) - \mathbb{E}[X(T)])/\sqrt{T}$ converges to a Gaussian distribution with a certain variance. The square root of this (constant) variance is then the limit for the flattening effect. Readers should be aware that this is not true for models where the variance is infinite. In such cases the central limit theorem cannot be applied and the flattening is not necessary.

Finally, we consider the short term skew/smile. We have already observed that jumps are used to model a pronounced smile for short dated options. This can also be modelled using exponential Lévy models.

3.3.1   The Variance Gamma Model

The Variance Gamma model was introduced in Madan, D. and Seneta, E. (1990) and Boyarchenko, S.I. and Levendorskii, S.Z. (2002). (For an overview see Kienitz, J. (2009)). The purpose in considering the Variance Gamma model was to provide a model for stock market returns which is practical and empirically more reasonable than the classic approach using Brownian motion. While Madan, D. and Seneta, E. (1990) considered a symmetric version of the model, Madan, D.B., Carr P.P. and Chang, E.C. (1998) extended the model to the general Variance Gamma model, which is the one we consider here.

The model allows for fat tails and retains the assumptions of independent stationary increments. There are two ways of expressing the Variance Gamma model:

(1) The difference of two Gamma processes $U(t)$ and $D(t)$, $X(t) := U(t) - D(t)$.
(2) A time-changed Brownian motion, $X(t) := W(Y(t))$, with a Gamma process $Y(t)$.

In the first case, (1), we refer to the C, G, M representation and in the second case, (2), to the σ, ν, θ representation. The choice of names will become apparent in the next paragraph.

```
function phi = cf(u,T,t_star,r,d, C, G, M)
% Variance Gamma CGM
phiX_u = C*log(G*M./(G*M+(M-G)*1i*u+u.*u));
phiX_i = C*log(G*M./(G*M+(M-G)-1));
phi =  1i*u*(lnS + (r-d-phiX_i)*T) + phiX_u*T;
end
```

Figure 3.13   Matlab implementation of the characteristic function of the Variance Gamma model. This corresponds to the C, G, M representation

The Characteristic Function

The representations considered in the last paragraph lead to different representations of the model's characteristic function:

$$\varphi_{VG}(u) \underset{(1)}{=} \left(\frac{GM}{GM + (M-G)iu + u^2} \right)^{Ct}$$

$$\underset{(2)}{=} \left(1 - iu\theta v + \frac{\sigma^2}{2}vu^2 \right)^{-t/v}.$$

Both representations (1) and (2) can be transformed into each other by using the following parameter transforms:

$$C = \frac{1}{v}$$

$$G = \left(\sqrt{\frac{1}{4}\theta^2 v^2 + \frac{1}{2}\sigma^2 v} - \frac{1}{2}\theta v \right)^{-1}$$

$$M = \left(\sqrt{\frac{1}{4}\theta^2 v^2 + \frac{1}{2}\sigma^2 v} + \frac{1}{2}\theta v \right)^{-1}.$$

We therefore implement the characteristic function in two ways. The implementation depends on the chosen parametrization (see Figures 3.13 and 3.14).

Lévy Measure

The Lévy measure, $v_{VG}^{C,G,M}$, for the Variance Gamma model using the CGM representation is given by

$$v_{VG}^{C,G,M}(dx) = \begin{cases} C \exp(Gx)|x|^{-1} dx & x < 0 \\ C \exp(-Mx)x^{-1}dx & x > 0 \end{cases} \tag{3.13}$$

and implemented in Matlab using the code shown in Figure 3.15.

```
function phi = cf_vg(u,lnS,T,r,d,sigma,nu,theta)
% Variance Gamma sigma, nu, theta
    omega = (1/nu)*( log(1-theta*nu-sigma*sigma*nu/2) );
    tmp = 1 - 1i * theta * nu * u + 0.5 * sigma * sigma * u .* u * nu;
    phi = 1i * u * (lnS + (r + omega - d) * T ) - T*log(tmp)/nu;
end
```

Figure 3.14   Matlab implementation of the characteristic function of the Variance Gamma model. This corresponds to the σ, v, θ representation

```
function y = levymvg_cgm(x,C,G,M)
    y = x;
    y(x<0) = C * exp( G * x(x<0)) ./ abs(x(x<0));
    y(x>0) = C * exp(-M * x(x>0)) ./ x(x>0);
    y(x==0) = inf;
end
```

Figure 3.15 Matlab code for implementing the Lévy measure for the Variance Gamma process using the C, G, M representation (see Equation 3.13)

The corresponding Lévy measure, $\nu_{VG}^{\sigma,\nu,\theta}$, in the σ, ν, θ representation is given by

$$\nu_{VG}^{\sigma,\nu,\theta} = \frac{\exp\left(\frac{\theta x}{\sigma^2}\right)}{\nu|x|} \exp\left(-\sqrt{\theta^2 + \frac{2\sigma^2}{\nu}}|x|\right) dx.$$

Since the integral with respect to the measure ν_{VG} is infinite, the Variance Gamma process jumps infinitely often in any finite time interval. Since $\int_{-1}^{1} |x|\nu(dx) < \infty$ the paths of the Variance Gamma model are of finite variation. Figure 3.16 illustrates the model's Lévy measure. We have chosen the CGM representation and consider the parameters $C = 1$, $G = 4$ and $M = 1$. Then, we both increase and decrease the corresponding parameters and record the effect on the jump structure and jump distribution. This is equivalent to the effect on the density of the Lévy measure. Changing the parameter C causes the Lévy measure to widen or tighten. Increasing the parameter G increases upward jumps, whereas increasing the parameter M increases downward jumps for the model.

We anticipate the same effect in the σ, θ and ν representation. Here, σ determines the overall scale of the volatility, θ determines the symmetry of the distribution and ν controls the tails.

Risk Neutral Density

The transition density, $f_t^{VG}(x)$, of the Variance Gamma model can be computed and has a closed form representation:

$$f_t^{VG}(x) = \frac{2\exp\left(\frac{\theta x}{\sigma^2}\right)}{\nu^{t/\nu}\sqrt{2\pi}\,\sigma\Gamma(t/\nu)}\left(\frac{x^2}{\frac{2\sigma^2}{\nu} + \theta^2}\right)^{t/2\nu - 1/4}$$

$$K_{\frac{t}{\nu}-\frac{1}{2}}\left(\frac{1}{\sigma^2}\sqrt{x^2\left(\frac{2\sigma^2}{\nu} + \theta^2\right)}\right). \tag{3.14}$$

with

$$z = x + (r - d)t + \frac{t}{\nu}\ln\left(1 - \theta\nu - \frac{\sigma^2\nu}{2}\right)$$

The function $K_a(\cdot)$ is the modified Bessel function of the third kind. It is also called a *MacDonald function*.

We remark that the naive application of the density in a numerical scheme often leads to instabilities since care has to be taken when using the modified Bessel function $K_\alpha(\cdot)$.

We have chosen the C, G, M representation to illustrate the effect of changing parameter values on the risk neutral density. The results are summarized in Figure 3.17.

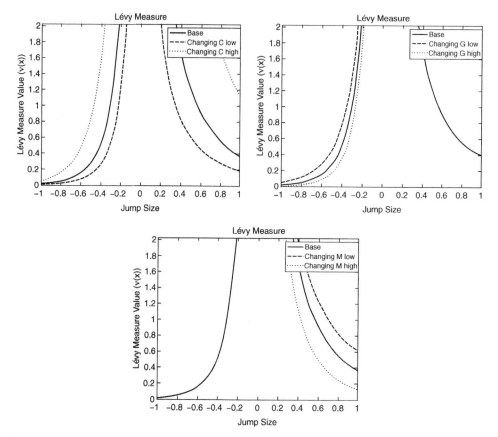

Figure 3.16 The Lévy measure of the VG model. The figure summarizes the effect on the Lévy measure of changing the model parameters. We consider $C = 0.5, 1, 3$ (top left), $G = 3, 4, 5$ (top right) and $M = 0.5, 1, 2$ (bottom)

Let us start the description by considering the effect of the parameter C. Decreasing its value leads to a more peaked distribution. This parameter therefore has a similar effect to the implied volatility for the Black–Scholes model. Increasing it leads to a flatter distribution while decreasing it leads to a wider distribution. The other two parameters, G and M, lead to asymmetric distributions. This is to be expected from our knowledge of the Lévy measure. The parameters determine the effect of upward and downward jumps and therefore increasing the parameters shifts mass to the corresponding tails of the distribution.

The moments of the Variance Gamma model which are useful for numerical applications are explicitly known. They are given by

$$\mathbb{E}[X(t)] = t\theta$$
$$\mathbb{V}[X(t)] = (\sigma^2 + v\theta^2)t$$
$$sk = \frac{2\theta^3 v^2 + 3\sigma^2 \theta v}{(\sigma^2 + v\theta^2)^{3t/2}}$$
$$ku = \frac{3}{t}(t + 2v - v\sigma^4(\sigma^2 + v\theta^2)^{-2}).$$

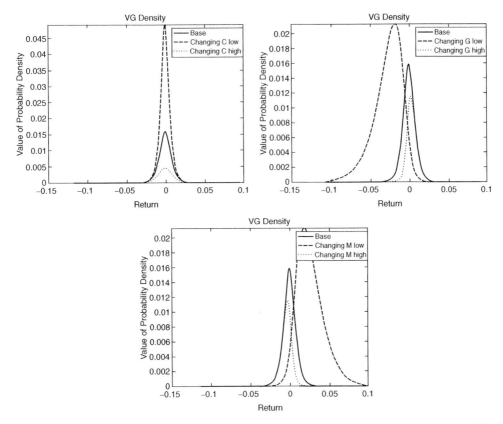

Figure 3.17 Risk neutral density for changing the values of the base scenario for $C = 2, 3, 4$ (top left), $G = 1, 3, 5$ (top right) and $M = 5, 10, 15$ (bottom)

The general formula to compute the n-th central moment is available and given by

$$\mathbb{E}[(X - \mu)^n] = \sum_{j=0}^{n} \binom{n}{j} (-1)^{n-j} \mathbb{E}[X^j] \mathbb{E}[X^{n-j}].$$

Skew and Smile

Since the smile is directly related to the risk neutral densities, in Figure 3.18 we only show the results on the shape of the implied volatility surface.

The parameter σ determines the overall level of volatility. Increasing σ leads to a higher level of implied volatility. The parameters θ and v affect the shape of the surface. While θ determines the skew, v reflects the convexity of the surface and therefore the smile. For all implied volatility surfaces we see that for high values of time to maturity and all parameters the surface is nearly flat.

Typical Paths and Returns

Finally, let us consider typical paths and the generated returns arrived at by applying the Variance Gamma model. Figures 3.19 and 3.20 show typical paths and the corresponding

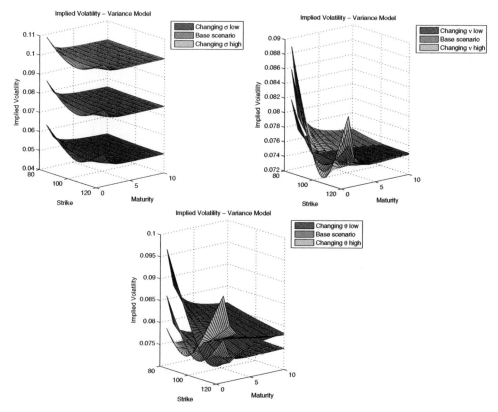

Figure 3.18 Variance Gamma. The implied volatility surface for different values of $\sigma =$ $0.05, 0.075, 0.3$ (top left), $\nu = 0.1, 0.2, 0.3$ (top right) and $\theta = -0.05, 0, 0.05$ (bottom)

returns for the parameters $C = 4.3574$, $G = 5.1704$ and $M = 5.6699$. One of the aims for introducing the model was to be able to generate realistic time series of returns. This feature can be observed when comparing the time series data of Figure 3.20.

The parameters C, G and M can be directly linked to the path structure. Increasing the value of C leverages all jumps. The parameters G and M determine the height of the upward and downward jumps, which is exactly what we expected knowing the Lévy measure of the Variance Gamma process. We implicitly observe the same effect when we consider the returns computed from simulated paths, given in Figure 3.20.

3.3.2   The Normal Inverse Gaussian Model

The *Normal Inverse Gaussian (NIG)* process was introduced in Barndorff-Nielsen, O.E. (1995) and Rydberg, T.H. (1997). It can be represented as a time-changed Brownian motion. The time change is an *Inverse Gaussian* process. The increments of an Inverse Gaussian process obey an Inverse Gaussian distribution. Let $X(t)$ denote the process, then, for time points $s \leq t$ and $a, b \in \mathbb{R}$ we have $X(t) - X(s) \sim \mathcal{IG}(a(t - s), b)$.

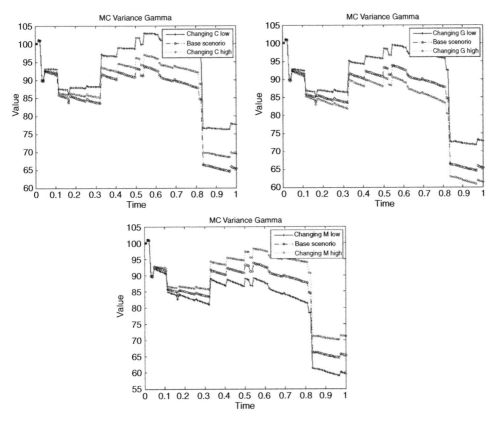

Figure 3.19 Typical paths generated by the Variance Gamma model. The parameters are $C = 0.5, 4.3574, 5$ (top left), $G = 5, 5.1704, 6$ (top right) and $M = 5, 5.6699, 6.5$ (bottom)

Characteristic Function

We have the following representation for the characteristic function:

$$\varphi_{\text{NIG}}(u) = \exp\left(-\delta t \left(\sqrt{\alpha^2 - (\beta + iu)^2} - \sqrt{\alpha^2 - \beta^2}\right)\right), \qquad (3.15)$$

with the implementation in Matlab given by Figure 3.21.

Lévy Measure

The Lévy measure determining the jumping behaviour when modelling with a Normal Inverse Gaussian model is given by

$$\nu_{\text{NIG}}(dx) = \frac{\delta \alpha}{\pi} \frac{\exp(\beta x) K_1(\alpha |x|)}{|x|} dx, \qquad (3.16)$$

where $K_1(\cdot)$ is the modified Bessel function of the second kind. We illustrated the effects of changing model parameters in Figure 3.22.

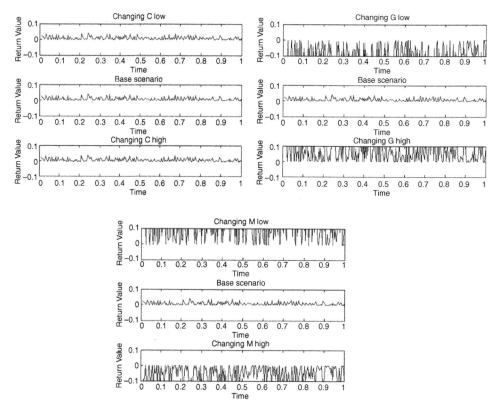

Figure 3.20 Logarithmic returns generated by the Variance Gamma model. The parameters are $C = 0.5, 4.3574, 5$ (top left), $G = 5, 5.1704, 6$ (top right) and $M = 5, 5.6699, 6.5$ (bottom)

Risk Neutral Density

The transition density for the Normal Inverse Gaussian model is known in closed form. It is given by

$$f_t^{NIG}(x) = \frac{\alpha}{\pi} \frac{K_1 \left(\alpha \delta t \sqrt{1 + \left(\frac{x - \mu t}{\delta t} \right)^2} \right)}{\sqrt{1 + \left(\frac{x - \mu t}{\delta t} \right)^2}} \exp \left(\delta t \left(\sqrt{\alpha^2 - \beta^2} + \beta \left(\frac{x - \mu t}{\delta t} \right) \right) \right). \qquad (3.17)$$

```
function phi = cf_nig(u,lnS,T,r,d,alfa,beta,mu,delta)
% Normal Inverse Gaussian
    m = delta*(sqrt(alfa*alfa-(beta+1)^2)-sqrt(alfa*alfa-beta*beta));
    tmp = 1i*u*mu*T-delta*T*(sqrt(alfa*alfa-(beta+1i*u).^2)...
        -sqrt(alfa*alfa-beta*beta));
    phi = 1i*u*(lnS + (r-d+m)*T) + tmp;
end
```

Figure 3.21 Matlab implementation of the logarithmic version of the characteristic function of the Normal Inverse Gaussian model

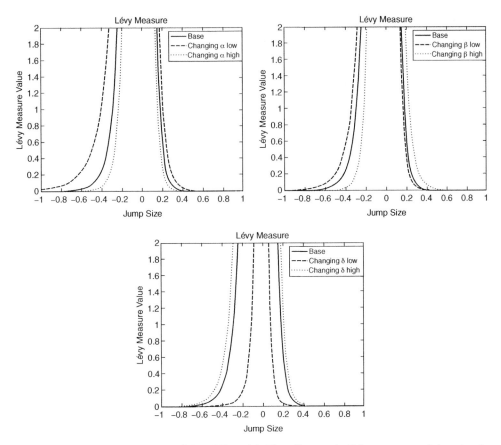

Figure 3.22 The Lévy measure of the NIG model. The effect on the Lévy measure of changing the model parameters. For $\alpha = 8, 12, 16$ (top left), $\beta = -6, -4, 1$ (top right) and $\delta = 0.05, 1, 2$ (bottom)

We have plotted the shape of the density when modifying the base scenario described by the parameter values $\alpha = 12$, $\beta = -4$ and $\delta = 1$. As for the previous models, we consider increasing and decreasing the parameters of the base scenario. Figure 3.23 summarizes our findings.

We now provide a brief overview of how the parameters affect the density. First, let us consider the parameter α. Increasing α leads to smaller variance and smaller kurtosis. The opposite effect is observed for decreasing α. The parameter β affects all moments of the distribution. Increasing β leads to higher expectation, variance, skewness and kurtosis, decreasing leads to a decrease in the expectation and the skewness, but this leads to larger values for the variance and the kurtosis. This is due to the fact that even powers of β determine variance and kurtosis. The parameter δ affects the even moments. In this case increasing δ leads to an increase in variance and kurtosis. Decreasing δ leads to the opposite observation. This interpretation can also be derived by considering the moments of the Normal Inverse Gaussian process. They are given by:

$$\mathbb{E}[X(t)] = \delta \beta t / \sqrt{\alpha^2 - \beta^2}$$
$$\mathbb{V}[X(t)] = t\alpha^2 \delta \gamma^{-3}$$

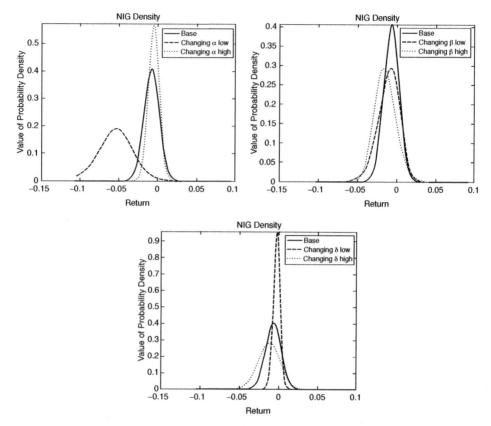

Figure 3.23 The probability density for the logarithmic returns for the NIG model. The effect on the density of changing the model parameters are summarized. We consider $\alpha = 1, 5, 10$ (top left), $\beta = -3, 0, 3$ (top right) and $\delta = 1, 5, 10$ (bottom)

$$sk = \frac{3\beta}{\alpha\sqrt{\delta t \sqrt{\alpha^2 - \beta^2}}}$$

$$ku = 3\left(1 + \frac{\alpha^2 + 4\beta^2}{\alpha^2 + \delta t \sqrt{\alpha^2 - \beta^2}}\right).$$

We used the abbreviation $\gamma = \sqrt{\alpha^2 - \beta^2}$.

We show the corresponding Figures 3.35 and 3.36 in the same order that we have chosen for the scenarios.

Skew and Smile

Let us consider the effect of changing the model parameters. Here we consider the shape of the implied volatility surface. To this end we look at the base scenario given by

- $S(0) = 100$
- $r = d = 0$
- $\alpha = 6.1882$
- $\beta = 0$
- $\delta = 0.1622.$

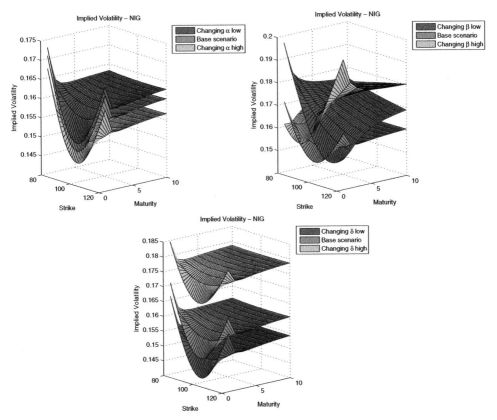

Figure 3.24 The shape of the implied volatility surfaces for the NIG model for different values of $\alpha = 6, 6.1882, 6.5$ (top left), $\beta = -2, 0, 2$ (top right) and $\delta = 0.15, 0.1622, 0.2$ (bottom)

Consider the maturities $T = 1, 2, \ldots, 10$ and the strike range $K = 80, 81, \ldots, 120$. Figure 3.24 summarizes the results. The parameter α determines the height of the implied volatility surface. Increasing α results in a higher volatility level. The parameter β determines the smile shape. $\beta = 0$ corresponds to a symmetric smile. Taking $\beta > 0$ steepens the smile for high strikes and $\beta < 0$ steepens the smile for low strikes. Finally, δ allows for a parallel shift of the whole surface.

As we did for the Variance Gamma model, we observe that the smile flattens out for large maturities.

Typical Paths and Returns

The last paragraph covered typical paths and returns calculated using a Normal Inverse Gaussian model. Figure 3.25 shows typical paths and the effect on the paths when changing the model parameters. The same procedure has been applied to generate Figure 3.26. It was our intention to introduce models based on Lévy processes to model realistic return time series and we do indeed see that the Normal Inverse Gaussian model is capable of this feature.

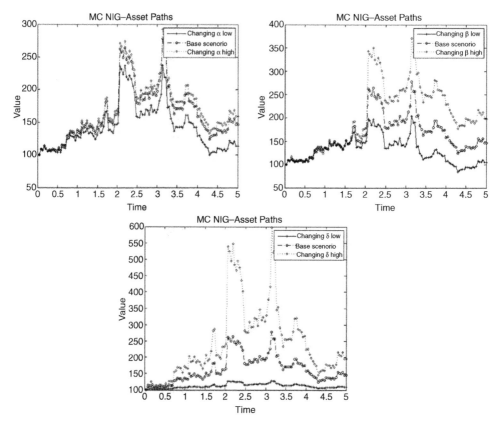

Figure 3.25   Typical paths for the NIG model and $\alpha = 5, 10, 15$ (top left), $\beta = -2, 0, 2$ (top right) and $\delta = 0.25, 1, 1.75$ (bottom)

For the Normal Inverse Gaussian model the effect of the parameters is more involved than in the Variance Gamma model due to the fact that we do not have a representation as the difference of two processes. Furthermore, each parameter affects several moments at once. Take, for instance, the parameter β. It mainly affects the overall variation of the paths but it also has higher order effects. But β seems to have a linear effect on the paths, whereas parameter values for α seem to have a non-linear effect. Decreasing the parameter as much as increasing it does not lead to the same absolute difference of the corresponding paths. This is what we mean here by *non-linear*. The same holds true for the parameter δ. The graph at the bottom of Figure 3.25 illustrates this issue.

3.4   OTHER MODELS

The *CGMY model* was introduced in Carr, P., Geman, H., Madan, D. and Yor, M. (2002). This model is also called the *KoBoL process*. The Variance Gamma model is a special case of the CGMY model. For discussion of this model, see Carr, P., Geman, H., Madan, D. and

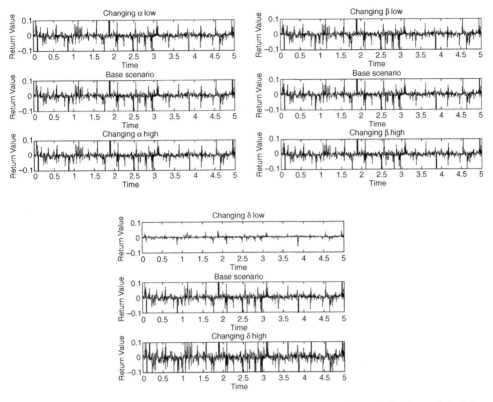

Figure 3.26 Logarithmic returns for the NIG model and $\alpha = 5, 10, 15$ (top left), $\beta = -2, 0, 2$ (top right) and $\delta = 0.25, 1, 1.75$ (bottom)

Yor, M. (2002) or Kienitz, J. (2009). The moments are given by

$$\mathbb{E}[X(t)] = tC(M^{Y-1} - G^{Y-1})\Gamma(1 - Y)$$
$$\mathbb{V}[X(t)] = tC(M^{Y-2} + G^{Y-2})\Gamma(2 - Y)$$
$$sk = \frac{tC(M^{Y-3} - G^{Y-3})\Gamma(3 - Y)}{(C(M^{Y-2} + G^{Y-2})\Gamma(2 - Y))^{3/2}}$$
$$ku = 3 + \frac{C(M^{Y-4} + G^{Y-4})\Gamma(4 - Y)}{(C(M^{Y} - 2 + G^{Y} - 2)\Gamma(2 - Y))^{2t}}.$$

The parameters are restricted to $C, G, M > 0$ and $Y < 2$. Compared to the Variance Gamma model, the CGMY model has an additional parameter Y. In fact, the Variance Gamma model is a special case and can be obtained from the general model by setting $Y = 1$.

First, let us consider the density of the CGMY model. To this end, let us take $C = 2, G = 3$, $M = 3$ and $Y = 1$ as the base scenario. Figure 3.27 shows the effect of the parameters on the probability density. The parameters allow for a variety of shapes of the density.

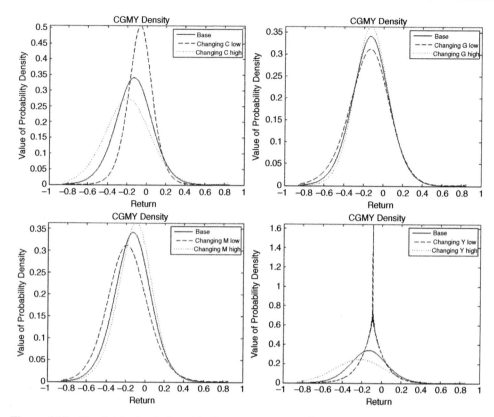

Figure 3.27 The density for the logarithmic returns corresponding to the CGMY model. The effect on the density when changing the model parameters is summarized. We consider $C = 0.5, 2, 3$ (top left), $G = 1, 3, 5$ (top right), $M = 1, 3, 5$ (bottom left) and $Y = 0.5, 1, 2$ (bottom right)

Next, let us consider the Lévy measure of the CGMY process. The Lévy measure is given by

$$v_{C,G,M,Y}(dx) = \begin{cases} C\dfrac{\exp(-G|x|)}{|x|^{1+Y}}dx & x < 0 \\[2mm] C\dfrac{\exp(-Mx)}{x^{1+Y}}dx & x > 0 \end{cases}. \tag{3.18}$$

The implementation is given in Figure 3.28.

Using the implementation given in Figure 3.28 we get the results displayed in Figure 3.29.

All the considerations are based on the characteristic function which is available for the CGMY model. The implementation in Matlab is presented in Figure 3.30. Please note that again we have given the implementation of the logarithm of the characteristic function.

```
function y = cgmylevydens(x,C,G,M,Y)
y=x;
    y(x<0) = C .* exp(-G.*abs(x(x<0)))./abs(x(x<0)).^(1+Y);
    y(x==0) = Inf;
    y(x>0) = C .* exp(-M.*x(x>0))./x(x>0).^(1+Y);
end
```

Figure 3.28   The Matlab implementation of the Lévy measure of the CGMY model

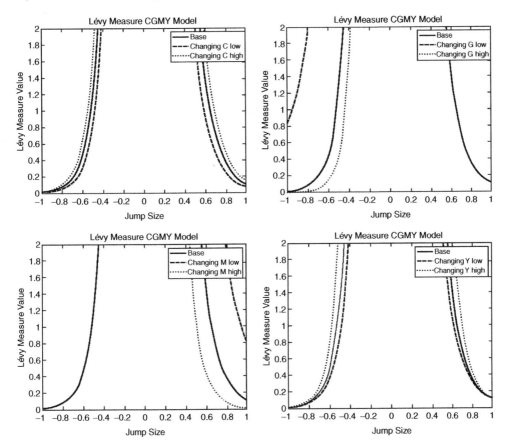

Figure 3.29   The Lévy measure of the CGMY model. The figure summarizes the effect on the Lévy measure of changing the model parameters. We consider $C = 4, 6, 8$ (top left), $G = 2, 6, 8$ (top right), $M = 2, 4, 6$ (bottom left) and $Y = 0.5, 1, 2$ (bottom right)

```
function phi = cf_cgmy(u,lnS,T,r,d,C,G,M,Y)
% CGMY
    m = -C*gamma(-Y)*((M-1)^Y-M^Y+(G+1)^Y-G^Y);
    tmp = C*T*gamma(-Y)*((M-1i*u).^Y-M^Y+(G+1i*u).^Y-G^Y);
    phi = 1i*u*(lnS + (r-d+m)*T) + tmp;
end
```

Figure 3.30   Matlab implementation of the logarithmic version of the characteristic function of the CGMY model

3.4.1 Exponential Lévy Models with Stochastic Volatility

The fit to empirical distributions obtained from time series data is reasonably good for models based on Lévy processes. Moreover, we saw that generating realistic return time series is also possible. One of the shortcomings is the floating smile property and the fit to option prices for the whole range of strikes and maturities. To address this, stochastic volatility extensions of Lévy process based models are considered.

To incorporate stochastic volatility into such a modelling framework we let the time be a (independent) stochastic process which can be seen as modelling business time. It may also reflect the stochastic movement in the volatility of the underlying.

The model we consider is given by

$$S(t) = S(0)\exp((r - d)t + L(Y(t)))$$
$$X(t) = X(0) + (r - d)t + L(Y(t)).$$

The process Y is the time-change of some Lévy process L. Y is not necessarily a Lévy process but it has to be an monotonically increasing process. Examples for stochastic clocks are

- Integrated Gamma Ornstein–Uhlenbeck process (GOU).
- Integrated Cox–Ingersoll–Ross process (CIR).

In the following section we review the concept of a stochastic clock which was introduced in Carr, P., Geman, H., Madan, D. and Yor, M. (2003). The resulting stochastic processes are not necessarily Lévy processes.

3.4.2 Stochastic Clocks

The literature and our considerations of models based on Lévy processes suggest that the calibration to option prices is not satisfactory. This is due to the fact that there are no parameters allowing for modifying the timely evolution of volatility. In realized time series of returns of indices we observe clusters with high and low activity. Therefore, the volatility cannot be constant or fixed at some level of time. The mathematical modelling put forward in Carr, P., Geman, H., Madan, D. and Yor, M. (2003) and enlarged upon in Carr, P. and Wu, L. (2004) is the method of time-change by a clock. This clock can change its speed. The underlying idea is simple. It assumes that business time does not flow linearly but is stochastic. On a trading day there might be high levels of activity but there might also be times when the activity is low. At peak times much information flows in and out and many trades are placed, leading to high market activity.

Once we have accepted this idea the question is how to choose the stochastic mechanism to model the business time. We consider two different concepts here. First, we suggest that new information and therefore activity appears like a jump and then peters out continuously until the next jump. Second, the information flow is continuous but displays some mean reverting behaviour. This corresponds to the average rate of the clock's speed. Let us consider two clocks, a generalized Ornstein–Uhlenbeck process and a square root or Cox–Ingersoll–Ross process (CIR).

- Gamma Ornstein–Uhlenbeck clock (GOU)

$$dz(t) = -\lambda z(t)dt + dZ(\lambda t), \quad \lambda > 0, \tag{3.19}$$

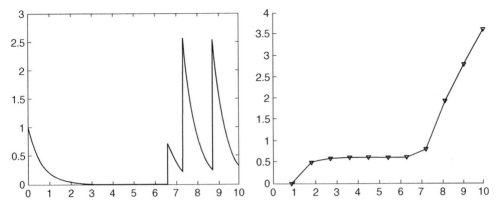

Figure 3.31 A typical path of a Gamma Ornstein–Uhlenbeck process with parameters $\lambda = 1.6790$, $a = 0.3484$ and $b = 0.7664$ (left) and the integrated path (right)

where the process Z is an increasing Lévy process. In this case it is a compound Poisson process with the jumps being exponentially distributed. If scaled with λ, this process is stationary and the limit distribution is a Gamma process.

$$\varphi_{GOU} = \exp\left(\frac{iuy_0}{\lambda}(1 - \exp(-\lambda t)) + \frac{\lambda a}{iu - \lambda b}\left(b\log\left(\frac{b}{b - \frac{iu}{\lambda}(1 - \exp(-\lambda t))}\right) - iut\right)\right).$$

- Cox–Ingersoll–Ross clock (CIR)

$$\varphi_{CIR} = \frac{\exp\left(\kappa^2\eta t/\lambda^2\right)\exp\left(2y_0 iu/(\kappa + \gamma\coth(\gamma t/2))\right)}{(\cosh(\gamma t/2) + \kappa\sinh(\gamma t/2)/\gamma)^{2\kappa\eta/\lambda^2}},$$

with $\gamma = \sqrt{\kappa^2 - 2\lambda^2 iu}$.

Let us comment on both clocks. First, let us consider a general Ornstein–Uhlenbeck process. Such a process is given in (3.19). Since it is driven by a Gamma process, a typical path is not continuous. Figure 3.31 shows the process and the integrated process. We observe that between jumps the process decays exponentially. This is a reasonable assumption.

The other choice, a CIR process, is continuous, and Figure 3.32 shows this process as well as the integrated process. Such a process is also a reasonable assumption for modelling business time.

We have plotted two versions of the integrated process. One uses a simple approximation of the integral using Riemann sums, whereas the second is computed using a numerical integration scheme. For both processes there is virtually no difference to be seen. The first method is much faster than the second. Therefore, we suggest computing the integrated process by approximating it using Riemann sums.

In what follows we investigate the Variance Gamma (VG) and the Normal Inverse Gaussian (NIG) model together with changing the business time using the clocks introduced above. We give the corresponding results, codes and figures for the four resulting models below.

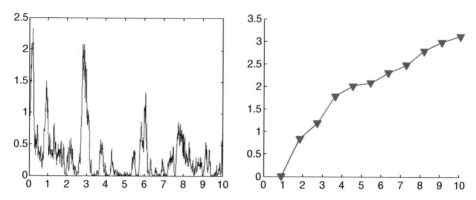

Figure 3.32 Typical path of the CIR process with parameters $\kappa = 1.2145, \eta = 0.5501$ and $\lambda = 1.7913$ (left) and the integrated path (right)

Pricing Formulae and Characteristic Function

In this section we give the characteristic functions for the Variance Gamma and the Normal Inverse Gaussian models with stochastic clocks. For the stochastic clocks we take the integrated GOU and the CIR clock.

NIG CIR/GOU   We have implemented the characteristic function for the NIG CIR/GOU model as outlined in Figure 3.33.

VG CIR/GOU   We give the implementation of the characteristic functions of the VG CIR and the VG GOU process in Figure 3.34. Again we assume that clock starts at $y0 = 1$.

Risk Neutral Density

Since the characteristic functions are available in closed form, it is possible to numerically compute the density. We consider the risk neutral density implied by the models under consideration and analyse the effect of the parameters governing the stochastic clock.

Using the scenarios defined in Table 3.1 we consider changes in the model parameters and summarize our findings by plotting the corresponding risk neutral densities. We show the corresponding figures in the same order we have chosen for the scenarios.

We see that the stochastic clock does affect the risk neutral density in a way which does not depend on the underlying model. For instance, taking the CIR clock we observe that the effect of changing the parameters governing the behaviour of the stochastic clock is to affect the risk neutral densities in the same way both for the NIG and for the VG model.

Table 3.1   Base scenarios for the analysis of stochastic volatility Lévy models

NIG CIR	$\alpha = 7$	$\beta = -3$	$\delta = 1$	$\lambda = 1$	$\kappa = 1$	$\eta = 0.5$
VG CIR	$C = 6$	$G = 3$	$M = 5$	$\lambda = 1$	$\kappa = 1$	$\eta = 0.5$
NIG GOU	$\alpha = 2$	$\beta = 0$	$\delta = 0.2$	$\lambda = 10$	$a = 1$	$b = 1$
VG GOU	$C = 4$	$G = 3$	$M = 3$	$\lambda = 10$	$a = 1$	$b = 1$

```
function phi = cf_nig_cir(u,lnS,T,r,d,alpha,beta,delta,lambda,kappa,eta)
% NIG CIR
y0 = 1;

psiX_u = (-1i) * (-delta)*(sqrt(alpha^2-(beta+1i*u).^2) ...
    -sqrt(alpha^2-beta^2));
psiX_i = (-1i) * (-delta)*(sqrt(alpha^2-(beta+1)^2) ...
-sqrt(alpha^2-beta^2));

gamma_u = sqrt(kappa^2-2*lambda^2*1i*psiX_u);
gamma_i = sqrt(kappa^2-2*lambda^2*1i*psiX_i);

f2_u = (kappa^2*eta*T/(lambda^2))'-log(cosh(0.5*gamma_u*T) ...
    +kappa*sinh(0.5*gamma_u*T)./gamma_u)*(2*kappa*eta*lambda^(-2));
f3_u = 2*psiX_u./(kappa+gamma_u.*coth(gamma_u*T/2));

f1_u = f2_u + 1i*f3_u*y0;

phi_T = kappa^2*eta*T*lambda^(-2) ...
    + 2*y0*1i*psiX_i./(kappa+gamma_i*coth(gamma_i*T/2)) ...
    -log( cosh(0.5*gamma_i*T) + kappa*sinh(0.5*gamma_i*T)/gamma_i ) ...
    *(2*kappa*eta/lambda^2);

phi = 1i*u*(lnS+(r-d).*T)- phi_T + f1_u;
end
%%%%
function phi = cf_nig_gou(u,lnS,T,r,d,alpha,beta,delta,lambda,a,b)
% NIG GOU
y0 = 1;

psiX_u = (-1i) * (-delta)*(sqrt(alpha^2-(beta+1i*u).^2) ...
    -sqrt(alpha^2-beta^2));
psiX_i = (-1i) * (-delta)*(sqrt(alpha^2-(beta+1)^2) ...
-sqrt(alpha^2-beta^2));

f2_u = 1i*psiX_u*T*lambda*a./(lambda*b-1i*psiX_u) ...
    + a*b*lambda./(b*lambda-1i*psiX_u) ...
    .*log(1 - 1i*psiX_u/(lambda*b)*(1-exp(-T*lambda)));
f3_u = 1/lambda*psiX_u*(1-exp(-lambda*T));

f1_u = f2_u + 1i*y0*f3_u + a*log((1-1i/b*f3_u)./(1-1i/b*f3_u));

phi_T = 1i*psiX_i*y0/lambda*(1-exp(-lambda*T)) ...
    + lambda*a./(1i*psiX_i-lambda*b) ...
    .*(b*log(b./(b-1i*psiX_i/lambda*(1-exp(-lambda*T))))) ...
    -1i*psiX_i*T);

phi = 1i*u*(lnS + (r-d).*T) - phi_T + f1_u;

end
```

Figure 3.33 Matlab implementation of the characteristic function corresponding to the NIG CIR/GOU model. By setting $y0 = 1$ we assume the clock starts at 1

```
function phi = cf_vg_cir(u,lnS,T,r,d,C,G,M,kappa,eta,lambda)
% VG CIR
y0=1;

v1 = -1i*C*(log(G*M)-log(G*M+(M-G)*1i*u + u.*u)));
v2 = -1i*C*(log(G*M)-log(G*M+(M-G)*1i*(-1i) + (-1i).*(-1i))));


gamma1 = sqrt(kappa^2 - 2*lambda^2*1i*v1);
gamma2 = sqrt(kappa^2 - 2*lambda^2*1i*v2);
phi1 = kappa^2*eta*T/lambda^2 + 2*y0*1i*v1 ...
    ./ (kappa + gamma1.*coth(0.5*gamma1*T))...
    - 2*kappa*eta/lambda^2*log(cosh(0.5*gamma1*T) ...
    + kappa*sinh(0.5*gamma1*T)./gamma1);
phi2 = kappa^2*eta*T/lambda^2 + 2*y0*1i*v2 ...
    / (kappa + gamma2*coth(0.5*gamma2*T))...
    - 2*kappa*eta/lambda^2*log(cosh(0.5*gamma2*T) ...
    + kappa*sinh(0.5*gamma2*T)/gamma2);

phi = 1i*u*(lnS + (r-d)*T) + phi1 - 1i*u*phi2;
end
%%%
function phi = cf_vg_gou(u,lnS,T,r,d,C,G,M,lambda,a,b)
% VG GOU
    psiX1 = (-1i)*log((G*M./(G*M+(M-G)*1i*u+u.*u)).^C);
    psiX2 = (-1i)*log((G*M/(G*M+(M-G)-1)).^C);
    phi1 - 1i*psiX1/lambda*(1-exp(-lambda*T)) ...
    + lambda*a./(1i*psiX1-lambda*b) ...
    .*(b*log(b./(b-1i*psiX1/lambda*(1-exp(-lambda*T))))) ...
    -1i*psiX1*T);
    phi2 = 1i*psiX2/lambda*(1-exp(-lambda*T)) ...
    + lambda*a./(1i*psiX2-lambda*b).*(b*log(b./(b-1i*psiX2/lambda ....
    *(1-exp(-lambda*T))))-1i*psiX2*T);
    phi = 1i*u*(lnS + (r-d)*T)+phi1 - 1i*u.*phi2;
end
```

Figure 3.34 Matlab implementation of the characteristic function corresponding to the VG CIR/GOU model. By setting $y0 = 1$ we assume that the clock starts at 1

Skew and Smile

In this section we consider implied volatility surfaces. Once more let us take the NIG and the VG model as the base models. Then, we consider the CIR and GOU clocks to model stochastic volatility. The base scenarios are given in Table 3.2.

Table 3.2 Base scenarios for the analysis of stochastic volatility Lévy models

NIG CIR					
$\alpha = 18.4815$	$\beta = -4.8412$	$\delta = 0.4685$	$\lambda = 1.8772$	$\kappa = 0.5391$	$\eta = 1.5746$
VG CIR					
$C = 11.9896$	$G = 25.8523$	$M = 35.5344$	$\lambda = 1.8772$	$\kappa = 0.5391$	$\eta = 1.5746$
NIG GOU					
$\alpha = 6.1882$	$\beta = 0$	$\delta = 0.1622$	$\lambda = 0.6282$	$a = 1.2517$	$b = 0.5841$
VG GOU					
$C = 11.9896$	$G = 25.8523$	$M = 35.5344$	$\lambda = 0.6282$	$a = 1.2517$	$b = 0.5841$

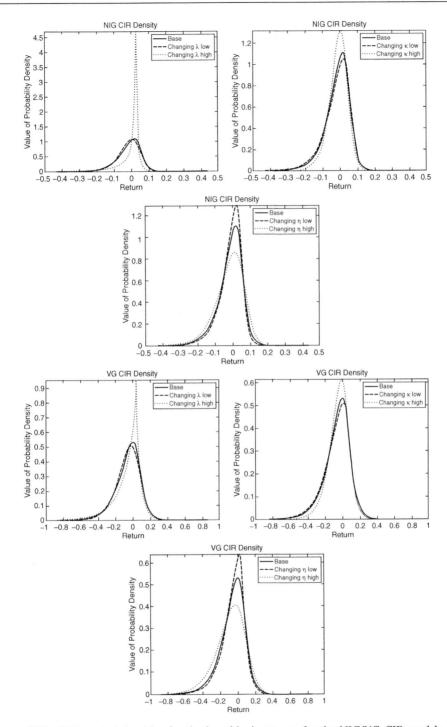

Figure 3.35 Risk neutral densities for the logarithmic returns for the NIG/VG CIR models. The base scenario is taken from Table 3.1. The values for the stochastic clock are changed by substituting $\lambda = 0.5, 1, 5, \kappa = 0.5, 1, 5$ and $\eta = 0.1, 0.5, 1.5$. The densities are for the NIG CIR model and λ (top left), κ (top right) and η (second row) and for the VG CIR model and λ (third row left), κ (third row right) and η (bottom)

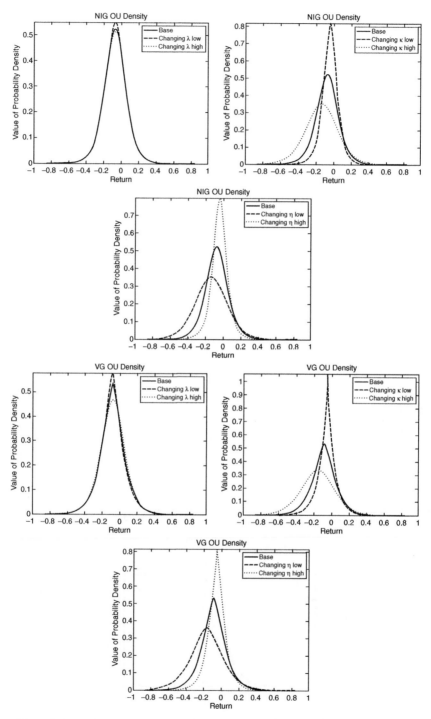

Figure 3.36 Risk neutral densities for logarithmic returns for the NIG/VG GOU models. The base scenario is taken from Table 3.1. The values for the stochastic clock are changed by substituting $a = 0.5, 1, 2, b = 0.5, 1, 5$ and $\lambda = 0.1, 10, 1000$. The densities are for the NIG CIR model and λ (top left), κ (top right) and η (second row) and for the VG CIR model and λ (third row left), κ (third row right) and η (bottom)

Table 3.3   Base scenarios for the analysis of stochastic volatility Lévy models

NIG CIR					
$\alpha = 10$	$\beta = 3$	$\delta = 1$	$\lambda = 2$	$\kappa = 1$	$\eta = 0.5$
NIG GOU					
$\alpha = 10$	$\beta = 3$	$\delta = 1$	$\lambda = 1$	$a = 1$	$b = 1$
VG CIR					
$C = 4.3574$	$G = 5.1304$	$M = 5.6699$	$\lambda = 5$	$\kappa = 5$	$\eta = 30$
VG GOU					
$\sigma = 0.1$	$\nu = 0.4$	$\theta = 0.2$	$\lambda = 1$	$a = 1$	$b = 1$

In what follows we provide the results for changing model parameters. Figures 3.37 and 3.38 summarize the results.

Typical Paths and Returns

Finally, let us look at typical paths generated by the models. To this end we consider the setting described by Table 3.3.

Figures 3.39 and 3.40 show the corresponding sample paths.

3.5 MARTINGALE CORRECTION

Let us revisit the exponential model considered at the beginning of this chapter. Thus, we consider some stochastic process $L(t)$ and

$$S(t) = S(0) \exp((r - d)t + L(t)).$$

To be able to use this model for pricing we need the discounted process to be a martingale. Thus, we have to adjust the dynamics to make the discounted asset price into a martingale. This means that we have to find a measure $\mathbb{Q}$ which is equivalent to the real-world measure $\mathbb{P}$. *Equivalent* means the measures have the same null sets. Under the measure $\mathbb{Q}$ the discounted asset price is a martingale.

For instance, in market models based on exponential Lévy processes there is no unique martingale measure and therefore no unique price of an option. In what follows we will consider two possible methods for adjusting the discounted asset price process to make it into a martingale:

 (i) Mean Correcting drift adjustment, (3.11)
 (ii) Multiplicative adjustment, (3.12)

Let us briefly review both concepts.

(i)   One way to make $S(t)$ into a martingale is to correct the mean of the stochastic process $L(t)$ by subtracting the expected value of L at time t. To this end we consider the stochastic process

$$S_{AM}(t) := S(0) \exp((r - d)t - \omega_L^a(t) + L(t)).$$

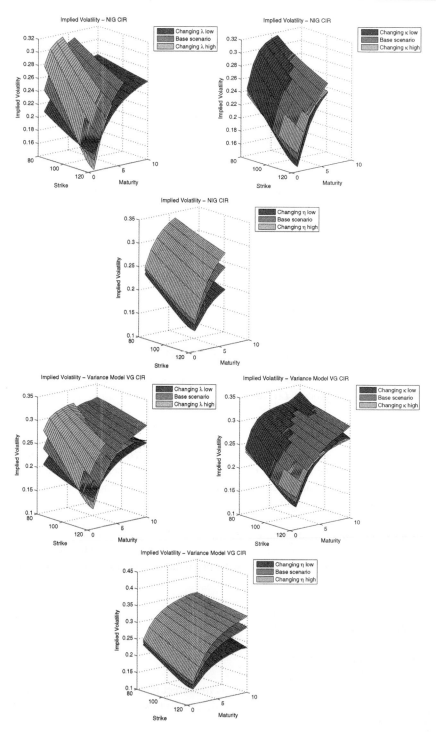

Figure 3.37 Volatility smiles for the NIG/VG CIR models. The base scenarios are given in Table 3.2. We take λ, κ and j. The corresponding results for the NIG case and λ (top left), κ (top right), η (second row) and the VG case with λ (third row left), κ (third row right) and η (bottom)

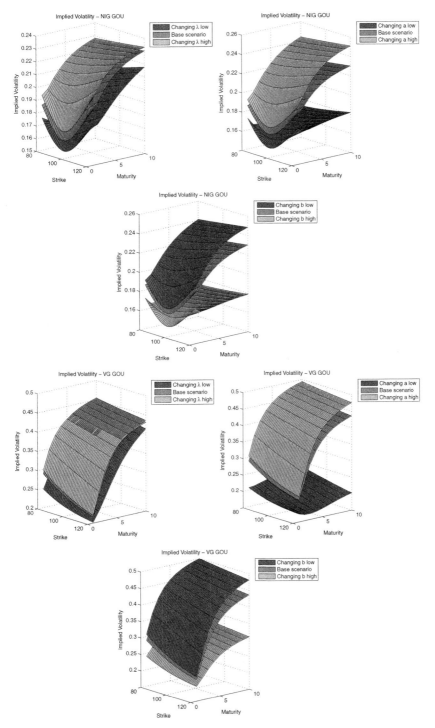

Figure 3.38 Volatility smiles for the NIG/VG GOU models. The base scenarios are given in Table 3.2. We take $\lambda = 0.25, 0.6282, 1.5, a = 0.25, 1.2517, 1$ and $b = 0.75, 0.5841, 1.5$. The corresponding results for the NIG case and λ (top left), a (top right) and b (second row) and for the VG case with λ (third row left), a (third row right) and b (bottom row)

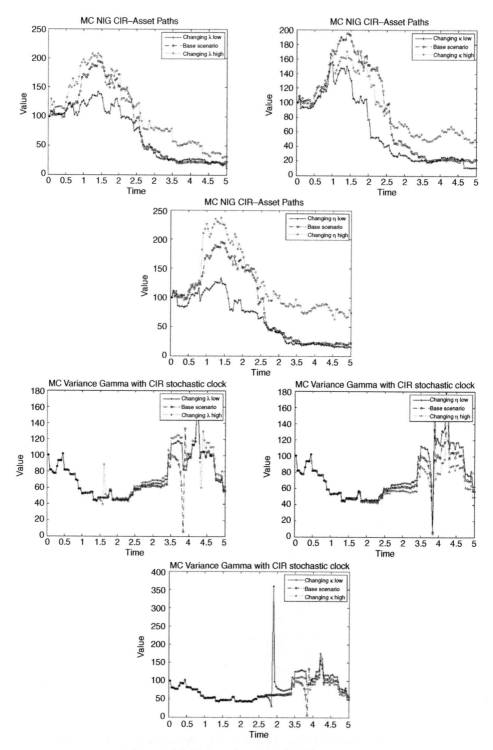

Figure 3.39   Typical paths for the NIG CIR model (upper half) and the VG GOU model (lower half) and the effect of increasing and decreasing respectively the CIR parameters for $\lambda = 1, 5, 10, \kappa = 1, 5, 10$ and $\eta = 1, 30, 60$

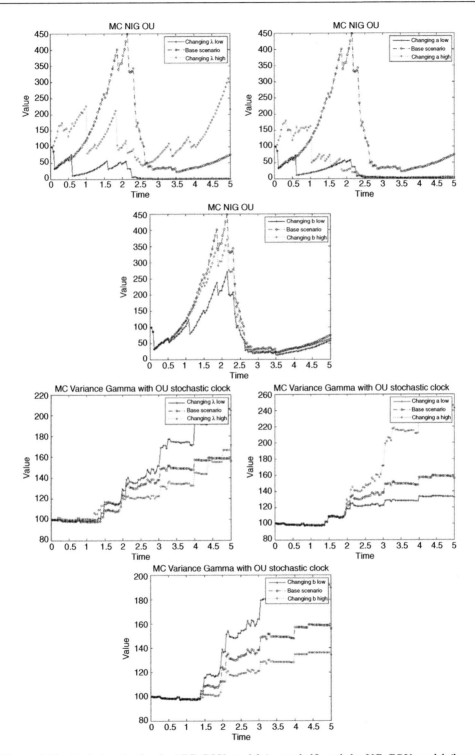

Figure 3.40 Typical paths for the NIG GOU model (upper half) and the VG GOU model (lower half) and the effect of increasing and decreasing respectively the GOU parameters for $\lambda = 0.5, 1, 50$, $a = 0.5, 1, 1.5$ and $b = 0.5, 1, 5$

We call the parameter ω_L^a the (additive) *martingale adjustment*. This adjustment is chosen such that the discounted and dividend adjusted price process $\exp(-(r-d)t)S$ is a martingale. This is given by $\omega_L^a(t) = \mathbb{E}[L(t)]$.

For instance, recall that in the setting of the Black–Scholes model $\omega_{BS}^a(t) = -\frac{\sigma^2}{2}t$. For other processes the correction can be found by considering the characteristic function φ_L of the stochastic process $L(t)$. We take

$$\omega_L^a(t) := \varphi_L(-i)t.$$

From the properties of the characteristic function we know that this adjustment corresponds exactly to the expectation of L at time t. If the process $L(t)$ is a Lévy process, $\omega(t)$ is a linear function. Table 3.4 lists some well-known models.

Table 3.4   Additive martingale adjustment for some models

Model	ω_L^a
BS	$\omega_{BS}^a(t) = -\frac{\sigma^2}{2}t$
VG	$\omega_{VG}^a(t) = Ct\log((M-1)(G+1)/MG)$
NIG	$\omega_{NIG}^a(t) = t\left(\delta\left(\sqrt{\alpha^2-(\beta+1)^2}-\sqrt{\alpha^2-\beta^2}\right)\right)$

For Lévy processes, $L(t)$ time changed by the integral of a subordination process $y(t)$, denoted by $Y(t)$, leads us to consider the price process

$$S_{AM}(t) = S(0)\exp((r-d)t - \omega_{LY}^a(t) + L(Y(t))).$$

The martingale adjustment can be computed and we find, $\omega_{LY}^a(t) = Y(t)\varphi_L(-i)$.

(ii)   Another way to make the process $\exp(-(r-d)t)S(t)$ into a martingale is to consider the ordinary exponential leading to a multiplicative adjustment. The guiding idea is that the forwards $S(t)$ are adjusted such that $\exp(-(r-d)t + L(t))$ is a martingale. Consider

$$S(t) = S(0)\exp((r-d)t + L(t)).$$

But in this case we take

$$S_{MM}(t) := S(0)\frac{\exp((r-d)t + L(t)}{\omega_L^m(t))}$$

and $\omega_L^m(t)$ is the expectation of $\exp(L(t))$. Let us consider the case of time changed Lévy processes $L(Y(t))$. We find that for the discounted logarithmic returns $\exp(-(r-d)t)\log(S(t)/S(0))$ is given in terms of the characteristic function. The adjustment is given by

$$\omega_L^m(t) := \frac{\varphi_{Y(t)}(-i\varphi_L(v))}{\varphi_{Y(t)}(-i\varphi_L(-i))}.$$

3.6 SUMMARY AND CONCLUSIONS

In this chapter we have reviewed methods which extend the class of financial models based on diffusion processes. First, we considered jump-diffusion processes and, second, models based on Lévy processes. The first extension is based on the assumption that jumps are rare events, and we modelled such events by some compound Poisson process. This process involved two stochastic mechanisms. A standard Poisson process generates the jump times using some intensity, and another stochastic mechanism specifies the size and the volatility of jumps. This extension led us to consider the Merton model, the Bates model and the Bates–Hull–White model.

The models based on Lévy processes can be driven by jumps alone. In this case jumps are no longer rare events. The method applied to specify the jump mechanism is the Lévy measure. We considered the Variance Gamma, the Normal Inverse Gaussian and the CGMY models as examples of this class of model. A further extension of this class allows for modelling business time by some increasing stochastic process. Using this concept it was possible to model stochastic volatility and therefore remove restrictions such as the floating smile property for pure Lévy models.

We have illustrated the main characteristics and features of the models by examining the effects of the model parameters on the distribution, the Lévy measure, the smile and on typical paths. Again, all the examples can be reproduced by the reader by applying the code provided as supporting material for this book.

4

Multi-Dimensional Models

4.1 INTRODUCTION AND OBJECTIVES

In this chapter we consider mathematical techniques for jointly modelling more than one underlying. In particular, we focus on methods which can be applied to calibrate such models.

We begin in Section 4.2 by considering baskets where the underlying assets are distributed according to a logarithmic normal distribution. Then, we look at Libor Market Models, focusing especially on a stochastic volatility version of the model introduced in Piterbarg, V. (2006). In Section 4.3 we introduce multi-dimensional versions of the Heston and SABR models. We introduce these models because we have built some of our numerical examples on these models. In Sections 4.4 and 4.5 we review techniques for the calibration of multi-dimensional models with stochastic volatility. We focus on *parameter averaging* and *Markovian projection*. Here we first give some mathematical details and then apply the methods to numerically price *Constant Maturity Spread options*. This pricing is fast and can be used for calibration purposes. All our illustrations include working Matlab code such that the reader can reproduce the results and experiment with the models.

In Section 4.6 we introduce the notion of a *copula*. This is a powerful tool for multi-dimensional modelling since by using this approach it is possible to separate the marginal distributions from the dependency structure. We review some of the copulae that are applied throughout financial modelling. For those copulae here we provide details on the implementation and on the applications to financial problems such as option pricing and asset allocation.

Section 4.7 considers multi-dimensional models based on jump processes and introduces the subordinator approach to model dependency for Lévy processes.

4.2 MULTI-DIMENSIONAL DIFFUSIONS

4.2.1 GBM Baskets

In this section we apply the standard model of a geometric Brownian motion to model $d \in \mathbb{N}$ assets S_i with weights ω_i in a basket, $\sum_{i=1}^{d} \omega_i S_i$. Since the covariance matrix, which implicitly determines the correlation matrix, controls the dependence structure, in this model we need to be able to simulate correlated normal distributed variables. We consider methods for generating correlated normal random variates. To this end we introduce the *Cholesky* and the *spectral decompositions*.

Suppose $\underline{Z} = (Z_1, \ldots, Z_d)^\top$ is a vector of uncorrelated Gaussian random variables, that is $\underline{Z} \sim \mathcal{N}(\underline{0}, I_d)$. Let A be a positive definite $d \times d$ matrix and L such that $LL^\top = A$. Then, $\underline{Y} := L\underline{Z}$ is a correlated Normal random vector with $\underline{Y} \sim \mathcal{N}(\underline{0}, A)$.

Cholesky Decomposition The function chol(A) gives the Cholesky decomposition of a matrix $A = (A_{i,j})_{i,j=1,\ldots,d}$ and leads to an upper triangular matrix $U = (U_{i,j})_{i,j=1,\ldots,d}$ such that $U_{i,j} = 0$ for $i > j$. The command chol(A, 'lower') leads to a lower triangular matrix $L = (L_{i,j})_{i,j=1,\ldots,d}$, that is the matrix with $L_{i,j} = 0$ if $i < j$.

```
function y = SpectralDecomposition(A)
    [evecs, evals] = eig(A);              % eigenvalues and vectors

    evals(evals<0) = 0;                   % truncate neg eigvalues
    evals(evals>0) = sqrt(evals(evals>0)); % sqrt of pos eigvalues

    y = evecs * evals;                    % return spectral decomp
end
```

Figure 4.1   Matlab code for computing the spectral decomposition of an input matrix A

Spectral Decomposition   For the spectral decomposition of a symmetric matrix $A \in \mathbb{R}^{d \times d}$ we consider the eigenvalues and eigenvectors of A. If

$$\lambda \underline{v} = A \underline{v}$$

holds, we call $\lambda \in \mathbb{R}$ an eigenvalue and $\underline{v} \in \mathbb{R}^d$ an eigenvector of A. The code to implement the spectral decomposition is given in Figure 4.1.

Examples   For illustrating the functions we consider the matrices A_1 and A_2,

$$A_1 := \begin{pmatrix} 1 & 0.748733508 & 0.888524896 & 0.821526502 \\ 0.748733508 & 1 & 0.726662801 & 0.683150423 \\ 0.888524896 & 0.726662801 & 1 & 0.878266274 \\ 0.821526502 & 0.683150423 & 0.878266274 & 1 \end{pmatrix} \quad (4.1)$$

and

$$A_2 := \begin{pmatrix} 1 & 0.9 & 0.7 \\ 0.9 & 1 & 0.4 \\ 0.7 & 0.4 & 1 \end{pmatrix}.$$

The Cholesky decompositions C_1 and C_2 as well as the spectral decompositions S_1 and S_2 are given by

$$C_1 = \begin{pmatrix} 1.0000 & 0 & 0 & 0 \\ 0.7487 & 0.6629 & 0 & 0 \\ 0.8885 & 0.0926 & 0.4494 & 0 \\ 0.8215 & 0.1027 & 0.3089 & 0.4681 \end{pmatrix}$$

$$C_2 = \begin{pmatrix} 1.0000 & 0 & 0 \\ 0.9000 & 0.4359 & 0 \\ 0.7000 & -0.5277 & 0.4812 \end{pmatrix}$$

$$S_1 = \begin{pmatrix} 0.9434 & 0.1481 & -0.2903 & 0.0618 \\ 0.8532 & -0.0086 & 0.0793 & -0.5155 \\ 0.9536 & -0.2463 & -0.0522 & 0.1649 \\ 0.9228 & 0.1111 & 0.2775 & 0.2430 \end{pmatrix}$$

$$S_2 = \begin{pmatrix} 0.1319 & 0.0872 & 0.9874 \\ -0.1002 & 0.4554 & 0.8846 \\ -0.0539 & -0.6333 & 0.7720 \end{pmatrix}.$$

4.2.2   Libor Market Models

Let us consider the Libor Market Model and extend it so that it is capable of modelling the skew and the smile observed in interest rate option data. To this end we add a local volatility function to the volatility and then consider the extension to stochastic volatility. We use the models to introduce a skew effect by the local volatility component and add convexity, this means a smile, by adding an uncorrelated stochastic volatility process of CIR type.

The standard Libor Market Model corresponds to setting the parameters to constant values or even to 0.

CMS and CMS Spread Options

We briefly considered constant maturity swaps (CMS) in Chapter 1, Subsection 1.4.2 and showed how to apply static hedging for calculating the convexity adjustment. Once the convexity adjustment for the swap rates is available we are in a position to price constant maturity swaps, caps and floors. Now, let us consider options on two CMS rates. Of particular interest are CMS spread options. If K denotes the strike level, the payoff h_{Spread} of a spread option is given by

$$h_{\text{Spread}}(S_1, S_2, K) := \max(S_1 - S_2 - K, 0). \tag{4.2}$$

Taking, for instance, S_1 to be the 10 year swap rate and S_2 the 2 year swap rate we can take a position in the slope of the yield curve. For this reason, such options are very popular among traders and risk managers.

Libor Market Models with Local Volatility and Stochastic Volatility

Next we consider a method to calibrate time-dependent stochastic volatility models. The method is called *parameter averaging* and was introduced in Piterbarg, V. (2006).

The *Libor rate* for the period $[T_i, T_{i+1}]$, that is fixed in T_i and paid in T_{i+1}, is defined by

$$L_i(t) := \frac{1}{\tau_i} \left(\frac{P(t, T_{i+1})}{P(t, T_i)} - 1 \right). \tag{4.3}$$

The function $\tau_i := \tau(T_{i+1}, T_i)$ denotes the year fraction which measures the distance of T_{i+1} and T_i with respect to the given market conventions. In this case it is the day count convention for the currency and the Libor. Now let us consider a stochastic volatility Libor Market Model. To do so we assume the following SDE for each Libor rate:

$$dL_i(t) = \mu_i(t)dt + (\beta_i(t)L_i(t) + (1 - \beta_i(t))L_i(0)) + \sigma_i(t)\sqrt{V(t)}dW(t) \tag{4.4}$$

$$dV(t) = \kappa(1 - V(t))dt + v\sqrt{V(t)}dZ(t). \tag{4.5}$$

Then, considering the swap rate, fixing at T_n and last payment at T_m, given by

$$S_{n,m}(t) := \frac{P(t, T_n) - P(t, T_m)}{\sum_{i=n}^{m-1} \tau_i P(t, T_{i+1})}. \tag{4.6}$$

The sum in the denominator is called *annuity* and we define

$$A_{n,m}(t) := \sum_{i=n}^{m-1} P(t, T_{i+1}).$$

Denoting $S_{n,m}(t)$ simply by $S(t)$, it is standard market practice to approximate the swap rate dynamics by

$$dS(t) = (\beta(t)S(t) + (1 - \beta(t))S(0))\sigma(t)\sqrt{V(t)}dW(t) \tag{4.7}$$
$$dV(t) = \kappa(1 - V(t))dt + v\sqrt{V(t)}dZ(t).$$

The coefficients in Equation (4.7) can be calculated explicitly. They are given by

$$\sigma(t) = \sum_{i=n}^{m-1} q_i \sigma_i(t) \tag{4.8}$$

$$\beta(t) = \sum_{i=n}^{m-1} p_i \beta_i(t) \tag{4.9}$$

$$q_i = \frac{L_i(0)}{S(0)} \frac{\partial S(0)}{\partial L_i(0)} \tag{4.10}$$

$$p_i = \frac{\sigma_i(t)^\top \sigma(t)}{(m-n)|\sigma(t)|^2}. \tag{4.11}$$

The parametrization of the Libor Market Model depends on the correlation and the volatility structure we choose. It is very popular to use a parametric structure. To this end we consider the version suggested in Lutz, M. (2010) and we assume that the number of Libors is n.

$$\rho_{ij} = \beta_1 + (1 - \beta_1)\left[e^{-\beta_3(i^{\beta_2} + j^{\beta_2})} + \frac{\vartheta_{ij}}{\vartheta_{jj}\vartheta_{ii}}\sqrt{\left(1 - e^{-2\beta_3 j^{\beta_2}}\right)\left(1 - e^{-2\beta_3 i^{\beta_2}}\right)}\right].$$

The variables ϑ_{ij} are specified by setting

$$\zeta_i = \exp\left(-\frac{1}{i}\left(\frac{i-1}{n-2}\beta_4 + \frac{n-1-i}{n-2}\beta_5\right)\right),$$

and the definition

$$\vartheta_{ij} := \begin{cases} 1 & \min(i, j) = 0 \\ \min(i, j) & \min(i, j) > 0; \zeta_i\zeta_j = 1 \\ \dfrac{\zeta_i\zeta_j}{1 - 1/\zeta_i\zeta_j} & \min(i, j) > 0; \zeta_i\zeta_j \neq 0 \end{cases}.$$

We pose the constraints $\beta_1 \in (0, 1)$, $\beta_2, \beta_3 > 0$ and $\beta_4, \beta_5 \in \mathbb{R}$. The parameter β_1 controls the asymptotic level of the correlation matrix. The parameters β_2 and β_3 control the decay from the diagonal and, finally, the parameters β_4 and β_5 allow for adjustment of the elements far from the diagonals.

For the parametric volatility we choose the following parametrization suggested in Brigo, D. and Mercurio, F. (2006):

$$\sigma(t) = ((T_{i-1} - t)\beta_1 + \beta_4)e^{-(T_i - t)\beta_2} + \beta_3.$$

4.3 MULTI-DIMENSIONAL HESTON AND SABR MODELS

Below we consider two multi-dimensional stochastic volatility models, namely the Heston and the SABR model. These models have been chosen because we wish to illustrate the general ideas of parameter averaging and Markovian projection using these models.

Since in a stochastic volatility model it is not obvious how to choose a valid correlation structure, we describe possible choices in the following subsection. Let S_i denote the assets and V_i, $i = 1, \ldots, d$, the corresponding stochastic variances. The correlation of S_i and V_j as well as the correlation for V_i and V_j, $i \neq j$, are not observable, nor are there enough quoted option prices from which the values can be calibrated.

4.3.1 Stochastic Volatility Models

The Heston Model

We wish to model a basket consisting of assets S_i, $i = 1, \ldots, N$. Furthermore, we assume that each asset is described by a Heston model, (2.49) and (2.50). The asset and the variance are correlated, (2.51). Thus, the multi-dimensional model is given by

$$dS_i(t) = (r - d)S_i(t)dt + \sqrt{V_i(t)}S_i(t)dW_i(t)$$
$$dV_i(t) = \kappa_i(\Theta_i - V_i(t))dt + v_i\sqrt{V_i(t)}dZ_i(t)$$
$$S_i(0) = S_{i,0}$$
$$V_i(0) = V_{i,0}$$
$$\langle dW_i, dZ_i \rangle = \rho_i dt.$$

The only thing missing in the above description is the full correlation structure of the model. Thus, we have to specify a positive definite matrix $\rho_{\text{Heston}} = (\rho_{ij})_{i,j}$ such that $\rho_{n+i,i} = \rho_i$ and $\rho_{i,i} = 1$ for $i = 1, \ldots, N$. In what follows we consider possible choices for ρ_{Heston}.

Simple Correlation Structure First, let us take the simple correlation structure such that we assume $\rho_{\text{Heston}} = \rho_{\text{Simple}}$ with

$$\rho_{\text{simple}} := \begin{pmatrix} 1 & 0 & \cdots & 0 & \rho_1 & 0 & \cdots & 0 \\ 0 & 1 & \cdots & 0 & 0 & \rho_2 & \cdots & 0 \\ \vdots & 0 & \ddots & \vdots & 0 & 0 & \cdots & 0 \\ 0 & 0 & \cdots & 1 & 0 & 0 & \cdots & \rho_N \\ \rho_1 & 0 & \cdots & 0 & 1 & 0 & \cdots & 0 \\ 0 & \rho_2 & \cdots & 0 & 0 & 1 & \cdots & 0 \\ \vdots & \ddots & \cdots & \vdots & 0 & 0 & \ddots & 0 \\ 0 & 0 & \cdots & \rho_N & 1 & 0 & \cdots & 1 \end{pmatrix}. \tag{4.12}$$

In fact, we assume that the Brownian motions driving the underlyings and/or the variances are independent. We have N Heston models. For this reason we have termed this correlation structure the *simple correlation structure*.

Full Correlation Structure In practice we wish to allow correlation between all assets S_i, $i = 1, \ldots, N$ and their corresponding variances, V_i, $i = 1, \ldots, N$. In subsequent chapters we see that these parameters can be inferred from quoted market prices but the other parameters, that is the correlations between S_i and V_j, $i, j = 1, \ldots, N$, $i \neq j$ and between V_i and V_j, $i, j = 1, \ldots, N$, $i \neq j$, cannot. If we assume that the correlations between S_i and V_i are given and that they are denoted by ρ_i, $i = 1, \ldots, N$, then we can define a valid correlation matrix by applying the algorithm derived in Günther, M. and Kahl, C. (2004). We arrange the correlation matrix such that the asset correlation matrix ρ_{ij}, $i, j = 1, \ldots, N$ is the $N \times N$ upper matrix

$$ A = a_{ij} = \begin{pmatrix} \rho & B \\ B & C \end{pmatrix}, $$

with $\text{diag}(B) = (\rho_1, \ldots, \rho_N)^\top$ and $\text{diag}(C) = (1, \ldots, 1)^\top$. Then, setting

$$ a(i + N, j) = \rho_i \rho_{ij} $$
$$ a(i + N, j + N) = \rho_i \rho_{ij} \rho_j $$

leads to a valid correlation matrix. Thus, we obtain the matrix

$$ \begin{pmatrix} 1 & \rho_{1,2} & \cdots & \rho_{1N} & \rho_1 & \rho_2\rho_{12} & \cdots & \rho_N\rho_{1N} \\ \rho_{21} & \cdots & & \vdots & \rho_1\rho_{21} & \rho_2\rho_{22} & \cdots & \rho_N\rho_{2N} \\ \vdots & \ddots & \ddots & \vdots & \vdots & \cdots & \ddots & \vdots \\ \rho_{N1} & \cdots & \cdots & \rho_{NN} & \rho_1\rho_{N1} & \rho_2\rho_{N2} & \cdots & \rho_N \\ \rho_1 & \rho_1\rho_{21} & \cdots & \rho_1\rho_{N1} & 1 & \rho_1\rho_{12}\rho_2 & \cdots & \rho_1\rho_{1N}\rho_N \\ \rho_2\rho_{2N} & \rho_2\rho_{21} & \vdots & \rho_2\rho_{N2} & \rho_1\rho_{21}\rho_2 & \rho_2\rho_{22}\rho_2 & \cdots & \rho_2\rho_{2N}\rho_N \\ \vdots & \vdots & \ddots & \cdots & \vdots & \vdots & \vdots & \vdots \\ \rho_N\rho_{1N} & \rho_N\rho_{21} & \cdots & \rho_N & \rho_1\rho_{N1}\rho_N & \rho_1\rho_{21}\rho_2 & \cdots & 1 \end{pmatrix}. \tag{4.13} $$

The SABR Model

In this section we introduce a multi-dimensional version of the SABR model which we call the *displaced SABR model*. The stochastic dynamic for S_i, and α_i $i = 1, \ldots, N$ is given in terms of the following set of SDEs:

$$ dS_i(t) = \alpha_i(t)S_i(t)^{\beta_i} dW_i(t) $$
$$ d\alpha_i(t) = v_i\alpha_i(t)dZ_i(t) $$
$$ S_i(0) = s_i^0 $$
$$ \alpha_i(0) = \alpha_i^0 $$
$$ \langle dW_i(t), dW_j(t) \rangle = \rho_{ij}dt $$
$$ \langle dW_i(t), dZ_j(t) \rangle = \gamma_{ij}dt $$
$$ \langle dZ_i(t), dZ_j(t) \rangle = \xi_{ij}dt, \quad i, j = 1, \ldots, N. \tag{4.14} $$

where ρ_{ij} is the correlation, γ_{ij} the *cross-skew* and ξ_{ij} the *de-correlation* between the stochastic volatilities.

4.4 PARAMETER AVERAGING

Usually fitting a model for a fixed maturity T works reasonably well. However, the story is different when considering the whole range of maturities at once. We observe from the application of Equations (4.7) and (4.8) that the implied volatility surface given a maturity T allows a good fit. If we fit to another maturity, the corresponding parameters may be very different.

To address this, from a modelling point of view it would be helpful to allow for time-dependent parameters. But for the additional flexibility we have to pay a price. Time-dependent models in general do not allow pricing of derivatives using closed form solutions. Thus, to overcome the difficulties with time-dependent parameters we first assume that the model parameters are given in terms of a function instead of a single parameter. We consider

$$\sigma \to \sigma(t), \quad \kappa \to \kappa(t), \quad \eta \to \eta(t).$$

The idea introduced in Piterbarg, V. (2006) is to use non-time-dependent methods for the time-dependent case. To do so we need some method to approximate the time-dependent model for a given maturity T using a constant parameter model. The method of choice, introduced in Piterbarg, V. (2006) and outlined in Andersen, L. and Piterbarg, V. (2010a), is called *parameter averaging*.

First, we need to average the volatility. To this end we replace $\sigma(t)$ by some constant $\bar{\sigma}$ such that the quoted swaption volatilities are matched well for fixed maturity T. We take

$$\mathbb{E}\left[(S(T) - S(0))^+\right] = \mathbb{E}\left[\mathbb{E}\left[(S(T) - S(0))^+ | (V_t)_{t \in [0,T]}\right]\right]. \tag{4.15}$$

If we assume $\rho = 0$, we find that the left side of (4.15) is equal to

$$\mathbb{E}[h(I_{\sigma,V}(T))],$$

where we have denoted

$$I_{\sigma,V}(T) := \int_0^T \sigma(s)^2 V(s) ds$$

$$h(x) := \frac{bS(0) + (1-b)L}{b} \left(\mathcal{N}(b\sqrt{x}/2) - 1\right).$$

In the case $\rho \neq 0$ the above equation can serve as an approximation.

Assuming that we wish to match the ATM prices – approximate them to a good extent – we have to solve for $\bar{\sigma}$ appearing in Equation (4.16),

$$\mathbb{E}\left[h\left(\int_0^T \sigma(t)^2 V(t) dt\right)\right] = \mathbb{E}\left[h\left(\bar{\sigma} \int_0^T V(t) dt\right)\right]. \tag{4.16}$$

Both expressions are not available in closed form but the characteristic functions are. With the help of these functions a system of ordinary differential equations is specified and we try the ansatz

$$h(x) \approx a + b \exp(cx).$$

Next, we proceed with the other parameters. For the average skew, $\bar{b}$, Andersen, L. and Piterbarg, V. (2010a) suggest taking

$$\bar{b} := \int_0^T b(t) \omega_T(t) dt,$$

with

$$\omega_T(t) := \frac{v(t)\sigma(t)^2}{\int_0^T v(t)^2 \sigma(t)^2 dt}$$

$$v(t)^2 := V(0)^2 \int_0^t \sigma(s)^2 ds + V(0)\eta^2 \exp(-\kappa t) \cdot \int_0^t \sigma(s)^2 \frac{e^{\kappa s} - e^{-\kappa s}}{2\kappa} ds.$$

Then,

$$\mathbb{E}\left[\left(\int_0^T \sigma(t)^2 \hat{V}(t) dt\right)^2\right] = \mathbb{E}\left[\left(\int_0^T \sigma(t)^2 V(t) dt\right)^2\right],$$

with the dynamics for $V(t)$ and $\hat{V}(t)$:

$$dV(t) = \kappa(V(0) - V(t))dt + \eta(t)\sqrt{V(t)}dZ(t)$$

$$d\hat{V}(t) = \kappa(\hat{V}(0) - \hat{V}(t))dt + \bar{\eta}\sqrt{\hat{V}(t)}dZ(t).$$

For pricing complex options, for instance a CMS spread option on two different swap rates, we have to take the correlation into account. To this end we consider two swap rates $S_1(t) := S_{n_1,m_1}(t)$ and $S_2(t) := S_{n_2,m_2}(t)$. The dynamics is derived from a Libor Market Model using the standard approximation. We have

$$dS_1(t) = S_1(t)(\mu_1(t)dt + \sigma_1(t)\sqrt{V(t)}dW_1(t)) \qquad (4.17)$$

$$dS_2(t) = S_2(t)(\mu_2(t)dt + \sigma_2(t)\sqrt{V(t)}dW_2(t)) \qquad (4.18)$$

$$dV(t) = \kappa(1 - V(t))dt + v\sqrt{V(t)}dZ(t) \qquad (4.19)$$

$$\langle dW_1(t), dW_2(t)\rangle = \rho dt \qquad (4.20)$$

$$\langle dW_i(t), dZ(t)\rangle = 0. \qquad (4.21)$$

The correlation driving the dependence of the underlying swap rates also has to be averaged and so we take

$$\bar{\rho} = \frac{\int_0^T \sigma_1(t)\sigma_2(t)^\mathsf{T} dt}{\sqrt{\int_0^T |\sigma_1(t)|^2 dt}\sqrt{\int_0^T |\sigma_2(t)|^2 dt}}. \qquad (4.22)$$

$\bar{\rho}$ in Equation 4.22 is called the *averaged correlation*.

4.4.1 Applications to CMS Spread Options

In this subsection we show the efficient use of transform methods together with the concepts introduced above. To do this we consider the pricing of *constant maturity swap spread options*. The results and the implementation are based on Kiesel, R. and Lutz, M. (2010). Our considerations are based on the model (4.7)–(4.8).

Using results obtained from Andersen, L. and Piterbarg, V. (2010b) it can be shown that the swap rate dynamic in the model is reasonably well approximated by

$$dS_{n,m}(t) \approx \mu_{n,m}(t)dt + (\beta_{n,m}(t)S_{n,m}(t) + (1 - \beta_{n,m}(t))S_{n,m}(0)) \cdot \sigma_{n,m}(t)\sqrt{V(t)}dW^{n,m}(t),$$

$$(4.23)$$

with V given by Equation (4.8).

```
fix=fixingTime/Basis;
end1=fix+endTime1/Basis; end2=fix+endTime2/Basis;

N=max(N,max(end1+1,end2+1));
% yield curve
dates=daysadd(today,(TimeGrid)*360);
curve=IRDataCurve('discount',today,dates,discountRates,...
    'Basis',2,'InterpMethod','spline');

% yield curve calcualtion
T = Basis:Basis:(N)*Basis;                % tenor structre
L = curve.getForwardRates(today+T*360)';  % Libor rates
P = curve.getDiscountFactors(today+T*360)'; % discounts
tau = Basis.*ones(size(P));               % year fraction

% determine the coefficients for computing sigmaSR and sigmaSRsquared
annuity=cumsum(tau.*P);
annuity1=annuity(end1)-annuity(fix);
annuity2=annuity(end2)-annuity(fix);

S1=(P(fix)-P(end1))/annuity1; S2=(P(fix)-P(end2))/annuity2;

endmax = max(end1,end2);

tmp  = P(fix:endmax-1); tmp2 = P(fix+1:endmax);
q1 = zeros(1,endmax-1); q2 = zeros(1,endmax-1);

q1(fix:max(end1,end2)-1)=(tmp-tmp2)./tmp.*(P(end1)/(P(fix)-P(end1)))...
    +(annuity(end1)-annuity(fix:endmax-1))/annuity1);
q2(fix:max(end1,end2)-1)=(tmp-tmp2)./tmp.*(P(end2)/(P(fix)-P(end2)))...
    +(annuity(end2)-annuity(fix:endmax-1))/annuity2);
```

Figure 4.2 Matlab code for transforming the input parameters

The swap rate dynamic can be approximated using a one-dimensional model. The corresponding model is specified by the SDE

$$dS_{n,m}(t) \approx (\bar{\beta}_{n,m}S_{n,m}(t) + (1 - \bar{\beta}_{n,m})S_{n,m}(0))\bar{\sigma}_{n,m}\sqrt{V(t)}dU(t), \tag{4.24}$$

where $\bar{\beta}_{n,m}, \bar{\sigma}_{n,m} \in \mathbb{R}$ and $U(t)$ is a one-dimensional Brownian motion.

In what follows we consider the pricing of CMS spread options in this model. To this end we have to calculate the averaged values of β, σ and ρ for two swap rates with different tenors. Let us start with some preliminary calculations. The input parameters are the current yield curve and the tenor structure from which all the necessary data, including the forward rates and the swap rates, are calculated (Figure 4.2).

First, we show how to implement the averaging for β. To do this let us examine the implementation for determining the averaged value $\bar{\beta}_1$ in Figure 4.3. For $\bar{\beta}_2$ the result can be applied with modified parameters.

In order to determine the averaged value $\bar{\sigma}_1$ we have to use (4.8) and (4.9). To this end we have applied two functions sigmaSRsquared, Figure 4.4, and betaSR, Figure 4.5, to implement these equations. Within the functions we compute the coefficients given in Equations (4.10) and (4.11).

Finally, we can also consider the averaged ρ. The implementation is provided in Figure 4.6.

```
tmp=@(t) (V^2 ...
    * quadv(@(t) sigmaSRsquared(t,fix,end1,T,q1,a,b,c,d),0,t)...
    + V*xi^2*exp(-kappa*t)* quadv(@(t) sigmaSRsquared(t,fix,...
      end1,T,q1,a,b,c,d)*(exp(kappa*t)-exp(-kappa*t))...
      /(2*kappa),0,t))*sigmaSRsquared(t,fix,end1,T,q1,a,b,c,d);
tmp2=@(t) tmp(t)*betaSR(t,fix, end1,T,q1,a,b,c,d);
% averaged beta_1
betaQuer1=quadv(tmp2,realmin,T(fix))/quadv(tmp,realmin,T(fix));
```

Figure 4.3 Matlab implementation of the averaging procedure for calculating β in a swap rate model

For establishing the pricing algorithm we consider the swap rate model

$$dS_i(t) = \mu_i(t) + (\beta_i^{SR}(t)S_i(t) + (1 - \beta_i^{SR})S_i(0))\sigma_i^{SR}\sqrt{V(t)}dW^{T_n+\delta}. \tag{4.25}$$

The drift, that is the convexity adjustment, in this setting is given by

$$\mu_i(t)dt = -\frac{P(t, T_n + \delta)}{A_i(t)}d\left(S_i(t), \frac{A_i(t)}{P(t, T_n + \delta)}\right).$$

We write $S_i(t)$ and $A_i(t)/P(t, T_n + \delta)$ as functions F_i and G_i of the Libor rates L_i. We have

$$S_i(t) = F_i(L(t))$$

$$\frac{A_i(t)}{P(t, T_n + \delta)} = G_i(L(t)).$$

The convexity adjustment can then be computed and we have

$$\mu_i(t) = -\frac{P(t, T_n + \delta)}{A_i(t)}\nabla F_i(L(t))D(t)\Sigma(t)D(t)\nabla G_i(L(t))^\top V(t), \tag{4.26}$$

```
tmp=@(t) sigmaSRsquared(t,fix,end1,T,q1,a,b,c,d);
zeta1=V*quadv(tmp,realmin,T(fix));

tmp2=@(t,y)odefkt(y,kappa,xi,1/(2*zeta1)+betaQuer1^2/8, ...
    sigmaSRsquared(t,fix,end1,T,q1,a,b,c,d),V);
lsg=ode23(tmp2,[0,T(fix)],[0 0]);

tmp2=exp(lsg.y(1,length(lsg.x))-V*lsg.y(2,length(lsg.x)));
tmp=@(x) fHut(x.^2.*(1/(2*zeta1)+betaQuer1^2/8),...
    kappa,xi,T(fix),V)-tmp2;
xval = 0:0.01:1; yval = tmp(xval);
lowval = max(xval(yval<0)); highval = max(xval(yval>0));

sigmaQuer1=fzero(tmp,[lowval,highval]);        % averaged sigma_1
```

Figure 4.4 Matlab implementation of the averaged σ in a swap rate model

```
function y = betaSR( t,fix, ausz,T,q,a,b,c,d , coeff1, coeff2)

J=fix:ausz-1;

qsigma = q(J).*sigma(T(J)-t,a,b,c,d);
sigmabeta = sigma(T(J)-t,a,b,c,d) ...
        .* beta(T(J)-t,T(length(T)-1),coeff1, coeff2);

rhomat = rho_new(T(J),T(J),t);

qsigmamat = repmat(qsigma',1,length(J));

y = sum(sum(qsigmamat .* rhomat).*sigmabeta) ...
        /((ausz-fix)*sigmaSRQuadrat(t,fix,ausz,T,q,a,b,c,d));
end
```

Figure 4.5 Matlab implementation of the averaged β in a swap rate model

with the $(N-1) \times (N-1)$ dimensional matrices

$$D(t) = \text{diag}\left(\beta_k(t)L_k(t) + (1-\beta_k(t))L_k(0)\right)$$
$$\Sigma(t) = \left(\sigma_k(t)\sigma_l(t)^{\top}\right)_{k,l=0}^{N-1}.$$

To determine the convexity adjustment we compute the derivatives of $S_i(t) = F_i(L(t))$ and $\frac{A_i(t)}{P(t,T_n+\delta)} = G_i(t)$ with respect to the Libor rates. Thus,

$$F(L(0)) = \frac{1 - \prod_{k=n}^{m-1} \frac{1}{1+\tau(k)L(k)}}{\sum_{k=n}^{m-1} \tau(k) \prod_{j=n}^{k} \frac{1}{1+\tau(j)L(j)}}$$

and the corresponding derivative is given by

$$\frac{\partial F(L(0))}{\partial L_i} = \frac{\tau_{i-1}P(0,T_{i+1})}{P(T_i)\sum_{k=n+1}^{m}\tau_k P(0,T_k)}$$
$$\times \left(P(0,T_m) + \frac{(P(0,T_n) - P(0,T_m))\sum_{k=i+1}^{m}\tau_k P(0,T_k)}{\sum_{k=n+1}^{m}\tau_k P(0,T_k)}\right).$$

```
rhoQuer=0;
J=fix:end2-1;

for i=fix:end1-1
    tmp=@(t) q1(i).*sigma(T(i)-t,a,b,c,d).* q2(J) ...
        .*sigma(T(J)-t,a,b,c,d).*rho(T(i),T(J),t);
    tmp = sum(quadv(tmp,0,T(fix)));
    rhoQuer = rhoQuer + tmp;
end

rhoQuer=rhoQuer/(sqrt(zeta1*zeta2)/V);        % averaged rho
```

Figure 4.6 Matlab implementation of the averaged ρ in a swap rate model

For the other function we have

$$G(L(0)) = -\frac{A_{n,m}(0)}{P(n+\delta)} = \frac{\sum_{k=n+1}^{m} \tau_k P(T_k)}{P(T_{n-1}+\delta)}$$

$$= \frac{\sum_{k=n+1}^{m} \tau_k P(T_{n+1}+\delta) \prod_{j=n+1+\delta}^{k} \frac{1}{1+\tau_j L(j)}}{P(T_n+\delta)}$$

and for the derivative

$$\frac{\partial G(L(0))}{\partial L_i} = \frac{\tau_{i-1} P(T_{i+1})}{P(T_i)P(T_n+\delta)} \sum_{k=i+1}^{m} \tau_k P(0, T_k).$$

Using the representation (4.26), we approximate the convexity adjustment μ_i by

$$\mu_i(t) \approx \nabla F_i(L(0)) D \bar{\Sigma} D \nabla G_i(L(0))^\top V(t) \left(\frac{P(0, T_n+\delta)}{A(0)} \right),$$

with the parameters

$$D := D(0) = \mathrm{diag}(L_k(0)), k = 0, \dots, N-1$$

$$\bar{\Sigma} := \left(\frac{1}{T_n} \int_0^{T_n} \sigma_k(t) \sigma_l(t)^\top dt \right)_{k,l=0}^{N-1}$$

$$\bar{\rho} := \frac{\int_0^{T_n} \sigma_1^{SR}(t) \sigma_2^{SR}(t)^\top dt}{\sqrt{\int_0^{T_n} |\sigma_1^{SR}(t)|^2} \sqrt{\int_0^{T_n} |\sigma_2^{SR}(t)|^2}}.$$

The Matlab implementation is presented in Figure 4.7.

The averaging method suggests that they need to replace the time-dependent dynamic (4.25) by the averaged dynamic

$$dS_i(t) \approx \bar{\mu}_i V(t) dt + \left(\bar{\beta}_i S_i(t) + (1 - \bar{\beta}_i) S_i(0) \right) \bar{\sigma}_i \sqrt{V(t)} dU_i(t),$$

with

$$\langle dU_1, dU_2 \rangle = \bar{\rho} dt.$$

Setting

$$X_i(t) := \bar{\beta}_i S_i(t) + (1 - \bar{\beta}_i) S_i(0)$$

and using the Itô formula the dynamic of $X_i(t)$ can be calculated. We have

$$dX_i(t) = \frac{\bar{\beta}_i \bar{\mu}_i}{X_i(t)} V(t) X_i(t) dt + X_i(t) \bar{\beta}_i \bar{\sigma}_i \sqrt{V(t)} dU_i(t),$$

with

$$\tilde{\sigma}_i = \bar{\beta}_i \bar{\sigma}_i; \quad \tilde{\mu}_i \approx \frac{\bar{\beta}_i \bar{\mu}_i}{S_i(0)} = \frac{\bar{\beta}_i \bar{\mu}_i}{X_i}.$$

Then, we have

$$X_i(T_n) \approx X_i(0) \exp \left(\left(\tilde{\mu}_i - \frac{\tilde{\sigma}_i}{2} \right) \bar{V}_{T_n} + \tilde{\sigma}_i \sqrt{\bar{V}_{T_n}} Z_i \right) =: \tilde{X}_i(T_n)$$

```
% numerically determine the gradients
gradF1 = zeros(1,(max(end1,end2)-fix));
gradG1 = gradF1; gradF2=gradF1; gradG2=gradF1;

gradF1(1:end1-fix) = tau(1-1+(fix-1):end1-fix-1+(fix-1)) ...
    .* P(1 +1+(fix-1):end1-fix +1+(fix-1)) ...
    ./(P(1 +(fix-1):end1-fix +(fix-1))*annuity1) ...
    .* (P(end1)+(P((fix))-P(end1))) ...
    .*(annuity(end1)-annuity(1 +(fix-1):end1-fix +(fix-1)))/annuity1);
gradF2(1:end2-fix) = tau(1-1+(fix-1):end2-fix-1+(fix-1)) ...
    .*P(1 +1+(fix-1):end2-fix +1+(fix-1)) ...
    ./(P(1 +(fix-1):end2-fix +(fix-1))*annuity2) ...
    .* (P(end2)+(P((fix))-P(end2))) ...
    .*(annuity(end2)-annuity(1 +(fix-1):end2-fix +(fix-1)))/annuity2);
gradG1(delta+1:end1-fix) = tau(1+delta-1+(fix-1):end1-fix-1+(fix-1)) ...
    .*P(1+delta+1+(fix-1):end1-fix+1+(fix-1)) ...
    ./(P(1+delta+(fix-1):end1-fix+(fix-1)).*P(fix+delta)) ...
    .* (annuity(end1)-annuity(1+delta+(fix-1):end1-fix+(fix-1)));
gradG2(delta+1:end2-fix) = tau(1+delta-1+(fix-1):end2-fix-1+(fix-1)) ...
    .*P(1+delta+1+(fix-1):end2-fix+1+(fix-1)) ...
    ./(P(1+delta+(fix-1):end2-fix+(fix-1)).*P(fix+delta)) ...
    .* (annuity(end2)-annuity(1+delta+(fix-1):end2-fix+(fix-1)));

% convexity correction
muQuer1 = P((fix)+delta)/annuity1*gradF1*D*Sigma*D*gradG1'; % convex SR1
muQuer2 = P((fix)+delta)/annuity2*gradF2*D*Sigma*D*gradG2'; % convex SR2
```

Figure 4.7 Matlab implementation of the computation of the convexity correction μ_i

$$S_i(T_n) \approx \frac{1}{\bar{\beta}_i}\left(\tilde{X}_i(T_n) - (1 - \bar{\beta}_i)S_i(0)\right).$$

The results are applied to price and calibrate CMS spread option prices in a multi-dimensional Libor Market Model. We have

$$\mathbb{E}\left[(S_1(T) - S_2(T) - K)^+\right] = \mathbb{E}\left[\mathbb{E}\left[(S_1(T) - S_2(T) - K)^+\right]|\bar{V}_{T_n}\right]$$

$$\approx \mathbb{E}\left[\mathbb{E}\left[\left(\frac{1}{\bar{\beta}_1}\left(\tilde{X}_1(T_n) - (1 - \bar{\beta}_1)S_1(0)\right)\right.\right.\right.$$

$$\left.\left.\left. - \frac{1}{\bar{\beta}_2}\left(\tilde{X}_2(T_n) - (1 - \bar{\beta}_2)S_2(0)\right) - K\right)^+|\bar{V}_{T_n}\right]\right],$$

with $\tilde{K} = \frac{1-\bar{\beta}_1}{\bar{\beta}_1}S_1(0) - \frac{1-\bar{\beta}_2}{\bar{\beta}_2}S_2(0)$.

The CMS caplet price is finally given by

$$\mathbb{E}\left[(S_1(T) - S_2(T) - K)^+\right] = \mathbb{E}\left[\mathbb{E}\left[\left(\frac{1}{\bar{\beta}_1}\tilde{X}_1(T_n) - \frac{1}{\bar{\beta}_2}\tilde{X}_2(T_n) - \tilde{K}\right)^+|\bar{V}_{T_n}\right]\right]$$

$$= P(0, T_n + \delta)\int_0^\infty \int_{-\infty}^\infty g(u, v)\frac{e^{\frac{u^2}{2}}}{\sqrt{2\pi}}du f(v)dv. \quad (4.27)$$

The function g is given in closed form:

$$
g(u, v) = \begin{cases}
\dfrac{S_1(0)}{\bar{\beta}_1} \exp(h(u, v) - \hat{K}(u, v)) & \hat{K}(u, v) \le 0 \\[2em]
\dfrac{S_1(0)}{\bar{\beta}_1} \exp(h(u, v)) \mathcal{N}\left(\dfrac{\frac{S_1(0)}{\bar{\beta}_1 \hat{K}(u,v)} + h(u, v) - \frac{\tilde{\sigma}^2}{2}(1 - \bar{\rho})v}{\tilde{\sigma}_1 \sqrt{v(1 - r\bar{h}o^2)}} \right) \\[2em]
\quad - \hat{K}(u, v) \mathcal{N}\left(\dfrac{\frac{S_1(0)}{\bar{\beta}_1 \hat{K}(u,v)} + h(u, v) - \frac{\tilde{\sigma}^2}{2}(1 - \bar{\rho})v}{\tilde{\sigma}_1 \sqrt{v(1 - r\bar{h}o^2)}} \right) & \hat{K}(u, v) > 0
\end{cases},
$$

with

$$
\hat{K}(u, v) = \frac{S_2(0)}{\bar{\beta}_2} \exp\left(\left(\tilde{\mu}_2 - \frac{\tilde{\sigma}_2^2}{2} \right) v + \tilde{\sigma}_2 \sqrt{vu} \right) + \tilde{K}
$$

$$
h(u, v) = \left(\tilde{\mu}_1 - \frac{\bar{\rho}^2 \tilde{\sigma}_1^2}{2} \right) v + \bar{\rho} \tilde{\sigma}_1 \sqrt{vu},
$$

with $\mu_i \in \mathbb{R}$ and $\sigma_i \in \mathbb{R}^+$ and $i = 1, 2$.

The Matlab code to implement the function g is presented in Figure 4.8.

Let us now show how to obtain the function g and how to efficiently compute the integral of Equation (4.27). With respect to the integrated variance in the model,

$$
\bar{V}_T = \int_0^T V(t)dt. \tag{4.28}
$$

```matlab
function fval = g_new( u,v,betaQuer1,betaQuer2, sigmaTilde1, ...
    sigmaTilde2, muTilde1,muTilde2, rhoQuer, S1,S2, KTilde, w)
%Implements the function g(u,v)
logKHut = (muTilde2-.5*sigmaTilde2^2)*v+sigmaTilde2*sqrt(v).*u ...
    + log(S2) - log(betaQuer2);
KHut = exp(logKHut) + KTilde;
h = (muTilde1-.5*rhoQuer^2*sigmaTilde1^2)*v ...
    + rhoQuer*sigmaTilde1*sqrt(v).*u;

fval = zeros(size(KHut));

arg1 = w*(log(S1./(betaQuer1*KHut(KHut > 0))) ...
    + h(KHut > 0) + .5*sigmaTilde1^2*(1-rhoQuer^2).*v(KHut > 0))...
    ./(sigmaTilde1*sqrt(v(KHut > 0)*(1-rhoQuer^2)));
arg2 = arg1 - w*sigmaTilde1*sqrt(v(KHut > 0)*(1-rhoQuer^2));

fval(KHut > 0) = w*(S1*exp(h(KHut > 0)).*normcdf(arg1)/betaQuer1 ...
    - KHut(KHut > 0).*normcdf(arg2));
if w == 1
    fval(KHut <= 0) = (S1/betaQuer1.*exp(h(KHut<=0))-KHut(KHut<=0));
end
fval = fval.*exp(-.5*u.^2);

end
```

Figure 4.8 Matlab code for the implementation of the function g

The swap rate processes S_i, $i = 1, 2$ are log-normally distributed with variance $\bar{V}_T$ and, furthermore, jointly log-normally distributed. Using the integrated variance, Equation (4.28), the pricing problem is given by the following equation:

$$\mathbb{E}\left[\left(S_1(0)e^{U_1} - S_2(0)^{U_2} - K\right)^+ |\bar{V}_T = v\right] = \frac{1}{2\pi}\int_{-\infty}^{\infty} g(u, v)e^{-\frac{u^2}{2}}du, \qquad (4.29)$$

with

$$g(u, v) = S_1(0)\exp\left(m(u) + \frac{s^2}{2}\right)\mathcal{N}\left(\frac{\log\left(\frac{S_1(0)}{h(u)}\right) + m(u) + s^2}{s}\right)$$

$$- h(u)\mathcal{N}\left(\frac{\log\left(\frac{S_1(0)}{h(u)}\right) + m(u)}{s}\right).$$

The functions and parameters appearing in the latter formula are given by

$$h(u) = S_2(v)\exp\left(\mu_2 T - \frac{\sigma_2^2 v}{2} + \sigma_2\sqrt{vu}\right) + K$$

$$m(u) = \mu_1 T - \frac{\sigma_1^2 v}{2} + \rho\sigma_1\sqrt{vu}$$

$$s^2 = \sigma_1^2(1 - \rho)v.$$

Thus, the CMS spread option price is given by the integral

$$\mathbb{E}\left[(S_1(T) - S_2(T) - K)^+\right] = \int_0^{\infty}\int_{-\infty}^{\infty} g(u, v)\frac{e^{-\frac{u^2}{2}}}{\sqrt{2\pi}}f(v)dv. \qquad (4.30)$$

To efficiently compute the density f we first have to consider the Laplace transform $\hat{f}$ of a displaced Heston model with $\rho = 0$, $\lambda = 1$ and $a = 1$. This transform is given by

$$\hat{f}(\mu) = \exp\left(\frac{2\kappa}{v^2}A(\mu) + B(\mu)\right), \qquad (4.31)$$

with the functions A and B

$$A(\mu) := \log\left|2\gamma e^{-\gamma T/2}\right| + i\left(\text{Arg}(2\gamma e^{-\gamma T/2}) + 2\pi n\right) - \log\left(\gamma + \kappa + (\gamma - \kappa)e^{-\gamma T}\right)$$

$$B(\mu) := \frac{\kappa^2 T}{v^2} + \left(\frac{2\gamma e^{-\gamma T}}{\gamma + \kappa + (\gamma - \kappa)e^{-\gamma T}} - 1\right)\frac{V(0)(\gamma - \kappa)}{v^2}$$

$$= \left\lfloor\frac{\text{Arg}(\gamma) - \frac{T}{2}|\gamma|\sin(\text{Arg}(\gamma)) + \pi}{2\pi}\right\rfloor$$

$$\gamma := \sqrt{\kappa^2 + 2\mu v^2}.$$

The implementation of $\hat{f}$ is given in Figure 4.9.

The density f can be recovered by using the inversion formula for Laplace transforms $\hat{f}$. It is given by the integral

$$f(x) = \frac{1}{2\pi i}\int_{a-i\infty}^{a+i\infty} e^{xs}\hat{f}(s)ds, \qquad (4.32)$$

```
function y = fHut ( mu,kappa,xi,T,V)
% the transform of f
    gamma = sqrt(kappa^2+2.*mu*xi^2);
    n = floor( (angle(gamma)-T/2*abs(gamma) ...
        .*sin(angle(gamma))+pi)/(2*pi) );

    A = log( abs(2.*gamma.*exp(-gamma.*T/2)) ) ...
        + 1i.*(angle(2.*gamma.*exp(-gamma.*T/2))+2*pi*n) ...
        -log(gamma+kappa+(gamma-kappa).*exp(-gamma.*T));
    B = kappa^2*T/(xi^2)+(2*gamma.*exp(-gamma*T) ...
        ./( gamma+kappa+(gamma-kappa).*exp(-gamma*T) ) -1) ...
        .*V.*(gamma-kappa)./(xi^2);

    y = exp(2*kappa/(xi^2).*A + B);
end
```

Figure 4.9   Implementation of the transform $\hat{f}$ of the function f

with $a > \mathcal{R}(s)$ the real part of the singularity s of $\hat{f}$. It can be shown that all singularities lie on the negative real axis, which implies $a \geq 0$.

Using symmetry we find for the density f

$$f(x) = \frac{1}{\pi} \int_0^\infty \mathcal{R}\left(e^{x(a+iu)} \hat{f}(a + iu)\right) du.$$

The integrand is in general a highly oscillatory function and $\hat{f}$ decays slowly for $\mathcal{I}(z) \to \infty$. Therefore, the integration is in general not manageable using standard techniques. Kiesel, R. and Lutz, M. (2010) have developed a method to efficiently calculate f. This method is applied and implemented in Matlab. Figure 4.10 illustrates the oscillatory nature of the integrand and shows why standard built-in numerical integration methods may not work properly.

Now let us look at the density for the variance. For each value of v we have to find the value where the function is equal to 0. To this end we use a Newton iteration for large values of x and the `fzero` function of Matlab for small values of x. By *small values* we mean values smaller than 10. We have included a maximum iteration variable `maxiter` of 20 and a stopping level eps which is set to 10^{-20}.

In order to compute the derivative necessary for the Newton iteration we have to rely on finite differences. We have chosen a value of `eps1` to control the stepping in the finite differences. The value is set to 10^{-10}. The code can be found in Figure 4.11. In practice, we observe that the iteration stops after 5 steps and the maximum number of iterations is never reached.

To speed things up we have also included a Gauss-Legendre integration, with the variables `lowerbound`, `upperbound` and `NumberPoints`. This is faster than the built-in Matlab quadrature formula which relies on adaptive integration.

The Cauchy theorem is applied by deforming the half line contour such that $\mathcal{R}(s) \to -\infty$. Thus, the integrand is forced to decay fast. This approach can be traced back to techniques proposed in Talbot, A. (1979). The standard method is to use the contour

$$s(\phi) = a + b\phi(\cot(\phi) + ic), \quad 0 \leq \phi < \pi.$$

Kiesel, R. and Lutz, M. (2010) propose use of the contour

$$s(u) = a + u(bi - a), \quad 0 \leq u < \infty, \quad a, b > 0. \tag{4.33}$$

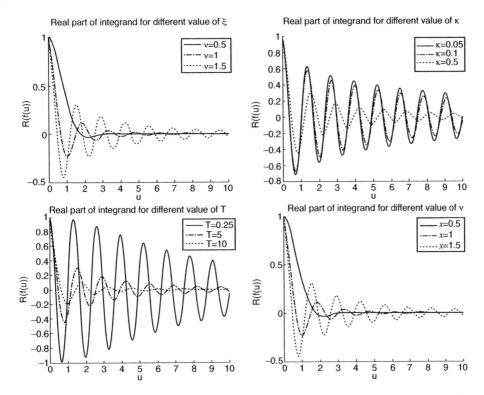

Figure 4.10 The integrand for $a = 0$, $V(0) = 1$ and $v = 0.5, 1.5, 3$ (top left), $\kappa = 0.05, 0.1, 0.5$ (top right), $T = 0.25, 1, 5, 10$ (bottom left) and $x = 1, 5, 10$, (bottom right)

For this contour (4.33), all singularities are to the left of it. As $u \to \infty$ the imaginary part of $s(u) \to \infty$ and therefore singularities are avoided, which makes the integration more stable and efficient.

Using the contour (4.33) the integrand becomes

$$f(x) = \frac{1}{\pi} \int_0^\infty \mathcal{I} \left(e^{x(a+u(bi-a))} \hat{f}(a + u(bi - a))(bi - a) \right) du.$$

We find

- For large x the density f gets large very fast due to the exponential function.
- To avoid the blow up, a can be chosen reciprocal to x, $a = 1/x$.
- b is the only free parameter.
- Choosing b too large leads to many oscillations.
- Choosing b too small gets too close to the singularities.

Figures 4.12–4.15 illustrate the optimal path integration. For different values of time to maturity, T, we consider three different paths. For the integration range we have plotted both the real and the imaginary part of the integrand.

From the figures it can be seen that the optimal paths avoid regions with high oscillations of the integrand. Sub-optimal choices can lead to significant oscillations. If we choose not to use the optimal path, we may use instead special integration schemes adapted to such integrands.

```
function [ out ] = DichteVar_new( v,T,kappa,xi,V )
    eps = 1e−20;        % stopping the Newton search level
    maxiter = 20;       % max iterations for Newton search
    eps1 = 1e−10;       % used for approx the derivative

    b = .125*ones(size(v,2),1)/pi;   % starting values
    b(1) = 0;
    x = v(1,:)';
    a = 1./x;
    a(isnan(a))=100000;

    % Zero search starts here
    N = length(x(x<10));
    for k = 2:N
        h = @(u)  x(k)*u+imag(eta(u*1i,kappa,xi,T,V))−.5*pi;
        b(k) = fzero(h,[0,10^3]);
    end
    N = N+1;
    h = @(u)  x(N:end).*u+imag(eta(u*1i,kappa,xi,T,V))−.5*pi;
    for i =1:maxiter
        b(N:end) = b(N:end) − h(b(N:end)) * eps1 ...
              ./ (h(b(N:end)+eps1)−h(b(N:end))));
        if min(abs(h(b(N:end)))) < eps
            break;
        end
    end
    % Gauss Legendre Integration
    lowerBound = 1e−6; upperBound = 1; NumberPoints = 64;
    [points, weights] = ...
            GaussLegInput(lowerBound,upperBound,NumberPoints);

    mat_a = repmat(a,1,NumberPoints);
    mat_b = repmat(b,1,NumberPoints);
    mat_x = repmat(x,1,NumberPoints);

    points_mat = repmat(points',length(x),1);
    weights_mat = repmat(weights',length(x),1);

    arg1 = mat_a−3*log(points_mat).*(mat_b*1i−mat_a);
    integral_val = sum(weights_mat.*imag(exp(mat_x.*arg1) ...
      .*fHut(arg1,kappa,xi,T,V).*(3./points_mat).*(mat_b*1i−mat_a)),2);

    out = repmat(max(integral_val,0)',size(v,1),1)/pi;
end
```

Figure 4.11 Matlab code for implementing the density f. The calculation relies on zero finding as well as numerical integration

Usually such schemes are costly in terms of time and thus the evaluation of derivatives is rendered slow.

Look at the integrand and consider

$$\exp(\mathcal{R}(\eta(ui)))\,(\cos(xu + \mathcal{I}(\eta(ui))) + i\,\sin(xu + \mathcal{I}(\eta(iu)))\,.$$

Take as a measure for the frequency of oscillations and compute the optimal b by considering:

$$\cos(bx + \mathcal{I}(\eta(bi))) = 0.$$

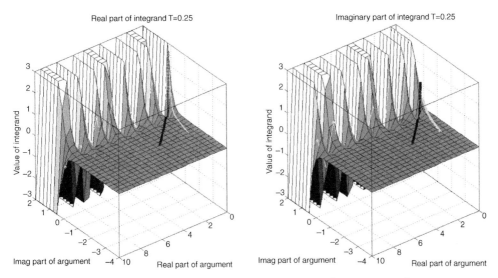

Figure 4.12   Integrand 1. The real and the imaginary part of $\mathcal{R}(e^{xz}\hat{f}(z))$ and $\mathcal{R}(e^{xz}\hat{f}(z))$ with different paths $b = 15$ (white), $b = 0.09$ (grey) and optimal b (black). We have used the values $x = 3$, $V(0) = 1$, $\kappa = 0.15$, $\nu = 1.3$, $T = 0.25$

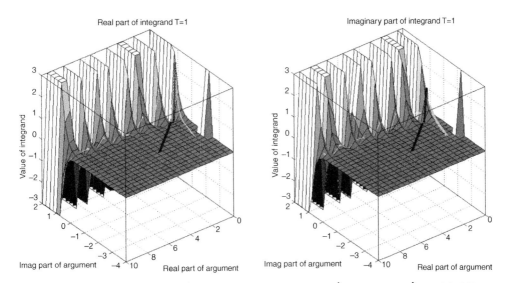

Figure 4.13   Integrand 2. The real and the imaginary part of $\mathcal{R}(e^{xz}\hat{f}(z))$ and $\mathcal{R}(e^{xz}\hat{f}(z))$ with different paths $b = 15$ (white), $b = 0.09$ (grey) and optimal b (black). We have used the values $x = 3$, $V(0) = 1$, $\kappa = 0.15$, $\nu = 1.3$, $T = 1$

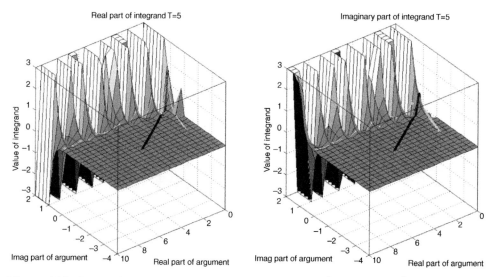

Figure 4.14 Integrand 3. The real and the imaginary part of $\mathcal{R}(e^{xz}\hat{f}(z))$ and $\mathcal{R}(e^{xz}\hat{f}(z))$ with different paths $b = 15$ (white), $b = 0.09$ (grey) and optimal b (black). We have used the values $x = 3$, $V(0) = 1$, $\kappa = 0.15$, $v = 1.3$, $T = 5$

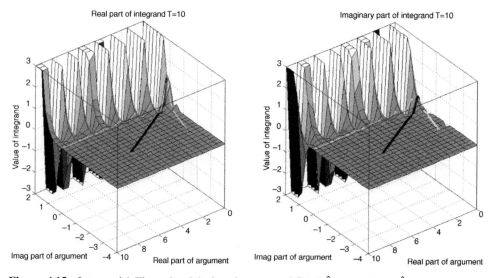

Figure 4.15 Integrand 4. The real and the imaginary part of $\mathcal{R}(e^{xz}\hat{f}(z))$ and $\mathcal{R}(e^{xz}\hat{f}(z))$ with different paths $b = 15$ (white), $b = 0.09$ (grey) and optimal b (black). We have used the values $x = 3$, $V(0) = 1$, $\kappa = 0.15$, $v = 1.3$, $T = 10$

Thus, we need to have

$$bx + \mathcal{I}(\eta(bi)) = \frac{\pi}{2}.$$

To solve this equation for each x at which the density is evaluated we use a search procedure such as the Newton iteration. We transform the integration range to $[0, 1]$. This enables us to use adaptive integration methods. This can be accomplished, for instance, by using $u \mapsto -3 \log(\tilde{u})$ which leads to the representation

$$f(x) = -\frac{1}{\pi} \int_0^1 \mathcal{I}\left(\exp(xs(u))\hat{f}(s(u))s'(u)\right) ds,$$

with $s(u) = a - 3\log(u)(bi - a)$ and $s'(u) = -3/u(bi - a)$. For different time to maturity, $T = 0.25, 1, 5, 10$, we consider the integrand in Figure 4.16. For all integrands we observe that they are smooth functions and therefore numerical integration can be performed reasonably well. Figure 4.16 show the integrands for different values of x.

Finally, let us consider the densities used for the numerical integration. Figure 4.17 gives the densities for different time to maturity, $T = 0.25, 1, 5, 10$. We use the optimal path and the densities for the computation of option prices for CMS options in the last paragraph of this section.

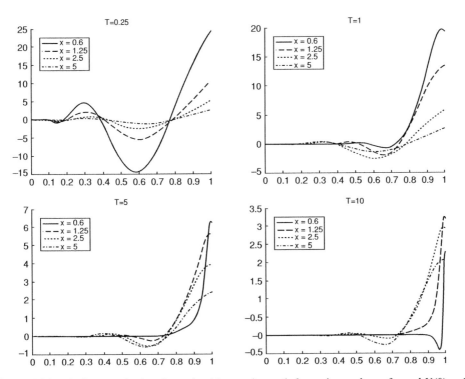

Figure 4.16 The integrand using the optimal integration path for various values of x and $V(0) = 1$, $\kappa = 0.15$, $\nu = 1.3$ and $T = 0.25$ (top left), $T = 1$ (top right), $T = 5$ (bottom left) and $T = 10$ (bottom right)

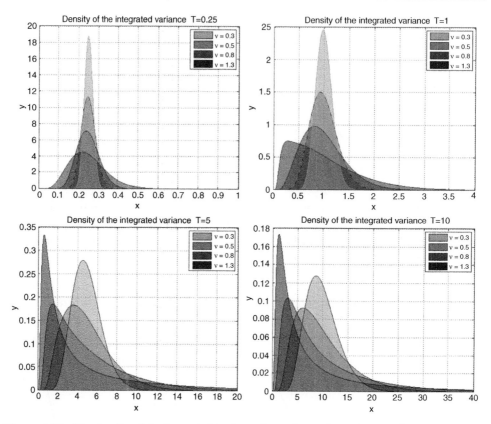

Figure 4.17 The density of the integrated variance for various values of v and $\bar{V}_T$ and $V(0) = 1$, $\kappa = 0.15$ and $T = 0.25$ (top left), $T = 1$ (top right), $T = 5$ (bottom left) and $T = 10$ (bottom right)

Numerical Example Let us consider a stochastic volatility Libor Market Model with the volatility, skew and correlation structure. The functions correspond to Kiesel, R. and Lutz, M. (2010):

- $|\sigma_i(t)| = (a + b(T_i - t))e^{-c(T_i - t)}$, $a = 0.04$, $b = 0.32$, $c = 1.1$, $d = 0.17$

```
function y = sigma( x,a,b,c,d )
%    Parametric Volatility of the volatility
    y=(a+b*x).*exp(-(c*x))+d;
end
```

- $\beta_i(t) = (1 - \frac{T_i - t}{T_{N-1}})a + \frac{T_i - t}{T_{N-1}}b$, $a = 0.4$, $b = 0.9$

```
function y = beta( x,T, a, b)
% the function beta_i(t)
% call: beta_i(t)=b(T(i)-t,lastTenor - 1)
    y = (1-(x)/T).*a+(x)/T.*b;
end
```

- $\rho_{i,j}(t) = \exp(-|T_i - T_j|\nu\exp(-\eta\min(T_i - t, T_j - t)))$, $\nu = 0.11$ and $\eta = 0.22$

```
function y = rho( Ti,Tj,t,nu,eta)
% call: rho(T(i),T(j),t,nu,eta) to calculate rho_ij(t)
    y = exp(-abs(Ti-Tj) .*nu.* exp(-eta*min(Ti-t,Tj-t)));    %Lutz
end
```

We consider the effect on the CMS prices when changing the model parameters (Figure 4.18).

The implementation is fast and can thus be used to calibrate a stochastic volatility Libor Market Model to all quoted swaption prices, CMS and CMS spread options. To summarize the parameter averaging technique:

- We have considered time-dependent models and techniques for calibration.
- We have considered basket dynamics and techniques for calibration.
- We have applied the methods to CMS spread options.
- We have presented several numerical experiments in order to show the validity of the methods.

The code for producing the figures as well as for the pricing, including time-averaging, can be found in the supporting material of this book.

4.5 MARKOVIAN PROJECTION

In this section we provide an introduction to the method called *Markovian projection*. This method is usually applied for multi-dimensional calibration. It was invented by Piterbarg, V. (2006) and was applied to financial problems (see, for instance, Andersen, L. and Piterbarg, V. (2010a), Antonov, A., Arneguy, M. and Audet, N. (2008), Antonov, A. and Misirpashaev, T. (2009) and Kienitz, J. and Wittke, M. (2010)).

The method is based on a result obtained by Gyoengy, I. (1986) and Brunick, G. (2008).

Basket dynamics are increasingly popular and multi-dimensional models are frequently used for modelling interest rates. The parameters of the model have to be calibrated. Furthermore, it is desirable to calibrate all the parameters jointly. The calibration should be stable and fast. Let us start by describing the method.

To this end let the process $X(t)$ be given as the solution to the SDE

$$dX(t) = \mu(t)dt + \sigma(t)dW(t),$$

where μ and σ are adapted bounded stochastic processes such that the SDE admits a unique solution. Then, define

$$m(t, x) := \mathbb{E}[\mu|X(t) = x]$$
$$s(t, x) := \mathbb{E}[\sigma|X(t) = x].$$

The SDE

$$dY(t) = m(t, Y(t))dt + s(t, Y(t))dW(t),$$

with $Y(0) = X(0)$ admits a weak solution $Y(t)$ that has the same one-dimensional distributions as $X(t)$ for fixed time t.

Let us assume $m = 0$, then, using results from Dupire, B. (1994) we have for a Call option, C,

$$\frac{\partial}{\partial t}C(t, K) = \frac{1}{2}\frac{\partial^2}{\partial K^2}C(t, K)s^2(t, K). \qquad (4.34)$$

By applying the Itô–Tanaka formula for discontinuous functions we get

$$\begin{aligned}\frac{\partial}{\partial t}C(t, K) &= \frac{1}{2}\mathbb{E}[\delta(X(t) - K)dX^2(t)] \\ &= \frac{1}{2}\mathbb{E}[\delta(X(t) - K)]\mathbb{E}[dX^2(t)|X(t) = K] \\ &= \frac{1}{2}\frac{\partial^2}{\partial K^2}C(t, K)\mathbb{E}[dX^2(t)|X(t) = K].\end{aligned}$$

The local variance of Y and that of X can be related by

$$\mathbb{E}[X^2(t)|X(t) = K] = s^2(t, K).$$

Thus, the process $Y(t)$ can be used to price a basket option instead of the process $X(t)$.

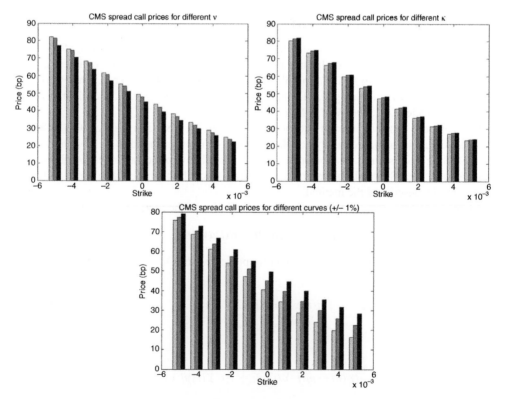

Figure 4.18 CMS spread call pricing. We consider changing the volatility of variance v (top left), Changing the mean reversion speed κ (top right) and the overall level of the curve by $\pm 1\%$ (bottom)

Let us consider two normally distributed random variables $X \sim \mathcal{N}(\mu_X, \sigma_X^2)$ and $Y \sim \mathcal{N}(\mu_Y, \sigma_Y^2)$. Then,

$$\mathbb{E}[Y|X] = \mathbb{E}[X] + \frac{\mathbb{C}[X, Y]}{\mathbb{V}[Y]}(Y - \mathbb{E}[Y]).$$

This can be used as a base for general Gaussian approximation. To this end we assume

$$dS(t) = \sigma(t)S(t)dW(t)$$
$$d\sigma(t) = \eta(t)dt + \epsilon(t)dZ(t).$$

Then,

$$\mathbb{E}[\sigma^2(T)|S(T) = s] = \int_0^T \mathbb{E}[\eta(s)]ds + a(x - S(0)).$$

Our plan is then as follows:

- We consider $S(t) = S_1(t) - S_2(t)$ where S_1 and S_2 are SABR dynamics.
- We apply Gaussian approximation to compute the conditional expectations.
- We choose an adequate model on which to project the dynamics.
- We need a result which is an extension of the result by Gyoengy.

The method can be extended to multi-dimensional dynamics. We consider X with

$$dX(t) = \underline{\sigma}d\underline{W}(t),$$

where $\underline{W}$ is a d-dimensional Brownian motion and $\underline{\sigma}$ a d-dimensional adapted process with bounded norm uniformly bounded away from 0. Then, there exists a process Y

$$dY(t) = s(t, Y(t))dZ(t),$$

with Z a one-dimensional Brownian motion and

$$s(t, x)^2 = \mathbb{E}[\sigma(t)^\top \sigma(t)|X(t) = x]$$

admits a weak solution $Y(t)$ that has the same one-dimensional distributions as $X(t)$.

This poses rather severe restrictions on the volatility which are not accommodated by, for example, the Heston or SABR model.

The result obtained by Gyoengy can be extended to the multi-dimensional case. To this end let $\underline{X}(t) = (X_1(t), \ldots, X_d(t))$ be a vector of d stochastic processes such that

$$dX_i(t) = \mu_i(t)dt + \sigma_i(t) \cdot d\underline{W}(t), \quad i = 1, \ldots, d.$$

The process $\underline{X}(t)$ can be mimicked with a d-dimensional Markovian process $\underline{Y}(t)$ with the same joint distribution for all components at a given maturity T. It satisfies

$$d\underline{Y}(t) = \underline{m}(t)dt + \underline{s}(t) \cdot d\underline{W}(t),$$

with

$$m(t) = \mathbb{E}[\mu_i(t)|\underline{X}(t) = \underline{y}]$$
$$s_i(t)^\top \cdot s_j(t) = \mathbb{E}[\sigma_i^\top \cdot \sigma_j(t)|\underline{X}(t) = \underline{y}].$$

4.5.1 Baskets with Local Volatility

In this section we give some examples for applying the Markovian projection method. To this end we consider the pricing of baskets in multi-dimensional stochastic volatility models. First, we consider a basket of $n \in \mathbb{N}$ assets each following a geometric Brownian motion or a Displaced Diffusion (DD) Heston model. Since such models have already been considered in Piterbarg, V. (2006), Antonov, A. and Misirpashaev, T. (2009) and Antonov, A., Arneguy, M. and Audet, N. (2008), we will touch upon them only briefly here. Next, we look at a multi-dimensional SABR model of the type considered in Kienitz, J. and Wittke, M. (2010). We give the projection as well as the implementation for this model.

4.5.2 Markovian Projection on Local Volatility and Heston Models

Here we briefly review two settings. First, we consider a basket of N assets given by

$$B(t) = \sum_{i=1}^{N} \omega_i S_i(t). \tag{4.35}$$

The asset dynamic for each S_i, $i = 1, \ldots, N$ of (4.35) is governed by a local volatility model (see Section 2.2).

Defining

$$\sigma^2(t) := \sum_{i,j=1}^{N} \omega_i \omega_j \varphi_i(S_i(t)) \varphi_j(S_j(t)) \rho_{ij}$$

$$dW(t) := \frac{1}{\sigma(t)} \sum_{i=1}^{N} \omega_i \varphi_i(S_i(t)) dW_i(t),$$

we find for the basket dynamic

$$dB(t) = \sigma(t) dW(t). \tag{4.36}$$

Using the Itô formula, on the other hand we have

$$dB(t) = \sum_{i=1}^{N} \omega_i \varphi_i(S_i(t)) dW_i(t). \tag{4.37}$$

We use both representations, (4.36) and (4.37), of the basket dynamic to determine a dynamic of the form

$$dB(t) = \varphi(t, S(t)) dW(t). \tag{4.38}$$

To this end we compute the local variance

$$s^2(t, x) = \mathbb{E}[\sigma^2(t) | S(t) = x]$$

$$= \sum_{i,j=1}^{N} \omega_i \omega_j \rho_{ij} \mathbb{E}[\varphi^2(S_i(t)) \varphi(S_j(t)) | S(t) = x].$$

Applying a Gaussian approximation for the conditional expectation, we find that the dynamic of the basket is approximated by

$$dB(t) = \varphi(S(t))dW(t). \tag{4.39}$$

The approximation procedure leads us to set

$$\rho_i := \frac{1}{p} \sum_{i=1}^{N} \omega_i p_i \rho_{ij}, \quad p_i := \varphi_i(S_i(0)), \quad q_i := \varphi'(S_i(0)).$$

Then, with $p = \sqrt{\sum_{i,j=1}^{N} \omega_i \omega_j p_i p_j \rho_{ij}}$ and $q = \frac{1}{p} \sum_{i=1}^{N} \omega_i p_i \rho_i^2 q_i$ the local volatility has to fulfil

$$\varphi(S(0)) = p, \quad \varphi'(S(0)) = q. \tag{4.40}$$

Thus, some local volatility function such as displacement can be applied to guarantee (4.40).

The same mechanism works for the Heston model. Let us assume that we have two assets following a Heston dynamics. To this end we take for $i = 1, 2$

$$dS_i(t) = \varphi_i(S_i(t))\sqrt{V_i(t)}dW_i(t)$$
$$dV_i(t) = \theta(1 - V_i(t))dt + \eta_i\sqrt{V_i(t)}dW_{2+i}$$
$$\langle dW_j(t), dW_k(t)\rangle = \rho_{jk}dt, \quad j, k = 1, \dots, 4.$$

In this case we find that the dynamic of the spread can be projected onto

$$dS(t) = \varphi(S(t))\sqrt{V(t)}dW(t), \tag{4.41}$$

with

$$\varphi(S(0)) = p, \quad \varphi'(S(0)) = q$$

and

$$p = \sqrt{p_1^2 - 2p_1 p_2 \rho_{12} + p_w^2}, \quad q = \frac{p_1 \rho_1^2 q_1 - p_2 \rho_2^2 q_2}{p}.$$

The parameters p_i, q_i and ρ_i, $i = 1, 2$ are given by

$$p_i = \varphi_i(S_i(0)), \quad q_i = \varphi_i'(S_i(0))$$
$$\rho_1 = \frac{p_1 - p_w \rho_{12}}{p}, \quad \rho_2 = \frac{p_1 \rho_{12} - p_2}{p}.$$

For the variance process $V(t)$ we find the SDE which approximates it to be

$$dV(t) = \theta\left(1 - \frac{\gamma}{\theta} - V(t)\right)dt + \sqrt{V(t)}d\tilde{W}(t), \tag{4.42}$$

with

$$\gamma = \frac{p_1 p_2 \rho_{12}}{4p^2} \left(v_1^2 - 2v_1 v_2 \rho_{34} + v_2^2 \right)$$

$$d\tilde{W}(t) = \frac{1}{\eta} (p_1 \eta_1 \rho_1 dW_3 - p_2 \eta_2 \rho_2 dW_4)$$

$$\rho = \frac{1}{p^2 v} \left(p_1^2 v_1 \rho_1 \rho_{13} - p_1 p_2 (v_1 \rho_1 \rho_{23} + v_2 \rho_2 \rho_{14}) + p_2^2 v_2 \rho_2 \rho_{24} \right)$$

$$v^2 = \frac{1}{p^2} \left((p_1 v_1 \rho_1)^2 - 2p_1 v_1 \rho_1 p_2 v_2 \rho_2 \rho_{34} + (p_2 v_2 \rho 2)^2 \right).$$

This result can now be used for the numerical studies in the next section.

4.5.3   Markovian Projection onto DD SABR Models

A displaced SABR diffusion is given by the following set of SDEs:

$$dS(t) = \alpha(t)F(S(t))dW(t)$$
$$d\alpha(t) = v\alpha(t)dZ(t)$$
$$\langle dW(t), dZ(t) \rangle = \gamma dt$$
$$F(S(t)) = (S(t) + a)q$$
$$= p + q(S(t) - S(0))$$
$$p = F(S(0))$$
$$q = F'(S(0)). \tag{4.43}$$

We project the basket dynamcis, $\sum_{i=1}^{d} \omega_i S_i$, where each $S_i(t)$ follows a one-dimensional SABR model, to a displaced SABR model. This is a reasonable choice since the basket can become negative, which is for instance the case if we consider a spread option. The parameters are $d = 2$, $\omega_1 = 1$ and $\omega_2 = -1$.

We propose to use a multi-dimensional SABR model. We have split the computation of the approximation into several steps.

First, we rewrite the original SABR diffusion (2.46)–(2.48) as a single diffusion with stochastic volatility driven by some Brownian motion. Then, we re-scale the volatility to preserve starting values of the process:

$$u_i(t) = \frac{\alpha_i(t)}{\alpha_i(0)}$$
$$\varphi(S_i(t)) = \alpha_i(0)S_i(t)^{\beta_i}$$
$$\Rightarrow dS_i(t) = u_i(t)\varphi(S_i(t))dW_i(t).$$

Next, we introduce the notation:

$$p_i := \alpha_i(0)S_i(0)^{\beta_i} = \varphi(S_i(0))$$
$$q_i := \alpha_i(0)\beta_i S_i(0)^{\beta_i - 1} = \varphi'(S_i(0)).$$

Finally, we apply the results from the previous section and compute the approximation formulae. The methods applied to the SABR model can also be used for deriving the results for other stochastic volatility models such as the Heston model, for example.

Let us start with the SDE for the individual assets. We find

$$dS(t) = \sum_{i=1}^{N} \epsilon_i dS_i(t) = \sum_{i=1}^{N} \epsilon_i u_i(t)\varphi(S_i(t))dW_i(t).$$

Choose the Brownian motion to drive the basket, according to the Lévy characterization, such that

$$dW(t) = \sigma^{-1}(t) \sum_{i=1}^{N} \epsilon_i u_i \varphi(S_i(t))dW_i(t). \tag{4.44}$$

Now, let us write the basket dynamics as

$$dS(t) = \sigma(t)dW(t), \tag{4.45}$$

with $\epsilon_{ij} := \epsilon_i \cdot \epsilon_j$ and $\sigma^2(t) := \sum_{i=1}^{N} \epsilon_i u_i^2 \varphi^2(S_i(t)) + 2\sum_{i<j}^{N} \epsilon_{ij}\rho_{ij}u_i u_j \varphi(S_i(t))\varphi(S_j(t))$.
To compute the conditional expectation we need to compute the variance of $S(t)$. We compute the variance $u^2(t)$ and get

$$u^2(t) = \frac{1}{p^2}\left(2\sum_{i<j}^{N} p_i p_j u_i(t)u_j(t)\rho_{ij}\epsilon_{ij} + \sum_{i=1}^{N} p_i^2 u_i(t)^2\right) \tag{4.46}$$

$$p = \sqrt{\sum_{i=1}^{N} p_i^2 + 2\sum_{i<j}^{N} \rho_{ij}p_i p_j \epsilon_{ij}}. \tag{4.47}$$

The factor $1/p$ is necessary to ensure $u(0) = 1$. For $t = 0$ we find $\sigma(0) = p$.
We set $s(t, x) := \mathbb{E}[\sigma^2(t)|S(t) = x]$ and then we also have $s(t, x) = \mathbb{E}[u^2(t)|S(t) = x] \cdot F^2(x)$. Thus, we have

$$F^2(x) = \frac{\mathbb{E}[\sigma^2(t)|S(t) = x]}{\mathbb{E}[u^2(t)|S(t) = x]}. \tag{4.48}$$

To compute the conditional expectations of the nominator and the denominator, we observe that $\sigma^2(t)$ and $u^2(t)$ are linear combinations of the form

$$\sigma^2(t) = \sum_{i=1}^{N} f_{ii}(t) + 2\sum_{i<j}^{N} f_{ij}(t)\rho_{ij}\epsilon_{ij}$$

$$u^2(t) = \sum_{i=1}^{N} g_{ii}(t) + 2\sum_{i<j}^{N} g_{ij}(t)\rho_{ij}\epsilon_{ij}.$$

with

$$f_{ij}(t) = \varphi(S_i)\varphi(S_j)u_i(t)u_j(t)$$
$$g_{ij}(t) = \frac{p_i p_j u_i(t)u_j(t)}{p^2}. \tag{4.49}$$

Now we are in a position to determine σ^2 and u^2.

We approximate the summands by a first order Taylor expansion:

$$f_{ij} \approx p_i p_j \left(1 + \frac{q_i}{p_i}(S_i(t) - S_i(0)) + \frac{q_j}{p_j}(S_j(t) - S_j(0)) + (u_i(t) - 1) + (u_j(t) - 1)\right)$$

(4.50)

$$g_{ij} \approx \frac{p_i p_j}{p^2}\left(1 + (u_i(t) - 1) + (u_j(t) - 1)\right).$$

(4.51)

To compute the conditional expectations of (4.48) we need simple expressions for the conditional expectations:

$$\mathbb{E}[S_i(t) - S_i(0)|S(t) = x]$$
$$\mathbb{E}[u_i(t) - 1|S(t) = x].$$

(4.52)

To find a simple formula we apply Gaussian approximation, which means we approximate the dynamic of S_i by a stochastic differential equation without drift and constant volatility. This leads us to the following approximations:

$$dS_i(t) \approx d\bar{S}_i(t) = p_i dW_i(t)$$
$$du_i(t) \approx d\bar{u}_i(t) = v_i dZ(t)$$
$$dS(t) \approx d\bar{S}(t) = pd\bar{W}(t)$$
$$d\bar{W} = p^{-1}\sum_{i=1}^{N} p_i \epsilon_i dW_i(t).$$

Using these approximations, we find the correlation structure of W, W_i and W, Z_i respectively:

$$\langle d\bar{W}(t), dW_i(t)\rangle = p^{-1}\sum_{j=1}^{N} p_j \epsilon_j \rho_{ji} dt = \rho_i dt$$

$$\langle d\bar{W}(t), dZ_i(t)\rangle = p^{-1}\sum_{j=1}^{N} p_j \epsilon_j \gamma_{ji} \rho_{j+N} dt = \rho_{i+N} dt.$$

The expected values can now be computed using the approximating processes $\bar{S}_i$. We have

$$\mathbb{E}[\bar{S}_i(t) - S_i(0)|\bar{S}(t) = x] = \frac{\langle \bar{S}_i(t), \bar{S}(t)\rangle}{\langle \bar{S}(t), \bar{S}(t)\rangle}(x - S(0)) = p_i \rho_i \frac{x - S(0)}{p}$$

$$\mathbb{E}[\bar{u}_i(t) - 1|\bar{S}(t) = x] = v_i \rho_{i+N}\frac{x - S(0)}{p}.$$

Using both expressions we can compute $F(t, x)$. Denoting the coefficient that appears in the denominator by A_d and the numerator by A_u, we find

$$F^2(x) = \frac{\mathbb{E}[\sigma^2(t)|S(t) = x]}{\mathbb{E}[u^2(t)|S(t) = x]} \approx \frac{p^2 + A_u(x - S(0))}{1 + A_d(x - S(0))},$$

(4.53)

with

$$A_u = \frac{2}{p} \left\{ \sum_{i=1}^{N} p_i^2 (q_i \rho_i + v_i \rho_{i+N}) + \sum_{i<j}^{N} \epsilon_{ij} \rho_{ij} p_i p_j (q_i \rho_i + q_j \rho_j + v_i \rho_{i+N} + v_j \rho_{j+N}) \right\},$$

$$A_d = \frac{2}{p^3} \left\{ \sum_{i=1}^{N} p_i^2 v_i \rho_{i+N} \sum_{i<j}^{N} \epsilon_{ij} \rho_{ij} p_i p_j (v_i \rho_{i+N} + v_j \rho_{j+N}) \right\}.$$

Given $F(S(0))$ and $F'(S(0))$ we find

$$F(S(0)) = p \qquad F'(S(0)) = q,$$

with p given by (4.47) and q given by

$$q = \frac{\sum_{i=1}^{N} \left(p_i^2 q_i \rho_i + \sum_{i \neq j}^{N} p_i q_i \rho_{ij} \rho_i \epsilon_{ij} p_j \right)}{p^2}.$$

Finally, we need to derive a SABR-like diffusion for the stochastic volatility. To do this we apply the Itô formula to derive the SDE for $u(t)$. Using only first order approximations and replacing the quotients $\frac{u_i(t)u_j(t)}{u^2(t)}$ with the expected value and setting

$$\mathbb{E}\left[\frac{u_i^2(t)}{u^2(t)}\right] = 1 = \mathbb{E}\left[\frac{u_i(t)u_j(t)}{u^2(t)}\right] \tag{4.54}$$

we get

$$\frac{du(t)}{u(t)} = \frac{1}{p^2} \sum_{i=1}^{N} \left(p_i^2 \frac{u_i^2}{u^2} + \sum_{i \neq j}^{N} \epsilon_{ij} \rho_{ij} p_i p_j \frac{u_i u_j}{u^2} \right) v_i dZ_i(t)$$

$$\overset{(4.54)}{=} \frac{1}{p^2} \sum_{i=1}^{N} \left(p_i^2 + \sum_{i \neq j}^{N} \epsilon_{ij} p_i p_j \right) v_i dZ_i(t). \tag{4.55}$$

More accurate approximations when keeping higher order terms result in drift terms. In this case results for the λ-SABR model (see Henry-Labordere, P (2005)) can be applied.

Computing the (simple) approximation, for $u(t)$ we obtain

$$du(t) = \eta u(t) dZ(t).$$

For the Brownian motion $Z(t)$, (4.56), we have

$$dZ(t) = \frac{\sum_{i=1}^{N} \left(p_i^2 v_i + \sum_{i \neq j}^{N} \epsilon_{ij} \rho_{ij} p_i p_j v_i \right) dZ_i(t)}{\eta p^2},$$

$$\eta^2 = Var \left(\frac{\sum_{i=1}^{N} \left(p_i^2 v_i + \sum_{i \neq j}^{N} \epsilon_{ij} \rho_{ij} p_i p_j v_i \right) dZ_i(t)}{p^2} \right),$$

where η is chosen such that the quadratic variation of $Z(t)$ scales to $\langle Z(t) \rangle = t$.

We determine the correlation between the dynamics of the forward price process and the stochastic volatility as

$$
\begin{aligned}
\gamma &= \frac{\langle dW(t), dZ(t)\rangle}{dt} \\
&\approx \frac{\langle d\bar{W}(t), dZ(t)\rangle}{dt} \\
&= \frac{1}{\eta p^3} \sum_{i=1}^{N} \sum_{k=1}^{N} \left(p_i^2 v_i + \sum_{i \neq j}^{N} \epsilon_{ij} \rho_{ij} p_i p_j v_i \right) p_k \epsilon_k \gamma_{ik}.
\end{aligned}
\tag{4.56}
$$

The dynamics of the spread is approximated by the solution to the SDE

$$
dS(t) = u(t)F(S(t))dW(t)
$$
$$
du(t) = \eta u(t)dZ(t),
$$

with $u(t)$ and $p(t)$ given by (4.46) with $d = 2$ and the function $F(.)$ satisfying

$$
F(S(0)) = p, \qquad F'(S(0)) = q = \frac{p_1 q_1 \rho_1^2 - p_2 q_2 \rho_2^2}{p},
$$

where the parameters are

$$
\eta = \sqrt{\frac{(p_1 v_1 \rho_1)^2 + (p_2 v_2 \rho_2)^2 - 2\xi_{12} p_1 v_1 \rho_1 p_2 v_2 \rho_2}{p^2}}
$$

$$
\gamma = \frac{1}{\eta p^2} \left(p_1^2 v_1 \rho_1 \gamma_{11} + p_2^2 v_2 \rho_2 \gamma_{22} - p_1 p_2 v_2 \rho_2 \gamma_{21} - p_1 p_2 v_1 \rho_1 \gamma_{12} \right),
$$

with

$$
A_u = \frac{2}{p} \left(p_1^2 (q_1 \rho_1 + v_1 \rho_3) + p_2^2 (q_2 \rho_2 + v_2 \rho_4) - p_1 p_2 \rho_{12} (q_1 \rho_1 + q_2 \rho_2 + v_1 \rho_3 + v_2 \rho_4) \right),
$$

and

$$
\mathbb{E}\left[u^2(t) | S(t) = x \right] \approx 1 + (x - S(0))A_d,
$$

with

$$
A_d = \frac{2}{p^3} \left(v_1 p_1 (p_1 - p_2 \rho_{12}) \rho_3 + v_2 (p_2 - p_1 \rho_{12}) \rho_3 \right).
$$

Next, we compute the approximating SDE for $S(t)$. To compute the dynamics of $u(t)$, we apply Equation (4.55) to get

$$
\begin{aligned}
du(t) &= \frac{1}{p^2} \left(p_1^2 v_1 \frac{u_1^2}{u^2} - \rho_{12} p_1 p_2 v_1 \frac{u_1 u_2}{u^2} \right) u(t)dZ_1(t) \\
&\quad + \frac{1}{p^2} \left(p_2^2 v_2 \frac{u_2^2}{u^2} - \rho_{12} p_1 p_2 v_2 \frac{u_1 u_2}{u^2} \right) u(t)dZ_2(t).
\end{aligned}
$$

The latter expression is equivalent to

$$
\frac{du(t)}{u(t)} = \left(\frac{p_1 v_1 \rho_1}{p} dZ_1(t) + \frac{p_2 v_2 \rho_2}{p} dZ_2(t) \right).
$$

We finally get the SDE by setting

$$Z(t) = \frac{1}{\eta p}(p_1 v_1 \rho_1 dZ_1 - \rho_2 v_2 \rho_2 dZ_2)$$

$$\eta^2 = \frac{1}{p^2}\left[(p_1 v_1 \rho_1)^2 + (p_2 v_2 \rho_2)^2 - 2\xi_{12}p_1 v_1 \rho_1 p_2 v_2 \rho_2\right].$$

To arrive at the pricing using the above dynamics we can use either Monte Carlo simulation or the SABR formula for implied Black volatilities using for the local volatility the one for displaced diffusions.

Numerical Examples   To illustrate the application of Markovian projection, let us examine a spread option on two assets, S_1 and S_2, with payoff

$$h_{\text{Spread}}(T, K) := \max(S_1(T) - S_2(T) - K, 0). \tag{4.57}$$

We consider the two-dimensional Heston and SABR models. The numerical example can be reproduced by running the source code. We use the parameters from Table 4.1.

We take the correlation matrices

$$\rho_{\text{Heston}} := \begin{pmatrix} 1 & 0.7 & -0.25 & -0.25 \\ 0.7 & 1 & -0.25 & -0.25 \\ -0.25 & -0.25 & 1 & 0.9 \\ -0.25 & -0.25 & 0.9 & 1 \end{pmatrix}$$

$$\rho_{\text{SABR}} := \begin{pmatrix} 1 & -0.4 & -0.2 & -0.2 \\ -0.4 & 1 & -0.2 & -0.3 \\ -0.2 & -0.2 & 1 & 0.3 \\ -0.2 & -0.3 & 0.3 & 1 \end{pmatrix}.$$

First, we consider the Heston model for maturities $T = 1, 5, 10$ and calculate the values obtained by simulation using the two-dimensional setting as well as applying the projected dynamics. We furthermore consider the relative error for European Call option prices. Here we have applied the results derived in Subsection 4.5.2. The results are shown in Figure 4.19.

Figure 4.20 summarizes the results for the SABR model. Again, we have considered $T = 1, 5, 10$ and the values as well as the relative errors.

Table 4.1   Parameter sets building the base for the numerical tests for the Heston and the SABR stochastic volatility models

Heston	Value	SABR	Value
$S_1(0)$	0.1	$S_1(0)$	0.03
$S_2(0)$	0.09	$S_2(0)$	0.026
$V_1(0)$	1	β_1	0.75
$V_2(0)$	1	β_2	0.85
κ	0.1	α_1	0.23
β_1	0.7	α_2	0.2
β_2	0.5	nu_1	0.2
σ_1	0.1	v_2	0.25
σ_2	0.09		
η_1	1		
η_2	1		

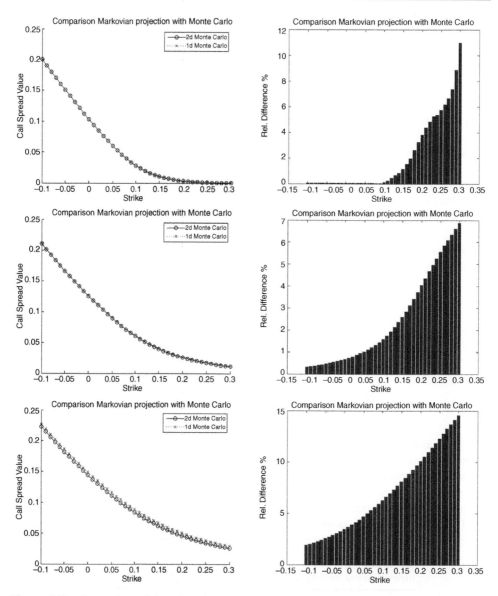

Figure 4.19 Comparison of the values for a European Call spread in the Heston model using Monte Carlo simulation. We consider the value for different strikes by discretizing the two-dimensional model labelled *2d Monte Carlo* and the one-dimensional model obtained using Markovian projection labelled *1d Monte Carlo*. The time to maturity is $T = 1$ (top), $T = 5$ (mid) and $T = 10$ (bottom)

We have compared the results for pricing a European Call spread option using a multi-dimensional Heston as well as a SABR model and the prices computed from the approximation obtained by applying the Markovian projection method.

In general, we observe that, no matter which model we apply, the approximation is reasonable up to five years. For longer maturities the approximation is far off the real spread option prices.

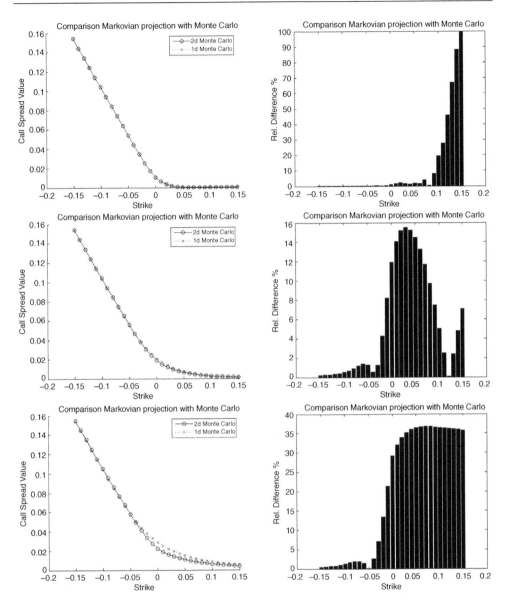

Figure 4.20   Comparison of the values for a European Call spread in the SABR model using Monte Carlo simulation. We consider the value for different strikes by discretizing the two-dimensional model labelled *2d Monte Carlo* and the one-dimensional model obtained using Markovian projection labelled *1d Monte Carlo*. The time to maturity is $T = 1$ (top), $T = 5$ (mid) and $T = 10$ (bottom)

In particular, we have observed that the parameters determining the cross-skew and the decorrelation of volatility cannot be neglected when pricing options on a basket of assets. In fact using only a multi-dimensional Brownian motion does not take into account the effects caused by the cross-skew and the decorrelation.

We have used simulation to compare the results of the projection. The option pricing problem for the projected model often significantly simplifies and therefore speeds up the pricing. Hence, the Markovian projection method is shown to be suitable for calibration purposes.

4.6 COPULAE

In this section we define the notion of a *copula*. A copula is a statistical tool for financial engineering and risk management. In fact, it is nothing other than a probability distribution on the d-dimensional unit interval $[0, 1]^d$.

Let us consider a function

$$C : [0, 1]^d \rightarrow [0, 1]. \tag{4.58}$$

C is a copula if

- C is increasing
- $C(1, \ldots, 1, u_i, 1, \ldots, 1) = u_i$ for all $i = 1, \ldots, d$
- For all $\underline{a}, \underline{b} \in [0, 1]^d$ such that for all $a_i \leq b_i$ we have

$$\sum_{i_1=1}^{2} \cdots \sum_{i_d=1}^{2} (-1)^{i_1 + \ldots i_d} C(u_{1i_1}, \ldots, u_{di_d}) \geq 0,$$

where $u_{j1} = a_j$ and $u_{j2} = b_j$.

Now consider two random variables X and Y with cumulative distributions F_1 and F_2. The joint distribution F is specified by a copula C since for continuous distributions the representation $F = C(F_1, F_2)$ is unique.

Conditional distributions can be written in terms of the copula and have a representation as a derivative. Let us consider the case in two dimensions by way of illustration.

$$
\begin{aligned}
\mathbb{P}(X \leq x | Y = y) &= \lim_{h \to 0} \mathbb{P}(X \leq x | y \leq Y \leq y + h) \\
&= \lim_{h \to 0} \frac{F(x, y + h) - F(x, y)}{F_2(y + h) - F_2(y)} \\
&= \lim_{h \to 0} \frac{C(F_1(x), F_2(y + h)) - C(F_1(x), F_2(y))}{F_2(y + h) - F_2(y)} \\
&= \lim_{h \to 0} \frac{C(F_1(x), F_2(y) + h) - C(F_1(x), F_2(y))}{\Delta_h} \\
&= \frac{\partial}{\partial u_2} C(u_1, u_2)|_{(F_1(x), F_2(y))} .
\end{aligned}
$$

Thus, conditional probability and the conditional expectation can be computed by differentiation. We have

$$
\begin{aligned}
D_1 C(F(X), F(Y)) \quad &\text{is a version of} \quad \mathbb{P}(Y \leq y | X) \\
D_2 C(F(X), F(Y)) \quad &\text{is a version of} \quad \mathbb{P}(X \leq x | Y).
\end{aligned}
$$

To extend the results to multiple dimensions let C be a d-dimensional copula. The density c of C is given by

$$c(u_1, \ldots, u_d) = \frac{\partial^d C(u_1, \ldots, u_d)}{\partial u_1 \cdots \partial u_d}. \tag{4.59}$$

If f denotes the density of a d-dimensional distribution function F with marginals F_i, $i = 1, \ldots, d$, then f and c are related by

$$f(x_1, \ldots, x_d) = c(F_1(x_1), \ldots, F_d(x_d)) \prod_{n=1}^{d} f_n(x_n). \tag{4.60}$$

Given two copulae C_1 and C_2, we say that C_1 is smaller than C_2, denoted by $C_1 \prec C_2$ if for all $\underline{u} = (u_1, \ldots, u_d)^\top \in [0, 1]^d$ we have

$$C_1(u_1, \ldots, u_d) \prec C_2(u_1, \ldots, u_d). \tag{4.61}$$

The following functions are called *lower Fréchet bound*, (4.62), *upper Fréchet bound*, (4.63) and *independence copula*, (4.64):

$$C^-(\underline{u}) = \max\left(\sum_{i=1}^{d} u_i - 1, 0\right) \tag{4.62}$$

$$C^+(\underline{u}) = \min(u_i, i = 1, \ldots, d) \tag{4.63}$$

$$C^\perp(\underline{u}) = \prod_{i=1}^{d} u_i. \tag{4.64}$$

First, the function appearing in (4.62) is not a copula if the dimension d is bigger than 2. Moreover, for any copula C we have

$$C^- \prec C \prec C^+.$$

To further illustrate the setting, Figure 4.21 provides simulated realizations and the functions given by (4.62)–(4.64) for $d = 2$.

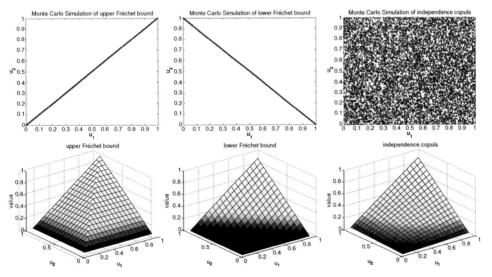

Figure 4.21 We have simulated 10000 realizations corresponding to the distributions C^- (left), C^+ (mid) and $C^\perp$ (right). The corresponding distribution functions are given in the same order on the bottom

Let F be a d-dimensional distribution function with margins $F_1, \ldots, F_d$. Then there exists a copula C such that for all $\underline{x} = (x_1, \ldots, x_d)^\top \in \mathbb{R}^d$

$$F(x_1, \ldots, x_d) = C(F_1(x_1), \ldots, F_d(x_d)).$$

If the margins are continuous the copula is unique.

Tail Dependence   The concept of *tail dependence* relates to the amount of dependence in the upper or the lower quadrant of a bivariate distribution. It is a concept that is relevant to dependence in the extreme values. Furthermore, tail dependence between two random variables X and Y is a property of the copula and hence the amount of tail dependence is invariant under strictly increasing transformations of X and Y. Suppose (X, Y) is a random vector with marginals F_1 and F_2 and joint distribution $F = C(F_1, F_2)$, where C is a copula. Then,

$$\lambda_U := \lim_{u \to 1-} \mathbb{P}[Y > F_2^{-1}(u) | X > F_1^{-1}(u)] \tag{4.65}$$

is called the *coefficient of upper tail dependence* provided the limit exists. We have a representation for λ_U in terms of the copula

$$\lambda_U = \lim_{u \to 1-} \frac{1 - 2u + C(u, u)}{1 - u}. \tag{4.66}$$

The *coefficient of lower tail dependence*, λ_L, can be defined in the same way.

$$\lambda_L := \lim_{u \to 0+} \frac{C(u, u)}{u}. \tag{4.67}$$

4.6.1   Measures of Concordance and Dependency

Let X and Y be two random variables with continuous marginal distributions and unique copula C. Measures of concordance and dependence have been introduced. We define a measure of concordance c. A function taking as input two random variables X and Y and fulfils

- $-1 \leq c(X, Y) \leq 1$
- $c(X, Y) = c(Y, X)$
- $c(X, Y) = 0$ if X and Y are independent
- $c(-X, Y) = c(X, -Y) = -c(X, Y)$
- Two copulae $C_1 \prec C_2$ inducing concordance measures $c_1 := c_{C_1}$ and $c_2 := c_{C_2}$ imply $c_1 \leq c_2$
- For sequences of random variables $X_n, Y_n, n \in \mathbb{N}$ and let a copula C_n be defined by the concordance measure $c(X_n, Y_n)$. Then the sequence C_n converges to a copula C, that is $C_n \to C$ and it holds $c(X_n, Y_n) \to c(X, Y)$.

A measure of dependence $\bar{\rho}$ has additionally to fulfil

- $\bar{\rho}(X, Y) = 0$ is equivalent to X and Y are independent
- For any copula C the induced concordance measure $\bar{\rho}$ fulfils $0 = \bar{\rho}_C^\perp \leq \bar{\rho}_C \leq \bar{\rho}_{C^+} = 1$.

Some of the most popular concordance measures are

- Kendall τ

$$\rho_\tau(X, Y) := 4 \int_0^1 \int_0^1 C(u_1, u_2) dC(u_1, u_2) - 1.$$

- Spearman ρ

$$\rho_S(X, Y) := 12 \int_0^1 \int_0^1 (C(u_1, u_2) - u_1 u_2) \, du_1 du_2.$$

For dependence measures we give as examples

- Hoeffding β

$$3\sqrt{10 \int_0^1 \int_0^1 (C(u_1, u_2) - u_1 u_2)^2 du_1 du_2}.$$

- SW-σ

$$12 \int_0^1 \int_0^1 |C(u_1, u_2) - u_1 u_2| du_1 du_2.$$

Since we do not apply these formulae in this book we do not provide the code.

4.6.2 Examples

Before we proceed we give some examples of copulae which are applied in financial modelling. For each copula we illustrate the dependence structure and show realizations.

4.6.3 Elliptical Copulae

A d-dimensional random variable X has an elliptical distribution if there exists a vector $\mu \in \mathbb{R}^d$ and a $d \times d$ positive definite matrix Σ such that the characteristic function of $X - \mu$ is given by

$$\varphi_{X-\mu}(\underline{x}) = \phi(\underline{x}^\top \Sigma \underline{x}),$$

with some function $\phi : \mathbb{R}^+ \to \mathbb{R}$.

The Gaussian Copula

Let ρ be a symmetric positive definite matrix with $\rho_{ii} = 1, i = 1, \ldots, d$. We denote by F_{N_d} the cumulative normal distribution and by $F_{N_d}^{-1}$ its inverse. Then the *Gaussian copula* or *normal copula* is defined by

$$C^G = (u_1, \ldots, u_d; \rho) = F_{N_d}\left(F_{N_1}^{-1}(u_1), \ldots, F_{N_1}^{-1}(u_d)\right). \qquad (4.68)$$

The copula density is given by

$$c^G(u_1, \ldots, u_d; \rho) = \frac{1}{\det(\rho)} \exp\left(-\frac{1}{2}x^\top(\rho^{-1} - 1)x\right),$$

where $x_i = F_{N_d}^{-1}(u_i)$ and *det* denotes the determinant of a matrix. The Gaussian copula

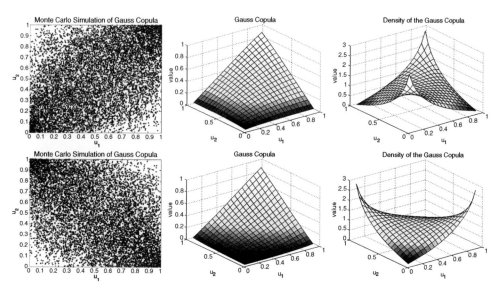

Figure 4.22   We have simulated 10000 realizations (left), the cumulative density (mid) and the density (right) for the Gaussian copula. We consider $\rho = -0.5$ (top) and $\rho = 0.5$ (bottom)

- exhibits no upper tail dependence
- exhibits no lower tail dependence
- is symmetric.

To illustrate the definition of the Gaussian copula we have included simulations, the cumulative density and the density in two dimensions. To this end we have chosen two different correlations, namely $\rho = -0.5$ and $\rho = 0.5$. The illustration is given in Figure 4.22.

The t-Copula

Let ρ be a symmetric positive definite matrix with $\rho_{ii} = 1$, $i = 1, \ldots, d$. Let t_ν denote the cumulative distribution function of the t-distribution with ν degrees of freedom and t_ν^{-1} its inverse, then the *t-copula* is given by

$$C_{\rho,\nu}^t(u_1, \ldots, u_d) = t_{\rho,\nu}\left(t_{nu}^{-1}(u_1), \ldots, t_\nu^{-1}(u_d)\right). \tag{4.69}$$

The corresponding density $c_{\rho,\nu}$ is then

$$c_{\rho,\nu}^t = \frac{1}{\sqrt{\det(\rho)}} \frac{\Gamma\left(\frac{\nu+d}{2}\right)\Gamma\left(\frac{\nu}{2}\right)^d \left(1 + \frac{1}{\nu}x^\top\rho^{-1}x\right)^{(d-\nu)/2}}{\Gamma\left(\frac{\nu+1}{2}\right)^d \Gamma\left(\frac{\nu}{2}\right)\prod_{n=1}^d \left(1 + x_n^2/\nu\right)^{(d-\nu)/2}},$$

where $x_n = t_\nu^{-1}(u_n)$. The t-copula

- exhibits upper tail dependence
- exhibits lower tail dependence
- is not symmetric.

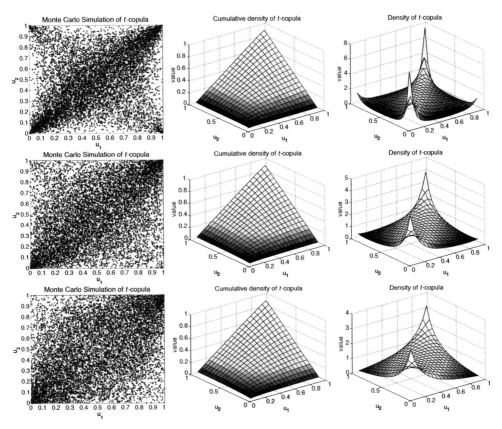

Figure 4.23 We have plotted 10000 simulations, the cumulative density and the density for the t-copula with correlation parameter $\rho = 0.5$ and different degrees of freedom n. We have chosen $n = 1$ (upper), $n = 3$ (mid) and $n = 7$ (bottom)

4.6.4 Archimedean Copulae

An *Archimedean copula* is a function, $C : [0, 1]^d \to [0, 1]$ given by

$$C(u_1, \ldots, u_d) = \phi\left(\phi^{(-1)}(u_1) + \ldots + \phi^{(-1)}(u_d)\right),$$

with a d monotone function ϕ. We call a function k monotone if $(-1)^k \frac{d^k\phi}{dx^k}(x) \geq 0$ for $x \geq 0$ and $k = 0, 1, \ldots, d-2$ and $(-1)^{d-2} \frac{d^{d-2}\phi(x)}{dx^{d-2}}$ is non-increasing and convex.

For the t-copula we consider the effect of the degrees of freedom on the dependence structure. We have plotted simulations, the cumulative density as well as the density for different degrees of freedom in Figure 4.23.

Clayton Copula

For $\theta \in (0, \infty)$ consider the following mapping $C_\theta : [0, 1]^2 \to \mathbb{R}$:

$$C_\theta(u, v) = \left(u^{-\theta} + y^{-\theta} - 1\right)^{-\frac{1}{\theta}}. \tag{4.70}$$

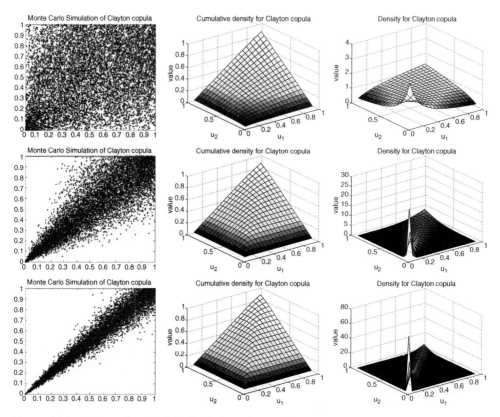

Figure 4.24   We have plotted 10000 simulations, the cumulative density and the density for the Clayton copula for different parameter values θ. We have chosen $\theta = 0.5$ (top), $\theta = 5$ (mid) and $\theta = 15$ (bottom)

C_θ is called the *Clayton copula* and the parameter θ determines the dependency structure. We have

$$\lim_{\theta \to \infty} C_\theta = C^+$$

$$\lim_{\theta \to 0} C_\theta = C^\perp.$$

We wish to complete the review by showing the effect of the parameter θ on the dependence structure. This parameter is the only parameter that allows us to control the dependency structure. Figure 4.24 shows simulations, the cumulative density plots and the density for different values of this parameter.

The Clayton copula can be generalized to d dimensions. In this case we consider the function $C_\theta : [0, 1]^d \to [0, 1]$ given by

$$C_\theta(u_1, \ldots, u_d) = \left(\sum_{k=1}^{d} u_k^{-\theta} - d + 1 \right)^{-\frac{1}{\theta}} . \tag{4.71}$$

4.6.5   Building New Copulae from Given Copulae

This section introduces two methods for building copulae from other copulae. We consider *convex combinations* and *product copulae*.

Convex Combinations

For $d \in \mathbb{N}$, let $\underline{u} \in [0, 1]^d$. We consider N copulae $C_1, \ldots, C_N$ and weights, $\omega_i, i = 1, \ldots, N$ such that $\sum_{i=1}^N \omega_i = 1$. The convex combination C_{convex} of $C_1, \ldots, C_N$ given by

$$C_{\text{convex}}(\underline{u}) = \sum_{i=1}^N \omega_i C_i(\underline{u}). \tag{4.72}$$

C_{convex} is called the *convex combination copula*.

Product Copulae

Let $d \in \mathbb{N}$ and consider $N \in \mathbb{N}$ copulae, $C_1, \ldots, C_N$. Let $f_{n,i}, n = 1, \ldots, N, i = 1, \ldots, d$ such that

$$f_{n,i} : [0, 1] \to [0, 1]$$
$$u \mapsto f_{n,i}(u)$$

are strictly increasing functions or $f_{n,i} = 1$ such that

$$\prod_{n=1}^N f_{n,i}(u) = u \text{ for } u \in [0, 1]^d, \quad i = 1, \ldots, d \text{ and } \lim_{u \to 0} f_{n,i}(u) = q_{n,i}(0).$$

Then, we consider for $\underline{u} \in [0, 1]^d$,

$$C_{\text{prod}}(\underline{u}) := \prod_{n=1}^N C_n(f_{n,1}(u_1), \ldots, f_{n,d}(u_d)). \tag{4.73}$$

C_{prod} is called the *product copula*.

4.6.6   Asymmetric Copulae

Asymmetric copulae have been shown to be useful for option pricing and risk management. For instance, when applied to pricing CMS spread options asymmetric copulae fit the observed market prices much better than do standard symmetric ones.

The Power Gauss Copula

The *Power Gauss copula* (see Andersen, L. and Piterbarg, V. (2010c)) is an example of a product copula. To see this, take $N = 2$ and consider for $\underline{u} = (u_1, \ldots, u_d)^\top$

$$C_1(\underline{u}) := C^\perp(\underline{u}) = \prod_{i=1}^d u_i \text{ and } C_2(\underline{u}) = C^G(\underline{u}, \rho).$$

We consider the independence copula and the Gaussian copula. Then let $\theta_i \in [0, 1]$, $i = 1, 2$, and get

$$q_{1,i} = u^{1-\theta_i} \text{ and } q_{2,i} = u^{\theta_i}.$$

The copula C^{PG} given by

$$C^{PG} := \left(\prod_{i=1}^{d} u_i^{1-\theta_i} \right) C^G(\underline{u}^\theta, \rho), \tag{4.74}$$

with $\underline{u}^\theta = (u_1^{\theta_1}, \ldots, u_d^{\theta_d})^\top$ is called the *Power Gauss copula*.

4.6.7 Applying Copulae to Option Pricing

Let us assume we have a vector $\underline{S} = (S_1, \ldots, S_d)^\top$ which consists of d assets. If the joint distribution $F_{\underline{S}}$ is given in terms of a copula C and it has density f, we find for the price an option $V(0)$ on $\underline{S}$ with payoff function h:

$$V(0) = \int_{-\infty}^{\infty} \cdots \int_{-\infty}^{\infty} h(s_1, \ldots, s_d) f(s_1, \ldots, s_d) ds_1 \ldots ds_d.$$

Let c be the copula density so that we can transform the latter equation to

$$V(0) = \int_{-\infty}^{\infty} \cdots \int_{-\infty}^{\infty} h(s_1, \ldots, s_d) c(F_{S_1}(s_1), \ldots, F_{S_d}(s_d)) \prod_{j=1}^{d} f_{S_j}(s_j) ds_1 \ldots ds_d.$$

Furthermore, we can transform the equation to restrict the integration to a bounded interval by applying the inverse of the $F_{S_j}^{-1}$, $j = 1, \ldots, d$, of the marginal distribution functions F_{S_j} and we have

$$V(0) = \int_0^1 \cdots \int_0^1 h(F_{S_1}^{-1}(u_1), \ldots, F_{S_d}^{-1}(u_d)) c(u_1, \ldots, u_d) du_1 \ldots du_d. \tag{4.75}$$

Equation (4.75) is a reasonable choice for applying numerical integration since it is on a bounded region.

4.6.8 Applying Copulae to Asset Allocation

Here we give a brief introduction to asset allocation and how the methods detailed in this book can be applied. We consider an economy modelled by d assets $S_1, \ldots, S_d$. A portfolio is a weighted sum of the assets and its value at time t is given by

$$V(t) = \underline{w} \cdot \underline{S} = \sum_{j=1}^{d} w_i S_i(t).$$

If $\underline{\mu}$ denotes the yield of $\underline{S}$, we find for the yield r of the portfolio

$$r = \underline{w}\underline{\mu} = \sum_{j=1}^{d} w_i \mu_i.$$

We call a portfolio a *fully invested* one if $\underline{w}\underline{1} = 1$. The measure for the yield is simply a vector. But we are also concerned about how to measure the risk of a portfolio. To this end we need to find some adequate risk measure. Risk can be measured in terms of quantiles of a distribution as it is reflected by the risk measures *VaR* or *CVaR*. Another measure would simply be the variance or the volatility of the portfolio. Once we have fixed a risk measure we can optimize the portfolio in terms of the weights $\underline{w}$ by

- Minimizing the risk.
- Maximizing the yield given some risk.
- Minimizing the risk given some yield.

All the above considerations have related to a fully invested portfolio. This assumption can, of course, be relaxed by allowing money to be invested in some risk free asset such as the bank account. Such optimization problems are analysed by applying asset allocation.

Gaussian Approaches   Classical asset allocation dates back to the work of Markowitz, H. (1952). The basic model assumes a d-dimensional market. Let $\mu \in \mathbb{R}^d$ and denote by $\Sigma \in \mathbb{R}^{d \times d}$ a positive definite matrix. The market is then modelled as a random variable with $X \sim \mathcal{N}(\mu, \Sigma)$. The vector μ, the expected yield and the matrix Σ, the market risk and correlation denote the model parameters. The parameters have to be estimated from real market data and this is usually done by deriving estimators from time series data. The financial toolbox function `ewstat` can, for instance, be used to perform the necessary calculations. The asset allocation is then an optimization problem.

Let us consider three optimization problems. The Gaussian setting is fully determined by μ and Σ. To this end the optimization problems are given in terms of equations

$$\underline{w}\Sigma\underline{w}^{\top} = \min, \underline{w}\underline{1} = 1$$
$$\underline{w}\mu = \max, \underline{w}\Sigma\underline{w}^{\top} = \sigma, \underline{w}\underline{1} = 1$$
$$\underline{w}\Sigma\underline{w}^{\top} = \min, \underline{w}\mu = r, \underline{w}\underline{1} = 1.$$

The latter equations can be solved using the methodology of Lagrange multipliers. This mean variance approach is implemented in Matlab. The function which has to be applied is `portopt` from Matlab's financial toolbox. Using this function it calculates `NPort` portfolios using `mu` and `Cov` as input parameters. For each of the `NPort` portfolios the weights for each asset, the yield, `mu_p` and the risk `sigma_p` are calculated and given as output. It is also possible to handle constraints. For our illustration we do not specify constraints (Figure 4.25).

Despite the fact that this approach is fast and constraints can be handled very easily, it has several shortcomings. One relevant shortcoming is the sensitivity with respect to the input parameters. Small changes sometimes lead to completely different portfolio weights for the constituting assets. In this case the sensitivity with respect to the expected yield is even more influential than that of the covariance matrix Σ. In practice we need to restrict the model parameters or put other constraints on the model.

To overcome some of the difficulties, Black, F. and Litterman, R. (1992) propose to include another set of parameters, called *views*, into the setting. The views reflect the opinion of an asset manager or research department on the market. For instance, it might be the case that some firm has recently achieved a breakthrough but that this is not reflected in the historical time series data. Thus, a positive view might be taken of this firm.

```
function [weights, mu_p, sigma_p] = meanVarianceOpt(mu, Cov, NPort)
    [sigma_p, mu_p, weights] = portopt(mu, Cov, NPort);
end
```

Figure 4.25 Matlab implementation of the Mean Variance portfolio optimization using the Matlab function portopt

Let us take the same setting as for the last example. To this end let $\mu \in \mathbb{R}^d$ and $\Sigma \in \mathbb{R}^{d \times d}$. Now, we consider linear combinations of the form

$$g(\underline{x}) = P\underline{x}, P \in \mathbb{R}^n \times \mathbb{R}^d, \quad n < d,$$

such that this random variable has a normal distribution $g(\underline{x}) \sim \mathcal{N}(\underline{v}, \Sigma^*)$. We call the linear combinations $g(\underline{x})$ views. For the views we have

$$V|P\underline{x} \sim \mathcal{N}(P\underline{x}, \Sigma^*).$$

The matrix P is called the *pick matrix*. The views can either be relative or absolute in terms of the yields. We only consider absolute views here. In this approach we could reduce the sensitivity but we have kept the assumption of the Gaussian distribution. We use the notation

$$\Omega := \left(\frac{1}{c} - 1 \right) P\Sigma P^\top$$

and consider the random variable $X|v$, which is distributed according to

$$X|v \sim \mathcal{N}(\mu_{\mathrm{BL}}, \Sigma_{\mathrm{BL}}).$$

If we denote $A := \Sigma P^\top \left(P\Sigma P^\top + \Omega \right)^{-1}$, we have for the mean vector μ_{BL} and the covariance matrix Σ_{BL}:

$$\mu_{\mathrm{BL}} = \mu + A(v - P\mu)$$
$$\Sigma_{\mathrm{BL}} = \Sigma - AP\Sigma.$$

An interesting observation is that the matrix Σ_{BL} does not depend on the views. We have implemented the basic Black–Litterman approach in Matlab. The code is presented in Figure 4.26.

```
function [mu_BL, Sigma_BL, sigma_BL, corr_BL] = ...
    blackLitterman(mu, Cov, c, P, V)

Omega=(1/c-1)*P*Cov*P';          % matrix including confidence level

mu_BL=mu+Cov*P'*inv(P*Cov*P'+Omega) * (V-P*mu);   % mu_BL
Sigma_BL=Cov-Cov*P'*inv(P*Cov*P'+Omega)*P*Cov;    % Sigma_BL

[sigma_BL, corr_BL] = cov2corr(Sigma_BL);         % sigma and correlation

end
```

Figure 4.26 Implementation of the basic Black–Litterman approach in Matlab

```
clear; clc; simulate = false;

if simulate
    NSim = 10000;
    NAssets = 6;

    mu = [0.003; 0.004; -0.001; 0.0034; -0.0004; 0.0002];
    Cov =    1.0e-003 * ...
    [0.7359     0.3339     0.3280     0.4046     0.4707     0.3175;
     0.3339     0.4698     0.1950     0.2931     0.3335     0.2196;
     0.3280     0.1950     0.7352     0.2695     0.3268     0.2097;
     0.4046     0.2931     0.2695     0.5070     0.4047     0.2324;
     0.4707     0.3335     0.3268     0.4047     0.8643     0.3450;
     0.3175     0.2196     0.2097     0.2324     0.3450     0.4625];
    [std, corr] = cov2corr(Cov);
    ccorr = chol(corr);

    Sample = repmat(mu',NSim,1) + randn(NSim,NAssets) * ccorr;
else
    load 'Simulation';
end

mu_mv = mean(Sample,1)';
Cov_mv = cov(Sample);

NPort = 10;
legenddata = ['A1'; 'A2'; 'A3'; 'A4'; 'A5'; 'A6'];

vol = 0;

[weightsp_mv, mup_mv, sigmap_mv] = ...
    meanVarianceOpt(mu_mv', Cov_mv, NPort);
PortComposition(mup_mv,sigmap_mv,weightsp_mv,vol, ...
    'Mean Variance',legenddata);

P = [1 0 0 0 0 0; 0 0 0 1 0 0; 0 0 0 0 0 1];
V = [0.00065; 0.00075; .0002];
Confidence = 0.25;

[mu_bl, Cov_bl, sigma_bl, corr_bl] = ...
    blackLitterman(mu_mv, Cov_mv, Confidence, P, V);


[weightsp_bl, mup_bl, sigmap_bl] = meanVarianceOpt(mu_bl, Cov_bl, 10);
PortComposition(mup_bl,sigmap_bl,weightsp_bl,vol,...
    'Black Litterman',legenddata);
```

Figure 4.27 Test script for running a mean variance and a Black–Litterman adjusted asset allocation using either simulated data or a pre-defined sample

Now, let us apply the code to the following set of parameters. We take as a test programme that given in Figure 4.27.

The output is generated by the functions meanVarianceOpt. For the second call we do not use the plain input data but the Black–Litterman adjusted data which are obtained by applying the function blackLitterman to the plain input data. The output is a sample due to the

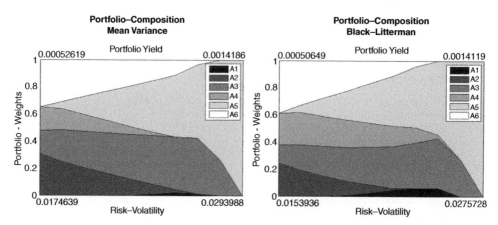

Figure 4.28 Output of the weights, yields and risk figures after performing an asset allocation of 6 assets. Plotted are the simple mean variance output (left) and the Black–Litterman adjusted (right)

posterior distribution. Finally, the function `PortComposition` performs the visualization. Figure 4.28 gives the output for the test script.

The reader can experiment using the confidence level and the views for asset allocation.

Non-Gaussian Approaches   In practice, we need to be more flexible. For instance, we wish to consider high-yield bonds, emerging market indices or indices corresponding to trading strategies as investment possibilities. To this end we have to relax the assumption of the Gaussian distribution. To realistically model the historical distributions or to be able to consider complex (fat tailed) distributions or dependence structures modelled by copulae, we have to find another way for computing the risk. This is necessary for advanced risk management and for asset allocation purposes. Several approaches and methods relaxing the assumption of a Gaussian setting are considered in Meucci, A. (2007). Here we have chosen to outline the *copula opinion pooling approach.*

The full generality does not come for free. We have to compute risk measures and, in this case, it is not possible to use all the nice features of the Gaussian distribution for optimization. For our illustration we apply the method for computing the *expected shortfall,* also called conditional value at risk (CVaR). This approach works as long as we are able to simulate the market vector for some future time T. Then, we apply the numerical optimization method introduced by Uryasev, S. (2000). We will consider the implementation and the applicability when we consider optimization issues in Chapter 11.

The copula opinion pooling approach, together with Matlab code, can be found in Meucci, A. (2006). We assume that the market $\underline{S}$ is modelled by some cumulative distribution F_S. We call F_S the prior and S often does not denote the assets but rather the invariants. In this case we can think of $\underline{S}$ as being the yields of the corresponding assets. Since for a general model it is not appropriate to consider parameters of the distribution, we work directly with the realizations. To this end, S is an $N Sim \times d$ matrix. Views can be integrated by considering some $k \times d$ matrix P. Consider $P^\perp$ such that

$$\hat{P} = \begin{pmatrix} P \\ P^\perp \end{pmatrix}.$$

```
function MPost = COP_GView(MPrior, Conf, P_mat,mu_v, sigma_v)

NSim = size(MPrior,1);              % get NSim
NViews = size(P_mat,1);             % get NViews

P_bar=[P_mat; null(P_mat)'];        % compute P_bar
V=MPrior*P_bar';                    % transform input

[W,C]=sort(V(:,1:NViews));          % for empirical copula
Grid =1:NSim;                       % for emprirical copula

for k=1:NViews                      % loop through views for copula
    C(:,k) =interp1(C(:,k),Grid,Grid)/(NSim+1);
end

F = zeros(NSim,NViews); F_hat = F; F_tilda = F; V_tilda = F;

for k=1:NViews          % determine the posterior marginal per view
    F(:,k)=Grid'/(NSim+1);
    % Gaussian view
    F_hat(:,k)=normcdf(W(:,k),mu_v(k),sigma_v(k));
    F_tilda(:,k)=(1-Conf(k))*F(:,k) ...
        + Conf(k)*F_hat(:,k);       % weighted distribution
    % joint posterior
    V_tilda(:,k) = interp1(F_tilda(:,k),W(:,k),C(:,k),'linear','extrap');
end

V_tilda=[V_tilda V(:,NViews+1:end)];% joint posterior distribution
MPost=V_tilda*inv(P_bar');          % new distribution incl. views
```

Figure 4.29 Implementation of the copula opinion pooling approach using a scenario generated for an arbitrary distribution and applying Gaussian views

The only condition on $P^\perp$ is that the matrix $\hat{P}$ should be invertible. Now, we consider the new variable V given by

$$V = \hat{P}S.$$

We get two different distributions for the vector V. First, we take the marginals, $\hat{F}_i, i = 1, \ldots, d$ with respect to the subjective probability measure. Alternatively, we can take the marginals with respect to the prior. We denote these marginals by F_i. For each $i = 1, \ldots, d$ we consider some confidence level c_i and determine a distribution G_i by

$$G_i = c_i F + (1 - c_i)\hat{F}, i = 1, \ldots, d.$$

This is a generalization of the Black–Litterman model but for general distributions. The distribution is supposed to obey the same dependence structure as the prior. In practical terms it can be achieved by taking the *NSim* scenarios and inferring the empirical copula from the data for G. Then, we are able to calculate the marginal posterior distribution and then the joint posterior, which is denoted by $\tilde{V}$. Finally, we get the market scenarios by transforming the new scenarios back using the matrix $\hat{P}$ by

$$\tilde{S} = \tilde{V}\hat{P}^{-1}.$$

```
clear; clc;
load 'Simulation.mat';

P = [1 0 0 0 0 0;
     0 0 0 0 0 1];
beta = [0.45; 0.3];
mu_v = [0.0006; 0.0007];
sigma_v = [0.05; 0.075];

legenddata = ['A1'; 'A2'; 'A3'; 'A4'; 'A5'; 'A6'];

MPost = COP_GView(Sample, beta, P,mu_v, sigma_v);
NPort = 10;

quantile = 0.97;
[w,y,var,cvar,exitflag]=CVaROpt_nonNormal(Sample, NPort,quantile);

PortComposition(y,cvar,w,2,'Copula Opinion Pooling', legenddata)
```

Figure 4.30 Test script for testing the copula opinion pooling approach on given samples. Version with Gaussian views

Using numerical methods on the new scenarios $\tilde{S}$ we are able to calculate the risk measures. Let us consider a numerical example for this approach. Figure 4.29 gives the Matlab code for implementing the procedure described.

To apply other than Gaussian views we have to replace the second loop in Figure 4.29. For instance, we can consider uniform views (Figure 4.30), which are implemented using the following piece of code:

```
for k=1:NViews          % determine the posterior marginal per view
    F(:,k)=Grid'/(NSim+1);
    % Uniform view
    F_hat(:,k)=unifcdf(W(:,k),range(k,1),range(k,2));
    F_tilda(:,k)=(1-Conf(k))*F(:,k) ...
        + Conf(k)*F_hat(:,k);
    % joint posterior
    V_tilda(:,k) = interp1(F_tilda(:,k),W(:,k),C(:,k),'linear',
    'extrap');
end
```

Numerical Example Let us take as an example the Workspace MPrior, which is included in the supporting material for this book. We wish to apply Gaussian views. To this end we take the function Cop_GView and provide as input data the sample matrix from the workspace MPrior. Then, we have to specify the matrix P, the confidence of the view and the parameters. For our example we take the following test script and the same input data as for the mean variance and Black–Litterman allocation.

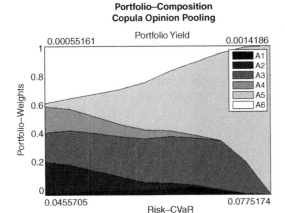

Figure 4.31 Output of the weights, yields and risk figures after performing an asset allocation of 6 assets. Plotted are the results for the copula opinion pooling approach

The output of the test script is again visualized by using the function `PortComposition`. Figure 4.31 shows the final allocation for 10 portfolios.

4.7 MULTI-DIMENSIONAL VARIANCE GAMMA PROCESSES

In this section we take another approach to model multi-dimensional processes. We consider the notion of a subordinator again. In general there are two possibilities to apply this concept to multi-dimensional processes:

- Multi-dimensional Brownian motion with one-dimensional subordinator.
- Multi-dimensional Brownian motion with multi-dimensional subordinator.

For further information see Semerano (2009), Luciano, E. and Semerano, P. (2007; 2008) and Luciano, E. and Schoutens, W. (2005).

- An increasing Lévy process is called a *subordinator*.
- A subordinator has no Brownian part, that is $\sigma = 0$.
- It has a non-negative drift.
- It has a Lévy measure which is zero on the negative half-line (it has only positive increments).
- A subordinator is non-decreasing and always of finite variation.

Let us consider a *subordinator process* which is an increasing process $G(t)$ together with a d-dimensional Brownian motion $\underline{W}$ and two vectors $\underline{\mu}, \underline{\sigma}$, that is the process

$$X_i(t) = \mu_i(G(t)) + \sigma_i W_i(G(t)), \quad i = 1, \ldots, d, \tag{4.76}$$

or in vector notation

$$\underline{X}(t) = \begin{pmatrix} X_1(t) \\ \cdots \\ X_d(t) \end{pmatrix} = \begin{pmatrix} \mu_1(G(t)) + \sigma_1 W_1(G(t)) \\ \cdots \\ \mu_d(G(t)) + \sigma_d W_n(G(t)) \end{pmatrix}.$$

The correlation in this case is given by

$$\rho(i, j) = \frac{\mu_i \mu_j \mathbb{V}[G(t)]}{\mathbb{V}[X_i(t)] \mathbb{E}[X_j(t)]}.$$

Next we look at the approach suggested in Leoni, P. and Schoutens, W. (2008), where the authors consider a model with d Variance Gamma processes Y_l, each having a martingale adjustment given by

$$\mu_l = (r - q_l) + \frac{1}{\nu} \log \left(1 - \frac{1}{2}\nu (\omega_l \sigma_l)^2 - \theta_l \nu \right).$$

In vector notation

$$\underline{\mu} = (\mu_1, \ldots, \mu_d)^{\mathsf{T}},$$

where r is the interest rate and q_l specifies the dividends. Thus the stock price model is given by

$$S_l(t) = S_l(0) \exp(Y_l(t)), \quad Y_l(t) = \mu_l t + \theta_l G(t) + \omega_l \sigma_l W(G(t)).$$

The characteristic functions of the single processes are computable:

$$\varphi(t, u) = \varphi(1, u)^t = \left(1 - iu\theta_l \nu + \frac{1}{2}(\omega_l \sigma_l)^2 \nu u^2 \right)^{-\frac{t}{\nu}} \exp(iu\mu_l t),$$

with

$$\Sigma_W = \begin{pmatrix} \sigma_1 & 0 & 0 \\ 0 & \ddots & 0 \\ 0 & 0 & \sigma_d \end{pmatrix} \begin{pmatrix} \rho_{11} & \cdots & \rho_{1d} \\ \vdots & \ddots & \vdots \\ \rho_{d1} & \cdots & \rho_{dd} \end{pmatrix} \begin{pmatrix} \sigma_1 & 0 & 0 \\ 0 & \ddots & 0 \\ 0 & 0 & \sigma_d \end{pmatrix}.$$

Now let us take two different stocks S_k and S_l and analyse the dependency of the corresponding Variance Gamma processes. To this end, we consider the two-dimensional characteristic function

$$\varphi(\underline{u}) = \mathbb{E}[\exp(i \langle \underline{u}, \underline{Y} \rangle)].$$

Since in this context the subordinator is independent of the Brownian motion, we compute the characteristic function

$$\varphi(\underline{u}) = \int_{\mathbb{R}} \int_{\mathbb{R}} f_W(z_k, z_l) \int_0^\infty f_{\Gamma(1/\nu, 1/\nu)}(x) \exp(i \langle \underline{u}, \underline{\mu} + \underline{\theta} + \underline{\omega}\sigma_W W \rangle) dx dz_k dz_l,$$

with $\underline{\mu} = (\mu_k, \mu_l)$, $\underline{\theta} = (\theta_k, \theta_l)$, $\underline{\omega} = (\omega_k, \omega_l)$ and $\underline{\omega}\sigma_W W = (\omega_k \sigma_k W_k, \omega_l \sigma_l W_l)$.
Thus, the characteristic function is given by

$$\varphi(\underline{u}) = \exp(i \langle \underline{u}, \underline{\mu} \rangle) \left(1 - i\nu\langle \underline{u}, \underline{\theta} \rangle + \frac{1}{2}\nu\langle \underline{u}, (\underline{\omega}^{\mathsf{T}}\underline{\omega} . * \Sigma_W)\underline{u} \rangle \right)^{-1/\nu}.$$

The multiplication $*$ means that for two matrices $A, B \in \mathbb{R}^{n \times m}$ the product $(A. * B)_{n,m} := a_{n,m} b_{n,m}$. From this we are able to calculate the assets covariance:

$$
\begin{aligned}
\Sigma_{S,k,l} &= \mathbb{E}[Y_k(t)Y_l(t)] - \mathbb{E}[Y_k(t)]\mathbb{E}[Y_l(t)] \\
&= -\frac{\partial^2}{\partial u_k \partial u_l} \varphi(\underline{u})\Big|_{\underline{u}=0} + \frac{\partial}{\partial u_k}\varphi(\underline{u})\Big|_{\underline{u}=0} \frac{\partial}{\partial u_l}\varphi(\underline{u})\Big|_{\underline{u}=0} \\
&= (\underline{\omega}^{\mathsf{T}}\underline{\omega}. * \Sigma_W)_{k,l} + v(\underline{\theta}^{\mathsf{T}}\underline{\theta})_{k,l} \\
&= \omega_k \omega_l \Sigma_{W,k,l} + v \theta_k \theta_l.
\end{aligned}
\tag{4.77}
$$

We consider two situations in which we need to apply the model. In the first instance, we wish to use the model when there are enough liquid options for the single assets in the basket, in which case it is possible to infer the marginals from the option prices. If, moreover, exotic options which depend on the correlation are available, it is possible to include these in the calibration. If this is not the case, we have to rely on an exogenous correlation matrix.

In the second instance we wish to apply the model when only time series data are available, but we have no option data available for calibration. Thus, we describe two calibration methods:

- Calibration to liquid options.
- Calibration in illiquid markets.

In the case of a liquid options market we can apply the valuation formulae for simple options to infer the model parameters from market prices.

For example, in the case of Variance Gamma processes the processes are specified by the corresponding Variance Gamma parameters (σ_i, v, θ_i), $i = 1, \ldots, d$.

To calibrate the model we have to find the common parameter v and the correlation. The latter can be obtained if exotic options are available for calibration or if they can be specified exogenously.

To reduce the number of parameters we assume $\sigma_k = 1$ for all k since ω_k and σ_k cannot be inferred for single asset calibration. Then, we proceed as follows:

1. Fix a starting parameter for v.
2. Calibrate the marginals, that is determine ω_k and θ_k.
3. If an overall error criterion or a maximum iterations criterion is met, stop or else go to (1).

The correlation matrix can be inferred from calibration if enough quoted correlation sensitive instruments are available, or can be computed from time series. The transform from asset to model correlation, that is to the instantaneous correlation of the driving Brownian motion, is as follows (for a two-factor model, for instance):

$$
\rho w = \frac{\rho s - v\theta_1 \theta_2}{\sqrt{(1 - v\theta_1^2)}\sqrt{(1 - v\theta_2^2)}}.
$$

We may assume that the volatility for the basket is available but not for the single stocks. Historical data might be used to create a valid correlation matrix. Leoni, P. and Schoutens, W. (2008) provide an outline of a numerical calibration algorithm based on Monte Carlo simulation. Suppose we wish to calibrate to N assets:

- Choose $n \ll N$.
- Choose starting values for the selected asset, i.e. $(\omega_k, \theta_k, v_k)$, $k = 1, \ldots, n$.

- Optimize with respect to the n assets and using a small number of Monte Carlo paths.
- Keep the m best parameter values.
- Start in (1) with $N \geq n_{\text{new}} > n$ until $n_{\text{new}} = N$.

Now let us suppose we have the volatilities and the correlation structure of a basket of asset returns. For example, we take $d = 3$ and the volatilities

$$\underline{\sigma}_S = (0.15, 0.2, 0.25)$$

as well as the correlation matrix

$$\rho_S = \begin{pmatrix} 1 & 0.7 & -0.5 \\ 0.7 & 1 & 0.1 \\ -0.5 & 0.1 & 1 \end{pmatrix} \quad \Sigma_S = \begin{pmatrix} 0.0225 & 0.0210 & -0.0187 \\ 0.0210 & 0.040 & 0.0050 \\ -0.0187 & 0.0050 & 0.0625 \end{pmatrix}.$$

In practice the volatilities and the correlation are given either from time series analysis or from calibration to liquid option prices as described above. We have taken the example from Leoni, P. and Schoutens, W. (2008).

Using Equation (4.77) we find the model correlation, that is the correlation for the Brownian motion:

$$\Sigma_S = \underline{\omega}^{\mathsf{T}} \underline{\omega}. * \Sigma_W + v \underline{\theta}^{\mathsf{T}} \underline{\theta}.$$

Thus, for our example

$$\Sigma_W = \begin{pmatrix} 0.0139 & 0.0157 & -0.028 \\ 0.0157 & 0.0375 & 0.0042 \\ -0.0208 & 0.0042 & 0.0764 \end{pmatrix},$$

which gives the model parameters

$$\sigma_W = \begin{pmatrix} 0.1181 \\ 0.1936 \\ 0.2764 \end{pmatrix} \quad \rho_W = \begin{pmatrix} 1 & 0.6857 & -0.6368 \\ 0.6857 & 1 & 0.0778 \\ -0.6368 & 0.0778v & 1 \end{pmatrix}.$$

For illustration we show correlated Variance Gamma processes using the following model parameters:

$$v = 0.2570 \quad \underline{\theta} = \begin{pmatrix} -0.2094 \\ -0.2301 \end{pmatrix}, \quad \underline{\omega} = \begin{pmatrix} 0.1325 \\ 0.1406 \end{pmatrix}.$$

Both assets have spot value 100.0 and we use a rate $r = 0.042$ and no dividends. We simulate 250 business days with a maturity of $T = 1$. Typical paths are shown in Figure 4.32.

Now let us look at an example of a two-dimensional Brownian motion $W(t) = (W_1(t), W_2(t))$ with $\langle W_1(t), W_2(t) \rangle = 0$. The subordinator is a Gamma process $G(t)$. Then,

- $W_1(G(t))$ and $W_2(G(t))$ are not independent.
- The dependence structure is linked to marginal parameters.
- The model accounts for excess kurtosis and skew.
- The model links complex marginals.

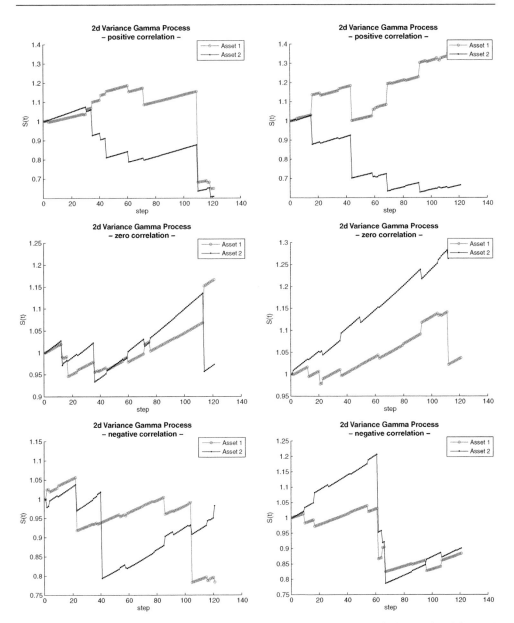

Figure 4.32 Two positively correlated (top), zero correlated (mid) and negatively correlated (bottom) Variance Gamma processes

One way of dealing with these shortcomings is to take a multi-dimensional subordinator process with a common and an individual component!

Let us take an increasing process $\underline{G}(t) = (G_1(t), \ldots, G_d(t))$ and model a d-dimensional random vector by considering

$$X_i(t) = \mu_i G_i(t) + \sigma_i W_i(G_i(t)). \tag{4.78}$$

We consider the idiosyncratic and common part of the subordinator process $\underline{G}$

$$\underline{G} = \begin{pmatrix} G_1 \\ \vdots \\ G_d \end{pmatrix} = \begin{pmatrix} Y_1(t) + a_1 Z(t) \\ \cdots \\ Y_d(t) + a_d Z(t) \end{pmatrix}.$$

In vector notation the process is given by

$$\underline{X}(t) = \begin{pmatrix} X_1(t) \\ \cdots \\ X_d(t) \end{pmatrix} = \begin{pmatrix} \mu_1 G_1(t) + \sigma_1 W_1(G_1(t)) \\ \cdots \\ \mu_d G_1(t) + \sigma_d W_n(G_d(t)) \end{pmatrix}.$$

The correlation in this case is given by

$$\rho(i, j) = \alpha_i \alpha_j \frac{\mu_i \mu_j \mathbb{V}[Z]}{\sqrt{\mathbb{V}[X_i(t)]}\sqrt{\mathbb{V}[X_j(t)]}}.$$

We assume Z, $Y_k(t)$, $k = 1, \ldots, d$ to be $d + 1$ Variance Gamma processes with parameters $(\tilde{\theta}_i, \tilde{\sigma}_i, \tilde{\nu}_i)$ and $(\tilde{\theta}_Z, \tilde{\sigma}_Z, \tilde{\nu}_Z)$ and Z to be independent of Y_k for all k.

The process

$$\underline{X}(t) = \begin{pmatrix} Y_1(t) + a_1 Z(t) \\ \vdots \\ Y_d(t) + a_d Z(t) \end{pmatrix}$$

is a Variance Gamma process if

$$\begin{cases} \tilde{\nu}_k \tilde{\theta}_k = \tilde{\nu}_Z a_k \tilde{\theta}_Z & k = 1, \ldots, d \\ \tilde{\nu}_k \tilde{\sigma}_k^2 = \tilde{\nu}_Z a_i^2 \tilde{\sigma}_Z^2 & k = 1, \ldots, d \end{cases}.$$

Each component X_k from $\underline{X}$ is a Variance Gamma process with parameters $(\theta_k, \sigma_k, \nu_k)$ with

$$\theta_k = \tilde{\theta}_k + a_i \tilde{\theta}_Z$$
$$\sigma_k^2 = \tilde{\sigma}_k^2 + a_k^2 \tilde{\sigma}_Z^2$$
$$\nu_k = \tilde{\nu}_k \tilde{\nu}_Z / (\tilde{\nu}_k + \tilde{\nu}_Z).$$

The characteristic function of $\underline{X}$ is given by

$$\varphi_{\underline{X}} = \left(1 - i\tilde{\theta}_Z \nu_Z \sum_{j=1}^{d} a_j u_j + \frac{\tilde{\sigma}_Z^2}{2} \tilde{\nu}_Z \left(\sum_{j=1}^{d} a_j u_j \right)^2 \right)^{-t/\nu_Z}$$

$$\prod_{j=1}^{d} \left(1 - i u_j a_j \theta_j \nu_j + u_j^2 \frac{a_j^2 \tilde{\theta}_j^2}{2} \nu_j \right)^{-t/\nu_j}.$$

The dependence structure in terms of the pairwise correlation can be computed and is given by

$$(\rho_{\underline{X}})_{kl} = \frac{a_k a_l (\tilde{\sigma}_Z + \tilde{\theta}_Z^2 \tilde{\nu}_Z)}{\sqrt{\sigma_k^2 + \theta_k^2 \nu_i}\sqrt{\sigma_l^2 + \theta_l^2 \nu_l}}.$$

4.8 SUMMARY AND CONCLUSIONS

In this chapter we have considered multi-dimensional models. After describing the model structure and the mechanism for modelling dependency, we introduced two standard methods for calibrating multi-dimensional stochastic volatility models. Parameter averaging was applied to handle time-dependent parameters and Markovian projection to derive a simple one-dimensional model from a complex multi-dimensional one. The resulting model can then be used to approximately price plain Vanilla options for calibration purposes.

Another technique for multi-dimensional modelling, the copula, was also introduced. We showed how to implement some widely applied copulae in finance and illustrated their use to model financial problems. First, we considered the use of copulae for option pricing and, second, for solving asset allocation problems.

Finally, we introduced a methodology for considering multi-dimensional models based on subordination. Using this technique it is possible to consider high-dimensional models based, for instance, on Lévy processes. The chosen subordinator was used to model the dependency. To help explain the application of the various approaches, we gave several numerical examples and illustrations.

Part II

NUMERICAL METHODS
AND RECIPES

5

Option Pricing by Transform Techniques and Direct Integration

5.1 INTRODUCTION AND OBJECTIVES

In this chapter we consider numerical methods based on Fourier transform and direct integration. In particular, we focus on the pricing of European Call and Put options since these are the most liquid instruments quoted by market participants.

Each one of the proposed methods can be applied to price such options efficiently and fast. Therefore, the numerical methods of this chapter can be applied to infer model parameters from quoted prices. This calibration procedure is an optimization problem and it is common that within a calibration many thousands of option prices have to be calculated. Thus, fast and efficient techniques are all-important.

Some of the methods can be extended to other European option payoffs or can even be applied to path-dependent options or options with early exercise features. We consider the following techniques:

- Carr–Madan method (CM), Carr, P. and Madan, D. (1999).
- Lewis method (LM), Lewis, A. (2000).
- Attari method (AM), Attari, M. (2004).
- Tankov method (CM-BS), Tankov, P. (2006).
- Convolution method (CONV), Lord, R., Fang, F., Bervoets, G. and Oosterlee, C.W. (2008).
- Cosine method (COS), Fang, F. and Oosterlee, K. (2008).
- Fourier Space Time-Stepping method (FST), Jaimungal, S. and Surkov, V. (2008).

The proposed methods are numerically fast and are not restricted to a single model class. The methods are applicable to all the models reviewed in Chapters 2 and 3 except the SABR model. We show that whenever the characteristic function of the model is available the above methods apply.

Since we apply the Fourier Space Time Stepping method directly to Bermudan style options, we also review that method in the next chapter.

5.2 FOURIER TRANSFORM

In this section we consider integrals of the form

$$\varphi(u) = \int_{-\infty}^{+\infty} e^{iux} f(x) dx. \tag{5.1}$$

Using inversion of the Fourier transform we are able to recover the transformed function f from φ using

$$f(x) = \frac{1}{2\pi} \int_{-\infty}^{+\infty} e^{-iux} \varphi(u) du. \tag{5.2}$$

Before we consider numerical methods we review the connection of Equations (5.1) and (5.2) in terms of financial modelling.

Let us suppose the characteristic function φ is given for some stochastic process $X(t)$, which is the logarithm of an asset price process $S(t)$. The characteristic function φ_X is related to the random variable X by

$$\varphi_X(u) = \int_{-\infty}^{+\infty} e^{iux} p_X(x) dx, \tag{5.3}$$

with p_X being the risk neutral density for the random variable X. Equation (5.3) is the starting point for further analysis. We consider two methods already introduced in Chapter 2 which we summarize here for the reader's convenience. To this end let φ be the model's characteristic function which is bounded and analytic in a strip $\mathcal{S}_z = \{z \in \mathbb{C} | a < \mathcal{I}(z) < b, a, b \in \mathbb{R}\}$.

- Generalized Black–Scholes formulae (see Equations (2.42) and (2.43))
  Consider $\varphi_1(z) = e^{-X_t - (r-d)(T-t)} \varphi(z - i)$ and $\varphi_2(z) = \varphi(z)$. Let $y = \log(K)$ and consider

$$\mathcal{D}_j = \frac{1}{2} + \frac{1}{\pi} \int_0^\infty \mathcal{R}\left(\frac{\varphi_j(z) e^{-izy}}{iz}\right) dz, \quad j = 1, 2. \tag{5.4}$$

  Then, the price of a European Call/Put option $C(K, T)/P(K, T)$ with strike K and maturity T is

$$C(K, T) = e^{-dT} S(0) \mathcal{D}_1 - e^{-rT} K \mathcal{D}_2 \tag{5.5}$$
$$P(K, T) = e^{-rT} K(1 - \mathcal{D}_2) - e^{-dT} S(0)(1 - \mathcal{D}_1). \tag{5.6}$$

- Direct Integration I
  Let $X(T)$ denote the logarithmic asset price at T and assume that the characteristic function φ is analytic in a strip $\mathcal{S}_z$ and the damped payoff function $e^{-cx} f(x)$ is integrable with $c \in \mathcal{S}_f$. Here $\mathcal{S}_f$ is the strip on which the payoffs Fourier transform, $\hat{f}$, exists and is analytic. If $\mathcal{S}_F := \mathcal{S}_f \cap \mathcal{S}_z$ is not empty, the option value $C(K, T)$ is given by

$$C(K, T) = \frac{e^{-rT}}{2\pi} \int_{ic-\infty}^{ic+\infty} \varphi(-z) \hat{f}(z) dz, \tag{5.7}$$

  with $c = \mathcal{I}(z), z \in \mathcal{S}_F$.
- Direct Integration Approach II (see Equation (2.44))
  A European option with payoff h can be evaluated by an integral formula. The option value $V_h(t_0, S(0))$ for a given spot price $S(0)$ and risk neutral density f is given by

$$V(h, T) = \int_0^\infty h(S(T)) f(S(T)) dS(T) \tag{5.8}$$

$$V(h, T) = \int_0^\infty h(x) f(x) dx. \tag{5.9}$$

In what follows we apply a transformed version of the integral equation. We consider the transform

$$g : \mathbb{R} \to \mathbb{R}$$
$$x \mapsto g(x).$$

For our purposes let us take the logarithmic transform $g(\cdot) = \log(\cdot)$ or mean correcting logarithmic transform $g(\cdot) = \log(\cdot) - \log(S(0))$. Then, the integration formula with $y = \log(S)$ becomes

$$V(T, h) = \int_{-\infty}^{\infty} h(y) f(y) dy. \tag{5.10}$$

5.2.1 Discrete Fourier Transform

Since for an implementation we have to work in a discrete setting, here we consider N grid points and the vectors $\underline{F}, \underline{f} \in \mathbb{C}^N$:

$$\underline{F} = \begin{pmatrix} F_1 \\ F_2 \\ \vdots \\ F_N \end{pmatrix}, \quad \underline{f} = \begin{pmatrix} f_1 \\ f_2 \\ \vdots \\ f_N \end{pmatrix},$$

and the $N \times N$ matrix

$$M := \begin{pmatrix} 1 & 1 & 1 & \cdots & 1 \\ 1 & \omega_N^1 & \omega_N^2 & \cdots & \omega_N^{N-1} \\ 1 & \omega_N^2 & \omega_N^4 & \cdots & \omega_N^{2(N-1)} \\ \vdots & \vdots & \vdots & \ddots & \vdots \\ 1 & \omega_N^{N-1} & \omega_N^{N(N-1)} & \cdots & \omega_N^{(N-1)(N-1)} \end{pmatrix},$$

with $\omega_N = e^{-\frac{2\pi i}{N}}$.

The vectors $\underline{F}$ and $\underline{f}$ are related by

$$\underline{F} = M\underline{f} \to F_k = \sum_{n=1}^{N} f_n e^{-\frac{2\pi}{N}(n-1)(k-1)} = \sum_{n=1}^{N} f_n \omega_N^{(n-1)(k-1)}. \tag{5.11}$$

Utilizing the properties of Fourier transforms (see Chapter 13), we are able to recover the probability density function p_X from its characteristic function φ_X by the formula

$$p_X(x) = \frac{1}{\pi} \mathcal{R} \left(\int_0^{\infty} e^{-itx} \varphi_X(t) dt \right). \tag{5.12}$$

Thus, it is possible to use direct integration methods to determine the density. For implementation we consider the x-domain and the t-domain. We divide the interval $[0, T]$ into N subintervals of length Δ_t. For the x-domain we consider the step size Δ_x. To be able to recover the density we have to compute the integral on the right side of Equation (5.12). To this end take a function g for which we wish to compute its integral and consider the following approximation:

$$I_g(T) := \int_0^T g(t)dt \approx \frac{\Delta_t}{2}\left[g(t_1) + 2\sum_{n=2}^{N-1} g(t_n) + g(t_N) \right]$$

$$= \Delta_t \left[\sum_{n=2}^{N-1} g(t_n) + \frac{g(t_1) + g(t_N)}{2} \right].$$

Setting $T := N\Delta$, $t_n := (n-1)\Delta_t$, $x := -b + \Delta_x(u-1)$, $u = 1, \ldots, N$. The number b can be chosen, but for simplicity we set $b := N\Delta_x/2$. Then, $I_g(T)$ can be approximated by

$$I_g(T) \approx \Delta_t \left[\sum_{n=2}^{N} e^{-i[(n-1)\Delta_t][-b+\Delta_x(u-1)]}\varphi(t_n) - \frac{g(t_1) + g(t_N)}{2} \right]$$

$$\approx \Delta_t \left[\sum_{n=2}^{N} e^{-i\Delta_x\Delta_t(n-1)(u-1)} e^{i(n-1)b\Delta_t}\varphi(t_n) - \frac{g(t_1) + g(t_N)}{2} \right].$$

Setting $\Delta_x\Delta_t := \frac{2\pi}{N}$ – the Nyquist condition – we finally obtain

$$I_g(T) \approx \Delta_t \left[\sum_{n=1}^{N} e^{-i\frac{2\pi}{N}(n-1)(u-1)} e^{i(n-1)\Delta_t b}\varphi(t_n) - \frac{e^{ixt_1}\varphi(t_1) + e^{ixt_N}\varphi(t_N)}{2} \right].$$

The latter equation shows that we can approximate the integral and therefore the density p_X by

$$p_X(x) \approx \frac{1}{\pi}\mathcal{R}\left(\Delta_t \left[\sum_{n=2}^{N} e^{-i\frac{2\pi}{N}(n-1)(u-1)} e^{i(n-1)\Delta_t b}\varphi(t_n) - \frac{e^{ixt_1}\varphi(t_1) + e^{ixt_N}\varphi(t_N)}{2} \right] \right).$$

The latter equation is in fact a matrix multiplication which requires N^2 complex multiplications and N^2 complex additions. Thus, the number of arithmetical operations is of the order N^2. However, Cooley, J. W. and Tukey, J.W. (1967) introduced a method for computing such expressions where the number of arithmetical operations is of the order $N\log_2(N)$. This method is known as the *fast Fourier transform (FFT)*.

Although there is a wide range of FFT algorithms, involving deep mathematics from number theory, algebra or polynomial algebras, in practice the majority of FFT implementations employ some variation of the Cooley–Tukey algorithm.

5.2.2 Fast Fourier Transform

The basic algorithm can be easily derived using only elementary algebra. It can be implemented almost as easily. Numerous textbooks list short FFT subroutines using only power-of-two sized grids. This means the number of points is given by 2^N for some $N \in \mathbb{N}$. The implementation of the Cooley–Tukey algorithm seems to be a long-solved problem but there are many optimizations and tricks to tune the basic algorithm.

Let X be an array of n complex numbers. For $k = 0, \ldots, n-1$ we define an array Y by

$$Y(k) = \sum_{l=0}^{n-1} X(l)\omega_n^{lk}, \quad \omega_n = \exp(-w\pi i/n).$$

Direct implementation would require $= O(n^2)$ operations to compute the sum. The Cooley–Tukey algorithm in practice, as all FFT algorithms in practice, computes the above sum in $O(n \log(n))$ steps. In fact, the algorithm was already known to Gauss. The basic idea is that a discrete Fourier transform of a composite of size $n = n_1 n_2$ can be re-expressed in terms of smaller discrete Fourier transforms of size n_1 and n_2 in practice, in fact a two-dimensional discrete Fourier transform of size $n_1 \times n_2$ with transposed output. The choice of factorizations of n combined with many different ways to implement the data re-ordering led to numerous implementation strategies.

Suppose that $n = n_1 n_2$ and $l = l_1 n_2 + l_2$ and $k = k_1 + k_2 n_1$. We then have

$$Y(k_1 + k_2 n_1) = \sum_{l_2=0}^{n_2-1} \left[\left(\sum_{l_1=0}^{n_1-1} X(l_1 n_2 + l_2) \omega_{n_1}^{l_1 k_1} \right) \omega_n^{l_2 k_1} \right] \omega_{n_2}^{l_2 k_2}.$$

As stated above, the algorithm computes n_2 discrete Fourier transforms of size n_1, multiplies with the unit roots ω_n^{lk} and finally computes n_1 transforms of size n_2. This decomposition can then be applied recursively.

A key difficulty in the implementation is that the n_1 dimension corresponds to discontiguous inputs l_1 in X but contiguous outputs k_1 in Y and vice versa for n_2. This is a matrix transpose for a single decomposition stage, and the composition of all such transpositions is a (mixed-base) digit-reversal permutation (or bit-reversal, for radix 2). The resulting necessity of discontiguous memory access and data re-ordering hinders efficient use of hierarchical memory architectures, for instance of caches, so that the optimal execution order of an FFT for given hardware is non-obvious, and various approaches have been proposed.

For implementation of the discrete Fourier transform we can use FFTW. The software FFTW is a C library for computing the discrete Fourier transform in one or more dimensions of arbitrary input size, and of both real and complex data. FFTW is free software and is the basis of many commercial implementations of discrete Fourier transform, for example Matlab. Its source can be found via the link www.fftw.org.

In this section we survey several applications of the *Fourier transform* for pricing options.

Finally, recall that the moments of the random variable X can be computed from the characteristic function. The k-th moment is given by

$$\mathbb{E}\left[X^k\right] = i^{-k} \frac{d}{du^k} \varphi(u) \Big|_{u=0}. \tag{5.13}$$

The *cumulant*, *moment generating* and *cumulant characteristic* functions are

$$k(u) = \log\left(\mathbb{E}[\exp(-uX)]\right) = \log(\varphi(iu))$$
$$\theta(u) = \mathbb{E}[\exp(uX)] = \varphi(-iu)$$
$$\psi(u) = \log\left(\mathbb{E}[\exp(iuX)]\right) = \log(\varphi(u)),$$

with

$$\mathbb{E}\left[X^k\right] = \frac{d}{du^k} \theta(u) \Big|_{u=0}.$$

5.3 THE CARR–MADAN METHOD

The first application of Fourier transform based evaluation methods for the integral (5.9) is given in Carr, P. and Madan, D. (1999). We denote $x_T := \log(S_T)$ the log asset price at time T, $k := \log(K)$ the log strike, $f(\cdot|x)$ risk neutral density at maturity T with logarithmic spot value x. The Call price is then given by

$$C(K, T) = \int_k^{\infty} e^{-rT} \left(e^y - e^k\right) f(y|x) dy. \tag{5.14}$$

In general, for a given maturity T the Call option price $C(\cdot, T)$ is not integrable since

$$C(K, T) \to S(0) \text{ as } K \to 0 (\text{or } k \to -\infty). \tag{5.15}$$

To assure integrability we need to introduce a parameter $\alpha \in \mathbb{R}$. This parameter is called a *dampening parameter*. We consider a modified Call price or damped Call price $c(k, T)$:

$$c(k, T) := e^{\alpha k} C(k, T). \tag{5.16}$$

Figure 5.1 illustrates the dampening on the payoff. We consider the payoff without dampening which corresponds to $\alpha = 0$ and for different values of α. In what follows we will see that there is an optimal value for choosing α. This value leads to the most stable numerical results (see Subsection 5.3.1).

For fixed T the function $c(\cdot, T)$ is square integrable if its Fourier transform

$$\varphi_{\text{Call}}(v) = \int_{-\infty}^{\infty} e^{ivk} c(k, T) dk$$

is finite for $v = 0$. To keep $\varphi_{\text{Call}}(0)$ finite we choose $\alpha > 0$ such that the expectation $\mathbb{E}[S_T^{\alpha+1}]$ is finite.

To keep $\varphi(0)$ finite we choose α such that $\varphi(-(\alpha + 1)i)$ is finite. This induces an upper bound on the dampening factor α. We give two examples for the upper bound. To this end we take the Variance Gamma model and the Variance Gamma model with Gamma Ornstein–Uhlenbeck

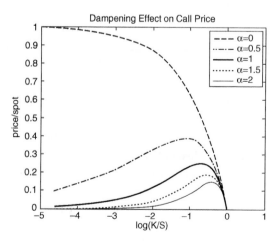

Figure 5.1 The effect of dampening on a Call payoff for $\log(S/K) = 0, 0.01, \ldots, 2$ and $\alpha = 0, 0.5, 1, 1.5, 2$. We assume $r = d = 0$

stochastic clock. The corresponding upper bounds are

$$
\alpha_{\text{sup}}^{\text{VG}} = -\frac{\theta}{\sigma^2} + \sqrt{\frac{\theta^2}{\sigma^4} + \frac{2}{\sigma^2 v}} - 1
$$

$$
\alpha_{\text{sup}}^{\text{VGGOU}} = -\frac{\theta}{\sigma^2} + \sqrt{\frac{\theta^2}{\sigma^4} + \frac{2}{\sigma^2 v}\left(1 - \exp\left(\frac{v b \lambda}{1 - e^{-vt}}\right)\right)} - 1.
$$

The latter integral expression for φ can be evaluated in the case of a European Call option and we get

$$
\varphi_{\text{Call}}(v) = \int_{-\infty}^{\infty} e^{ivk} \int_{k}^{\infty} e^{-rT + \alpha k}(e^y - e^k) f(y|x) dy dk \tag{5.17}
$$

$$
= \int_{-\infty}^{\infty} e^{-rT} f(y|x) \int_{-\infty}^{s} (e^{\alpha k + y} - e^{(\alpha+1)k}) e^{ivk} dk dy
$$

$$
= \int_{-\infty}^{\infty} e^{-rT} f(y|x) \left(\frac{e^{(\alpha+1+iv)y}}{\alpha + iv} - \frac{e^{(\alpha+1+iv)y}}{\alpha + 1 + iv}\right) dy
$$

$$
= \frac{e^{-rT} \varphi(v - (\alpha + 1)i)}{\alpha^2 + \alpha - v^2 + i(2\alpha + 1)v}. \tag{5.18}
$$

The Call option price formula with $k = \log(K)$ is

$$
C(k, T) = \frac{e^{-\alpha k}}{\pi} \int_{0}^{\infty} e^{-ivk} \varphi_{\text{Call}}(v) dv. \tag{5.19}
$$

We numerically evaluate Equation (5.19) by approximating the integral in terms of a sum by applying the trapezoidal integration rule:

$$
C(k, T) \approx \frac{e^{-\alpha k}}{\pi} \sum_{j=0}^{N-1} e^{-iv_j k} \varphi_{\text{Call}}(v_j) \eta.
$$

For $\eta > 0$ we set $b = \frac{N\lambda}{2}$ and use $v_j = \eta j, j = 0, \ldots, N - 1$; $k_u = -b + \lambda u, u = 0, \ldots, N - 1$. This leads to

$$
C(k_u, T) \approx \frac{e^{-\alpha k_u}}{\pi} \sum_{j=0}^{N-1} e^{-i\lambda\eta j u} e^{i\left(\frac{N\lambda}{2} v_j\right)} \varphi_{\text{Call}}(v_j) \eta. \tag{5.20}
$$

For the Put price $P(K, T)$ we consider a damped version $p(K, T) := e^{-\alpha K} P(K, T)$ as well. The Fourier transform for the damped Put price is then given by

$$
\varphi_{\text{Put}}(u) = \frac{\varphi_{\text{Call}}(u - (-\alpha + 1)i)}{\alpha^2 - \alpha - u^2 + i(-2\alpha + 1)u}.
$$

As we have outlined at the beginning of this chapter, the FFT is a method that efficiently computes sums of the form

$$
\sum_{j=0}^{N-1} e^{-i\frac{2\pi}{N} j u} x_j, u = 0, \ldots, N - 1
$$

only requiring $O(N/\log(N))$ arithmetic operations. We rewrite Equation (5.20) in a slightly different form to see that the FFT algorithm can be applied. In so doing we also use weights

```
function Call_price_fft = price_cm(model,imethod,S,K,T,r,d,varargin)

lnS = log(S);                      % log spot
lnK = log(K);                      % log strike

% compute the optimal alpha or set alpha directly
%alpha = optimalAlpha(model,lnS,lnK,T,r,d,varargin{:});
alpha = .5;

DiscountFactor = exp(-r*T); % discounting due to rate r

% predefined parameters for fft
FFT_N = 2^18;                      % must be a power of two (2^14)
FFT_eta = 0.05;                    % spacing of psi integrand

% effective upper limit for integration
% uplim = FFT_N * FFT_eta;

FFT_lambda = (2 * pi) / (FFT_N * FFT_eta);   % spacing for log strike
FFT_b = (FFT_N * FFT_lambda) / 2;            %

uvec = 1:FFT_N;                    % create all indices up to FFT_N
%log strike levels ranging from -b to +b
ku = - FFT_b + FFT_lambda * (uvec - 1);
jvec = 1:FFT_N;
vj = (uvec-1) * FFT_eta;

%applying FFT
tmp = DiscountFactor * psi(model,vj,alpha,lnS,T,r,d,varargin{:}) ...
       .* exp(1i * vj * (FFT_b)) * FFT_eta;
%applying simpson's rule
tmp = (tmp / 3) .* (3 + (-1).^jvec - ((jvec - 1) == 0) );
% Call price vector
cpvec = real(exp(-alpha .* ku) .* fft(tmp) / pi);

indexOfStrike = floor((lnK + FFT_b)/FFT_lambda + 1);

% create x and y vectors for interpolation
xp = [ku(indexOfStrike) ku(indexOfStrike+1)];
yp = [cpvec(indexOfStrike) cpvec(indexOfStrike+1)];

Call_price_fft = real(interp1(xp,yp,lnK,imethod));  % output prices
end
```

Figure 5.2 Matlab implementation of the method proposed by Carr and Madan for computing Call option prices using the FFT and the characteristic function

coming from the Simpson integration rule to increase the accuracy. This leads to

$$C(k_u, T) \approx \frac{e^{-\alpha k_u}}{\pi} \sum_{j=0}^{N-1} e^{-i\frac{2\pi}{N}ju} \underbrace{e^{ibv_j} \varphi_{\text{Call}}(v_j)\frac{\eta}{3}(3 + (-1)^{j+1} - \delta_j)}_{=:x_j}. \tag{5.21}$$

The approximation (5.24) can be computed efficiently using the FFT in Matlab.

We use the characteristic function in the code displayed in Figure 5.2 for the dampened Call option payoff given by Figure 5.3.

```
function ret = psi(model,v,alpha,varargin)
% function given for the modified Call option payoff
  ret = exp(feval(@CharacteristicFunctionLib, model, ...
    v - (alpha + 1) * 1i,varargin{:})) ...
    ./ (alpha.^2 + alpha - v.^2 + 1i * (2 * alpha + 1) .* v);
end
```

Figure 5.3 The function psi is called by the function $price\_cm$ which implements the Carr–Madan evaluation method

There is a modification of the basic pricing formula. This modification has been developed to keep the option prices bounded since high option prices could lead to numerical instabilities. We define the following option payoffs for European Calls and Puts such that the option is always out of the money. This means that the strike is smaller than the assets forward price for Calls and larger for Puts. We consider

$$z_T(k) = \begin{cases} (e^k - e^y)1_{\{y<k,k<0\}} & \text{if} \quad k < \log(S(0)) \\ (e^y - e^k)1_{\{y>k,k>0\}} & \text{if} \quad k > \log(S(0)) \end{cases}.$$

The transform ζ_T and z_T as the inverse transform are given by

$$\zeta_T(v) = \int_{-\infty}^{\infty} e^{ivk} z_T(k)dk; \quad z_T(k) = \frac{1}{2\pi} \int_{-\infty}^{\infty} e^{-ivk} \zeta_T(v)dv.$$

We scale the asset spot price and take $S(0) = 1$. Then, we have

$$z_T(k) = e^{-rT} \int_{-\infty}^{\infty} \zeta_T(y)f(y|x)dy.$$

To ensure integrability we use the transform $\sinh(\alpha k)z_T(k)$, $\alpha > 0$ and get

$$z_T(k) = \frac{1}{2\pi \sinh(\alpha k)} \int_{-\infty}^{\infty} e^{-ivk} \gamma_T(v)dv, \tag{5.22}$$

with characteristic function

$$\gamma_T(v) = \int_{-\infty}^{\infty} e^{ivk} \sinh(\alpha k)z_T(k)dk = \frac{\zeta_T(v-i\alpha) - \zeta_T(v+i\alpha)}{2}. \tag{5.23}$$

The integrals appearing in the function ζ can be solved in closed form and we get

$$\zeta_T(v) = \int_{-\infty}^{0} dk e^{ivk} e^{-rT} \int_{-\infty}^{k} (e^k - e^y)f(y|x)dy$$

$$+ \int_{0}^{\infty} dk e^{ivk} e^{-rT} \int_{k}^{\infty} (e^y - e^k)f(y|x)dy$$

$$= \int_{-\infty}^{0} ds e^{-rT} f(y|x) \int_{y}^{0} (e^{(1+iv)k} - e^{y+ivk})dk$$

$$+ \int_{0}^{\infty} dy e^{-rT} f(y|x) \int_{0}^{y} (e^{y+ivk} - e^{(1+iv)k})dk$$

$$= e^{-rT} \left[\frac{1}{1+iv} - \frac{e^{rT}}{iv} - \frac{\varphi(v-i)}{v^2 - iv} \right].$$

The explicit formula suitable for implementation can be obtained by adjusting with a multiplicative factor $\frac{1}{2\pi}\frac{1}{\sinh(\alpha k)}$ and replacing the characteristic function by γ_T, (5.23). We finally have

$$C(k_u, T) \approx \frac{1}{2\pi \sinh(\alpha k_u)} \sum_{j=0}^{N-1} e^{-i\frac{2\pi}{N} ju} \underbrace{e^{ibv_j} \gamma(v_j)\frac{\eta}{3}(3 + (-1)^{j+1} - \delta_j)}_{=:x_j}. \tag{5.24}$$

Greeks   The Carr–Madan method can be applied to the calculation of Δ and Γ. We find by differentiation with respect to the spot price $S(0)$

$$\Delta = \frac{\exp(-\alpha \log(K) - (r-d)T)}{S(0)\pi} \int_0^\infty \frac{e^{iu \log(K)}(iu + (\alpha+1))\varphi(u - (\alpha+1))}{\alpha^2 + \alpha - u^2 + (2\alpha+1)iu} du. \tag{5.25}$$

For Γ a similar formula can be derived.

$$\Gamma = \frac{\exp(-\alpha \log(K) - (r-d)T)}{S(0)^2\pi} \int_0^\infty \mathcal{R}\left(e^{iu \log(K)}\varphi(u - (\alpha+1)i)\right) du. \tag{5.26}$$

The Greeks can then be calculated by using direct integration or FFT methods.

Black–Scholes Modification   Look once more at the Carr–Madan formulation of pricing of a Call option, Equation (5.19).

We considered a dampened Call price such that we ensure integrability. A modification of the Call price, subtracting the Black–Scholes price for some given implied volatility σ_{BS}, can be considered. The idea is that the difference is so small that integrability is ensured. The choice of σ_{BS} is discussed later. Thus, the modified option price, $c(k, T)$, is given as the difference

$$c(k, T) = e^{-rT}\mathbb{E}[(e^x - e^k)^+] - C_{BS}^\sigma(k, T). \tag{5.27}$$

The Fourier transform is derived in terms of the characteristic function of the underlying model and is given by

$$\varphi_{\text{Call}}(u) = e^{iurT} \frac{\varphi(u-i) - \overbrace{\exp\left(-\frac{\sigma_{BS}^2 T}{2}(u(u+i))\right)}^{\varphi_{BS}}}{iu(1+iu)}. \tag{5.28}$$

Let us consider Equation (5.27). We compute a Black–Scholes-wise expectation Call_{M-BS} of the modified call option price using FFT as

$$\mathcal{D}_1 = \frac{\varepsilon}{2\pi} \int_{-\infty}^\infty \frac{e^{-iu\kappa}\left[\varphi(u)e^{i(u-i)\omega T} - \varphi_{BS}e^{-\frac{\sigma^2}{2}T}\right]}{iu} du$$

$$\mathcal{D}_2 = \frac{\varepsilon}{2\pi} \int_{-\infty}^\infty \frac{e^{-iu\kappa}\left[\varphi(u)e^{iu\omega T} - \varphi_{BS}(u)\right]}{iu} du$$

$$\text{Call}_{M-BS}(K, T) = \varepsilon\left[e^{-dT}S(0)\mathcal{D}_1 - e^{-rT}K\mathcal{D}_2\right],$$

where $\kappa = \log(K/S) - (r-d)T$, $\varphi_{BS}(u) = e^{-\sigma_{BS}^2 T/2u^2}$ and $\varphi(-i) = e^{-\omega T}$ and $\varepsilon = 1$ if it is a Call and $\varepsilon = -1$ if it is a Put.

For the special case of the Variance Gamma model we find

$$\mathcal{D}_1 = \varphi(u)e^{iu\omega T} - \varphi_{BS}(u) = T\left(\theta + \omega + \frac{\sigma_{BS}^2}{2}\right)iu + O(u^2)$$

$$\mathcal{D}_2 = \varphi(u - i)e^{i(u-i)\omega T} - \varphi_{BS}(u - i)e^{\frac{-\sigma_{BS}^2}{2}T}$$

$$= -\left(\sigma_{BS}^2 + \frac{\theta + \sigma_{BS}^2}{-1 + v(\theta + \sigma_{BS}^2/2)} - \omega\right)iu + O(u^2).$$

For this approach it is necessary to choose σ_{BS}. We show possible choices. First, we take

$$\sigma_{BS} := \sqrt{-\left.\frac{\partial^2 \varphi(x)}{\partial x^2}\right|_{x=0} + \left.\frac{\partial \varphi(x)}{\partial x}\right|_{x=0}}$$

or in terms of the characteristic function

$$\sigma_{BS} = \sqrt{-\mathcal{R}(\varphi''(0)) - \mathcal{I}(\varphi'(0))}.$$

Thus, σ_{BS} can be determined numerically using finite differences.

Another way is to employ cumulants. The cumulants are related to the moments of a distribution. Due to the fact that certain financial models for short maturities and some parameters have sharp peaks and fat tails it is often necessary to include the fourth cumulant and we set

$$\sigma_{BS} := \sqrt{|c_2| + \sqrt{|c_4|}}.$$

The cumulants are determined numerically using the characteristic function, but for many models the cumulants are known in closed form.

Furthermore, it is possible to combine the standard Carr–Madan pricing approach with dampening α with the method discussed in this subsection. This reduces the dependence on optimal values for α and σ_{BS}.

5.3.1 The Optimal α

In this subsection we consider the choice of the parameter α in Equation (5.16). We base or exposition on Lord, R. and Kahl, C. (2007).

To determine the optimal exponent α we have to specify an optimality criterion. To this end, and as suggested in Lord, R. and Kahl, C. (2007), we take the quadratic difference between the exact and the approximated price. We then note that in a neighbourhood of the optimal value for α the slope of the quadratic difference is close to 0. Thus, solving for the optimal α leads us to consider

$$\underset{(\alpha_{min}, \alpha_{max})}{\arg\min}\left|\frac{\partial}{\partial\alpha}e^{-\alpha\log(K)}\int_0^\infty \psi(u,\alpha)du\right| \quad \text{with } \psi(u,\alpha) := \mathcal{R}(e^{-iuk}\varphi_{Call}(u)).$$

Further simplification of the problem leads us to consider only the maximum of the latter expression, which is attained at $u = 0$. Thus,

$$\underset{(\alpha_{min}, \alpha_{max})}{\arg\min}\left|e^{-\alpha\log(K)}\psi(-(\alpha+1)i)\right|.$$

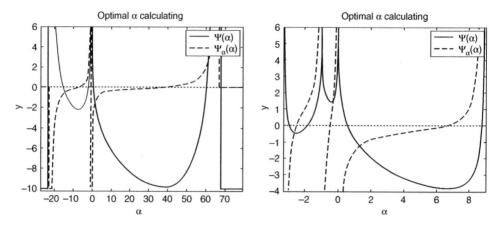

Figure 5.4   The functions Ψ and Ψ_α for $\tau = 0.1; K = 1.2$ (left) and $\tau = 1; K = 1.2$ (right)

or in other notation, denoting $k := \log(K)$ and

$$\Psi(\alpha, k), \quad \Psi(\alpha, k) := -\alpha k + \frac{1}{2}\log[\psi(-(\alpha + 1)i)^2].$$

the optimal value can be expressed as

$$\alpha_{\mathrm{opt}} = \operatorname*{arg\,min}_{(\alpha_{\min}, \alpha_{\max})} \Psi(\alpha, k).$$

For the function Ψ we denote the derivative with respect to α by $\Psi_\alpha := \frac{\partial \Psi_\alpha}{\partial \alpha}$ we have to solve the equation $\Psi_\alpha = 0$ to obtain the optimal value.

In order to illustrate the result numerically, we have chosen different values of α and the Heston model with parameters $S = 1; r = 0; V_0 = \theta = 0.1; \kappa = 1; \nu = 1; \rho = -0.9$ to generate the graphs given in Figure 5.4, which show the values of the functions Ψ and Ψ_α for different time to maturity.

The corresponding code is given in Figure 5.5 and uses an optimizer based on the *SQP* method. This method will be analysed, explained and illustrated in Chapter 9.

In fact we consider three possibilities:

- $\alpha \in (\alpha_{\min}, -1)$.
- $\alpha \in (-1, 0)$.
- $\alpha \in (0, \alpha_{\max})$.

It is possible to numerically approximate the minimum, $\alpha_{\min}$, and the maximum value, $\alpha_{\max}$. We note that Ψ is not finite at $\alpha = -1$ and $\alpha = 0$. The function value tends to $\pm\infty$.

We consider the integrand and show that, dependent on the parameter α, the corresponding graph shows that the oscillatory behaviour is reduced if we approach the optimal value of α. Taking some arbitrary α might cause serious trouble using a standard numerical integration scheme since the integrand can oscillate significantly. Figure 5.6 illustrates the phenomenon using the code shown in Figure 5.7. Furthermore, it suggests that for small time to maturity the effect is significant and much care has to be taken when choosing α. The computation of the optimal α, of course, takes CPU time and therefore it is problematic to apply this approach when considering the calibration to option prices. In this case we have to rely on some average value which we apply for all the option prices.

```
% Specification of the parameters first
% ...
% Computing starts here
zetaDm = (omega - 2*kappa*rho - sqrt((omega - 2*kappa*rho)^2 ...
    + 4*(1-rho^2)*kappa^2))/(2*omega*(1-rho^2));
zetaDp = (omega - 2*kappa*rho + sqrt((omega - 2*kappa*rho)^2 ...
    + 4*(1-rho^2)*kappa^2))/(2*omega*(1-rho^2));

fun = @(x)Tstar(x,kappa,omega,rho,tau);
tmpVal = zetaDp + 0.2;
lb = fun(zetaDp+0.1);ub = fun(tmpVal);   % bounds
while lb*ub > 0      %maxImum zeta : zetaMax > zetaDp > 1
    tmpVal = tmpVal+.1;
    ub = fun(tmpVal);
end
zetaMax = fzero(fun,[tmpVal,zetaDp+0.1]);

tmpVal = zetaDm-0.2;
lb = fun(tmpVal); ub = fun(zetaDm-0.1);   % bounds
while lb*ub > 0      %minimum zeta : zetaMin < zetaDp < 0
    tmpVal = tmpVal-.1;
    lb = fun(tmpVal);
end
zetaMin = fzero(fun,[tmpVal,zetaDm-0.1]);

alfaMax = zetaMax-1; alfaMin = zetaMin-1;

[alfaOpt,fmin] = modifiedSQP(@alfaOptimal,(zetaDp-1)/2,...
    @ConstraintsOptimalAlfa,0,alfaMax,[],0,[vInst;kappa;omega;rho],...
    [S,K,0,0,tau],vLong,[0;tau],alfaMax);   % opt alpha

price = priceHestonCarrMadan([vInst;kappa;omega;rho;alfaOpt],...
    [S,K,0,0,tau],vLong,[0;tau]);            % CarrMadan price

alfa1 = (7/6*alfaMin:0.005:-1.0001); alfa2 = (-0.9995:0.0001:-0.0001);
alfa3 = (0.0001:0.0005:alfaMax*7/6);

h = 1e-6;               % for finite differences
n1 = length(alfa1); n2 = length(alfa2); n3 = length(alfa3);

alfa = [alfa1, alfa2, alfa3];
psi1 = zeros(1,n1+n2+n3); psi2 = psi1;

for k = 1:(n1 + n2 + n3)
    psi1(k)=funcCarrMadan(0,F,K,kappa,vLong,rho,omega,vInst,...
        [0;tau],alfa(k));
    psi2(k)=funcCarrMadan(0,F,K,kappa,vLong,rho,omega,vInst,...
        [0;tau],alfa(k)+h);
end

Psi1 = -alfa*log(K) + 0.5*log(psi1.^2);
Psi2 = -(alfa+h)*log(K) + 0.5*log(psi2.^2); DPsi = (Psi2-Psi1)/h;

% plotting and Cut off for big values goes here ...
```

Figure 5.5 Matlab implementation of the calculation of the optimal dampening parameter α used for pricing options in the framework introduced by Carr and Madan

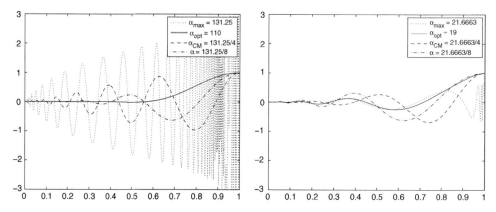

Figure 5.6 Integrand for the optimal α for $\tau = 0.1; K = 2$ (left) and $\tau = 1; K = 2$ (right)

5.4 THE LEWIS METHOD

In this section we consider a method for pricing options which was introduced in Lewis, A. (2001). The derivation of the option pricing formula is based on the Plancharel/Parseval theorem and the generalized Fourier transform. Let us consider the price $V(K, T)$ of an option with payoff v. We consider some complex number w.

$$V(K, T) = e^{-rT} \mathbb{E}[v] = \frac{e^{-rT}}{2\pi} \mathbb{E}\left[\int_{i\mathcal{I}(w)-\infty}^{i\mathcal{I}(w)+\infty} e^{izx} \mathcal{F}(v)(z)dz\right]$$

$$= \frac{e^{-rT}}{2\pi} \int_{i\mathcal{I}(w)-\infty}^{i\mathcal{I}(w)+\infty} \Phi(-z)\mathcal{F}(v)dz.$$

Thus, to apply the formula we have to compute the transform $\hat{v}$ of the payoff. This can be done for many European options including the Call and the Put option (see Section 5.1). The standard Fourier transform would not be possible but if we apply the generalized transform in a strip in the complex plane, the transform exits.

For the price of a European Call option, denoting $k = \log(S/K) + (r - d)T$ we have

$$C(K, T) = S(0)e^{-dT} - \frac{Ke^{-rT}}{2\pi} \int_{iv_1-\infty}^{iv_1+\infty} e^{-iuk} \frac{\Phi(-u)}{u^2 - iu} du. \tag{5.29}$$

This can be transformed to

$$C(K, T) = S(0)e^{-dT} - \frac{S(0)^{v_1}}{K^{v_1-1}\pi} e^{-rT} e^{(r-d)T v_1} \int_0^\infty \mathcal{R}\left(e^{iuk} \frac{\Phi(u - iv_1)}{u^2 - 2iuv_1 + iu - v_1(nu_1 + 1)}\right).$$

We introduced characteristic functions of several models in Chapters 2 and 3. To apply the function with the method reviewed in this chapter we have to adjust the Matlab implementation of the characteristic function. This is due to the definition of k. To this end we have to remove the term including the logarithmic spot, the rate r and the dividend yield d. This adjustment is made for our implementation of the characteristic function in `CharacteristicFunction-Lib_Lewis`.

```
% Specification of the parameters first
% ...
F=S*exp((r-d)*tau);  %Forward

%roots of D(-i*zeta)
zetaDm = (omega - 2*kappa*rho - sqrt((omega - 2*kappa*rho)^2 ...
    + 4*(1-rho^2)*kappa^2))/(2*omega*(1-rho^2));
zetaDp = (omega - 2*kappa*rho + sqrt((omega - 2*kappa*rho)^2 ...
    + 4*(1-rho^2)*kappa^2))/(2*omega*(1-rho^2));

%maximum zeta : zetaMax > zetaDp > 1
fun = @(x) Tstar(x,kappa,omega,rho,tau);
lb = fun(zetaDp+0.1);
tmpVal = zetaDp + 0.2;
ub = fun(tmpVal);
while lb*ub > 0
   tmpVal = tmpVal+.1;
   ub = fun(tmpVal);
end
zetaMax = fzero(fun,[tmpVal,zetaDp+0.1]);

%maximum zeta : zetaMin < zetaDp < 0
tmpVal = zetaDm-0.2;
lb = fun(tmpVal);
ub = fun(zetaDm-0.1);
while lb*ub > 0
   tmpVal = tmpVal-.1;
   lb = fun(tmpVal);
end
zetaMin = fzero(fun,[tmpVal,zetaDm-0.1]);

alfaMax = zetaMax-1; alfaMin = zetaMin-1;    % alfa max and min

%optimal alfa
[alfaOpt,fmin] = modifiedSQP(@objFunctionAlphaOptimal,(zetaDp-1)/2, ...
    @constraintsAlphaOptimal,0,alfaMax,[],0, ...
    [vInst;vLong;kappa;omega;rho],[S,K,r,d,tau],alfaMax);

alfaVec = (0.0001:0.0005:(alfaOpt+alfaMax)/2)';
funcval = objFunctionAlphaOptimal(alfaVec,[vInst;vLong;kappa;omega; ...
    rho],[S,K,r,d,tau]);

plot(alfaVec,funcval)

x = (0.0001:0.002:0.99999)';       % integration range
% transforms range [0,1] -> [0,+infinity)
Cinf = sqrt(1-rho^2)*(vInst+kappa*vLong*tau)/omega;
u = -log(x)/Cinf;

% plotting goes here ...
```

Figure 5.7 Matlab code for computing the integrand for the numerical integration and the Heston model. This piece of code was used to create Figure 5.6

```
function cpl = price_lewis_z0 (model,z0,S,K,T,r,d,varargin)
% computes the call price due to the method introduced by Alan Lewis
% this time we use general 0 < z0 < 1 instead of z0 = 0.5

k=log(S./K)+(r-d)*T;           % adjusted strike

  % the integrand to the Lewis integration scheme at z0 i
  lint = @(u) tmpintegrand(u,k,z0,model,T,varargin{:});
  lewisintegral=quad(lint,0,100);

  cpl  = S*exp(-d*T)- K*(S/K)^z0 * exp(-r*T)*exp((r-d)*T*z0)/pi ...
      * lewisintegral;      % final call price
end



function ret = tmpintegrand(u,k,z0,model,varargin)
% integrand for applying Lewis integration method
  ret=real(exp(1i*u.*k) ...
        .*exp(feval(@CharacteristicFunctionLib_Lewis, model, ...
        u-z0*1i,varargin{:}))./(u.*u - 2*u*1i*z0+1i*u-z0^2+z0)));
end
```

Figure 5.8 Straightforward implementation of the Lewis pricing method. We have used the integration range from 0 to 100. The integration range can also be a variable which can be passed to the function. The integrand is denoted by `tmpintegrand`. We have applied it using the `feval` command to be able to specify the model using a function handle

This is the general form of the integration formula. The value v_1 can take any value in $\mathcal{S}_w$ which denotes a strip in the complex plane. We implement this integration in Matlab by using the algorithm outlined in Figure 5.8.

Lewis suggests that we take $v_1 = \frac{1}{2}$ and argues that this value lies in the middle of the singularities at 0 and 1. Then, the pricing formula becomes

$$C(K,T) = S(0)e^{-dT} - \frac{1}{\pi}\sqrt{SK}e^{-(r+d)T/2} \int_0^\infty \mathcal{R}\left(e^{iuk}\Phi\left(u - \frac{i}{2}\right)\frac{1}{u^2 + \frac{1}{4}}\right)du. \quad (5.30)$$

The latter integration is implemented in Matlab by the function described in Figure 5.9. The corresponding integrand is given at the end of the code.

The role of v_1   Now let us choose different values $v_1 = 0.1, 0.3, 0.5, 0.7, 0.9$ for the Heston stochastic volatility model as well as for the Variance Gamma model. Figures 5.10 and 5.11 illustrate the real and the imaginary parts of the corresponding integrands.

For both examples we observe that the choice of the integration range determined by the value of v_1 impacts the shape of the integrand. The recommended choice $v_1 = \frac{1}{2}$ in all the cases considered gives reasonable results.

Greeks   It is possible to evaluate Δ and Γ numerically. The use of finite difference methods is possible but there exist semi-analytic formulae which can be evaluated very fast. We have (leaving dividends aside)

$$\Delta = 1 - \frac{Ke^{-rT}}{S(0)\pi}\int_0^\infty \frac{\mathcal{R}\left[\left(iu + \frac{1}{2}\right)\exp\left(\left(iu + \frac{1}{2}\right)k\right)\Phi\left(u - \frac{i}{2}\right)\right]}{u^2 + \frac{1}{4}}du$$

$$\Gamma = \frac{Ke^{-rT}}{S(0)^2\pi}\int_0^\infty \mathcal{R}\left[\exp\left(\left(iu + \frac{1}{2}\right)k\right)\Phi\left(u - \frac{i}{2}\right)\right]du.$$

```
function cpl = price_lewis(model,S,K,T,r,d,varargin)
% computes the call price due to the method introduced by Alan Lewis
tstart=tic;

k=log(S./K)+(r-d)*T;                          % adjusted strike

 % the integrand to the Lewis integration scheme at 0.5i
lint = @(u) tmpintegrand(u,k,model,T,varargin{:});
lewisintegral=quad(lint,0,100);

cpl = S*exp(-d*T)-(sqrt(S*K)/pi) ...
      * exp(-(r+d)*T*0.5) * lewisintegral;    % final call price
toc(tstart)
end

function ret = tmpintegrand(u,k,model,varargin)
% integrand for applying Lewis integration method
   ret=real(exp(1i*u.*k) ...
        .*exp(feval(@CharacteristicFunctionLib_Lewis,model, ...
        u-0.5*1i,varargin{:}))./(u.*u+.25));
end
```

Figure 5.9   Straightforward implementation of the Lewis method. We have used the integration range from 0 to 100. The integration range can also be a variable which can be passed to the function

Remarks   The integrals appearing in Equations (5.29) or (5.30) are easier to approximate at infinity than the integral appearing in the Carr–Madan setting, Equation (5.19). The integrand decays exponentially due to the presence of characteristic function.

The price to pay is the choice of v_1 which is not an easy task. Choosing it too big leads to slower decay at infinity and larger truncation errors. Yet, if we choose it too close to 1, the denominator diverges and the discretization error increases.

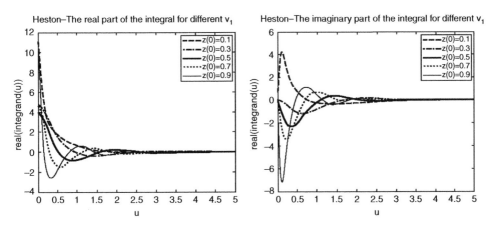

Figure 5.10   The integrands for the Heston model used to compute Call option prices in the Lewis model. We consider the real part of the integrand (left) and the imaginary part of it (right) for $v_1 = 0.1, 0.3, 0.5, 0.7, 0.9$. We have chosen $S(0) = 100$, $K = 100$, $r = d = 0$, $V(0) = \Theta = 0.02$, $\kappa = 0.1$, $v = 0.5$ and $\rho = -0.6$

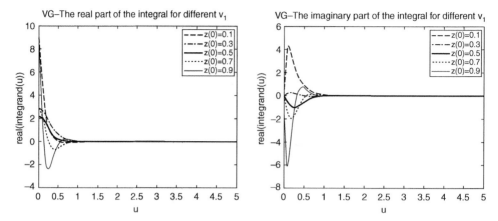

Figure 5.11 The integrands for the Variance Gamma model used to compute Call option prices in the Lewis model. We consider the real part of the integrand (left) and the imaginary part of it (right) for $v_1 = 0.1, 0.3, 0.5, 0.7, 0.9$. We have chosen $S(0) = 100$, $K = 100$, $r = d = 0$, $\sigma = 0.7$, $\theta = 0.1$ and $v = 0.7$.

For models with exponentially decaying tails of Lévy measure, c cannot be chosen a priori and must be adjusted depending on the model parameters.

In Sepp, A. (2003) it is reported that the method using the Black–Scholes adjusted method (5.27) is approximately three times faster than that of the Lewis method.

The method may blow up for certain parameter values. For example, for the Variance Gamma model we need

$$\alpha < \sqrt{\frac{\theta^2}{\sigma^4} + \frac{2}{\sigma^2 v} - \frac{\theta}{\sigma^2} - 1}.$$

Finally, in Lipton, A. (2002) another formula is derived. A European Call option can be valued using

$$C(K, T) = S(0) - \frac{Ke^{-rT}}{\pi} \int_{-\infty}^{\infty} e^{(iu+\frac{1}{2})} \frac{\Phi(u - i/2)}{u^2 + \frac{1}{4}} du. \tag{5.31}$$

This formula is the same as Equation (5.30) since $k = \log(S(0)/K)$ and therefore

$$\exp\left(\frac{1}{2}k\right) = \sqrt{\frac{S(0)}{K}}.$$

5.4.1 Application to Other Payoffs

In Lewis, A. (2000) several payoffs apart from the standard Call and Put options are considered. We have summarized these option payoffs in Table 5.1.

For illustration we calculate the transform of a European Call option.

$$\mathcal{F}(c(K, T))(z) = \int_{-\infty}^{\infty} e^{izx} (e^x - K)^+ dx$$

$$= \int_{\log(K)}^{\infty} e^{izx} (e^x - K) dx$$

Table 5.1   Payoffs, payoff transforms and the strip of regularity

Type	Payoff	Payoff Transform	Strip of Regularity
Call	$(e^x - K)^+$	$-\dfrac{K^{iz+1}}{z^2 - iz}$	$\mathcal{I}(w) > 1$
Put	$(K - e^x)^+$	$-\dfrac{K^{iz+1}}{z^2 - iz}$	$\mathcal{I}(w) < 1$
Covered Call	$\min(e^x, K)$	$\dfrac{K^{iz+1}}{z^2 - iz}$	$0 < \mathcal{I}(w) < 1$
Cash-or-Nothing Call	$1_{e^x \geq K}$	$-\dfrac{K^{iz}}{iz}$	$\mathcal{I}(w) > 0$
Cash-or-Nothing Put	$1_{e^x \leq k}$	$\dfrac{K^{iz}}{iz}$	$\mathcal{I}(w) < 0$
Asset-or-Nothing Call	$e^x 1_{e^x \geq K}$	$-\dfrac{K^{iz+1}}{iz + 1}$	$\mathcal{I}(w) > 1$
Asset-or-Nothing Put	$e^x 1_{e^x \leq K}$	$\dfrac{K^{iz+1}}{iz + 1}$	$\mathcal{I}(w) < 0$
Arrow–Debreu	$\delta(x - \log(K))$	K^{iz}	$\mathbb{C}$
Money Market	1	$2\pi \delta(z)$	$\mathcal{I}(w) = 0$

$$= \left[\frac{e^{(iz+1)x}}{iz + 1} - K\frac{e^{izx}}{iz} \right]_{\log(K)}^{\infty}$$

$$= -\frac{K^{iz+1}}{z^2 - iz}. \tag{5.32}$$

For other payoff functions the calculation proceeds along the same lines.

5.5 THE ATTARI METHOD

In Attari, M. (2004) a particular method is considered. First, it reduces the number of integrations to compute option prices when applying the general Black formula to only one integration. Second, it reduces the number of evaluation of the model's characteristic function. We give the pricing formulae for European Call and Put options.

$$C(K, T) = S(0) - e^{-rT} K \left[\frac{1}{2} + \frac{1}{\pi} \int_0^\infty I_A(x) dx \right] \tag{5.33}$$

$$P(K, T) = S(0) - e^{-rT} K \left[\frac{1}{2} - \frac{1}{\pi} \int_0^\infty I_A(x) dx \right], \tag{5.34}$$

with

$$I_A(x) = \frac{\left(\left[\mathcal{R}(\varphi(x)) + x^{-1}\mathcal{I}(\varphi(x)) \right] \cos(\beta x) + \left[\mathcal{I}(\varphi(x)) - x^{-1}\mathcal{R}(\varphi(x)) \right] \sin(\beta x) \right)}{1 + x^2}$$

and $\beta = \log(\frac{e^{-rT}K}{S(0)})$. Since we do not use the Attari method for pricing options, we do not give the Matlab code here. But because it is a simple numerical integration the reader can modify some other piece of source code to implement the Attari method.

5.6 THE CONVOLUTION METHOD

Let us consider Equation (5.8) to price a European Call option. If we take a general payoff function h, the equation can be written as

$$V_h(K,T) = e^{-rT} \int_{-\infty}^{\infty} h(y)f(y|S(t_0))dy, \qquad (5.35)$$

with f being the probability density for the asset price with spot value $S(t_0)$. Therefore, it can also be seen as a transition density. To this end let us take the transition density f as a function of two variables, thus

$$f : \mathbb{R} \times \mathbb{R} \to [0, 1]$$
$$(y, x) \mapsto f(y, x).$$

The *convolution method*, CONV for short, is based on the assumption that the value of the transition density does not directly depend on the values of x and y but on the difference $y - x$. Thus, the main assumption is that

$$f(y|x) = f(y - x). \qquad (5.36)$$

Many financial models to which we apply the CONV method later fulfil (5.36). If the assumption holds we write (5.35) in slightly different form. Applying the change of variable rule for a translation of coordinates we get

$$C(K,T) = e^{-rT} \int_{-\infty}^{\infty} h_C(x + y)f(y)dy. \qquad (5.37)$$

The integral in Equation (5.37) is nothing but a convolution. Starting from Equation (5.37) we can use the characteristic function of the underlying model to bring the equation into a form which is very suitable for numerical evaluation. Using that, the characteristic function of a convolution is nothing other than the product of the constituting characteristic functions. Thus, having the characteristic function of the payoff as well as for the financial model pricing can be done numerically by applying the FFT.

The CONV method was introduced by Lord, R., Fang, F., Bervoets, G. and Oosterlee, C.W. (2008). For illustration purposes we consider the case of a European Call option but note that more general payoffs can also be considered.

For integration purposes we take the dampened Call price

$$c_\alpha(k, t) := \exp(\alpha k)C(k, t), \quad \alpha \in \mathbb{R}.$$

Using the same methods applied in Section 5.3 and similar calculations we find for the Call option price

$$C(K,T) = \exp(-rT - \alpha k)\mathcal{F}^{-1}\left(\mathcal{F}(c_\alpha(y, T)\varphi(-(u - i\alpha)))\right)(k), \qquad (5.38)$$

where $\mathcal{F}$ denotes the Fourier transform and $\mathcal{F}^{-1}$ its inverse (see Chapter 13, Section 13.5, for details).

With respect to the valuation formula it is necessary to compute

$$\mathcal{F}(u) = \int_{-\infty}^{\infty} e^{iux}c_\alpha(x)dx \qquad (5.39)$$

$$c_\alpha(K,T) = e^{-rT} \int_{-\infty}^{\infty} e^{-iux} \underbrace{\int_{-\infty}^{\infty} e^{iux} c_\alpha(x) dx \, \varphi(-(u-i\alpha))}_{\mathcal{F}(u)} du. \qquad (5.40)$$

We have to find a suitable discrete representation for (5.39) and (5.40). To arrive at the approximation we show how the variables u, x and y are discretized.

Discretization – Grid Construction

For the implementation of the CONV method we have to discretize the state space of u, x and y. To this end we define a discrete grid. For pricing European options a standard method for the construction is appropriate. For more advanced applications, such as extending the method to early exercise possibilities, we consider a more involved grid construction. We start by describing the standard grid.

The Standard Grid   First, we observe that (5.40) and (5.39) correspond to the Fourier transform and its inverse transform. To construct the standard grid we consider the three-dimensional grid where each dimension is of length N. We denote the grids representing the variables u, x and y by $\{u\}$, $\{x\}$ and $\{y\}$. This takes account of the fact that x represents the log price at time t_0, y the log price at T and u the frequency domain variable of the Fourier transform. To ensure a good performance of the implemented algorithm we must hope that the grids for x and y coincide. Therefore, we consider the grids with grid points

$$u_j = u_0 + j\Delta_u; \quad x_j = x_0 + j\Delta_x; \quad y_j = y_0 + j\Delta_y; \quad j = 1, \dots, N. \qquad (5.41)$$

We assume $\Delta_x = \Delta_y$ and the *Nyquist condition* to hold for the grid size Δ_u, which is the relation

$$\Delta_u \Delta_y = \frac{2\pi}{N}. \qquad (5.42)$$

The grid needs to be chosen such that the errors from applying the discrete method can be neglected for pricing. To this end we control the discretization as well as the truncation error. While we do not reproduce the derivation of the results from Lord, R., Fang, F., Bervoets, G. and Oosterlee, C.W. (2008) here, we do their results and consider $y_0 = -\frac{L}{2}$ and $\Delta_y = \frac{L}{N}$ with L chosen such that we have covered most of the mass for the underlying density in the interval $[-\frac{L}{2}, \frac{L}{2}]$. The choice of L has to be made with care. Choosing too small values leads to unstable results since we do not cover the important range of the probability distribution. Taking too large values may imply smaller errors resulting from truncation. Larger values of L, in fact, lead to a smaller range of the grid used in the Fourier domain. A reasonable choice and a rule-of-thumb for determining the correct value of L is to take a certain amount of the standard deviation of $X = \log(S)$. To this end for some positive δ we use

$$L := \delta \sqrt{ -\frac{\partial^2 \varphi}{\partial u^2}\Big|_{u=0} + \left(\frac{\partial \varphi}{\partial u}\Big|_{u=0} \right)^2 }.$$

In the literature it is suggested that we take $L = 10$. We show the dependence on the parameter L by plotting the option price for different models against the value L.

For pricing European options the adjusted grid is easy to construct. We simply include the current log asset price, $\log(S_0/S_0) = 0$ on the grid. This is to ensure that the current ATM price lies on the grid. In fact, this corresponds to using the grid points

$$u_j = \left(j - \frac{N}{2}\right)\Delta_u; \quad x_j = y_j = \left(j - \frac{1}{2}\right)\Delta_y; \quad j = 0, \ldots, N - 1. \tag{5.43}$$

The Approximation

We apply the trapezoidal rule for integration. Thus, the transform of the dampened Call option value, (5.39), is approximated by the following discrete sum:

$$\mathcal{F}(u_j) = \exp(ijy_0(\Delta_u))\exp(iu_0y_0)\Delta_y\left(A_0 + A_{N-1} + \sum_{k=1}^{N-2} A_k\right), \tag{5.44}$$

where A_0, A_{N-1} and A_k are given by

$$A_0(y_j) = \frac{c_\alpha(y_0)}{2}$$

$$A_{N-1}(y_j) = \frac{\exp\left(ij(1 - \frac{2\pi}{N})\right)\exp(iu_0(N-1)\Delta_y)c_\alpha(y_{N-1})}{2}$$

$$A_k(y_j) = \exp\left(ij\frac{2\pi k}{N}\right)\exp(iu_0k\Delta_y)c_\alpha(y_k).$$

It is possible to use the exact value for the dampened Call option price which is given by Equation (5.32). Now, we give the discrete approximation for the value of Equation (5.40).

$$c_\alpha(x_p, T) \approx \exp(-rT + iu(y_0 - x_0))(-1)^p \text{fft}\left[e^{ij(y_0 - x_0)\Delta_u}\varphi(-u_j - i\alpha)\text{fft}\left((-1)^n w_n c_\alpha(y_n)\right)\right]$$

using $w_0 = w_N = \frac{1}{2}$ and $w_k = 1$ for $k = 1, \ldots, N - 1$. Finally, we give the corresponding implementation of (5.18) in Matlab (see Figure 5.12). The implementation can be applied to a whole range of strikes at once. We apply the repmat function used to multiply arrays. In this way it is possible to create a grid with columns representing one particular strike.

Finally, we illustrate the impact of the two parameters α and L on the option values. The parameter α is the dampening parameter and can be chosen by the modeller. Figures 5.13 and 5.14 summarize our findings. To this end we have taken the Black–Scholes model with a constant volatility $\sigma_{BS} = 0.25$, the Variance Gamma model with $\sigma = 0.125$, $\theta = -0.15$ and $\nu = 0.21$ as well as the Normal Inverse Gaussian model with $\alpha = 6.1882$, $\beta = -3.8941$, $\nu = 1$ and $\delta = 0.1622$. The choice of α has virtually no effect on the prices generated using the CONV method and the Black–Scholes model, whereas we see a strong dependence for the other two models. The reader should try out other models using the characteristic function library provided in the source code.

To illustrate the dependence of the chosen cut-off for integration we have varied the parameter L and plotted European Call option prices for the models and parameters given above. It is interesting to observe that the chosen truncation does affect the Black–Scholes model and the Variance Gamma model in the same way. For the Normal Inverse Gaussian model we observe another effect. While the prices seems to converge for large values of L in the Black–Scholes and the Variance Gamma model, there seems to be a maximum value for the Normal Inverse

```
function price = FFTCONV_E(n, L, alpha, cp, model, S0, t, r, q, ...
    strike, varargin)

Ngrid = 2^n;                              % number of grid points
Nstrike = length(strike);                 % number of strikes
rdt = r * t;                              % riskfree times t

Delta_y = L/Ngrid;                        % Delta_y
Delta_x = Delta_y;                        % Delta_x = Delta_y
Delta_u = 2 * pi / L;                     % Delta_u

% Grids
Grid_i = repmat((0:Ngrid-1)',1,Nstrike);  % Gridindex
Grid_m = (-1).^Grid_i;                    % (-1)^Grid_i

x = (Grid_i .* Delta_x) - (Ngrid/2 * Delta_x);   % adjusted x-grid
y = repmat(log(strike / S0)',Ngrid,1) ...
    + (Grid_i .* Delta_y) - (Ngrid/2 * Delta_y);% adjusted y-grid
u = (Grid_i .* Delta_u) - (Ngrid/2 * Delta_u);   % u-grid

V = max(cp .* (S0*exp(y) - repmat(strike',Ngrid,1)), 0);% payoff
v = V .* exp(alpha .* y);                 % dampened value

w = ones(Ngrid,Nstrike); w(1,:) = 0.5; w(Ngrid,:) = 0.5; % coeff

FT_Vec = ifft( (Grid_m) .* w .* v );             % inner transform
FT_Vec_tbt=exp( 1i .* Grid_i * (diag(y(1,:)-x(1,:))) .* Delta_u ) ...
    .* exp(feval(@CF, model,-(u-(1i*alpha)), t,r,q,varargin{:})) ...
    .* FT_Vec;                            % vector to be transf.

C = abs(exp(-rdt-(alpha .* x)+(1i .* u*(diag(y(1,:) - x(1,:)))))) ...
    .* (Grid_m) .* fft(FT_Vec_tbt));      % final value
price = double(C(Ngrid/2 + 1, :));        % return price
end
```

Figure 5.12 Matlab code for pricing European Call and Put options with the CONV method

Gaussian model. Thus, the modeller has to take care in choosing an appropriate value for the truncation range. Figure 5.14 summarizes our findings.

The Greeks   The CONV method can be applied to calculate Greeks. We use the formulae

$$\Delta = \frac{e^{-rT} - \alpha x}{S(0)} \left(-\alpha \mathcal{F}^{-1}(A(u))(x) - \mathcal{F}^{-1}(iu A(u))(x) \right)$$

$$\Gamma = \frac{e^{-rT-\alpha x}}{S(0)^2} \left(\alpha(\alpha + 1)\mathcal{F}^{-1}(A(u))(x) + (2\alpha + 1)\mathcal{F}^{-1}(iu A(u))(x)\mathcal{F}^{-1}(u^2 A(u))(x) \right).$$

Here we set

$$A(u) := \mathcal{F}(e^{\alpha y} C(y, T)(u)\varphi(-(u - i\alpha))).$$

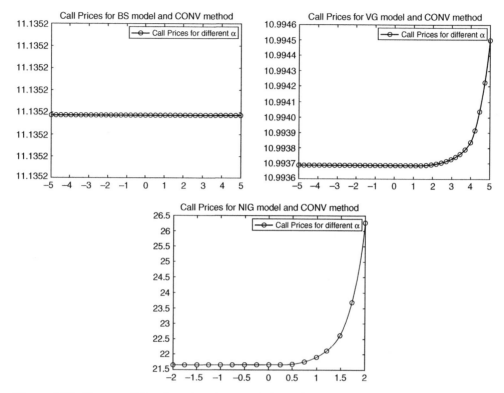

Figure 5.13 European Call option values for numerical test of CONV method with different dampening parameters for α. Considered are the Black–Scholes (top left), the Variance Gamma (top right) and the Normal Inverse Gaussian models (bottom) with the dampening parameter α varied

5.7 THE COSINE METHOD

The cosine method was introduced in Fang, F. and Oosterlee, K. (2008). The price of a European option v is approximated by

$$v(x, T) \approx e^{-rT} \left(\frac{1}{2} \mathcal{R}(\varphi(0)V_0) + \sum_{k=1}^{N-1} \mathcal{R}\left(\varphi\left(\frac{k\pi}{b-a}; x \right) e^{-ik\pi \frac{a}{b-a}} \right) V_k \right). \quad (5.45)$$

The coefficients V_k depend on the option payoff. The real numbers a and b have to be chosen appropriately.

We show how to apply the method to different options and models.

Let $g : [0, \pi] \to \mathbb{R}$, then the cosine expansion is given by

$$g(\theta) = \frac{A_0}{2} + \sum_{k=1}^{\infty} A_k \cos(k\theta), \quad A_k = \frac{2}{\pi} \int_0^\pi g(\theta) \cos(k\theta) d\theta.$$

For a function with domain of definition being the interval $[a, b]$ different from $[0, \pi]$, $f : [a, b] \to \mathbb{R}$. It is still possible to expand the function into a cosine series. Setting $\theta := \frac{y-a}{b-a}$

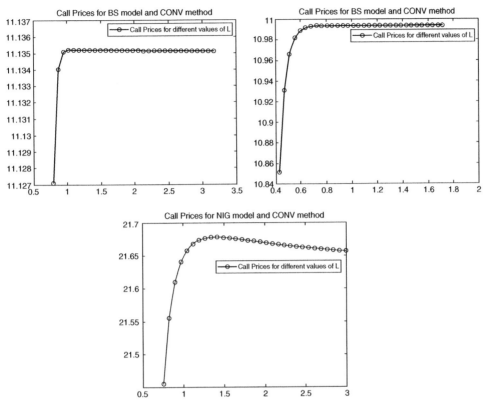

Figure 5.14 European Call option values computed applying the CONV method with different truncation parameters L. Considered are the Black–Scholes (top left), the Variance Gamma (top right) and the Normal Inverse Gaussian models (bottom)

and $x = \frac{b-a}{\pi}\theta + a$, the expansion is

$$f(y) = \frac{A_0}{2} + \sum_{k=1}^{\infty} A_k \cos\left(k\pi \frac{y-a}{b-a}\right) \qquad (5.46)$$

$$A_k = \frac{2}{b-a} \int_a^b f(y) \cos\left(k\pi \frac{y-a}{b-a}\right) dy.$$

Since the option pricing problem under consideration involves the evaluation of an infinite integral we truncate this infinite integral. If we choose a, $b \in \mathbb{R}$ such that the resulting approximation error is small, this leads to

$$v(x, T) \approx e^{-rT} \int_a^b v(y, T) f(y|x) dy.$$

The density $f(\cdot)$ is in general not known in closed form or is not easy to compute since special functions, for instance Bessel functions, have to be evaluated. In contrast, the characteristic function corresponding to the density often is. To this end we replace the density f by its approximated cosine expansion, Equation (5.46), in y:

$$f(y|x) = \frac{A_0(x)}{2} + \sum_{k=1}^{N-1} A_k(x) \cos\left(k\pi \frac{y-a}{b-a}\right).$$

Using the latter expression and interchanging summation and integration for the approximated price we obtain

$$v(x, T) \approx \frac{b-a}{2} e^{-rT} \left(\frac{A_0(x)}{2} V_0 + \sum_{k=1}^{N-1} A_k(x) V_k\right) \qquad (5.47)$$

$$V_k = \frac{2}{b-a} \int_a^b v(y, T) \cos\left(k\pi \frac{y-a}{b-a}\right) dy. \qquad (5.48)$$

Since the option price is given by an indefinite integral, we have to approximate the finite integral appearing in A_k by the infinite one. Thus, we take the coefficients

$$\tilde{A}_k = \frac{2}{b-a} \mathcal{R}\left(\varphi\left(\frac{k\pi}{b-a}\right) \exp\left(-i\frac{ka\pi}{b-a}\right)\right),$$

where φ is the characteristic function of the underlying model.

A detailed analysis of the approximation error is given in Fang, F. and Oosterlee, K. (2008). The following errors are analysed:

- Truncation error of the integral approximation, $\int_{-\infty}^{\infty} \approx \int_a^b$
- Truncating the series $\sum_{k=1}^{\infty} \approx \sum_{k=1}^{N-1}$
- Using the characteristic function $\varphi = \int_{-\infty}^{\infty} e^{-i\omega x} f(x) dx$ instead of the integral $\int_a^b e^{-i\omega x} f(x) dx$.

To keep the approximation error small we have to choose the truncation range appropriately. We choose for the range of integration $[a, b]$, such that

$$[a, b] := \left[c_1 - L\sqrt{|c_2| + \sqrt{|c_4|}}, c_1 + L\sqrt{|c_2| + \sqrt{|c_4|}}\right]. \qquad (5.49)$$

In Equation (5.49) c_n, $n = 1, \ldots, 4$, denote the n-th cumulant of $\log(S(T)/K)$. Cumulants of higher order such as c_4 have to be included to account for sharp peaks of the density for short maturities ($T \approx 0.1$). For shorter maturities one may have to include further cumulants such as c_6 or even higher-order cumulants to accurately price options. High-order cumulants are difficult to derive either in closed form or using numerical differentiation of the characteristic function.

For some of the considered models the cumulants are not available in closed form. Using the characteristic function it is possible to calculate the cumulants numerically by using finite differences. We give the corresponding equations for the first four cumulants. First, we define the cumulant generating function

$$k(u) := \log\left(\varphi(iu)\right).$$

Then, the n-th cumulant is given by the n-th derivative of k with respect to u evaluated at $u = 0$, $\frac{\partial k}{\partial u}\big|_{u=0} = c_n$. Therefore, we need the first four finite differences denoted by $d_n f(\cdot)$ of

Table 5.2   Cumulants for the GBM, Merton, Heston, NIG, VG and CGMY models

GBM	$c_1 = \mu T$
	$c_2 = \sigma^2 T$
	$c_4 = 0$
	$w = 0$
Merton	$c_1 = T(\mu + \lambda \mu_j)$
	$c_2 = T\lambda \left(\dfrac{\sigma^2}{\lambda} + \mu_j^2 + \sigma_j^2 \right)$
	$c_4 = T\lambda \left(\mu_j^4 + 6\sigma_j^2 \mu_j^2 + 3\sigma_j^4 \right)$
Heston	$c_1 = \mu T + (1 - e^{-\lambda T}) \dfrac{u - u_0}{2\lambda} - \dfrac{1}{2} uT$
	$c_2 = \dfrac{1}{8\lambda^3}(\eta T \lambda e^{-\lambda T}(u_0 - u)(8\lambda\rho - 4\eta) + \lambda\rho\eta(1 - e^{-\lambda T})(16u - 8u_0)$
	$\qquad + 2u\lambda T(-4\lambda\rho\eta + \eta^2 + 4\lambda^2) + \eta^2((u - 2u_0)e^{-2\lambda T} + u(6e^{-\lambda T} - 7) + 2u_0)$
	$\qquad + 8\lambda^2(u_0 - u)(1 - e^{-\lambda T}))$
	$w = 0$
NIG	$c_1 = \left(\mu - \dfrac{\sigma^2}{2} + \omega \right) t + \delta T \beta / \sqrt{\alpha^2 - \beta^2}$
	$c_2 = \delta T \alpha^2 (\alpha^2 - \beta^2)^{-3/2}$
	$c_4 = 3\delta T \alpha^2 (\alpha^2 + 4\beta^2)(\alpha^2 - \beta^2)^{-7/2}$
	$\omega = -\delta(\sqrt{\alpha^2 - \beta^2} - \sqrt{\alpha^2 - (\beta + 1)^2})$
VG	$c_1 = (\mu + \theta)T$
	$c_2 = (\sigma^2 + v\theta^2)T$
	$c_4 = 3(\sigma^4 v + 2\theta^4 v^3 + 4\sigma^2\theta^2 v^2)T$
	$w = \dfrac{1}{v} \log(1 - \theta v - \sigma^2 v/2)$
CGMY	$c_1 = \mu T + CT\Gamma(1 - Y)(M^{Y-1} - G^{Y-1})$
	$c_2 = \sigma^2 T + CT\Gamma(2 - Y)(M^{Y-2} + G^{Y-2})$
	$c_4 = CT\Gamma(4 - Y)(M^{Y-4} + G^{Y-4})$
	$\omega = -C\Gamma(-Y)((M - 1)^Y - M^Y + (G + 1)^Y - G^Y)$

some function f. For some small value $h > 0$, for instance $h = 10^{-6}$, we find

$$d_1 f(x) = \frac{f(x + h) - f(x - h)}{2h}$$

$$d_2 f(x) = \frac{f(x - h) - 2f(x) + f(x + h)}{h^2}$$

$$d_3 f(x) = \frac{f(x + 2h) - 2f(x + h) + 2f(x - h) - f(x - 2h)}{2h^3}$$

$$d_4 f(x) = \frac{f(x + 3h) - 2f(x + 2h) + 4f(x)}{4h^4}$$
$$\frac{-f(x + h) - f(x - h) - 2f(x - 2h) + f(x - 3h)}{4h^4}$$

and $d_1k(0), \ldots, d_4k(0)$ are the cumulants up to order 4. Thus, using the finite differences $d_1 f, \ldots, d_4 f$ we are able to compute the cumulants when the function k is given.

Evaluation of Option Payoffs   We have outlined how to apply the cosine expansion to approximate integrals appearing in option valuation problems. The key to price different options are the coefficients V_k. The option payoff determines these coefficients. For European Call and Put options the corresponding coefficients V_k can be derived using (5.48). They are

$$V_k^{\text{Call}} = \frac{2}{b-a} K(\xi_k(0, b) - \psi_k(0, b)) \tag{5.50}$$

$$V_k^{\text{Put}} = \frac{2}{b-a} K(-\xi_k(a, 0) + \psi_k(a, 0)), \tag{5.51}$$

with the functions ξ_k and ψ_k

$$\xi_k(c, d) = \int_c^d e^y \cos\left(k\pi \frac{y-a}{b-a}\right) dy$$

$$= \begin{cases} \dfrac{1}{1 + \left(\dfrac{k\pi}{b-a}\right)^2} \left[\cos\left(k\pi\dfrac{d-a}{b-a}\right) e^d - \cos\left(k\pi\dfrac{c-a}{b-a}\right) e^c \right. \\ \left. + \dfrac{k\pi}{b-a}\left(\sin\left(k\pi\dfrac{d-a}{b-a}\right)e^d - \sin\left(k\pi\dfrac{c-a}{b-a}\right)e^c\right)\right] \end{cases} \tag{5.52}$$

$$\psi_k(c, d) = \int_c^d \cos\left(k\pi \frac{y-a}{b-a}\right) dy$$

$$= \begin{cases} \left[\sin\left(k\pi\dfrac{d-a}{b-a}\right) - \sin\left(k\pi\dfrac{c-a}{b-a}\right)\right]\dfrac{b-a}{k\pi} & k \neq 0 \\ d - c & k = 0 \end{cases}. \tag{5.53}$$

We map the formulae (5.50) and (5.51) taking into account the analytic formulae (5.52) and (5.53) to Matlab by utilizing the code given in Figure 5.15.

Before we consider the application to other European options we give a brief numerical study of the effect of the parameter L which we have not as yet specified. It is used to determine the truncation. To this end we consider three models, namely the Black–Scholes model with $\sigma_{\text{BS}} = 0.2$, the Variance Gamma model with $\sigma = 0.18$, $\theta = -0.13$ and $\nu = 0.25$ and the Normal Inverse Gaussian model with $\alpha = 24.12154$, $\beta = -17.6234$, $\nu = 1$ and $\delta = 0.635434$. We take the spot value $S(0) = 100$ and compute the price of a European Call option with strike $K = 90$. Figure 5.16 illustrates the dependence of truncation for small times to maturity. We have chosen $T = 0.1$, and Figure 5.17 shows the results for maturity $T = 5$. For short time to maturity the dependence on L is significant and an inappropriate choice leads to unstable and unreliable option prices. This is shown in the graph which is a curved line; it does not appear to converge. For longer time to maturity the choice is more stable in the sense that there is a larger interval for L, which leads to stable prices. We also tested the dependence for European Put options. We observed the same behaviour. The reader can try out different models and other payoffs, maturities and ranges for L. The source code for further experiments is included in the supporting material for this book.

```
function [chi, psi] = cosine_coeff_Vanilla(a,c,d,tmp,cp)
% coefficients for Call option prices; cp = 1 (Call), cp = -1 (Put)
    x1 = (d-a)*tmp;                 % arg for cosine and sine
    x2 = (c-a)*tmp;                 % arg for cosine and sine

    exp_c = exp(c);                 % coeff - lower bound integration
    exp_d = exp(d);                 % coeff - upper bound integration

    % formula for analytic coefficients for Call options
    chi = ( cos(x1)*exp_d - cos(x2)*exp_c ...
          + tmp.*(sin(x1)*exp_d-sin(x2)*exp_c) ) ./ ( 1 + tmp.^2 );

    psi = (sin(x1)-sin(x2))./tmp;%tmp = k*pi/(b-a);
    psi(k == 0) = d-c;

    psi = cp * psi;                 % adjust due to Call or Put
    chi = cp * chi;                 % adjust due to Call or Put
end
```

Figure 5.15 Matlab function to compute the coefficients necessary to use the cosine expansion for option pricing

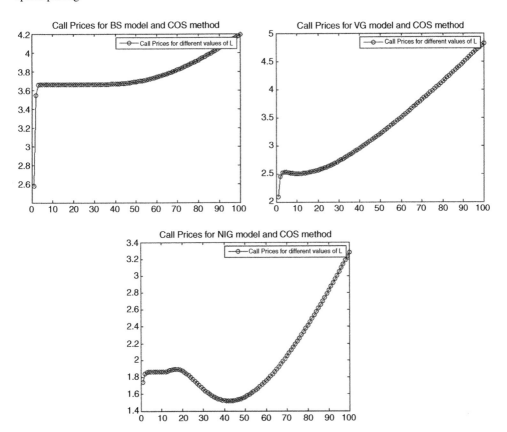

Figure 5.16 European Call option values computed applying the COS method with different truncation parameters L and a short time to maturity $T = 0.1$. Considered are the Black–Scholes (top left), the Variance Gamma (top right) and the Normal Inverse Gaussian models (bottom)

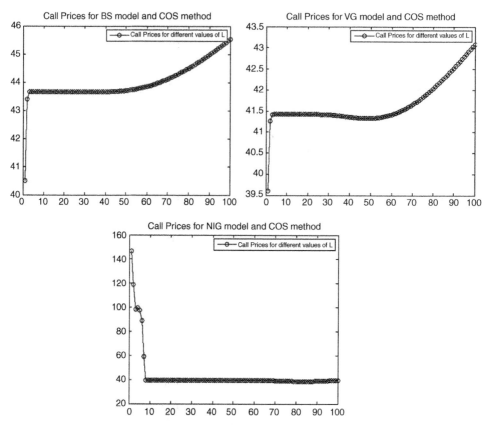

Figure 5.17   European Call option values computed applying the COS method with different truncation parameters L for maturity $T = 5$. Considered are the Black–Scholes (top left), the Variance Gamma (top right) and the Normal Inverse Gaussian models (bottom)

It is possible to extend the method to other option payoffs. For instance, coefficients V_k for the payoff of a *cash-or-nothing*, h_{con} and a *gap option*, h_{go}, can be calculated. The payoffs are given respectively by

$$h_{\text{con}}(T, K) = \begin{cases} 0 & \text{if } S(T) \leq K \\ K & \text{if } S(T) > K \end{cases}$$

$$h_{\text{go}}(T, K, R) = \begin{cases} S(T) - K - R & \text{if } S(T) < H \\ R & \text{if } S(T) \geq K \end{cases}.$$

The corresponding coefficients are

$$V_k^{\text{con}} = \frac{2}{b - a} K \psi_k(0, b) \tag{5.54}$$

$$V_k^{\text{go}} = \frac{2K(\xi_k(0, \log(H/K)))}{b - a} - \psi_k(0, \log(H/K))) + \frac{2R\psi_k(\log(H/K), b)}{b - a}.$$

Simplification For models based on Lévy processes the cosine expansion can be simplified and is given by

$$v(K, T) = e^{-rT} \mathcal{R} \left(\frac{\Phi(0)V_0}{2} + \sum_{k=1}^{N-1} \Phi\left(\frac{k\pi}{b-a} \right) V_k e^{ik\pi \frac{x-a}{b-a}} \right),$$

with $V_k = U_k K$. Thus, it is possible to separate the computation of the coefficients from the multiplication and we get

$$v(x, t_0) = K e^{-rT} \mathcal{R} \left(\frac{\Phi(0)U_0}{2} + \sum_{k=1}^{N-1} \Phi\left(\frac{k\pi}{b-a} \right) U_k e^{ik\pi \frac{x-a}{b-a}} \right), \tag{5.55}$$

with the scalars U_k

$$U_k := \begin{cases} \dfrac{2}{b-a}(\xi_k(0, b) - \psi_k(0, b)) & \text{Call} \\ \dfrac{2}{b-a}(-\xi_k(a, 0) + \psi_k(a, 0)) & \text{Put} \end{cases}.$$

For the Heston model the cosine expansion can be obtained as well and it is given by

$$v(x, t_0) = K e^{-rT} \mathcal{R} \left(\frac{\Phi(0)U_0}{2} + \sum_{k=1}^{N-1} \Phi\left(\frac{k\pi}{b-a}; V(0) \right) U_k e^{ik\pi \frac{x-a}{b-a}} \right). \tag{5.56}$$

Again, we have the same formula for the calculation of the coefficients and the multiplication with the strike are separated. In the latter equation $V(0)$ is the spot variance from the Heston model.

Greeks We compute Greeks Δ and Γ. They are given by

$$\Delta = \frac{\partial V}{\partial S(0)} = \frac{\partial v}{\partial x} \frac{\partial x}{\partial S(0)} = \frac{1}{S(0)} \frac{\partial v}{\partial S(0)}$$

$$\Gamma = \frac{\partial^2 V}{\partial S(0)^2} = \frac{1}{S(0)^2} \left(-\frac{\partial v}{\partial S(0)} + \frac{\partial^2 v}{\partial S(0)^2} \right).$$

Thus, using the cosine expansion we find

$$\Delta = \frac{V_0 \Phi(0)}{2S(0)} + e^{-rT} \sum_{k=1}^{N-1} \mathcal{R} \left(\varphi\left(\frac{k\pi}{b-a} \right) \exp\left(ik\pi \left(\frac{x-a}{b-a} \right) \right) \frac{ik\pi}{b-a} \frac{V_k}{S(0)} \right)$$

$$\Gamma = \frac{V_0 \Phi(0)}{2S(0)^2} + e^{-rT} \sum_{k=1}^{N-1} \mathcal{R} \left(\varphi\left(\frac{k\pi}{b-a} \right) \exp\left(ik\pi \left(\frac{x-a}{b-a} \right) \right) \left[-\frac{ik\pi}{b-a} + \left(\frac{ik\pi}{b-a} \right)^2 \right] \frac{V_k}{S(0)^2} \right).$$

For the COS method we have the following implementation in Matlab (see Figure 5.18). This implementation can be applied to a whole range of strikes at once. To this end we have used the command `repmat` which replicates and tiles arrays. The implementation uses the functions `calcvkp` and `coeff` which are given in Figures 5.19 and 5.20.

```
function y = FFTCOS_E(n, L, c, cp, model, S0, t, r, q, strike, varargin)

Ngrid = 2 ^ n;                          % number of grid points
Nstrike = size(strike,1);               % number of strikes

x = repmat(double(log(S0 ./ strike))',Ngrid,1);        % center

a = double(c(1) + x - L * sqrt(c(2) + sqrt(c(3))));    % low bound
b = double(c(1) + x + L * sqrt(c(2) + sqrt(c(3))));    % up bound

Grid_i = repmat((0:Ngrid-1)',1,Nstrike);       % Grid index

vk_p = @(x) vkPutTermEuCOS(x,b,a,strike);      % coefficients for Put

fk_i = exp(feval(@CF, model,Grid_i.*pi./(b-a), t,r,q,varargin{:}));
fk_i = double(2./(b - a) .* real( fk_i ...
       .* exp(1i .* pi .* Grid_i .* x ./ (b - a)) ...
       .* exp(-1i .* (pi .* Grid_i .* a ./ (b - a))) ));

Vk = vk_p(Grid_i);
y = double(exp(-r .* t) ...
           .* (sum(fk_i .* Vk) - 0.5 * (fk_i(1,:) .* Vk(1,:)) ))';

if cp  == 1    % European Call price using pu-Call-parity
    y = y + S0 * exp(-q * t) - strike * exp(-r * t);
end

end
```

Figure 5.18   Matlab code for implementing the COS method to price European Call and Put options

5.8 COMPARISON, STABILITY AND PERFORMANCE

In this section we compare all the methods described in this chapter in terms of stability, speed and performance. To this end we take the Heston and Variance Gamma models as our benchmark models. Our tests are

(I) Take as a reference value $N_{ref} = 13$ and compute option prices along a given strike range using different methods and different values for N. Also compare the computed values for N and the strike range for the models

(II) Take the reference value $N_{ref} = 18$ to construct the grid and consider $\log(|(C_{18} - C_N)/C_{18}|$ for different models

(III) CPU time and accuracy comparison for option pricing of a whole grid of options for different models.

```
function y = calcvkp(k, b, a, strike)

[chi, psi] = coeff(k,a,0,a,b);
y = (psi - chi)*diag(strike);

end
```

Figure 5.19   Matlab implementation for determining the values for χ and ψ to be used with the COS method

```
function [chi, psi] = coeff(k, c, d, a, b)

chi = (exp(d)-exp(c));
psi = (d-c);

auxVar = double((b - a) ./ (k .* pi) ...
        .* ( sin(k .* pi .* (d - a) ./ (b - a)) - ...
        sin(k .* pi .* (c - a) ./ (b - a)) ));

psi(2:end,:) = auxVar(2:end,:);

chi1 = 1 ./ ( 1 + ( k .* pi ./ (b - a) ) .^ 2 );
chi2 = exp(d) .* cos(k .* pi .* (d - a) ./ (b - a)) ...
        - exp(c) .* cos(k .* pi .* (c - a) ./ (b - a));
chi3 = k .* pi ./ (b - a) .* ...
        ( exp(d) .* sin(k .* pi .* (d - a) ./ (b - a)) ...
        - exp(c) .* sin(k .* pi .* (c - a) ./ (b - a)) );

auxVar = chi1 .* (chi2 + chi3);

chi(2:end,:) = auxVar(2:end,:);

end
```

Figure 5.20   Matlab code for determining the coefficients in the cosine expansion

(I)   For the first numerical experiment we consider a benchmark value for the number of grid points. To this end we take Ngrid = 8192. In order to compare the stability of the suggested valuation algorithms we consider the percentage differences in prices for the Heston model and the Variance Gamma model. We choose the following parameter sets:

- Heston: $S(0) = 100, r = d = 0, T = 1, V(0) = \theta = 0.04, \kappa = 0.5, v = 0.2$ and $\rho = -0.8$
- Variance Gamma: $S(0) = 100, r = d = 0, T = 1, \sigma = 0.25, v = 2.0$ and $\theta = -0.1$.

For both models we calculate the prices with respect to the strikes $1, 2, \ldots, 200$. Our findings are summarized in Figures 5.21 to 5.24. Our observation is that the cosine method shows the best performance in terms of stability, whereas the other methods show the same stability.

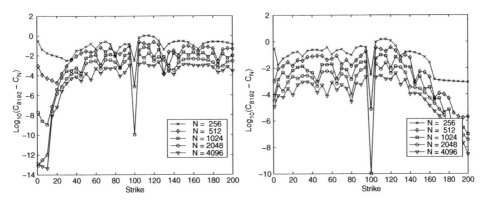

Figure 5.21   Relative differences in the option prices obtained by applying the Black–Scholes (left) extended method and the Carr–Madan (right) method to illustrate the stability of the methods for the Heston model. Considered are the percentage differences taking Ngrid = 8192 and grids with Ngrid = 4096, 1024, 512, 256

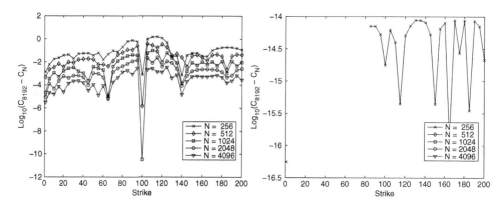

Figure 5.22 Relative differences in the option prices obtained by applying the Lewis extended method (left) and the COS method (right) to illustrate the stability of the methods for the Heston model. Considered are the percentage differences taking Ngrid = 8192 and grids with Ngrid = 256, 512, 1024, 2048, 4096

(II) For this test we have chosen two different number of grid points, Ngrid = 4096 and Ngrid = 8192. We consider the Variance Gamma model with the parameters given above. Then, we price European Call options for the strike range $K = 1, 2, \ldots, 200$ with different methods. Figure 5.25 summarizes our findings. We see that the COS method is the most stable method and that for deep OTM European Calls the stability is less accurate than for ITM/ATM and slightly OTM European Call options.

Now, let us consider a fixed strike value K and the percentage difference using different values for Ngrid. Our reference value is Ngrid = 26214. We perform this computation for $K = 50, 100, 150$ and display the results in Figure 5.26.

(III) We consider the pricing of 110 option prices. The current spot price is $S(0) = 2781$, the risk neutral rate is 4% and we assume that the underlying pays no dividends. The strikes

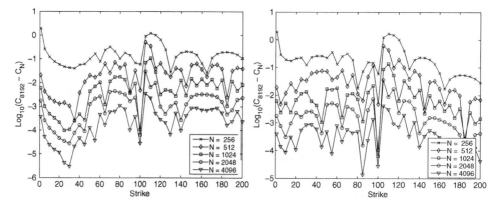

Figure 5.23 Relative differences in the option prices obtained by applying the Black–Scholes extended method (left) and the Carr–Madan method (right) to illustrate the stability of the methods for the Variance Gamma model. Considered are the percentage differences taking Ngrid = 8192 and grids with Ngrid = 256, 512, 1024, 2048, 4096

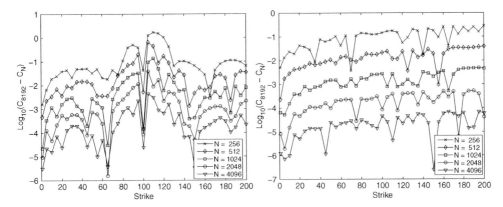

Figure 5.24 Relative differences in the option prices obtained by applying the Lewis extended method (left) and the COS method (right) to illustrate the stability of the methods for the variance gamma model. Considered are the percentage differences taking Ngrid = 8192 and grids with Ngrid = 256, 1024, 2048, 4096

$k = 0.5, \ldots, 1$, quoted as moneyness, and the maturity T as well as the quoted volatilities are given by Figure 5.27.

The results we observed are summarized in Tables 5.3 and 5.4.

We see that the runtime does not depend on the strike price but that the accuracy of the methods differs considerably. However, it needs to be said that it might be possible to increase the accuracy of the CONV method as well as of the Carr–Madan method by choosing different values for the dampening parameter α. Furthermore, we observe that the number of grid points does not impact the Lewis method. This is due to the fact that we calculate one single integral.

As a final example we consider the methods and show the results for pricing a European Call option in the Variance Gamma model with parameters $\sigma = 0.12$, $v = 0.2$ and $\theta = -0.14$.

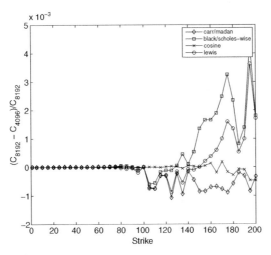

Figure 5.25 Percentage difference of values for European Call option prices computed with Ngrid = 8192 and Ngrid = 4096 grid points along a strike range $1, 2, \ldots, 200$

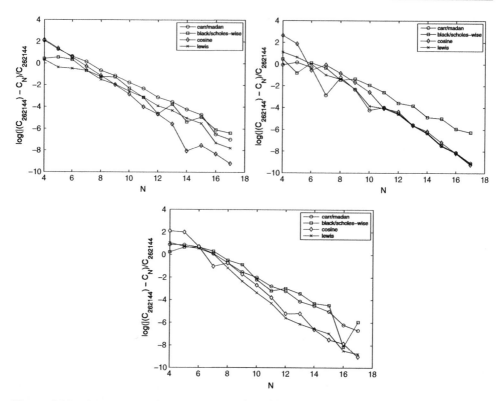

Figure 5.26 The percentage difference between the value of a European Call option with strike 50 (top left), 100 (top right) and 150 (bottom) calculated with a different number of grid points. The reference value is Ngrid = 26214

We take $S(0) = 100$ and $K =$ and two different maturities. One is a short dated option with $T = 0.1$ and the other is a long dated option with $T = 5$. To illustrate our results we have plotted the grid size 2^n against the logarithmic relative error given by

$$\log \text{rel. error} = \log\left(\left|\frac{V - V_{\text{ref}}}{V_{\text{ref}}}\right|\right),$$

the grid size against the CPU time and, finally, the CPU time against the logarithmic relative error. The results are displayed in Figures 5.28, 5.29 and 5.30. Our results suggest that the COS method is the most effective method for pricing the options and is especially well suited for calibration.

K/T	0.52	1.02	1.52	2.02	2.52	3.02	3.52	4.02	4.52	5.02
0.5	39.29%	36.44%	34.64%	33.52%	32.50%	31.93%	31.57%	31.35%	31.15%	31.05%
0.6	37.37%	34.31%	32.68%	31.79%	30.99%	30.59%	30.37%	30.28%	30.17%	30.16%
0.7	34,61%	31.90%	30.59%	30.01%	29.46%	29.26%	29.18%	29.21%	29.20%	29.28%
0.8	31.13%	29.27%	28.42%	28.20%	27.94%	27.93%	28.00%	28.15%	28.25%	28.42%
0.9	27.15%	26.50%	26.22%	26.41%	26.43%	26.62%	26.84%	27.11%	27.31%	27.56%
1.0	22.97%	23.70%	24.03%	24.64%	24.97%	25.34%	25.70%	26.10%	26.39%	26.73%
1.1	19.06%	20.97%	21.90%	22.94%	23.55%	24.10%	24.60%	25.12%	25.50%	25.91%
1.2	17.00%	18.75%	19.98%	21.33%	22.19%	22.91%	23.54%	24.16%	24.63%	25.12%
1.3	16.75%	17.50%	18.54%	19.97%	20.97%	21.79%	22.52%	23.25%	23.79%	24.35%
1.4	16.75%	17.13%	17.68%	18.93%	19.94%	20.80%	21.60%	22.39%	22.99%	23.60%
1.5	16.75%	17.12%	17.31%	18.23%	19.13%	19.97%	20.78%	21.61%	22.25%	22.90%

Figure 5.27 Volatility matrix for the numerical performance test of the different integration methods

Table 5.3   CPU times (msec) for pricing options for different $N = 10, \ldots, 16$ and applying the methods reviewed in Chapter 5

Method	$N = 10$	$N = 11$	$N = 12$	$N = 13$	$N = 14$	$N = 15$	$N = 16$
Strike = 80							
COS	1.4040	2.1840	3.9000	6.8640	11.8561	27.1442	59.7484
CONV	1.0920	2.0280	3.9000	7.3320	14.0401	31.6682	64.5844
Lewis	1.0920	1.8720	3.1200	6.3960	11.7001	24.3362	52.7283
CM	1.0920	1.7160	3.1200	5.6160	12.4801	24.8042	50.3883
Strike = 100							
COS	1.4040	2.0280	3.4320	6.2400	11.5441	23.5562	54.4443
CONV	0.9360	1.7160	3.1200	6.3960	10.6081	25.5842	55.0684
Lewis	1.0920	1.8720	3.2760	6.0840	12.0121	24.8042	55.3804
CM	1.0920	1.8720	3.2760	5.6160	10.9201	20.4361	49.9203
Strike = 120							
COS	1.4040	2.1840	3.7440	6.8640	13.2601	26.8322	61.3084
CONV	1.0920	2.1840	4.0560	7.6440	13.4161	31.0442	62.8684
Lewis	1.0920	2.0280	3.7440	6.0840	12.3241	24.1802	54.2883
CM	1.0920	1.8720	3.1200	5.7720	10.9201	24.0242	48.0483

5.8.1   Other Issues

There are other issues apart from choosing the semi-analytic method for option pricing. Since we only compute the prices at discrete points, the option price to a given strike might not be part of the discrete set of points. To this end we have to apply interpolation. Thus, the choice of the interpolation scheme impacts the calculated price.

For numerical integration there exist numerous methods. We consider the impact of the choice of an integration scheme on option prices. We do not consider the *fractional Fourier*

Table 5.4   Error to option prices for different $N = 10, \ldots, 16$ and the methods reviewed in Chapter 5

Method	$N = 10$	$N = 11$	$N = 12$	$N = 13$	$N = 14$	$N = 15$	$N = 16$
Strike = 80							
COS	0	0	0	0	0	0	0
CONV	0.0157	0.0039	0.0010	0.0002	0.0001	0	0
Lewis	−0.3172	0.0067	−0.0106	−0.0033	−0.0033	−0.0032	−0.0031
CM	30.3327	8.4634	−1.2634	−0.4965	0.1215	0.0313	0.0074
Strike = 100							
COS	0	0	0	0	0	0	0
CONV	0.3697	0.3697	0.3697	0.3697	0.3697	0.3697	0.3697
Lewis	−0.008	−0.008	−0.008	−0.008	−0.008	−0.008	−0.008
CM	−180.1	−180.1	−180.1	−180.1	−180.1	−180.1	−180.1
Strike = 120							
COS	0	0	0	0	0	0	0
CONV	3.7657	0.9413 0.	0.2353	0.0588	0.0147	0.0037	0.0009
Lewis	−82.3409	−39.1081	−18.0904	−7.8295	−2.7731	−0.2650	−0.1502
CM	−105.1592	−59.6296	−30.6053	−14.8230	−6.6811	−2.5572	−0.4833

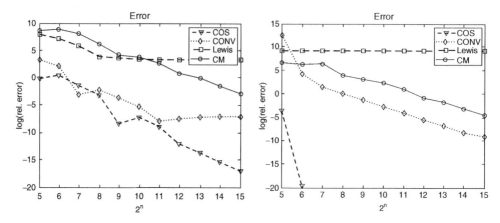

Figure 5.28 Number of grid points against the logarithmic absolute percentage error when pricing a European Call option in the Variance Gamma model for different valuation methods with maturities $T = 0.1$ (left) and $T = 5$ (right)

transform technique or discuss its relevance for solving option pricing problems here, since we have observed that the results obtained by standard techniques are very reasonable.

Interpolation

Matlab provides six standard interpolation methods:

- `nearest`; the interpolation is given by the value of the nearest neighbour
- `linear`; the standard method
- `cubic`; same as `pchip`
- `spline`; cubic spline
- `pchip`; piecewise cubic Hermite interpolation
- `v5cubic`; cubic interpolation of Matlab V5.

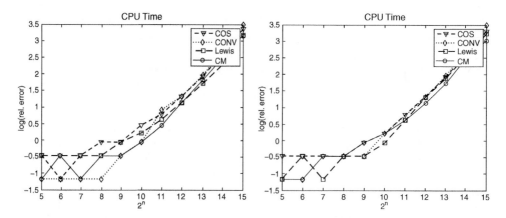

Figure 5.29 Number of grid points against the CPU time in milliseconds when pricing a European Call option in the Variance Gamma model for different valuation methods with maturities $T = 0.1$ (left) and $T = 5$ (right)

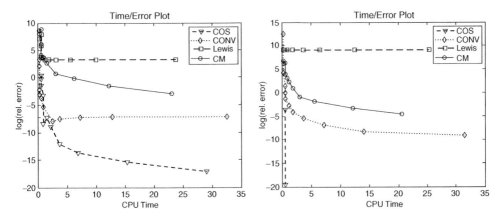

Figure 5.30 CPU time in milliseconds against the logarithmic absolute percentage error when pricing a European Call option in the Variance Gamma model for different valuation methods with maturities $T = 0.1$ (left) and $T = 5$ (right)

When we were looking at the methods introduced in this chapter, we assumed some interpolation method when computing the option value at a given strike.

Let us consider the case of the Variance Gamma model with $S(0) = 100, T = 1, r = d = 0$. The model parameters we have chosen are $\sigma = 0.12$, $\theta = -0.14$ and $v = 0.2$. As the pricing algorithm we have chosen the Carr–Madan method for the strikes 80.76, 100.09, ..., 120.5. The results are shown in Table 5.5.

Integration Scheme

We expect that the numerical integration scheme will impact the final price. Using a poor integration method is not appropriate and leads to instabilities. We do not give the results obtained by using different integration schemes here since we observed that the differences are small. We applied the Matlab built-in integration schemes, but our considerations using several Gaussian quadrature rules always led to reasonable results.

5.9 EXTENDING THE METHODS TO FORWARD START OPTIONS

For many models it is possible to extend the applicability of the methods provided in this chapter to forward start options. Such options are basic building blocks of *Cliquet options*. To

Table 5.5 The standard interpolation methods of Matlab applied to value a Call option within the Variance Gamma model with $\sigma = 0.12$, $\theta = -0.14$ and $v = 0.2$. The strikes are 80.76, 100.09 and 120.5. The relative difference is plotted in basis points. The reference value is the value computed using the Lewis method

Strike	nearest	linear	spline	pchip	cubic	v5cubic
80.76	92.2409	0.1360	−0.0021	−0.0022	−0.0022	−0.0021
100.09	218.0903	−0.7211	−0.0366	−0.0384	−0.0384	−0.0366
120.5	296.9527	−8.9003	0.1124	0.0199	0.0199	0.1124

fix ideas and to define the general Cliquet option on one underlying we introduce the return R_n, which is also known as the performance of an asset S over the time interval $[t_{n-1}, t_n]$, by

$$R_n := \frac{S(t_n)}{S(t_{n-1})} - 1. \tag{5.57}$$

The value $S(t_n)$ represents the closing price at time t_n. Typically, the time period differs from values of one month to one year. Thus, typical values for $t_n - t_{n-1}$ are $1/12, 0.25, 0.5$ or 1.

The maximum loss to be taken is reflected by a *local floor, LF*. The maximum gain is reflected by a *local cap, LC*:

$$U_n := \mathrm{Min}\,(\mathrm{Max}\,(LF, R_n), LC). \tag{5.58}$$

Since the Cliquet is an average over such periods, we have to glue all components together to compute the price. We consider the arithmetic or the geometric Cliquet, depending on the averaging technique we apply. We can further control the overall payoff by introducing a maximum loss level, the global floor, denoted by GF, and a maximal upside level, the global cap, denoted by GC. The arithmetic Cliquet option pays

$$\mathrm{Min}\left(\mathrm{Max}\left(GF, \sum_{n=1}^{N} U_n\right), GC\right). \tag{5.59}$$

The geometric Cliquet option is represented by the payoff

$$\mathrm{Min}\left(\mathrm{Max}\left(GF, \prod_{n=1}^{N} U_n\right), GC\right). \tag{5.60}$$

For such options the relevant risk factor is the dynamic of the forward implied volatility surface of the model.

In what follows we show that the methods described in this chapter can be applied to price forward starting options in affine models and for a class of (stochastic volatility) Lévy models. To this end we consider the *forward characteristic function*. We explain how to derive it for affine models such as the Heston model and stochastic volatility Lévy model (see Beyer, P. and Kienitz, J. (2009)).

Affine Models   Suppose the characteristic function φ of a model is given by

$$\varphi = e^{A+BX},$$

where A and B are matrices. Thus, $A + BX$ is an affine linear function in X. Utilizing the results in Duffie, D., Pan, J. and Singleton, K. (2000) the characteristic function of $X(T) - X(t)$ is given in closed form and we can apply it to the derivation of the forward characteristic function.

$$
\begin{aligned}
\mathbb{E}[e^{iu_1(X(T)-X(t))}] &= \mathbb{E}[e^{-iu_1 X(t)}\mathbb{E}[e^{iu_1 X(T)}|\mathcal{F}_t]] \\
&= \mathbb{E}[e^{-iu_1 X(t)}\varphi(u1, 0, \tau, x(t), v(t))] \\
&= e^{A(u_1,0,\tau)}\mathbb{E}[e^{B(u1,0,\tau)v(t)}] \\
&= e^{A(u_1,0,\tau)}\mathbb{E}[e^{i(-iB(u1,0,\tau)v(t))}] \\
&= e^{A(u_1,0,\tau)}\varphi(0, -iB(u1,0,\tau), t, v(0), x(0)) \\
&= e^{A(u_1,0,\tau)}e^{A(0,-iB(u_1,0,\tau),t)+B(0,-iB(u_1,0,\tau),t)v(0)}.
\end{aligned}
$$

Thus, for an affine model the forward characteristic function can be derived and it is possible to price forward start options using the numerical methods described in this chapter.

For the Heston stochastic volatility model we have the forward characteristic function as in Chapter 2, Equation (2.56) but with the quantity G replaced by:

$$\tilde{G} = \frac{k - \rho v u i - D - i u_2 \omega}{k - \rho v u i + D - i u_2 \omega}.$$

(Time Changed) Lévy Models   Below, we review the results obtained by Beyer, P. and Kienitz, J. (2009) for time-changed Lévy models. To fix notation we take $0 \le t^* < T$ to be the forward start time t^* and T the maturity of the option. We consider the Lévy process $X(t)$ and an integrated time change $Y(t)$. The time change process is the integral of a positive process $y(t)$ which is not necessarily a Lévy process; it can, for instance, be a deterministic process. We assume $X(t)$ and $Y(t)$ to be independent. For the characteristic function of $Z_t \equiv X_{Y_t}$ we derive an expression of the form

$$\varphi_{Z_t}(u) \equiv \mathbb{E}[\exp(iu Z_t)] = \varphi_{Y_t}(-i\psi_X(u)). \tag{5.61}$$

The above expression ψ_X denotes the *characteristic exponent* of X which is $\varphi_{X_t}(u) = \exp(t\psi_X)$.

For the particular examples we assume that the process Y is either a CIR process or a generalized Ornstein–Uhlenbeck process.

The log forward returns are defined by

$$s_{t^*,T} := \log\left(\frac{S_T}{S_{t^*}}\right). \tag{5.62}$$

Using $\mathbb{E}[\exp(X_{Y_t})] = \varphi_{Z_t}(-i)$ we have

$$\begin{aligned}
\varphi_{s_{t^*,T}}(u) &= \mathbb{E}[\exp(iu s_{t^*,T})] \\
&= \exp\left(iu\left[r(T - t^*) - \log\frac{\varphi_{Z_T}(-i)}{\varphi_{Z_{t^*}}(-i)}\right]\right) \\
&\quad \times \underbrace{\mathbb{E}[\exp(iu(Z_T - Z_{t^*}))]}_{=f_1(u)}.
\end{aligned} \tag{5.63}$$

Thus, the characteristic function of the time change processes can be computed if there is an explicit expression for f_1. Let us assume that the stochastic clock starts at $y_0 = 1$. To calculate $\varphi_{s_{t^*,T}}(u)$ we set

$$f_1(u) := \mathbb{E}[\exp(iu(Z_T - Z_{t^*})).$$

Based on the tower property of conditional expectations we set

$$\begin{aligned}
f_1(u) &= \mathbb{E}\left[\mathbb{E}\left[\exp(iu(X_{t_1} - X_{t_2}))\right]\big|_{t_1=Y_T, t_2=Y_{t^*}}\right] \\
&= \mathbb{E}\left[\mathbb{E}\left[\exp(iu(X_{t_1-t_2}))\right]\big|_{t_1=Y_T, t_2=Y_{t^*}}\right].
\end{aligned}$$

Further simplification gives

$$
\begin{aligned}
f_1(u) &= \mathbb{E}\left[\exp((Y_T - Y_{t^*})\psi_X(u))\right] \\
&= \mathbb{E}\left[\mathbb{E}\left[\exp\left(i(-i)\psi_X(u)\int_{t^*}^{T} y(s)\mathrm{d}s\right)\bigg| y_{t^*}\right]\right] \\
&= \mathbb{E}\left[\varphi_{Y_{T-t^*}}^{y_{t^*}}(-i\psi_X(u))\right],
\end{aligned}
$$

where $\varphi_{Y_{T-t^*}}^{y_{t^*}}$ is the characteristic function of Y evaluated at $T - t^*$ with initial value y_{t^*}. We assume that the latter expression is of the form

$$
\varphi_{Y_{T-t^*}}^{y_{t^*}}(u) = f_2(u)\exp(if_3(u)y_{t^*}).
$$

Finally, we get the expression suitable for presenting the results for the models.

$$
\begin{aligned}
f_1(u) &= f_2(-i\psi_X(u))\mathbb{E}\left[\exp(if_3(-i\psi_X(u))y_{t^*})\right] \\
&= f_2(-i\psi_X(u))\varphi_{y_{t^*}}(f_3(-i\psi_X(u))).
\end{aligned} \tag{5.64}
$$

In what follows we give the representation for (5.64) for some well-known financial models. We use the same notation as in Chapter 3.

5.9.1 Forward Characteristic Function for Lévy Processes and CIR Time Change

Set $\gamma(u) = \sqrt{\kappa^2 - 2\lambda^2 iu}$. Depending on the Lévy process X we have

$$
\begin{aligned}
f_1(u) &= f_2(-i\psi_X(u))\left(1 - \frac{1}{2}if_3(-i\psi_X(u))\frac{\lambda^2}{\kappa}\left(1 - \exp\left(-\kappa t^*\right)\right)\right)^{-2\kappa\eta/\lambda^2} \\
&\quad \times \exp\left(\frac{if_3(-i\psi_X(u))y_0\exp(-\kappa t^*)}{1 - \frac{1}{2}if_3(-i\psi_X(u))\frac{\lambda^2}{\kappa}(1 - \exp(-\kappa t^*))}\right)
\end{aligned} \tag{5.65}
$$

$$
f_2(u) = \frac{\exp(\kappa^2\eta(T - t^*)/\lambda^2)}{(\cosh(\gamma(u)(T - t^*)/2) + \kappa\sinh(\gamma(u)(T - t^*)/2)/\gamma(u))^{2\kappa\eta/\lambda^2}} \tag{5.66}
$$

$$
f_3(u) = \frac{2u}{\kappa + \gamma(u)\coth(\gamma(u)(T - t^*)/2)}. \tag{5.67}
$$

The characteristic function for $Z(t) = X_{Y_t}$ at time T evaluated at $-i$ is

$$
\begin{aligned}
\varphi_{Z(T)}^{(X-\mathrm{CIR})}(-i) &= \exp(\kappa^2\eta T/\lambda^2) \\
&\quad \exp\left(\frac{2y_0 i(-i)\psi_X(-i)}{\kappa + \gamma((-i)\psi_X(-i))\coth(\gamma((-i)\psi_X(-i))T/2)}\right) \\
&\quad \Big/ \left[\cosh\left(\frac{1}{2}\gamma((-i)\psi_X(-i))T\right)\right. \\
&\quad \left. + \frac{\kappa}{\gamma((-i)\psi_X(-i))}\sinh\left(\frac{1}{2}\gamma((-i)\psi_X(-i))T\right)\right]^{2\kappa\eta/\lambda^2}.
\end{aligned} \tag{5.68}
$$

and finally we get

$$
\varphi_{S_{t^*},T}^{(X-\mathrm{CIR})}(u) = \exp\left(iu\left[r(T - t^*) - \log\frac{\varphi_{Z(T)}(-i)}{\varphi_{Z(t^*)}(-i)}\right]\right)f_1(u). \tag{5.69}
$$

```
function phi = cf_vgcir_fwd_start(u,T,t_star,r,d, varargin)
y0 = 1;          % clock start
% characteristic exponents
psiX_u = (-1i)*C*log(G*M./(G*M+(M-G)*1i*u+u.*u));   %-i * psi(u)
psiX_i = (-1i)*C*log(G*M/(G*M+(M-G)-1));            %-i * psi(-i)

% calculating f2, f3 and f1
gamma_u = sqrt(kappa^2-2*lambda^2*1i*psiX_u); %gamma(u)
gamma_i = sqrt(kappa^2-2*lambda^2*1i*psiX_i); %gamma(-i)

f2_u=exp(kappa^2*eta*(T-t_star)/(lambda^2))...
     ./((cosh(0.5*gamma_u*(T-t_star))  ...
     + kappa * sinh(0.5*gamma_u * (T-t_star))  ...
     ./ gamma_u).^(2*kappa*eta/lambda^2));%f2(-i psi(u))
f3_u=2*psiX_u./(kappa+gamma_u...
     .*coth(gamma_u*(T-t_star)/2));%f3(-i psi(u))
%f_1(-ipsi(u))
f1_u=f2_u .* (1-0.5*1i*f3_u*lambda^2/kappa*(1-exp(-kappa*t_star)))...
     .^(-2*kappa*eta/lambda^2).* exp(1i*f3_u*y0*exp(-kappa*t_star)  ...
     ./(1-0.5*1i*f3_u*lambda^2/kappa*(1-exp(-kappa*t_star)))));
%phi_Z(t)(-i)
phi_T = exp(kappa^2*eta*T*lambda^(-2))...
     *exp(2*y0*1i*psiX_i/(kappa+gamma_i*coth(gamma_i*T/2)))  ...
     ./ ( cosh(0.5*gamma_i*T) + kappa*sinh(0.5*gamma_i*T)./gamma_i )...
     .^(2*kappa*eta*lambda^(-2));

%phi_Z(t^*)(-i)
phi_tstar = exp(kappa^2*eta*t_star*lambda^(-2))...
     *exp(2*y0*1i*psiX_i/(kappa+gamma_i*coth(gamma_i*t_star/2)))  ...
     ./ ( cosh(0.5*gamma_i*t_star)...
     + kappa*sinh(0.5*gamma_i*t_star)./gamma_i ).^(2*kappa*eta/lambda^2);

%phi_st^*,T(u), s_t^*,T = ln(S_T/S_t^*)
phi = exp(1i*u*(r*(T-t_star)-log(phi_T/phi_tstar))) .* f1_u;
end
```

Figure 5.31 Matlab code for the forward start characteristic function of the Variance Gamma model with CIR stochastic time change

Matlab Code   We only list the corresponding Matlab code for the Variance Gamma model in Figure 5.31 and the Normal Inverse Gaussian model in Figure 5.32 with a stochastic clock driven by a square root process, CIR clock.

5.9.2 Forward Characteristic Function for Lévy Processes and Gamma-OU Time Change

We consider the forward characteristic function of a Lévy process being time-changed with the process from Equation (3.19). In this case the characteristic functions for ΓOU process and the integrated process are

$$\varphi_{y_t}^{(\Gamma-\text{OU})}(u) = \exp\left(iy_0 \exp(-\lambda t)u + a \log\left(\frac{1 - i/b \exp(-\lambda t)u}{1 - i/bu}\right)\right) \tag{5.70}$$

```
function phi = cf_nigcir_fwd_start(u,T,t_star,r,d,varargin)
y0 = 1;                    % clock start
% characteristic exponents
psiX_u = (-1i) * (-delta)*(sqrt(alpha^2-(beta+1i*u).^2)...
    -sqrt(alpha^2-beta^2));  % -i * psi(u)
psiX_i = (-1i) * (-delta)*(sqrt(alpha^2-(beta+1)^2)...
-sqrt(alpha^2-beta^2));       % -i * psi(i)

% calculating f2, f3 and f1
gamma_u = sqrt(kappa^2-2*lambda^2*1i*psiX_u);  %gamma(u)
gamma_i = sqrt(kappa^2-2*lambda^2*1i*psiX_i);  %gamma(-i)

f2_u = (kappa^2*eta*(T-t_star)/(lambda^2))...
    -log(cosh(0.5*gamma_u*diag(T-t_star))...
    +kappa*sinh(0.5*gamma_u*(T-t_star))./gamma_u)...
    *(2*kappa*eta*lambda^(-2));  %f2(-i psi(u))
%f3(-i psi(u))
f3_u = 2*psiX_u./(kappa+gamma_u.*coth(gamma_u*(T-t_star)/2));
%f_1(-ipsi(u))
f1_u = f2_u + log(1-0.5*1i*f3_u*lambda^2/kappa...
    *(1-exp(-kappa*t_star)))*(-2*kappa*eta*lambda^(-2)) ...
    + 1i*f3_u*y0*exp(-kappa*t_star)...
    ./(1-0.5*1i*f3_u*lambda^2/kappa*(1-exp(-kappa*t_star))));
%phi_Z(t)(-i)
phi_T = kappa^2*eta*T*lambda^(-2) ...
    + 2*y0*1i*psiX_i./(kappa+gamma_i*coth(gamma_i*T/2)) ...
    - log( cosh(0.5*gamma_i*T) ...
    + kappa*sinh(0.5*gamma_i*T)/gamma_i )*(2*kappa*eta/lambda^2);
%phi_Z(t^*)(-i)
phi_tstar = kappa^2*eta*t_star*lambda^(-2)    ...
    + 2*y0*1i*psiX_i/(kappa+gamma_i*coth(gamma_i*t_star/2)) ...
    - log( cosh(0.5*gamma_i*t_star) ...
    + kappa*sinh(0.5*gamma_i*t_star)/gamma_i )*(2*kappa*eta/lambda^2);

%phi_st^*,T(u), s_t^*,T = ln(S_T/S_t^*)
phi = exp(1i*u*((r-d).*(T-t_star)-(phi_T - phi_tstar)) + f1_u);

end
```

Figure 5.32 Matlab code for the forward start characteristic function of the Normal Inverse Gaussian model with CIR stochastic time change

and

$$\varphi_{Y_t}^{(\Gamma-\text{OU})}(u) = \exp\left(iy_0\lambda^{-1}(1-\exp(-\lambda t))u\right.$$

$$\left. + \frac{\lambda a}{iu-\lambda b}\left(b\log\left(\frac{b}{b-iu\lambda^{-1}(1-\exp(-\lambda t))}\right)-iut\right)\right). \quad (5.71)$$

Finally, we obtain

$$f_1(u) = \exp\left(\frac{i(T-t^*)u\lambda a}{\lambda b - iu}\right) \quad (5.72)$$

$$\times \exp\left(\frac{ab\lambda}{b\lambda-iu}\log\left(1-\frac{iu}{\lambda b}(1-\exp(-(T-t^*)\lambda))\right)\right)$$

$$f_2(u) = \frac{1}{\lambda}(1 - \exp(-\lambda(T - t^*)))u \tag{5.73}$$

$$f_3(u) = f_1(-i\Psi_X(u))\exp\left(iy_0\exp(-\lambda t^*)f_2(-i\Psi_X(u))\right)$$

$$\times \exp\left(a\log\left(\frac{1 - i/b\exp(-\lambda t^*)f_2(-i\Psi_X(u))}{1 - i/bf_2(-i\Psi_X(u))}\right)\right). \tag{5.74}$$

Again, we use the characteristic exponent and the characteristic function corresponding to Z and we find

$$\varphi_{Z(T)}^{(X-\Gamma-OU)}(-i) = \exp(i\psi_X(-i)y_0\lambda^{-1}(1 - \exp(-\lambda T))) \tag{5.75}$$

$$+ \left[\frac{\lambda a}{i\psi_X(-i) - \lambda b}\left(b\log\left(\frac{b}{b - i\psi_X(-i)\lambda^{-1}(1 - \exp(-\lambda T))}\right) - i\psi_X(-i)T\right)\right].$$

Finally, we get

$$\varphi_{S_{t^*},T}^{(X-\Gamma-OU)}(u) = \exp\left(iu\left[r(T - t^*) - \log\frac{\varphi_{Z(T)}(-i)}{\varphi_{Z(t^*)}(-i)}\right]\right)f_1(u). \tag{5.76}$$

For the sake of completeness we give the forward characteristic functions of the Variance Gamma (VG) and the Normal Inverse Gaussian (NIG) model.

VG and NIG Model without Time Change   For the VG model we have

$$\varphi_{X_1}^{(VG)}(u) = \left(\frac{GM}{GM + (M - G)iu + u^2}\right)^C$$

$$\varphi_{X_1}^{(VG)}(-i) = \left(\frac{GM}{GM + (M - G) - 1}\right)^C$$

and

$$\varphi_{S_{t^*},T}^{(VG)}(u) = \exp\left(iu\left[r(T - t^*) - \log\frac{\varphi_{X_1}(-i)^T}{\varphi_{X_1}(-i)^{t^*}}\right]\right)\varphi_{X_1}(u)^{T-t^*} \tag{5.77}$$

$$= \exp\left(iu(T - t^*)\left[r - \Psi_X^{(VG)}(-i)\right]\right)\varphi_{X_{T-t^*}}^{(VG)}(u).$$

For the NIG model we have

$$\varphi_{X_1}^{(NIG)}(u) = \exp\left((-\delta)\left(\sqrt{\alpha^2 - (\beta + iu)^2} - \sqrt{\alpha^2 - \beta^2}\right)\right)$$

$$\varphi_{X_1}^{(NIG)}(-i) = \exp\left((-\delta)\left(\sqrt{\alpha^2 - (\beta + 1)^2} - \sqrt{\alpha^2 - \beta^2}\right)\right)$$

and

$$\varphi_{S_{t^*},T}^{(NIG)}(u) = \exp\left(iu(T - t^*)\left[r - \Psi_X^{(NIG)}(-i)\right]\right)\varphi_{X_{T-t^*}}^{(NIG)}(u). \tag{5.78}$$

Matlab Code   Again, we give the Matlab code for the forward start characteristic function (Figures 5.33 and 5.34).

```
function phi = cf_vgou_fwd_start(u,T,tstar,r,d,varargin)
y0 = 1;                        % clock start
% characteristic exponents
psiX_u = (-1i)*C*log(G*M./(G*M+(M-G)*1i*u+u.*u));    %-i * psi(u)
psiX_i = (-1i)*C*log(G*M/(G*M+(M-G)-1));             %-i * psi(-i)

% Deriving f2, f3 and f1
f2_u = 1i*psiX_u*(T-tstar)*lambda*kappa./(lambda*eta-1i*psiX_u) ...
         + kappa*eta*lambda./(eta*lambda-1i*psiX_u) ...
         .*log(1-1i*psiX_u/(lambda*eta)) ...
         *(1-exp(-(T-tstar)*lambda)));              %f2(-i psi(u))
f3_u = 1/lambda*psiX_u*(1-exp(-lambda*(T-tstar)));  %f3(-i psi(u))
f1_u = f2_u + 1i*y0*exp(-lambda*tstar)*f3_u ...
         + kappa*log((1-1i/eta*exp(-lambda*tstar)*f3_u) ...
         ./(1-1i/eta*f3_u));                        %f_1(-ipsi(u))

% Computing the forward characteristic function
%phi_Z(t)(-i)
phi_T = 1i*psiX_i*y0*lambda^(-1)*(1-exp(-lambda*T)) ...
         + lambda*kappa./(1i*psiX_i-lambda*eta) ...
         .*(eta*log(eta./(eta-1i*psiX_i*lambda^(-1)*(1-exp(-lambda*T)))))...
         -1i*psiX_i*T);
%phi_Z(t^*)(-i)
phi_tstar = 1i*psiX_i*y0*lambda^(-1)*(1-exp(-lambda*tstar)) ...
         + lambda*kappa./(1i*psiX_i-lambda*eta) ...
         .*(eta*log(eta./(eta-1i*psiX_i/lambda ...
         *(1-exp(-lambda*tstar))))-1i*psiX_i*tstar);

%phi_st^*,T(u), s_t^*,T = ln(S_T/S_t^*)
phi = exp(1i*u*((r-d).*(T-tstar)-(phi_T-phi_tstar)) + f1_u);
end
```

Figure 5.33 Matlab code for the forward start characteristic function of the Variance Gamma model with Gamma Ornstein–Uhlenbeck stochastic time change

5.9.3 Results

Below we illustrate the use of the forward characteristic function for pricing forward start Call options. Later we verify the prices by comparing them to values obtained by applying Monte Carlo simulation. We have chosen to price a Call option with maturity of one year starting today, in one, two, three and five years' time. Since we base our pricing on the moneyness, S/K,

Table 5.6 Prices with respect to moneyness of a Call option. For the Merton process the forward prices are all the same. The columns refer to the prices for forward starting Calls at $t^* = 0, 1, 2, 5$ years

Moneyness	Price 1	Price 2	Price 3	Price 4
0,7	0,34695	0,34695	0,34695	0,34695
0,8	0,25929	0,25929	0,25929	0,25929
0,9	0,17634	0,17634	0,17634	0,17634
1	0,10603	0,10603	0,10603	0,10603
1,1	0,05551	0,05551	0,05551	0,05551
1,2	0,0253	0,0253	0,0253	0,0253
1,3	0,01015	0,01015	0,01015	0,01015

```
function phi = cf_nigou_fwd_start(u,T,tstar,r,d,varargin)
y0 = 1;                         % clock start
% characteristic exponents
psiX_u = (-1i) * (-delta)*(sqrt(alpha^2-(beta+1i*u).^2)...
        -sqrt(alpha^2-beta^2));                   %-i * psi(u)
psiX_i = (-1i) * (-delta)*(sqrt(alpha^2-(beta+1)^2)...
        -sqrt(alpha^2-beta^2));                   %-i * psi(-i)

% Deriving f2, f3 and f1
f2_u = 1i*psiX_u*(T-tstar)*lambda*a./(lambda*b-1i*psiX_u) ...
     + a*b*lambda./(b*lambda-1i*psiX_u).*log(1 - 1i*psiX_u/(lambda*b)...
     *(1-exp(-(T-tstar)*lambda)));                %f2(-i psi(u))
f3_u = 1/lambda*psiX_u*(1-exp(-lambda*(T-tstar)));   %f3(-i psi(u))
%f_1(-ipsi(u))
f1_u = f2_u + 1i*y0*exp(-lambda*tstar)*f3_u ...
     +a*log((1-1i/b*exp(-lambda*tstar)*f3_u)./(1-1i/b*f3_u));

% Computing the forward characteristic function
%phi_Z(t)(-i)
phi_T = 1i*psiX_i*y0*lambda^(-1)*(1-exp(-lambda*T)) ...
    + lambda*a./(1i*psiX_i-lambda*b).*(b*log(b./(b-1i*psiX_i*lambda^(-1)...
    *(1-exp(-lambda*T)))))-1i*psiX_i*T);
%phi_Z(t^*)(-i)
phi_tstar = 1i*psiX_i*y0*lambda^(-1)*(1-exp(-lambda*tstar)) ...
    + lambda*a./(1i*psiX_i-lambda*b).*(b*log(b./(b-1i*psiX_i*lambda^(-1)...
    *(1-exp(-lambda*tstar)))))-1i*psiX_i*tstar);

%phi_st^*,T(u),  s_t^*,T = ln(S_T/S_t^*)
phi = exp(1i*u*((r-d).*(T-tstar)-(phi_T-phi_tstar)) + f1_u);

end
```

Figure 5.34 Matlab code for the forward start characteristic function of the Normal Inverse Gaussian model with Gamma Ornstein–Uhlenbeck stochastic time change

the process starts at 1. We have chosen $r = 4\%$ and $d = 0\%$. The corresponding prices are labelled as Price1, Price2, Price3 and Price4. We have applied the standard Fourier transform method together with the derived characteristic functions to price the options.

Merton Jump We use the model parameters $\sigma = 0, 152861$, $\mu_J = -0, 88229$, $\sigma_J = 0, 000271941$ and $\lambda = 0, 0813494$.

VG We use the parameters $C = 1, 2022$, $G = 4, 2276$ and $Y = 18, 2317$. We expect that the prices *Price1*, ..., *Price4* are the same for a given moneyness since the floating smile property holds. The numerical results in Table 5.7 verify this.

NIG We use the model parameters $\alpha = 8, 72609$, $\beta = -6, 90168$ and $\delta = 0, 169428$.

We expect that the prices *Price1*, ..., *Price4* are the same for a given moneyness since the floating smile property holds. The numerical results in Table 5.8 verify this.

VG Stochastic Volatility We use the model parameters $C = 6, 47043$, $G = 11, 1021$, $M = 33, 4128$, $\lambda = 0, 939691$, $a = 0, 629078$ and $b = 1, 46587$ for the Variance Gamma

Table 5.7 Prices with respect to moneyness of a Call option for the VG process with parameters $C = 1,2022$, $G = 4,2276$ and $Y = 18,2317$. The columns refer to the prices for forward starting Calls at $t^* = 0, 1, 2, 5$ years

Moneyness	Price 1	Price 2	Price 3	Price 4
0,7	0,33989	0,33989	0,33989	0,33989
0,8	0,25567	0,25567	0,25567	0,25567
0,9	0,17895	0,17895	0,17895	0,17895
1	0,11261	0,11261	0,11261	0,11261
1,1	0,05989	0,05989	0,05989	0,05989
1,2	0,02409	0,02409	0,02409	0,02409
1,3	0,00718	0,00718	0,00718	0,00718

Table 5.8 Prices with respect to moneyness of a Call option. For the NIG process the forward prices are all the same

Moneyness	Price 1	Price 2	Price 3	Price 4
0,7	0,34241	0,34241	0,34241	0,34241
0,8	0,25761	0,25761	0,25761	0,25761
0,9	0,17946	0,17946	0,17946	0,17946
1	0,11133	0,11133	0,11133	0,11133
1,1	0,05788	0,05788	0,05788	0,05788
1,2	0,0236	0,0236	0,0236	0,0236
1,3	0,00765	0,00765	0,00765	0,00765

Table 5.9 Prices with respect to moneyness of a Call option. For the VG GOU and VG CIR process the forward prices are all the same

Moneyness	Price 1	Price 2	Price 3	Price 4
VG GOU				
0,7	0,33639	0,33169	0,32527	0,32026
0,8	0,25081	0,24659	0,24021	0,23509
0,9	0,1738	0,16869	0,16218	0,15685
1	0,1092	0,10131	0,09421	0,08848
1,1	0,06025	0,04873	0,0405	0,034
1,2	0,02807	0,0155	0,00765	0,00326
1,3	0,01066	0,0028	0,00087	0,00039
VG CIR				
0,7	0,3354	0,32847	0,32468	0,32474
0,8	0,24966	0,24388	0,23952	0,23923
0,9	0,17242	0,1667	0,16171	0,16101
1	0,10734	0,10017	0,09479	0,09377
1,1	0,05783	0,04852	0,04358	0,0425
1,2	0,02566	0,01625	0,0132	0,01253
1,3	0,00909	0,0036	0,00268	0,00249

Table 5.10 Prices with respect to moneyness of a Call option. For the NIG GOU and NIG CIR process the forward prices are all the same. The columns refer to the prices for forward starting Calls at $t^* = 0, 1, 2, 5$ years

Moneyness	Price 1	Price 2	Price 3	Price 4
NIG GOU				
0,7	0,33741	0,33275	0,32622	0,32034
0,8	0,25214	0,2477	0,24113	0,23506
0,9	0,17507	0,16969	0,1629	0,15653
1	0,10992	0,10196	0,09456	0,08773
1,1	0,06027	0,04899	0,04058	0,03312
1,2	0,0278	0,01601	0,00864	0,00366
1,3	0,01053	0,00328	0,00108	0,00045
NIG CIR				
0,7	0,33556	0,32846	0,32518	0,32532
0,8	0,24984	0,24382	0,24001	0,23986
0,9	0,17256	0,16657	0,16216	0,16169
1	0,10737	0,09999	0,09523	0,09449
1,1	0,05778	0,04844	0,0441	0,0433
1,2	0,02567	0,01651	0,01386	0,01336
1,3	0,00917	0,00381	0,00295	0,0028

model with GOU clock and $C = 58, 1151, G = 50, 4954, M = 69, 3685, \kappa = 1, 23294, \eta = 0, 64976$ and $\lambda = 1, 43335$ for the corresponding model with CIR clock (Table 5.9).

NIG Stochastic Volatility We use the model parameters $\alpha = 15, 9532, \beta = -10, 6732, \delta = 0, 412095, \lambda = 0, 855302, a = 0, 68104$ and $b = 1, 52999$ for the NIG GOU model and $\alpha = 538, 311, \beta = -9, 58059, \delta = 17, 9022, \kappa = 1, 32756, \eta = 0, 656748$ and $\lambda = 1, 50423$ for the NIG CIR model (Table 5.10).

5.10 DENSITY RECOVERY

The density recovery is an application of the inversion theorem for Fourier transforms. This theorem can be applied to compute the risk neutral density from the characteristic function of the model. The methods described in this chapter can then be used to recover the risk neutral density numerically. To this end we do not have to apply numerical differentiation of European Call or Put option prices since we can use the characteristic function directly. The equations we employ to recover the density are (1.3) and (5.2), respectively. The piece of Matlab code is given in Figure 5.35. We have applied this method for computing the densities we have provided in Chapters 2 and 3.

It is also possible to apply the cosine expansion to the generation of the density. To this end we consider

$$F_j = \frac{2}{b-a} \varphi \left(\frac{j\pi}{b-a} \exp \left(\frac{ij a\pi}{b-a} \right) \right) \text{ and } C_j(x) = \cos \left(ij \frac{x-a}{b-a} \right).$$

```
function y = fftdensity(cf,a,N)
% calculate the density from a given characteristic function

b = a/N;
u = ( (0:N−1) − N/2 ) * b;          % create the grid
h2 = ((−1).^(0:N−1)) .* cf(u);      % discret points due to charfunc
g = fft(h2);                        % inverse charfunc = probdist
y = real( ((−1).^(0:N−1)) .* g ...  
     * b / (2*pi) );                % transform to values

end
```

Figure 5.35   Matlab code for computing the risk neutral density from the characteristic function

The value of the density at x is given by the scalar product of the vectors F and C as follows:

$$pdf(x) = \sum_{j}^{N} = F_j C_j(x) - \frac{1}{2} F_0.$$

Since the evaluation can be done for a whole range of values x the method is very fast. We can calculate the cumulative density since

$$F(x) = \int_{-\infty}^{x} pdf(y)dy \approx \int_{b}^{x} pdf(y)dy$$

$$\approx \int_{b}^{x} \sum_{k=1}^{N-1} \frac{2}{b-a} \mathcal{R}\left(\varphi\left(\frac{k\pi}{b-a}\right)\right) \cos\left(k\pi \frac{x-a}{b-a}\right) + \frac{1}{b-a} \mathcal{R}(\varphi(0))$$

$$= \sum_{k=1}^{N-1} \frac{2}{b-a} \mathcal{R}\left(\frac{k\pi}{b-a}\right) \psi_k(b,x) + \frac{1}{b-a} \mathcal{R}(\varphi(0)),$$

with

$$\psi_k(x,y) = \begin{cases} \sin\left(k\pi \frac{y-a}{b-a}\right) - \sin\left(k\pi \frac{x-a}{b-a}\right) \frac{b-a}{k\pi}, & k \neq 0 \\ b-a, & k = 0 \end{cases}.$$

Let us expand on the method in the sequel to underpin the relationship. The characteristic function and the probability density of random variable Z are related by

$$\hat{f}(u) = \int_{\mathbb{R}} \exp(iux) f(x)dx$$

$$f(x) = \frac{1}{2\pi} \int_{\mathbb{R}} \exp(-iux) \hat{f}(u)du.$$

We consider an interval $S = [-A, A]$ and f on the discrete set

$$u_k = \pi/A \,(k - N/2), k = 0, \ldots, N-1,$$

which leads to

$$\hat{f}(u_k) = \int_{S} \exp(iu_k x) f(x)dx \approx \Delta x \sum_{j=0}^{N-1} \exp(iu_k x_j) f(x_j) \quad k = 0, \ldots, N-1.$$

Using conjugate symmetry we find

$$
\begin{aligned}
\exp(-iu_k x_j)\phi_t(u_k) + \exp(-iu_{N-k}x_j)\phi_t(u_{N-k}) &= \exp(-iu_k x_j)\phi_t(u_k) + \overline{\exp(iu_k x_j)\phi(u_k)} \\
&= \exp(-iu_k x_j)\phi_t(u_k) + \overline{\exp(-iu_k x_j)\phi_t(u_k)} \\
&= 2\mathcal{R}\left(\exp(-iu_k x_j)\phi_t(u_k)\right).
\end{aligned}
$$

The latter equation is used to implement the inversion technique we apply for the proxy simulation if only the characteristic function is given.

Error Bounds   For the error bound we use Theorem 7 from Hughett, P. (1998). To this end let d denote a probability distribution and ϕ the corresponding characteristic function. If there exist positive numbers $B, C, \alpha > 1$ and some constant $\beta > 1/2$ with

$$
|d(x)| \le B|x|^{-\alpha}, \quad \text{for all } |x| > A,
$$

and

$$
|\phi(u)| \le C|u/(2\pi)|^{-\beta}, \quad \text{for all } |u| > \frac{\pi N}{2A}
$$

then,

$$
\frac{1}{\sqrt{2A}}\|d - d_s\| \le \frac{B}{A^\alpha}\frac{2\alpha - 1}{\alpha - 1}
$$

and

$$
\frac{1}{\sqrt{2A}}\|\| \le \frac{C(2A)^{\beta-1/2}}{\sqrt{\beta - 1/2}}\left(\frac{2}{N}\right)^{\beta-1/2},
$$

where we denote by d_s the periodified density d as in Hughett, P. (1998).

The Algorithm   We consider a basic algorithm for pedagogical purposes. To this end let $S = [-A, A]$. We assume that the interval is chosen such that $d(-A) = d(A)$. Let M be a positive integer. To determine the value of the probability density at x we proceed by

- Set $N = 2^M$
- $u_j = j\pi(1/A - N/(2A))$, $\quad j = 0, \ldots, N - 1$
- Set $\delta_u = \pi/A$
- return $\sum_{j=0}^{N-1} 2(\mathcal{R}(\exp(-iu_j x)f(u_j)))\Delta_u/(4\pi)$.

We denote by $\mathcal{R}(\cdot)$ the real part of a complex number.

Note that the interval S need not be symmetric; we have assumed symmetry just for convenience.

In Fang, F. and Oosterlee, K. (2008), the authors state that their methods lead to stable and robust results and are specially suited to reduce computational effort.

Source of Error   The choice of the interval S may lead to unreasonable behaviour if A is too small. Since the algorithm produces a periodic function especially using asymmetric distribution, functions may suffer from an inappropriate value of A. We identify two errors affecting the approximation:

- Truncation Error (choosing A).
- Discretization Error (choosing M).

We could ask ourselves how to choose an appropriate constant A. For example, we have applied the following choices in practical experiments:

The first choice is based on the observation that

$$\mathbb{E}[X] = -i \frac{d}{du} \Phi_X(u) \Big|_{u=0}$$

$$\mathbb{V}[X] = (-i)^2 \frac{d^2}{du^2} \Phi_X(u) \Big|_{u=0} .$$

Then, computing the first and second order finite differences,

$$\bar{\mu} = -i \frac{\Phi_X(\epsilon) - \overline{\Phi_X(\epsilon)}}{2\epsilon}$$

$$\bar{\sigma} = \sqrt{\frac{\Phi_X(\epsilon) - 2 + \overline{\Phi_X(\epsilon)}}{\epsilon^2} - \bar{\mu}^2}.$$

We can take

$$[-n\bar{\sigma}, n\bar{\sigma}]$$

to include approximately n standard deviations for the numerical inversion.

Another choice is motivated by the fact that we are dealing with probability densities. Thus, the integral of the density is equal to 1. We may compute the integral starting from the expected value to the left and to the right and stop if we have reached a certain boundary, i.e. we take $A = \mu - \tilde{A}$ such that

$$\int_{\mu - \tilde{A}}^{\mu + \tilde{A}} f(x)dx \approx 1.$$

Applying the Method to the VG model   As a benchmark model we take the VG model. To this end we consider the following parameter sets for our numerical tests (Table 5.11):

Table 5.11   Parameter sets for numerical experiments

Set	C	G	M
Set 1	6.161	9.6443	16.026
Set 2	8.88	24.95	48.19
Set 3	6.47	11.10	33.41

For each of the parameter sets we plot the density which is given in closed form for the VG model and compare it to our approximation using the characteristic function. Set1 is motivated by the choice of parameters by Schoutens, W., Simons, E. and Tistaert, J. (2004). The sets Set 2 and Set 3 are obtained by calibrating the model to index data for the STOXX50 and DAX indices (Figure 5.36).

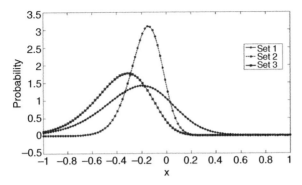

Figure 5.36 Difference of the analytic and the FFT values between the probability distributions obtained by using the characteristic function and the closed form solution. The lines indicate the values computed using the closed form solution and the indicated points show the values obtained using the characteristic function

We consider the approximation for different times. Figures 5.37 and 5.38 illustrate the probability distribution computed using the closed form solution (upper left), the method using the characteristic function (upper right), the absolute error (lower left) and both distributions (lower right). We see that the approximation error is less for longer time to maturity T.

Applying the Method to the VG GOU model   For the Variance Gamma model with Gamma Ornstein–Uhlenbeck stochastic clock a closed form of the transition density is not known, but

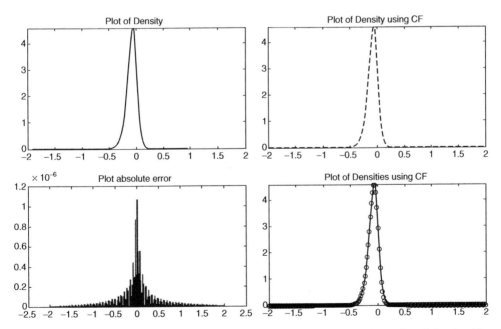

Figure 5.37 Density for the Variance Gamma model for $T = 0.5$. We have plotted the densities obtained by the analytic expression (top left) and the numeric method applying FFT (top right). The absolute errors are shown (bottom left) and both densities in one diagram (bottom right)

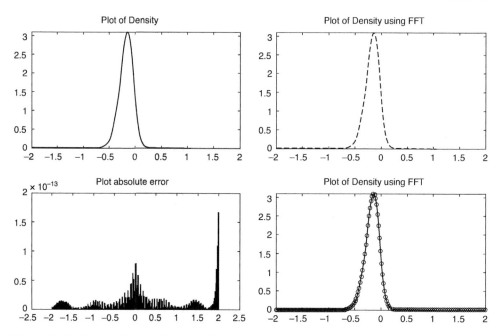

Figure 5.38 Density for the Variance Gamma model for $T = 1.0$. We have plotted the densities obtained by the analytic expression (top left) and the numeric method applying FFT (top right). The absolute errors are shown (bottom left) and both densities in one diagram (bottom right)

the characteristic function is given in closed form. We apply the inversion technique discussed earlier to this model. We consider the parameter sets given in Table 5.12 for our numerical test.

For each of the parameter sets we plot the density obtained by using the characteristic function (Figure 5.39).

5.11 SUMMARY AND CONCLUSIONS

In this chapter we reviewed a range of modern techniques for pricing options. All the methods rely on the characteristic function of the underlying stochastic process. The methods are efficient and fast. Furthermore, since we can re-use the numerical implementation of the pricing algorithm and change only the characteristic function (i.e. the input), it is possible to set up one pricer and apply it to stochastic volatility, jump diffusions, Lévy processes and Lévy models with stochastic volatility.

Table 5.12 Parameter sets for testing the numerical density method with the VG GOU model

Set	C	G	M	λ	a	b
Set 1	6.161	9.6443	16.026	1.679	0.3484	0.7664
Set 2	8.88	24.95	48.19	3.3	0.715	1.031
Set 3	6.47	11.10	33.41	0.94	0.63	1.47

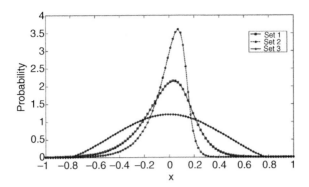

Figure 5.39 Probability density functions obtained using the characteristic function. Indicated are the sampled points. The lines are interpolated values

After introducing the numerical methods CM, LM, CM-BS, CONV and COS, we compared them in terms of stability and speed. Our findings suggest that the COS method is the most stable one. To show this, we have discussed this method in great detail and have included the source code together with all the steps involved. The code can be found in the supporting material of this book. Thus, the reader can set up proprietary applications using this method.

Finally, we extended the pricing methods to forward starting options. This is very convenient since options based on the future shape of the implied volatility surface such as Cliquet options can now be priced using semi-analytical methods. Furthermore, the methods enabled us to compute forward implied volatility surfaces.

As a final application we applied the methods to the recovery of the risk neutral density of the model.

6
Advanced Topics Using Transform Techniques

6.1 INTRODUCTION AND OBJECTIVES

In this section we consider further applications of the fast Fourier transform (FFT). We extend the numerical methods so that they are applicable to exotic option pricing problems. First, we modify the well-known and stable Lewis integration method to make it applicable to a whole range of strikes at once. Second, we implement a method which allows us to incorporate early exercise possibilities into an option. We study the pricing of Bermudan options and use extrapolation techniques to approximate the price of an American option. The application of Fourier transform methods is fast and can thus be used for calibrating to quoted market prices. For instance, quoted single stock options are American options. We also extend the range of methods by considering Fourier Space Time-Stepping (FST), which is a variant of FFT based pricing methods. Third, we extend the pricing method to handle some exotic payoffs such as Barrier options or Digital options. In particularly, we address the COS method and show that the option payoff determines the coefficients in the cosine series' representation. Finally, we address the task of calculating hedge sensitivities. Using the methods presented in Chapter 5 together with the results obtained in this chapter we give algorithms for calculating Greeks for all considered options including Bermudan, American and some exotic options. We apply the method to the calculation of Δ, Γ or *Vega* and also to study mean variance hedges.

6.2 PRICING NON-STANDARD VANILLA OPTIONS

We fix a maturity T and a strike K. The price of a European option with payoff f, strike K and maturity T is given by

$$\mathbb{E}[f(S(T)] = \int f(x)p(x)dx = \int f(x)\frac{\partial^2 C(S(0), T, K)}{\partial K^2}dK.$$

For any twice continuously differentiable function f the value of a European option with payoff f can thus be priced using

$$\mathbb{E}[f(S(T))] = f(K) + f'(K)(S(0) - K) \tag{6.1}$$

$$+ \int_{-\infty}^{K} P(S(0), T, x)f''(x)dx + \int_{K}^{\infty} C(S(0), T, x)f''(x)dx.$$

This formula can be efficiently implemented using Fourier transformation since for a given maturity the Call and the Put prices are calculated for the whole range of strikes.

6.2.1   FFT with Lewis Method

In this section we show how we can combine the method for pricing options given in Lewis, A. (2001) with FFT to be able for a given maturity T to evaluate the option prices for a given strike range at once. To this end we employ the characteristic function

$$\varphi(u) = e^{iu(\log(S)+(r-d)T)+\Phi(X_T)}$$

and observe

$$C(K,T) = Se^{-dT} - \frac{1}{\pi}\sqrt{SK}e^{-(r+d)T/2}\int_0^\infty \mathcal{R}\left(e^{iuk}\Phi\left(u-\frac{i}{2}\right)\frac{1}{u^2+\frac{1}{4}}\right)du$$

$$= Se^{-dT} - \frac{1}{\pi}\sqrt{K}e^{-rT}\int_0^\infty \mathcal{R}\left(e^{-iu\log(K)}\frac{\varphi(u-\frac{i}{2})}{u^2+\frac{1}{4}}du\right)$$

$$\approx Se^{-dT} - \frac{1}{\pi}\sqrt{K}e^{-rT}\sum_{j=1}^N \mathcal{R}\left(e^{-iv_j\log(K)}\frac{\varphi(v_j-\frac{i}{2})}{v_j^2+\frac{1}{4}}\eta\right).$$

In the last equation we used the Trapezoidal rule and $v_j = \eta(j-1)$ to approximate the integral on the right side. Repeating the calculations detailed in Section 5.3 the Call price $C(k_u, T)$ for $k_u = -b + \lambda(u-1)$, $u = 1, \ldots, N$ can be approximated by the following equation:

$$C(k_u,T) = Se^{-dT} - \frac{1}{\pi}e^{\frac{k_u}{2}}e^{-rT}\underbrace{\sum_{j=1}^N \mathcal{R}\left(e^{-i\frac{2\pi}{N}(j-1)(u-1)}e^{ibv_j}\frac{\varphi(v_j-\frac{i}{2})}{v_j^2+\frac{1}{4}}\eta\right)}_{(*)}, \qquad (6.2)$$

where we can apply the FFT method to compute the sum $(*)$ in (6.2). Thus,

$$C(k_u,T) = Se^{-dT} - \frac{1}{\pi}e^{\frac{k_u}{2}}e^{-rT}\mathcal{R}\left(\text{fft}\left(e^{ibv_j}\frac{\phi\left(v_j-\frac{i}{2}\right)}{v_j^2+\frac{1}{4}}\eta\right)\right). \qquad (6.3)$$

The Matlab code is presented in Figure 6.1.

6.3   BERMUDAN AND AMERICAN OPTIONS

Before we explain how to apply the methods introduced in Chapter 5, we will first outline the general valuation method. To this end we consider the time points at which exercising the option is possible. Let the current time be t_0 and the maturity T. Then,

$$\mathcal{T} = \{t_1, \ldots, t_{Nex}\}, \quad t_0 < t_1 < \ldots < t_{Nex} = T. \qquad (6.4)$$

In general, the spacing between the consecutive time points need not be equal but for simplicity we assume $t_n - t_{n-1} = \Delta_t$, $n = 1, \ldots, Nex$. The value of an option with payoff function h and early exercise schedule $\mathcal{T}$ is given by

$$V(t_0, S(0)) = \sum_{\tau \text{ Stopping time}} \mathbb{E}\left[e^{-r\tau}h(S(\tau))\right]. \qquad (6.5)$$

```
function [call_price_fft, call_delta_fft,call_gamma_fft] = ...
                LewisCallPricingFFT(N,eta,model,S,K,T,r,d,varargin)

lnS = log(S); lnK = log(K);
% predefined parameters
FFT_N = N;% must be a power of two (e.g. 2^14)
FFT_eta = eta; % spacing of psi integrand
FFT_lambda = (2 * pi) / (FFT_N * FFT_eta); %spacing for log strike
FFT_b = (FFT_N * FFT_lambda) / 2;
uvec = 1:FFT_N;

%log strike levels ranging from -b to +b
ku = - FFT_b + FFT_lambda * (uvec - 1);
jvec = 1:FFT_N;
vj = (jvec-1) * FFT_eta;

%applying FFT
tmp = psi(model,vj,r,d,T,varargin{:}).*exp(1i * vj* (FFT_b)) * FFT_eta;

%applying simpson's rule
tmp = (tmp / 3) .* (3 + (-1).^jvec - ((jvec - 1) == 0) );

%discrete fourier transform of integrand
price_vec = real(exp(0.5*ku).*fft(tmp))/pi;

call_price_fft = S*exp(-d*T)-exp(-r*T)...
    .*interp1(ku,price_vec,lnK);
end

function ret = psi(model,v,varargin)
   ret = exp(feval(@CharacteristicFunctionLib, model, v - 0.5 * 1i,...
            varargin{:})) ./ (v.^2 + 0.25);
end
```

Figure 6.1 Matlab code for implementing the Lewis method combined with FFT extended to price a given strike range at once

The general valuation method to compute (6.5), also known as *backward induction*, proceeds as follows:

Algorithm 6.1: Bermudan valuation

---

1 Start: Compute the value $V(t_{\text{Nex}}, S(t_0))$ by evaluating the payoff at t_{Nex}
2 Backward Induction:
  for Nex $- 1$ *to* 0 **do**
2a   Compute the *continuation value*

$$C(t_n, S(t_n)) = e^{-r\Delta}\mathbb{E}_{t_n}[V(t_{n+1}, S(t_{n+1}))].$$ (6.6)

2b   Compute the option value at t_n by

$$V(t_n, S(t_n)) = \max[C(t_n, S(t_n)), h(S(t_n))].$$

3 Final Step:
  Compute the option value $V(t_0, S(0)) = e^{-r\Delta}\max(C(t_1, S(t_1)), h(S(t_1)))$.

Thus, we need to be able to evaluate (6.6). In this chapter we assess the CONV, COS and FST methods for achieving this goal.

American Options   In contrast to the options considered so far, American options can be exercised anytime in $[t_0, T]$. To value such options we consider two approaches. The first approach is to increase the number of exercise possibilities in the set $\mathcal{T}$ and consider the limit. The other, more advanced, method is to consider *Richardson Extrapolation*, the application which is discussed in Chang, C., Chung, S. and Stapelton, R.C. (2007). We briefly review the method and consider the application to option pricing problems using the Heston and the Variance Gamma model in Subsection 6.3.3. Let $V_\Delta(t_0, S(t_0))$ denote the value of a Bermudan option with the exercise times equally spaced. The time between two such exercise dates is Δ. We denote $\mathcal{T}_\Delta := \{t_1, \ldots, t_N\}$, such that $t_n - t_{n-1} = \Delta$ for $n = 1, \ldots, N$. Let $A(t_0, S(t_0))$ denote the price of the American option, then

$$\lim_{\Delta \to 0} V_\Delta(t_0, S(t_0)) = A(t_0, S(t_0)).$$

The method assumes that the Bermudan price $V_\Delta(t_0, S(t_0))$ can be expanded to the price of the American options with respect to Δ as

$$V_\Delta(t_0, S(t_0)) = A(t_0, S(t_0)) + \sum_{k=1}^{\infty} a_k \Delta^{\beta_k}, \quad 0 < \beta_k < \beta_{k+1}.$$

We wish to add exercise opportunities to a Bermudan contract. To do this we take a sequence $\Delta_k, k = 1, \ldots$ such that $\Delta_1 > \Delta_2 > \ldots$. Using this construction the number of exercise opportunities increases. If T is the maturity we have for the number N_{Δ_k} of exercise opportunities, $N_{\Delta_1} < N_{\Delta_2} < \ldots$. Then, we recursively define a sequence $A_{j,k}, j, k = 0, \ldots$ by

$$A_{0,k} := V_{\Delta_k}(t_0, S(t_0))$$

$$A_{j,k} := A_{j+1,k-1} + \frac{A_{j+1,k-1} + A_{j,k-1}}{\left(\frac{\Delta_j}{\Delta_{j+k}}\right)^\beta - 1}.$$

Once we fix the exponent β we are in a position to compute the sequence in terms of the time steps and the corresponding Bermudan option prices. For instance, Fang, F. and Oosterlee, K. (2008) suggest taking the four-point Richardson extrapolation with $\beta = 1$ as an approximation to the value of the corresponding American option. This approximation is given for $\Delta_k := 2^{-k}$, $k = n, n+1, n+2, n+3$ by

$$\frac{64V_{\Delta_{n+3}}(t_0, S(t_0)) - 56V_{\Delta_{n+2}}(t_0, S(t_0)) + 14V_{\Delta_{n+2}}(t_0, S(t_0)) - V_{\Delta_n}(t_0, S(t_0))}{21}. \tag{6.7}$$

We use this approach when we present results on American options in what follows.

6.3.1 The Convolution Method

In order to apply the CONV method to the pricing of Bermudan options we specialize the general algorithm, Algorithm 6.1, to

---

Algorithm 6.2: Pseudo algorithm for pricing a Bermudan option using the CONV method

---

1 Input: Let x be a grid point, t_{Nex} the maturity
2 Start: Compute the value $C(t_{Nex}, x)$ by evaluating the payoff at t_{Nex}
3 Backward induction:
　for $m = \text{Nex} - 1$ *to* 0 **do**
3a　　Apply dampening to $C(t_{m+1}, x)$ to get $c_\alpha(t_{m+1}, x)$
3b　　Take the Fourier transform of $c_\alpha(t_{m+1}, x)$
3c　　Numerically evaluate

$$e^{-r\Delta} \mathcal{F} \left[e^{\alpha y} V(t_{Nex}, S(t_0)) \right] (u)\varphi(-(u - i\alpha), \Delta).$$

3d　　Compute the *continuation value*

$$C(t_m, x) = e^{-r\Delta - \alpha x} \mathcal{F}^{-1} \left[\mathcal{F} \left(e^{\alpha y} C(t_{m+1}, y) \right) (u)\varphi(-(u - i\alpha)) \right](x). \qquad (6.8)$$

3e　　Compute the option value at t_n by

$$V(t_n, x) = \max \left[C(t_n, x), h(x) \right].$$

4 Final Step: Compute the option value $V(t_0, S(0)) = C(t_0, 0)$

The Adjusted Grid　When we applied the convolution method for pricing European options (see Section 5.6), we constructed a grid. For pricing of Bermudan options we have to compute the option value as the maximum of the continuation value and the intrinsic value at each time step where early exercise is possible. To do this it may be necessary to shift the grid accordingly due to the option value being non-continuous at early exercise points. We describe the modification of the grid below.

Let $\mathcal{T}_{ex} := \{t_1, \ldots, t_{Nex}\}$ denote the time points where early exercise is possible. Then let $\{x\}^n$ denote a log-price grid with $Ngrid$ points at time-step t_n, $0 \le n \le Nex$ and $\{u\}$ a grid in the frequency domain consisting of $Ngrid$ points.

First, we compute $C(t_{Nex-1}, x_p), 0 \le p \le Ngrid - 1$. For European options at $\log(S(0)/K)$ the integrand is not continuous. We therefore apply a grid shift. For Bermudan options the problem is more severe. First, this phenomenon occurs at any $t_n \in \mathcal{T}_{ex}$ at the early exercise point. Second, the early exercise point is not known in advance and has to be determined at each step. To construct appropriate grids we have implemented the method suggested in Lord, R., Fang, F., Bervoets, G. and Oosterlee, C.W. (2008). We describe a backward algorithm for the pricing problem in the sequel.

We start at the options maturity, t_{Nex} with the standard grid $\{x\}^{Nex}$. Suppose we are at time step t_{m+1}. Now, we proceed as follows to time step t_m:

Algorithm 6.3: Pseudo algorithm for creating the grid for applying the CONV method to the pricing of Bermudan options

---

1 Start: Set x-grid equal to y-grid at time step t_{m+1}
2 Compute the continuation value $C(t_m, x)$ for grid points x on the x-grid
3 Consider the x-grid and derive j such that x_j and x_{j+1} are grid points such that the discontinuity is located between x_j and x_{j-1}
4 Set

$$x^* = \frac{x_{j+1}(C(t_m, x_j) - I(x_j)) - x_j(C(t_m, x_{j+1}) - I(x_{j+1}))}{(C(t_m, x_j) - I(x_j)) - (C(t_m, x_{j+1} - I(x_{j+1}))}.$$

5 Shift the x-grid to included the point x^*
6 Recalculate $C(t_m, x)$ for all $x \in x$-grid
7 Set the y-grid equal to the new x-grid since both grids should coincide

---

We apply Algorithm 6.3 until we reach $n = 0$. In this case we choose the grid such that $0 = \log(S(0)/S(0))$ is one of the grid points. The Matlab implementation is given in Figure 6.2.

We used the function cv to compute the continuation value. The implementation is shown in Figure 6.3.

Remark We can gain more speed if we calculate the continuation value in the main algorithm and do not call a function cv (see Figure 6.3). This is an often observed phenomenon when working with Matlab. Calling functions is computationally expensive. To this end we tuned the algorithm, see Figures 6.4 and 6.5.

6.3.2 The Cosine Method

In this section we review the application of the COS method to price Bermudan options. We keep the notation close to Fang, F. and Oosterlee, K. (2008). From the calculations considered in Section 5.7, where we applied the method to price European options, we know that the coefficients of the cosine expansion have to be calculated. We denote the indices of the expansion by k. Then, we have at the m-th exercise opportunity

$$V_k(t_m) = \frac{2}{b-a} \int_a^b v(y, t_m) \cos\left(k\pi \frac{x-a}{b-a}\right).$$

Recall that if $g(x, t_m)$ is the value of the payoff evaluated on the grid points x and t_m, we have for the continuation value and the option value

$$c(x, t_m) = \exp(-r\Delta_t) \int_{-\infty}^{\infty} v(y, t_{m+1}) f(y|x) dy \tag{6.9}$$

$$v(x, t_m) = \max(g(x, t_m), c(x, t_m)). \tag{6.10}$$

```
function price = FFTCONV_B(n, L, alpha, cp, model, S0, t, ...
    r, q, strike, Nex, varargin)

Ngrid = 2^n;                      % num grid points
dt = t / Nex;                     % time step
rdt = r * dt;                     % riskfree times dt

Delta_y = L/Ngrid;                % discrete y
Delta_x = Delta_y;                % discrete x
Delta_u = 2 * pi / L;             % discrete u

adj_y = log(strike/S0) ...
    - (ceil(log(strike/S0)/Delta_y) * Delta_y); % adjustment y-grid

% Construct the Grids
Grid_i = (0:Ngrid-1)';            % index nums for grids

y = adj_y + (Grid_i .* Delta_y) ...
    - (Ngrid/2 * Delta_y);        % Adjusted y-grid
x = y;                            % x-grid from y-grid

u = zeros(Ngrid, 1);              % the base u-grid
u = u + (Grid_i .* Delta_u) ...
    - (Ngrid/2 * Delta_u);        % Set u-grid
% coefficients
w = ones(Ngrid,1); w(1) = 0.5; w(Ngrid) = 0.5;

V = max(cp .* (S0*exp(y) - strike), 0); % option value at t_Nex
v = V .* exp(alpha .* y);              % dampened option value

cval = @(v,x,y) cv(Grid_i, rdt, w, v, Delta_u, model, u, x, y, ...
    alpha, dt, r, q, varargin{:});       % calc cont val

for m = Nex-1:-1:1                      % backward induction
    C = cval(v,x,y);                    % continuation value
    h = max(cp .* (S0*exp(x) - strike), 0);% payoff at t_m
    V = max(C, h);                      % option value at t_m

    l = find(V==h,1,'last');            % find exercise boundary
    if cp == 1                          % case of a call
        l = l-1;
    end
    % x^star
    xstar = ( x(l+1)*(C(l) - h(l)) - x(l)*(C(l+1) - h(l+1)) ) ...
        / ( (C(l) - h(l)) - (C(l+1) - h(l+1)) );
    % adjust x-grid
    adj_x = xstar-(ceil(xstar/Delta_x)*Delta_x);
    x = adj_x + (Grid_i .* Delta_x) ...
        - (Ngrid/2 * Delta_x);          % new x-grid

    C = cval(v,x,y);                    % continuation value
    V = max(C,max(cp .* (S0*exp(x) - strike), 0));
    y = x;                              % y-grid = x-grid
    v = V .* exp(alpha .* y);           % dampened option value
end
% Last Step
x = (Grid_i .* Delta_x) ...
    - (Ngrid/2 * Delta_x);              % final x-grid

C = cval(v,x,y);                        % final value
price = C(Ngrid/2 + 1, 1);              % return price
end
```

Figure 6.2 Matlab code for the CONV method and the pricing of Bermudan Call and Put options

```
function y = cv(Grid_i, rdt, w, v, Delta_u, model, u, x, y, alpha, ...
    dt, r, q, varargin)
% calculate continuation value
    % inner transform
    FT_Vec = ifft( ((-1) .^ Grid_i) .* w .* v );
    % outer transform
    FT_Vec_tbt = exp( 1i .* Grid_i .* (y(1) - x(1)) .* Delta_u ) ...
        .* exp(feval(@CF, model,-(u - (1i*alpha)), dt,r,q,...
        varargin{:})) .* FT_Vec;
    % calculation of value using above transforms
    y = abs(exp(-rdt-(alpha .* x) + (1i .* u .* (y(1) - x(1))) ) ...
        .* ((-1).^Grid_i) .* fft(FT_Vec_tbt));
end
```

Figure 6.3 Matlab code for the CONV method and for computing the continuation value which is
called by the function *FFTCONV_B*

Finally, we obtain for the last step the option value at t_0.

$$v(x, t_0) = \exp(-r\Delta_t) \int_{-\infty}^{\infty} v(y, t_1) f(y|x) dy.$$

Since the determination of the continuation value c, (6.9), is a pricing problem to which we
apply the cosine method, we denote the corresponding approximation by $\hat{c}$ and the current
option value by v, (6.10).

Suppose we are able to determine the early exercise boundary at t_m and denote it by x_m^*.
Once x_m^* is determined it is possible to split the expression for the k-th coefficient $V_k(t_m)$ into
two parts which correspond to the sum of two integrals. One integral ranges from a to x_m^* and
the other one ranges from x_m^* to b. If we let C_k and G_k represent these two parts, we have

$$V_k(t_m) = \begin{cases} C_k(a, x_m^*, t_m) + G_k(x_m^*, b), & \text{Call} \\ C_k(x_m^*, b) + G_k(a, x_m^*, t_m), & \text{Put} \end{cases}, \qquad (6.11)$$

with

$$C_k(x_1, x_2, t_m) = \frac{2}{b-a} \int_{x_1}^{x_2} \hat{c}(x, t_m) \cos\left(k\pi \frac{x-a}{b-a}\right) dx \qquad (6.12)$$

$$G_k(x_1, x_2, t_m) = \frac{2}{b-a} \int_{x_1}^{x_2} g(x, t_m) \cos\left(k\pi \frac{x-a}{b-a}\right) dx. \qquad (6.13)$$

In Fang, F. and Oosterlee, K. (2008) expressions for C, (6.12), and G, (6.13), are determined.
In fact, the value of G is given as an analytic expression but C has to be derived numerically.
We have

$$G_k(x_1, x_2) = \begin{cases} \frac{2}{b-a} K [\chi_k(x_1, x_2) - \psi_k(x_1, x_2)], & \text{Call} \\ \frac{2}{b-a} K [\psi_k(x_1, x_2) - \chi_k(x_1, x_2)], & \text{Put} \end{cases} \qquad (6.14)$$

and

$$C(x_1, x_2, t_m) = \frac{e^{-r\Delta}}{\pi} \mathcal{I}((M_c + M_s)u). \qquad (6.15)$$

```
function price = FFTCONV_B_Fast (n, L, alpha, cp, model, S0, t, ...
    r, q, strike, Nex, varargin)

Ngrid = 2^n;                                    % num grid points
dt = t / Nex;                                   % time step
rdt = r * dt;                                    % riskfree times dt

Delta_y = L/Ngrid;                              % discrete y
Delta_x = Delta_y;                              % discrete x
Delta_u = 2 * pi / L;                           % discrete u

adj_y = log(strike/S0) ...
    - (ceil(log(strike/S0)/Delta_y) * Delta_y); % adjustment y-grid

% Construct the Grids
Grid_i = (0:Ngrid-1)';                          % index for grids
Grid_m = (-1).^(0:Ngrid-1)';                    % (-1)^Grid_i

y = adj_y + (Grid_i .* Delta_y) ...
    - (.5*Ngrid * Delta_y);                     % Adjusted y-grid
x = y;                                          % x-grid from y-grid
u = zeros(Ngrid, 1);                            % the base u-grid
u = u + (Grid_i .* Delta_u) ...
    - (.5*Ngrid * Delta_u);                     % Set u-grid
w = ones(Ngrid,1); w(1) = 0.5; w(Ngrid) = 0.5; % coefficients

V = max(cp .* (S0*exp(y) - strike), 0);        % opt value at t_Nex
v = V .* exp(alpha .* y);                        % dampened opt value

for m = Nex-1:-1:1                               % backward induction
    FT_Vec = ifft( (Grid_m) .* w .* v );% direct FFT for v
    FT_Vec_tbt = exp( 1i .* Grid_i .* (y(1) - x(1)) .* Delta_u ) ...
    .* exp(feval(@CF, model,-(u - (1i*alpha)), dt,r,q,varargin{:})) ...
    .* FT_Vec;                                   % vector to be transf.
    C = abs(exp(-rdt-(alpha .* x) + (1i .* u .* (y(1) - x(1))) ) ...
    .* (Grid_m) .* fft(FT_Vec_tbt));% continuation value
    h = max(cp .* (S0*exp(x) - strike), 0);     % payoff at t_m
    V = max(C, h);                               % opt value at t_m

    l = find(V==h,1,'last');                     % find ex boundary
    if cp == 1                                   % case of a call
        l = l-1;
    end
    xstar = ( x(l+1)*(C(l) - h(l)) - x(l)*(C(l+1) - h(l+1)) ) ...
        / ( (C(l) - h(l)) - (C(l+1) - h(l+1)) );% x^star
    adj_x = xstar-(ceil(xstar/Delta_x)*Delta_x);% adjust x-grid
    x = adj_x + (Grid_i .* Delta_x) ...
        - (.5*Ngrid * Delta_x);                 % new x-grid

    % calculate with new x-grid
    FT_Vec_tbt = exp( 1i .* Grid_i .* (y(1) - x(1)) .* Delta_u ) ...
    .* exp(feval(@CF, model,-(u - (1i*alpha)), dt,r,q,varargin{:})) ...
    .* FT_Vec;                                   % vector to be transf.

    % use new grid
    C = abs(exp( -rdt - (alpha .* x) + (1i .* u .* (y(1) - x(1))) ) ...
        .* (Grid_m) .* fft(FT_Vec_tbt));         % continuation
    V = max(C,max(cp .* (S0*exp(x) - strike), 0));% option value
    y = x;                                        % y-grid = x-grid
    v = V .* exp(alpha .* y);                     % dampened opt value
end

% Last Step
x = (Grid_i .* Delta_x)-(.5*Ngrid * Delta_x);  % final x-grid
```

Figure 6.4 Matlab code for the CONV method and the pricing of Bermudan Call and Put options –
Fast method

```
% final transforms
FT_Vec = ifft( (Grid_m) .* w .* v );
FT_Vec_tbt = exp( 1i .* Grid_i .* (y(1) - x(1)) .* Delta_u ) ...
    .* exp(feval(@CF, model,-(u - (1i*alpha)), dt,r,q,varargin{:})) ...
    .* FT_Vec;          % vector to be transf.

C = abs(exp( -rdt - (alpha .* x) + (1i .* u .* (y(1) - x(1))) ) ...
    .* (Grid_m) .* fft(FT_Vec_tbt));          % final value

price = C(.5*Ngrid + 1, 1);                   % return price
end
```

Figure 6.5 Matlab Code – CONV method Bermudan (fast version) continued from Figure 6.4

The corresponding functions in (6.14) are given by

$$\chi_k(x_1,x_2) = \frac{1}{1+\left(\frac{k\pi}{b-a}\right)^2}\left[\cos\left(\frac{x_2-a}{b-a}\right)e^{x_2} - \cos\left(\frac{x_1-a}{b-a}\right)e^{x_1}\right.$$

$$\left. + \frac{k\pi}{b-a}\left(\sin\left(\frac{x_2-a}{b-a}\right)e^{x_2} - \sin\left(k\pi\frac{x_1-a}{b-a}\right)e^{x_1}\right)\right] \quad (6.16)$$

$$\psi_k(x_1,x_2) = \begin{cases} \frac{b-a}{k\pi}\left(\sin\left(\frac{x_2-a}{b-a}\right) - \sin\left(\frac{x_1-a}{b-a}\right)\right), & k\neq 0 \\ x_2-x_1, & k=0 \end{cases} \quad (6.17)$$

The matrices in (6.15), $M_c := \left(M_{k,j}^c(x_1,x_2)\right)_{k,j=0}^{\text{Nex}}$, are given by

$$M_{k,j}^C(x_1,x_2) = \begin{cases} i\pi\frac{x_2-x_1}{b-a}, & k=j=0 \\ \frac{\exp\left(i(j-k)\pi\frac{x_1-a}{b-a}\right)-\exp\left(i(j+k)\pi\frac{x_1-a}{b-a}\right)}{j+k}, & \text{otherwise} \end{cases} \quad (6.18)$$

$$M_{k,j}^s(x_1,x_2) = \begin{cases} i\pi\frac{x_2-x_1}{b-a}, & k=j \\ \frac{\exp\left(i(j-k)\pi\frac{x_1-a}{b-a}\right)-\exp\left(i(j-k)\pi\frac{x_1-a}{b-a}\right)}{j+k}, & k\neq j \end{cases} \quad (6.19)$$

Let us briefly comment on the derivation of the formulae (6.18) and (6.19). Starting with the representation of $M_{k,j}(x_1,x_2)$ and for a real number u we apply the formula $\exp(iu) = \cos(u) + i\sin(u)$, then we have

$$M_{k,j}(x_1,x_2) = \int_{\frac{x_1-a}{b-a}}^{\frac{x_2-a}{b-a}} \cos(j\pi x)\cos(k\pi x)dx + 2i\int_{\frac{x_1-a}{b-a}}^{\frac{x_2-a}{b-a}} \sin(j\pi x)\sin(k\pi x)dx. \quad (6.20)$$

The integrals appearing in Equation (6.20) can be computed analytically and we find

$$
M_{k,j} = \begin{cases}
-\dfrac{i}{\pi}\left[\dfrac{1}{j+k}\exp(i(j+k)\pi u)+\dfrac{1}{j-k}\exp(i(j-k)\pi u)\right]_{\frac{x_1-a}{b-a}}^{\frac{x_2-a}{b-a}}, & j+k\neq 0,\, j-k\neq 0 \\[2ex]
2\dfrac{x_2-x_1}{b-a}, & j,k=0 \\[2ex]
\left(\dfrac{x_2-x_1}{b-a}+\left[\dfrac{1}{j+k}\exp(i(j+k)\pi u)\right]_{\frac{x_1-a}{b-a}}^{\frac{x_2-a}{b-a}}\right), & j=k,\, j,k\neq 0
\end{cases}
\tag{6.21}
$$

Using Equation (6.21), Fang, F. and Oosterlee, K. (2008) show that

$$
M_{k,j} = -\frac{i}{\pi}\left(M_{k,j}^{c}+M_{k,j}^{s}\right)
\tag{6.22}
$$

and, therefore, Equation (6.15) holds. The matrices M^{c} and M^{s} are known as *Hankel* and *Toeplitz matrices*.

The following representation is useful for the implementation:

$$
M^{c}=(m_{ij}^{c})=\begin{pmatrix}
m_0 & m_1 & m_2 & \cdots & m_{N-1} \\
m_1 & m_2 & \cdots & \cdots & m_N \\
\vdots & \vdots & \ddots & \ddots & \vdots \\
m_{N-2} & m_{N-1} & \cdots & \cdots & m_{2N-3} \\
m_{N-1} & \cdots & \cdots & m_{2N-3} & m_{2N-2}
\end{pmatrix}
\tag{6.23}
$$

$$
M^{s}=(m_{ij}^{s})=\begin{pmatrix}
m_0 & m_1 & \cdots & m_{N-2} & m_{N-1} \\
m_{-1} & m_0 & m_1 & \cdots & m_{N-2} \\
\vdots & \vdots & \ddots & \ddots & \vdots \\
m_{2-N} & \cdots & m_{-1} & m_0 & m_1 \\
m_{1-N} & m_{2-N} & \cdots & m_{-1} & m_0
\end{pmatrix}.
\tag{6.24}
$$

For the values m_j we have

$$
m_j=\begin{cases}
\dfrac{(x_2-x_1)\pi}{b-a}i, & j=0 \\[2ex]
\dfrac{\exp\left(ij\frac{(x_2-a)\pi}{b-a}\right)-\exp\left(ij\frac{(x_1-a)\pi}{b-a}\right)}{j}, & j\neq 0
\end{cases}
\tag{6.25}
$$

Then, the multiplication of the matrices M_s and M_c with a vector u can be done very efficiently. The product $M_s u$ is equal to the first N elements of $\mathcal{F}^{-1}(\mathcal{F}(m_s)\mathcal{F}(u_s))$ with $m_s=(m_0,\ldots,m_{1-N},0,m_{N-1},\ldots,m_1)^T$, $u_s=(u_0,u_1,\ldots,u_{N-1},0,\ldots,0)^T$. $M_c u$ is equal to the first N elements of $\mathcal{F}^{-1}(\mathcal{F}(m_c)\mathcal{F}(u_c))$ with $m_c=(m_{2N-1},m_{2N-2},\ldots,m_0)^T$, $u_c=(0,\ldots,0,u_0,u_1,\ldots,u_{N-1})^T$.

We consider the pricing of Bermudan options using the cosine expansion method. To this end we summarize the general algorithm, Algorithm 6.2, modified to apply the COS method. The notation used in the description of the algorithm is adopted from the formulae in this section.

Algorithm 6.4: Pseudo algorithm for pricing Bermudan options using the COS method

1 Compute the coefficients $V_k(t_{Nex})$ which are $G_k(0, b)$ for a Call and $G_k(a, 0)$ for a Put
2 Backward induction
   for $m = \text{Nex} - 1$ *to* 0 **do**
2a   Compute the early exercise boundary x^*
2b   Compute $V_k(t_m)$ using the following algorithm:
    2ba   Calculate m_j using (6.25)
    2bb   Calculate u, $u_j := \varphi\left(\frac{j\pi}{b-a}\right) V_j(t_{m+1})$, $u_0 = 0.5\varphi(0)V_0(t_{m+1})$
    2bc   Calculate $M_s u$ by using the first N elements of $\mathcal{F}^{-1}(\mathcal{F}(m_s)\mathcal{F}(u_s))$
    2bd   Calculate $M_c u$ by using the first N elements of $\mathcal{F}^{-1}(\mathcal{F}(m_c)\text{sign}\mathcal{F}(u_c))$ and reverse the order
    2be   Set $C(x_1, x_2, t_m) = e^{-r\Delta}\mathcal{I}((M_c + M_s)u)$
2c   Determine the continuation value $C(x_1, x_2, t_0)$
3 Final Step: Compute $v(x, t_0)$ using the coefficients $V_k(t_1)$

Greeks It is straightforward to calculate Δ and Γ for Bermudan options. The main difficulty lies in the determination of the relevant coefficients V_k in the backward algorithm and in finding the exercise boundary. In what follows we present the Matlab code which can compute the Bermudan prices for a range of strikes at once. It can also be used efficiently for calibration purposes. As indicated, it is essentially a backward algorithm. The coefficients necessary to give the cosine expansion are computed from the continuation value and the current value of the option. To do so we call a function *xstark* computing the optimal exercise strategy by a Newton root finding algorithm.

Let us now consider the functions involved in determining the Bermudan price. First, we give the implementation of the coefficients necessary to derive the cosine expansion. These are the function `calcv` and `coeff_b` given in Figures 6.7 and 6.8. To save time we can implement the calculating of the coefficients in the function `calcv`. Then, we do not have the function call to `coeff_b`.

While the function `calcv` essentially does the multiplication, the coefficients for the cosine expansion and thus the important ingredients for calculating the value are determined in the function `coeff_b`.

The following code snippet, Figure 6.9, illustrates the Matlab implementation of the continuation value. At this stage we have to apply the FFT and to compute the Hankel and Toeplitz matrices discussed earlier in this section.

Let us consider the root finding. For most applications we have observed that the algorithm converges very fast and that only fewer than 10 steps are necessary. However, we set the maximal number of iteration to 50 and include a convergence criterion. To this end we set the threshold `eps` to some small number, for instance $1e - 6$, and exit the `for` loop if the accuracy is better or equal to `eps`. The root finding is presented in Figure 6.10.

```
function price = FFTCOS_B(n, Nex, L, c, cp, type, S0, t, r, q, ...
    strike, varargin)

dt = t / Nex;                    % time interval
Ngrid = 2 ^ n;                   % Grid points
Nstrike = size(strike,1);        % number of strikes

x = double(log(S0 ./ strike));       % center

a = double(c(1) + x - L * sqrt(c(2) + sqrt(c(3))));    % lower trunc
b = double(c(1) + x + L * sqrt(c(2) + sqrt(c(3))));    % upper trunc

Grid_i = repmat((0:Ngrid-1)',1,Nstrike);    % Grid index

% Set up function handles
if cp == 1
    vk = @(x) calcv(Grid_i, x, b, a, b, cp, strike);
    cv = @(x,y) cvalue(a, x, a, b, Ngrid, y, type, dt, ...
        r, q, varargin{:});

else
    vk = @(x) calcv(Grid_i, a, x, a, b, cp, strike);
    cv = @(x,y) cvalue(x, b, a, b, Ngrid, y, type, dt, ...
        r, q, varargin{:});
end

initialGuess = 0;                % guess for x^*(t_Nex-1)
V = vk(0);                       % coeff V in t_Nex-1

xstark = zeros(Nstrike, Nex-1);
for m = Nex-1:-1:1                    % backward induction
    % could be fzero but Newton with some number of iteration is fine!
    xstark(:,m) = xstar(initialGuess,cp, a, b, 50, Grid_i, type, ...
            V, dt, r, q, strike, varargin{:}); % early exercise point
    C = cv(xstark(:,m),V);           % Cont value at t_m
    V = vk(xstark(:,m)) + C;       % Coeff V in t_m
    initialGuess = xstark(:,m);
end


cfval = exp(feval(@CF, type,pi*Grid_i*diag(1./(b-a)), dt, ...
    r,q,varargin{:}));

pF = cfval .* exp( 1i * pi * Grid_i * diag((x - a) ./ (b - a)) );

pF(1,:) = 0.5*pF(1,:);

price = exp(-r * dt) * sum(real(pF) .* V) ;   % Option value at t_0
end
```

Figure 6.6 Matlab code for computing Bermudan Call and Put option values using the COS method

```
function result = calcv(k, x1, x2, a, b, cp, strike)

[chi, psi] = coeff_b(k,x1,x2,a,b);
result = 2 .* cp .* strike ./ (b - a) .* ( chi - psi);
```

Figure 6.7 Matlab code for computing the coefficients V to be used with the COS method

```
function [chi, psi] = coeff_b(k, x1, x2, a, b)
% compute chi and psi for cosine method

arg2 = k .* pi * diag((x2 - a) ./ (b - a));     % arg trig func
arg1 = k .* pi * diag((x1 - a) ./ (b - a));     % arg trig func

term1 = cos( arg2 ) * diag(exp(x2));
term2 = cos( arg1 ) * diag(exp(x1));

term3 = pi * k .* sin( arg2 ) * diag(exp(x2)./ (b-a));
term4 = pi * k .* sin( arg1 ) * diag(exp(x1)./ (b-a));

chi = 1 ./ ( 1 + ((k .* pi) *diag(1./ (b - a))).^2 ) ...
      .* ( term1 - term2 + term3 - term4 );

chi(1,:) = (exp(x2)-exp(x1));  % calc chi

psi = ((sin(arg2) - sin(arg1)) ./ (k .* pi)) *diag(b-a);

psi(1,:) = (x2-x1);            % calc psi

end
```

Figure 6.8   Matlab code for computing the coefficients of the COS method for a Bermudan option

6.3.3   Numerical Results

In this section we apply the CONV and the COS methods to the pricing of Bermudan and American options. The models we have chosen for the numerical tests are the Heston stochastic volatility model and the Variance Gamma model. For this numerical test let us fix the model parameters. For the Heston stochastic volatility model we consider $V(0) = 0.02$, $\theta = 0.02$, $\kappa = 0.2$, $v = 0.5$ and $\rho = -0.8$. We consider $S(0) = 100$, $r = 0.1$, $d = 0$ and $\sigma = 0.17$, $\theta = -0.19$ and $v = 0.24$ for the Variance Gamma model. We analyse the methods and models by:

1. Performance of the COS and CONV methods for pricing Bermudan options with daily and monthly exercise and dependence on the grid size.
2. Convergence of the Bermudan option prices to the American option price by increasing the exercise possibilities.
3. Dependence of the American option price on the size of the grid.

Heston Model – CONV and COS   First, we consider the Heston model. For this numerical test we price Bermudan and American Put options with $T = 1/12$, $K = 110$. We consider daily exercise and different sizes of the grid. Figure 6.11 shows the results. We observe that the COS method converges for lower values of n and thus allows for fewer grid points without losing accuracy. In relation to the CPU time/accuracy plot, both methods show a stable convergence behaviour. Considering the CPU time we observe that the performance of the COS method for a given grid size, that is fixed n, is slightly worse than the performance of the CONV method, but since the COS method leads to the same accuracy of option prices for smaller grids, it outperforms the CONV method.

```
function result = cvalue(x1, x2, a, b, N, V, ...
    model, t, r, q, varargin)

exp2 = exp( 1i .* (1:N)' .* (x2 - a) ./ (b - a) .* pi );  % init
exp1 = exp( 1i .* (1:N)' .* (x1 - a) ./ (b - a) .* pi );  % init

m = zeros(3*N-1, 1);    % init base

m(N, 1) = 1i * pi * (x2 - x1) / (b - a);
m(N+1:2*N, 1) = 1 ./ (1:N)' .* ( exp2 - exp1 );
m(1:N-1, 1) = - conj(flipud(m(N+1:2*N-1, 1)));
m(2*N+1:3*N-1, 1) = ( exp2(1:N-1, 1) .* exp2(N,1) - exp1(1:N-1, 1) ...
    .* exp1(N, 1) ) ./ ( (N+1:2*N-1)' );

Grid_j = (0:N-1)';                                       % fix grid

% compute u values
u = exp(feval(@CF, model,Grid_j.*pi./(b-a), t,r,q,varargin{:})) .* V;
u(1) = 0.5*u(1);

m_s = [m(N:-1:1, 1); 0; m(2*N-1:-1:N+1, 1)];
u_s = [u; zeros(N, 1)];
m_c = m(3*N-1:-1:N, 1);

shortCut = 1;

% apply fft five times
if shortCut == 1
    zeta = -ones(2*N, 1);
    zeta(2 .* (1:N)' - 1) = 1;

    fft_u_s = fft(u_s);
    xi_s = ifft((fft(m_s)) .* fft_u_s);
    xi_c = ifft((fft(m_c)) .* (zeta .* fft_u_s));

    result = exp(-r * t) / pi .* imag( xi_s(1:N) ...
        + flipud(xi_c(1:N)) );
else
    M_c = zeros(N, N);
    M_s = zeros(N, N);

    for n = 0:N-1
        M_c(:, n+1) = m(N+n:2*N-1+n);
        M_s(:, n+1) = m(N+n:-1:1+n);
    end

    result = exp(-r*t) / pi .* imag((M_c + M_s) * u);
end

end
```

Figure 6.9 Matlab code for computing a Bermudan option value using the COS method

We now apply the same test setting $T = 1$ and we take 12 exercise opportunities, which makes it possible to exercise the option monthly. Figure 6.12 again verifies the results for the short dated option and shows the superior performance of the COS method.

Variance Gamma Model – CONV and COS For this numerical test we again price Bermudan and American Put options with $T = 0.1$, $K = 110$ but this time we choose the Variance

```
function result = xstar(ival, cp, a, b, iter, Grid_k, ...
    model, V, t, r, q, strike, varargin)

cfvals = exp(feval(@CF, model, Grid_k.*pi ./ (b-a), ...
    t,r,q,varargin{:}));

x = ival;
eps = 1e-6;
for n = 1:iter
    exp_t = exp( 1i .* Grid_k .* pi .* (x - a) ./ (b - a) );
    vec = real( cfvals .* exp_t ) .* V;
    vec(1) = 0.5*vec(1);

    g = (exp(-r * t) * sum(vec, 1)) ...
            - cp .* strike .* (exp(x) - 1);

    vec = imag(cfvals .* Grid_k .* exp_t) .* V;
    vec(1) = 0.5*vec(1);

    dg = - exp(-r * t) .* pi / (b - a) .* sum(vec, 1) ...
            - cp .* strike .* exp(x);

    x = x - (g / dg);
    if abs(g) < eps
        break;
    end
end

result = x;

end
```

Figure 6.10   Matlab code for computing the exercise boundary x^* for applying the COS method

Gamma model. We allow for daily exercise of the option and therefore the number of exercise opportunities is set to $Nex = 30$. Then, we consider the dependence of the Bermudan option price on the number of grid points. Figure 6.13 illustrates the results. In the case of the Variance Gamma model the superior performance of the COS method against the CONV method is clearly visible. Not only is a high accuracy obtained for small sized grids but for the CPU time/ accuracy plot the COS method also outperforms the CONV method. Therefore, it does not matter that for a fixed number n the performance in terms of CPU time is slightly better when the CONV method is applied.

We have also carried out the test again with $T = 1$ and 12 exercise opportunities, suggesting that it is possible to exercise the option monthly. Figure 6.14 again verifies the results for the short dated option for the Variance Gamma model and those for the Heston model and shows the superior performance of the COS method.

Heston Model – Bermudan and American   In this paragraph we consider the Heston model. For the numerical test we increase the number of possible exercise opportunities and measure the change in price, the CPU time and display the error of the approximation of an American option. We take 10, 20, ..., 200 exercise possibilities. To measure the accuracy we compute a reference value which is the American option price obtained by Richardson extrapolation and

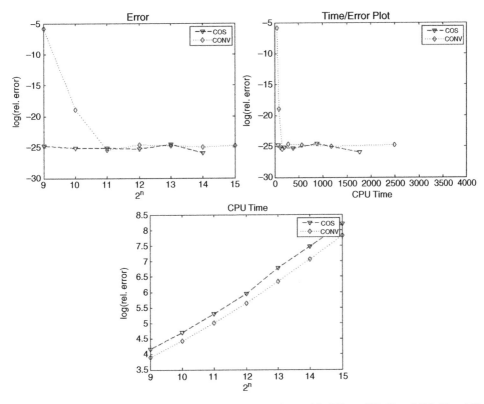

Figure 6.11 Pricing of Bermudan and American Put options with $S(0) = 100$, $T = 1/12$, $K = 110$, $r = 0.1$ and $q = 0$ in the Heston model. We have 30 exercise opportunities. The upper left graph shows the pricing error increasing the number of possible exercise times. The upper right graph shows the CPU time in msec against the error from approximating an American option and, finally, the lower graph shows the CPU time in msec against the number of exercise possibilities

measure the relative error to the Bermudan price. Figure 6.15 illustrates our findings for the Heston model.

In this case we see that the COS method leads to smooth and stable convergence with the corresponding reference value price. However, the convergence of the CONV method in this case is not stable. The graph illustrates erratic behaviour. The CPU time / accuracy plot confirms this. Therefore, it does not matter that the performance in terms of pure CPU time is in favour of the CONV method.

Variance Gamma Model – Bermudan and American   We consider the approximation of an American Put option by increasing the number of exercise opportunities of a Bermudan Put option. As the price of the American Put we take the values applying Richardson extrapolation. Then, we consider $10, 20, \ldots, 200$ exercise opportunities and the relative error to the reference value. Figure 6.16 summarizes the results.

For the Variance Gamma model both methods show a smooth and stable convergence behaviour. The convergence of the COS method is faster than that of the CONV method. Thus, we can confirm that the COS method outperforms the CONV method for pricing Bermudan options.

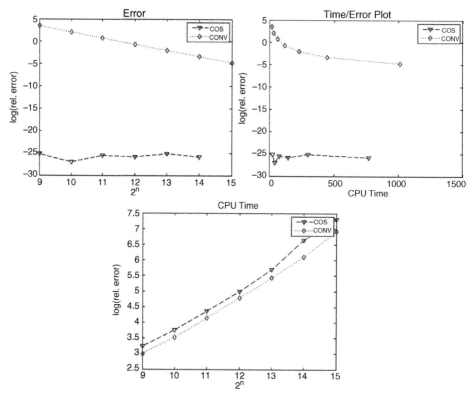

Figure 6.12 Pricing of Bermudan and American put options with $S(0) = 100$, $T = 1$, $K = 110$, $r = 0.1$ and $q = 0$ in the Heston model. The upper left graph shows the pricing error increasing the number of possible exercise times. The upper right graph shows the CPU time in msec against the error from approximating an American option and, finally, the lower graph shows the CPU time in msec against the number of exercise possibilities

We perform the same numerical test and take two reference values for the American Put option price. The reference values are calculated as the American option prices within the model by applying Richardson extrapolation and a large number of grid points. We then apply the same test as above and compare the convergence of the Bermudan options in the corresponding model. The results are summarized in Figure 6.17.

Again, we observe that the COS method outperforms the CONV method but that both methods lead to smooth and stable convergence when applied to pricing Bermudan and American options.

6.3.4 The Fourier Space Time-Stepping

Now let us look at another method for solving the pricing problem. We follow Jackson, K., Jaimungal, S. and Surkov, V. (2007).

The main idea is to use the representation of the solution of the pricing problem as a *partial integro differential equation (PIDE)*. Then, the problem is transformed to Fourier space. The transformation leads to a simpler problem since in Fourier space the solution is given in terms of *ordinary differential equations (ODE)*. Another advantage of this approach is that the

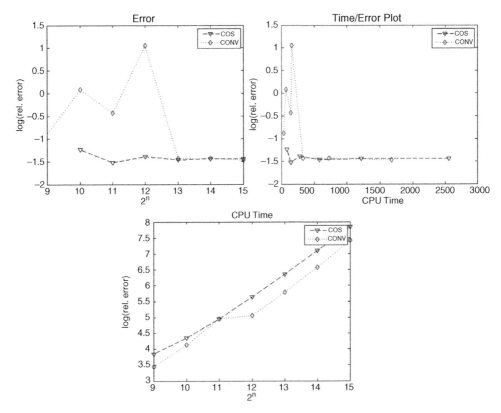

Figure 6.13 Pricing of Bermudan and American Put options with $S(0) = 100$, $T = 0.1$, $K = 110$, $r = 0.1$ and $q = 0$ in the Variance Gamma model. We have 30 exercise opportunities. The upper left graph shows the pricing error increasing the number of possible exercise times. The upper right graph shows the CPU time in msec against the error from approximating an American option and, finally, the lower graph shows the CPU time in msec against the number of exercise possibilities

Fourier transformed payoff is not needed, something which makes the method attractive for applying it to path-dependent and early exercise options.

For the presentation of the algorithm we fix some notation. We denote by $\underline{S}(t) = (S_1(t), \ldots, S_d(t))^\top$ the vector of underlyings and by $V(t, \underline{S}(t))$ the price at time t of an option with payoff h. To simplify the notation we write $S(t)$ despite the fact that it can actually be a d-dimensional vector. Then, we have

$$V(t, S(t)) = \mathbb{E}[\exp(-r(T - t))h(S)].$$

Using the logarithmic transform and calculating in terms of the forward price, we find

$$v(t, S(t)) := e^{-r(T-t)}V(t, S(t))\exp(X(t)).$$

This representation has no drift and $S(t) = S(0)\exp(X(t))$. For what follows we denote by (γ, Σ, ν) the Lévy triplet for $X(t)$. The pricing PDE is given by

$$\begin{cases} (\partial_t + \mathcal{L})v &= 0 \\ V(T, x) &= \varphi(S(0)e^x) \end{cases} \tag{6.26}$$

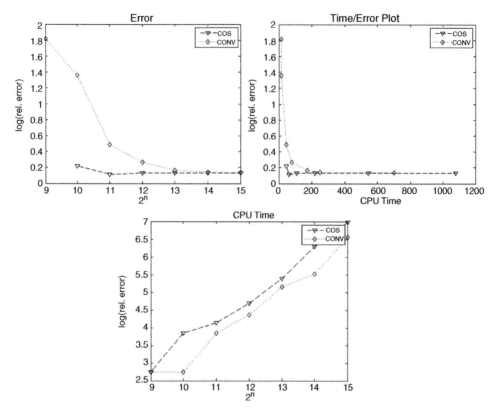

Figure 6.14 Pricing of Bermudan and American Put options with $S(0) = 100$, $T = 1$, $K = 110$, $r = 0.1$ and $q = 0$ in the Variance Gamma model. The upper left graph shows the pricing error increasing the number of possible exercise times. The upper right graph shows the CPU time in msec against the error from approximating an American option and, finally, the lower graph shows the CPU time in msec against the number of exercise possibilities

If $\mathcal{L}$ denotes the generator of the Lévy process, we have for a differentiable function f

$$\mathcal{L}f(x) = \left(\gamma\partial_x + \frac{\partial_x \Sigma \partial_x^T}{2}\right) f(x) \tag{6.27}$$

$$+ \int_{\mathbb{R}^d\setminus 0} (f(x+y) - f(x) - y\partial_x(x)1_{\{|y|<1\}})v(dy).$$

Using the Fourier transform we reduce the order of differentiation using

$$\mathcal{F}[\partial_x^d f(x)](w) = iw\mathcal{F}[\partial_x^{d-1} f](w).$$

Thus, we have

$$\mathcal{F}(\mathcal{L}v)(t, w) = \left(i\gamma w - \frac{w\Sigma w^T}{2} + \int_{\mathbb{R}^d} \left(e^{iwy} - 1 - iyw1_{\{|y|<1\}}\right) v(dy)\right)\mathcal{F}(v)(t, w)$$

$$= \psi(w)\mathcal{F}(v)(t, w). \tag{6.28}$$

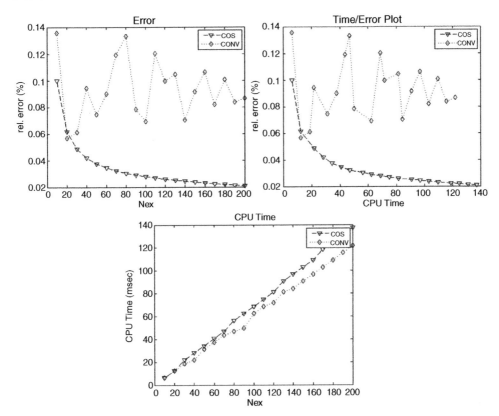

Figure 6.15 Pricing of Bermudan and American Put options with $S(0) = 100$, $T = 1$, $K = 110$, $r = 0.1$ and $q = 0$ in the Heston model. The upper left graph shows the pricing error when increasing the number of possible exercise times. The upper right graph shows the CPU time in msec against the error from approximating an American option and, finally, the lower graph shows the CPU time in msec against the number of exercise possibilities. We have taken the reference value as a model intrinsic calculated value

Applying the transform approach to (6.26) we find

$$
\begin{cases}
\partial_t \mathcal{F}[v](t, w) + \varphi(w)\mathcal{F}[v](t, w) &= \quad 0 \\
\mathcal{F}[v](T, w) &= \quad \mathcal{F}[h](w)
\end{cases}. \tag{6.29}
$$

Given $\mathcal{F}[v](t, w)$ at some time $t_2 < T$ for some time $t_1 < t_2$ we find

$$
\mathcal{F}(v)(t_1, w) = \mathcal{F}(v)(t_2, w)e^{\psi(w)(t_2 - t_1)}. \tag{6.30}
$$

Applying the inverse transform to (6.30) leads to

$$
v(t_1, x) = \mathcal{F}^{-1}\left(\mathcal{F}(v)(t_2, .)e^{\psi(w)(t_2 - t_2)}\right)(x). \tag{6.31}
$$

To numerically solve (6.31) we proceed by considering a grid for the set $[0, T] \times [x_{min}, x_{max}]$ which is

$$
\mathcal{T} \times \mathcal{X}, \quad \mathcal{T} = \{t_m | m = 0, \ldots, M\}, \quad \mathcal{X} = \{x_n | n = 0, \ldots, N - 1\} \tag{6.32}
$$

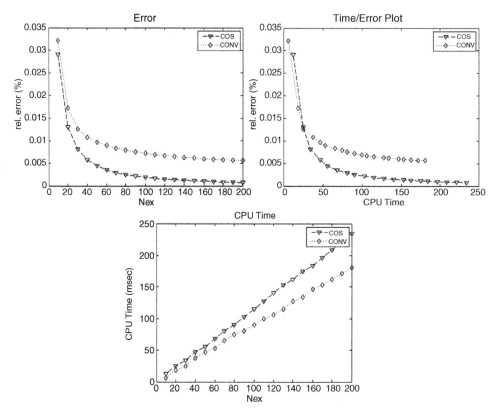

Figure 6.16 Pricing of Bermudan and American Put options with $S(0) = 100$, $T = 1$, $K = 110$, $r = 0.1$ and $q = 0$ in the Variance Gamma model. The upper left graph shows the pricing error increasing the number of possible exercise times. The upper right graph shows the CPU time in msec against the error from approximating an American option and, finally, the lower graph shows the CPU time in msec against the number of exercise possibilities

the grid points are given by

$$t_m = m\Delta_t, \quad x_n = x_{\min} + \Delta_x,$$

with $\Delta_t = T/M$ and $\Delta_x = (x_{\max} - x_{\min})/(N - 1)$. For the frequency domain we take the grid

$$w_n = -w_{\max} + n\Delta_w, \quad n = 0, 1, \ldots, N \tag{6.33}$$

with $\Delta_w = 2w_{\max}/N$ and $w_{\max} = \pi/\Delta_w$. Choosing the grid is no easy task and is discussed in Jackson, K., Jaimungal, S. and Surkov, V. (2007). For this section we use a standard grid which is constructed as described above. For the implementation see the code in Figure 6.18.

The boundary points $x_{\max}$ and $x_{\min}$ are chosen such that the interval is large enough to capture all information necessary for determining the option value but at the same time small enough to maintain numerical accuracy. The same holds true for choosing $w_{\max}$. Let us fix some notation for the option value and the transform on the grid

$$v_n^m := v(t_m, x_n), \quad \tilde{v}_n^m := \tilde{v}(t_m, w_n).$$

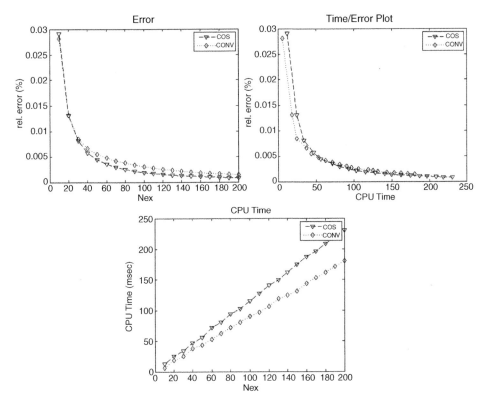

Figure 6.17 Pricing of Bermudan and American Put options with $S(0) = 100$, $T = 1$, $K = 110$, $r = 0.1$ and $q = 0$ in the Variance Gamma model. The parameters we have chosen are $\sigma = 0.17$, $\theta = -0.19$ and $\theta = -0.19$. The upper left graph shows the pricing error increasing the number of possible exercise times. The upper right graph shows the CPU time in msec against the error from approximating an American option and, finally, the lower graph shows the CPU time in msec against the number of exercise possibilities. We have taken the reference value as a model intrinsic calculated value

Using this notation we have

$$\mathcal{F}(v)(t_m, w_n) \approx \sum_{k=0}^{N-1} v_k^m e^{-w_n x_k} \Delta_x$$

$$= e^{-i\omega_n x_{\min}\Delta_x} \sum_{k=0}^{N-1} v_k^m e^{-ink/N}$$

$$= e^{-i\omega_n x_{\min}\Delta_x} \text{fft}(v^m)(n).$$

Thus, we have

$$v_n^m = \text{ifft}\left(\frac{V^m}{\alpha}\right)(n).$$

For one step backwards in time we find

$$V^{m-1} = \text{ifft}\left(\alpha^{-1} V^{m-1}\right) = \text{ifft}\left(\alpha^{-1} V^m e^{\psi \Delta t}\right)$$

$$= \text{ifft}\left(\alpha^{-1} \alpha \text{fft}\left(V^m\right) e^{\psi \Delta t}\right) = \text{ifft}\left(\text{fft}\left(V^m\right) e^{\psi \Delta t}\right).$$

```
function y = FST_MertonJumpDiffusion(S, K, sigma, rate, div, ...
    T, lambdaj, muj, sigmaj,cp)
% [0,T] x [x_min,x_ax]
M = 2^9;     % number of grid points time
N = 2^13;    % number of grid points space

dt = T/M;                          % Delta_t
x_min = -8; x_max = 8;             % x_min and x_max
dx =(x_max-x_min)/(N-1);           % Delta_x
x  = x_min:dx:x_max;               % x Grid

s = K*exp(x);                      % Values on Grid

% [0,T] x [0,w_max]
w_max = pi/dx;                     % w_max
dw = 2*w_max/N;                    % Delta_w
w = [0:dw:w_max, -w_max+dw:dw:-dw]; % w grid

fftw('planner', 'measure');        % init fftw

payoff = max(cp*(s-K),0);          % Time T payoff
val_opt = payoff;                  % init opt price for backward algo

% Characteristic function (could be from lib for other models)
cf = @(x) exp((1i*(rate-div-0.5*sigma*sigma ...
    -lambdaj*(exp(muj+0.5*sigmaj^2)-1)) ...
    .*w-0.5*(sigma*w).^2 ...
    +lambdaj*(exp(1i*muj*w-0.5*(sigmaj*w).^2)-1)-rate)*x);

for index_t = M-1:-1:0 % backward algorithm
    t_dt = (index_t+1-index_t)*dt;
    char_func = cf(t_dt);                            % char func

    val_opt = real(ifft(fft(val_opt).*char_func));   % FST method
    val_opt = max(val_opt, payoff);                  % for American
end

y = interp1(s,val_opt,S,'cubic'); % interpolate for getting opt value
```

Figure 6.18 Matlab implementation of the FST method for the Merton model to pricing European and Bermudan options

The parameter α incorporating boundary information such as $e^{-i\omega_n x_{\min}}$ cancels out in the end.

For certain payoff functions there might be singularities on the real axis. To overcome this problem we shift the frequency domain $w \to w + i\varepsilon$. Then, the backward step in time also has to be adjusted and we have for $\bar{v}_k^m := e^{\varepsilon x_k} v_k^m$ and $\bar{\varphi}(w) = \varphi(w + i\varepsilon)$, that is the points at time t_{m-1}:

$$v^{m-1} = \text{ifft}(\text{fft}(\bar{v}^m)e^{\bar{\varphi}\Delta_t}).$$

We do not provide implementation details here since a software package for Matlab can be obtained from Surkov, V. (2009). Furthermore, in their papers Jaimungal, S. and Surkov, V. (2008), Surkov, V. (2009), Jaimungal, S. and Surkov, V. (2010) and Davison, M. and Surkov, V. (2010) provide further applications of the method. However, we do give some sample code for pricing an option with early exercise opportunities in Figure 6.18.

European Options   The algorithm given in Figure 6.18 can be applied to price European options by using a single time step. We have observed that for certain parameter sets, for instance applying it to short rate models, more than one step for European options is necessary. This is due to the fact that the FST method uses a transformation to avoid extrapolation. But using this transformation can cause numerical instabilities when applied to large time steps.

American Options   To apply the FST method of this section to American options we simply modify the backward time step by

$$v^{m-1} = \max \left\{ \text{ifft}(\text{fft}(v^m)e^{\varphi \Delta_t}), v^m \right\}.$$

6.4 THE COSINE METHOD AND BARRIER OPTIONS

Below we illustrate the numerical application of the COS method to price discretely monitored Barrier options. The results have been presented in Fang, F. and Oosterlee, C. W. (2008b) and are closely related to the pricing of Bermudan options. For Barrier options the exercise is triggered if a predefined level, the barrier level, is breached. This is also the case for Bermudan options. In that case the level at which the exercise is triggered is the early exercise boundary, denoted by x^*, which had to be computed. In order to price Barrier options we can basically apply the same methodology we used for pricing Bermudans. But as we do not have to solve the trigger level the valuation of Barrier options should be faster.

Let us consider the payoffs of European Barrier Call and Put options. Let $R \in \mathbb{R}^+$ denote the rebate value. Then, the payoffs are given by

$$V_C(T, K) = (\max(S(T) - K, 0) - R) \, 1_{\{S(t_i) < h\}} + R \tag{6.34}$$

$$V_P(T, K) = (\max(K - S(T), 0) - R) \, 1_{\{S(t_i) < h\}} + R. \tag{6.35}$$

For some $M \in \mathbb{N}$ let $\mathcal{T} := \{t_1, t_2, \ldots, t_M\}$ denote the discrete set of time points where the option is monitored. To be able to apply the COS method we have to find the coefficients in the corresponding cosine expansion. For the option under consideration they are given by

$$V_k(t_m) = C_k(a, h, t_m) + e^{-r(T - t_{m-1})} R \frac{2}{b-a} \psi_k(h, b). \tag{6.36}$$

The expression $C_k(a, h, t, m)$ is the same as in (6.12) and $h = \log(H)$. We take two different cases, $h < 0$ and $h \geq 0$, and give the corresponding formulae.

$$V_k^{h<0}(t_M) = \begin{cases} 2R \frac{\psi_k(h,b)}{b-a}, & \text{Call} \\ G_k(a, b) + 2R \frac{\psi_k(h,b)}{b-a}, & \text{Put} \end{cases} \tag{6.37}$$

$$V_k^{h\geq0}(t_m) = \begin{cases} G_k(0, h) + 2R \frac{\psi_k(h,b)}{b-a}, & \text{Call} \\ G_k(a, 0) + 2R \frac{\psi_k(h,b)}{b-a}, & \text{Put} \end{cases}. \tag{6.38}$$

With the given coefficients the algorithm is now closely related to the one for Bermudan options (see Figure 6.6). Applying the pseudo algorithm from Figure 6.6 we can modify the implementation used for pricing Bermudan options. The corresponding Matlab code can be found in Figure 6.19 for Down-and-Out and Figure 6.20 for Up-and-Out options. The only thing which changes here is the initialization.

Algorithm 6.5: Pseudo code for pricing Up-and-Out and Down-and-Out discretely monitored Barrier options

---

1 Compute the coefficients $V_k(t_{Nex})$ which are $G_k(0, b)$ for a call and $G_k(a, 0)$ for a put
2 Down-and-Out: Set $x_1 = h$ and $x_2 = b$, $c = a$ and $d = h$
3 Up-and-Out: Set $x_1 = a$ and $x_2 = h$, $c = h$ and $d = b$
4 Compute m_s and m_c
5 Set $\mathcal{F}_s = \mathcal{F}(m_s)$ and $\mathcal{F}_c = \mathcal{F}(m_c)$
6 Set $G = \frac{2}{b-a}\psi_k(c, d)$
7 Backward induction
  for $m = \text{Nex} - 1$ *to* 0 **do**

7a	Compute u, $u_j := \varphi\left(\frac{j\pi}{b-a}\right) V_j(t_{m+1})$ and $v_0 = \frac{\varphi(0)}{2} V_0(t_{m+1})$
7b	Compute u_s by extending the vector u with zeros
7c	Calculate $M_s u$ by using the first N elements from $\mathcal{F}^{-1}(\mathcal{F}_s \mathcal{F}(u_s))$
7d	Calculate $M_c u$ by using the first N elements from $\mathcal{F}^{-1}(\mathcal{F}_c \mathcal{F}(u_s))$ and reversing them
7e	Determine the continuation value $C(x_1, x_2, t_0) = \frac{e^{-r\Delta t}}{\pi}\mathcal{I}(M_s u + M_c u)$ and V

8 Compute $v(x, t_0)$ using the coefficients $V_k(t_1)$

We illustrate the performance of the algorithm with a numerical example.

To do so we have chosen to price Down-and-Out Calls and Puts, as well as Up-and-Out Calls and Puts. The financial model is the CGMY model with parameters $C = 4$, $G = 50$, $M = 60$ and $Y = 0.7$. The current spot price $S(0)$ is 100, the upper barrier level is 120 and the lower one 80. We have chosen a rebate of 0. Table 6.1 shows the computed option prices. The computation along all strikes for all the different options took 1728 msec.

6.5 GREEKS

In this section we consider the implementation and comparison of all the approaches for calculating the Greeks. We are addressing these processes here since, with respect to Subsection 6.2.1, we now have each method available for a given strike range.

European Options We consider the Matlab code for pricing options using the Carr–Madan, the Lewis, the Convolution and the Cosine method. To compute Δ and Γ we can extend the code such that it can handle the corresponding pricing. The formulae have been provided in Chapter 5, Sections 5.3, 5.4, 5.6 and 5.7. The code is displayed in Figures 6.21, 6.22, 6.23 and 6.24.

For each model listed in Table 6.2 we compute Δ and Γ for the strike range $K = 20, 21, \ldots, 180$. When choosing a large number of grid points we see virtually no difference between the different methods. Figure 6.25 shows the Greeks for the Black–Scholes model calculated using these methods.

Since we have a benchmark result for the Black–Scholes model we can compute the relative error for calculating the Greeks by a given numerical method. We have calculated the relative

```
function price = FFTCOS_DownAndOut(n, Nex,H,Rb, L, c, cp, type, S0, ...
              t, r, q, strike, varargin)

% Nex := number of examination points
% H := Barrier, Rb := Rebate

dt = t / Nex;                  % time interval
Ngrid = 2 ^ n;                 % Grid points
Nstrike = size(strike,1);      % number of strikes

x = double(log(S0 ./ strike));        % center
h = double(log(H ./ strike));

a = double(c(1) + x - L * sqrt(c(2) + sqrt(c(3))));   % lower trunc
b = double(c(1) + x + L * sqrt(c(2) + sqrt(c(3))));   % upper trunc

Grid_i = repmat((0:Ngrid-1)',1,Nstrike);      % Grid index

% Set up function handles
if cp == 1
    vk = @(x) calcv(Grid_i, x, b, a, b, cp, strike);
    if h >= 0
        V = vk(h);
    else
        V = vk(0);
    end
else
    vk = @(x) calcv(Grid_i, x, 0, a, b, cp, strike);
    if h >= 0
        V = vk(a);
    else
        V = vk(h);
    end
end

cv = @(y) cvalue(h, b, a, b, Ngrid, y, type, dt, r, q, varargin{:});

aux = pi * Grid_i * diag(1./(b-a));
G = (sin(aux * diag(h-a))./aux);
G = exp(-r * dt) * 2 * Rb * [((h-a)./(b-a))';G(2:end,:)] ...
    * diag(1./(b-a));

V = V + G;
for m = Nex-1:-1:1              % backward induction
    V = cv(V) + G;
end

cfval = exp(feval(@CF, type,aux, dt,r,q,varargin{:}));

pF = cfval .* exp( 1i * aux * diag(x - a) );
pF(1,:) = 0.5*pF(1,:);
price = exp(-r * dt) * sum(real(pF) .* V) ;   % Option value at t_0

end
```

Figure 6.19 Matlab code for pricing a discretely monitored Down-and-Out Barrier option with the COS method

```
function price = FFTCOS_UpAndOut(n, Nex,H,Rb, L, c, cp, type, S0, ...
        t, r, q, strike, varargin)

% Nex := number of examination points; H := Barrier; Rb := Rebate

dt = t / Nex;                       % time interval
Ngrid = 2 ^ n;                      % Grid points
Nstrike = size(strike,1);           % number of strikes

x = double(log(S0 ./ strike));      % center
h = double(log(H ./ strike));

a = double(c(1) + x - L * sqrt(c(2) + sqrt(c(3))));   % lower trunc
b = double(c(1) + x + L * sqrt(c(2) + sqrt(c(3))));   % upper trunc

Grid_i = repmat((0:Ngrid-1)',1,Nstrike);    % Grid index

% Set up function handles
if cp == 1
    vk = @(x) calcv(Grid_i, x, h, a, b, cp, strike);
    if h >= 0
        V = vk(0);
    end
else
    vk = @(x) calcv(Grid_i, a, x, a, b, cp, strike);
    if h >= 0
        V = vk(0);
    else
        V = vk(h);
    end
end

cv = @(y) cvalue(a, h, a, b, Ngrid, y, type, dt, r, q, varargin{:});

aux = pi * Grid_i * diag(1./(b-a));
G = ((sin(aux * diag(b-a))-sin(aux*diag(h-a)))./aux);
G = exp(-r * dt) * 2 * Rb * [((b-h)./(b-a))';G(2:end,:)]* diag(1./(b-a));

V = V + G;
for m = Nex-1:-1:1                   % backward induction
    V = cv(V) + G;
end

cfval = exp(feval(@CF, type,aux, dt,r,q,varargin{:}));

pF = cfval .* exp( 1i * aux * diag(x - a) );
pF(1,:) = 0.5*pF(1,:);
price = exp(-r * dt) * sum(real(pF) .* V) ;   % Option value at t_0
end
```

Figure 6.20 Matlab code for pricing a discretely monitored Up-and-Out Barrier option with the COS method

```
delta_vec = real(exp(-0.5*ku).*fft((-1i*vj+0.5).*tmp))/pi;
gamma_vec = real(exp(-0.5*ku).*fft((vj.^2+0.25).*tmp))/pi;

call_delta_fft = (exp(-d*T) - exp(-r*T).*interp1(ku,delta_vec,kappa));
call_gamma_fft = exp(-r*T)/S.*interp1(ku,gamma_vec,kappa);
```

Figure 6.21 Matlab code for computing Δ and Γ using the Lewis method

Table 6.1 Prices of Down-and-Out Calls, Put and Up-and-Out Calls and Puts for the CGMY model with $C = 4$, $G = 50$, $M = 60$ and $Y = 0.7$. The current spot price is 100, the upper barrier level 120 and the lower one 80. We have chosen a rebate of 0

Strike	DOC	DOP	UOC	UOP
80	3,92881648297515	0	3,3891274885609	7,825933389741980
81	3,65245058368482	0,00509000676799516	3,07953169240885	8,4369934976911881
82	3,38696226194441	0,0210575910854376	2,79155353345055	9,0696712428342582
83	3,13324340694865	0,0487946421479752	2,52434676358557	9,723120377070683
84	2,89196268168595	0,0889698229437369	2,27702844827698	10,396457965863484
85	2,66356133796108	0,142024385276819	2,04868850196458	11,088773923652385
86	2,4482656117842	0,208184565157808	1,83839867680053	11,799140002589686
87	2,24610979784534	0,28748465727696	1,64522092473914	12,526618154629687
88	2,05696456551095	0,37979533100099	1,46821507557829	13,2702682095788
89	1,88056641779575	0,484853089344828	1,30644579396087	14,02915483205489
90	1,71654568611064	0,602288263718477	1,15898879628197	14,802353738476490
91	1,5644516831011	0,731650166766235	1,02493632413128	15,588957170427191
92	1,4237744839902	0,872428873713842	0,903401884659115	16,388078635056292
93	1,29396332019772	1,0240736159797	0,793524280069574	17,19885693456893
94	1,17444184135973	1,18600804319977	0,694470958060318	18,020459516660194
95	1,06462061596184	1,35764272385982	0,605440722252524	18,852085184953795
96	0,963907258117092	1,53838527207379	0,525665846671537	19,69296621347496
97	0,871714535589947	1,72764845560481	0,454413641632056	20,542369912535997
98	0,787466766446205	1,92485659251913	0,390987520411497	21,399599695416698
99	0,710604768600172	2,1294505007312	0,334727617069721	22,263995696176399
100	0,640589593116213	2,34089123130519	0,285011005662181	23,13493498887100
101	0,576905244504458	2,55866278875185	0,241251569854803	24,011831457164101
102	0,519060564224303	2,78227401453028	0,202899569798368	24,8941353612088102
103	0,466590425867711	3,01125978223174	0,169440950485367	25,7813326459972103
104	0,419056364696267	3,24518162711835	0,140396433211288	26,6729440328245104
105	0,376046743610261	3,48362791209077	0,115320429530309	27,5685239332448105
106	0,337176543157262	3,72621361769644	0,0937998153165811	28,4676592231325106
107	0,302086852924361	3,97257983352137	0,0754526011041802	29,3699679130214107
108	0,270444132507886	4,22239301916294	0,0599265335962526	30,2750977496148108
109	0,241939300271032	4,47534409298506	0,0468976619093074	31,1827247820293109
110	0,216286697319952	4,73114739609147	0,0360689004411934	32,0925519246624110
111	0,193222964129989	4,98953956896021	0,0271686177039531	33,0043075460266111
112	0,172505859601094	5,25027837048957	0,0199492763252353	33,9177441087492112
113	0,15391304726123	5,51314146420751	0,0141861429532478	34,8326368794785113
114	0,137240870254641	5,77792519325922	0,0096760777103789	35,748782718337114
115	0,122303134039675	6,04444336310183	0,00623640157429171	36,6659989463022115
116	0,108929912496729	6,31252604761825	0,00370382807722653	37,5841222769065116
117	0,0969663892960267	6,58201843047525	0,00193343515302284	38,5030077880837117
118	0,0862717423936391	6,8527796896307	0,000797646192919949	39,4225279032248118
119	0,0767180764643127	7,12468192975967	0,000185188197400594	40,3425713493307119
120	0,0681894061177463	7,39760916547166	0	41,2630420652347120

error and found that the COS method is the one which performs best. The relative errors of the numerical methods considered have been computed for 2^{13} grid points and plotted along the strike range 30, 21, ..., 180. Figure 6.26 displays the results.

If we decrease the number of grid points the situation changes dramatically. Then the only method to perform well is the COS method. Figure 6.27 summarizes the results. Thus, we have to take care when we apply the different methods to the derivation of Δ and Γ.

```
deltavec = real(exp(-optAlpha .* ku) ...
  .* fft((1i*vj+(optAlpha+1)).*tmp) / S / pi);
gammavec = real(exp(-optAlpha .* ku) ...
  .* fft((1i*vj+(optAlpha+1)).*((1i*vj+(optAlpha+1))-1).*tmp)/S/S/ pi);

delta_fft = real(interp1(ku,deltavec,lnK));
gamma_fft = real(interp1(ku,gammavec,lnK));
```

Figure 6.22   Matlab code for computing Δ and Γ using the Carr–Madan method

```
call_delta_fft = exp(-r*T)*K.*real((mat.*mat_tmp) ...
  * (phi.*U_k))/S + exp(-d*T);
call_gamma_fft=exp(-r*T)*K.*real((mat.*(mat_tmp.*(mat_tmp-1))) ...
  * (phi.*U_k))/S^2;
```

Figure 6.23   Matlab code for computing Δ and Γ using the COS method

```
invFFT_delta = fft(repmat(-1i*u,1,M) ...
  .*exp(1i*matN*diag(y(1,:)-x(1,:))*du).*phi.*FFT);
% delta vector conv method
delta_conv = exp(-r*T)*real(repmat(exp(1i*u(1)*(y(1,:)-x(1,:))),N,1) ...
  .*Ivec.*invFFT_delta)/S;

invFFT_gamma = fft(repmat((-1i*u).^2,1,M) ...
  .*exp(1i*matN*diag(y(1,:)-x(1,:))*du).*phi.*FFT);
% gamma vector conv method
gamma_conv = exp(-r*T)*real(repmat(exp(1i*u(1)*(y(1,:)-x(1,:))),N,1) ...
  .*Ivec.*(invFFT_gamma-invFFT_delta))/S^2;

call_delta_fft = delta_conv(N/2+1,:)';
call_gamma_fft = gamma_conv(N/2+1,:)';
```

Figure 6.24   Matlab code for computing Δ and Γ using the CONV method

Table 6.2   Models and parameters for calculating the Greeks Δ and Γ

Black–Scholes
$\sigma = 0.2$

Heston
$V(0) = 0.04$ $\Theta = 0.04$ $\kappa = 0.5$ $\nu = 0.2$ $\rho = -0.8$

Variance Gamma
$\sigma = 0.125$ $\nu = 0.375$ $\theta = 0.2$

CGMY
$C = 0.1$ $G = 0.75$ $M = 1$ $Y = 0.25$

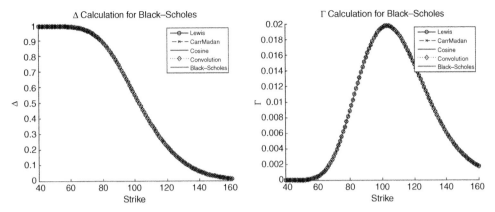

Figure 6.25 Values for Δ and Γ in the Black–Scholes model for strikes $20, 21, \ldots, 180$ calculated using the analytic solution as well as the Lewis, Carr–Madan, CONV and COS methods with 2^{13} grid points. The volatility $\sigma_{BS} = 0.2$, $r = 0.1$ and the spot value is $S(0) = 100$

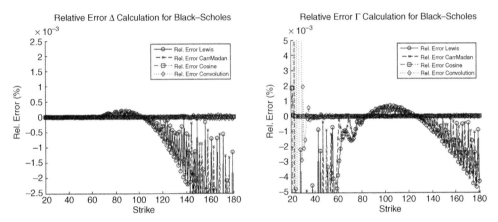

Figure 6.26 Relative errors to the analytic solution for Δ and Γ in the Black–Scholes model for strikes $20, 21, \ldots, 180$ calculated using the Lewis, Carr–Madan, CONV and COS methods, with 2^{13} grid points. The volatility $\sigma_{BS} = 0.2$, $r = 0.1$ and the spot value is $S(0) = 100$

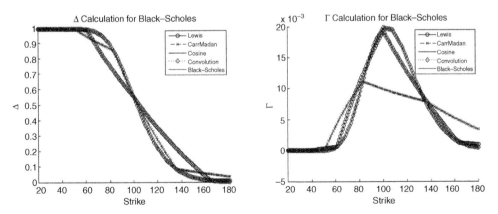

Figure 6.27 Values for Δ and Γ in the Black–Scholes model for strikes $20, 21, \ldots, 180$ calculated using the analytic solution as well as the Lewis, Carr–Madan, CONV and COS methods with 2^8 grid points. The volatility $\sigma_{BS} = 0.2$, $r = 0.1$ and the spot value is $S(0) = 100$. The values differ according to the pricing method

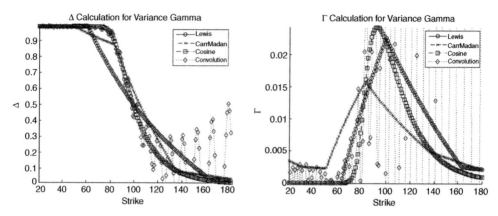

Figure 6.28   Values for Δ and Γ in the Variance Gamma model for strikes 20, 21, . . . , 180 calculated using the Lewis, Carr–Madan, CONV and COS methods with 2^8 grid points. The parameters are given in Table 6.2, $r = 0.1$ and the spot value is $S(0) = 100$

Considering the other models and keeping the number of grid points equal to 2^8, we observe significant differences between the methods considered. Figure 6.28 gives the results for the Variance Gamma mode and Figure 6.29 those for the Heston model.

Finally, we consider a large number of grid points and the CGMY model. To this end we take $N = 2^{13}$. We consider the relative error taking the results from the COS method as the benchmark. First, Figure 6.30 shows that even for 2^{13} grid points only the COS method leads to reliable results.

This fact can be further illustrated by considering the relative error. For a comparison we have chosen to compute the relative error against the values computed using the COS method. The results are displayed in Figure 6.31. We conclude that, even with a large number of grid points, some methods are not suited for computing hedge sensitivities.

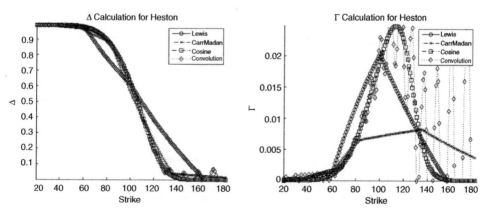

Figure 6.29   Values for Δ and Γ in the Heston model for strikes 20, 21, . . . , 180 calculated using the Lewis, Carr–Madan, CONV and COS methods with 2^8 grid points. The parameters are given in Table 6.2, $r = 0.1$ and the spot value is $S(0) = 100$

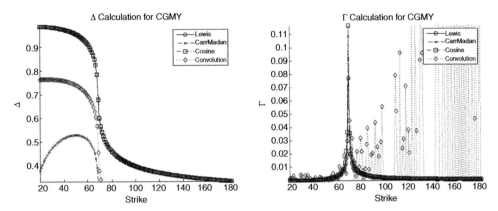

Figure 6.30 Values for Δ and Γ in the CGMY model for strikes $20, 21, \ldots, 180$ calculated using the Lewis, Carr–Madan, CONV and COS methods with 2^{13} grid points. The parameters are given in Table 6.2, $r = 0.1$ and the spot value is $S(0) = 100$

Bermudan Options For computing the Greeks corresponding to Bermudan options we show the modification of the COS method. The implementation is given in Figure 6.32. The code is essentially the same as the one presented in Figure 6.6.

Let us give some numerical illustration for the Greeks of Bermudan options. We consider the CGMY model with $C = 0.5$, $G = 3$, $M = 3$ and $Y = 0.5$. The current spot price is $S(0) = 100$, the risk free rate $r = 0.1$ and the dividend yield $d = 0$. For our illustration we consider the strike range $K = 10, 11, \ldots, 190$. For each strike we calculate the Δ and the Γ. The time to maturity is set to $T = 1$ with 10 possible exercises. Figure 6.33 shows the results in terms of increasing the number of grid points for the cosine expansion. We consider 2^N points with $N = 4, 5, \ldots, 9$ and the reference value calculated using 2^{15} points. The reference values are marked by 'o'.

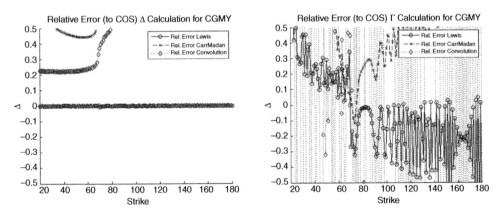

Figure 6.31 Relative errors for Δ and Γ in the CGMY model for strikes $20, 21, \ldots, 180$ calculated using the Lewis, Carr–Madan and CONV methods with 2^{13} grid points. The relative errors are calculated with the values computed using the COS method as the reference values. The parameters are given in Table 6.2, $r = 0.1$ and the spot value is $S(0) = 100$

```matlab
function [price, delta, gamma] = FFTCOS_B(n, Nex, L, c, cp, type, S0, ..
    t, r, q, strike, varargin)
dt = t / Nex;                       % time interval
Ngrid = 2 ^ n;                      % Grid points
Nstrike = size(strike,1);           % number of strikes

x = double(log(S0 ./ strike));          % center

a = double(c(1) + x - L * sqrt(c(2) + sqrt(c(3))));     % lower trunc
b = double(c(1) + x + L * sqrt(c(2) + sqrt(c(3))));     % upper trunc
Grid_i = repmat((0:Ngrid-1)',1,Nstrike);    % Grid index

% Set up function handles
if cp == 1
    vk = @(x) calcv(Grid_i, x, b, a, b, cp, strike);
    cv = @(x,y) cvalue(a, x, a, b, Ngrid, y, type, dt, ...
        r, q, varargin{:});
else
    vk = @(x) calcv(Grid_i, a, x, a, b, cp, strike);
    cv = @(x,y) cvalue(x, b, a, b, Ngrid, y, type, dt, ...
        r, q, varargin{:});
end
    initialGuess = 0;                   % guess for x^*(t_Nex-1)

V = vk(0);                          % coeff V in t_Nex-1

xstark = zeros(Nstrike,Nex-1);
for m = Nex-1:-1:1                   % backward induction
    xstark(:,m) = xstar(initialGuess,cp, a, b, 5, Grid_i, type, ...
        V, dt, r, q, strike, varargin{:});      % early ex point
    C = cv(xstark(:,m),V);              % Cont value at t_m
    V = vk(xstark(:,m)) + C;            % Coeff V in t_m
    initialGuess = xstark(:,m);
end

cfval = exp(feval(@CF, type,pi*Grid_i*diag(1./(b-a)), dt,...
    r,q,varargin{:}));

aux = 1i* pi * Grid_i * diag(1./(b-a));
pF = cfval .* exp( 1i * pi * Grid_i * diag((x - a) ./ (b - a)) );
dF = pF.*aux;
gF = dF.*(aux-1);

pF(1,:) = 0.5*pF(1,:); dF(1,:) = 0.5*dF(1,:); gF(1,:) = 0.5*gF(1,:);

price = exp(-r * dt) * sum(real(pF) .* V) ;             % price
delta = exp(-r * dt) * 2./(b-a)'.*sum(real(dF) .* V)/S0 ;  % delta
gamma = exp(-r * dt) * 2./(b-a)'.*sum(real(gF) .* V)/S0/S0 ;% gamma

end
```

Figure 6.32 Matlab code for computing the Greeks of a Bermudan option and sensitivities using the COS method

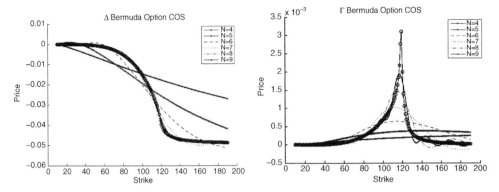

Figure 6.33   Values for Δ and Γ for the Greeks of a Bermudan option with 10 exercise possibilities in the CGMY model for strikes $10, 11, \ldots, 190$ calculated using the COS method using 2^N points. The parameters are $C = 0.5$, $G = 3$, $M = 3$ and $Y = 0.5$. The other parameters are $r = 0.1$, $d = 0$, $T = 1$ and the spot value is $S(0) = 100$

In the next case we consider $T = 1/12$ and allow 10 exercises. We compute the Δ and the Γ of the option. Figure 6.34 summarizes the results. The dependence of the number of grid points is illustrated. The circles represent the reference value calculated with 2^{15} grid points.

6.6 SUMMARY AND CONCLUSIONS

This chapter has shown how to extend methods applied to plain Vanilla European options to be applicable to exotic options and options with early exercise opportunities. To this end we have shown how to generalize some of the pricing algorithms discussed in Chapter 5. Another method, FST, is introduced. We illustrated our results by pseudo algorithms as well as usable Matlab source code. The examples we applied can all be found in the supporting material for

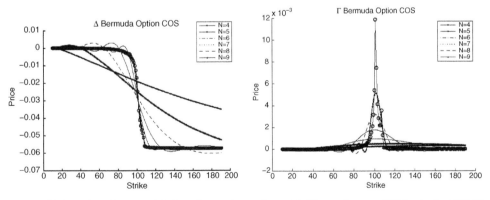

Figure 6.34   Values for Δ and Γ for a Bermudan option with 10 exercise possibilities in the CGMY model for strikes $10, 11, \ldots, 190$ calculated using the COS method using 2^N points. The parameters are $C = 0.5$, $G = 3$, $M = 3$ and $Y = 0.5$. The other parameters are $r = 0.1$, $d = 0$, $T = 1/12$ and the spot value is $S(0) = 100$

this book. Thus, it is possible for the reader to test the algorithms, modify them and try out proprietary methods for pricing and hedging.

Numerical examples included a comparison of the CONV and the COS methods in terms of accuracy and speed for pricing Bermudan and American options. Moreover, we considered convergence issues when deriving American option prices.

Finally, we showed how to obtain stable and fast algorithms for calculating hedge sensitivities for advanced models. To this end it is possible to use advanced models for dynamic hedges. We proposed to use the numerical methods of this chapter to study dynamical hedge strategies. This issue will be considered in Chapter 10.

7
Monte Carlo Simulation and Applications

7.1 INTRODUCTION AND OBJECTIVES

In Chapters 5 and 6 we considered the pricing of options using integration methods. In particular, we focused on the fast Fourier method. Despite the fact that such methods can be applied to path-dependent options, the derivation – if possible – is often cumbersome and other methods have to be considered. One such method is the *Monte Carlo Simulation*. To be able to apply it to a stochastic model we must be able to sample paths of the model under consideration. Using the sampled paths we then evaluate a payoff or a risk measure. Using results given in Chapter 13, where the rationale of Monte Carlo simulation is outlined, we derive an estimator of the price or risk measure.

We consider the sampling of stochastic processes and review special purpose schemes for the models introduced in Chapters 2 and 3. First, we start with standard schemes based on (stochastic) Taylor expansion. The schemes considered are the (Log-)Euler scheme, the Predictor-Corrector scheme and the Milstein scheme. Then, we proceed by sampling from stochastic volatility models, Lévy processes based models and stochastic volatility Lévy models. We provide Matlab code for all the schemes considered. The source code can be used and modified by the user.

Bridge sampling to extend the method for using Quasi Random Numbers is detailed and a corresponding technique for Lévy processes is described. A short introduction to sampling in the Libor Market Model and multi-dimensional Lévy models is presented. Since copulae are a widespread tool for multi-dimensional modelling we, finally, present some sampling methods and some examples.

7.2 SAMPLING DIFFUSION PROCESSES

The first section is about sampling from a diffusion process. If reasonably easy, robust and fast methods for exact simulation are available, we advise readers to rely on such methods. If not we consider three discretization methods, namely, the *Euler scheme*, the *Predictor-Corrector scheme* and the *Milstein scheme*. The different schemes are often the method of choice when implementing Monte Carlo simulation. We consider the general setup in Matlab in this section.

First, we give the basic discretization methods for diffusion processes. To this end we assume that the dynamic is given in terms of the SDE on some probability space Ω,

$$ds = \mu(t, S)dt + \sigma(t, S)dW(t), \quad t \in [t_0, T] \tag{7.1}$$

or equivalently in integral notation

$$S(t) = S(t_0) + \int_{t_0}^{t} \mu(u, S(u))du + \int_{t_0}^{t} \sigma(u, S(u))dW(u), t \in [t_0, T]. \tag{7.2}$$

For fixed $\omega \in \Omega$ the functions μ and σ are given by

$$\mu : [t_0, T] \times \mathbb{R} \to \mathbb{R}, \quad \sigma : [t_0, T] \times \mathbb{R} \to \mathbb{R}^+.$$

For an interval $[t_0, T]$ we fix a discretization $\mathcal{T} := \{t_0, t_1, \ldots, t_{Nt} = T\}$ and denote $\Delta_k :=$ $t_k - t_{k-1}, k = 1, \ldots, Nt$. We denote the number of time steps by Nt. This does not mean that they are time-dependent but it is to distinguish the number from the number of simulations N.

7.2.1 The Exact Scheme

For certain models it is possible to find an exact solution for (7.1) and (7.2). For instance, if $\sigma(t, S(t)) = \sigma S(t)$ and $\mu(t, S(t)) = r S(t)$, the exact solution is known.

$$S(t_k) = S(t_{k-1}) \cdot \exp\left(\left(r - \frac{\sigma^2}{2}\right) \Delta_k + \sigma \sqrt{\Delta_k} Z\right), \quad Z \sim \mathcal{N}(0, 1).$$

In the following subsections we review standard numerical schemes applicable whenever an exact solution is not available.

7.2.2 The Euler Scheme

The Euler scheme approximates the integrals in (7.2) by taking the values of μ and σ at t_{k-1} of an interval $[t_{k-1}, t_k]$, and multiplying with the time step Δ_k, and $\sqrt{\Delta_k} Z_k$ with $Z_k \sim \mathcal{N}(0, 1)$ respectively, thus

$$\int_{t_{k-1}}^{t_k} \mu(u, S(u)) du \approx \mu(t_{k-1}, S(t_{k-1})) \Delta_k$$

$$\int_{t_{k-1}}^{t_k} \sigma(u, S(u)) dW(u) \approx \sigma(t_{k-1}, S(t_{k-1})) \sqrt{\Delta_k} Z_k.$$

This leads to the following sample scheme:

$$S(t_k) \approx S(t_{k-1}) + \mu(t_{k-1}, S(t_{k-1})) \Delta_k + \sigma(t_{k-1}, S(t_{k-1})) \sqrt{\Delta_k} \cdot Z_k. \tag{7.3}$$

If we consider the logarithm of $S(t)$, denoted by $X(t)$, thus $S(t) = \exp(X(t))$, and apply the Euler scheme, we have

$$X(t_k) \approx X(t_{k-1}) + \mu(t_{k-1}, S(t_{k-1})) \Delta_k + \sigma(t_{k-1}, S(t_{k-1})) \sqrt{\Delta_k} \cdot Z_k. \tag{7.4}$$

The latter scheme is called the *log-Euler scheme*. In this case we do not have to evaluate an exponential function at each time step and we can apply summation instead of multiplication. This scheme is much faster to compute and more stable than (7.3). Finally, we note that if the process $(S(t))_t$ is a martingale, $(S(t_k))_k$ is also a martingale.

7.2.3 The Predictor-Corrector Scheme

Here we look at a general Predictor-Corrector scheme. Special versions of this scheme exist in the literature and appear in practical applications. For instance, the drift correcting Predictor-Corrector scheme is a scheme which is applied if the contribution resulting from the drift of (7.1) is relevant, which is for instance the case when a Libor Market Model is discretized.

For this scheme, first, a predictor S_p is sampled by the following equation and denoting $Z_k \sim \mathcal{N}(0, 1)$:

$$S_p(t_k) := S(t_{k-1}) + \mu(t_{k-1}, S(t_{k-1})) \Delta_k + \sigma(t_{k-1}, S(t_{k-1})) \sqrt{\Delta_k} \cdot Z_k. \tag{7.5}$$

Define $\hat{\mu}(t_1, t_2, x_1, x_2, \alpha) := \alpha \mu(t_2, x_2) + (1 - \alpha)\mu(t_1, x_1)$ and $\hat{\sigma}(t_1, t_2, x_1, x_2, \beta) := \beta \sigma$
$(t_2, x_2) + (1 - \beta)\sigma(t_1, x_1)$. Then, the corrector S_c specified by (7.6) is used as the approxima-
tion to the dynamics of S. The variates Z_k are the same as in (7.5). The corrector is given by

$$S_c(t_k) := S(t_{k-1}) + \hat{\mu}(t_{k-1}, t_k, S(t_{k-1}), S_p(t_k))\Delta_k$$
$$+ \hat{\sigma}(t_{k-1}, t_k, S(t_{k-1}), S_p(t_k))\sqrt{\Delta_k} \cdot Z_k. \qquad (7.6)$$

This scheme can also be applied to the logarithmic spot price $X(t)$ and we call it the *log
Predictor-Corrector* scheme. The advantage is the same as for the Log-Euler scheme.

7.2.4   The Milstein Scheme

The Milstein scheme is a refinement of the Euler scheme. It approximates the integrals
appearing in (7.2) by

$$\int_{t_{k-1}}^{t_k} \sigma(u, S(u))dW(u) \approx \sigma(t_{k-1}, S(t_{k-1}))\sqrt{\Delta_k}Z_k$$
$$+ \frac{\sigma(t_{k-1}, S(t_{k-1}))'\sigma(t_{k-1}, S(t_{k-1}))}{2}\Delta_k(Z_k^2 - 1), \quad Z_k \sim \mathcal{N}(0, 1).$$

This leads to the following numerical scheme, again denoting $Z_k \sim \mathcal{N}(0, 1)$:

$$S(t_k) = S(t_{k-1}) + \mu(t_{k-1}, S(t_{k-1}))\Delta_k + \sigma(t_{k-1}, S(t_{k-1}))\sqrt{\Delta_k} \cdot Z_k$$
$$+ \underbrace{\frac{1}{2}\sigma'(t_{k-1}, S(t_{k-1}))\sigma(t_{k-1}, S(t_{k-1}))\Delta_k(Z_k^2 - 1)}_{SII}. \qquad (7.7)$$

The Milstein scheme does not preserve the martingale property. The second summand SII of
(7.7) destroys this property.

7.2.5   Implementation and Results

We have implemented the schemes in Matlab for which the code is given in Figure 7.2. We
only consider the one-dimensional setting for fixing the ideas. The generalization to several
underlyings is possible by multiplying a vector of independent Gaussian variables with the
Cholesky or the Spectral decomposition of a correlation matrix. The volatility σ and the drift
μ are functions of time and space. To this end we have coded function handles to implement

$$\mu : \mathbb{R}^+ \times \mathbb{R} \to \mathbb{R}, \mu = \mu(t, S)$$
$$\sigma : \mathbb{R}^+ \times \mathbb{R} \to \mathbb{R}^+, \sigma = \sigma(t, S).$$

We first compute the volatilities and the drifts and then the values are passed into the path
construction schemes. The exact scheme can only be used for SDE which has an exact solution.
   We have to initialize several constants such as the spot value $S(0)$, the volatility matrix Σ,
the maturity T and the function handles for diffusion and drift, called `diffusion` and `drift`.
Furthermore, to apply the Milstein scheme we need the derivative of the volatility; the corresponding function is named `ddiff`. We use the function for presenting the code in Figure 7.1.
   Let us examine the code given in Figure 7.1. First, we consider the computation of the
volatility, which is done using the function handle `diffusion`. We provide a volatility matrix
of dimension time and space and we used the Matlab interpolation function `intern`. Of

```
S0 = 100;                    % spot
r = 0.03; d = 0.005;         % rate and dividend yield
T= 2;                        % maturity

sigma = 0.15;                % constant volatility
Sigma = [    0.35 0.34 0.3 0.285 0.27;
             0.25 0.24 0.23 0.21 0.19;
             0.21 0.20 0.19 0.18 0.15;
             0.19 0.16 0.15 0.18 0.21;
             0.15 0.11 0.10 0.12 0.15;
             0.21 0.2 0.19 0.18 0.15];
Sgrid = [0 80 100 120 200]; % has to be number of columns of Sigma
Tgrid = 0:0.5:T+0.5;        % has to be number of rows of Sigma


% diffusion functions as handels
% local volatility using a grid of quoted volatilities
diffusion_exact = @(S,t) interpn(Tgrid,Sgrid,Sigma,t,S);
diffusion_euler = @(S,t) S.*(interpn(Tgrid,Sgrid,Sigma,t,S))';
diffusion_logeuler = @(S,t) interpn(Tgrid,Sgrid,Sigma,t,exp(S));
diffusion_milstein = @(S,t) S.*interpn(Tgrid,Sgrid,Sigma,t,S);

% drift functions as handles
% could include martingale adjustment into the drift!!!
drift_euler = @(S,t) (r-d) * S;
drift_exact = @(S,t) (r-d);
drift_logeuler = @(S,t) (r-d);
drift_milstein = @(S,t) (r-d)*S;

% for Milstein scheme since it uses derivative of diffusion coeff
eps = 1;
ddiffusion = @(S,t) 0.5*(diffusion_euler(S+eps,t) ...
    - diffusion_euler(S-eps,t))./eps;

NSim = 1;                    % Number of simulations
Nt = 24;                     % Number of time steps
delta = T/Nt;                % distance of consec steps
sdelta = sqrt(delta);        % square root of delta
Timegrid = cumsum(0:delta:delta*Nt);
lnS = zeros(NSim,Nt+1);      % the log spots
lnS(:,1) = log(S0);          % init first since it is the log-spot
```

Figure 7.1   Input data used to discretize diffusion models

course, other functions such as parametric functions are feasible. For instance, we can take the constant function which leads to the Black–Scholes model.

7.3   SPECIAL PURPOSE SCHEMES

After reviewing standard schemes we turn to special purpose schemes in this section. Such schemes are developed to be applicable to classes of models or even only to a certain model. We implement schemes for all models considered in Chapters 2 and 3. The schemes we consider closely resemble the dynamic of the underlying model. We start with the Heston stochastic volatility model and the SABR model. We proceed by considering the simulation of compound

```
dW = randn(NSim,Nt);          % Gaussians

% Exact, Euler, Log-Euler, Milstein, PC
S_Exact = zeros(NSim,Nt+1);   % spots for exact solution
S_Exact(:,1)=S0;              % init first since it is the spot
S_Euler = S_Exact;            % spots for Euler
S_Milstein = S_Exact;         % spots for Milstein
S_C = S_Exact;                % spot for Predictor-Corrector

gamma1 = 0.5; gamma2 = 0.5;   % parameters for Predicotr-Corrector

for t=2:Nt+1
    vol_logeuler = diffusion_logeuler(lnS(:,t-1),delta*(t-1));
    mu_logeuler = drift_logeuler(lnS(:,t-1),delta*(t-1));

    vol_exact = diffusion_exact(S_Exact(:,t-1),delta*(t-1));
    mu_exact = drift_exact(S_Exact(:,t-1),delta*(t-1));

    vol_euler = diffusion_euler(S_Euler(:,t-1),delta*(t-1));
    mu_euler = drift_euler(S_Euler(:,t-1), delta*(t-1));

    vol_c = diffusion_euler(S_C(:,t-1),delta*(t-1));
    mu_p = drift_euler(S_C(:,t-1), delta*(t-1));

    vol_milstein = diffusion_milstein(S_Milstein(:,t-1),delta*(t-1));
    mu_milstein = drift_milstein(S_Milstein(:,t-1),delta*(t-1));

    S_Exact(:,t) = S_Exact(:,t-1) ...
        .* exp(mu_exact * delta ...
        - 0.5 * vol_exact.^2 * delta + sdelta * vol_exact .* dW(:,t-1));

    lnS(:,t) = lnS(:,t-1) + delta * (-0.5 * vol_logeuler.^2 ...
        + mu_logeuler) + sdelta * vol_logeuler .* dW(:,t-1);

    S_Euler(:,t) = S_Euler(:,t-1) ...
        + mu_euler * delta ...
        + sdelta * vol_euler .* dW(:,t-1);

    S_P = S_C(:,t-1)  + mu_p*delta ...
        + sdelta * vol_c .* dW(:,t-1);
    mu_c = drift_euler(S_P,delta*(t-1));

    S_C(:,t) = S_C(:,t-1) ...
        + (gamma1*mu_c+gamma2*mu_p)*delta ...
        + sdelta * vol_c .* dW(:,t-1);

    diff1 = ddiffusion(S_Milstein(:,t-1),delta*(t-1));
    S_Milstein(:,t) = S_Milstein(:,t-1) ...
        + mu_milstein * delta ...
        + sdelta * vol_milstein .* dW(:,t-1); ...
        + 0.5 * vol_milstein * diff1 .* (dW(:,t-1).^2-1)*delta;
end
S_LogEuler = exp(lnS);
```

Figure 7.2 Matlab implementation of the schemes based on (stochastic) Taylor expansion, namely the Euler, the log-Euler, the Milstein, the Predictor-Corrector and the exact schemes

Poisson processes on a fixed grid and on a stochastic grid. After presenting the schemes for jump-diffusion models we consider schemes for discretizing models based on Lévy processes.

7.3.1 Schemes for the Heston Model

Let us take the Heston stochastic volatility model. We apply the same notation as in Chapter 2, Subsection 2.3.3, where the model was introduced. First, we apply a Euler scheme to discretize the variance process V. We assume we have already simulated $V(t)$ and now we wish to simulate $V(t+\Delta)$ by

$$V(t+\Delta) = V(t) + \kappa(\Theta - V(t))\Delta + v\sqrt{V(t)\Delta}Z, \quad Z \sim \mathcal{N}(0, 1).$$

A realization z of the random variable $Z \sim \mathcal{N}(0, 1)$ can lead to negative values of V when

$$z < -\frac{V(t) + \kappa(\Theta - V(t))\Delta}{v\sqrt{V(t)\Delta}}.$$

Since to compute the volatility we have to take the square root, this leads to an error. Taking smaller time steps, Δ, the probability of such variates decreases, since $-\frac{c_1}{\sqrt{\Delta}} - c_2\sqrt{\Delta} \to -\infty$ for some constants $c_1, c_2 \in \mathbb{R}^+$ but simulating the process using smaller time steps needs more computational time. Several authors have proposed sampling schemes for this model. We consider the exact sampling (Broadie, M. and Kaya, O. (2006)) and the Quadratic Exponential (QE) scheme (Andersen, L. (2008)). The Zhu, the non-central χ^2 inversion scheme (van Haastrecht, A. and Pelsser, A. (2010)) and the Γ expansion scheme (Glasserman, P. and Kim, K.-K. (2008)) are not considered since we have observed that the QE scheme is the most reliable simulation scheme and thus this scheme is market standard.

Exact Sampling / The Broadie–Kaya Scheme

Broadie, M. and Kaya, O. (2006) introduced an exact sampling procedure for the Heston stochastic volatility model. The scheme is termed the *Broadie–Kaya scheme*. Since they apply the numerical inversion of a cumulative distribution using the characteristic function, the scheme is computationally expensive and not applicable for the sampling. The time required to evaluate the function and invert the corresponding probability distribution numerically is too long.

If W_1 and W_2 are the correlated driving Brownian motions of the Heston model driving the underlying and the variance, we can replace these Brownian motions with two uncorrelated Brownian motions W and Z such that $W_2 = W$ and $W_1 = \rho Z + \sqrt{1 - \rho^2}W$. The logarithm of the underlying $X(t)$ and the variance process $V(t)$ are then given by

$$X(t+\Delta) = X(t) - \frac{1}{2}\int_t^{t+\Delta} V(s)ds + \rho\int_t^{t+\Delta}\sqrt{V(s)}dZ(s)$$

$$+\sqrt{1-\rho^2}\int_t^{t+\Delta}\sqrt{V(s)}dW(s) \tag{7.8}$$

$$V(t+\Delta) = V(t) + \kappa\int_t^{t+\Delta}(\theta - V(s))ds + v\int_t^{t+\Delta}\sqrt{V(s)}dZ(s).$$

Using the integrated square root process for the variance

$$\int_t^{t+\Delta}\sqrt{V(s)}dZ(s) = \frac{V(t+\Delta) - V(t) - \kappa\theta\Delta + \kappa\int_t^{t+\Delta}V(s)ds}{v}V(t) \tag{7.9}$$

and substituting (7.9) into (7.8) leads to

$$X(t + \Delta) = X(t) + \frac{\rho \kappa}{\nu} \int_t^{t+\Delta} V(s)ds - \frac{1}{2} \int_t^{t+\Delta} V(s)ds$$

$$+ \frac{\rho}{\nu}(V(t + \Delta) - V(t) - \kappa \theta \Delta) + \sqrt{1 - \rho^2} \int_t^{t+\Delta} \sqrt{V(s)}dW(s).$$

First, for time $t + \Delta$ the simulation of $V(t + \Delta)$ with known variance $V(t)$ can be achieved by sampling from a non-central χ^2 distribution. We denote by χ_n the χ^2 distribution with n degrees of freedom and by χ_{nc}^2 the χ^2 distribution with n degrees of freedom and non-centrality parameter λ. We have

$$\chi_{nc}^2(n, \lambda) = \begin{cases} (Z_1 + \sqrt{\lambda})^2 + \chi_{n-1}, & n > 1 \\ \chi_{n+2Z_2}^2, & 0 < n \leq 1 \end{cases}.$$

With $Z_1 \sim \mathcal{N}(0, 1)$ and a Poissonian random variable $Z_2 \sim \mathcal{P}\left(\frac{\lambda}{2}\right)$. Since the χ^2 distribution is a special case of a Γ distribution, we can rely on sampling from that distribution using acceptance-rejection or inversion methods.

For the next step the integrated variance $I_V := \int_t^{t+\Delta} V(s)ds$ is sampled with known values for $V(t + \Delta)$ and $V(t)$. The cumulative distribution is not known in closed form. If $\varphi(\cdot)$ denotes the characteristic function of I_V and $\mathcal{R}(\cdot)$ is the real part of some complex number, then

$$F(x) := \mathbb{P}\left(\int_t^{t+\Delta} V(s)ds \leq x\right) \sim \frac{2}{\pi} \int_0^\infty \frac{\sin(ux)}{u} \mathcal{R}(\varphi(u))du. \qquad (7.10)$$

Applying numerical integration, it is possible to compute the integrals appearing in Equation (7.10). In Broadie, M. and Kaya, O. (2006) the trapezoidal rule with N steps of size Δ_N is applied, thus

$$F(x) \approx \frac{\Delta_N x}{\pi} + \frac{2}{\pi} \sum_{j=1}^N \frac{\sin(j x \Delta_N)}{j} \mathcal{R}(\varphi(j \Delta_N)). \qquad (7.11)$$

Therefore, the cumulative probability can be computed and inverted numerically. To this end let u be a realization of $U \sim \mathcal{U}(0, 1)$, we derive $F^{-1}(u)$ using a zero finding algorithm such as Newton iteration or the `fzero` function from Matlab.

The logarithmic asset price $X(t + \Delta)$ is sampled given $V(t)$, $V(t + \Delta)$ and $\int_t^{t+\Delta} V(s)ds$ and using the fact that $\int_t^{t+\Delta} \sqrt{V(s)}ds$ is normally distributed.

The simulation is bias free except for the applied approximations for numerically inverting the integral and solving for the inverse cumulative density. The parameters N and thus Δ_N determine the accuracy of the applied approximation.

The scheme used the function `FourierInversion` which was proposed by Broadie, M. and Kaya, O. (2006). This function given in Figure 7.4 must be implemented since we apply the Matlab function `fzero` to find the quantile which leads to the value `uniforms(j)` in Figure 7.3.

The QE Scheme

Observing that the first two moments of the conditional expectation and the conditional variance of the variance, (2.54) and (2.55), are given in closed form, Andersen, L. (2008) suggests applying moment matching to sample $V(t + \Delta)$ when $V(t)$ is known. As we outlined

```
function [Price S t] = ...
    ExactSampling_Heston(S0,V0,K,r,T,kappa,theta,nu,rho,Nt,NSim)

dt = T/Nt;                                           % equidistant step
t = 0:dt:T;                                          % time grid
N = 800;                                             %
h = 0.5;
start = 1;
V = ones(NSim,Nt+1);
V = V0 * V(:,1);                                     % init variance
S = ones(NSim,Nt+1);
S = S0 * S(:,1);                                     % init asset
Inverse = zeros(NSim,1);                             % for num inversion
options = optimset('TolX',1e-6);                     % for num inversion

    for i = 2:Nt+1
        dt = t(i)-t(i-1);                            % time step
        A = 4*kappa*theta/(nu^2);                    % parameter chi^2
        B = (4*kappa*exp(-kappa*dt)*V(:,i-1)) ...
            /((nu^2)*(1-exp(-kappa*dt)));             % parameter chi^2
        C = (((nu^2)*(1-exp(-kappa*dt)))/(4*kappa)); % parameter chi^2
        V(:,i) = C*ncx2rnd(A,B,NSim,1);              % variate for V

        uniforms = rand(NSim,1);                     % uniforms

        % apply numerical inversion
        for j = 1:NSim
            Inverse(j) = fzero(@(x) FourierInversion(h,V(j),V(j,i),...
                dt,nu,kappa,theta,N,x,start)-uniforms(j),0.05,options);
        end
        % integral
        Integral = (1/nu)*(V(:,i)-V(:,i-1) ...
            -kappa*theta*(dt)+kappa*Inverse);
        mu = log(S(:,i-1))+r*dt-0.5*Inverse+rho*Integral;
        sig = (1-rho^2)*Inverse;
        S(:,i) = exp(mu+randn(NSim,1).*sqrt(sig));   % variate from path
    end
    Price = mean(max(S(:,end)-K,0))*exp(-r*T);
end
```

Figure 7.3 Matlab implementation of the Exact Sampling scheme of Broadie and Kaya for the Heston stochastic volatility model

```
function y = FourierInversion(h,Vs,Vt,dt,nu,kappa,theta,N,x,start)
    A = h*x/pi;
    vec = (start:N)*h;
    B = sum((2/pi)*(sin(vec.*x)./(start:N)).* ...
        exp(CharFun(vec,Vs,Vt,dt,nu,kappa,theta)));
    y = A+B;
end
```

Figure 7.4 Matlab implementation of the FourierInversion function used to invert the characteristic function needed to apply the exact sampling numerically

in Chapter 2, the distribution of the variance in the Heston model is a non-central χ^2 distribution with n degrees of freedom; the moment matching is only well suited to approximate the distribution if n is large. If the Feller condition (2.52) is not fulfilled, then $n = 4\kappa\Theta/v^2$ is small and therefore the moment matching is not suited for approximating the density. To this end for small n another sampling method has to be considered. Furthermore, a rule for switching between this sampling technique and the one applying moment matching has to be established.

The Quadratic Exponential scheme, or QE scheme for short, was introduced in Andersen, L. (2008). It applies two different sampling techniques for simulating the variance process due to the fact that we consider two different distributions for approximating the distribution of the variance. In addition a switching rule is established to obtain a reasonable approximation for small values of the variance.

Suppose we have already simulated $V(t)$ and we choose $\Psi_C \in [1, 2]$, the proposed choice is $\Psi_C = 1.5$. The scheme is given by

---

Algorithm 7.1: QE sampling algorithm for the Heston model

---

1 Compute

$$m = \Theta + (V(t) - \Theta)\exp(-\kappa\Delta), \quad s^2 = \frac{V(t)v^2 e^{-\kappa\Delta}}{\kappa}\left(1 - e^{-\kappa\Delta}\right) + \frac{\Theta v^2}{2\kappa}\left(1 - e^{-\kappa\Delta}\right)^2$$

2 For comparison compute Ψ

$$\Psi = \frac{s^2}{m^2} = \frac{\frac{V(t)v^2 \exp(-\kappa\Delta)}{\kappa}\frac{(1-\exp(-\kappa\Delta))\Theta v^2}{2\kappa}(1 - \exp(-\kappa\Delta))^2}{(\Theta + (V(t) - \Theta)\exp(-\kappa\Delta))^2}$$

3 Generate $u \sim \mathcal{U}(0, 1)$

4 Compute $V(t + \Delta)$ by the Switching Rule
   if $\Psi \leq \Psi_C$ **then**
      Use a non-central χ^2 distribution for approximation. Apply:

A   For the moment-matching compute
      $b^2 = 2\Psi^{-1} - 1 + \sqrt{2/\Psi^{-1}}\sqrt{2\Psi^{-1} - 1} \geq 0$ and $a = \frac{m}{1+b^2}$

B   Let z_1 denote a variate of $Z_1 \sim \mathcal{N}(0, 1)$

C   Set $V(t + \Delta) = a(b + z_1)^2$

   if $\Psi > \Psi_C$ **then**
      In this case we use an exponential distribution to approximate the true distribution.
      To generate variates of this distribution we apply the following rule:

A   Set $p = \frac{\Psi-1}{\Psi+1}$

B   Set $\beta = \frac{1-p}{m} = \frac{2}{m(\Psi+1)} > 0$

C   Set $V(t + \Delta) = \Psi^{-1}(u; p, \beta)$
      with

$$\Psi^{-1}(u) = \Psi^{-1}(u; p, \beta) = \begin{cases} 0 & 0 \leq u \leq p \\ \beta^{-1}\log\left(\frac{1-p}{1-u}\right) & p < u \leq 1 \end{cases}.$$

5 Denoting by z_2 a realization of $Z \sim \mathcal{N}(0, 1)$, we set

$$X(t + \Delta) = X(t) + K_0 + K_1 V(t) + K_2 V(t + \Delta) + \sqrt{K_3 V(t) + K_4 V(t + \Delta)}z_2. \tag{7.12}$$

Since $K_0, \ldots, K_4$ depend on the time step $\Delta_i, i = 1, \ldots, N$ it is only possible to pre-compute the constants for equidistant time steps. Then, they are given by

$$K_0 = -\frac{\rho \kappa \Theta}{v} \Delta$$

$$K_1 = \gamma_1 \Delta \left(\frac{\kappa \rho}{v} - \frac{1}{2} \right) - \frac{\rho}{v} ; \quad K_2 = \gamma_2 \Delta \left(\frac{\kappa \rho}{v} - \frac{1}{2} \right) + \frac{\rho}{v}$$

$$K_3 = \gamma_1 \Delta (1 - \rho^2) ; \quad K_4 = \gamma_2 \Delta (1 - \rho^2).$$

For a non-equidistant grid with $\Delta_i, i = 1, \ldots, N$ we define

$$K_{i0} = -\frac{\rho \kappa \Theta}{v} \Delta_i ; \quad K = \frac{\rho}{v}$$

$$K_{i1} = \gamma_1 \Delta_i \left(\frac{\kappa \rho}{v} - \frac{1}{2} \right) - K ; \quad K_{i2} = \gamma_2 \Delta_i \left(\frac{\kappa \rho}{v} - \frac{1}{2} \right) + K$$

$$K_{i3} = \gamma_1 \Delta_i (1 - \rho^2) ; \quad K_{i4} = \gamma_2 \Delta_i (1 - \rho^2).$$

for $j = 1, \ldots, 4$ and $i = 1, \ldots, N$. Before we proceed by improving the standard QE scheme, we consider its implementation in Matlab. The basic QE scheme given in Figure 7.5 is already

```
function [pathS, pathV] = MC_QE(S0,r,d,T,Vinst,Vlong, ...
    kappa,epsilon,rho,NTime,NSim,NBatches)
% discretization for the Heston model
% using QE scheme

dT = T/NTime;                        % time step

pathS = zeros(NSim,NTime+1,NBatches);   % output pathS
pathV = zeros(NSim,NTime+1,NBatches);   % output pathV

lnS1 = zeros(NSim,NTime+1);          % logspot price path
lnS1(:,1)=log(S0*exp(-d*T));         % set S(0) adjust with dividend

V2 = zeros(NSim,NTime+1);            % Variance path
V2(:,1) = Vinst;                     % set V0

k1 = exp(-kappa*dT);
k2 = epsilon^2*k1.*(1-k1)/kappa;
k3 = exp(kappa*dT)*0.5.*k2.*(1-k1).*Vlong;

psiC = 1.5;                          % psiC in (1,2)
gamma1 = .5;                         % For PredictorCorrector
gamma2 = .5;                         % For PredictorCorrector

c1 = (r-d)*dT;                       % adjustment due to drift
c2 = -rho*kappa*Vlong*dT/epsilon;    % used to determine K0

K0 = c1 + c2;                        % drift adjusted K0
K1 = gamma1*dT*(kappa*rho/epsilon - .5)-rho/epsilon;  % K1
K2 = gamma2*dT*(kappa*rho/epsilon - .5)+rho/epsilon;  % K2
K3 = gamma1*dT*(1-rho^2);                              % K3
K4 = gamma2*dT*(1-rho^2);                              % K4
```

Figure 7.5 Matlab implementation of the QE scheme for the Heston stochastic volatility model. This code is continued in Figure 7.6

```
for l = 1:NBatches
    UV1 = rand(NSim,NTime);      % uniforms
    dW2 = randn(NSim,NTime);     % Gaussians

    for i=2:NTime+1                  % time loop
        m = Vlong + (V2(:,i-1)-Vlong)*k1; % mean (moment matching)
        s2 = V2(:,i-1)*k2 + k3;           % var (moment matching)
        psi = s2./m.^2;                   % psi compared to psiC

        psihat = 1./psi;
        b2 = 2*psihat - 1 + sqrt(2*psihat.*(2*psihat-1));
        a = m ./ (1 + b2);

        I1 = find(psi<=psiC); % Non-Central Chi^2 approx for psi < psiC
        if isempty(I1)
        else
            V2(I1,i) = a(I1).*(sqrt(b2(I1)) + norminv(UV1(I1,i-1))).^2;
        end
        p = (psi - 1)./(psi + 1);                % for switching rule
        V2((UV1(:,i-1)<=p) & (psi>psiC),i) = 0; % case u<=p & psi>psiC
        I1b = find((UV1(:,i-1)>p) & (psi>psiC));% find is faster here!

        beta = (1 - p)./m;                       % for switching rule
        if isempty(I1b)
        else     %Psi^(-1)
            V2(I1b,i) = log((1-p(I1b))./(1-UV1(I1b,i-1)))./beta(I1b);
        end
        % log Euler Predictor-Corrector step
        lnS1(:,i) = lnS1(:,i-1) + K0 + K1.*V2(:,i-1) + K2.*V2(:,i) ...
                    + sqrt(K3.*V2(:,i-1) + K4.*V2(:,i)).*dW2(:,i-1);
    end
    pathS(:,:,l) = exp(lnS1);
    pathV(:,:,l) = V2;
end
```

Figure 7.6 Matlab implementation of the QE scheme for the Heston stochastic volatility model (continued)

stable and produces reliable results. The input parameters are the spot value $S0$, the strike K, the riskless rate r, the dividend yield d, the maturity T as well as the model parameters Vinst, Vlong, kappa, epsilon, rho denoting the instantaneous variance, the long term variance, the mean reversion speed, the volatility of variance and the correlation of the Brownian motions driving the underlying and the variance process. For the Monte Carlo method we have to supply the number of batches, *NBatches*, the simulations per batch, *NSim* and the number of time steps, *NTime*.

However, improvements and extensions can be made. For instance, we consider

- Martingale Correction.
- Refinement for small values of the variance process.
- Time-dependent parameters.
- Displacement.

We take the QE scheme adjusted by a martingale correction.

The Martingale Correction   Replace the constant K_0 in Equation (7.12) by

$$K_0^* = -\log(M) - (K_1 + 0.5K_3)\, V_n. \tag{7.13}$$

The constant M can be computed explicitly and we have in the first case, namely $\Psi \leq \Psi_c$,

$$M = \frac{\exp\left(\frac{Ab^2a}{1-2Aa}\right)}{\sqrt{1-2Aa}}, \quad A < 1/2a.$$

For the second case it is given by

$$M = p + \frac{\beta(1-p)}{\beta - A}, \quad A < \beta$$

where

$$A = K_2 + 0.5K_4 = \frac{\rho}{\omega}(1 + \kappa\gamma_2\Delta) - 0.5\gamma_2\Delta\rho^2.$$

The martingale correction approach imposes a restriction on the discretization in terms of the correlation and the volatility of variance. For negative correlation there is no restriction but if $\rho > 0$, then we have to guarantee that

$$\Delta < \frac{2}{\rho\omega}.$$

Let $f(\rho, \omega) = \frac{2}{\rho\omega}$ denote the upper bound. The function is monotone decreasing in ρ and ω, that is $f(\rho, \omega_1) > f(\rho, \omega_2)$ for $\omega_1 < \omega_2$ and fixed ρ and $f(\rho_1, \omega) > f(\rho_2, \omega)$ for $\rho_1 < \rho_2$ for fixed ω. The value at $\rho = 0.999$ and $\omega = 200\%$ is greater than 1 and we recommend that Δ is less than 1. Therefore, for practical problems this is not a serious restriction.

The martingale corrected QE scheme is given in Figures 7.7 and 7.8.

Numerical Results and Comparison

For a numerical test we employ our implementation of the QE scheme to price European Call options and test it against the test cases in Andersen, L. (2008). The spot price is $S(0) = 100$ and $r = d = 0$. For the model parameters we take:

The prices t which we compare the MC prices corresponding to $K = 70$, 100 and 140 we find using the parameters for Table 7.1 by semi-analytic methods, see Table 7.2.

First, we take the standard QE scheme and price the European Call options. We display the difference to the option prices from Table 7.3. Now, we consider the QE scheme extended by the martingale correction, see Table 7.4.

7.3.2   Unbiased Scheme for the SABR Model

In this section we consider the discretization of the SABR model (see Subsection 2.3.4). The main difficulties lie in the simulation of the integrated variance and establishing an exact simulation of a CEV type dynamic. Since for a CEV variable $S(t)$

$$\mathbb{P}_{\text{CEV}}[S(\Delta) \leq x] = 1 - \chi^2(a, b, c) = \chi^2(c, 2-b, a) + \mathbb{P}[\inf\{t : S(t) = 0\} < \Delta],$$

we can apply the approximation

$$\mathbb{P}[S(\Delta) \leq x] \approx \chi^2(c, 2-b, a)$$

only if $S(0)$ is not too small. For small values of $S(0)$ we have to rely on a zero search mechanism to invert (2.66).

```
function [pathS,pathV] = MC_QE_m(S0,r,d,T,Vinst,Vlong, ...
    kappa,epsilon,rho,NTime,NSim,NBatches)
% discretization for the Heston model
% using QE scheme and martingale correction

dT = T/NTime;                              % time step

pathS = zeros(NSim,NTime+1,NBatches);      % output pathS
pathV = zeros(NSim,NTime+1,NBatches);      % output pathV

lnS1 = zeros(NSim,NTime+1);                % logspot price path
lnS1(:,1)=log(S0*exp(-d*T));               % set S(0) adjust with dividend

V2 = zeros(NSim,NTime+1);                  % variance path
V2(:,1) = Vinst;                           % set V0

k1 = exp(-kappa*dT);
k2 = epsilon^2*k1.*(1-k1)/kappa;
k3 = exp(kappa*dT)*0.5.*k2.*(1-k1).*Vlong;

psiC = 1.5;                                % psi in (1,2)
gamma1 = .5;                               % for PredictorCorrector
gamma2 = .5;                               % for PredictorCorrector

c1 = (r-d)*dT;                             % adjustment due to drift

K1 = gamma1*dT*(kappa*rho/epsilon - .5)-rho/epsilon;  % K1
K2 = gamma2*dT*(kappa*rho/epsilon - .5)+rho/epsilon;  % K2
K3 = gamma1*dT*(1-rho^2);                  % K3
K4 = gamma2*dT*(1-rho^2);                  % K4

A= K2+0.5*K4;                              % further adjustment
```

Figure 7.7 Matlab implementation of the QE scheme together with martingale correction

Unbiased Scheme We give the algorithm introduced in Chen, B., Oosterlee, C.W. and van der Weide, H. (2010) for unbiased simulation within a SABR model. The Matlab implementation is presented in Figures 7.9 and 7.10.

The zero search can be implemented using a Newton approach. To this end we use the iteration

$$c_{n+1} = c_n - \frac{h(c_n)}{q(c_n)}, \quad n = 1, \dots \text{ and } c_0 = 0,$$

Table 7.1 Model parameters for the numerical test of the QE scheme for the Heston model

Parameter	Value		
ν	1	0.9	1
κ	0.5	0.3	1
ρ	-0.9	-0.5	-0.3
T	10	15	5
$V(0) = \theta$	0.04	0.04	0.09

```
for l= 1:NBatches
    UV1 = rand(NSim,NTime);          % uniforms
    dW2 = randn(NSim,NTime);         % Gaussians

    K0 = zeros(NSim,1);              % K0 for martingale adjust

    for i=2:NTime+1                  % time loop
        m = Vlong + (V2(:,i-1)-Vlong)*k1; % mean (moment matching)
        s2 = V2(:,i-1)*k2 + k3;           % var (moment matching)
        psi = s2./m.^2;                   % psi compared to psiC

        psihat = 1./psi;
        b2 = 2*psihat - 1 + sqrt(2*psihat.*(2*psihat-1));
        a = m ./ (1 + b2);

        % Non-central chi squared approximation for psi< psiC
        I1 = find(psi<=psiC);
        I2 = ~I1;
        V2(I1,i) = a(I1).*(sqrt(b2(I1)) + norminv(UV1(I1,i-1))).^2;

        p = (psi - 1)./(psi + 1);                % for switching rule
        V2((UV1(:,i-1)<=p) & (psi>psiC),i) = 0;  % case u<= p & psi>psiC
        I1b = find((UV1(:,i-1)>p) & (psi>psiC)); % find is faster here!

        beta = (1 - p)./m;                       % for switching rule
        if isempty(I1b)
        else      % Psi^(-1)
            V2(I1b,i) = log((1-p(I1b))./(1-UV1(I1b,i-1)))./beta(I1b);
        end
        % K0 for martingale adjustment
        K0(I1)= c1-A*b2(I1).*a(I1)./(1-2*A*a(I1)) + 0.5*log(1-2*A*a(I1));
        K0(I2)= c1-log(p(I2)+beta(I2).*(1-p(I2))./(beta(I2)-A));

        % log Euler Predictor-Corrector step
        lnS1(:,i) = lnS1(:,i-1) + K0 - (K1+0.5*K3).*V2(:,i-1) ...
            + K1.*V2(:,i-1) + K2.*V2(:,i) ...
            + sqrt(K3.*V2(:,i-1) + K4.*V2(:,i)).*dW2(:,i-1);
    end
    pathS(:,:,l) = exp(lnS1);
    pathV(:,:,l) = V2;
end
```

Figure 7.8 Matlab implementation of the QE scheme together with martingale correction (continued)

Table 7.2 Prices for European Call options using the Heston model for strike $K = 70$, 100 and 140 and the test cases given in Table 7.1

	I	II	III
$K=70$	35.8498	37.1697	38.7720
$K=100$	13.0847	16.6492	21.7953
$K=140$	0.2958	5.1382	9.9831

Table 7.3 Relative differences of the Monte Carlo prices for different numbers of time-steps using the standard QE scheme and the analytic prices, computed using FFT methods introduced in Chapter 3 and displayed in Table 7.2

Steps					
1	2	4	8	16	32
$K = 70$					
0.0199	0.0047	0.0015	0.0009	0.0018	0.0003
0.0100	0.0011	0.0003	0.0133	0.0003	0.0022
0.0032	0.0115	0.0011	0.0022	0.0027	0.0107
$K = 100$					
0.0724	0.0259	0.0071	0.0001	0.0034	0.0005
0.0177	0.0083	0.0021	0.0254	0.0007	0.0047
0.0197	0.0070	0.0016	0.0039	0.0017	0.0208
$K = 140$					
0.2887	0.0289	0.0014	0.0051	0.0133	0.0111
0.0532	0.0105	0.0025	0.0562	0.0006	0.0097
0.0590	0.0019	0.0021	0.0056	0.0022	0.0407

with q being the function

$$q(c) = \frac{1}{2} \left(\frac{c}{a}\right)^{\frac{b-a}{4}} \exp\left(-\frac{a+c}{2}\right) I_{|\frac{s-2}{2}|}(\sqrt{ac}).$$

Should the search algorithm not converge after a predefined number of steps we perform another one. For this search the step size applied for the iterating is smaller. For the implementation we used the factor 0.5. The initial step size is therefore multiplied by one-half. At this stage there is room for improvement. Either a clever guess of the starting point or an approximation of the function can be used, of which the latter is numerically cheaper to compute. When computing the absorbtion probability and using the `gammainc` function of

Table 7.4 Relative differences of the Monte Carlo prices for different numbers of time steps using the martingale adjusted QE scheme and the semi-analytic prices given in Table 7.2

Steps					
1	2	4	8	16	32
$K = 70$					
0.0016	0.0009	0.0023	0.0002	0.0036	0.0022
0.0021	0.0023	0.0101	0.0007	0.0033	0.0037
0.0030	0.0032	0.0047	0.0014	0.0010	0.0044
$K = 100$					
0.0139	0.0103	0.0004	0.0018	0.0051	0.0053
0.0318	0.0120	0.0234	0.0003	0.0081	0.0073
0.0193	0.0026	0.0090	0.0019	0.0014	0.0065
$K = 140$					
0.2999	0.1107	0.0107	0.0103	0.0182	0.0098
0.0673	0.0096	0.0858	0.0098	0.0286	0.0140
0.0494	0.0059	0.0214	0.0076	0.0021	0.0078

Matlab we have to take care. In contrast to the material presented in Chen, B., Oosterlee, C.W. and van der Weide, H. (2010), the arguments are interchanged and a normalization is implicitly applied, which means that the division using the factor $\Gamma(1/(2(2 - \beta)))$ is already implemented in `gammainc`.

We have indicated the steps just described in the implementation given in Figure 7.9. This should suffice to find the value for each step of the algorithm in our implementation.

Algorithm 7.2: Algorithm to sample from the SABR terminal distribution

---

1 Let z_1 be a sample from $Z_1 \sim \mathcal{N}(0, \sqrt{\Delta})$. Set $\sigma(\Delta) := \exp\left(\alpha z_1 - \frac{\alpha^2 \Delta}{2}\right)$

2 Compute the conditional mean m and conditional variance v by

$$m = \sigma(0)^2 \Delta \left(1 + \alpha z_1 + \frac{\alpha^2}{3}\left(2z_1^2 - \frac{\Delta}{2}\right) + \frac{\alpha^3}{3}\left(z_1^3 - z_1\Delta\right)\right)$$

$$v = \frac{\sigma(0)^4 \alpha^2 \Delta^3}{3}.$$

Set the corresponding values for the moment-matched log-normal distribution $\sigma^2 = \log\left(1 + \frac{v}{m^2}\right)$, $\mu = \log(m) - \frac{\sigma^2}{2}$.

3 Take a uniform u_1 variate drawn from $U \sim \mathcal{U}(0, 1)$ and determine the inverse according to the logarithmic normal distribution by setting for the integrated variance

$$A(\Delta) := \exp\left(\sigma \mathcal{N}^{-1}(u_1) + \mu\right), \quad v(\Delta) := (1 - \rho^2)A(\Delta).$$

4 Case $\beta = 1$: Set for z_1 and z_2 drawn from $Z \sim \mathcal{N}(0, 1)$

$$S(\Delta) = S(\Delta)(1 + \sigma_0(\rho z_1 + \sqrt{(1 - \rho^2)}\sqrt{(\Delta)}z_2)));$$

Case $\beta < 1$: Compute

$$a = \frac{1}{v(\Delta)}\left(\frac{S(0)^{1-\beta}}{1 - \beta} + \frac{\rho}{\alpha}(\sigma(\Delta) - \sigma(0))\right), \quad b = 2 - \frac{1 - 2\beta - \rho^2(1 - \beta)}{(1 - \beta)(1 - \rho^2)}.$$

Draw u_2 from $U_2 \sim \mathcal{U}(0, 1)$ and compute $p := \mathbb{P}[S(\Delta) = 0|S(0)]$.

a) If $S(0) = 0$ or $u_2 < p$ set $S(\Delta) = 0$

b) If $S(0) > 0$ and $u_2 \geq p$ go to step 5.

5 Compute $\Psi = \frac{s^2}{m_1^2}$ using $m_1 = 2 - b + a$ $s^2 = 2(2 - b + 2a)$.

6 If $\Psi > 0$ and $\Psi < \Psi_C$ and $m_1 \geq 0$ then

$$e^2 = 2/\Psi - 1 + \sqrt{2/\Psi}\sqrt{2/\Psi - 1}; \quad d = \frac{m_1}{1 + e^2}$$

$$S(\Delta) = \left((1 - \beta)^2 v(\Delta)d(\sqrt{e^2} + z_2)^2\right)^{\frac{1}{2(1-\beta)}}, \quad z_2 \sim \mathcal{N}(0, 1).$$

If Case $\Psi > \Psi_c$ and $m_1 < 0$ then
   Find c^* such that $0 = h(x) := 1 - \chi^2(a; b, x) - u_2$ and set

$$S(\Delta) = \left(c^*(1 - \beta)^2 v(\Delta)\right)^{2(\beta-1)}.$$

```
function  [price_unbiased, std_unbiased] = ...
  sabr_mc_unbiased(S_0,alfa,beta,rho,sigma_0,K,NSim,Delta,NSteps)

S_Delta = repmat(S_0,NSim,1);       % S
TOL = 1e-6;                         % tolerance
Psi_C = 1.5;                        % switching parameter
maxiter = 250;                      % maximum iteration number for 0 search

for i = 1:NSteps
    % Step 1
    Z = sqrt(Delta)*randn(NSim,1);                      % normal variates
    sigma_Delta = sigma_0.*exp(alfa*(Z-0.5*alfa*Delta));% sigma Delta
    % Step 2
    m = sigma_0.^2*Delta.*(1 + alfa*(Z + alfa*((2*Z.^2-0.5*Delta)/3 ...
        + alfa*((Z.^3-Z*Delta)/3 ...
        + alfa*(2/3*Z.^4-1.5*Z.^2*Delta+2*Delta^2)/5))));
    v = sigma_0.^4*alfa^2*Delta^3/3;
    % Step 3
    sigma2 = log(1+v./m.^2);            % sigma^2
    mu = log(m) - 0.5*sigma2;           % mu

    Z2 = sqrt(sigma2).*randn(NSim,1);   % normal variates
    A_Delta = exp(Z2 + mu);             % integrated variance
    v_Delta = (1-rho^2)*A_Delta;        % nu(Delta)

    if beta == 1    % special case: beta = 1
        S_Delta = S_Delta.*(1 + sigma_0.*(rho*Z ...
            + sqrt(1-rho^2)*sqrt(Delta)*randn(NSim,1)));
    else
        a = (S_Delta.^(1-beta)/(1-beta) ...
            + rho*(sigma_Delta-sigma_0)/alfa).^2./v_Delta;
        b = 2 - (1-2*beta-rho^2*(1-beta))/(1-beta)/(1-rho^2);

        U = rand(NSim,1);               % uniforms
        P_absorb = 1 - chi2cdf(a,b);    % Step 2

        I1 = S_Delta == 0; S_Delta(I1) = 0;             % (a)
        I2 = S_Delta ~= 0 & U <= P_absorb; S_Delta(I2) = 0; % (b)
        I3 = S_Delta ~= 0 & U > P_absorb;               % (c)

        if sum(I3) > 0
            m1 = 2-b+a;
            s2 = 2*(2-b+2*a);
            Psi = s2./m1.^2;                            % Step 5

            I4 = ((Psi > 0 & Psi <= Psi_C) & m1 >= 0) & I3 == true;
            if sum(I4) > 0                  % moment matching
                e2 = 2./Psi-1+sqrt(2./Psi).*sqrt(2./Psi-1);
                d = m./(1+e2);
                % update the asset price as quadratic gaussian
                S_Delta(I4) = ((1-beta)^2*v_Delta(I4).*d(I4) ...
                    .*(sqrt(e2(I4)) ...
                    +randn(sum(I4),1)).^2).^(1/(2*(1-beta)));  % (A)
            end
        end
```

Figure 7.9   Matlab implementation of the unbiased scheme for the SABR model

```
                I5 = ((Psi > Psi_C | m1 < 0) & I3 == true);
                if sum(I5) > 0                    % zero search
                    H = @(c,IVec)(1-ncx2cdf(a(IVec),b,c)-U(IVec));
                    qbar = @(c,IVec) (0.5*(c./a(IVec)).^(0.25*(b-2))) ...
                        .* exp(-0.5*(a(IVec)+c)) ...
                        .* besseli(abs(0.5*(b-2)),sqrt(a(IVec).*c)));

                    nVec = (1:length(a))'; indexVec = nVec(I5);

                    IndOfInterest = H(0,indexVec) < 0;
                    iVec = indexVec(IndOfInterest);

                    c_star = a(iVec); c_old = c_star;    % initial guess
                    k = 0;                               % counter

                    % identify values for which the tolerance is not reached
                    I6 = abs(H(c_star,iVec)) > TOL;
                    while k < maxiter && sum(I6) > 0
                     k = k+1;
                     step = 1;
                     % a full Newton step
                     c_star(I6) = c_old(I6) ...
                         - H(c_old(I6),iVec(I6))./qbar(c_old(I6),iVec(I6));
                     %reduced stepsize if c* becomes negative
                     while step > TOL && sum(c_star < 0) > 0
                      I7 = c_star < 0;
                      step = 0.5*step;
                      % reduced Newton step
                      c_star(I7) = c_old(I7) ...
                          -step*H(c_old(I7),iVec(I7))./qbar(c_old(I7),iVec(I7));
                     end
                     c_old(I6) = c_star(I6);
                     I6 = abs(H(c_star,iVec)) > TOL;
                    end

                    S_Delta(iVec) = (c_star.*(1-beta)^2 ...
                        .*v_Delta(iVec)).^(1/(2-2*beta)); % (B)
                    % for values of c* < 0 we set S_delta = 0
                    S_Delta(indexVec(~IndOfInterest)) = 0.0;
                end
            end
        end
    sigma_0 = sigma_Delta;
end

price_unbiased = mean(max(S_Delta - K,0));
std_unbiased = std(max(S_Delta - K,0))/sqrt(NSim);

end
```

Figure 7.10 Matlab implementation of the unbiased scheme for the SABR model (continued)

Numerical Examples For the numerical test we consider the test cases III and IV from Chen, B., Oosterlee, C.W. and van der Weide, H. (2010). These cases correspond to the following sets of model parameters:

Table 7.5 Model parameters for the numerical test of the unbiased scheme for the SABR model

Parameter	Scenario III	Scenario IV
$S(0)$	0.005	0.07
$\alpha(0)$	0.2	0.4
ν	0.3	0.8
β	0.7	0.4
ρ	−0.3	−0.6

For the parameter sets from Table 7.5 the results are displayed in Figure 7.11 and Table 7.7. Furthermore, we reproduce the results from Chen, B., Oosterlee, C.W. and van der Weide, H. (2010). Thus, for the first test we verify the martingale property as shown in Table 7.6 for different maturities and time steps, denoted by Δ, per year.

For further illustration we consider the SABR model with parameters and price Call options for different strikes and $T = 5$ in Figure 7.12.

Numerical Inversion We apply the numerical inversion of the cumulative density for the SABR model. To this end we first introduce an extrapolation technique for the density, Kienitz, J. (2011). Applying the standard SABR implied volatility approximation formula (2.64) and differentiating it twice to extract the probability density leads to poor results especially for far in-the-money or out-of-the-money strikes. This has consequences for applying SABR to the pricing of CMS and CMS spread options.

Possible solutions to overcome this problem have been proposed and include

1. Constant extrapolation.
2. Regimes of volatility of volatility.
3. Price extrapolation.
4. Density extrapolation.

Using the results given in Subsection 2.3.4, method 4, leads to a representation allowing us to smoothly fit the modified density at cut-off points k_l and k_u. Furthermore, it is possible to directly control the tail behaviour using constants $\mu_l > 0$ and $\mu_u < 0$. Suppose the parameters are given, then the Matlab implementation is that provided in Figure 7.13.

Table 7.6 We consider the parameters from Table 7.5 and that $T = 5, 10$ and 15. We simulate the forward prices which corresponds to setting $K = 0$

Δ	Unbiased	Δ	Unbiased	Δ	Unbiased
	$T = 5$		$T = 10$		$T = 15$
0.5	0.0402	0.5	0.0401	0.5	0.0399
0.25	0.0402	0.25	0.0399	0.25	0.0399
0.125	0.0400	0.125	0.0400	0.125	0.0401
0.0625	0.0401	0.0625	0.0400	0.0625	0.0400

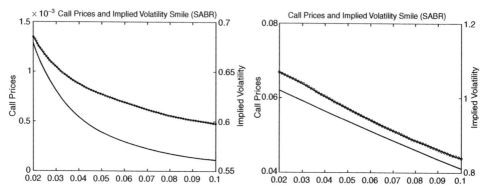

Figure 7.11   We have chosen the model parameters from Table 7.5 and consider $T = 5$ and the strike range from 0.5% to 15%. The figure shows the Call prices and the corresponding implied volatilities

Table 7.7   Unbiased SABR simulation results for Test Case IV computed using our implementation of the algorithm. We used N time steps per year and 100000 simulations. For comparison we use a logarithmic Euler scheme. The results are given in the last three columns. We have not reproduced the results of the reference Chen, B., Oosterlee, C.W. and van der Weide, H. (2010) exactly

	K = 40%			K = 40%		
N	2	5	10	2	5	10
1	0.0568	0.0580	0.0584	0.0601	0.0643	0.0630
2	0.0554	0.0577	0.0579	0.0637	0.0600	0.0600
4	0.0566	0.0575	0.0583	0.0583	0.0618	0.0617
8	0.0575	0.0585	0.0588	0.0611	0.0612	0.0626
16	0.0583	0.0597	0.0604	0.0596	0.0618	0.0630
32	0.0591	0.0602	0.0605	0.0604	0.0621	0.0624
	K = 100%			K = 100%		
N	2	5	10	2	5	10
1	0.0447	0.0480	0.0492	0.0526	0.0578	0.0569
2	0.0425	0.0469	0.0478	0.0541	0.0518	0.0524
4	0.0434	0.0465	0.0480	0.0475	0.0525	0.0530
8	0.0441	0.0474	0.0484	0.0491	0.0510	0.0533
16	0.0448	0.0484	0.0498	0.0470	0.0510	0.0530
32	0.0454	0.0488	0.0499	0.0472	0.0510	0.0520
	K = 160%			K = 160%		
N	2	5	10	2	5	10
1	0.0345	0.0392	0.0409	0.0471	0.0527	0.0521
2	0.0316	0.0374	0.0388	0.0466	0.0451	0.0459
4	0.0322	0.0368	0.0387	0.0386	0.0446	0.0454
8	0.0328	0.0375	0.0390	0.0391	0.0421	0.0450
16	0.0333	0.0383	0.0403	0.0363	0.0415	0.0440
32	0.0338	0.0387	0.0404	0.0359	0.0410	0.0426

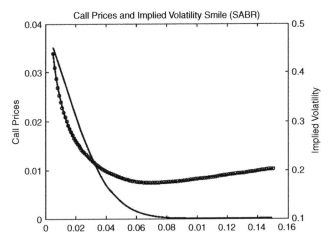

Figure 7.12 We have chosen the model parameters $\alpha = 0.2$, $\beta = 1$, $\nu = 0.3$, $\rho = -0.5$ and $f = 0.04$ and consider $T = 5$ and the strike range from 0.5% to 15%. The figure shows prices for European Call options and the corresponding implied volatilities

In what follows we examine the density construction for all the methods and two parameter sets. The first set, $\alpha = 0.1339 f^{1-\beta}$, $\beta = 0.5$, $\nu = 0.3843$, $\rho = -0.1595$ and $f = 0.0495$, leads to a reasonable, that is a convex, shape of the Call option prices. The second, $\alpha = 0.9 f^{1-\beta}$, $\beta = 0.5$, $\nu = 0.2$, $\rho = -0.2$ and $f = 0.03$, leads to concave Call option prices when the standard implied volatility formula is applied. Thus, this causes negative densities. The corresponding scripts with the applied parameters as well as the code to generate the figures is included in the supporting material.

While Figure 7.14 shows that all methods except the constant extrapolation method lead to reasonable densities, this is completely different for the second case. In the second case, illustrated in Figure 7.15, only our method, the Kienitz method, based on density extrapolation is working properly. All the other methods show severe shortcomings and do not represent

```
function y = psabr_5(a, b, r, n, f, k, t, ...
    kl, ku, mu, cl, bl,al, nu, cu,bu,au)
% sabr prices using an admissible region kl <= k <= ku
% for kl<k<ku apply standard sabr
% for 0 <= k <= kl    use   f(x) = K^mu exp(a + bx + cx^2)
% for ku < k < +infty use   f(x) = K^(-nu) exp(a + bx^(-1) + cx(-2)
% a big range (small kl and big ku) guarantee prices to be in line
% with the observed calls and puts

yl = real(k(k<kl).^mu .* exp(al + bl .* k(k<kl) + cl * k(k<kl).^2));
ym = real(psabr(a,b,r,n, f,k((kl<=k)&(k<=ku)),t));
yu = real(k(k>ku).^(-nu) .* exp(au+bu./k(k>ku)+cu./k(k>ku).^2));

y = [yl ym yu];              % output
end
```

Figure 7.13 Matlab implementation of the extrapolation technique for the SABR model if the parameters k_1, k_u, mu, nu and al, bl, cl and au, bu, cu are given

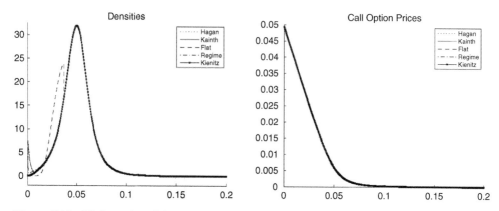

Figure 7.14   We have plotted the SABR densities and the Call option prices using different methods. The parameters are $\alpha = 0.1339 f^{1-\beta}$, $\beta = 0.5$, $v = 0.3843$, $\rho = -0.1595$ and $f = 0.0495$

a probability density. For Figure 7.14 the names displayed in the legend correspond to the names of the method's originators.

Let us now take a brief look at the effect of the parameters used for extrapolating the SABR density. Figures 7.16 and 7.17 summarize the effects. The attachment points k_l and k_u specify the strikes from which the extrapolation is applied. Choosing these parameters appropriately leads to a close fit to the option prices.

The parameters μ and v control the tail behaviour of the density. These parameters can be specified in advance but can also be the output of a calibration procedure for the model.

- Since the probability density can be easily calculated it is also suitable for Monte Carlo applications.
- The inverse of the cumulative density can be efficiently evaluated.
- We compared the results to Chen, B., Oosterlee, C.W. and van der Weide, H. (2010) and found that our method leads to comparable results but is faster since we can apply one step sampling.

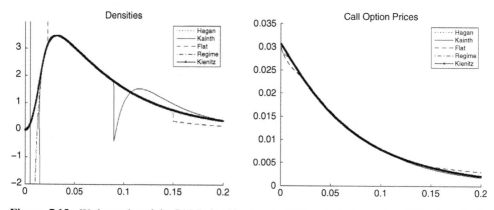

Figure 7.15   We have plotted the SABR densities and the Call option prices using different methods. The parameters are $\alpha = 0.9 f^{1-\beta}$, $\beta = 0.5$, $v = 0.2$, $\rho = -0.2$ and $f = 0.03$

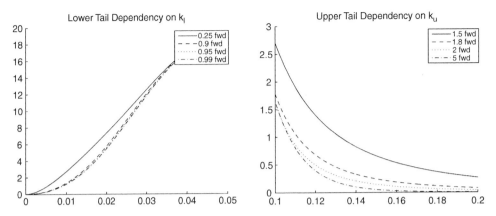

Figure 7.16 Using the attachment points as multiple of the forward to construct the distribution for the lower (left) and the upper (right) tail of the SABR density

Having implemented the density function, and observing that it is a smooth function, we can efficiently compute the cumulative density and the inverse cumulative density. This is done by approximating the integral using sums.

If f denotes the function we wish to integrate, we consider a discretization $\mathcal{T} = \{t_0, t_1, \ldots, t_N = T\}$ of the interval $[0, T]$ and the sum

$$\sum_{i=1}^{N} f(t_{i-1})(t_i - t_{i-1}).$$

We implement this approach in Matlab by coding the function `FSABR2_1`, shown in Figure 7.18. The approximation is reliable since the functions are smooth and the computation is both fast and efficient.

The input f is a function handle and makes the function work with any representation of the SABR density. In our case we use the function `psabr5`.

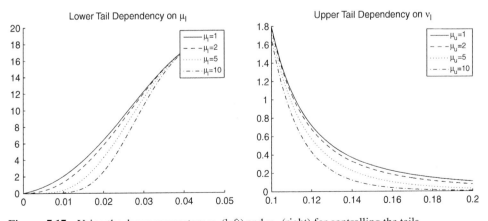

Figure 7.17 Using the decay parameters μ_l (left) and μ_u (right) for controlling the tails

```
function y = FSABR2_1(x, f)
% P(f<x) based on sum instead of integration makes it fast!

% create range
eps = 0.001;
y = zeros(1,length(x));
for j=1:length(x)
    k = 0:eps:x(j);
    yi = f(k);
    yis = sum(yi) * eps;
    y(j) = yis;
end

end
```

Figure 7.18   Matlab implementation of the cumulative density of the SABR model

The inverse function to generate random variates is a simple and fast bracketing algorithm to solve the Equation (7.14) for $u \in (0, 1)$

$$F_X(u) - u = 0. \tag{7.14}$$

This algorithm enables us to determine a quantile u corresponding to the random input $U \sim \mathcal{U}(0, 1)$ sampled from the uniform distribution. This implements the inverse method for the SABR model.

```
function [c,fc] = FInvSABR4_2(x,x_sabr,y_sabr)
% This function computes the inverse of a SABR cumulative distribution
% Since it is based on FSABR2 it is very fast and works for vectors!
f2 = @(t) (x - FSABR2_2(t,x_sabr,y_sabr));

% Use simple bisection
a = 0.00001 * ones(1,length(x));   % left starting points
b = 1*ones(1,length(x));           % right starting points

eps = 1e-3;                        % accuracy level
k = 0;                             % init iteration counter

c=(b+a)/2;
fc = f2(c);

while(k <= 200)
    k = k+1;                                % increase iteration counter

    if( (-eps <= min(fc)) & (max(fc) <= eps))
        break;                              % end if all values have been found
    else
        b(fc<0) = 0.5*(b(fc<0)+a(fc<0));    % update right boundary
        a(fc>=0) = 0.5*(b(fc>=0)+a(fc>=0)); % update left boundary
    end
    c = 0.5*(b+a);
    fc = f2(c);                             % evaluate function at new c
end
end
```

Figure 7.19   Matlab implementation of the inverse cumulative density of the SABR model

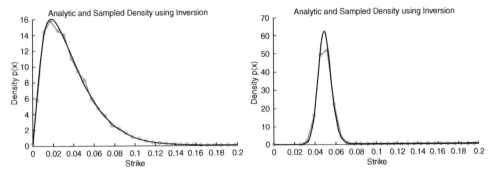

Figure 7.20 Application of the numerical inversion to the SABR model. The results are for parameter sets 1 (left) and 2 (right). The continuous line indicates the density, and the line marked with dots indicates the sampled density

We have applied this method (Figure 7.19) for sampling 100000 random variates for the SABR model which takes about 8.782 seconds whereas for the same accuracy applying the unbiased simulation scheme the authors report running times in Chen, B., Oosterlee, C.W. and van der Weide, H. (2010). The results are shown in Figure 7.20. The results for the stressed test case, 2, show that indeed more samples are necessary to obtain accurate results. The Matlab code is provided.

7.4 ADDING JUMPS

In this section we consider the simulation of jump-diffusion models. We examine two sampling methods:

- Fixed grid sampling (FGS).
- Stochastic grid sampling (SGS).

For FGS we choose a fixed time grid, $\mathcal{T}$ by

$$\mathcal{T} := \{t_0, t_1, \ldots, t_{Nt} = T\} \tag{7.15}$$

and propose a scheme which accounts for the jumps appearing between the consecutive grid points t_k, $k = 0, 1, \ldots, Nt$. For SGS we simulate a grid due to the jump distribution for each try in the simulation. If $i = 1, \ldots, NSim$ and let $N(i)$ denote the number of times the process jumps in scenario i, we denote the corresponding grid by

$$\mathcal{T}(i) = \{t_0, t_1^i, \ldots, t_{N(i)}^i, T\}. \tag{7.16}$$

Therefore, we term this procedure *stochastic grid sampling*.

7.4.1 Jump Models – Poisson Processes

Paths corresponding to a diffusion process are continuous. But there are processes with a completely different stochastic movement. In general we distinguish between two kinds of movement. On the one hand, the movement can be a small movement with high probability;

alternatively it can be a large movement with low probability. The latter movement is called a *jump*. For a more detailed discussion see Kienitz, J. (2007a).

This stochastic movement can be illustrated by taking a simple example, namely the *Poisson process*. In contrast to a diffusion process it has discontinuous sample paths and takes values in the positive integers.

To introduce the basic process we consider a sequence of independent exponentially distributed random variables $(\tau_n)_{n \in \mathbb{N}}$ where the probability for each τ_n being equal to $k \in \mathbb{N}$ is given by $\mathbb{P}(\tau_n = k) = (\exp(1)/k!)$. For $n \in \mathbb{N}$ we take the sum $T_n := \sum_{i=1}^{n} \tau_i$ and consider the following mapping:

$$N : \mathbb{R}^+ \times \Omega \to \mathbb{N}; \quad N(t) = \sum_{n \geq 1} 1_{\{t \geq \tau_n\}}. \tag{7.17}$$

$(N(t))_{t \in [0,T]}$ is called the Poisson process. This process is also known as a *counting process*. It counts the random times τ_n that occur between 0 and t. The modelling assumptions are:

(P1) it starts at zero, $N(0) = 0$
(P2) it has stationary, independent increments
(P3) the distribution of $N(t)$ is a Poisson distribution, that is $N(t) \sim \mathcal{P}(t)$
(P4) the mapping $t \mapsto N(t)$ is piecewise constant and increases by jumps of size 1.

The sequence $(\tau_n)_n$ models the random times at which jumps occur. We may introduce another parameter, $\lambda > 0$, called the *jump intensity*. The exponentially distributed random variables τ_n, $n \in \mathbb{N}$, describing the times at which jumps occur, are now exponentially distributed with parameter λ, that is $\mathbb{P}(\tau_n = k) = \exp(-\lambda)\frac{\lambda^k}{k!}$.

Proceeding as above the only thing that changes is assumption (P3), the random variable $N(t)$ is now distributed due to $N(t) \sim \mathcal{P}(\lambda t)$. The resulting process is called *Poisson process with intensity* λ.

One may be tempted to generalize the above setting by allowing general increasing sequences of random times $(\tau_n)_n$ having any distribution. This leads to general counting processes, but the Poisson process is special since it is the only counting process which fulfils assumption (P2).

The Poisson process does not obey the martingale property since its expected value is λt. To make it into a martingale we subtract its mean at time t. The mean and variance are those of a Poisson distributed random variable and are thus equal to λt.

This leads to the *compensated Poisson process*, given by $\tilde{N}(t) = N(t) - \lambda t$.

A *compound Poisson process* with intensity λ and jump size distribution J is a stochastic process given by

$$X(t) = \sum_{i=1}^{N(t)} Y_i(t) \tag{7.18}$$

where Y_i, $i \in \mathbb{N}$ is a sequence of random variables that are independent and identically distributed and $N(t)$ being a Poisson process independent of Y_i.

7.4.2 Fixed Grid Sampling (FGS)

To sample from a compound Poisson process on a fixed grid, (7.15), we apply the following algorithm, denoting $\Delta_k := t_k - t_{k-1}$ and the jump distribution by $\mathcal{D}$:

Algorithm 7.3: Sampling a compound Poisson process using the FGS method

---

1 Simulate $N_k \sim \mathcal{P}(\lambda \Delta_k)$ for each $k = 1, \dots, Nt$
2 Simulate N_k random variables $U_i \sim \mathcal{U}(0, (t_k - t_{k-1})), i = 1, \dots, Nt$
3 Simulate N_k random variables $Y_i \sim \mathcal{D}(\cdot), i = 1, \dots, Nt$
4 Set $X(t_k) = \sum_{i=1}^{N_k} Y_i 1_{\{U_i \leq t_k\}}$

We considered the Merton model in Subsection 3.2.2 and the Bates model in Subsection 3.2.3. Since the jump component is independent of the diffusion part and the jumps are distributed due to a logarithmic normal distribution with parameters μ_J and σ_J, we apply the following scheme for independent normally distributed random variables Z_1, Z_2 and a Poisson random variable N with intensity λ:

$$X(t + \Delta) = X(t) + (r - d - m)\Delta + \sigma\sqrt{\Delta}Z_1 + N\mu_J + \sqrt{N}\sigma_J Z_2.$$

Here, m denotes the martingale adjustment, which is given by $m = \sigma^2/2 + \lambda(\exp(\mu_J + \sigma_J^2/2) - 1)$, and $N\mu_1 + \sqrt{N}\sigma_J Z_2$ reflects the changes due to jumps on $[t, t + \Delta]$.

Suppose we wish to state the scheme for the logarithm of $S(t)$ and we have already simulated $X(t_{k-1}) = \log(S(t_{k-1}))$. We proceed by simulating the diffusion and the jump component. The pseudo code for a general jump-diffusion model is given by Algorithm 7.4.

Algorithm 7.4: Sampling a logarithmic: Normal jumps needed for applying the FGS method

---

1 Simulate $Z \sim \mathcal{N}(0, 1)$
2 Simulate $N_k \sim \mathcal{P}(\lambda \Delta_k)$
3 Simulate N_k random variables $\log(Y_k) \sim \mathcal{D}(\cdot)$
4 Set $M_k = \log(Y_1) + \dots + \log(Y_{N_k})$
5 Set $X(t_k) = X(t_{k-1}) - \sigma^2/2\Delta_k + \sigma\sqrt{\Delta_k} \cdot Z + M_k$

Let us give the Matlab code for simulating using the Merton model together with FGS simulation in Figure 7.21.

7.4.3 Stochastic Grid Sampling (SGS)

The sampling algorithm for a stochastic grid first samples the jump times which constitute the basic grid points and then variates from the jump distribution again denoted by $\mathcal{D}$.

To do this we generate the time steps Δ_i as long as $\sum_{i=0} \Delta_i <= T$ and we sample the values $X(\Delta_1), X(\Delta_2), \dots$ for each path. To this end set $X(t_0) = X(0)$. We now apply the SGS to the pricing of continuously monitored Barrier options.

Algorithm 7.5: Sampling using the SGS method

---
1 Set $\Delta_i = 0$
2 Simulate $\Delta_i \sim \mathcal{E}(1/\lambda)$, $\mathcal{E}$ denotes exponential distribution
3 Set $\tau_{i+1} = \tau_i + \Delta_i$
  if $\tau_{i+1} \geq T$ **then**
  a   Set $\tau_{i+1} = T$
  b   Stop
    else
  a   Simulate $Z \sim \mathcal{N}(0, 1)$
  b   Simulate $\log(Y_i) \sim \mathcal{D}(\cdot)$
  c   Set $X(\tau_{i+1}) = X(\tau_i) - \sigma^2/2\Delta_i + \sigma\sqrt{\Delta_i} \cdot Z + \log(Y_i)$

Next, we combine this method with a variance reduction method called *importance sampling*. We give the code for SGS in the Merton model (Figure 7.22). In this case we cannot provide a set of paths since the grid changes for each path and so we only give the terminal value here.

Application to Pricing Continuously Monitored Barrier Options

The probability distribution is adjusted such that only relevant paths are simulated. Relevant paths are those on which the payoff is not 0. We give two examples for applying this technique. To this end we implement the algorithm from Joshi, M. and Leung, T. (2007).

```
function y = MC_merton_fgs (S, r, sigma, T, ...
      a, b, lambda, NSim, Nt)
% Implements the FGS sampling for the Merton model

    nu = r - lambda*(exp(a+0.5*b^2)-1) - 0.5*sigma^2;
% adjustment
        dt = T/Nt;                            % dt
        X = log(S)*ones(NSim,1);              % X log price process

        for i = 1:Nt
            P = poissrnd(lambda*dt, NSim, 1);  % randoms for jump part
            lnJ = a*P + b*sqrt(P) ...
                .*randn(NSim,1);               % jump part
            X = X + nu*dt ...
                + sigma*sqrt(dt)*randn(NSim,1) ...
                + lnJ;                         % diff part + jump part
        end

    y = exp(X);                               % price process
end
```

Figure 7.21 Matlab implementation of the FGS method for path discretization in the Merton model

```
function y = MC_merton_sgs(S,r,sigma,T, a,b,lambda,NSim)
%Implements the SGS method for the Merton model
nu = r - lambda*(exp(a+0.5*b^2)-1)-0.5*sigma^2; % martingale correction

X = log(S)*ones(NSim,1);              % X is the log price path

for k=1:NSim
    t = 0;
    tau = [];
    %simulate the jump times first
    while t < T
        dt = -log(rand)/lambda;  % jump time
        t = t + dt;              % add the jump times
        tau = [tau; dt];                % not good matlab but works!
    end
    tau(end) = T-(t-dt);
    N = length(tau);                  % N number of jumps + 1
    W1 = randn(1,N);                  % uniforms for diffusion
    if N > 1
        W2 = randn(1,N-1);            % uniforms for jumps
        for i = 1:N-1
            Z = nu*tau(i) + sigma*sqrt(tau(i)) * W1(i);
            lnY = a+b*W2(i);
            X(k) = X(k) + Z + lnY;
        end
    end

    dt_end = tau(end);
    Z = nu * dt_end + sigma * sqrt(dt_end) * W1(end);
    X(k) = X(k) + Z;
end
y = exp(X);
end
```

Figure 7.22 Matlab implementation of the SGS method for path discretization in the Merton model

First, we split the problem into two parts since the option price of a continuously monitored Barrier option can be separated with respect to the paths where no jump occurs and the paths where at least one jump occurs. Let us examine the cases where the barrier is breached until T. Then we weight the Monte Carlo estimators for both sets of paths with the corresponding probabilities. This is the probability of the event that there is no jump until T, $\mathbb{P}(t_1 > T)$ and the probability where there is at least one jump until T, $\mathbb{P}(t_1 \leq T)$. The option price is given by

$$C = \mathbb{P}(t_1 > T)C^{NJ} + \mathbb{P}(t_1 \leq T)C^J. \tag{7.19}$$

The following algorithm is based on adjusting a likelihood ratio due to jump times and hitting the barrier. The likelihood ratio is a measure and is the percentage of the relevant paths contributing to the payoff.

Algorithm 7.6: Pricing of continuously monitored Barrier options by advanced Monte Carlo simulation

---

1 Set the likelihood ratio equal to 1.
2 Draw the first jump time t_1, using importance sampling such that $t_1 < T$.
3 Draw the succeeding jump times t_j such that the increments are exponentially distributed.
4 Main step:
   Draw increments of the stochastic dynamics across the current time step insuring that it is above or below the barrier.
   Multiply the likelihood ratio accordingly.
   Compute the probability that the barrier was breached using Brownian bridge formula. Multiply it to the likelihood ratio.
   Draw the jump sizes such that the stock stays above or below the barrier.
5 Calculate the expected value of the option using the pricing formula (7.19) and add the no-jump contribution and the contribution from the Monte Carlo sample multiplied by the final likelihood ratio.
6 Draw increments of the stochastic dynamics across the current time step ensuring that it is above / below the barrier and multiply the likelihood ratio accordingly.
7 Compute the probability that the barrier was breached using Brownian bridge formula and multiply it by the likelihood ratio.
8 Draw the jump sizes such that the stock stays above / below the barrier.

To ensure that we only sample in a region where a payoff is non-zero, as may be the case for *knock-in* or *knock-out* options, we take the following equation which is implemented by considering

$$\psi = \begin{cases} \mathbb{P}(X \geq h)^{-1}, & x \geq h \\ 0, & \text{otherwise} \end{cases}$$

and the equation

$$\int f(x)\varphi(x)dx = \int_{\{x \geq h\}} f(x)\varphi(x)dx = \mathbb{P}(X \geq h)\int f(x)\psi(x)dx. \tag{7.20}$$

If the stock price follows a geometric Brownian motion we can sample a variate by

$$\mathcal{N}^{-1}(1 - \mathbb{P}(X \geq h) \cdot u)$$

to ensure that the variate is above the value h and

$$\mathcal{N}^{-1}(\mathbb{P}(X \geq h) \cdot u)$$

to ensure that it is below the level h. Simulating within a jump-diffusion model, to ensure that at least one jump occurs in the path, we apply importance sampling to the stochastic grid based, SGS, method as follows. Simulate $u \sim \mathcal{U}(0, 1)$ and consider

$$\tilde{u} = \mathbb{P}(t_1 < T) \cdot u.$$

Thus, we can simulate the first time at which a jump occurs by setting

$$t_1 = -\log((1 - \tilde{u})/\lambda).$$

```
function [CallPrice, CJumpstd] = MC_merton_barrier_is(S,K,r,sigma,T, ...
    a,b,lambda,H,NSim)
% Implements the algorithm given in Joshi and Leung
if(H>S) % nothing to compute
    CallPrice = 0.0; CJumpstd = 0.0; return;
end

if lambda > 0 % the case of jumps
    sigma2 = sigma^2;                       % variance
    mj = log(a);
    nu = r + lambda*(1-a)-0.5*sigma2;       % martingale correction
    p = 1-exp(-T*lambda);                   % p = P(t < T)
    t = -log(1-p*rand(NSim,1))/lambda;      % First jump at t<T
    dt = t;                                 % updated wrt jump time

    X = log(S)*ones(NSim,1);                % log price path
    Likelihood = ones(NSim,1);              % likelihood = 1
    V = ones(NSim,1);
    if t == 0
        CJump = 0; CJumpstd = 0;
    else
        for k=1:NSim
            tau = [];
            while t(k) < T                  % Apply SGS
                tau = [tau;dt(k)];          % append to tau
                dt(k) = -log(1-rand)/lambda; % paths with >= 1 jump
                t(k) = t(k) + dt(k);        % add the jump times
            end

            N = length(tau);               % N jumps
            U1 = rand(1,N); U2 = rand(1,N); % uniforms

            for i = 1:N
                theta1 = 1-normcdf(log(H),X(k)+nu*tau(i), ...
                    sigma*sqrt(tau(i))); % P(Z>x) for BB part Z
                % IS, choose variate such that barrier is not breached
                Z=norminv(1-theta1.*U1(i),nu*tau(i),sigma*sqrt(tau(i)));

                %compute P(Z>x) for the jump size
                theta2 = 1-normcdf(log(H),X(k)+Z+(mj-0.5*b^2),b);
                % IS, choose variate such that barrier is not breached
                lnY = norminv(1-theta2.*U2(i),(mj-0.5*b^2),b);
                % Update Likelihood
                Likelihood(k)=theta1.*theta2.*(1-exp(-2*(log(H)-X(k))...
                    .*(log(H)-X(k)-Z)/(sigma2*tau(i)))).*Likelihood(k);
                X(k) = X(k) + Z + lnY;                  % update sample
            end
            Tend = min(max(T-(t(k)-dt(k)),0),1);        % time to T
            V(k) = BS_DownOutCall(exp(X(k)),K,r, ...
                -lambda*(1-a),sigma,Tend,H);            % option price
        end
        CJump = mean(exp(-r*(t-dt)).*Likelihood .*V);   % MC estimate
        CJumpstd = std(exp(-r*(t-dt)).*Likelihood .* V)...
            /sqrt(NSim);                                % std error
    end
    % Black Formula for no jumps
    NoJump = BS_DownOutCall(S,K,r,-lambda*(1-a),sigma,T,H);
    CallPrice = (1-p)*NoJump + p*CJump;     % final price
else
    CallPrice = BS_DownOutCall(S,K,r,0,sigma,T,H); CJumpstd = 0.0;
end
end
```

Figure 7.23 Matlab function for computing the price of continuously monitored Barrier options in the Merton model using Monte Carlo sampling

```
function y = MC_merton_barrier_standard(S,K,r,sigma,T, ...
    a,b,lambda,H,paths,steps)

    nu = r + lambda*(1-a)-0.5*sigma^2;  % adjustment
    dt = T/steps;                                    % dt

    X = log(S)*ones(paths,1);              % X log price process
    lnH = log(H);                          % the log barrier level
    %A indicates values where asset price process is above the barrier
    A = X > lnH;

    for i = 1:steps
        P = poissrnd(lambda*dt,paths,1);
% randoms for jump
        lnJ = (log(a)-b^2/2)*P + b*sqrt(P).*randn(paths,1);% jump part
        X = X + nu*dt ...
            + sigma*sqrt(dt)*randn(paths,1) ...  % diff part
            + lnJ;                               % jump part

        A = A + (X > lnH);
    end

    ST = exp(X);                     % price process
    Ind = A==(steps+1);              % select paths that contribute
    payDOC = max(ST(Ind)-K,0);       % payoff (down-and-out-call)
    y = sum(exp(-r*T)*payDOC)/paths;% MC estimator

end
```

Figure 7.24 Matlab implementation for pricing continuously monitored Barrier options in a jump-diffusion model

For continuously monitored Barrier options there is a probability of the asset price crossing the barrier between two consecutive points of a given discretization T.

We can account for this probability by considering the sampling procedure using

$$\mathbb{P}\left(\max_{t\in(u,v)} S(t)|S(u), S(v)\right) = 1 - \exp\left(-2\frac{(h-S(u))(h-S(v))}{\sigma^2(v-u)}\right).$$

We describe the details of bridge sampling later in this book (see Section 7.5). Then, we also consider general bridge sampling for Lévy processes. For applications to subordinated Lévy processes see Ribeiro, C. and Webber, N. (2007a) or Ribeiro, C. and Webber, N. (2007b).

To be complete we also show the standard implementation. While Figure 7.23 shows the enhanced algorithm, Figure 7.24 shows the Matlab code.

The method of importance sampling can be applied to compute stable Greeks using the Mont Carlo method. This method was introduced in the context of Libor Market Models by Fries, C. and Kampen, J. (2006), Fries, C. and Joshi, M. (2008) and Fries, C. (2007) and has been generalized to the setting of Lévy processes, respectively processes from which the characteristic function is known by Kienitz, J. (2010) and Kienitz, J. (2008). The method is referred to as *The Proxy Method* in the literature.

We employ this method when we tackle the problem of computing Greeks using Monte Carlo methods.

Numerical Example   To illustrate the difference between the sampling schemes we give a numerical example. To this end we take

- $S(0) = 100$
- $K = 110$
- $H = 95$
- $r = 0.05$
- $\sigma = 0.25$
- $\mu_J = 1.005$
- $\sigma_J = 0.1$
- $\lambda = 0.2$
- $T = 1$.

Before we compare the scheme based on importance sampling with the standard scheme we check the accuracy of the method against the number obtained in Joshi, M. and Leung, T. (2007). To this end we take different values for $\lambda = 0.1, 0.2, 0.5, 1.0, 2.0, 4.0$ and 8.0. Table 7.8 compares the results using our implementation against the quoted prices from Joshi, M. and Leung, T. (2007).

To carry out another test we compare the scheme based on importance sampling with the standard simulation. The results are summarized in Table 7.9.

Looking at Table 7.9 we observe that a standard implementation does not lead to reasonable price, but it is fast. The importance sampling method is accurate even for a small number of sample paths. Furthermore, we see that the accuracy of the standard scheme increases when we increase the number of time steps for large values of the jump intensity λ.

Now, let us consider another value for λ. We wish to investigate how many time steps we need for the standard simulation scheme to obtain accurate results for $\lambda = 0.2$. We observe that we need $NSim = 1000000$ and $Nt = 9600$ steps to get near the range of the prices. The corresponding prices and standard errors are 4.0614(0.0684) and 4.1427(0.0249). The computational time is 657 seconds. For the scheme based on importance sampling to reach the same level of accuracy only needs 16 seconds.

It is, however, possible to increase the speed for the importance sampling scheme. To sample the jump times and the likelihood ratio it is necessary to use `while` or `for` loops. This is known

Table 7.8   We consider different values of $\lambda =$ and compare the prices to the ones quoted in Joshi, M. and Leung, T. (2007). We have also given the standard errors

Value of λ	Implementation	Std.Error	Benchmark
0.1	4.0461	0.0618	4.0396
0.2	4.0614	0.0634	4.0651
0.5	4.1878	0.0674	4.1384
1.0	4.2204	0.0700	4.2475
2.0	4.4599	0.0785	4.4623
4.0	4.8435	0.0944	4.8480
8.0	5.4338	0.1234	5.4585

Table 7.9 Simulation of the price of continuously monitored Barrier options. We varied the number of simulations $NSim = 10000, 50000, 100000, 150000, 250000, 500000$ and the number of time steps from 12 to 72. The table shows the price and the elapsed time in seconds for the standard and the methods based on *importance sampling*. For varying the time steps we see that this does not impact the importance sampling algorithm

NSim ($\times 10^3$)	10	50	100	150	250	500
Price						
Method						
IS	5.3408	5.4334	5.4459	5.4562	5.4584	5.4565
Standard	7.6663	7.6630	7.7397	7.8183	7.6710	7.6784
Time (sec. $\times 10^3$)						
IS	0.0263	0.1306	0.2615	0.3920	0.6550	1.3085
Standard	0.0002	0.0002	0.0005	0.0008	0.0013	0.0029
Nt	12	24	36	48	60	72
Price						
IS	5.4566					
Standard	8.6993	7.6241	7.2937	7.1646	6.8518	6.6240
Time (sec.)						
IS	83.0370					
Standard	0.3530	0.5857	0.8101	1.0276	1.2491	1.4753

to be slow in Matlab. The performance where vector and matrix based implementations can be used is much better. Therefore, the SGS method for jump diffusion explains the speed of the standard sampling scheme.

7.4.4 Simulation – Lévy Models

To apply Lévy processes to financial problems we should be able to simulate such processes. This section covers the simulation of Lévy models by

- Subordination.
- Approximation using a jump diffusion.
- Direct simulation.
- Series representation.

We describe each method in detail and focus on the Variance Gamma model for illustration. For further information the reader may consult Duffy, D. and Kienitz, J. (2009), Schoutens, W. (2003), Cont, R. and Tankov, P. (2004) or Glasserman, P. (2004).

Subordination

Let $W(t)$ be a standard Brownian motion and take the stochastic process h. For fixed $\omega \in \Omega$, let

$$h(\omega, \cdot) : \mathbb{R}^+ \to \mathbb{R}^+, \quad t \mapsto h(\omega, t). \tag{7.21}$$

We call h from (7.21) a *subordinator* if $h(t)$ is increasing. Then, $W(h(t))$ is a Brownian motion. For illustration we consider two stochastic processes, the Gamma process and the Inverse Gaussian process, which can be applied as subordinator processes. The Gamma process (X_t)

is specified by the Lévy triplet

$$\left(\frac{a}{b}\left(1 - e^{-b}\right), 0, \frac{a}{x}e^{-bx}1_{\{x>0\}}dx\right). \tag{7.22}$$

The Inverse Gaussian process is given in terms of its Lévy triplet

$$\left(\frac{a}{b}\left(2\mathcal{N}(b) - 1\right), 0, \frac{1}{\sqrt{2\pi}}\frac{a}{x^{3/2}}1_{\{x>0\}}dx\right). \tag{7.23}$$

Applying the processes specified by (7.22) and (7.23) lead to Variance Gamma and to Normal Inverse Gaussian (NIG) processes respectively.

Suppose we wish to simulate from a Variance Gamma process with parameters θ, σ and ν. For a given time grid, (7.15), denoting $\Delta_i = t_{i+1} - t_i$ let h be a Gamma process and we proceed by the following algorithm:

- Simulate $h_i \sim \Gamma(\Delta_i/\nu, \nu)$
- Simulate $Z \sim \mathcal{N}(0, 1)$
- Set $X(t_i) = X(t_{i-1}) + \theta h(t_i) + \sigma \sqrt{h(t_i)} \cdot Z$.

For financial modelling we have to include the martingale correction. Thus, since we have already shown how to sample from a diffusion process we only have to find a method to sample from the subordinator's distribution. Thus, we denote the model parameters by *sigma*, *theta* and *nu*, the market parameters by *S0* for the spot, *r* for the riskless rate and *d* for the dividend yield and *T* for the maturity.

Using the Monte Carlo parameter for the number of batches, *NBatches*, the number of simulations per batch, *NSim*, and the number of time steps by *Nt*, the discretization is given by Figure 7.25.

```
function pathS = MC_VG_S(S0,r,d,T,nu,theta,sigma,NTime,NSim,NBatches)
% discretisation of Variance Gamma process
% using subordination

pathS = zeros(NSim,NTime+1,NBatches);      % create the output
lnS = zeros(NSim,NTime+1);                 % used per batch
dT = T / NTime;                            % delta time
omegaT = -1/nu * log(1-theta(1)*nu ...
    - nu*sigma(1)^2/2);                    % martingale correction
lnS(:,1) = log(S0);                        % Set starting spot price

for l = 1 : NBatches                       % batch loop
%    G = nu * gamrnd(dT/nu,1,NSim,NTime);
%    dW = randn(NSim,NTime);
    for m=2:NTime+1                        % time loop
        G = nu * gamrnd(dT/nu,1,NSim);     % Gamma subordinator
        dW = randn(NSim,1);                % Gaussians
        lnS(:,m) = lnS(:,m-1) ...          % log VG
            + (r-d-omegaT) * dT ...
            + theta(1) * G + sqrt(G) * sigma .* dW;
    end

    pathS(:,:,l) = exp(lnS);               % simulated paths
end
```

Figure 7.25 Matlab implementation of the subordinator approach for the Variance Gamma model using the σ, θ and ν representation and subordination of a Brownian motion

```
function pathS = MC_NIG(S0,r,d,T,alpha,beta,delta,NTime,NSim,NBatches)
% discretisation of NIG process
% using IG subordinator

pathS = zeros(NSim,NTime+1,NBatches);    % create output
lnS = ones(NSim,NTime+1);                % used during batches
lnS(:,1) = log(S0);                      % set spot

omega = delta*(sqrt(alpha^2-(beta+1)^2) ...
    -sqrt(alpha^2-beta^2));              % martingale correction
dT = T/NTime;                            % delta time
b_par = delta*sqrt(alpha^2-beta^2);      % par for IG subordinator
theta = dT/b_par;                        % par for IG subordinator
chi = dT^2;
% method based on loops
for l = 1 : NBatches                     % batch loop
    for m = 2:NTime+1                    % time loop
        chisq1 = randn(NSim,1).^2;
        Yvec = theta + 0.5*theta./chi .* ( theta.*chisq1 - ...
        sqrt(4*theta.*chi.*chisq1 + theta.^2.*chisq1.^2) );
        Ind = find(rand(NSim,1) >= theta./(theta+Yvec));
        Yvec(Ind) = theta.^2./Yvec(Ind);% IG subordinator
        dW = randn(NSim,1);              % Gaussians
        lnS(:,m) = lnS(:,m-1) + (r-d)*dT + omega*dT ...
            + beta*delta^2*Yvec + delta*sqrt(Yvec).*dW;
    end

    pathS(:,:,l) = exp(lnS);             % simulated paths
end
```

Figure 7.26 Matlab implementation for the discretization of the NIG model using the representation as subordinated Brownian motion. The path set pathS can be used to evaluate a given payoff

We also consider the NIG model. Again, we denote the market parameters by *S0*, *r*, *d* and *T* and the Monte Carlo parameters by *NBatches*, *NSim* and *Nt*. The model parameters are *alpha*, *beta* and *delta*. As for the Variance Gamma model we have included a purely vectorized version and a version using loops. The reader can take the code and comment on the particular version in or out. Then the discretization is given by Figure 7.26.

Approximation with Jump Diffusions

To apply an approximation procedure using jump-diffusion processes we have to specify a jump size ε to specify small jumps. We call a jump a small jump if its jump size is smaller than ε. Then, we approximate the small jumps with a Brownian motion and the large jumps, that is jumps of size bigger than ε, by a compound Poisson process.

Consider a Lévy process with triplet $(a, 0, v)$. We decomposed this process into two parts:

$$X(t) := X^{\varepsilon}(t) + X_{\varepsilon}(t)$$

where $X^{\varepsilon}(t)$ is a compound Poisson process with a drift and the distribution of jumps proportional to the measure $v^{\varepsilon} = v_{|\{|x|>\varepsilon\}}$. The process $X_{\varepsilon}(t)$ has mean 0 and Lévy measure

$v_\varepsilon = v_{|\{|x|\le\varepsilon\}}$. The latter process reflects the small jumps. Considering very small ε we may take

$$X(t) \approx X^\varepsilon(t). \qquad (7.24)$$

If the intensity of small jumps is high we may rely on another approximation. The simplest one would be to replace the small jumps by the expected value. A more sophisticated albeit not universally applicable method is to approximate the small jumps by a Brownian motion using

$$X(t) \approx X^\varepsilon(t) + \sigma_\varepsilon W(t). \qquad (7.25)$$

Neglecting the small jumps would require an enormous number of jumps to be simulated to obtain a reasonable approximation accuracy using (7.24). To select ε and determining σ_ε numerically in (7.25) ideally requires a series representation of $X(t)$.

Suppose we wish to simulate from a Lévy process with Lévy the density of the Lévy measure denoted by k. For a fixed time grid $\mathcal{T} = \{t_0, t_1, \ldots, t_{Nt}\}$ set

$$\sigma_\varepsilon^2 := \int_{-\varepsilon}^{\varepsilon} x^2 k(x) dx \qquad (7.26)$$

$$\lambda_\varepsilon^+ := \int_{\varepsilon}^{\infty} k(x) dx \quad ; \quad \lambda_\varepsilon^- := \int_{-\infty}^{-\varepsilon} k(x) dx$$

$$k_\varepsilon^+(x) := k(x) 1_{\{x\ge\varepsilon\}}/\lambda_\varepsilon^+ \quad ; \quad k_\varepsilon^-(x) := k(x) 1_{\{x\le-\varepsilon\}}/\lambda_\varepsilon^- .$$

The simulation algorithm can be summarized as follows:

Algorithm 7.7: Algorithm for approximating a pure jump process with a jump-diffusion process

---

Assume we already simulated the value $X(t_{k-1})$.
1 Simulate $N_k^+ \sim \mathcal{P}(\lambda_\varepsilon^+, \Delta_k)$, $N_k^- \sim \mathcal{P}(\lambda_\varepsilon^-, \Delta_k)$
2 Simulate $X_{k,j}^+ \sim \{k_\varepsilon^+\}, \quad j = 1, \ldots, N_k^+$, $X_{k,j}^- \sim \{k_\varepsilon^-\}, \quad j = 1, \ldots, N_k^-$
3 Simulate $Z \sim \mathcal{N}(0, 1)$
4 Set $X(t_k) = X(t_{k-1}) + Z\sigma_\varepsilon\sqrt{\Delta_k} + \sum_{j=1}^{N_k^+} X_{k,j}^+ + \sum_{j=1}^{N_k^-} X_{k,j}^-$

In general, if the jump-diffusion parameters are given by (7.26), we can apply either FGS or SGS simulation methods.

Now let us reconsider the jump-diffusion approximation. We apply a more sophisticated method. This is based on a partition of $\mathbb{R}\backslash(-\varepsilon, \varepsilon)$. Let P_i, $i = 1, \ldots, N$ be this partition and choose

$$\lambda_i := k(P_i) \qquad (7.27)$$

$$c_i^2 \lambda_i := \int_{P_i} x^2 k(x) dx. \qquad (7.28)$$

This consideration leads to an approximation using N compound Poisson processes $N_i(t)$ and

$$X(t) \approx \sum_{i=1}^{N} c_i \left(N_i(t)\lambda_i 1_{\{|c_i|<1\}} \right)$$

with c_i chosen such that the second moments are matched.

Table 7.10 $\sigma_\varepsilon, \frac{\sigma_\varepsilon}{\varepsilon}, \lambda_\varepsilon^+$ and λ_ε^- for different values of ε for the Variance Gamma model with $C = 11.1111$, $G = 7.1845$ and $M = 6.9595$

ε	1	0.1	0.01	0.001	0.0001	0.00001	0.000001
σ_ε	0.664525679	0.265224623	0.032559002	0.003325485	0.000333255	3.33325E-05	3.33332E-06
$\frac{\sigma_\varepsilon}{\varepsilon}$	0.664525679	2.652246234	3.255900237	3.325485463	3.332546005	3.33325309	3.333323809
λ_ε^+	0.001042419	4.01074877	23.62890438	48.50867736	74.02122745	99.59829765	125.1818325
λ_ε^-	0.001343235	4.18506415	23.95830422	48.85972248	74.37451383	99.95180895	125.5353663

However, it has been proven that this approximation is not valid for all Lévy processes. Rosinski, J. (2001) rigorously proves when the approximation is feasible. It is shown that for some $\lambda > 0$

$$\lim_{\varepsilon \to 0} \frac{\lambda \min(\sigma_\varepsilon, \varepsilon)}{\sigma_\varepsilon} = 1. \tag{7.29}$$

Schoutens, W. (2003) gives a condition which implies (7.29). It holds if

$$\lim_{\varepsilon \to 0} \frac{\sigma_\varepsilon}{\varepsilon} = \infty. \tag{7.30}$$

Example: Variance Gamma Process Let us consider the Variance Gamma process with parameters $C = 11.1111$, $G = 7.1845$ and $M = 6.9595$. We wish to determine σ_ε, λ_ε^+ and λ_ε^-. To this end we have to fix $\varepsilon > 0$ and perform a numerical integration with respect to the Lévy measure ν_{VG}. This leads to the results presented in Table 7.10.

The jump-diffusion approximation incorporating a Brownian component is not valid since the Variance Gamma process can be represented by the difference of two Gamma processes, U and D. Let a_l and b_l, $l = U, D$ be the parameters of the Gamma processes U and D. Then, using Equation (7.30), we have

$$\lim_{\varepsilon \to 0} \frac{\sigma_\varepsilon}{\varepsilon} \to \frac{1}{2}(a_U - a_D)$$

and therefore the condition (7.30) cannot be fulfilled.

Example: Normal Inverse Gaussian Process Let us now take the NIG process with parameters $\alpha = 1.8$, $\beta = -0.3$ and $\delta = 0.2$. We wish to determine σ_ε, λ_ε^+ and λ_ε^-. To this end we have to fix $\varepsilon > 0$ and perform a numerical integration with respect to the Lévy measure ν_{VG}. This leads to the results shown in Table 7.11.

Table 7.11 $\sigma_\varepsilon, \frac{\sigma_\varepsilon}{\varepsilon}, \lambda_\varepsilon^+$ and λ_ε^- for different values of ε for the NIG model with $\alpha = 1.8$, $\beta = -0.3$ and $\delta = 0.2$

ε	1	0.1	0.01	0.001	0.0001	0.00001	0.000001
σ_ε	0.291115021	0.112029195	0.035677724	0.01128377	0.003568248	0.001128379	0.000356825
$\frac{\sigma_\varepsilon}{\varepsilon}$	0.291115021	1.12029195	3.56777236	11.28376961	35.6824814	112.8379167	356.8248232
λ_ε^+	0.01035402	0.52883463	6.273624557	63.60840686	636.6094678	6366.231303	63662.05478
λ_ε^-	0.004576042	0.45767279	6.11536983	63.36221529	636.2753242	6365.809207	63661.54473

The jump-diffusion approximation incorporating a Brownian component is valid since

$$\sigma_\varepsilon \approx \sqrt{\frac{2\alpha\delta}{\pi}}\sqrt{\varepsilon}$$

and therefore for $\varepsilon \to 0$ we find $\frac{\sigma_\varepsilon}{\varepsilon} \to \infty$ which leads to (7.29).

Direct Simulation

Sometimes it is possible to directly simulate the distribution either by decomposing the distribution of the process into two processes with known distributions or by numerically inverting the cumulative distribution.

Numerical Inversion   We use the *Lévy inversion formula* to numerically compute the inverse of the cumulative distribution. The inversion formula (see Subsection 13.3.2) is given by

$$F(x_1) - F(x_2) = \frac{1}{2\pi} \lim_{A \to \infty} \int_{-A}^{A} \frac{e^{-itx_2} - e^{-itx_1}}{it} \varphi(t) dt. \tag{7.31}$$

The function F denotes the cumulative distribution function at x_1 and x_2, $x_2 < x_1$. The function φ is the characteristic function corresponding to the cumulative distribution F.

To numerically invert the cumulative distribution function for fixed spot price s, we consider the function arg given by

$$arg(z) := -s^{-iz}/iz + \varphi(z).$$

Then, for a real number c the cumulative distribution is given by

$$F(x) = \frac{1}{\pi} \int_{-\infty}^{x} \mathcal{R}\left(arg(z + ic)\right) dx.$$

The constant c can be chosen such that the integral can be evaluated conveniently. It corresponds to shifting the integration path into the complex plane. Finally, the inversion can be done by a zero search. The inverse cumulative distribution F^{-1} is given by

$$F^{-1}(y) = inf_x\{x : F(x) - y = 0\}.$$

We have applied this procedure to the Variance Gamma process. The result is shown in Figure 7.27.

Decomposition   We sample the Variance Gamma process as the difference of two Gamma processes, $U(t)$ and $D(t)$. U represents the upward jumps and D the downward jumps. The Variance Gamma process, $X(t)$, is then given by

$$X(t) = U(t) - D(t).$$

We fix the discrete set $\mathcal{T} = \{t_0, t_1, t_2, \ldots, t_N\} \subset [0, T]$, denote $\Delta_i = t_i - t_{i-1}$ and we assume we have simulated $X(t_{i-1}) = \log(S(t_{i-1}))$.

Suppose we wish to simulate from a Variance Gamma process with parameters C, G and M, then we apply the rule

- $U(t_i) \sim \Gamma(\Delta_i/C, CG)$ and $D(t_i) \sim \Gamma(\Delta_i/C, CM)$
- Set $X(t_i) = X(t_{i-1}) + U(t_i) - D(t_i)$.

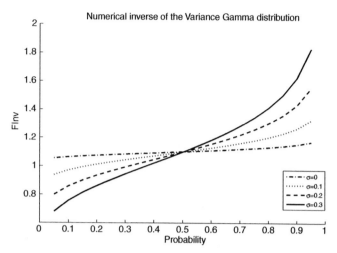

Figure 7.27 The inverse of the Variance Gamma cumulative distribution calculated numerically. We used $T = 1, \theta = 0.1$ and $\nu = 0.1$. The parameter σ varies

We denote the model parameters by C, G and M, the market parameters by $S0$ for the spot, r for the riskless rate and d for the dividend yield and T for the maturity. Denoting the number of batches, *NBatches*, the number of simulations per batch, *NSim*, and the number of time steps by Nt, the discretization is given by Figure 7.28.

```
function pathS = MC_VG_CGM(S0,r,d,T,C,G,M,NTime,NSim,NBatches)
% discretisation of Variance Gamma process
% using the cgm representation

pathS = zeros(NSim,NTime+1,NBatches);       % create the output
lnS = zeros(NSim,NTime+1);                  % used per batch

dT = T / NTime;                             % delta time
omegaT = -C*log((G*M /(G*M + (M-G)-1)));    % martingale correction
lnS(:,1) = log(S0);                         % set spot price

for l = 1 : NBatches                        % batch loop
    for m=2:NTime+1                         % time loop
        Gvec1 = gamrnd(dT*C , 1/M, NSim,1); % Gamma process1
        Gvec2 = gamrnd(dT *C , 1/G, NSim,1); % Gamma process2
        lnS(:,m) = lnS(:,m-1) + (r-d + omegaT) * dT ...
                     + Gvec1 - Gvec2;        % log VG
    end

    pathS(:,:,l) = exp(lnS);                % output sim result
end
```

Figure 7.28 Matlab implementation of the Variance Gamma process represented as the difference of two Gamma processes and using the C, G, M representation. The generated path `pathS` can then be used to compute a Monte Carlo estimator for some payoff

Series Representation

The *series representation* provides an approximation along a sample path of the process. We use the fact that any Lévy process $(X(t))$ can be represented by an almost surely convergent series (uniformly in t) of the form

$$X(t) = \sum_{j=1}^{\infty} \left[H(\Gamma_j, V_j) 1_{\{U_j \leq t\}} - t a_j \right], \quad 0 \leq t \leq T, \tag{7.32}$$

$\Gamma_j, i = 1, \ldots$ are the arrival times of a Poisson process with intensity 1, V_j are independent, identically distributed random variables and $U_j \sim \mathcal{U}(0, T)$ are independent.

Furthermore, the sequences Γ, V and U are independent of each other. The function $H \to \mathbb{R}$ is measurable, non-increasing and $a_j \in \mathbb{R}$. The functions H and V are not unique.

$$\int_{\mathbb{R}} f(x) \nu(dx) = \frac{1}{T} \int_0^{\infty} \mathbb{E}[f(H(r, V))] dr$$

for any Borel measurable function f such that $f(0) = 0$.

Let V_j be an independent identically distributed sequence of exponential random variables with parameter $\lambda > 0$. Then,

$$X(t) = \sum_{j=1}^{\infty} \exp(-\Gamma_j)/(\alpha T) V_j 1_{\{U_j \leq t\}}, \quad 0 \leq t \leq T,$$

represents a Gamma process with parameters α and λ, using the fact that a Variance Gamma process can be represented by the difference of two Gamma processes. This, then, leads to the series representation of this process.

Example: General OU process   Let us consider the case of a GOU process with parameters a, b and λ. Let $y(t)$ be this process then it is a solution to the SDE

$$dy(t) = -\lambda y(t) dt + dz(\lambda t).$$

It can be shown that the process $(z(t))_t$ is of the form

$$z(t) = \sum_{n=1}^{N(t)} X(n),$$

with $N(t)$ being a Poisson process with intensity $\mathbb{E}[N(t)] = at$ and $X(n) \sim \mathcal{G}(1, b)$. Thus, since it is a compound Poisson process it jumps only finitely often on a given compact interval. If we consider the solution $y(t)$ we find

$$y(t) = e^{-\lambda t} \left(y(0) + \int_0^{\lambda t} e^s dz(s) \right).$$

For the simulation we choose to use series representation to simulate from $e^{-\lambda t} \int_0^t e^s dz(s)$ directly.

Direct Simulation   Let ν_z denote the Lévy measure of the process $z(t)$. Define

$$\nu_z^{-1}(x) := \inf \left\{ y > 0 | \int_x^{+\infty} \nu_z(t) dt \leq x \right\}.$$

In this case we explicitly determine v_z^{-1}. It is given by

$$v_z^{-1}(x) = \max\left(0, -\frac{\log\left(\frac{x}{a}\right)}{b}\right).$$

Then, we have

$$\int_0^t f(s)dz(s) = \sum_{i=1}^{\infty} v_z^{-1}(a_i/t)f(tu_i), \quad a_1 < a_2 < \dots \text{ and } u_i \sim \mathcal{U}(0,1)$$

and a_i being the arrival time of a Poisson process with intensity 1. Thus,

$$e^{-\lambda t}\int_0^{\lambda t} e^s dz(s) = \frac{\exp(-\lambda t)}{b}\sum_{i=1}^{N(1)}\log(c_i)\exp(\lambda t u_i)$$

with $c_1 < c_2 < \dots$ are the arrival times of a Poisson process $N(t)$ with intensity $a\lambda t$ and $N(1)$ is the number of arrivals until $t = 1$.

Series Representation   Another approach is to use series representation. Then, the scheme is given as follows:

$$y(t_n) = (1 - \lambda\Delta)y(t_{n-1}) + \sum_{n=N(t_{n-1})+1}^{N(t_n)} X(n)$$

with $X(n) \sim \Gamma(1, b)$.

7.4.5   Schemes for Lévy Models with Stochastic Volatility

The final section considers sampling from Lévy processes with stochastic time change which models the stochastic volatility for Lévy processes. In this case we only describe the subordination approach. We wish to simulate the process $Z(t) := X(Y(t))$ where X is a given Lévy process and Y is the integral of some positive stochastic process y. We split the simulation into three steps:

1. Simulate $y(t)$.
2. Compute $Y(t) = \int_0^t y(s)ds$.
3. Simulate $Z(t) = X(Y(t))$.

Thus, we need efficient sampling schemes for y. Moreover, to compute Y we need sufficiently many steps. If Y can be sampled directly this is a good way to save running time and we can use step 3 directly. We focus on two particular examples, the integrated Gamma Ornstein–Uhlenbeck process and the integrated Cox–Ingersoll–Ross process. In the following two sections we provide the code for VG GOU, NIG GOU, VG CIR and NIG CIR models (Figures 7.29, 7.30, 7.31, 7.32 and 7.33). First, we provide all the parameters needed for the model and the option. Then, the code for the path generation is given and, finally, the option payoff can be evaluated by using the output of the path generating functions.

```
function pathS = MC_VGGOU(S0,r,d,T,C,G,M,lambda,a,b,NTime,NSim,NBatches)
    intNt = 20;                    % steps in between orginial grid points
    allsteps = intNt * NTime;      % grid containing all necessary steps
    dT = T / NTime;                % time step
    time = 0 : dT : T;             % time for martingale correction

    pathS = zeros(NSim,NTime+1,NBatches); % output
    lnS = zeros(NSim,NTime+1);            % used in batch
    lnS(:,1) = log(S0*exp(-d*T));         % set S(0) dividend adjusted

    %precompute the constants used for martingale correction
    y0 = 1;
    psiVG = (-1i)*C*log(G*M/(G*M+(M-G)-1));
% char exp                                        %characteristic exponent
    phiGOU = 1i*psiVG*y0/lambda*(1-exp(-lambda*time)) + ...
        lambda*a./(1i*psiVG-lambda*b).* ...
        (b*log(b./(b-1i*psiVG/lambda* ...
        (1-exp(-lambda*time)))))-1i*psiVG*time; % char func
    omegaT = -phiGOU;              % martingale correction
%martingale correction value
    omegaT(1) = 0;                 % martingale correction in 0

for l = 1:NBatches                 % batch loop
    yy = ones(NSim,allsteps+1);    % init stochastic clock
    Np = poissrnd(a*lambda/allsteps*T,[NSim,allsteps]);

    for k = 1 : NSim
        for j = 1 : allsteps       % generating OU process
            if Np(k,j) > 0
                Ex = -log(rand(Np(k,j),1))/b; % exponential law
                U = exp(-lambda * T / allsteps * rand(Np(k,j),1));
% Uniforms
                yy(k,j+1) = (1-lambda*T/allsteps)*yy(k,j) ...
                    + sum(Ex .* U);
            else
                yy(k,j+1) = (1-lambda*T/allsteps)*yy(k,j);
            end
        end
    end

    ZZ = T*cumsum(yy,2)/allsteps;            %Integrated Time
    Y = zeros(NSim,NTime+1);
    for m = 2:NTime+1
        Y(:,m) = ZZ(:,(m-1)*intNt);
    end

    Intensity = C * (Y(:,2:end)-Y(:,1:end-1));       % intensity
    DGam = gamrnd(Intensity,1/M) - gamrnd(Intensity,1/G);
    diffomegaT = omegaT(2:end) - omegaT(1:end-1);    % martingale corr

    for m=2:NTime+1                % time loop
        lnS(:,m) = lnS(:,m-1) + (r-d)*dT ...
            + diffomegaT(m-1) + DGam(:,m-1);
    end
    pathS(:,:,l) = exp(lnS);
end
```

Figure 7.29 Matlab implementation of the discretization of the VG GOU model. The function returns the asset paths and can then be used as an input to a pricing function for Monte Carlo simulation

```
function pathS = MC_NIGGOU(S0,r,d,T,alpha,beta,delta, ...
    lambda,a,b,NTime,NSim,NBatches)
% discretization of Normal Inverse Gaussian process with
% Gamma Ornstein–Uhlenbeck clock

intNt = 10;                     % steps in between orginial grid points
allsteps = intNt * NTime;       % All Nts that have to be simulated
dT = T / NTime;                 % Delta for time discretisation
time = 0 : dT : T;              % dummy for martingale correction

pathS = zeros(NSim,NTime+1,NBatches); % output
lnS = zeros(NSim,NTime+1);            % used in batch
lnS(:,1) = log(S0*exp(-d*T));         % set S(0) dividend adjusted

% precompute constants
y0 = 1;
psiNIG = (-1i)*(-delta)*(sqrt(alpha^2-(beta+1)^2) ...
    -sqrt(alpha^2-beta^2));                      % char exp
phiGOU = 1i*psiNIG*y0/lambda*(1-exp(-lambda*time)) ...
        + lambda*a./(1i*psiNIG-lambda*b) ...
        .*(b*log(b./(b-1i*psiNIG/lambda ...
        *(1-exp(-lambda*time))))-1i*psiNIG*time);% char func
omegaT = -phiGOU;               % martingale correction
omegaT(1) = 0;                  % martingale correction in 0


for l = 1 : NBatches            % batch loop
    yy = ones(NSim,allsteps+1);                  % spot clock
    Np = poissrnd(a*lambda/allsteps*T,[NSim,allsteps]);  % Poissonians

    for k = 1 : NSim
        for j = 1 : allsteps                     % generating OU process
            if Np(k,j) > 0
                Ex = -log(rand(Np(k,j),1))/b; % RVs with exponential law
                U = exp(-lambda * T / allsteps * rand(Np(k,j),1));
% Uniforms
                yy(k,j+1) = (1-lambda*T/allsteps)*yy(k,j) + sum(Ex .* U);
            else
                yy(k,j+1) = (1-lambda*T/allsteps)*yy(k,j);
            end
        end
    end

    ZZ = T*cumsum(yy,2)/allsteps;        % integrated Gamma O–U process
    Y = zeros(NSim,NTime+1);             % intergrated time
    % compute the integrated time at discretisation steps
    for m=2:NTime+1
        Y(:,m) = ZZ(:,(m-1)*intNt);
    end
```

Figure 7.30 Matlab implementation of the discretization of the NIG GOU model. The function returns the asset paths and can then be used as an input to a pricing function for Monte Carlo simulation

```
    for m=2:NTime+1       % time loop
        a_par = Y(:,m)-Y(:,m-1);           % IG param
        b_par = delta*sqrt(alpha^2-beta^2);  % IG param
        theta = a_par/b_par;
        chi = a_par.^2;
        chisq1 = randn(NSim,1).^2;
        Yvec = theta + 0.5*theta./chi .* ( theta.*chisq1 - ...
            sqrt(4*theta.*chi.*chisq1 + theta.^2.*chisq1.^2) );
        Ind = find(rand(NSim,1) >= theta./(theta+Yvec));
        Yvec(Ind) = theta(Ind).^2./Yvec(Ind);   % subordinator

        Zvec = randn(NSim,1);          % Gaussian
        lnS(:,m) = lnS(:,m-1) + (r-d)*dT + omegaT(m)-omegaT(m-1) ...
                     + beta*delta^2*Yvec + delta*sqrt(Yvec).*Zvec;
    end

    pathS(:,:,1) = exp(lnS);     % spot paths
end
```

Figure 7.31 Matlab implementation of the discretization of the NIG GOU model. The function returns the asset paths and can then be used as an input to a pricing function for Monte Carlo simulation (continued)

The Gamma Ornstein–Uhlenbeck Time Change

For integrating the stochastic clock we choose *intstep* steps, *step* time steps and *NBatches* as well as *NSim* simulations per batch. The model parameters are given in terms of the parameters C, G, M for the Variance Gamma part and a, b and λ for the Ornstein–Uhlenbeck part. Again, the market parameters are denoted by $S0$, r, d and T. The model parameters are denoted by *alpha*, *beta*, *delta*, *a*, *b* and *lambda*.

The CIR Time Change

In this section we present the Matlab code for generating paths with respect to NIG and VG models which are time changed using a CIR clock. We denote the model parameters for the CIR clock by *kappa*, *eta* and *lambda*. The generated paths can then be used to price options applying the Monte Carlo method.

Numerical Results

First, let us consider the results obtained in Subsection 5.9.3. We have used integration methods to derive the prices of forward starting Call options. In this section we apply the simulation schemes to verify the prices obtained.

VG We use the parameters $C = 1.2022$, $G = 4.2276$ and $Y = 18.2317$ and apply the simulation schemes and find the prices given in Table 7.12 and the differences to the semi-analytic results in Table 7.13.

NIG We use the model parameters $\alpha = 8.72609$, $\beta = -6.90168$ and $\delta = 0.169428$. The results are shown in Tables 7.14 and 7.15.

```
function pathS = MC_VGCIR(S0,r,d,T,C,G,M,kappa,eta,...
    lambda,NTime,NSim,NBatches)
intNt = 20;                       % steps in between orginial grid points
allsteps = intNt * NTime;         % grid containing all necessary steps
dT = T / NTime;                   % time step
daT = T/allsteps;                 % time step
time = 0 : T/NTime : T;           % Variable time for the mart corr

pathS = zeros(NSim,NTime+1,NBatches);% output
lnS = ones(NSim,NTime+1);              % used for each batch
lnS(:,1) = log(S0*exp(-d*T));          % set S(0) dividend adjusted

% precompute constants
psiVG = (-1i)*C*log(G*M/(G*M+(M-G)-1));   % char exp
gamma = sqrt(kappa^2-2*lambda^2*1i*psiVG);% CIR par
denom = ( cosh(0.5*gamma*time) ...        % denom
    + kappa*sinh(0.5*gamma*time)./gamma ).^(2*kappa*eta*lambda^(-2));
% coth is inf at 0
phiCIR(time>0) = kappa^2*eta*time(time>0)*lambda^(-2) ...
    + 2*1i*psiVG./(kappa+gamma.*coth(gamma*time(time>0)/2)) ...
    - log(denom(time>0));                % char func
phiCIR(1) = log(denom(1));               % char func start
omegaT = -phiCIR;                        % martingale correction
omegaT(1) = 0;                           % maringale correction in 0


deg = 4*eta*kappa/lambda^2;
fac1 = 4*kappa*exp(-kappa*daT)/lambda^2/(1-exp(-kappa*daT));
fac2 = lambda^2*(1-exp(-kappa*daT))/4/kappa;
Y = zeros(NSim,NTime);                   % Integrated clock

for l = 1 : NBatches                     % batch loop
    % Generating time change
    yy = ones(NSim,allsteps+1);              % stochastic clock
    for n = 1 : allsteps
        Nvec = poissrnd(0.5 * fac1 * yy(:,n));  % Poissonians
        yy(:,n+1) = fac2 * chi2rnd(deg+2*Nvec); % stochastic time
    end

    for m=1:NTime
        Y(:,m+1) = Y(:,m) + daT * sum(yy(:,1+(m-1)*intNt:m*intNt),2);
    end

    Intensity = C * (Y(:,2:end)-Y(:,1:end-1));      % intensity
    DGam = gamrnd(Intensity,1/M) - gamrnd(Intensity,1/G);% two gamma proc
    diffomegaT = omegaT(2:end) - omegaT(1:end-1);    % Mart correct

    for m=2:NTime+1                          % time loop
        lnS(:,m) = lnS(:,m-1) + (r-d)*dT + diffomegaT(m-1) + DGam(:,m-1);
    end
    pathS(:,:,1) = exp(lnS);
end
```

Figure 7.32 Matlab implementation of the discretization of the VG CIR model. The function returns the asset paths and can then be used as an input to a pricing function for Monte Carlo simulation

```
function pathS = MC_NIGCIR(S0,r,d,T,alpha,beta,delta,...
    kappa,eta,lambda,NTime,NSim,NBatches)
% discretisation for the NIG - CIR model

intNt = 10;                      % steps in between the org grid points
allsteps = intNt * NTime;        % grid containing all necessary steps
dT = T / NTime;                  % time step
daT = T/allsteps;                % time step
time = 0 : dT : T;               % used to determine martingale correction

pathS = zeros(NSim,NTime+1,NBatches);  % output
lnS = ones(NSim,NTime+1);        % used for each batch
lnS(:,1) = log(S0*exp(-d*T));    % S(0) dividend adjusted

% precompute parameters
psiNIG = (-1i)*(-delta)*(sqrt(alpha^2-(beta+1)^2)...
    -sqrt(alpha^2-beta^2));
gamma = sqrt(kappa^2-2*lambda^2*1i*psiNIG);  % char exp
denom = ( cosh(0.5*gamma*time)...            % CIR par
    + kappa*sinh(0.5*gamma*time)./gamma ).^(2*kappa*eta*lambda^(-2));  % denom
% coth is inf at 0
phiCIR(time>0) = kappa^2*eta*time(time>0)*lambda^(-2)...
        + 2*1i*psiNIG./(kappa+gamma.*coth(gamma*time(time>0)/2))...
        - log(denom(time>0));                % char func
phiCIR(1) = log(denom(1));       % char func at 0
omegaT = -phiCIR;                % martingale correction
omegaT(1) = 0;                   % martingale correction at 0

deg = 4*eta*kappa/lambda^2;
fac1 = 4*kappa*exp(-kappa*daT)/lambda^2/(1-exp(-kappa*daT));
fac2 = lambda^2*(1-exp(-kappa*daT))/4/kappa;
Y = zeros(NSim,NTime+1);         % Integrated clock

for l = 1 : NBatches             % batch loop
    % Generating time change
    yy = ones(NSim,allsteps+1);          % spot clock
    for n = 1 : allsteps
        Nvec = poissrnd(0.5 * fac1 * yy(:,n));  % Poissonians
        yy(:,n+1) = fac2 * chi2rnd(deg+2*Nvec); % stochastic time
    end

    for m=1:NTime
        Y(:,m+1) = Y(:,m) + daT * sum(yy(:,1+(m-1)*intNt:m*intNt),2);
    end

    for m=2:NTime+1              % time loop
        a_par = Y(:,m)-Y(:,m-1);              % param of IG distribution
        a_par(a_par<=0) = realmin;            % security check
        b_par = delta*sqrt(alpha^2-beta^2);   % param of IG distribution
        theta = a_par/b_par;
        chi = a_par.^2;

        chisq1 = randn(NSim,1).^2;
        Yvec = theta + 0.5*theta./chi .* ( theta.*chisq1 - ...
            sqrt(4*theta.*chi.*chisq1 + theta.^2.*chisq1.^2) );
        Ind = find(rand(NSim,1) >= theta./(theta+Yvec));
        Yvec(Ind) = theta(Ind).^2./Yvec(Ind);   % Subordinator

        Zvec = randn(NSim,1);                    % Gaussians
        lnS(:,m) = lnS(:,m-1) + (r-d)*dT + omegaT(m)-omegaT(m-1) ...
            + beta*delta^2*Yvec + delta*sqrt(Yvec).*Zvec;
    end

    pathS(:,:,l) = exp(lnS);     % spot paths
end
```

Figure 7.33   Matlab implementation of the discretization of the NIG CIR model

Table 7.12   Prices and standard error using the Monte Carlo method for VG

Moneyness	Price 1	Price 2	Price 3	Price 5
0.7	0.33945 (0.00021)	0.33975 (0.00021)	0.33953 (0.00021)	0.33992 (0.00021)
0.8	0.25562 (0.00019)	0.25568 (0.00019)	0.25541 (0.00019)	0.25534 (0.00019)
0.9	0.17893 (0.00016)	0.17905 (0.00016)	0.17887 (0.00016)	0.17894 (0.00016)
1	0.11245 (0.00013)	0.11231 (0.00013)	0.11277 (0.00013)	0.11261 (0.00013)
1.1	0.05973 (0.00009)	0.05992 (0.00009)	0.05984 (0.00009)	0.05993 (0.00009)
1.2	0.02425 (0.00006)	0.02398 (0.00006)	0.02401 (0.00006)	0.02409 (0.00006)
1.3	0.00716 (0.00003)	0.00717 (0.00003)	0.00719 (0.00004)	0.00718 (0.00003)

Table 7.13   The relative errors for comparing the price computed using FFT and the forward characteristic function and Monte Carlo simulation

Moneyness	Price 1	Price 2	Price 3	Price 5
0.7	0.0013	0.00041	0.00108	−0.00009
0.8	0.0002	−0.00003	0.00102	0.00128
0.9	0.0001	−0.00055	0.00046	0.00006
1	0.00143	0.00265	−0.00143	0.00003
1.1	0.00275	−0.00046	0.00078	−0.00071
1.2	−0.00675	0.00468	0.00349	−0.00005
1.3	0.00284	0.00137	−0.00128	0.00093

VG OU   We use the model parameters $C = 6.47043$, $G = 11.1021$, $M = 33.4128$, $\lambda = 0.939691$, $a = 0.629078$ and $b = 1.46587$. The results are shown in Tables 7.16 and 7.17.

VG CIR   We use the model parameters $C = 58, 1151$, $G = 50, 4954$, $M = 69, 3685$, $\kappa = 1, 23294$, $\eta = 0, 64976$ and $\lambda = 1, 43335$. The results are shown in Tables 7.18 and 7.19.

NIG OU   We use the model parameters $\alpha = 15, 9532$, $\beta = -10, 6732$, $\delta = 0, 412095$, $\lambda = 0, 855302$, $a = 0, 68104$ and $b = 1, 52999$. The results are shown in Tables 7.20 and 7.21.

NIG CIR   We use the model parameters $\alpha = 538, 311$, $\beta = -9, 58059$, $\delta = 17, 9022$, $\kappa = 1, 32756$, $\eta = 0, 656748$ and $\lambda = 1, 50423$. The results are shown in Tables 7.22 and 7.23.

Table 7.14   Prices computed using the Monte Carlo method for NIG

Moneyness	Price 1	Price 2	Price 3	Price 5
0.7	0.34242 (0.0002)	0.34219 (0.0002)	0.34224 (0.0002)	0.34234 (0.0002)
0.8	0.25746 (0.00018)	0.25758 (0.00018)	0.25775 (0.00018)	0.25743 (0.00018)
0.9	0.17941 (0.00016)	0.17932 (0.00016)	0.17949 (0.00016)	0.17967 (0.00016)
1	0.11157 (0.00013)	0.11155 (0.00013)	0.11128 (0.00013)	0.11157 (0.00013)
1.1	0.05786 (0.00009)	0.05778 (0.00009)	0.05794 (0.00009)	0.05777 (0.00009)
1.2	0.02367 (0.00006)	0.02353 (0.00006)	0.02362 (0.00006)	0.02367 (0.00006)
1.3	0.00767 (0.00004)	0.00764 (0.00004)	0.00761 (0.00004)	0.00765 (0.00004)

Table 7.15 The relative errors for comparing the price computed using FFT and the forward characteristic function and Monte Carlo simulation

Moneyness	Price 1	Price 2	Price 3	Price 5
0.7	−0.00003	0.00063	0.0005	0.00021
0.8	0.00059	0.00015	−0.00054	0.00071
0.9	0.0003	0.00079	−0.00018	−0.00114
1	−0.00216	−0.00199	0.00047	−0.00215
1.1	0.00036	0.0019	−0.00094	0.00198
1.2	−0.00271	0.003	−0.00069	−0.003
1.3	−0.00338	0.00059	0.00561	−0.00024

Table 7.16 Prices computed using the Monte Carlo method for VG GOU

Moneyness	Price 1	Price 2	Price 3	Price 5
0.7	0.33674 (0.00021)	0.33258 (0.00019)	0.32599 (0.00018)	0.32071 (0.00017)
0.8	0.25122 (0.00019)	0.24721 (0.00017)	0.24082 (0.00016)	0.23584 (0.00015)
0.9	0.17428 (0.00017)	0.16917 (0.00014)	0.16277 (0.00013)	0.15727 (0.00012)
1	0.10959 (0.00014)	0.10183 (0.00011)	0.09467 (0.0001)	0.08873 (0.00009)
1.1	0.06034 (0.0001)	0.04897 (0.00008)	0.04068 (0.00006)	0.03416 (0.00005)
1.2	0.02812 (0.00007)	0.01564 (0.00004)	0.0076 (0.00003)	0.00324 (0.00002)
1.3	0.01072 (0.00004)	0.00276 (0.00002)	0.00086 (0.00001)	0.0004 (0.00001)

Table 7.17 The relative errors for comparing the price computed using FFT and the forward characteristic function and Monte Carlo simulation

Moneyness	Price 1	Price 2	Price 3	Price 5
0.7	−0.00104	−0.00266	−0.00221	−0.0014
0.8	−0.00163	−0.00254	−0.00255	−0.00315
0.9	−0.00273	−0.00286	−0.00362	−0.00266
1	−0.00348	−0.0051	−0.00484	−0.00274
1.1	−0.00158	−0.00488	−0.00433	−0.00454
1.2	−0.00189	−0.00919	0.00665	0.00647
1.3	−0.0052	0.01282	0.00839	−0.02205

Table 7.18 Prices computed using the Monte Carlo method for VG CIR

Moneyness	Price 1	Price 2	Price 3	Price 5
0.7	0.33548 (0.0002)	0.32825 (0.00019)	0.3247 (0.00018)	0.32461 (0.00018)
0.8	0.24958 (0.00019)	0.24408 (0.00017)	0.23947 (0.00017)	0.23913 (0.00016)
0.9	0.17253 (0.00016)	0.16654 (0.00015)	0.16192 (0.00014)	0.16119 (0.00014)
1	0.1073 (0.00013)	0.10015 (0.00011)	0.09494 (0.00011)	0.09387 (0.00011)
1.1	0.0579 (0.0001)	0.04852 (0.00008)	0.04354 (0.00007)	0.04244 (0.00007)
1.2	0.02568 (0.00006)	0.01628 (0.00004)	0.01316 (0.00004)	0.0125 (0.00004)
1.3	0.0091 (0.00004)	0.0036 (0.00002)	0.00268 (0.00002)	0.00252 (0.00002)

Table 7.19   The relative errors for comparing the price computed using FFT and the forward characteristic function and Monte Carlo simulation

Moneyness	Price 1	Price 2	Price 3	Price 5
0.7	−0.00023	0.00065	−0.00006	0.0004
0.8	0.00033	−0.00084	0.00025	0.00039
0.9	−0.00063	0.00096	−0.00131	−0.00109
1	0.00033	0.00027	−0.0016	−0.00109
1.1	−0.00108	−0.00004	0.00082	0.00154
1.2	−0.00086	−0.00167	0.00319	0.00238
1.3	−0.00169	0.00229	0.00043	−0.0085

Table 7.20   Prices computed using the Monte Carlo method for NIG GOU

Moneyness	Price 1	Price 2	Price 3	Price 5
0.7	0.33777 (0.00021)	0.33336 (0.00019)	0.32661 (0.00018)	0.32056 (0.00017)
0.8	0.25238 (0.00019)	0.24785 (0.00017)	0.24175 (0.00016)	0.23545 (0.00015)
0.9	0.17531 (0.00017)	0.17005 (0.00014)	0.16344 (0.00013)	0.15693 (0.00012)
1	0.11028 (0.00014)	0.10233 (0.00011)	0.09483 (0.0001)	0.08787 (0.00009)
1.1	0.0604 (0.0001)	0.04925 (0.00008)	0.04083 (0.00006)	0.03324 (0.00005)
1.2	0.02783 (0.00007)	0.01606 (0.00004)	0.00864 (0.00003)	0.00363 (0.00002)
1.3	0.01051 (0.00004)	0.00328 (0.00002)	0.00109 (0.00001)	0.00044 (0.00001)

Table 7.21   The relative errors for comparing the price computed using FFT and the forward characteristic function and Monte Carlo simulation

Moneyness	Price 1	Price 2	Price 3	Price 5
0.7	−0.00105	−0.00183	−0.00121	−0.0007
0.8	−0.00093	−0.00062	−0.00259	−0.00166
0.9	−0.00134	−0.00215	−0.00334	−0.00258
1	−0.00327	−0.00368	−0.00282	−0.00156
1.1	−0.00204	−0.00539	−0.00625	−0.00362
1.2	−0.00118	−0.00325	−0.00031	0.00766
1.3	0.00187	−0.00009	−0.0064	0.01716

Table 7.22   Prices computed using the Monte Carlo method for NIG CIR

Moneyness	Price 1	Price 2	Price 3	Price 5
0.7	0.33603 (0.0002)	0.32839 (0.00019)	0.3249 (0.00018)	0.32524 (0.00018)
0.8	0.25001 (0.00019)	0.24355 (0.00017)	0.24002 (0.00017)	0.23998 (0.00016)
0.9	0.17262 (0.00016)	0.16683 (0.00015)	0.16232 (0.00014)	0.16148 (0.00014)
1	0.10753 (0.00013)	0.09997 (0.00011)	0.09536 (0.00011)	0.09443 (0.00011)
1.1	0.05772 (0.0001)	0.04845 (0.00008)	0.04412 (0.00007)	0.04324 (0.00007)
1.2	0.02556 (0.00006)	0.01642 (0.00005)	0.01386 (0.00004)	0.01336 (0.00004)
1.3	0.00918 (0.00004)	0.00378 (0.00002)	0.00295 (0.00002)	0.00282 (0.00002)

Table 7.23   The relative errors for comparing the price computed using FFT and the forward characteristic function and Monte Carlo simulation

Moneyness	Price 1	Price 2	Price 3	Price 5
0.7	−0.00138	0.00022	0.00084	0.00026
0.8	−0.00066	0.00113	−0.00004	−0.0005
0.9	−0.00036	−0.00156	−0.00098	0.00134
1	−0.00148	0.0002	−0.00135	0.00058
1.1	0.00113	−0.00028	−0.0005	0.00144
1.2	0.004	0.00536	−0.00056	−0.00028
1.3	−0.00059	0.00685	−0.00048	−0.00803

Table 7.24   Prices computed using the Monte Carlo method for Merton

Moneyness	Price 1	Price 2	Price 3	Price 5
0.7	0.34723 (0.00019)	0.34711 (0.00019)	0.3475 (0.00019)	0.34692 (0.00019)
0.8	0.25906 (0.00018)	0.25915 (0.00018)	0.25938 (0.00018)	0.2593 (0.00018)
0.9	0.17641 (0.00016)	0.17617 (0.00016)	0.17627 (0.00016)	0.17639 (0.00016)
1	0.10595 (0.00013)	0.10604 (0.00013)	0.10599 (0.00013)	0.10608 (0.00013)
1.1	0.05554 (0.0001)	0.05568 (0.0001)	0.0555 (0.0001)	0.05546 (0.0001)
1.2	0.0254 (0.00007)	0.0253 (0.00007)	0.02528 (0.00007)	0.02532 (0.00007)
1.3	0.01016 (0.00004)	0.01012 (0.00004)	0.01012 (0.00004)	0.01014 (0.00004)

Table 7.25   The relative errors for comparing the price computed using FFT and the forward characteristic function and Monte Carlo simulation

Moneyness	Price 1	Price 2	Price 3	Price 5
0.7	−0.0008	−0.00044	−0.00158	0.00008
0.8	0.0009	0.00057	−0.00032	−0.00002
0.9	−0.00039	0.00096	0.00037	−0.0003
1	0.00083	−0.0001	0.00043	−0.00044
1.1	−0.00055	−0.00306	0.00011	0.00093
1.2	−0.00412	0.00005	0.00073	−0.00085
1.3	−0.00152	0.00294	0.00239	0.00071

Merton Jump   We use the model parameters $\sigma = 0,152861$, $\alpha_j = -0,88229$, $\sigma_j = 0,000271941$ and $\lambda = 0,0813494$. The results are shown in Tables 7.24 and 7.25.

7.5   BRIDGE SAMPLING

In this section we consider methods for efficiently sampling from stochastic processes. To this end we consider *Bridge Sampling*. This method of sampling can significantly reduce the statistical error in Monte Carlo methods, in particular if it is combined with other variance reduction methods or when applied in conjunction with quasi random numbers such as Sobol numbers. In this section we look at the general principle of Bridge sampling and give the implementation of the Brownian and the Gamma bridges.

Suppose $X(t)$ is a stochastic process. To apply the bridge construction method we suppose $t_1 < t_2$ and consider $x \sim F_{X(t_1)}$ and $y \sim F_{X(t_2)}$ with densities f_{t_1} and f_{t_2}. Denote by $f_{x,y}$ the joint density.

If $z = x + y$ with density f_z, then the density of $x|z$ is given by

$$f_{x|z} = \frac{f_{x,z}(x, z - x)}{f_z(z)}. \tag{7.33}$$

Let us take a Brownian motion $W(t)$ and consider three time points $t_i < t_j < t_k$ and assume that $W(t_i)$ and $W(t_k)$ are given. For the expectation and the variance at t_j we have

$$\mathbb{E}[W(t_j)] = \left(\frac{t_k - t_j}{t_k - t_i}\right) W(t_i) + \left(\frac{t_j - t_i}{t_k - t_i}\right) W(t_k) \tag{7.34}$$

$$\mathbb{V}[W(t_j)] = \frac{(t_j - t_i)(t_k - t_j)}{(t_k - t_i)}. \tag{7.35}$$

For a fixed time grid $\mathcal{T} := \{t_0, \ldots, t_n\}$ it is possible to compute the expected values and the variance in advance. Using (7.33) we find

$$f_{x|z}(x) = \frac{1}{\sqrt{\frac{(t_k - t_j)(t_j - t_i)}{t_k - t_i}}\sqrt{2\pi}} \exp\left(-\frac{1}{2}\left(\frac{(x - \frac{t_j - t_i}{t_k - t_i}z)}{\sqrt{\frac{(t_k - t_j)(t_j - t_i)}{t_k - t_i}}}\right)^2\right).$$

The aim of the bridge construction method is to use the first variate to determine the endpoint of the path and then successively fill in the other points. For instance, using high-dimensional *low discrepancy numbers*, the lower dimensions are more suitable for simulation and are applied for the most important step, which often is the maturity.

Now, we wish to apply this observation to some *Markov process* $X(t)$. If x and y are realizations of increments of the process $X(t)$, for instance, $x = X(t_j) - X(t_i)$ and $y = X(t_k) - X(t_j)$, then the densities depend on the time increments determined by t_i, t_j and t_k.

Simulating the conditional distribution requires these time points, $t_i < t_j < t_k$ and two weights ω_1, ω_2 as well as a number c_j for the current point.

The time point t_j is called the *current bridge index* abbreviated by bI and t_i, t_k the left, lI, and right index, rI. For the description of the general bridge algorithm we call the arrays used to store all the numbers by bI, lI, rI, lW, rW and bS for the coefficients.

For a given simulation step l in the bridge construction we update the entries $bI(l), lI(l), rI(l), lW(l), rW(l)$ and $bS(l)$ as well as an array called *done* which keeps track of the constructed indexes up to the current simulation step.

Suppose we wish to construct a bridge corresponding to the discrete time set $\mathcal{T}$. Initialize the first step by setting

$$bI(1) = n, lI(1) = 0, rI(1) = n, lW(1) = 0, rW(1) = 0 \text{ and } bS = c,$$

c is chosen with respect to the distribution of the bridge.

We discuss the implementation of the *Brownian Bridge* as well as the *Gamma Bridge* in what follows. The first bridge is used to construct the Brownian motion, whereas the second is used to construct the Variance Gamma process.

For the i-th step we apply the following algorithm:

Algorithm 7.8: Bridge sampling

1 Find the smallest unset entry and denote it by j
2 Find the smallest already set entry and denote it by k
3 Update the current bridge index $l = j + (k-j) - \text{remainder}((k-j)/2)$
4 Find the index of set entries which is smaller than l and call it j
5 Set

$$rI(i) = k, \quad lI(i) = \begin{cases} 0 & \text{if } l = 1 \\ j & \text{otherwise} \end{cases}$$

6 Set

$$v = \begin{cases} 0 & j = 0 \\ t_j & \text{otherwise} \end{cases}$$

Furthermore, set $lW(i) = t_k - t_l$, $rW(i) = t_l - v$
7 Set the current value j using

$$\begin{cases} j = k+1 & j < n \\ j = 0 & \text{otherwise} \end{cases}$$

The corresponding Matlab code is given in Figure 7.34. It creates the bridge indices as well as the corresponding left and right indices and the weights. This is the basic bridge which constitutes the fundamental part of all the bridge constructions we apply.

It is often convenient to create a Brownian bridge from a given set of Gaussian variates. To this end we first populate a matrix with realizations from a standard normal distribution and denote it by W. This matrix is the input to the function `buildpathbbW` which than creates a Brownian bridge. The code is given in Figure 7.35. It calls the basic bridge building procedure `createbridge`.

We apply the construction method for Brownian paths by comparing the results for pseudo as well as for quasi random numbers since bridging techniques are often combined with quasi random sampling also called *quasi Monte Carlo simulation*. We apply the standard path generation techniques and the Brownian bridge construction. The test programme applied is given in Figure 7.36.

For the quasi random numbers we use Sobol numbers. The results are for $S(0) = 100$, $K = 100$, $r = 0.03$, $T = 1$, $NSim = 100000$, $Nt = 12$. The results are given in Table 7.26 and Figure 7.37.

To be complete we give the code for generating the Brownian bridge for prescribed time points. To this end we have to apply a different weighting. Figure 7.38 gives this modification of the code displayed in Figure 7.34.

Gamma Bridge For the Gamma process $G(t)$ we find for the conditional density from Equation (7.33) with Γ being the Gamma function

$$f_{x|z}(x) = \frac{1}{z} \frac{\Gamma\left(\frac{t_j - t_i}{v} + \frac{t_k - t_j}{v}\right)}{\Gamma\left(\frac{t_j - t_i}{v}\right)\Gamma\left(\frac{t_k - t_j}{v}\right)} \left(\frac{x}{z}\right)^{\frac{t_j - t_i}{v} - 1} \left(1 - \frac{x}{z}\right)^{\frac{t_k - t_j}{v} - 1}.$$

```
function [bI, lI, rI, lW, rW, bS] = createbridge(n)
% function creates a standard brownian bridge
% the output are bridgeindex (bI), leftindex (lI),
% rightindex (rI), leftweight (lW), rightweight (rW)
% and bridgevalue (bS)

done = zeros(1,n+1);
done(n) = 1;

bI = zeros(1,n); bI(1) = n;      % bI -> bridge index
lI = bI; lI(1) = 1;              % lI -> left index
rI = bI; rI(1) = 1;              % rI -> right index
lW = bI; lW(1) = 0;              % lW -> left weight
rW = bI; rW(1) = 0;              % rW -> right weight
bS = bI; bS(1) = sqrt(n);        % bS -> value of variance

j = 1;

for i=2:1:n
    if(done(j+1)>0)
        ind = find(done==0);     % find all indices not done
        j = ind(1)-1;            % take smallest - 1 as left index
    end
    ind = find(done > 0);        % find all indices already done
    ind = ind(ind > j+1);        % find all indices already done > j+1
    k - ind(1)-1;                % take k+1 as right index
    l = j + (k-1-j - rem((k-1-j),2)) / 2; % l+1 is bridge index
    done(l+1) = i;               % indicate as done
    bI(i) = l+1;                 % set bridge index
    lI(i) = j+1;                 % set left index
    rI(i) = k+1;                 % set right index
    lW(i) = (k-l) / (k+1-j);     % left weight
    rW(i) = (l+1-j)/(k+1-j);     % right weight
    bS(i) = sqrt((l+1-j)*(k-l) ...
            / (k+1-j));          % compute value
    j = k+1;
    if(j>=n)
        j = 0;
    end
end
end
```

Figure 7.34 Matlab code for computing the bridge indices and weights to be used for the bridge construction

The quotient x/z has a beta distribution, $\mathcal{B}(a, b)$, and if we denote $\beta(t_j)$ a random variable with distribution $\mathcal{B}\left(\frac{t_j - t_i}{v}, \frac{t_k - t_j}{v}\right)$ we find for the Gamma process G

$$G(t_j) = G(t_i) + \beta(t_j)(G(t_k) - G(t_i)), \quad t_i < t_j < t_k. \tag{7.36}$$

Using Equation (7.36) we are able to implement bridge sampling from a Variance Gamma process since it can be represented by the difference of two Gamma processes, U and D.

To this end suppose $U(0) = D(0) = 0$,

$$U(t_N) \sim \Gamma(t_N v, Gv) \text{ and } D(t_N) \sim \Gamma(t_N v, Mv).$$

```
function path = buildpathbbW(W)
% Brownian bridge using W as the Gaussians
n = size(W,2);                                  % determine size cols
m = size(W,1);                                  % determine size rows
[bI, lI, rI, lW, rW, bS] = createbridge(n);% creates the bridgeinput
path = zeros(m,n);                              % init paths for output
path(:,end) = bS(1) * W(:,end);                 % set final value
for i=1:1:n-1
    j = lI(i+1);                                    % left index
    k = rI(i+1);                                    % right index
    l = bI(i+1);                                    % bridge index
    if j<n
        % standard value
        path(:,l) = lW(:,i+1)*path(:,j) ...
            + rW(:,i+1)*path(:,k) + bS(i+1) * W(:,i+1);
    else
        % final value
        path(:,l) = rW(:,i+1) * path(:,k) + bS(i+1) * W(:,i+1);
    end
end
end
```

Figure 7.35   Matlab implementation of the Brownian bridge using an input of a matrix of Gaussians W

We proceed as follows for sampling using the Gamma bridge:

Algorithm 7.9: Pseudo algorithm for generating the Gamma bridge

---

1 **for** $k = 1$ *to* M **do**
   Setting $n = 2^{M-k}$
   for $j = 1$ *to* 2^{k-1} **do**
      $i = (2j - 1) \cdot n$
      Simulate $Y_i^+, Y_i^- \sim \mathcal{B}\left(\frac{(t_i - t_{i-n})}{v}, \frac{(t_{i+1} - t_i)}{v}\right)$ independently
      Set $U(t_i) = U(t_{i-n}) + [U(t_{i+n}) - U(t_{i-n})]Y_i^+$ and
      $D(t_i) = D(t_{i-n}) + [D(t_{i+n}) - D(t_{i-n})]Y_i^-$
      Set $X(t_i) = U(t_i) - D(t_i)$

The pseudo code can be translated into Matlab code. Figure 7.39 gives the implementation of the sampling of a Gamma processeses using the Gamma bridge technique. To use bridge sampling to build a Variance Gamma process two standard Gamma processes have to be sampled and subtracted using the code in Figure 7.39.

For coding the Gamma bridge we have applied the function createbridgetg, which calculates the necessary indices and weights for the Gamma bridge application. The code is given in Figure 7.40. Numerical results for different options can be found in Ribeiro, C. and Webber, N. (2007a) and Ribeiro, C. and Webber, N. (2007b). The code can be applied and modified to set up similar simulation methods as in the abovementioned papers.

There is yet the subordinator representation of the Variance Gamma process. Bridge sampling is possible by combining the Gamma bridge and the Brownian bridge. To this end we sample using the Gamma bridge in combination with the Brownian bridge as follows:

```
function [yqmcs, stdqmcs, yqmcsbb, stdqmcbb, ymcs, stdmcs, ...
    ymcbb, stdmcbb] = qmc(S,K, sigma, r, T, NSim, Nt)
% different monte carlo estimators and standard errors
% first: qmc using low discrepancy numbers
% sec: qmc using low discrepancy numbers and Brownian bridge
% third: standard mc using pseudo random numbers
% fourth: standard mc using pseudo random and Brownian bridge

% precompute constants
delta = T / Nt;                                    % delta
mudt = delta*(r - sigma*sigma/2);                  % drift
sdt = sqrt(delta) * sigma;                         % root delta
deltaTMat = [zeros(NSim,1), ones(NSim,Nt) * mudt];
deltaTMat = cumsum(deltaTMat,2);

lnS0 = log(S) * ones(NSim,1);                      % spot prices

qrng = sobolset(Nt,'Leap', 100);                   % quasi random stream
%qrng = scramble(qrng, 'MatousekAffineOwen');      % scrambling
QR = net(qrng,NSim+1);
% get quasi random numbers

Q = norminv(QR(2:NSim+1,:),0,sdt);                 % inverse normal
lnSt = cumsum([lnS0, Q],2) + deltaTMat;            % asset price path

yqmcs = mean(payoff(exp(lnSt),K,r,T));             % mc estimator
stdqmcs = std(payoff(exp(lnSt),K,r,T))/NSim;       % standard error
plot(cumsum(payoff(exp(lnSt),K,r,T)) ...
    ./ cumsum(ones(NSim,1)),'Color', [.25 .25 .25]); hold on;

Q = buildpathbbW(Q);                               % apply Brownian bridge
lnSt = log(S) * ones(NSim, Nt+1) + [lnS0, Q] + deltaTMat;

yqmcsbb = mean(payoff(exp(lnSt),K,r,T));           % mc estimator
stdqmcbb = std(payoff(exp(lnSt),K,r,T))/NSim;      % standard error
plot(cumsum(payoff(exp(lnSt),K,r,T)) ...
        ./cumsum(ones(NSim,1)),'Color',[0 0 0]);

W = norminv(rand(NSim,Nt),0, sdt);                 % Gaussians
lnSt = cumsum([lnS0, W],2) + deltaTMat;            % log asset price path

ymcs = mean(payoff(exp(lnSt),K,r,T));              % mc estimator
stdmcs = std(payoff(exp(lnSt),K,r,T))/NSim;        % standard error
plot(cumsum(payoff(exp(lnSt),K,r,T)) ...
    ./ cumsum(ones(NSim,1)),'Color', [.5 .5 .5]);

W = buildpathbbW(randn(NSim,Nt));                  % apply Brownian bridge
lnSt = log(S) * ones(NSim,Nt+1) + [zeros(NSim,1), sdt*W] + deltaTMat;

ymcbb = mean(payoff(exp(lnSt),K,r,T));
stdmcbb = std(payoff(exp(lnSt),K,r,T))/NSim;
plot(cumsum(payoff(exp(lnSt),K,r,T)) ...
    ./ cumsum(ones(NSim,1)),'Color', [.75 .75 .75]);

hold off;
legend('qmc', 'qmcbb', 'mc', 'mcbb'); ylim([ymcbb-2 ymcbb+2]);
end

function poff = payoff(S,K,r,T)
    poff = exp(-r*T) * max(S(:,size(S,2)) - K, 0);
end
```

Figure 7.36 Test program for sampling paths for geometric Brownian motion using pseudo and quasi random numbers. The standard and the Brownian bridge path construction techniques are applied

---

Algorithm 7.10: Simulation of a Gamma bridge applying a Brownian bridge

1 Let $X(0) = 0$, $\gamma_0 = 0$, $\gamma_{t_N} \sim \Gamma(t_N/v, v)$ and $X(t_N) \sim \mathcal{N}(\theta \gamma_{t_N}, \sigma^2 \gamma_{t_N})$.

2 **for** $k = 1$ *To M* **do**

a   Set $n = 2^{M-k}$

b   **for** $j = 1$ *To* 2^{k-1} **do**

aa   Set $i = (2j - 1)n$

bb   Simulate $Y_i \sim \mathcal{B}\left(\frac{(t_i - t_{i-n})}{v}, \frac{(t_{i+n} - t_i)}{v}\right)$

cc $G_{t_i} = G(t_{i-n}) + [G(t_{i+n}) - G(t_{i-n})]Y_i$

dd   Simulate $Z_i \sim \mathcal{N}(0, [G(t_{i+n}) - G(t_i)]\sigma^2 Y_i)$

ee   Set $X(t_i) = Y_i X(t_{i+n}) + (1 - Y_i)X(t_{i-n}) + Z_i$

The corresponding code is given in Figure 7.41.

In particular working with Sobol sequences, the following path construction is used in finance.

Suppose we wish to simulate *NSim* times for a d dimensional model with *Nt* time steps.

- Generate a matrix of size $NSim \times (d \cdot Nt)$ Sobol numbers $u_{i,j}$.
- Transfer the numbers to standard normal distributed variates v by using $v_{i,j} = \mathcal{N}^{-1}(u_{i,j})$.
- Sort/scramble the Sobol numbers.
- Apply the Brownian bridge method which ensures that the first variate is used to determine the endpoint of the path.

We suggest the following sorting method for the application of Sobol sequences:

$$\begin{pmatrix} v_{1,1} & v_{1,2} & v_{1,3} & \cdots & v_{1,d \cdot Nt} \\ v_{2,1} & v_{2,2} & v_{2,3} & \cdots & v_{2,d \cdot Nt} \\ \vdots & \vdots & \vdots & \vdots & \vdots \\ v_{NSim,1} & v_{NSim,2} & v_{NSim,3} & \cdots & v_{NSim,d \cdot Nt} \end{pmatrix}$$

$$\downarrow$$

$$\begin{pmatrix} v_{1,1} & v_{1,d} & v_{1,d+1} & \cdots & v_{1,2d} & v_{1,2d+1} & \cdots & v_{1,nd} \\ v_{2,1} & v_{2,d} & v_{2,d+1} & \cdots & v_{2,2d} & v_{2,2d+1} & \cdots & v_{2,nd} \\ \vdots & \vdots & \vdots & \vdots & \vdots & & & \\ v_{N,1} & v_{N,d} & v_{N,d+1} & \cdots & v_{N,2d} & v_{N,2d+1} & \cdots & v_{N,nd} \end{pmatrix}.$$

Sobol sequences are often the method of choice when implementing Monte Carlo valuation methods for Libor Market Models (LMMs). In the next section we cover the simulation within an LMM. We outline which part has to be changed when Sobol sequences are applied.

Table 7.26 We priced a European Call option using $S(0) = 100$, $K = 100$, $r = 0.03$, $T = 1$, $NSim = 100000$, $Nt = 12$ and QMC, QMC with BB, MC and MC with BB

	QMC Seq	QMC BB	MC Seq	MC BB
PV	11.3742	11.3630	11.3488	11.2912
StdErr	0.0018	0.0018	0.0018	0.0018

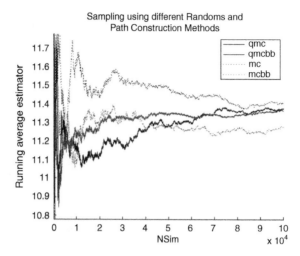

Figure 7.37   Running averages for different sampling methods, sequential and bridge, and using pseudo as well as quasi random numbers

7.6 LIBOR MARKET MODEL

Here we assess the Libor Market Model introduced in (4.4). The model can have a stochastic volatility of the form (4.5). In order to apply Monte Carlo simulation to the model we have to consider the drift calculation using different numeraires. To this end we write the Libor dynamic of the n-th Libor rate as

$$dL_n(t) = \sigma_n^\top(t)dW^{n+1}(t).$$

In the above equation the notation dW^{n+1} indicates that $W^{n+1}(t)$ is a Brownian motion with respect to the zero bond P_{T_n} paying one unit of currency at T_{n+1}. Now, let P_{T_k} be the zero bond maturing at $T_{k+1} < T_{n+1}$, then the Libor dynamic with respect to the new numeraire is given by

$$dL_n(t) = \sigma_n^\top(t) \left(\sum_{j=k}^{n} \frac{\tau_k \sigma_k(t)}{1 + \tau_k L_k(t)} dt + dW^k(t) \right).$$

Thus, L_n is a martingale under the measure associated with P_{T_k} if $\tilde{W}$ given via the SDE

$$d\tilde{W}(t) := \left(\sum_{j=k}^{n} \frac{\tau_k \sigma_k(t)}{1 + \tau_k L_k(t)} dt + dW^k(t) \right)$$

is chosen as the Brownian motion. Thus, by applying the change of numeraire mechanism it is possible to transform the Libor process into another measure and calculate the drift for this new setting. We consider two numeraires which are very important for interest rate modelling. The first is the *terminal measure* and the second the *spot measure*. We suppose that we simulate the Libor dynamics up to some final maturity T_N.

```
function [bI, lI, rI, lW, rW, bS] = createbridget(t)
% function creates a brownian bridge for time array t
% the output are bridgeindex (bI), leftindex (lI),
% rightindex (rI), leftweight (lW), rightweight (rW)
% and bridgevalue (bS)

n = size(t,2);                    % number of steps

done = zeros(1,n+1);              % indicates the steps already done
done(n) = 1;                      % the final point is done

bI = zeros(1,n); bI(1) = n;       % bI -> bridge index
lI = bI; lI(1) = 1;               % lI -> left index
rI = bI; rI(1) = 1;               % rI -> right index
lW = bI; lW(1) = 0;               % lW -> left weight
rW = bI; rW(1) = 0;               % rW -> right weight
bS = bI; bS(1) = sqrt(t(n));      % bS -> value of S

j = 0;

for i=2:1:n
    if(done(j+1)>0)
            ind = find(done==0);      % find all indices not done
            j = ind(1)-1;             % take smallest - 1 as left index
    end
    ind = find(done > 0);         % find all indices already done
    ind = ind(ind > j+1);         % find all indices already done > j+1
    k = ind(1)-1;                 % take k+1 as right index
    l = j + (k-1-j - rem((k-1-j),2)) / 2;   % l+1 is bridge index
    done(l+1) = i;                % indicate as done
    bI(i) = l+1;                  % set bridge index
    lI(i) = j+1;                  % set left index
    rI(i) = k+1;                  % set right index
    if j == 0
        leftval = 0;
    else
        leftval = t(j);
    end
    lW(i) = (t(k+1)-t(l+1)) / (t(k+1) - leftval);   % left weight
    rW(i) = (t(l+1)-leftval)/(t(k+1)-leftval);      % right weight
    bS(i) = sqrt((t(l+1)-leftval)*(t(k+1)-t(l+1)) ...
            / (t(k+1)-leftval));                    % compute value
    j = k+1;
    if(j>=n)
        j = 0;
    end
end
end
```

Figure 7.38 Implementation of the Brownian bridge for prescribed time grid which is the input variable t

Terminal Measure With respect to the zero bond paying exactly one unit of currency at time T_N the Libor dynamics is given by

$$dL_i(t) = \sigma_i^\top \left(- \sum_{j=i+1}^{N-1} \frac{\tau_j \sigma_j(t)}{1 + \tau_j L_j(t)} dt + dW^i(t) \right). \qquad (7.37)$$

```
function path = buildpathbbG(t,nu)
% gamma bridge standard representation

n = size(t,2);                                % size of time grid
[bI, lI, rI, lW, rW, bS] = createbridgetg(t,nu);  % init bridge
path = zeros(1,n);                            % init the path
path(end) = gamrnd(t(n)/nu, nu);              % set the endpoint
for i=2:1:n
    j = lI(i);                                % left index
    k = rI(i);                                % right index
    l = bI(i);                                % bridge index
    if j<n && j > 1   % general construction
        path(l) = path(j) + bS(l)*(path(k)-path(j));
    else              % left and rightmost steps are special
        path(l) = bS(l)* path(k);
    end
end
end
```

Figure 7.39   Matlab implementation of the Gamma bridge

Spot Measure   Now let us suppose we invest one unit of currency again and again using the fixed Libor rates. The associated measure is the spot measure, and the dynamics of the Libor rates are given by

$$dL_i(t) = \sigma_i^{\top}\left(\sum_{j=q(t)}^{i}\frac{\tau_j\sigma_j(t)}{1+\tau_jL_j(t)}dt + dW^i(t)\right). \tag{7.38}$$

Discretization   Once we know the computation of the drift and diffusion part of the model we can use a discretization to simulate paths corresponding to the model dynamic. We consider only the example of a Euler scheme together with a constant volatility function. We do not consider other and more sophisticated methods since these will be investigated in detail in Kienitz, J., Wetterau, D. and Wittke, M. (forthcoming). We fix a tenor structure

$$0 = T_1 < \ldots < T_m < T_{m+1}, \quad \tau_j := T_{j+1} - T_j, \ j = 1, \ldots, m$$

and consider the following mapping:

$$\eta : \mathbb{R}_+ \to \mathbb{N}$$
$$t \mapsto \eta(t)$$

where $\eta(t)$ is the smallest $T_i > t$. Let

$$(\sigma_1, \ldots, \sigma_m) \in \mathbb{R}_+^m$$

be a vector of constant volatilities and denote by $\sigma \in \mathbb{R}^{m \times m}$ the corresponding diagonal matrix. Define the drift

$$\tilde{\mu} : \mathbb{R}^m \times \mathbb{R}^m \to \mathbb{R}^m$$
$$(y, \sigma) \mapsto \tilde{\mu}(y, \sigma),$$

```
function [bI, lI, rI, lW, rW, bS] = createbridgetg(t,nu)
% function creates a gamma bridge with parameter nu and time array t
% the output are bridgeindex (bI), leftindex (lI),
% rightindex (rI), leftweight (lW), rightweight (rW)
% and bridgevalue (bS)

n = size(t,2);                      % determine the length of the time array

done = zeros(1,n);                  % map the indexes which are done already
done(n) = 1;                        % last point mapped to first of bridge

bI = zeros(1,n);                    % Init bI
lI = bI; lI(1) = 0;                 % Init lI and set first entry 0
rI = bI; rI(1) = n;                 % Init rI and set first entry n
lW = bI; lW(1) = 0;                 % Init lW and set first entry 0
rW = bI; rW(1) = 0;                 % Init rW and set first entry 0
bI(1) = n;                          % Set first enty to n
bS = bI; bS(1) = betarnd(0,t(n)/nu); %betarnd(t(1)/nu,t(n)/nu);
j=1;
for i=2:1:n
    ind = find(done == 0);          % find all unset entries
    j = ind(1);                     % take the smallest unset entry
    ind = find(done > 0);           % find all set entries
    ind = ind(ind > j);             % find all populatd entries
                                    % bigger than the smallest
                                    % unset entry, i.e. j

    k = ind(1);                     % smallest entry > j
    rI(i) = k;                      % right strut of the bridge is k
    l = j + (k-j - rem((k-j),2)) / 2;  % l is "midpoint" of the
                                    % j, j+1, j+2, ..., k
    done(l) = i;                    % l is set for the next go
    bI(i) = l;                      % set current bridge index to l
    ind = find(done>0);             % find all populated entries
    ind = find(ind<l);              % find all populated entries < l
    if size(ind,2) == 0
        lI(i) = 0;                  % no index exists left point 0
    else
        lI(i) = ind(end);           % if index exists take the max
    end
    if lI(i) == 0
        leftval = 0;                % no left index use star val = 0
    else
        leftval = t(lI(i));         % value at the left index lI(i)
    end
    lW(i) = (t(k)-t(l));            % left weight for gamma bridge
    rW(i) = (t(l)-leftval);         % right weight for gamma bridge
    bS(i) = betarnd(lW(i)/nu,rW(i)/nu);  % weight for gamma bridge
                                    % due to beta distribution
    j = k+1;
    if(j>=n)
        j = 1;                      % reset starting index
    end
end

end
```

Figure 7.40   Matlab implementation of the Gamma bridge mechanism

```
function path = buildpathbbGW(t,nu)
% Gamma bridge due to subordinator representation
n = size(t,2);                     % number of steps
path = buildpathbbG(t,nu);         % build a path due to Gamma bridge
path = cumsum(path);               % take the sums
[bI, lI, rI, lW, rW, bS] = createbridget(path); % create standard BB
W = normrnd(0,1,1,n);              % random number for path construction
path = zeros(1,n);                 % init the path
path(n) = bS(1) * W(n);            % terminal value of bridge gamma path
for i=1:1:n-1                      % create bridge gamma path11
    j = lI(i+1);
    k = rI(i+1);
    l = bI(i+1);
    if j<n
        path(:,l) = lW(i+1)*path(j) + rW(i+1)*path(k) + bS(i+1) * W(i+1);
    else
        path(:,l) = rW(i+1) * path(k) + bS(i+1) * W(i+1);
    end
end
path = [0 path];
end
```

Figure 7.41 Matlab implementation of the Variance Gamma model using Gamma and Brownian bridges. This approach is based on the representation of a Variance Gamma process as subordinated Brownian motion

where

$$\tilde{\mu}_i(y, \sigma) := \sigma_i \sum_{j=\eta(t)}^{i} \frac{\sigma_j \tau_j \tilde{y}_j}{1 + \tau_j y_j}.$$

The $\mathbb{R}^m$-valued diffusion

$$d\tilde{L}(t) = \tilde{\mu}(\tilde{L}(t), \sigma) + \sigma\, dW(t) \tag{7.39}$$

is called the *Libor Market Model*.

If one applies a Euler scheme to the logarithms of the $\tilde{L}_i(t)$, one obtains the following approximation to (7.39).

The following recursion is called the *Libor scheme*. For any $1 \leq n \leq m-1$

$$\forall 1 \leq i \leq n : L_i(n+1) := L_i(n),$$

$$n+1 \leq i \leq m : L_i(n+1) := L_i(n)\exp\left((\mu_i(n) - \frac{1}{2}\sigma_i^2)\tau_n + \sqrt{\tau_n}\sigma_i Z(n+1)\right),$$

$$\mu_i(n) := \sigma_i \sum_{j=n+1}^{i} \frac{\tau_j L_j(n)\sigma_j}{1 + \tau_j L_j(n)}. \tag{7.40}$$

These equations can also be expressed by

$$L(n+1) = F_n(L(n), \sigma),$$

where $F_n : \mathbb{R}^m \times \mathbb{R}^m_+ \to \mathbb{R}^m$ is a suitable map. Consequently (7.40) is an evolution equation as in (8.62).

If one defines $\eta(j) := \tilde{\eta}(T_j) = T_{j+1}$, it is intuitively clear that one can think of $L_i(n)$ as an approximation to $\tilde{L}_i(T_n)$. We use this representation to give the Matlab code in Figure 7.42.

```
function LD = LMM_Simulation(LD)

    LD.LIBORs = zeros(LD.m, LD.m, LD.paths);
    S = zeros(LD.m,1);

    for omega = 1:LD.paths
        LD.LIBORs(:,1,omega) = LD.L;
    end

    for omega=1:LD.paths
        for n = 1:LD.m-1
            S = LD.sigma .* LD.tau .* LD.LIBORs(:,n,omega) ...
                ./ ( 1 + LD.tau .* LD.LIBORs(:,n,omega) );
            S(1:n) = 0;
            S = cumsum(S);
            S = exp( LD.sigma .*( (S - LD.sigma*0.5)* LD.tau(n) ...
                + LD.Z(n,omega) *sqrt(LD.tau(n)) ) );
            LD.LIBORs(n+1:LD.m,n+1,omega)=LD.LIBORs(n+1:LD.m,n,omega) ..
                .* S(n+1:LD.m);
        end
    end
end
```

Figure 7.42   Basic Simulation of a Libor Market Model using the spot measure

Of course there are much more sophisticated approaches to simulate trajectories for Libor Market Models. Furthermore, the model introduced here is not capable of modelling the market observed smile. To this end the basic Libor Market Model has to be combined with a local volatility or a stochastic volatility model as demonstrated in Subsection 4.2.2.

7.7 MULTI-DIMENSIONAL LÉVY MODELS

Using the subordinator approach described in Section 4.7 we consider the two-dimensional version of the Variance Gamma model. To this end we let $S0$ be a two-dimensional vector of spot prices, r the riskless rate, d the vector of dividend yields and T the maturity. The model parameters are given in terms of the vectors σ, θ and v. For the dependence structure, we need a correlation matrix, which is denoted by $Corr$ (see Figure 7.43).

Numerical Results   We illustrated sampled paths for two-dimensional Variance Gamma processes using different correlation structures in Figure 4.32. To this end we have implemented a performance spread Call, a Worst-of-Call and a Best-of-Call option. The implementation is given in Figure 7.44.

We consider the correlation dependence on these products. The results are shown in Figure 7.45. To illustrate the effect of using a two-dimensional Variance Gamma model we have plotted the Black–Scholes prices for comparison. To this end we consider the range of correlation $\rho = -1, -0.0, \ldots, 1$. For the other parameters we use the same setting as those provided in Leoni, P. and Schoutens, W. (2008). Thus, we have $\underline{S}(0) = (1.0, 1.0), r = 0.0424$, $\underline{d} = (0.035, 0)$, $v = 0.257$, $\underline{\sigma} = (0.1325, 0.1406)$ and $\underline{\theta} = (-0.2094, -0.2301)$. We price all four options introduced in Figure 7.44.

We do not reproduce the results of Leoni, P. and Schoutens, W. (2008) exactly.

```
% Discretisation of a 2d Variance Gamma process
lnS1 = zeros(NSim, Nt+1);    % log spot prices asset 1
lnS2 = zeros(NSim, Nt+1);    % log spot prices asset 2
%
% parameter ...
%

omegaT = -1/nu * [log(1-theta(1)*nu ...
    - nu*sigma(1)^2/2) log(1-theta(2)*nu - nu*sigma(2)^2/2)];
drift = [r-d(1) r-d(2)];

R = chol(Corr);

% precomputed constants
deltaT = T / Nt;            % delta for time discretisation
lnS1(:,1) = log(S0(1));     % Set the starting spot price
lnS2(:,1) = log(S0(2));

oNs = ones(NSim,1);

% Start Monte Carlo here
for number = 1 : NBatches
    % Time discretisation
    for m=1:Nt
        G = nu * gamrnd(deltaT/nu,oNs);
        W = randn(NSim,2);
        W = W*R;
        lnS1(:,m+1) = lnS1(:,m) + (drift(1)-omegaT(1)) * deltaT ...
                    + theta(1) * G + sqrt(G) * sigma(1) .* W(:,1);
        lnS2(:,m+1) = lnS2(:,m) + (drift(2)-omegaT(2))* deltaT ...
                    + theta(2) * G + sqrt(G) * sigma(2) .* W(:,2);
    end

    S1 = exp(lnS1);         % Simulated prices for asset 1
    S2 = exp(lnS2);         % Simulated prices for asset 2
end
end
```

Figure 7.43 Matlab implementation of the two-dimensional Variance Gamma model. The output can be used to price options on two underlyings

7.8 COPULAE

We have introduced copulae earlier, in Section 4.6. To apply copulae to financial problems we can either rely on integration methods or find methods to simulate from copulae. This is especially important when simulation based optimization is applied for asset allocation. In this section we consider the sampling of some copulae. To this end we introduce two simulation techniques:

- Distributional Sampling Approach (DSA).
- Conditional Sampling Approach (CSA).

Convex combinations of copulae as well as product copulae will also be reviewed.

```
function y = WorstOfCall(S1,S2)
% implementation of a Worst-Of-Call option
    % compute the performance
    A = [(S1(:,end)-S1(:,1))./S1(:,1) (S2(:,end)-S2(:,1))./S2(:,1)];
    %val = [min(A,[],2) zeros(nsim,1)];   % taking the max
    val = max(min(A,[],2), 0);
    y = mean(max(val,[],2));                  % average
end

function y = BestOfCall(S1,S2)
% Implementation of a Best-Of-Call Option
    nsim = size(S1,1);                        % number of simulations
    % compute the performance from start to end
    A = [(S1(:,end)-S1(:,1))./S1(:,1) (S2(:,end)-S2(:,1))./S2(:,1)];
    val = [max(A,[],2) zeros(nsim,1)];   % take the max pos performance
    y = mean(max(val,[],2));                  % average
end

function y = Spread(S1,S2)
% Implementation of a performance spread option
    nsim = size(S1,1);                        % number of simulations
    % compute the performance
    A = S1(:,end)./S1(:,1) - S2(:,end)./S2(:,1);
    val = [max(A,[],2) zeros(nsim,1)];   % take the max
    y = mean(max(val,[],2));                  % average
end

function y = TwoAssetCorrel(S1,S2)
    nsim = size(S1,1);
    ind = S2(:,end)./S2(:,1)-1 >= 0.1;
    A = (S1(ind,end)-S1(ind,1))./S1(ind,1);
    val = max(A,0);
    y = sum(val)/nsim;
end
```

Figure 7.44   Implementation of a Spread Option, Worst-of-Call and a Best-of-Call payoff

7.8.1   Distributional Sampling Approach (DSA)

We outline the DSA in this section. Let $d \in \mathbb{N}$ and consider a vector $u = (u_1, \ldots, u_d)^\top \in \mathbb{R}^d$ as well as a copula C. Due to the one-to-one correspondence between copulae and multi-dimensional continuous distributions we have

$$C(u) = F(F_1^{-1}(u_1), \ldots, F_d^{-1}(u_d)). \qquad (7.41)$$

If the distribution function F as well as the inverse of the marginals F_i^{-1}, $i = 1, \ldots, d$ are available in closed form, we can apply the following algorithm for sampling from the copula C:

- Simulate $Y = (Y_1, \ldots, Y_d) \in \mathbb{R}^d$ with $Y \sim F$
- $(F_1(Y_1), \ldots, F_d(Y_d))^\top \in [0, 1]^d$ is a variate from C.

This approach can be applied to the Gaussian and the t-copula. We give the Matlab implementation in Figures 7.46 and 7.48.

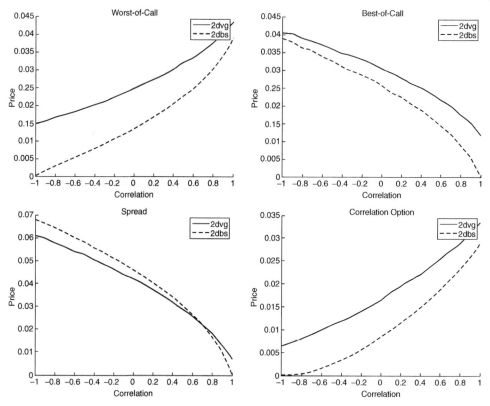

Figure 7.45 Worst-of-Call (top left), Best-of-Call (top right), Spread (bottom left) and Correlation Option (bottom right) priced within a two-dimensional Variance Gamma model

The input *Rho* is the correlation matrix denoted by ρ, Equation (7.42). The size of the matrix determines the dimensionality and *NSim* is the number of simulations. For the numerical illustration we take, for instance,

$$\rho = \begin{pmatrix} 1 & 0.5 & -0.9 \\ 0.5 & 1 & -0.34 \\ -0.9 & -0.34 & 1 \end{pmatrix}. \qquad (7.42)$$

The algorithm using the DSA method for the *t*-copula is given in Figure 7.48.

```
function u = S_GaussCopula(Rho, NSim)

d = size(Rho,2);        % dimension
y = randn(NSim,d);      % normal variates (independent)
A = chol(Rho);          % Cholesky
x = (y*A);              % normal variates (dependent)
u = normcdf(x);         % variates from Gauss copula
end
```

Figure 7.46 Matlab implementation of the DSA for generating variates of the Gaussian copula

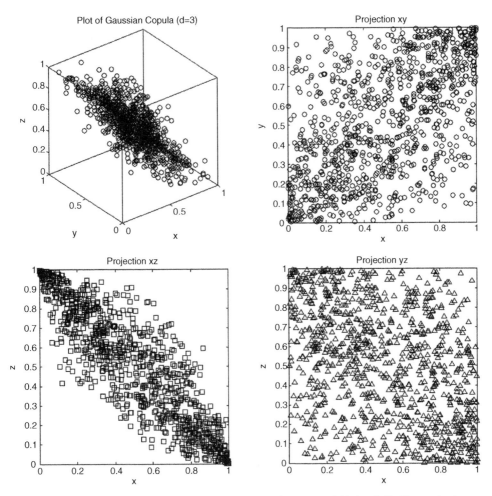

Figure 7.47 The Gaussian Copula for ρ from (7.42) and $NSim = 1000$ (top left). The projections to the xy-plane (top right), xz-plane (bottom left) and yz-plane (bottom right)

```
function u = S_TCopula(Rho, lambda, NSim)
d = size(Rho,2);                          % dimension
z = randn(NSim,d);                        % normal variates (independent)
A = chol(Rho);                            % Cholesky
y = (z*A);                                % normal variates (dependent)

s = chi2rnd(lambda,[1 NSim]);             % chi2 lambda degress of freedom
x = (sqrt(lambda./s)'*ones(1,d)).*y;      % d-dim student

u = tcdf(x,lambda);                       % t-copula variates
end
```

Figure 7.48 Matlab implementation of the DSA for generating variates of the t-copula

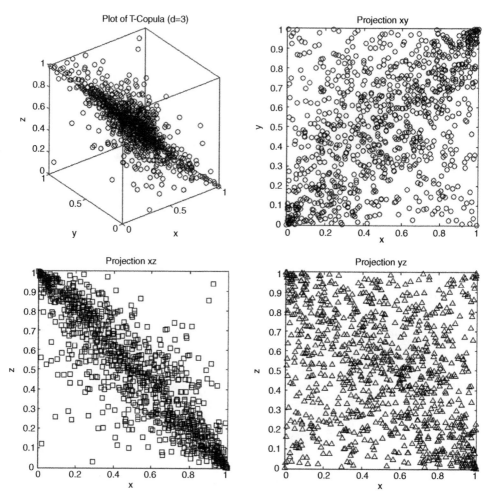

Figure 7.49 The *t*-copula for $\lambda = 3$, ρ from (7.42) (top left) and *NSim* = 1000. The projections to the *xy*-plane (top right), *xz*-plane (bottom left) and *yz*-plane (bottom right)

For the function S_TCopula the input *Rho* is the correlation matrix. The size of the matrix determines the dimensionality. The parameter *lambda* determines the degrees of freedom and *NSim* is the number of simulations. We applied the function to ρ from (7.42), $\lambda = 3$ and *NSim* = 1000. The result is displayed in Figure 7.49.

7.8.2 Conditional Sampling Approach (CSA)

There are copulae where the function F as well as the marginals F_i, $i = 1, \ldots, d$ from (7.41) are not available in closed form and therefore the DSA cannot be applied. There is yet another approach, called the *Conditional Sampling Approach*, or CSA for short, to simulate variates from a given copula. To this end for $d_1 \leq d$ we consider the marginals $C_{d_1} := C(u_1, \ldots, u_{d_1}, 1, \ldots, 1)$ of a copula C. The conditional distribution of U_{d_1} given

$U_1, \ldots, U_{d_1-1}$ is given by

$$F_{U_{d_1}|U_1,\ldots,U_{d_1-1}} = \frac{\partial^{(d_1-1)}_{u_1,\ldots,u_{d_1-1}} C_{d_1}(u_1,\ldots,u_{d_1})}{\partial^{(d_1-1)}_{u_1,\ldots,u_{d_1-1}} C_{d_1}(u_1,\ldots,u_{d_1-1})}. \qquad (7.43)$$

Then,

- Simulate a random variate u_1 from $U_1 \sim \mathcal{U}(0,1)$
- Simulate a random variate u_2 from $U_2 \sim F_{U_2|U_1}(U_2|u_1)$
- ...
- Simulate a random variate u_d from $U_d \sim F_{U_d|U_1,\ldots,U_{d-1}}(U_d|u_1,\ldots,u_{d-1})$.

To apply this approach sampling from the conditional distribution

$$F_{U_k|U_1,\ldots,U_{k-1}}(U_k|u_1,\ldots,u_{k-1})$$

has to be done. If the inverse distribution is not available in closed form, the equation

$$F_{U_k|U_1,\ldots,U_{k-1}}(u_k|u_1,\ldots,u_{k-1}) - u = 0$$

has to be numerically solved.

For the particular case of an Archimedean copula the sampling can be simplified consider-ably. Let φ denote the generator of the copula (see Subsection 4.6.4). Then, the conditional distribution is given in terms of the generator φ and its inverse $\psi := \varphi^{-1}$. For a given function f we denote by $f^{(d-1)}$ the d-th derivative, then we have

$$F_{U_k|U_1,\ldots,U_{k-1}}(U_k|u_1,\ldots,u_{k-1}) = \frac{\psi^{k-1}(\varphi(u_1)+\ldots+\varphi(u_k))}{\psi^{k-1}(\varphi(u_1)+\ldots+\varphi(u_{k-1}))}.$$

To this end the sampling from the class of Archimedean copulae is feasible once the function ψ as well as the derivatives are known in closed form. We illustrate the application of the CSA for the Clayton copula. The algorithm implemented in Matlab is presented in Figure 7.50. It uses as an input the number of simulations, the dimensionality as well as a parameter which determines the dependency structure for the Clayton copula.

We have applied S_ClaytonCopula to generate $NSim = 1000$ variates for $d = 3$ and $a = 4$. The result as well as the projections to xy-, xz- and yz-plane are presented in Figure 7.51.

```
function v = S_ClaytonCopula(NSim,d,a)
v = zeros(NSim,d);            % init copula variates
u = rand(NSim,d);            % uniforms

v(:,1)  = u(:,1);            % first variate set
for j=2:d                    % loop over dimensions
      u_mat = [v(:,1: j-1) u(:,j)];
      v(:,j) = ((sum(u_mat(:,1:j-1).^(-a),2) - j +2) .*...
               ((u_mat(:,j).^(a/((a* (1-j))-1)))) - 1) + 1).^(-1/a);
end

end
```

Figure 7.50 Matlab implementation of the CSA for the Clayton copula

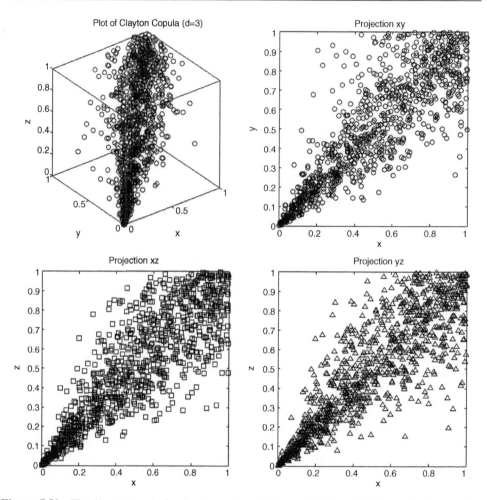

Figure 7.51 The Clayton copula for $d = 3$, $a = 4$ and $NSim = 1000$ (top left). The projections to the xy-plane (top right), xz-plane (bottom left) and yz-plane (bottom right)

7.8.3 Simulation from Other Copulae

We have considered convex combinations of copulae and product copulae. Let us now consider N copulae $C_1, \ldots, C_N$. Suppose we are able to sample from each C_i, $i = 1, \ldots, N$ then sampling from the convex combination $C = \omega_1 C_1 + \ldots + \omega_d C_d$ is simple by sampling variates $u_1, \ldots, u_d$ from $C_1, \ldots, C_d$ and setting $u = \omega_1 u_1 + \ldots + \omega_d u_d$.

For the product copula this is not so easy. To this end let $\underline{U}^n = (U_1^n, \ldots, U_d^n)$ denote a collection of independent samples from copula C_n, $\underline{U} = (U_1, \ldots, U_d)$ variates with $U_i \sim \max_{n=1,\ldots,N} \left(q_{n,i}^{-1}(U_i^n) \right)$ and $\underline{u} = (u_1, \ldots, u_d)^\top \in [0, 1]^d$. Then, using results from Liebscher, E. (2008) we have

$$\mathbb{P}(U_1 < u_1, \ldots, U_d < u_d) = \mathbb{P}(\max_{n=1,\ldots,N} q_{n,1}^{-1}(U_1^n) < u_1, \ldots, \max_{n=1,\ldots,N} q_{n,d}^{-1}(U_d^n) < u_d)$$

$$= \prod_{n=1}^{N} \mathbb{P}(U_1^n < q_{n,1}(u_1), \ldots, U_d^n < q_{n,d}(u_d)).$$

Using the latter equation we can sample from the corresponding probability distributions and multiply the samples.

7.9 SUMMARY AND CONCLUSIONS

In this chapter we considered simulation as the method of choice to price options, generate scenarios for a given financial model or calculate risk measures. Such considerations can serve as the basis for stress testing, asset allocation or scenario analysis.

To be in a position to price path-dependent options such as Barrier options or options involving the maximum/minimum for a certain time period it is necessary to sample a whole path and evaluate the payoff on this path. Thus, when applying Monte Carlo simulation it is necessary to consider a discrete approximation (in time).

We started by introducing the standard discretization techniques such as the (Log-)Euler scheme and extended the scope of the method to jump-diffusion models and special purpose discretization methods. We observed that it becomes necessary to consider sample schemes which are adapted to the underlying model since simple approximations such as the (Log-)Euler scheme do not work properly. To this end we introduced and compared different methods proposed for the Heston model or the SABR model.

For multi-dimensional models we considered the simulation of a Libor Market Model and applied it to the pricing options including early exercise rights, namely Bermudan swaptions.

Finally, we considered multi-dimensional models based on Lévy processes and general modelling of dependence. In particular, we introduced copulae and illustrated different sampling methods.

8

Monte Carlo Simulation – Advanced Issues

8.1 INTRODUCTION AND OBJECTIVES

In the last chapter we introduced methods for sampling paths from different model dynamics such as stochastic volatility models or Lévy process based models. The payoffs we considered were evaluated on either a pre-specified or a stochastic time grid and paid at maturity. In this chapter we consider the pricing of options with early exercise possibilities using Monte Carlo simulation. Such options can be exercised at any time point up to maturity (American options) or at a discrete set of prescribed time points up to maturity (Bermudan options). To be able to price such features we consider three different methods:

- The Regression method.
- The Policy Iteration method.
- The Upper Bound method.

We illustrate each method in the one-dimensional setting. We provide source code for each of the methods.

Finally, we look at the derivation of hedge sensitivities for derivatives with path-dependent or discontinuous payoffs using simulation. We present different methods and techniques and give several examples. In particular, we focus on non-Gaussian models here.

In addition, we examine early exercise opportunities in options and their corresponding Greeks for a multi-dimensional model. To this end we introduce a general technique based on adjoint methods and apply it to a Libor Market Model. The adjoint method has gained great popularity among quants since it can reduce the computing time immensely.

8.2 MONTE CARLO AND EARLY EXERCISE

We introduced American and Bermudan options in Chapter 6 and applied Fourier transform methods to option pricing problems. In this section we consider the application of Monte Carlo simulation to this problem. To this end we aim to determine an approximation to the option price V using the optimal stopping time τ^*. Thus, as in Chapter 6, we consider the price time zero price $V_\tau(h)$ depending on the payoff and a stopping time τ. We have

$$V_{\tau^*}(h) = essup_{\tau \, \text{stopping time}} V_\tau(h).$$

If Nx denotes the number of exercise opportunities and $NSim$ the number of paths, then we take a set of prices $P(i, j)$, $i = 1, \ldots, Nx$, $j = 1, \ldots, NSim$. For fixed j, $P(i)$ is a realization of a discrete time stochastic process. For instance, $P(i)$ can be values of an option with payoff h at the i-th exercise possibility t_i given a discretization of some stochastic process $S(t)$, $t \in [0, T]$ on fixed time points $t_1, \ldots, t_{Nx}$. The current value is denoted by h_i. We fix notation by considering a filtration $\mathcal{F}_i$, $i = t_1, \ldots, t_{Nx}$ and $\mathcal{T}_i$ the set of $\mathcal{F}_i$-stopping times taking values in $\{t_i, \ldots, t_{Nx}\}$. Thus, the optimal stopping problem can be formulated by looking at the following equation:

$$\mathbb{E}^{\mathcal{F}_i}[P(\tau_i)] = essup_{\tau \in T_i} \mathbb{E}^{\mathcal{F}_i}[P(\tau)] =: \mathcal{S}^P(t_i).$$

We call $\mathcal{S}^P(t_i)$ the *Snell envelope* of P. It is the smallest super-martingale that dominates P. An important observation for applying backward programming, which is important when setting up Monte Carlo, is that $\mathcal{S}^P$ can be constructed by

$$\mathcal{S}^P(t_{Nx}) = P(t_{Nx})$$
$$\mathcal{S}^P(t_i) = \max\left\{\mathcal{S}^P(t_i), \mathbb{E}_{\mathcal{F}_i}[\mathcal{S}^P(t_{i+1})]\right\}.$$

The value $c_i := \mathbb{E}_{\mathcal{F}_i}[\mathcal{S}^P(t_{i+1})]$ is called the *continuation value*.

8.2.1   Longstaff–Schwarz Regression

Let h be some payoff, that is for a fixed realisation ω we consider the function on the set of paths $\mathcal{P}$,

$$h : \mathcal{P} \to \mathbb{R}$$
$$S_t(\omega) \mapsto h(S_t(\omega)).$$

The option value V_i at a given time point t_i is the maximum of the current payoff value h_i and the continuation value c_i. To fix notation, the value V_i is given by

$$V_i = \begin{cases} e^{-r(t_{i+1}-t_i)}V_{i+1}, & \text{if } h_i < c_i \\ h_i, & \text{if } h_i \geq c_i \end{cases}.$$

The aim of the *Longstaff–Schwarz method* is to compute the continuation value using regression. To this end we generate a set of paths and use this set at each time point t_i and regression to determine the continuation value c_i. Thus, using an expected value of the form

$$c_i = e^{-r(t_{i+1}-t_i)}\mathbb{E}[V_{i+1}|S_{i+1}],$$

we are able to compute the continuation value using the simulated path set of *NSim* paths.

To apply regression we fix a set of *basis functions* $f_k, k = 0, \ldots, Nr$ and approximate the continuation value at time t_i using the values of the underlying path set P.

We have two choices for applying the regression method. We can either use the values generated for the underlying at time t_i or at time t_{i+1}. The expression *regression now* refers to the first and *regression later* to the second choice. In the following we consider the case of regression now. Thus, we apply the regression to $S(t_i)$.

$$c_i = e^{-r(t_{i+1}-t_i)}\mathbb{E}[v_{i+1}|S_{i+1}] \approx \sum_{k=0}^{Nr} a_k f_k(S_i).$$

The coefficients $a_k, k = 0, \ldots, Nr$ are real values and are yet to be determined. To determine the coefficients we solve for the least squares error $\varepsilon > 0$ determined by

$$c_i = \sum_{k=0}^{Nr} a_k f_k(S_i) + \varepsilon. \tag{8.1}$$

For $0 < i < Nx$ we minimise this expression in the sense of the least squares error. Using vectors V, A and $\mathcal{E}$ given by

$$V = \begin{pmatrix} v_1 \\ v_2 \\ \vdots \\ v_{NSim} \end{pmatrix}, \quad A = \begin{pmatrix} a_1 \\ a_2 \\ \vdots \\ a_{Nr} \end{pmatrix}, \quad \mathcal{E} = \begin{pmatrix} \varepsilon_1 \\ \varepsilon_2 \\ \vdots \\ \varepsilon_{NSim} \end{pmatrix} \in \mathbb{R}^{NSim}.$$

For the regression function f_k, $k = 1, \ldots, Nr$ from (8.1) we denote the value of the i-th time step in the n-th simulation by $f_k(S_i, n)$. We denote the matrix $F \in \mathbb{R}^{NSim \times Nr}$ by

$$F := \begin{pmatrix} f_1(S_i, 1) & f_2(S_i, 1) & \cdots & f_{Nr}(S_i, 1) \\ f_1(S_i, 2) & f_2(S_i, 2) & \cdots & f_{Nr}(S_i, 2) \\ \vdots & \vdots & \ddots & \vdots \\ f_1(S_i, NSim) & f_2(S_i, NSim) & \cdots & f_{Nr}(S_i, NSim) \end{pmatrix}.$$

Thus, we have

$$V = FA + \mathcal{E}.$$

For the least squares minimizer we finally find

$$F^\top F A = F^\top V.$$

This leads us to consider

$$A = (F^\top F)^{-1} F^\top V. \tag{8.2}$$

Let us consider the implementation in Matlab. We have created a function which takes the generated asset values for S as input. The other input variables are the payoff values g and the discount factors at the exercise dates, df. The object B is a cell array containing function handles. This object models the basis functions. Let us look at the definition of B. To model the basis functions, for instance 1, x and x^2, we create a cell array of function handles as shown in Figure 8.1.

This allows us to modify the basis functions $1, x, x^2$ outside the main function (see Figure 8.2) without modifying the actual implementation of the regression based pricing. Furthermore, we do not need the number of basis functions we use. The reader can modify the basis functions by taking proprietary functions or orthogonal polynomials such as Hermite or Laguerre functions.

Let us now consider the code for pricing the early exercise option, the corresponding function is called LongstaffSchwartz in Figure 8.2 using the code from Figure 8.3.

We observe that the current approach leads to a biased estimator. This bias can be removed. It is due to the fact that we use the path set P for calculating the regression coefficients A and for pricing. The above can be modified to calculate the regression coefficients for a path set P_1, to store the regression coefficients and to implement another path set P_2 for pricing. To this end a function RegCoeff is implemented which returns the regression coefficients

```
B = @(x) {{ones(length(x),1) x x.^2}};
```

Figure 8.1 Matlab implementation of the basis functions applied for calculating the Monte Carlo value of a Bermudan option using the Longstaff–Schwarz method

```
function [price, se, low, high] ...
     = LongstaffSchwartz(S, g, df, B, Nx, NSim, level)

v = g(:,end);    % start for backward induction

% backward induction and regression from t_{Nx-1} up to t_1
for i = Nx-1:-1:1
         index = find(g(:,i) > 0);  % all ITM paths
         s = S(index,i);                % values of S at given time point
         v = v * df(i+1);               % option value at t_i

         Acell = B(s);                  % eval basis function in cell array B
         A = cell2mat(Acell{:,:});  % convert to matrix

         f = inv(A'*A)*A'*v(index);  % determine coefficients
         c = A*f;                        % continuation value
         earlyexercise = g(index,i) >= c;    % early exercise
         v(index(earlyexercise)) = g(index(earlyexercise),i);
end

price = mean(v * df(1));    % final option value

% standard error and confidence interval
sv = sqrt(1/(NSim-1)*sum((v*100 - price * ones(NSim,1)).^2));
se = sv/sqrt(NSim);
low =  price - norminv(level) * sv/sqrt(NSim);
high = price + norminv(level) * sv/sqrt(NSim);

end
```

Figure 8.2 Matlab code for the implementation of the regression method of Longstaff and Schwarz. This function calculates the regression coefficients and uses these for pricing. Both the coefficients as well as the prices are calculated on the path set P

A calculated using the set P_1, and the function LongstaffSchwartz has to be modified by using A as an input argument. The corresponding functions are presented in Figure 8.4 for the pricing and Figure 8.5 for the coefficients.

Let us look at an example for exotic options with early exercise possibilities. We take a payoff which depends on the maximum on a path. Some Barrier options or Lookback options are of this type. The algorithm we implemented can be extended to include other variables, for instance the minimum or the average. Figure 8.5 implements the pricing, called LongstaffSchwartz_M, for payoffs g relying on the maximum.

Again, we separate the pricing from the determination of the regression coefficients. The corresponding code is named LongStaffSchwartz_M_2 and the calculation of the regression coefficients is called RegCoeff_M_2 and can be found in the source code examples. We test the methods for exotic options using the Matlab script given in Figure 8.6.

Bermudan Swaptions – LMM

To generalize to multi-factor models we provide a brief introduction to the case of the Libor Market Model and pricing Bermudan swaptions within this model. Let us recall the definition of

```
function f = RegCoeff(S, g, df, B, Nb, Nr)

v = g(:,end);    % start for backward induction

f = zeros(Nb, Nr-1);

% backward induction and regression from t_{Nr-1} up to t_1
for i = Nr-1:-1:1
        index = find(g(:,i) > 0);  % all ITM paths
        s = S(index,i+1);          % values of S at given time point
        v = v * df(i+1);           % option value at t_i

        Acell = B(s);              % eval basis function in cell array B
        A = cell2mat(Acell{:,:});  % convert to matrix

        f(:,i) = inv(A'*A)*A'*v(index);  % determine coefficients
        c = A*f(:,i);                    % continuation value
        exercise = g(index,i) >= c;      % early exercise
        v(index(exercise)) = g(index(exercise),i);
end

end
```

Figure 8.3 Matlab code for the calculation of the regression coefficients to be used with the Longstaff–Schwartz regression method

a Bermudan swaption. Mathematically this option is modelled as a tuple $B = (T, e, K, \mathcal{N}, \phi)$ consisting of

1. a *tenor structure*

$$0 = T_1 < T_2 < \ldots < T_m < T_{m+1}$$

with *tenor distances*

$$\tau_i := T_{i+1} - T_i, \quad i = 1, \ldots, m,$$

the *maturity* T_m (or the *maturity time index* m), the *first exercise time index* e, $1 \le e \le m$. Often in the market the notation $nNCm$ is used. This means for n years exercise is not possible but then, every m-th year,
2. a *strike rate* $K \in [0, 1]$,
3. a *nominal value* $\mathcal{N} \in \mathbb{R}_{>0}$,
4. a *payer-or-receiver-factor* $\phi \in \{-1, +1\}$.

We encapsulate all the structure into a Matlab class. The actual code and the implementation is presented in Section 12.8, when we introduce object oriented programming.

The payoff of a Bermudan swaption is formalized by specifying the *payments* at time index n by

$$X_n := X_n(L(n)) := X_n(L_n(n)) := \phi \mathcal{N} \tau_n (L_n(n) - K).$$

```
function [price, se, low, high]  ...
      = LongstaffSchwartz_2(S, g, df, B, f, Nr, NSim, level)

v = g(:,end);    % start for backward induction

% backward induction and regression from t_{Nr-1} up to t_1
for i = Nr-1:-1:1
        index = find(g(:,i) > 0);  % all ITM paths
        s = S(index,i+1);              % values of S at given time point
        v = v * df(i+1);               % option value at t_i

        Acell = B(s);                  % eval basis function in cell array B
        A = cell2mat(Acell{:,:});  % convert to matrix

        c = A*f(:,i);                         % continuation value

        exercise = g(index,i) >= c;    % early exercise
        v(index(exercise)) = g(index(exercise),i);
end

price = mean(v * df(1));      % final option value

% standard error and confidence interval
sv = sqrt(1/(NSim-1)*sum((v - price * ones(NSim,1)).^2));
se = sv/sqrt(NSim);
low =  price - norminv(level) * sv/sqrt(NSim);
high = price + norminv(level) * sv/sqrt(NSim);

end
```

Figure 8.4 Matlab code for the implementation of the regression method of Longstaff and Schwarz. This function takes the regression coefficients calculated using a path set S_1 different from a path set S_2 used for pricing

If the Bermudan swaption is exercised at time index r, the payment $X_n, r \leq n \leq m$, is calculated at time index n, but received at time index $m + 1$. Therefore, the *discount factor* back to T_1 is

$$PV_{n+1} := PV_{n+1}(L(n)) := \prod_{i=1}^{n} \frac{1}{1 + \tau_i L_i(i)}.$$

The *payoff* of a Bermudan swaption exercised at time index r is

$$g := g(L(m)) := \sum_{\mu=r}^{m} PV_{\mu+1} X_\mu.$$

For any $e \leq \mu \leq m$ define

$$g_\mu := g_\mu(L(\mu)) := PV_{\mu+1} X_\mu \tag{8.3}$$

to be the discounted payoff at time index μ.

We obtain the following facts that become useful when working with Bermudan payoffs and which enable us to use sophisticated methods for calculating the Greeks.

```
function [price, se, low, high] ...
    = LongstaffSchwartz_M(S, M, Ns, g, df, B, Nr, NSim, level)

v = g(:,end);    % start for backward induction

% backward induction and regression from t_{Nr-1} up to t_1
for i = Nr-1:-1:1
        index = find(g(:,i+1) > 0);  % all ITM paths
        s = S(index,i+1);            % values of S at given time points
        m = M(index,i+1);            % values of M at given time points
        v = v * df(i+1);             % option value at t_i

        Acell = B(s,m);              % eval basis function in cell array B
        A = cell2mat(Acell{:,:});    % convert to matrix

        if i == 1 % for this period A is singluar thus we only take S
            A=[A(:,1:Ns) A(:,7)];
        end

        f = inv(A'*A)*A'*v(index);   % determine coefficients
        c = A*f;                     % continuation value
        exercise = g(index,i+1) >= c;    % early exercise
        v(index(exercise)) = g(index(exercise),i+1);
end

price = mean(v * df(1));     % final option value

% standard error and confidence interval
sv = sqrt(1/(NSim-1)*sum((v - price * ones(NSim,1)).^2));
se = sv/sqrt(NSim);
low =   price - norminv(level) * sv/sqrt(NSim);
high =  price + norminv(level) * sv/sqrt(NSim);

end
```

Figure 8.5 Matlab implementation for calculating the regression coefficients for the Longstaff–Schwartz approach for pricing exotic options which also need the maximum denoted by M

1. The discounted payoff satisfies

$$g = g(L(m)) = \sum_{\mu=r}^{m} g_\mu(L(m)) = \sum_{\mu=r}^{m} g_\mu(L(\mu)) = \sum_{\mu=r}^{m} g_\mu \qquad (8.4)$$

2. The derivative with respect to $L(1)$ satisfies

$$\nabla(g)(L(m)) = \sum_{\mu=r}^{m} \nabla(g_\mu)(L(\mu)) \qquad (8.5)$$

Since g_μ depends on $L_1(1), \ldots, L_\mu(\mu)$, Equation (8.4) follows directly from the definition of the scheme for the Libor rates, L. Equation (8.5) follows from (8.4).

```
Nr = 13;          % exercise possibilities
NSim = 1000;      % number of simulations
S0 = 100;         % spot price
K = 100;          % strike price

ScaleFactor = 156;

T=1;
dt = T/Nr;        % equidistant time grid
r = 0.06;         % zero rate
d = 0.0;          % dividend yield
sigma = 0.15;
type = 0;

S0 = S0 * exp(-d*T);

S0 = S0 / ScaleFactor;
K = K / ScaleFactor;

gp = @(x,y,z) getPathsAsian(x, r, sigma, dt, y, z);    % Paths
pay = @(x) putpayoff(x,K);                             % Payoff

[S,M] = gp(S0, NSim, Nr);

h = [S(:,1) pay(M(:,2:end))];
%h = pay(M(:,2:end));

df = exp(-r*dt) * ones(Nr,1);   % discounts for all time points
% choose the basis functions
B = @(x,y) {{ones(length(x),1)   x   x.^2   y   y.^2   x.*y   (x.^2).*y
x.*(y.^2)}};

fprintf('Tree Value:');
BinTree_A(S0, K, r, T, sigma, 20, type)*ScaleFactor  % bin tree

fprintf('Asian Option:');
% Longstaff Schwarz - Arithmetic Asian option
[price, se, low, high] ...
    = LongstaffSchwartz_M(S, M, 3, h, df, B, Nr, NSim, 0.99);
price * ScaleFactor

RC = RegCoeff_M(S, M, 3, h, df, B, 8, Nr);

[price, se, low, high] = LongstaffSchwartz_M2(S, M, 3, h, df, RC, ...
    B, Nr, NSim, 0.99);
price * ScaleFactor

Bki = @(x) {{ones(length(x),1)   x   x.^2 }};  % choose the basis functions

Barrier = 95; Barrier = Barrier / ScaleFactor;

fprintf('Tree Value:');
price = BinTree_KI(S0, K, r, T, sigma, 20, Barrier, type);
price * ScaleFactor

fprintf('Barrier Options:');
payki = @(x) knockinpayoff(x,K,Barrier,type);
hki = payki(S(:,2:end));
% Longstaff Schwarz - Barrier option
[price, se, low, high]=LongstaffSchwartz(S, hki, df, Bki,Nr,NSim, 0.99);
price * ScaleFactor
```

Figure 8.6 Matlab test script for pricing Bermudan, Arithmetic Asian and Barrier options by applying the Longstaff–Schwarz regression method

8.2.2   Policy Iteration Methods

As we shall see below, the *Policy Iteration* method leads to lower bounds for the option value since we explicitly improve upon a given stopping rule approximating the optimal stopping rule.

We consider the Policy Iteration method for the pricing of early exercise options using Monte Carlo methods. This method is based on choosing an initial exercise strategy τ and then improving it iteratively. The method is described in Bender, D., Kolodko, A. and Schoenmakers, J. (2008) and we adhere closely to their notation here.

We say that a family of stopping times taking values in a discrete set is *consistent* if $t_i \leq \tau(i) \leq t_{Nx}$, $\tau(Nx) = t_{Nx}$ and for $\tau(i) > t_i$ follows $\tau(i) = \tau(i+1)$ for $1 \leq i \leq k$. We consider consistent stopping times. For the implementation and the application of the Policy Iteration method an important example for such a stopping time denoted by $\hat{\tau}$ is constructed using the maximum of *still-alive* European options. We have

$$\hat{\tau} := \inf \left\{ t_j : i \leq j \leq Nx, P(t_j) > \max_{j+1 \leq p \leq Nx} \mathbb{E}^{\mathcal{F}_i}[S(t_p)] \right\}.$$

An *adapted random set* is a set $\mathcal{A} \subset \{t_1, \ldots, t_{Nx}\}$ with $1_\mathcal{A}(t_i)$ is $\mathcal{F}_i$ adapted, and $t_{Nx} \in \mathcal{A}$ almost surely. For some consistent stopping family τ we consider a stopping family, $\tilde{\tau}$, given by

$$\tilde{\tau} := \inf \left\{ t_j : i \leq j \leq Nx, S(\tau_j) \geq \max_{j+1 \leq p \leq Nx} \mathbb{E}_{\mathcal{F}_j}[P(\tau_p)] \text{ and } j \in \mathcal{A} \right\}. \tag{8.6}$$

If there exists some optimal stopping family τ^* such that $\tau(i) \in \mathcal{A}$, $i = 1, \ldots, Nx$ almost surely we call $\mathcal{A}$ an *a priori set*. To link all this and apply it to the pricing of Bermudan options we assume that L is a lower bound on the Snell envelope. Thus, L can be some sub-optimal exercise strategy. We consider the a priori set together with L and we take

$$\mathcal{A}(\omega) := \left\{ t_j : 1 \leq j \leq N\dot{x}, P(t_j, \omega) \geq L(t_j, \omega) \right\}.$$

The stopping family $\tilde{\tau}$, (8.6), is called a *one-step improvement* of τ since it leads to a higher (or equal) option price and is thus closer to the Snell envelope. In the next paragraph we give the algorithm for setting up different constructions of the one-step improvement and the pricing of Bermudan options.

Let τ be the initially chosen stopping time. Denoting by V_0 the price of the Bermudan option with exercise schedule $\mathcal{T} := \{t_1, \ldots, t_{Nx}\}$ we have

$$e^{-r\tau} \mathbb{E}[h(\tau)] \leq V_0.$$

Thus, choosing some stopping times leads to a lower bound on the option price. Furthermore, it satisfies

$$e^{-r\tau(k)} \mathbb{E}_k[h(\tau(k))] \leq V_0.$$

For the stopping time $\tau(k)$ we have

$$k \leq \tau(k) \leq n, \quad \tau_{Nx} = Nx.$$

If we do not choose to exercise we have $\tau(k) > k$ and $\tau(k) = \tau(k+1)$. Now, we are outlining a procedure to determine an exercise strategy τ.

Choosing a Starting Point   To start, we take as the initial stopping time τ^0:

$$\tau^0(k) := \inf\{i : i = k, \ldots, Nx \in \mathcal{A}\}$$

by denoting $\mathcal{A}$ the set of points where the payoff is bigger or equal to the value B_i on the exercise boundary in t_i, thus,

$$\mathcal{A} = \{t_i : i = 1, \ldots, \text{Nx}, h(t_i) \geq B_i\}$$

with the obvious constraint $B_{Nx} = 0$. Since the maturity of the option is reached at t_{Nx}, to actually find a starting point for the iteration we have to specify τ^0 given $\mathcal{A}$.

Let $h^E(\cdot)$ denote the payoff of a European option with payoff h, thus we take $B_i := h^E(t_i)$ and get

$$\mathcal{A} = \{t_i : i = 1, \ldots, \text{Nx}, h(t_i) \geq h^E(t_i)\}.$$

Using the fact that a Bermudan option is at least as expensive as its European counterpart, we have

$$B_i^E = \begin{cases} \max_{k=i+1,\ldots,Nx} \mathbb{E}_i[e^{-r(t_k-t_i)}V_i^E(t_k - t_i)], & i = 1, \ldots, \text{Nx-1} \\ 0, & i = \text{Nx} \end{cases}.$$

We use the notation V_i^E for the price of the corresponding European option with time to maturity $t_k - t_i$ and spot value $S(t_i)$. The exercise strategy is to consider the still-alive European options and take the most expensive of these. We assume that the price can be calculated efficiently either by analytic, semi-analytic or by some accurate approximate formula.

Other choices for $\mathcal{A}$ are possible, for instance the exercise policy obtained from applying regression leads to the set $\mathcal{A}_{\text{reg}}$.

Longstaff and Schwarz   Let us take a set of regression functions f_k, $k = 1, \ldots, Nr$ with the corresponding regression coefficients A_k^i. The regressed price $\tilde{V}_i$ at time t_i is then given by

$$\tilde{V}_i = \sum_{k=1}^{Nr} A_k^i f_k(S_i).$$

At maturity, that is t_{Nx}, we have $\tilde{V}_{Nx} = 0$ and for the other time points at which exercising the option is possible

$$\mathcal{A} = \{t_i : i = 1, \ldots, Nx, \quad h_i \geq \tilde{V}_i\}.$$

We therefore modify the initial step by considering

$$\mathcal{A} = \{t_i : i = 1, \ldots, Nx, \quad h_i \geq \max(\tilde{v}_i, h_i^E)\}.$$

We consider the implementation of the Policy Iteration procedure using still-alive European options for which the Matlab code is presented in Figure 8.7. The nested simulation necessary for improving the stopping rule by computing a conditional expectation is shown in Figure 8.8.

The function *PIter_E* takes as input a set of paths S, a set of payoffs g computed from the payoff function and the path set. For computing the analytic values the values of the riskless rate r and the volatility $\texttt{sigma}$ are input data. The variables $\texttt{NSim}$, $\texttt{Nx}$, $\texttt{NSSim}$ refer to the

```
function [price_pi, se, conflevel_low, conflevel_high] = ...
  PIter_E(S, g, K, r, T, sigma, Nr, NSim, NSSim, type,getpaths, payoff)

dt = T/Nr;                    % equidistant spacing
tau = Nr*ones(NSim,1);        % exercise rule for each path
iVec = (1:NSim)';             % index vector
for i = 1:Nr-1
    i_nexercise = tau == Nr;          % only ex if not already done
    % paths (realisation) where the stopping rule needs improvement
    I_nexercise = iVec(i_nexercise);

    price = BlackScholesPrice(S(i_nexercise,i+1), K, r, (1:Nr-i)'*dt, ...
        sigma, type);                 % analytic price
    exbound0 = max(price, [],2);      % ex decision
    isubsim = g(i_nexercise,i) >= exbound; % index set indicating subsim

    if sum(I_nexercise(isubsim)) ~= 0         % if necessary
        Indicator = subsimulation(S(I_nexercise(isubsim),i+1), K, r, ...
            sigma, dt, NSSim, Nr-i, type,getpaths, payoff); % subsim

        Ind = iVec(I_nexercise(isubsim)); % index:payoff >=current rule
        % exercised before this time? Use Indicator
        ind2 = g(I_nexercise(isubsim),i) >= Indicator; % at ind2 and q
        Ind2 = iVec(ind2);
% ind set for ind2
        if sum(ind2) ~= 0
            tau(Ind(Ind2)) = i; % final exercise
        end
    end
end

f = zeros(NSim,1); % sum payoffs for exercise times
for j = 1:NSim
    f(j) = g(j,tau(j));
end
price_pi = mean(f .* exp(-r*dt*tau));

sv = sqrt(1/(NSim-1)*sum((f*100 - price_pi * ones(NSim,1)).^2));
se = sv/sqrt(NSim);
conflevel_low = price_pi - 1.96 * sv/sqrt(NSim);
conflevel_high = price_pi + 1.96 * sv/sqrt(NSim);

end
```

Figure 8.7 Matlab implementation of the Policy Iteration algorithm for pricing Bermudan options applying Monte Carlo simulation

number of simulations, the number of exercise opportunities and the number of simulations we apply within a subsimulation. The variables getpaths and payoff are function handles for accomplishing the simulation and payoff evaluation for the subsimulation.

Along each path of the set we start at the first time at which early exercise is possible. We determine the analytic prices using an analytical, a semi-analytical or an accurate approximation formula. Then, we apply these prices to determine whether early exercise could be an opportunity or if continuation would be best. At the index set which we have identified as being likely to continue to hold the option we perform a subsimulation. Within the subsimulation

```
function [price_local] = subsimulation(S, K, r, sigma, dt, NSim, Nr, ...
            type, getpaths, payoff)
    lenS = length(S);              % length of the path set S
    iVec = (1:NSim)';              % index set
    S2 = getpaths(S,NSim,Nr);      % new path set
    g2 = payoff(S2(:,2:end,:));    % evaluate option on path set S2

    price_local = zeros(lenS, 1);

    for k = 1:lenS
        payoff = zeros(NSim, Nr);
        for i=1:1:Nr-1
            for z=i:1:Nr-1
                i_nexercise = payoff(:,i) == 0; % check if exercised
                I_nexercise = iVec(i_nexercise);

                price = BlackScholesPrice(S2(I_nexercise,z,k),K,r, ...
                    (1:Nr-z)'*dt,sigma,type);   % analytic price
                exbound=max(price,[],2);        % bound for exercise

                exercise = g2(i_nexercise,z,k) >= exbound; % exercise
                payoff(I_nexercise(exercise),i) = ...
                    g2(I_nexercise(exercise),z,k) * exp(-r*dt*z);

            end

            finalexercise = payoff(:,i) == 0;   % finally not exercised
            payoff(finalexercise,i) = g2(finalexercise,Nr,k) ...
                * exp(-r*dt*Nr);                % final exercise

        end
        payoff(:,Nr) = g2(:,Nr,k) * exp(-r*dt*Nr);
        price_local(k) = max(mean(payoff));
    end

end
```

Figure 8.8 Matlab implementation for the subsimulation necessary when applying policy iteration

we check against the analytic prices again. Having determined the improvement at the current time step we proceed to the next step until we reach maturity.

The Policy Iteration procedure can be applied to several stopping times as starting values. We consider the still-alive European options and regression described so far. But the method is not limited to these choices. For instance, we can take the trivial stopping rule $\tau_i = t_i$ which is immediate stopping. Let us outline the implementation using regression in the sequel. The code for implementing this approach is given in Figures 8.9 and 8.10 and the corresponding code for the subsimulation in Figure 8.11.

The input to the function is slightly different since the basis functions, the cell array B, and the number of basis functions Nb are necessary inputs. This also holds true for the corresponding subsimulation. The main body of the algorithm is the same as in Figure 8.8; only a minor modification has to be made to use it in this situation. This modification is necessary to determine an exercise policy using regression.

```
function [price_pi, se, conflevel_low, conflevel_high] ...
    = PIter_R(S, g, r, T, Nr, B, Nb, NSim, NSSim, getpaths, payoff)

dt = T/Nr;                  % equidistant spacing

v = g(:, end);              % option value at maturity
beta = zeros(Nb, Nr-1);     % coefficients for regression
c = zeros(NSim,Nr-1);       % continuation value

for i=Nr-1:-1:1
        index = find(g(:,i)>0);

        s = S(index,i+1);
        v = v * exp(-r*dt*i);

        Acell = B(s);
        A = cell2mat(Acell{:,:});

        beta(:,i) = inv(A'*A)*A'*v(index);  % calc coeffs
        c(index,i) = A*beta(:,i);           % cont value itm paths

        earlyexercise = g(index,i) >= c(index,i);            % exercise
        v(index(earlyexercise)) = g(index(earlyexercise),i); % opt value
end

tau = Nr*ones(NSim,1);      % exercise rule for each path
iVec = (1:NSim)';           % index vector

for i = 1:Nr-1
    i_nexercise = tau == Nr; % only exercise if not already done
    % paths (realisation) where the stopping rule needs improvement
    I_nexercise = iVec(i_nexercise);

    s = S(I_nexercise,i+1);
    Acell = B(s);
    A = cell2mat(Acell{:,:});
    price = A * beta(:,i);
    exbound = max(price, [],2);   % ex decision
    isubsim = g(i_nexercise,i) >= exbound;  % ind set indicating subsim

    if sum(I_nexercise(isubsim)) ~= 0       % subsim necssary
        Indicator = subsimulation(S(I_nexercise(isubsim),i+1), r, ...
            beta, B, dt, NSSim, Nr-i,getpaths, payoff);  % subsim

        Ind = iVec(I_nexercise(isubsim));
% payoff >= current rule
        % exercised before this time? Use Indicator
        ind2 = g(I_nexercise(isubsim),i) >= Indicator; % at ind2 and q
        Ind2 = iVec(ind2);                   % index set ind2
        if sum(ind2) ~= 0
            tau(Ind(Ind2)) = i;              % final exercise
        end
    end
end
end
```

Figure 8.9 Matlab implementation of the Policy Iteration method using regression instead of the still-alive European options

```
f = zeros(NSim,1);
for j = 1:NSim
    f(j) = g(j,tau(j));                        % sum payoffs
end

price_pi = mean(f .* exp(-r*dt*tau));

% standard error and confidence level
sv = sqrt(1/(NSim-1)*sum((f*100 - price_pi * ones(NSim,1)).^2));
se = sv/sqrt(NSim);
conflevel_low = price_pi - 1.96 * sv/sqrt(NSim);
conflevel_high = price_pi + 1.96 * sv/sqrt(NSim);

end
```

Figure 8.10 Matlab implementation of the Policy Iteration method using regression instead of the still-alive European options (continued)

8.2.3 Upper Bounds

So far we have only considered lower bounds on the option price. We successfully applied regression and policy iteration to solve this problem. In this section we consider upper bounds for American/Bermudan options. We use the *duality relation* applied in Rogers, L.C.G. (1984) and Haugh, M. and Kogan, L. (2001). To compute the present value V_0 of the option with payoff h the key observation is that for a given martingale $(\pi_t)_t$ and τ being some stopping time we have

$$\mathbb{E}[h(\tau, S(\tau))] = \mathbb{E}[h(\tau, S(\tau)) - \pi_\tau] \le \mathbb{E}[\max_{k \in \tau} h(t_k, S(t_k)) - \pi_{t_k}]. \tag{8.7}$$

Equation (8.7) can be used to obtain

$$\mathbb{E}[h(\tau, S(\tau)] \le \inf_\pi \mathbb{E}[\max_{t_k \in \tau} h(t_k, S(t_k)) - \pi_{t_k}]. \tag{8.8}$$

Equation (8.8) allows us to express the option value as a minimization problem with respect to martingales. Since (8.8) holds for all stopping times τ, it holds for the supremum taken over all stopping times τ. The main issue when deriving upper bounds is to determine some martingale which is close to the minimizing martingale.

We consider two methods for implementing an upper bound. The first method (M1) is outlined in Broadie, M. and Cao, M. (2008), while the other (M2) can be found in Glasserman, P. (2004).

(M1) To give an explicit construction for a martingale process, π, to compute upper bounds we consider the super-martingale $df(i)V_i$. With respect to the Doob-Meyer decomposition we can find a process A_i such that

$$A_i \ge 0$$
$$A_0 = 0$$
$$\pi_i = df(i)V_i + A_i.$$

```
function [price_local] = subsimulation(S, r, beta, B, dt, NSim, Nx, ...
                                    getpaths, payoff)

    lenS = length(S);              % length of S
    iVec = (1:NSim)';              % for calculation of indices

    S2 = getpaths(S,NSim,Nx);      % generate paths

    S2 = S2(:,2:end,:);            % values without spot
    g2 = payoff(S2);

    price_local = zeros(lenS, 1);
    for k = 1:lenS                 % loop over spots
        payoff = zeros(NSim, Nx);
        for i=1:1:Nx-1             % loop over maturities
            for z=i:1:Nx-1         % loop over stopping
                % exercise if not already done
                i_nexercise = payoff(:,i) == 0;
                I_nexercise = iVec(i_nexercise);% corresp. index

                s = S2(i_nexercise,i);
                Acell = B(s);
                A = cell2mat(Acell{:,:});
                price = A * beta(:,i);

                exbound=max(price,[],2);            % europ. exbound

                exercise = g2(i_nexercise,z,k) >= exbound; % exercise
                payoff(I_nexercise(exercise),i) = ...
                    g2(I_nexercise(exercise),z,k) * exp(-r*dt*z);

            end

            finalexercise = payoff(:,i) == 0; % finally not exercise
            payoff(finalexercise,i) = g2(finalexercise,Nx,k) ...
                * exp(-r*dt*Nx);                % finally exercised

        end

        payoff(:,Nx) = g2(:,Nx,k) * exp(-r*dt*Nx);
        price_local(k) = max(mean(payoff));

    end
end
```

Figure 8.11 Matlab implementation for the `subsimulation` necessary for the Policy Iteration method using regression to determine a stopping time

If we consider some lower bound process for the option price L_i we have

$$df(i)L_i = \mathbb{E}[df(i)g(\tau_i)].$$

Using $\tau_i = \inf\{k : k = i, \ldots, Nx, \quad g_k \geq c_k\}$. Thus, the guiding idea is to use the lower bound L_i instead of the unknown option value V_i to derive π. We set

$$\pi_0 := L_0$$
$$\pi_1 := df(1)L_1.$$

For $2 \le i \le Nx$ we have

$$\pi_i := \pi_{i-1} + df(i)L_i - df(i-1)L_{i-1} - 1_{\{i-1\}}\mathbb{E}[df(i)L_i - df(i-1)L_{i-1}]$$
$$= \pi_{i-1} + df(i)L_i - Q_{i-1}$$

where we used the notation

$$Q_i := \begin{cases} df(i)L_i & 1_{\{i-1\}} = 0 \\ \mathbb{E}[df(i+1)L_{i+1}] & 1_{\{i-1\}} = 1 \end{cases}.$$

with $1_{\{i\}}$ is 1 if we exercise at time t_i and 0 if we do not exercise. The process defined using this ansatz is indeed a martingale. We do not show the derivation here.

(M2)   To fix the notation we let $df(i), i = 1, \ldots, Nx$ denote the discount factors for the time periods starting at t_{i-1} up to t_i. V_i denotes the value of the option at time t_i and h_i is the intrinsic payoff value at t_i.

Furthermore, let us denote $\Delta_k := df(i)V_i - \mathbb{E}_i[df(i)V_i]$. We define a martingale discretization by fixing $\pi_0 = 0$ and setting $\pi_i = \sum_{k=0}^{i} \Delta_k$. The martingale property can be checked by considering

$$\mathbb{E}_{\mathcal{F}_{i-1}}[\Delta_i] = \mathbb{E}_{\mathcal{F}_{i-1}}[df(i)V_i - \mathbb{E}_{\mathcal{F}_{i-1}}[df(i)V_i]]$$
$$= \mathbb{E}_{\mathcal{F}_{i-1}}[df(i)V_i] - \mathbb{E}_{\mathcal{F}_{i-1}}[df(i)V_i] = 0.$$

Thus, we obtain an upper bound on the option price V_0 by

$$V_0 \le \mathbb{E}[\max_{i=1,\ldots,Nx}(df(i)(h_i - \pi_i)]. \tag{8.9}$$

To apply this method for pricing early exercisable options we determine $\Delta_i, i = 1, \ldots, Nx$. Using the stopping time τ obtained by regression and since

$$\Delta_i = df(\tau_i)\mathbb{E}_{\mathcal{F}_i}[h_{\tau_i}] - df(\tau_i)\mathbb{E}_{\mathcal{F}_{i-1}}[h_{\tau_i}], \tag{8.10}$$

we need to simulate the conditional expectations given in (8.9). The code presented in Figure 8.14 is the Matlab code for deriving this conditional expectation.

The subsimulation necessary to compute the conditional expectations is displayed in Figure 8.15. We did not specify a particular model and payoff but we pass these to the function as function handles, `getpaths` and `payoff`. The handles can be adapted to a specific model and a specific payoff. Thus, the code is model independent.

8.2.4   Problems of the Method

Let us briefly comment on familiar problems arising when applying the Longstaff–Schwartz to the pricing of options.

We have suggested looking at ITM options only. This is a problem if we wish to price OTM options. There may be too few paths ending up ITM to apply the regression. For path-dependent options this issue becomes even more important since due to the path dependence there are even fewer paths ending up ITM.

We can transfer the problem by applying the *regression later* method and hope that the problem hits us one time step later.

Two other possible solutions are to use a related payoff for the regression and, in particular, for path-dependent options, consider only basic non-path-dependent options such as Calls or

```
function [lower, upper] = ...
  UpperBound1(S, g, df,B,beta,lower, Nr, NSim, NSSim, getpaths, payoff)
% method from Broadie
v = g(:, end);              % option value at maturity
c = zeros(NSim,Nr-1);       % continuation value

stoppingtime = Nr * ones(NSim,1);

 for i=Nr-1:-1:1
        index = find(g(:,i)>0);
        s = S(index, i+1);
        v = v * df(i+1);

        Acell = B(s);
        A = cell2mat(Acell{:,:});
        c(index,i) = A*beta(:,i);
% cont value itm paths

        earlyexercise = g(index,i) >= c(index,i);% exercise
        stoppingtime(index(earlyexercise)) = i;
        v(index(earlyexercise)) = g(index(earlyexercise),i);
 end

% Computing the martingale pi
L = zeros(NSim,1);
expectation = zeros(NSim,Nr);
expectation(:,1) = lower * ones(NSim,1);

pi = zeros(NSim,Nr+1);                          % martingale
pi(:,1) = lower * ones(NSim,1);                 % set pi(0)

% perform the subsimulation for each value of the path set
for i=1:1:Nr-1
    for j=1:NSim
        expectation(j,i+1) = subsimulation(S(j,i+1), df, B, NSSim, ...
        Nr-i,beta(:,i:end), getpaths, payoff) * prod(df(1:i));
    end
end

for i=1:1:Nr
    i_exercise = stoppingtime == i;      % check if early exercised

    if i < Nr
        L(i_exercise) = g(i_exercise, i) * prod(df(1:i));
        L(~i_exercise) = expectation(~i_exercise,i+1);
    else
        L(i_exercise) = g(i_exercise, i) * prod(df(1:i));
    end

    pi(:,i+1) = pi(:,i) + L - expectation(:,i);
end

maximum = zeros(NSim,1);

for j=1:1:NSim
    maximum(j) = L(j) + max(g(j,:) - pi(j,2:end));  % compute the max
end
upper = mean(maximum);

end
```

Figure 8.12 Matlab implementation for method (M1) to compute an upper bound given a stopping rule τ derived from applying regression. The function `subsimulation` is shown in Figure 8.13

```
function y = subsimulation(S0, df, B, NSim, Nr, beta, gp,payoff)
    S2 = gp(S0,NSim,Nr); S2 = S2(:,2:end);    % paths
    g2 = payoff(S2);                           % payoff
    iVec = 1:NSim;

    exercise = Nr * ones(NSim,1);              % exercise per path
    % determine exercise strategy for path set S2
    for i=1:1:Nr-1
        i_nexercised = exercise == Nr;
        I_nexercise = iVec(i_nexercised);

        s = S2(i_nexercised,i);
        Acell = B(s);
        A = cell2mat(Acell{:,:});
        c = A * beta(:,i);

        i_exercise = g2(i_nexercised,i) >= c & g2(i_nexercised,i) > 0;
        exercise(I_nexercise(i_exercise)) = i;
    end
    summe=0;
    for j=1:1:NSim
        summe = summe + g2(j,exercise(j)) * prod(df(1:exercise(j)));
    end
    y = summe / NSim;                          % MC value from subsimulation
end
```

Figure 8.13 Matlab implementation for the function subsimulation to compute an upper bound as presented in Figure 8.12. The function subsimulation is shown in Figure 8.15

Puts to determine the regression coefficients. When we price the option we then take into account the path dependency.

We can incorporate information about the problem when we choose the basis functions. For instance, we can include a function indicating when barriers are breached. This method can also lead to instabilities stemming from the basis functions involving the indicator levels. Such basis functions can take jointly the value 0 and therefore the regression matrix gets singular.

The final possibility is to try variance reduction methods, importance sampling in this case, to avoid singular regression matrices entirely. We have not applied the latter possibility here.

8.2.5   Financial Examples and Numerical Results

In this subsection we apply the methods to financial models and different option payoffs. We use the methods described in Chapter 7 to generate the path set P. Then, we use the paths sets to consider

- Put options
- Asian options
- Barrier options
- Bermudan swaptions and the Libor Market Model.

Let us denote the asset price dynamic by $S(t)$. In what follows we consider the options to which we apply the numerical methods.

```
function [lower, upper] = ...
    UpperBound2(S, g, df, B, Nb, Nr, NSim, NSSim, getpaths, payoff)
% method from Glasserman
v = g(:, end);                 % option value at maturity
beta = zeros(Nb, Nr-1);        % Regression coefficients
c = zeros(NSim,Nr-1);          % continuation value

iVec = 1:NSSim;

for i=Nr-1:-1:1
        index = find(g(:,i)>0);

        s = S(index,i+1);
        v = v * df(i+1);

        Acell = B(s);
        A = cell2mat(Acell{:,:});

        beta(:,i) = inv(A'*A)*A'*v(index);
        c(index,i) = A*beta(:,i);       % continuation value itm paths

        earlyexercise = g(index,i) >= c(index,i); % early exercise
        v(index(earlyexercise)) = g(index(earlyexercise),i);
end
lower = mean(v * df(1)); % lower bound using LongStaff Schwarz

% Computing the martingale numerically, martingale = pi
L = zeros(NSim,1);             % used to construct delta_i
expectation = zeros(NSim,Nr); % used to determine delta_i
expectation(:,1) = lower * ones(NSim,1);

for i=1:1:Nr-1
    for j=1:1:NSim
        expectation(j,i+1) = subsimulation(S(j,i+1), df, B, NSSim, ...
        Nr-i,beta(:,i:end), iVec(1:NSSim), getpaths, payoff) ...
        * prod(df(1:i));
    end
end

pi = zeros(NSim,Nr+1); % stores the values of the constructed martingale

for i=1:1:Nr-1
    % exercise in this case if not already exercised
    i_exercise = g(:,i) >= c(:,i) & c(:,i) > 0;
    i_nexercise = ~i_exercise;
    L(i_exercise) = g(i_exercise, i) * prod(df(1:i));
    L(i_nexercise) = expectation(i_nexercise,i+1);

    pi(:,i+1) = pi(:,i) + L - expectation(:,i);
end
pi(:,Nr+1) = pi(:,Nr) + g(:,Nr)* prod(df(1:Nr)) - expectation(:,Nr);

% upper bound using the martingale pi
maximum = zeros(NSim,1);

for j=1:1:NSim
    maximum(j) = max(g(j,:) - pi(j,2:end)); % compute max
end
upper = mean(maximum);

end
```

Figure 8.14 Matlab implementation for the method (M2) described in this section

```
function y = subsimulation(S0, df, B, NSim, Nr, beta, iVec, gp,payoff)

S2 = gp(S0,NSim,Nr); S2 = S2(:,2:end);    % paths
g2 = payoff(S2);                          % payoff

exercise = Nr * ones(NSim,1);             % exercise per path
for i=1:1:Nr-1
    i_nexercised = exercise == Nr;
    I_nexercise = iVec(i_nexercised);

    s = S2(i_nexercised,i);
    Acell = B(s);
    A = cell2mat(Acell{:,:});
    c = A * beta(:,i);

    i_exercise = g2(i_nexercised,i) >= c & g2(i_nexercised,i) > 0;
    exercise(I_nexercise(i_exercise)) = i;
end
summe=0;
for j=1:1:NSim
    summe = summe + g2(j,exercise(j)) * prod(df(1:exercise(j)));
end
y = summe / NSim;                         % MC value from subsimulation
end
```

Figure 8.15 Matlab implementation for the function subsimulation used in Figure 8.14

Put Options For a fixed time point t the payoff of a Put option is given by

$$\max(K - S(t), 0).$$

Let us fix the parameters $S(0) = K = 100$, the volatility $\sigma = 0.15$ and the rate $r = 0.06$. We assume that there are no dividends and the maturity is three-month. The values for the American Put are displayed in Table 8.1.

Asian Options Let us fix a grid $\mathcal{T} = \{t_1, \ldots, t_N = T\}$. For an Arithmetic Asian option we consider the arithmetic average on $\mathcal{T}$. It is given by

$$A(\mathcal{T}) = \frac{1}{N-1} \sum_{i=1}^{N} S(t_i). \tag{8.11}$$

Table 8.1 Values for the American Put option using a Monte Carlo estimator. We considered Regression with $n = 3$ and $n = 91$ exercise opportunities

Paths	$n = 13$	$n = 91$	Confidence
10000	2.3958	2.4193	[2.3920, 2.4286]
100000	2.3984	2.4247	[2.3945, 2.4378]

Table 8.2 Computed prices for Arithmetic Asian options. The value has been computed by Monte Carlo methods. The table shows the estimated mean, the standard deviation and the confidence interval

Paths	Value	StandardError	Confidence
Call			
10.000	2.3591	0.029	[2.3014, 2.4168]
100.000	2.3716	0.009	[2.3531, 2.3901]
1.000.000	2.3835	0.003	[2.3776, 2.3893]
Put			
10.000	1.6249	0.023	[1.5809, 1.6690]
100.000	1.6328	0.007	[1.6187, 1.6470]
1.000.000	1.6351	0.002	[1.6306, 1.6396]

Then, an Arithmetic Asian option is an option with payoff for the Call and the Put

$$A_C = \max(A(T) - K, 0)$$
$$A_P = \max(K - A(T), 0).$$

There is also an average strike version of the options. Here the payoffs are

$$A_C = \max(S(T) - A(T), 0)$$
$$A_P = \max(A(T) - S(T), 0).$$

We consider the basis functions $1, S, S^2, S_A, S_A^2, S^2 S_A, SS_A^2$ for applying the Longstaff–Schwarz method to the pricing of an American Arithmetic Asian option. We find for $S(0) = 100$, $K = 100$, $\sigma = 0.15$, $r = 0.06$, $T = 0.25$ and $N = 13$ the prices displayed in Table 8.2.

Barrier Options   For the numerical experiments we consider *Knock-In* and *Knock-Out* Barrier options. In general let us consider two functions lb and ub given by

$$lb, ub : [0, T] \to \mathbb{R}^+$$
$$t \mapsto lb(t), ub(t).$$

The functions lb and ub respectively are called the *lower barrier* and the *upper barrier*. A Knock-Out option is triggered once the asset moves below lb or above ub, whereas a Knock-In option is triggered when the asset moves below ub or above lb. The functions can be chosen to be constant. We consider the following types of option:

$$DIP = \begin{cases} \max(S(T) - K, 0) & T_{lb} \leq T \\ 0 & T_{lb} > T \end{cases}, \tag{8.12}$$

$$UIP = \begin{cases} \max(K - S(T), 0) & T_{ub} \leq T \\ 0 & T_{ub} > T \end{cases}, \tag{8.13}$$

$$DOP = \begin{cases} \max(S(T) - K, 0) & T_{lb} \geq T \\ 0 & T_{lb} < T \end{cases}, \tag{8.14}$$

$$UOP = \begin{cases} \max(K - S(T), 0) & T_{ub} \geq T \\ 0 & T_{ub} < T \end{cases}. \tag{8.15}$$

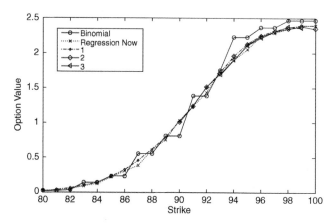

Figure 8.16 Pricing American Knock-In Put options applying different methods for calculating the price

In the above equations T_{lb} denotes the time when the lower barrier is breached and T_{ub} the time when the upper barrier is breached. Let us look at the pricing of an American Knock-In option applying different methods. We consider the strike range $80, \ldots, 120$ and take $S(0) = K = 100$, $\sigma = 0.15$ and $r = 0.06$. The maturity is set to $T = 0.2$ and we consider 13 exercise possibilities for $NSim = 100000$ paths. Figure 8.16 shows the results.

It is remarkable that the standard method, method 1, does not lead to prices for the whole range of option strikes. This is due to the fact that by applying regression we are not able to compute the regressed values since the matrices are no longer invertible. Too few paths end up ITM.

Bermudan Swaptions Using the Libor Market Model   The method presented in the last sections can be carried over to the multi-dimensional setting, for instance to price Bermudan swaption in a Libor Market Model. To this end we generate scenarios due to a given Libor Market Model. Take the early exercise set $T = \{t_1, \ldots, t_{Nx}\}$. The latter is often specified by stating the period where no early exercise is possible and then the period at which exercise is possible. For instance, 10NC2 half-yearly means that the maturity is 10 years and for the first 2 years early exercise is not possible but after 2 years it is possible to exercise every 6 months.

At each time point $t_k \in T$ we determine the swap rate S_k for the generated scenarios. Thus, we obtain a one-dimensional model. We can then directly apply the methodology described above.

Before we consider the implementation we introduce hedge sensitivities in the next section. Then, we apply this to Bermudan swaptions.

8.3 GREEKS WITH MONTE CARLO

This section discusses computing sensitivities (Greeks) for derivatives using Monte Carlo methods. A set of sample paths $S_{i,j}$, $i = 1, \ldots, NSim$, $j = 1, \ldots, Nt$ is used to approximate the expected value, that is the option price. This option price depends on several model parameters ϕ_k, $k \in \mathbb{N}$ since the evolution of a path and thus the set $(S_{i,j})_{i,j}$ depends on the parameters. For instance, the current spot price or the current level of volatility affects the price of an option since it changes the whole path set.

We indicate the dependence by denoting the sample path by $S_{\phi_1, \phi_2, \ldots,}$ or, where we consider a single parameter ϕ, we denote the dependence by S_ϕ or when we evaluate a payoff h we write h_ϕ.

We are interested in the effect changing one of the model parameters has on the option price. To this end we apply the partial derivative with respect to this parameter. The sensitivity, or *Greek*, with respect to the parameter ϕ is given by

$$\text{Greek}_\phi := \frac{\partial}{\partial \phi} \mathbb{E}[h_\phi(S)]. \tag{8.16}$$

Several methods to apply Monte Carlo simulation to compute the partial derivative (Equation (8.16)) have been suggested. Each of the approaches requires additional information which has consequences for the implementation. We review three methods for computing Greeks in a Monte Carlo framework:

- *Finite Difference method* (FDM) see Subsection 8.3.1.
- *Pathwise method* (PWM) see Subsection 8.3.2.
- *Likelihood Ratio method* (LRM) see Subsection 8.5.3.

We first describe the methods and then show how to implement these methods in Matlab. The problem entails either simulating another set of paths or evaluating the paths with a modified payoff. Finally, we summarize the properties of each method and give an overview when it is applicable.

8.3.1 The Finite Difference Method (FDM)

The *Finite Difference Method* or FDM for short approximates the partial derivative given by Equation (8.16) by a *difference estimator*. From real analysis it is known that a differentiable function can locally be approximated by a linear function. The finite difference estimator applies this concept to option values.

We take a payoff function h which may depend on the values of the asset $S = (S_1, \ldots, S_N)^\top$ at Nt times and on d model parameters, $\phi = (\phi_1, \ldots, \phi_d)^\top$.

$$h : \mathbb{R}^{N \times Nt} \times \mathbb{R}^d \to \mathbb{R}$$
$$S_1^1, \ldots, S_N^1, \ldots, \phi \mapsto h_\phi(S_1, \ldots, S_N).$$

To simplify notation we write $h_\phi(S)$ keeping in mind that this is a shorthand notation. For some $\varepsilon > 0$ we approximate Greek_ϕ from Equation (8.16) using the difference estimator

$$\text{Greek}_\phi^{FD} := \frac{\mathbb{E}[h_{\phi+\varepsilon}(S)] - \mathbb{E}[h_{\phi-\varepsilon}(S)]}{2\varepsilon}. \tag{8.17}$$

Equation (8.17) is called the *central difference estimator*. We may wish to apply other differences such as the *forward* or the *backward difference* estimator. For $\varepsilon > 0$ we have the following equations for the different estimators:

- central difference estimator: $\frac{f(x+\varepsilon)-f(x-\varepsilon)}{2\varepsilon}$
- forward difference estimator: $\frac{f(x+\varepsilon)-f(x)}{\varepsilon}$
- backward difference estimator: $\frac{f(x)-f(x-\varepsilon)}{\varepsilon}$.

Let us consider a set of simulated paths $S^i(\phi), i = 1, \ldots, NSim$ depending on the model parameter ϕ and the corresponding Monte Carlo estimator which is given by

$$\widehat{Greek}_{\phi}^{FD} := \frac{1}{N} \sum_{i=1}^{N} \frac{h(S^i(\phi + \varepsilon)) - h(S^i(\phi - \varepsilon))}{2\varepsilon}. \tag{8.18}$$

We have used the notation $\widehat{Greek}_{\phi}^{FD}$ to denote the sample estimate of Equation (8.18). To apply the FDM we do not need any further information on the model, the simulation scheme, the payoff or the nature of the model parameter ϕ. We generate two sets of paths using the disturbed model parameters and compute the finite difference estimator. The Monte Carlo estimator in this case shows a significant dependence on the parameter ε. Furthermore, it is not possible to handle discontinuous payoffs. The error for the latter case grows like $O(\varepsilon^{-1})$. If the expectation of the payoff is differentiable with respect to the parameter ϕ, the difference estimator converges if ε tends to 0. Often simultaneous movements, for instance that of $S(0)$ and σ, are of interest to traders. *Vanna* and *Volga* are two typical examples.

$$Vanna := \frac{\partial^2 \mathbb{E}[h(S(S(0), \sigma))]}{\partial S(0)\partial\sigma}; \quad Volga := \frac{\partial^2 \mathbb{E}[h(S(\sigma))]}{\partial\sigma^2}.$$

Another example are basket options. Such options generally depend on multiple assets. Therefore, a trader might be interested in the sensitivity of changes in the spot price of asset n_1 and asset n_2 simultaneously. Such sensitivities are called *Cross Gammas* and correspond to partial derivatives of second order:

$$Greek_{\phi_i,\phi_j}^{FD} = \frac{\partial^2}{\partial\phi_i\partial\phi_j}\mathbb{E}[h(S(\phi_i, \phi_j))]. \tag{8.19}$$

Let us consider a d factor model and that we wish to disturb the model parameters ϕ_i and ϕ_j by $\varepsilon_i > 0$ and $\varepsilon_j > 0, i, j = 1, 2, \ldots, d$. Then, the finite difference estimator is given by

$$Greek_{\phi_i,\phi_j}^{FD} = \frac{1}{4\varepsilon_1\varepsilon_2} \left(\mathbb{E}[h(S(\phi_i + \varepsilon_1, \phi_j + \varepsilon_2))] - \mathbb{E}[h(S(\phi_i - \varepsilon_1, \phi_j + \varepsilon_2))] \right.$$
$$\left. - (\mathbb{E}[h(S(\phi_i + \varepsilon_1, \phi_j - \varepsilon_2))] - \mathbb{E}[h(S(\phi_i - \varepsilon_1, \phi_j - \varepsilon_2))]) \right). \tag{8.20}$$

Pitfalls and Improvement   The determination of the parameter $\varepsilon > 0$ remains a challenge. We need stable results and do not want to run into numerical problems because we have chosen it too small or too big. There is, however, no general recipe for determining it in practice.

For a discussion on this subject see, for example, Jäckel, P. (2005). If V denotes the price of an option Jäckel suggests setting

$$\varepsilon := \sqrt{\sqrt{12\frac{V}{V^{(3)}}r_{min}}}$$

where $V^{(3)}$ denotes the third derivative with respect to the underlying parameter and r_{min} is the smallest number that can be represented on your computer. In Matlab this number is encoded in the variable `realmin`.

Furthermore, to reduce the pricing bias we also suggest using the same random variates for computing both disturbed prices for the central finite difference estimator. Then, both computed prices suffer from the same simulation bias which cancels out by taking the difference.

Complex Methods   We use complex variables to compute the derivative of a real function. This approach goes back to the paper by Lyness, J.N. and Moler, C.B. (1967). Another reference is Squire, W. and Trapp, G. (1998). In this paragraph we assume that it is possible to extend the defining range of a function

$$f : D \subset \mathbb{R} \to \mathbb{R}$$

to some subset of the complex plain, $\mathbb{C}$. Then, we find for its Taylor expansion

$$f(x + i\varepsilon) = f(x) + i\varepsilon f_x(x) - \frac{\varepsilon^2}{2} f_{xx}(x) + \frac{\varepsilon^3}{6} f_{xxx}(x) \pm \ldots$$

Taking the imaginary part of $f(x + i\varepsilon)$ we find

$$\mathcal{I}[f(x + i\varepsilon)] = \varepsilon f_x(x) \pm \ldots$$

We divide both parts of the latter equation by ε and get

$$f_x(x) = \frac{\mathcal{I}[f(x + i\varepsilon)]}{\varepsilon} + O(\varepsilon^2).$$

This approach has been applied to higher order derivatives. Now let us apply this method to a simple function. We take

$$f : \mathbb{R} \to \mathbb{R}$$
$$x \mapsto \sqrt{x^9} + \sin(x).$$

For some $x_0 \in \mathbb{R}$ the analytic value of the derivative is $\frac{9}{2}\sqrt{x^7} + \cos(x)$. Table 8.3 gives the first derivative at $x_0 = 0.2$ using the FDM and the complex method (CM) and different values for ε. We take $\underline{\varepsilon} = (10^{-1}, \ldots, 10^{-20})^\top$.

We observe that the FDM is only stable in the range 10^{-2}–10^{-16}, whereas the CM produces stable results from 10^{-2} onwards. This is due to numerical errors when calculating the function values necessary for applying difference methods.

8.3.2   The Pathwise Method

The Pathwise Method (PWM) approximates Equation (8.16) by an expression involving the derivative of the payoff and the derivative of the simulated path:

$$\text{Greek}_\phi^{PW} := \mathbb{E}\left[h'_\phi(S) \frac{\partial}{\partial \phi} S_\phi \right] \tag{8.21}$$

and the corresponding Monte Carlo estimator is given by

$$\widehat{\text{Greek}^{PW}}_\phi := \frac{1}{N} \sum_{i=1}^{N} h'_\phi(S^i) \cdot \frac{\partial (S_\phi^i)'}{\partial \phi}. \tag{8.22}$$

The PWM requires additional knowledge of the model, additional information on the payoff and the parameter set ϕ. It leads to an unbiased estimator of the corresponding derivative if the

Table 8.3 Derivatives calculation for a simple function using the $\underline{\varepsilon} = (10^{-1}, \ldots, 10^{-20})^{\top}$ and the finite difference (FD) and complex method (CM)

ε	FD	CM
10^{-1}	1.0057	0.9920
10^{-2}	0.9966	0.9961
10^{-3}	0.9962	0.9962
10^{-4}	0.9962	0.9962
10^{-5}	0.9962	0.9962
10^{-6}	0.9962	0.9962
10^{-7}	0.9962	0.9962
10^{-8}	0.9962	0.9962
10^{-9}	0.9962	0.9962
10^{-10}	0.9962	0.9962
10^{-11}	0.9962	0.9962
10^{-12}	0.9962	0.9962
10^{-13}	0.9964	0.9962
10^{-14}	0.9964	0.9962
10^{-15}	1.0270	0.9962
10^{-16}	1.3878	0.9962
10^{-17}	0	0.9962
10^{-18}	0	0.9962
10^{-19}	0	0.9962
10^{-20}	0	0.9962

stochastic dynamics and the model fulfil certain mathematical properties (see Subsection 13.2.3 for details). The method is not applicable to discontinuous payoff functions. The PWM is based on the following equation to hold

$$\frac{\partial}{\partial x}\mathbb{E}\left[f(x)\right] = \mathbb{E}\left[\frac{\partial}{\partial x}f(x)\right]. \tag{8.23}$$

The relation (8.23), and therefore (8.21), does not hold in general because interchanging the expectation with the differentiation is only possible under certain conditions. The conditions for interchanging both operators are based on Lebesgue's *convergence theorem.*

How to Apply the Pathwise Method   We consider two examples, namely an exact and an Euler discretized stochastic differential equation of the stochastic differential equation for a diffusion

$$dS(t) = \mu(S(t))dt + \sigma(S(t))dW(t)$$
$$S(0) = S(0).$$

The drift, $\mu : \mathbb{R}^+ \times \mathbb{R} \to \mathbb{R}$, and the volatility, $\sigma : \mathbb{R}^+ \times \mathbb{R} \to \mathbb{R}^+$, are functions of the time and the asset value. Denoting $\Delta_n := t_{n+1} - t_n$, we have

$$\hat{S}_{n+1} = \hat{S}_n + \mu(t_n, \hat{S}_n)\Delta_n + \sigma(t_n, \hat{S}_n)\sqrt{\Delta_n}Z_{n+1}, \quad Z_{n+1} \sim \mathcal{N}(0, 1) \tag{8.24}$$

and, alternatively,

$$\hat{S}_{n+1} = \hat{S}_n \exp\left(\mu(t_n, \hat{S}_n)\Delta_n + \sigma(t_n, \hat{S}_n)\sqrt{\Delta_n}Z_{n+1}\right), \quad Z_{n+1} \sim \mathcal{N}(0, 1), \tag{8.25}$$

since the asset price and therefore the scheme depends on the model parameter ϕ. For both cases the consideration is the same and we only examine Equation (8.24). The pathwise derivative with respect to some parameter ϕ, denoted by "'", is

$$\hat{S}'_{n+1} = \hat{S}'_n + \mu'(t_n, \hat{S}_n)\hat{S}'_n\Delta_n + \sigma'(t_n, \hat{S}_n)\hat{S}'_n\sqrt{\Delta_n}Z_{n+1}. \tag{8.26}$$

Applying it to all Nt time steps and taking the sum we find

$$\sum_{i=1}^{Nt} \frac{\partial h}{\partial \hat{S}_{i\phi}} \left(\hat{S}_{1\phi}, \ldots, \hat{S}_{N\phi}\right) \frac{\partial}{\partial \phi} \hat{S}_i, \tag{8.27}$$

with

$$\begin{cases} \dfrac{\partial}{\partial \phi}\hat{S}_{n+1} = \dfrac{\partial}{\partial \phi}\hat{S}_n + \mu'(S_n)\dfrac{\partial}{\partial \phi}\hat{S}_n\Delta_n + \sigma'(S_n)\dfrac{\partial}{\partial \phi}\hat{S}_n\sqrt{\Delta_n}Z_{n+1} \\ \dfrac{\partial}{\partial \phi}\hat{S}_0 = x \end{cases} \tag{8.28}$$

For example, if we denote the partial derivative with respect to the spot price and abbreviate the partial derivative $\frac{\partial}{\partial S(0)}\hat{S}_i$ by $\hat{\Delta}_{S_i}$, we obtain

$$\begin{cases} \hat{\Delta}_{S_{n+1}} = \hat{\Delta}_{S_n} + \mu'(t_n, S_n)\hat{\Delta}_{S_n}\Delta_n + \sigma'(t_n, S_n)\hat{\Delta}_{S_n}\sqrt{\Delta_n}Z_{n+1} \\ \hat{\Delta}_{S_0} = 0 \end{cases} \tag{8.29}$$

Despite the fact that this method can be applied to a wide range of stochastic dynamics it is computationally expensive because we have to compute the Monte Carlo estimator for each Greek. Therefore, we have to generate random variables and compute the numerical scheme. But if there are no analytic expressions available it may be the only possibility.

Example: Black–Scholes Call

As an example, we apply this method to compute the sensitivity with respect to the spot value $S(0)$ for the Black–Scholes model. Going back to Equation (8.24) the drift factor in the Black–Scholes model is $\mu(t, S) = rS(t)$ and the diffusion coefficient is $\sigma(t, S) = \sigma_{BS}S(t)$. Both, r and σ_{BS} are positive real numbers.

Since $\sigma'(t_i, S_i) = \frac{\partial}{\partial S_i}\sigma_{BS}S_i = \sigma_{BS}$ and $\mu'(t_i, S_i) = \frac{\partial}{\partial S_i}rS_i = r$ the dynamic in this case is

$$\begin{cases} \hat{\Delta}_{S_{n+1}} = \hat{\Delta}_{S_n} + r\hat{\Delta}_{S_n}\Delta_n + \sigma_{BS}\hat{\Delta}_{S_n}\sqrt{\Delta_n}Z_{n+1} \\ \Delta_{S(0)} = 0 \end{cases} \tag{8.30}$$

For practical purposes it should be possible to pre-compute the differential of the path with respect to a model parameter. The Greeks can then be computed by evaluating a payoff type function for the simulated path.

In fact, for the Black–Scholes model we can use the exact solution instead of the Euler approximation and do not need to evolve the sensitivity through time. Taking Equation (8.25)

```
function optval = PW_Delta_CallPut(S,K,C,r,T)
% S = NSim x 1 matrix of simulated prices
% K = Strike price
% C = 1 -> Call; C = 0 -> Put
    Indicator = S(:,end);

    if(C==1)
        Indicator(Indicator<=K) = 0;
        Indicator(Indicator>K) = 1;
        optval = mean(S(:,end)./S(:,1).*Indicator)*exp(-r*T);
    else
        Indicator(Indicator>=K) = 0;
        Indicator(Indicator<K) = 1;
        optval = mean(S(:,end)./S(:,1).*Indicator)*exp(-r*T);
    end
end
```

Figure 8.17 Matlab code for implementing the Δ for geometric Brownian motion for European Call and Put options

we see that the following equation holds true:

$$\frac{dV}{dS(0)} = \frac{dV}{dS(T)}\frac{dS(T)}{dS(0)}. \tag{8.31}$$

Using the exact solution, Equation (8.25) leads to

$$\left.\frac{d}{dS(0)}V\right|_{S(0)} = \frac{S(T)}{S(0)}1_{\{S(T)>K\}}. \tag{8.32}$$

Therefore, we can compute the pathwise estimator just by using another payoff given by Equation (8.32) and implemented in Figure 8.17.

Finally, we give the standard example where the pathwise method cannot be used. We consider a digital option and find

$$0 = \mathbb{E}\left[\left.\frac{d}{dS(0)}V\right|_{S(0)}\right] \neq \frac{d}{dS(0)}\mathbb{E}[V]. \tag{8.33}$$

We now consider the pathwise estimator with respect to the implied volatility σ_{BS}, the Vega of the option (Figure 8.18). It is given by

$$\text{Greek}_{\sigma_{BS}}^{PW} = \exp(-rT)\sigma_{BS}^{-1}\left(\log\left(\frac{S(T)}{S(0)}\right) - r + \frac{\sigma_{BS}^2}{2}T\right)S(T)1_{\{S(T)>K\}}. \tag{8.34}$$

In what follows we assess examples for computing the pathwise Greeks for path-dependent and multi-asset options. To this end we consider Arithmetic Average Asian options and spread options. However, we do not provide the Matlab code since it is a straightforward implementation of the corresponding formulae (8.35)–(8.38)

Example: Black–Scholes Asian Call

The same procedure can be applied to compute estimates for path-dependent options. To cover Arithmetic Asian options applying the pathwise method for the computation of the Greeks the

```
function optval = PW_Vega_CallPut(S,Z,K,C,r,sigma,T)
    % S = NSim x 1 matrix of simulated prices
    % K = Strike price
    % C = 1 -> Call; C = 0 -> Put
    Indicator = S(:,end);

    if(C==1)
        Indicator(Indicator<=K) = 0;
        Indicator(Indicator>K) = 1;
        optval =exp(-r*T) * ...
            mean(S(:,end).*Indicator .*(-sigma*T + sqrt(T)*Z) );
    else
        Indicator(Indicator>=K) = 0;
        Indicator(Indicator>K) = 1;
        optval =exp(-r*T) * ...
            mean(S(:,end).*Indicator .*(-sigma*T + sqrt(T)*Z) );
    end
end
```

Figure 8.18 Matlab code for implementing the Vega for geometric Brownian motion for European Call and Put options

following formulae have to be implemented:

$$\text{Greek}^{PW}_{S(0)} = \exp(-rT)\frac{\bar{S}(T)}{S(0)}1_{\{\bar{S}(T)>K\}} \tag{8.35}$$

$$\text{Greek}^{PW}_{\sigma_{BS}} = \exp(-rT)\frac{1}{\sigma_{BS}N}\sum_{i=1}^{N}\left(\log\left(\frac{S(t_i)}{S(0)}\right) - r + \frac{\sigma_{BS}^2}{2}T\right)\cdot\bar{S}(T)1_{\{\bar{S}(T)>K\}}. \tag{8.36}$$

The implementation does depend heavily on the chosen discretization. The discrete set t_i, $i = 1,\ldots,N$ therefore has to be known.

Example: Black–Scholes Spread Option

An example of an option with payoff depending on more than one underlying is a spread option with strike K. It has payoff $\max(S_2(T) - S_1(T) - K, 0)$. Since it depends on two assets we have two first order sensitivities. The sensitivities are calculated with respect to the initial spot values $S_1(0)$ and $S_2(0)$:

$$\text{Greek}^{PW}_{S_1(0)} = \exp(-rT)\frac{S_2(T)}{S_2(0)}1_{\{S_2(T)-S_1(T)>K\}}, \tag{8.37}$$

$$\text{Greek}^{PW}_{S_2(0)} = \exp(-rT)\frac{S_1(T)}{S_1(0)}1_{\{S_2(T)-S_1(T)>K\}}. \tag{8.38}$$

The implementation is easy once the necessary derivatives have been calculated.

8.3.3   The Affine Recursion Problem (ARP)

All the results in this section are based on Nowakcyk, N. and Kienitz, J. (2011), Giles, M. and Glasserman, P. (2006) and Leclerc, M., Liang, Q. and Schneider, I (2009).

To state the *Affine Recursion Problem (ARP)* we assume we are given the data $N, m, q \in \mathbb{N}$ and for any $n = 1, \ldots, N - 1$

$$A_1 \in \mathbb{R}^{m \times q}, \qquad D(n) \in \mathbb{R}^{m \times m}, \qquad C(n) \in \mathbb{R}^{m \times q}, \qquad v \in \mathbb{R}^{1 \times m}. \tag{8.39}$$

We use the following notation, A_0 is the initial matrix, $D(n)$ the factor matrices, $C(n)$ the translation matrices and v the start vector. Assume that $A(n) \in \mathbb{R}^{m \times q}$ is a sequence of matrices satisfying the *forward recursion*

$$\forall 1 \leq n \leq N - 1 : A(n + 1) = B(n)A(n) + C(n), \qquad A(1) = A_1. \tag{8.40}$$

The calculation of the result vector w

$$w := vA(N) \in \mathbb{R}^{1 \times q} \tag{8.41}$$

is called the Affine Recursion Problem or just an ARP. We say A is the *recursing matrix*, A_1 is the *initial matrix*, D are the *factors factor matrix*, C are the *translations translation matrix*, v is the *start vector* and v is the *result vector* of the ARP defined by the data (8.39).

The *forward method* can be specified by considering any ARP. In fact, for all $1 \leq n \leq N$ we find

$$A(n) = \left(\sum_{j=1}^{n-1} \left(\prod_{k=1}^{j-1} D(n-k) \right) C(n-j) \right) + \left(\prod_{j=1}^{n-1} D(n-j) \right) A_1. \tag{8.42}$$

Consequently

$$w = vA(N) = \left(\sum_{j=1}^{N-1} v \left(\prod_{k=1}^{j-1} D(N-k) \right) C(N-j) \right) + v \left(\prod_{j=1}^{N-1} D(N-j) \right) A_1. \tag{8.43}$$

We verify (8.42) using induction over n. In case $n = 1$ we have

$$A(1) = \left(\sum_{j=1}^{0} \left(\prod_{k=1}^{j-1} D(1-k) \right) C(1-j) \right) + \left(\prod_{j=1}^{0} D(n-j) \right) A_1 = A_1$$

and for general n we compute

$$A(n+1) = \left(\sum_{j=1}^{n} \left(\prod_{k=1}^{j-1} D(n+1-k) \right) C(n+1-j) \right) + \left(\prod_{j=1}^{n} D(n+1-j) \right) A_1$$

$$= C(n) + \left(\sum_{j=2}^{n} \left(\prod_{k=1}^{j-1} D(n-(k-1)) \right) C(n-(j-1)) \right)$$

$$+ \left(\prod_{j=1}^{n} D(n-(j-1)) \right) A_1$$

$$= C(n) + \left(\sum_{j=1}^{n-1} \left(D(n) \prod_{k=2}^{j} D(n-(k-1)) \right) C(n-j) \right)$$

$$+ B(n) \left(\prod_{j=2}^{n} D(n - (j - 1))) \right) A_1$$

$$= C(n) + \left(D(n) \sum_{j=1}^{n-1} \left(\prod_{k=1}^{j-1} D(n - k)) \right) C(n - j)) \right)$$

$$+ B(n) \left(\prod_{j=2}^{n} D(n - (j - 1))) \right) A_1$$

$$= C(n) + D(n)A(n).$$

A straightforward algorithm to calculate w would be to implement the forward recursion (8.40). The computational cost of calculating $A(n + 1)$ from $A(n)$ is the matrix multiplication $D(n)A(n)$ and the matrix addition $D(n)A(n) + C(n)$. A naive implementation of a matrix multiplication has complexity $\mathcal{O}(m^3)$ and the matrix addition has complexity $\mathcal{O}(m^2)$, which is therefore negligible. Since we have to calculate $N - 1$ of these recursions to obtain $A(N)$ and a final matrix-vector multiplication $A(N)v$ (which has complexity $\mathcal{O}(m^2)$ and is also negligible), the total computational cost to calculate w is in $\mathcal{O}(Nm^3)$, which is considerable. We call this method of calculating w the *forward method*. Its implementation in Matlab is given in Figure 8.19.

8.3.4 Adjoint Method

Due to the high computational cost of the forward method, we now develop an alternative approach.

The vectors $V(n) \in \mathbb{R}^{m \times 1}$ are called the *adjoint vector sequence* and they are defined by

$$V(n) := D(n)^\top V(n + 1), \qquad V(N) := v^\top, \tag{8.44}$$

and called the *sequence adjoint to the ARP*.

The vectors $\overline{V}(n) \in \mathbb{R}^{q \times 1}$ defined by

$$\overline{V}(n) := C(n)^\top V(n + 1) + \overline{V}(n + 1), \qquad \overline{V}(N) := 0, \tag{8.45}$$

```
function [w A] = forward(A1, B, C, v)
%Forward method
    [m, q, N] = size(C);          %calculate dimensions
    N = N+1;
    A = zeros(m,q,N);             %initialize A
    A(:,:,1)=A1;
    for n = 1:N-1                 %run forward recursion
        A(:,:,n+1) = B(:,:,n)*A(:,:,n) + C(:,:,n);
    end
    w = v * A(:,:,N);             %calculate result
end
```

Figure 8.19   General forward method

$(\overline{V}(n))_n$ is the total adjoint vector sequence and we call it the *total adjoint sequence* of the ARP described in Subsection 8.3.3. The importance of these definitions becomes clear in the next section when we consider the adjoint method to solve the calculation of Greeks.

Adjoint Method

The result vector of the ARP is given by

$$w = vA(N) = \sum_{n=1}^{N-1} V(n+1)^\mathsf{T} C(n) + V(1)^\mathsf{T} A_1 = \overline{V}(1)^\mathsf{T} + V(1)^\mathsf{T} A_1. \tag{8.46}$$

The sequences $V(n)$ and $\overline{V}(n)$ are explicitly given by

$$\forall 1 \le n \le N : V(n) = \left(\prod_{k=n}^{N-1} D(k)^\mathsf{T} \right) v^\mathsf{T}, \tag{8.47}$$

$$\forall 1 \le n \le N : \overline{V}(n) = \sum_{j=n}^{N-1} C(j)^\mathsf{T} V(j+1). \tag{8.48}$$

The Equations (8.47) and (8.48) follow directly from the definition. To prove the claim, we calculate w^T instead of w. This approach is the key idea for applying this method. Using re-indexation, we obtain

$$w^\mathsf{T} = \left(\sum_{j=1}^{N-1} C(N-j)^\mathsf{T} \left(\prod_{k=1}^{j-1} D(N-k) \right)^\mathsf{T} v^\mathsf{T} \right) + A_1^\mathsf{T} \left(\prod_{j=1}^{N-1} D(N-j) \right)^\mathsf{T} v^\mathsf{T}$$

$$= \left(\sum_{j=1}^{N-1} C(N-j)^\mathsf{T} \left(\prod_{k=N-j+1}^{N-1} D(k)^\mathsf{T} \right) v^\mathsf{T} \right) + A_1^\mathsf{T} \left(\prod_{j=1}^{N-1} D(j)^\mathsf{T} \right) v^\mathsf{T}$$

$$= \left(\sum_{n=1}^{N-1} C(n)^\mathsf{T} \left(\prod_{k=n+1}^{N-1} D(k)^\mathsf{T} \right) v^\mathsf{T} \right) + A_1^\mathsf{T} \left(\prod_{j=1}^{N-1} D(j)^\mathsf{T} \right) v^\mathsf{T}.$$

$$= \left(\sum_{n=1}^{N-1} C(n)^\mathsf{T} V(n+1) \right) + A_1^\mathsf{T} V(1)$$

$$= \overline{V}(1) + A_1^\mathsf{T} V(1). \tag{8.49}$$

Consequently, we find

$$w = (w^\mathsf{T})^\mathsf{T} = \overline{V}(1)^\mathsf{T} + V(1)^\mathsf{T} A_1.$$

The implementation of the adjoint method in Matlab is also straightforward and is given in Figure 8.20.

The tremendous numerical advantage of the adjoint method is the fact that (8.44) and (8.45) are vector recursions, where (8.40) is a matrix recursion. Therefore, the computational cost of calculating all the $V(n)$ and $\overline{V}(n)$ is of complexity $\mathcal{O}(Nm^2)$, which also is the complexity of the entire algorithm. The corresponding code runs significantly faster than the forward method, which has complexity $\mathcal{O}(Nm^3)$.

```
function w = adjoint(A1, D, C, v)
%Adjoint method
    [m, q, N] = size(C);      %calculate dimensions
    N = N+1;
    V=v.';                    %initialize V
    Vbar = zeros(q,1);        %initialize Vbar
    for n = N-1:-1:1          %run backward recursion
        Vbar = Vbar + C(:,:,n).' * V;
        V = D(:,:,n).' * V;
    end
    w = Vbar.' + V.' * A1;    %calculate result
end
```

Figure 8.20 General adjoint method

The name *adjoint method* stems from the following fact: if $f : V \to V$ is a linear map on an n-dimensional $\mathbb{R}$ vector space with inner product $\langle \cdot, \cdot \rangle$, the coordinate matrix $c_B(f^*)$ of the adjoint map f^* is defined by the relation

$$\langle f(v), w \rangle = \langle v, f^*(w) \rangle, \text{ for all } x, y \in V$$

with respect to a basis $B = (b_1, \ldots, b_n)$. The value $c_B(f^*)$ is related to $c_B(f)$ by

$$c_B(f^*) = c_B(f)^\top.$$

We do not need this algebraic context for our practical purposes. We only need the transpose operation, so we might equally well call this method the *transpose method*.

The Matlab implementations given for the forward and the adjoint method are of a most general type. For practical applications we sometimes get a better performance if we adapt the algorithms to the specific situation at hand. We illustrate the method for several examples later.

8.3.5 Bermudan ARPs

In this subsection we adapt the general adjoint method to a case that is only slightly more special and is needed for the application to calculate the Greeks of Bermudan swaptions. We consider Bermudan swaptions, and we see in (8.4) that they have a payoff function, which is given as a sum of payoffs. For financial applications of the adjoint method it might be more instructive to skip this subsection and come back to it later as and when needed. The ARP is *Bermudan with start index e* start index, if there exists $1 \le e \le N$ such that for all $e \le \mu \le N$ it exists

$$v_{(\mu)} \in \mathbb{R}^{1 \times m},$$

such that

$$w = vA(N) = \sum_{\mu=e}^{N} v_{(\mu)} A(\mu). \tag{8.50}$$

From a formal point of view any ARP is Bermudan with start index $e := N$, but this way of thinking is not helpful when aiming at a practical implementation.

Assume that the ARP is Bermudan with start index e. For any $e \le \mu \le N$ we think of $v_{(\mu)}$ as the new start vector of a recursion with the same matrices, that is for all $1 \le n \le \mu$

$$A^{(\mu)}(n+1) = D^{(\mu)}(n)A^{(\mu)}(n) + C^{(\mu)}(n), \qquad A^{(\mu)}(1) = A_1^{(\mu)},$$

and for any $1 \le n \le \mu$,

$$A^{(\mu)}(n) = A(n), \ D^{(\mu)}(n) = D(n), \ C^{(\mu)}(n) = C(n), \ A_1^{(\mu)} = A_1.$$

Let $V^{(\mu)}$ be vector sequence adjoint to recursion, that is

$$\forall 1 \le n \le \mu - 1 : V^{(\mu)}(n) = D(n)^\mathsf{T} V^{(\mu)}(n+1), \qquad V^{(\mu)}(\mu) = v_{(\mu)}, \tag{8.51}$$

and let $\overline{V}^{(\mu)}$ be the total adjoint vector sequence of this recursion, we have

$$\forall 1 \le n \le \mu - 1 : \overline{V}^{(\mu)}(n) := C(n)^\mathsf{T} V^{(\mu)}(n+1) + \overline{V}^{(\mu)}(n+1),$$
$$\overline{V}^{(\mu)}(\mu) := 0. \tag{8.52}$$

Then

$$w = \overline{W}(1)^\mathsf{T} + W(1)^\mathsf{T} A_1, \tag{8.53}$$

where $W(n) \in \mathbb{R}^{m \times 1}, \overline{W}(n) \in \mathbb{R}^{q \times 1}$ are the sequence of vectors defined by

$$W(n) := \sum_{\mu = \max(n,e)}^{N} V^{(\mu)}(n),$$

$$\overline{W}(n) := \sum_{\mu = \max(n,e)}^{N} \overline{V}^{(\mu)}(n). \tag{8.54}$$

These sequences satisfy the backward recursions

$$W(N) := v_{(N)}^\mathsf{T},$$
$$\forall r \le n \le N - 1 : W(n) := D(n)^\mathsf{T} W(n+1) + v_{(n)}^\mathsf{T},$$
$$\forall 1 \le n \le e - 1 : W(n) := D(n)^\mathsf{T} W(n+1), \tag{8.55}$$
$$\overline{W}(N) := 0,$$
$$\forall 1 \le n \le N - 1 : \overline{W}(n) := C(n)^\mathsf{T} W(n+1) + \overline{W}(n+1).$$

First we verify that (8.54) satisfies (8.55). By definition

$$W(N) = V^{(N)}(N) = v_N^\mathsf{T},$$
$$\overline{W}(N) = \overline{V}^{(N)}(N) = 0.$$

For any $e \le n \le N - 1$

$$W(n) = \sum_{\mu = n}^{N} V^{(\mu)}(n) = \sum_{\mu = n+1}^{N} V^{(\mu)}(n) + V^{(n)}(n)$$

$$= \sum_{\mu = n+1}^{N} D(n)^\mathsf{T} V^{(\mu)}(n+1) + V^{(n)}(n) = D(n)^\mathsf{T} W(n+1) + v_{(n)}^\mathsf{T}$$

and

$$\overline{W}(n) = \sum_{\mu=n}^{N} \overline{V}^{(\mu)}(n) = \sum_{\mu=n+1}^{N} C(n)^{\top} V^{(\mu)}(n+1) + \overline{V}^{(\mu)}(n+1)$$

$$= C(n)^{\top} \sum_{\mu=n+1}^{N} V^{(\mu)}(n+1) + \sum_{\mu=n+1}^{N} \overline{V}^{(\mu)}(n+1)$$

$$= C(n)^{\top} W(n+1) + \overline{W}(n+1).$$

In a similar fashion, for any $1 \le n \le e - 1$, we obtain

$$W(n) = \sum_{\mu=e}^{N} V^{(\mu)}(n) = \sum_{\mu=e}^{N} D(n)^{\top} V^{(\mu)}(n+1) = D(n)^{\top} W(n+1)$$

and

$$\overline{W}(n) = \sum_{\mu=e}^{N} \overline{V}^{(\mu)}(n) = \sum_{\mu=e}^{N} C(n)^{\top} V^{(\mu)}(n+1) + \overline{V}^{(\mu)}(n+1)$$

$$= C(n)^{\top} W(n+1) + \overline{W}(n+1).$$

Now we calculate

$$w = \sum_{\mu=e}^{N} v_{(\mu)} A(\mu) = \sum_{\mu=e}^{N} \overline{V}^{(\mu)}(1)^{\top} + V^{(\mu)}(1)^{\top} A_1 = \overline{W}(1)^{\top} + W(1)^{\top} A_1.$$

The sequences $W(n)$ and $\overline{W}(n)$ defined by (8.54) are the *Bermudan sequence* and the *total Bermudan sequence* of the ARP respectively.

Notice that this definition makes sense only for Bermudan ARPs. Also notice that the Bermudan sequence and the total Bermudan sequence have strong formal similarities to the sequence adjoint to the ARP and the total adjoint sequence. Nevertheless, the sequences themselves are not equal (unless in trivial cases), although they lead to the same numerical result.

Finally, we provide a criterion to verify that an ARP is Bermudan. Condition (8.50) is satisfied, if

$$v = \sum_{\mu=e}^{N} v_{(\mu)}, \qquad (8.56)$$

$$\forall e \le \mu \le N : \forall \mu + 1 \le i \le m : v_{(\mu)}^{i} = 0, \qquad (8.57)$$

$$\forall e \le \mu \le N : \forall 1 \le j \le m : \forall 1 \le i \le \mu : A_{ij}(N) = A_{ij}(\mu). \qquad (8.58)$$

We find by some algebra

$$w = v A(N) = \sum_{\mu=e}^{N} v_{(\mu)} A(N)$$

$$= \sum_{\mu=e}^{N} \sum_{j=1}^{q} (v_{(\mu)} A(N))_j e_j = \sum_{\mu=e}^{N} \sum_{j=1}^{q} \sum_{i=1}^{m} v_{(\mu)}^{i} A_{ij}(N) e_j$$

```
function w = adjoint_summation(A1, B, C, V, r)
%Adjoint Summation method
    [m, q, N] = size(C);        %calculate dimensions
    N = N+1;
    W = V(N,:).';               %initialize W
    Wbar = zeros(q,1);          %initialize Wbar

    for n = N-1:-1:r            %run backward recursion
        Wbar = Wbar + C(:,:,n).' * W;
        W = B(:,:,n).' * W + V(n,:).';
    end
    for n = r-1:-1:1
        Wbar = Wbar + C(:,:,n).' * W;
        W = B(:,:,n).' * W;
    end

    w = Wbar.' + W.' * A1;      %calculate result
end
```

Figure 8.21   Bermudan adjoint method

$$= \sum_{\mu=e}^{N} \sum_{j=1}^{q} \sum_{i=1}^{\mu} v_{(\mu)}^i A_{ij}(N) e_j = \sum_{\mu=e}^{N} \sum_{j=1}^{q} \sum_{i=1}^{\mu} v_{(\mu)}^i A_{ij}(\mu) e_j$$

$$= \sum_{\mu=e}^{N} v_{(\mu)} A(\mu).$$

These calculations lead to the algorithm described in Figure 8.21. We refer to this technique as the *Bermudan adjoint method*.

In the source code selection the reader will find applications of the adjoint method to a Trigger swap, but we do not describe the implementation here in detail.

8.4 EULER SCHEMES AND GENERAL GREEKS

In this section we briefly recapitulate the definition of diffusion processes and discuss how they are approximated by Euler schemes. The main difference here is that we work in a multidimensional setting. The primary purpose of this is merely to fix notation. The treatment of these topics is close to Giles, M. and Glasserman, P. (2006).

8.4.1 SDE of Diffusions

Let $(\Omega, \mathcal{F}, \mathbb{P})$ be a probability space equipped with a filtration $(\mathcal{F}_t)_t$ and let

$$\tilde{X} : \Omega \times \mathbb{R}_{\geq 0} \to \mathbb{R}^m$$

be a stochastic process adapted to the filtration $(\mathcal{F}_t)_t$. Assume that X is a *diffusion*, that is it satisfies the stochastic differential equation

$$d\tilde{X}_t = a(\tilde{X}_t, t)dt + b(\tilde{X}_t, t)dW(t), \tag{8.59}$$

where $a \in C^2(\mathbb{R}^m \times \mathbb{R}_{\geq 0}, \mathbb{R}^m)$ is the *drift*, $b \in C^2(\mathbb{R}^m \times \mathbb{R}_{\geq 0}, \mathbb{R}^{m \times d})$ is the *diffusion matrix* and W is a d-dimensional Brownian motion. Sometimes $a = a(y, \sigma)$ and $b = b(y, \sigma)$ also depend (differentiable) on a set of parameters $\sigma \in \mathbb{R}^q$. Here we think of X as being forward Libor rates and of σ as volatilities.

In addition, assume that $T > 0$ and that g is a function $g \in C^2(\mathbb{R}^m, \mathbb{R})$. We abbreviate its derivatives by considering $1 \leq j \leq m$

$$\partial_j(g) := \frac{\partial g}{\partial y_j}.$$

Consider the quantity

$$\tilde{p} := E[g(\tilde{X}_T)]. \tag{8.60}$$

For instance, g could be the discounted payoff of a derivative at time T, with underlying X. Then, $\tilde{p}$ is the fair price of that derivative.

The quantity $\tilde{p}$ can be thought of as a function of a lot of variables, namely $\tilde{X}_i(1)$, $i = 1, \ldots, m$ and σ. The derivatives

$$\tilde{\Delta} := \nabla_{\tilde{X}(1)}(\tilde{p}) \in \mathbb{R}^m,$$
$$\tilde{\Gamma} := \text{Hess}_{\tilde{X}(1)}(\tilde{p}) \in \mathbb{R}^{m \times m}, \tag{8.61}$$
$$\widetilde{\text{Vega}} := \nabla_{\sigma}(\tilde{p}) \in \mathbb{R}^m,$$

called *Delta*, *Gamma* and *Vega*, are the Greeks of $\tilde{p}$.

8.4.2 Approximation by Euler Schemes

We would like to develop a numerical framework to calculate approximations of $\tilde{p}$ in (8.60) and the Greeks in (8.61).

Choose any *time grid* $0 = T_1 < \ldots < T_N = T$ and define $\tau_n := T_{n+1} - T_n$, $n = 1, \ldots, N - 1$. For $1 \leq n \leq N - 1$ any sequence

$$X(n+1) := F_n(X(n), \sigma), \qquad X(1) := \tilde{X}_{T_1} = \tilde{X}_0, \tag{8.62}$$

where

$$F_n : \mathbb{R}^m \times \mathbb{R}^q \to \mathbb{R}^m$$
$$(y, \sigma) \mapsto F_n(y, \sigma)$$

is a C^2-map, is an *approximation to X*. We say (8.62) is the *evolution equation*.

We choose F_n in a way such that $X(n) \approx \tilde{X}(T_n)$. One standard choice is the *Euler scheme*, that is

$$F_n(y, \sigma) := y + a(y, \sigma)\tau_n + b(y, \sigma)Z(n+1)\sqrt{\tau_n}, \tag{8.63}$$

where $Z(n+1) \in \mathbb{R}^d$ is a sequence of random vectors following a standard normal distribution.

8.4.3 Approximating General Greeks Using ARP

We develop algorithms to approximate the Greeks Δ, Γ and Vega. The general idea is to express them as the result of an ARP and apply the general theory. We describe the objects of primary interest in what follows.

Let X be an approximation of $\tilde{X}$. Then, $p := g(X(N))$ is an approximation of $\tilde{p}$. The quantity p is a function of $X_i(n)$, $i = 1, \ldots, m$, $n = 1, \ldots, N-1$ and σ.

The derivatives

$$\Delta := \nabla_{X(1)}(p) \in \mathbb{R}^{1 \times m},$$

$$\Gamma := \text{Hess}_{X(1)}(p) \in \mathbb{R}^{m \times m},$$

$$\text{Vega} := \nabla_{\sigma}(p) \in \mathbb{R}^{1 \times q},$$

are the *approximated Greeks*.

In what follows we consider the application of the adjoint method to Bermudan swaptions in a Libor Market Model. Recall that the aim is to provide not an efficient implementation of a Libor Market Model but the application of the adjoint method.

Delta

First, we consider the Δ computed by adjoint techniques. To apply the general framework we have to specify the matrices in this case. The approximated Δ is given as the result vector

$$\Delta = v\Delta(N) \tag{8.64}$$

of an ARP with matrix recursion using $\Delta(n)$ as the recursing matrix, $D(n)$ as the factor matrix and the rule. For all $1 \leq n \leq N-1$ we have

$$\Delta(n+1) = D(n)\Delta(n), \qquad \Delta(1) = I, \tag{8.65}$$

The recursing matrix $\Delta(n)$ for $1 \leq i, j \leq m$, $1 \leq n \leq N$ is defined by

$$\Delta_{ij}(n) := \frac{\partial X_i(n)}{\partial X_j(1)}.$$

The factor matrix D is defined by

$$D_{ik}(n) := \frac{\partial F_n^i}{\partial y_k}(X(n), \sigma). \tag{8.66}$$

Finally, the start vector is defined by

$$v := \nabla g(X(N)) \in \mathbb{R}^{1 \times m}.$$

If $\tilde{X}$ is approximated using an Euler scheme (8.63) we have

$$D_{ik}(n) = \delta_{ik} + \partial_k(a_i)(X(n), \sigma)\tau_n + \sum_{l=1}^{d} \partial_k(b_{il})(X(n), \sigma)Z_l(n+1)\sqrt{\tau_n}.$$

Consequently, if V is the vector sequence adjoint to this recursion, that is

$$\forall 1 \leq n \leq N-1 : V(n) := D(n)^{\mathsf{T}}V(n+1), \qquad V(N) := \nabla g(X(N))^{\mathsf{T}},$$

the Δ can be calculated by using

$$\Delta = V(1)^{\mathsf{T}}.$$

Equation (8.64) is an application of the chain rule. Since by definition

$$X(n+1) = F_n(X(n), \sigma)$$

```
function Delta = adjoint_delta(D, v)
%calculates the delta using adjoint method
    m = size(D,1);                    %calculate dimensions
    N = size(D,3)+1;
    V=v.';                            %initialize V
    for n = N-1:-1:1                   %run backward recursion
        V = D(:,:,n).' * V;
    end
    Delta = V.';                      %return result
end
```

Figure 8.22 Calculating Δ using the adjoint method

applying the chain rule leads to

$$\Delta_{ij}(n) = \frac{\partial X_i(n+1)}{\partial X_j(1)} = \frac{\partial}{\partial X_j(1)}(F_n(X(n),\sigma))$$

$$= \sum_{k=1}^{m} \frac{\partial F_n^i}{\partial y_k}(X(n),\sigma)\frac{\partial X_k(n)}{\partial X_j(1)} = \sum_{k=1}^{m} D_{ik}(n)\Delta_{kj}(n) = (D(n)\Delta(n))_{ij}.$$

In the case of an Euler scheme we differentiate (8.63) to calculate $D_{ik}(n)$.

The claim concerning V follows from Equation (8.46), since all the translations in the matrix recursion (8.65) are zero and $\Delta(1)$ is the identity matrix.

We use the adjoint method to implement the calculation of Δ in Matlab as shown in Figure 8.22 and we give an implementation of the forward calculation of all $\Delta(n)$ in Figure 8.23.

Gamma

The second derivative with respect to the inital rates is the Γ. The application of the adjoint method is not straightforward and one application of the forward method is needed. Furthermore, we have to smooth the payoff since differentiating twice leads to a function with jumps.

```
function [w Delta] = forward_delta(D, v)
%Calculates the Delta using forward method
    m = size(D,1);                    %calculate dimensions
    N = size(D,3)+1;
    Delta = zeros(m,m,N);             %initialize Delta
    Delta(:,:,1)=eye(m);
    for n = 1:N-1                     %run forward recursion
        Delta(:,:,n+1) = D(:,:,n)*Delta(:,:,n);
    end
    w = v * Delta(:,:,N);             %calculate result
end
```

Figure 8.23 Calculating all $\Delta(n)$ using the forward method

Table 8.4   Symbols used in the sequel and their meaning

Symbol	Explanation
$G^{(j)}(n)$	recursing matrix
$E^{(i)}(n)$	parameter matrix
$C^{(j)}(n)$	translation matrix
H	Hessian of the payoff

For any $1 \leq i, j, k \leq m$, $1 \leq n \leq N$, define the following scalar quantities:

$$\Delta_{ij}(n) := \frac{\partial X_i(n)}{\partial X_j(1)}, \qquad D_{ik}(n) := \frac{\partial F_n^i}{\partial y_k}(X(n), \sigma),$$

$$G_{ik}^{(j)}(n) := \frac{\partial^2 X_i(n)}{\partial X_j(1)\partial X_k(1)} \qquad E_{jk}^{(i)}(n) := \partial_{jk}(F_n^i)(X(n), \sigma),$$

$$C_{ik}^{(j)}(n) := (\Delta(n)^\top E^{(i)}(n)^\top \Delta(n))_{kj}, \quad H_{ij} := \partial_{ij}(g)(X(N)).$$

We used the notation in Table 8.4.

This defines matrices $\Delta(n)$, $D(n)$, $G^{(j)}(n)$, $E^{(i)}(n)$, $C^{(j)}(n)$, $H \in \mathbb{R}^{m\times m}$ having certain properties which we summarize now.

1. For any $1 \leq j \leq m$ the matrices $G^{(j)}(n)$ for $1 \leq n \leq N - 1$ satisfy the recursion

$$G^{(j)}(n + 1) = D(n)G^{(j)}(n) + C^{(j)}(n), \qquad G^{(j)}(1) = 0. \tag{8.67}$$

2. Let

$$v := \nabla(g)(X(N)) \in \mathbb{R}^{1\times m} \tag{8.68}$$

be a start vector and let $U^{(j)}(n) \in \mathbb{R}^{m\times 1}$ be the vector sequences adjoint to these recursions. Then the corresponding result vectors $w_{(j)}$ are given by

$$w_{(j)} = vG^{(j)}(N) = \sum_{n=1}^{N-1} U^{(j)}(n + 1)^\top C^{(j)}(n) = \overline{U}^{(j)}(1)^\top \in \mathbb{R}^{1\times m}. \tag{8.69}$$

Let $w \in \mathbb{R}^{m\times m}$ be the matrix whose rows are formed by the $w_{(j)}$.
3. The matrices $\Delta(n)$ for $1 \leq n \leq N - 1$ satisfy the recursion

$$\Delta(n + 1) = D(n)\Delta(n), \qquad \Delta(1) = I.$$

4. Let $Y := \Delta(N)^\top H \Delta(N) \in \mathbb{R}^{m\times m}$. Then the Gamma is given by

$$\Gamma = w + Y.$$

5. Where F_n is an Euler scheme we have

$$E^i_{jk}(n) = \partial_{jk}(a_i)(X(n), \sigma)\tau_n + \sum_{l=1}^{d} \partial_{jk}(b_{il})(X(n), \sigma)Z_l(n + 1)\sqrt{\tau_n}.$$

1. Notice that $\Delta(n)$, $D(n)$ and v are the same as in Subsection 8.4.3. Therefore, using the results obtained there, we obtain

$$G_{ik}^{(j)}(n+1) = \frac{\partial}{\partial X_k(1)}\left(\frac{\partial}{\partial X_j(1)}X_i(n+1)\right) = \frac{\partial}{\partial X_k(1)}\left(\Delta_{ij}(n+1)\right)$$

$$= \frac{\partial}{\partial X_k(1)}\left((D(n)\Delta(n))_{ij}\right) = \sum_{s=1}^{m}\frac{\partial}{\partial X_k(1)}\left(D_{is}(n)\Delta_{sj}(n)\right)$$

$$= \sum_{s=1}^{m}\frac{\partial}{\partial X_k(1)}\left(D_{is}(n)\right)\Delta_{sj}(n) + D_{is}(n)\frac{\partial}{\partial X_k(1)}\left(\Delta_{sj}(n)\right)$$

$$= \sum_{s=1}^{m}\frac{\partial}{\partial X_k(1)}\left(\frac{\partial F_n^i}{\partial y_s}(X(n),\sigma)\right)\Delta_{sj}(n) + \sum_{s=1}^{m}D_{is}(n)G_{sk}^{(j)}$$

$$= \underbrace{\sum_{s=1}^{m}\sum_{t=1}^{m}E_{st}^{(i)}(n)\Delta_{tk}(n)\Delta_{sj}(n)}_{=:(*)} + (D(n)G^{(j)})_{ik} \qquad (8.70)$$

and

$$(*) = \sum_{s=1}^{m}(E^{(i)}(n)\Delta(n))_{sk}\Delta_{sj}(n) = \sum_{s=1}^{m}(\Delta(n)^{\top}E^{(i)}(n)^{\top})_{ks}\Delta_{sj}(n)$$

$$= (\Delta(n)^{\top}E^{(i)}(n)^{\top}\Delta(n))_{kj} = C_{ik}^{(j)}$$

since

$$G_{ik}^{j}(1) = \frac{\partial^2 X_i(1)}{\partial X_j(1)\partial X_k(1)} = \frac{\partial}{\partial X_j(1)}(\delta_{ik}) = 0.$$

Thus, we find Equation (8.67).
2. If the $U^{(j)}(n)$ are the vector sequences adjoint to the recursions (8.67) with start vector v, the result vectors $w^{(j)}$ are given by (8.69) as proven in (8.46).
3. This was already proven in Subsection 8.4.3.
4. For any $1 \leq j, k \leq m$:

$$\Gamma_{jk} = \frac{\partial^2(g(X(N)))}{\partial X_j(1)\partial X_k(1)} = \frac{\partial}{\partial X_j(1)}\left(\sum_{i=1}^{m}\partial_i(g)(X(N))\frac{\partial X_i(N)}{\partial X_k(1)}\right)$$

$$= \sum_{i=1}^{m}\frac{\partial}{\partial X_j(1)}(\partial_i(g)(X(N)))\Delta_{ik}(N) + \sum_{i=1}^{m}\partial_i(g)(X(N))\frac{\partial^2 X_i(N)}{\partial X_j(1)\partial X_k(1)}$$

$$= \sum_{i=1}^{m}\sum_{l=1}^{m}\partial_{li}(g)(X(N))\Delta_{lj}(N)\Delta_{ik}(N) + \sum_{i=1}^{m}v_i G_{ik}^{(j)}(N)$$

$$= \sum_{l=1}^{m}\sum_{i=1}^{m}H_{il}\Delta_{ij}(N)\Delta_{lk}(N) + (vG^{(j)}(N))_k$$

$$= \sum_{l=1}^{m} (H^\top \Delta(N))_{lj} \Delta_{lk}(N) + w_k^{(j)}$$

$$= (\Delta(N)^\top H \Delta(N))_{jk} + w_k^{(j)}$$

$$= Y_{jk} + w_{jk}. \tag{8.71}$$

5. We calculate

$$E^i_{jk}(n) = \partial_{jk}(F^i_n)(X(n), \sigma)$$

$$= \partial_j \left(\delta_{ik} + \partial_k(a)\tau_n + \sum_{l=1}^{d} \partial_k(b^i)Z_l(n+1)\sqrt{\tau_n} \right)(X(n), \sigma)$$

$$= \partial_{jk}(a)(X(n), \sigma)\tau_n + \sum_{l=1}^{d} \partial_{jk}(b^i)(X(n), \sigma)Z_l(n+1)\sqrt{\tau_n}.$$

Expressing Γ as a solution to an ARP is unfortunately more difficult than the Δ. There are two reasons for this. On the one hand, the matrix $\Delta(N)$ is necessary to calculate Y and, on the other, the calculation of the $C^{(j)}$ requires all the matrices $\Delta(n)$. To this end we have to use the forward method to calculate $\Delta(n)$.

If we wish to calculate Γ and Δ, we get the Δ as a by-product of calculating Γ. The vectors $w_{(j)}$ are calculated using the Bermudan adjoint method. This yields the following Matlab implementation presented in Figure 8.24. The function adjoint_noA1 is the same as adjoint, but it assumes that $A_1 = 0$.

```
function Gamma = adjoint_gamma (D, E, H, v)
%Calculates the Gamma using adjoint and forward methods

    m = size(D,1);                          %read dimensions
    N = size(D,3)+1;

    [w, Delta] = forward_delta(D,v);        %calculate forward Delta
    Y = Delta(:,:,N).' * H * Delta(:,:,N);  %calculate Y
    Gamma = Y;

    C = zeros(m,m,m,N-1);                   %build C
    for n = 1:N-1
        for i = 1:m
            C(i,:,:,n) = Delta(:,:,n).'  * E(:,:,i,n).' * Delta(:,:,n);
        end
    end

    W = zeros(m,m);                         %calculate W

    for j = 1:m
        W(j,:) = adjoint_noA1(D,squeeze(C(:,:,j,:)),v);
    end
    Gamma = Gamma + W;                      %calculate Gamma
end
```

Figure 8.24 Calculating Γ using adjoint and forward methods

Vega

The last application of the adjoint method we propose is the calculation of Vega. For $1 \le i \le m, 1 \le j \le q, 1 \le n \le N$ define

$$\text{Vega}_{ij}(n) := \frac{\partial X_i(n)}{\partial \sigma_j}$$

with Vega(n) being the recursing matrix and $B(n)$ the translation matrix.

1. Then Vega$(n) \in \mathbb{R}^{m \times q}$ satisfies the recursion

$$\text{Vega}(n+1) = D(n)\text{Vega}(n) + B(n), \qquad \text{Vega}(1) = 0,$$

where $D(n)$ is defined by (8.66) and for $1 \le i \le m; 1 \le j \le q; 1 \le n \le N-1$

$$B_{ij}(n) := \frac{\partial F_n^i}{\partial \sigma_j}(X(n), \sigma).$$

2. Let $V(n)$ be the sequence adjoint to this recursion with start vector

$$v = \nabla(g)(X(N)).$$

and $\overline{V}(n)$ be the total adjoint sequence. Then,

$$\text{Vega} = v\text{Vega}(N) = \sum_{n=1}^{N-1} V(n+1)^\top B(n) = \overline{V}(1)^\top.$$

3. In case F_n is an Euler scheme

$$B_{ij}(n) = \frac{\partial a^i}{\partial \sigma_j}(X(n), \sigma)\tau_n + \sum_{l=1}^{d} \frac{\partial b_{li}}{\partial \sigma_j}(X(n), \sigma)Z_l(n+1)\sqrt{\tau_n}.$$

1. Again using the evolution Equation (8.62), we obtain

$$\text{Vega}_{ij}(n+1) = \frac{\partial}{\partial \sigma_j}(X_i(n+1)) = \frac{\partial}{\partial \sigma_j}\left(F_n^i(X(n), \sigma)\right)$$

$$= \sum_{k=1}^{m} \partial_k(F_n^i)(X(n), \sigma)\frac{\partial X_k(n)}{\partial \sigma_j} + \frac{\partial F_n^i}{\partial \sigma_j}(X(n), \sigma)$$

$$= \sum_{k=1}^{m} D_{ik}(n)\text{Vega}_{kj}(n) + B_{ij}(n)$$

$$= (D(n)\text{Vega}(n))_{ij} + B_{ij}(n)$$

and finally

$$\text{Vega}_{ij}(1) = \frac{\partial X_i(1)}{\partial \sigma_j} = 0.$$

2. Consequently, the chain rule implies

$$\text{Vega} = \nabla_\sigma(g(X(N))) = \nabla(g)(X(N))\nabla_\sigma(X(N)) = v\text{Vega}(N)$$

$$= \sum_{n=1}^{N-1} V(n+1)^\top B(n) = \overline{V}(1)^\top.$$

3. In case F_n is an Euler scheme

$$B_{ij}(n) = \frac{\partial}{\partial \sigma_j}\left(y^i + a^i(y,\sigma)\tau_n + \sum_{l=1}^{d} b_{li}(y,\sigma)Z_l(n+1)\sqrt{\tau_n}\right)(X(n),\sigma)$$

$$= \frac{\partial a^i}{\partial \sigma_j}(X(n),\sigma)\tau_n + \sum_{l=1}^{d}\frac{\partial b_{li}}{\partial \sigma_j}(X(n),\sigma)Z_l(n+1)\sqrt{\tau_n}.$$

8.4.4 Greeks

In this section we apply the adjoint method to the calculation of Δ, Γ and Vega of a Bermudan swaption and a Trigger swap. Since we have already considered general Greeks in Subsection 8.4.3, we can use these results, so we just have to analyse the specific aspects of the aforementioned derivatives. In Chapter 12 we present the Matlab code necessary to implement the results since we use it to illustrate the object oriented programming paradigm in Matlab.

Delta

Consider a Bermudan swaption exercised at time index e. We consider g_μ as a discounted payoff of a single (virtual) derivative $B^{(\mu)}$ on $L(\mu)$ and denote by $\Delta^{(\mu)}(n)$ the corresponding recursing matrix as in Subsection 8.4.3 and by $\Delta^{(\mu)}$ the delta of that payoff g_μ. In addition, let $D(n)$ be as in Subsection 8.4.3 as well and denote the start vectors for $e \le \mu \le m$ by

$$v := \nabla(g)(L(m)), \qquad v_{(\mu)} := \nabla(g_\mu)(L(\mu)).$$

Then the following hold in addition to Subsection 8.4.3.

1. For any $1 \le i, j \le m$, $1 \le n \le m-1$, the factor matrices $D(n)$ are given by

$$D_{ik}(n) = \partial_k(F_n^i)(L(n),\sigma) = \begin{cases} 1, & i = k \le n, \\ \dfrac{L_i(n+1)}{L_i(n)} + \dfrac{L_i(n+1)\sigma_i^2\tau_i\tau_n}{(1+\tau_i L_i(n))^2}, & i = k \ge n+1, \\ \dfrac{L_i(n+1)\sigma_i\sigma_k\tau_k\tau_n}{(1+\tau_k L_k(n))^2}, & m \ge i > k \ge n+1, \\ 0, & \text{otherwise.} \end{cases}$$

2. For any $e \le n \le m$ the start vector $v_{(n)} \in \mathbb{R}^{1\times m}$ is given by

$$v_{(n)}^j = \alpha_n \cdot \begin{cases} \dfrac{\tau_j(K - L_n(n))}{1+\tau_j L_j(j)}, & 1 \le j \le n-1, \\ \left(1 - \tau_n\dfrac{L_n(n)-K}{1+\tau_n L_n(n)}\right), & j = n, \\ 0, & n+1 \le j \le m, \end{cases} \qquad (8.72)$$

where

$$\alpha_n := \phi \mathcal{N}\tau_n \prod_{i=1}^{n}\frac{1}{1+\tau_i L_i(i)}.$$

3. Employing the notation from Subsection 8.4.3, for $1 \leq n \leq \mu - 1$ the matrices $\Delta^\mu(n)$, $e \leq \mu \leq m$, satisfy

$$\Delta^\mu(n+1) = D(n)\Delta^\mu(n), \qquad \Delta^\mu(1) = I, \qquad \Delta^{(\mu)}(n) = \Delta(n).$$

Let $V^{(\mu)}$ be the vector sequence adjoint to this recursion, that is for $1 \leq n \leq \mu - 1$

$$V^{(\mu)}(n) = D(n)^\top V^{(\mu)}(n+1), \qquad V^{(\mu)}(\mu) := v_{(\mu)}^\top := \nabla g_{(\mu)}(L_\mu(\mu))^\top.$$

Then,

$$\Delta^{(\mu)} = v_{(\mu)}\Delta^{(\mu)}(\mu) = V^{(\mu)}(1)^\top.$$

In addition, for any $e \leq \mu \leq m, 1 \leq j \leq m, 1 \leq i \leq \mu$,

$$\Delta_{ij}(m) = \Delta_{ij}(\mu). \tag{8.73}$$

4. As usual let Δ be the delta of the payoff g of the Bermudan swaption. Then

$$\Delta = v\Delta(m) = \sum_{\mu=e}^{m} v_{(\mu)}\Delta(\mu) = W(1)^\top,$$

where $W(n)$ is the sequence from the considerations above. In particular the Δ of a Bermudan swaption is the solution of a Bermudan ARP.

1. This follows by directly calculating the derivative of the F_n defined by (7.40) in this case.
2. The functions $g_{(\mu)}$ are given by (8.3), so the claim follows by explicitly calculating the derivative.
3. The first part is a direct application of the results of Subsection (8.4.3) to $\Delta^{(\mu)}$. To see the second statement notice that Definition of L implies

$$\Delta_{ij}(m) = \frac{\partial L_i(m)}{\partial L_j(1)} = \frac{\partial L_i(\mu)}{\partial L_j(1)} = \Delta_{ij}(\mu).$$

4. We would like to apply the method for Bermudan swaptions with factor matrices equal to $D(n)$ and translation matrices equal to zero. In that case the sequence $\overline{W}(n)$ is identically zero as well. Furthermore, for any $1 \leq n \leq \mu, 1 \leq i, j \leq m$

$$\Delta_{ij}^{(\mu)}(n) = \frac{\partial L_i(n)}{\partial L_j(1)} = \Delta_{ij}(n).$$

It remains to check condition (8.50). This is done by verifying the three conditions (8.56), (8.57), (8.58). The first condition was already proven in (8.5), the second one was shown in (8.72) and the third one was just verified in (8.73). Therefore, by the conclusion of lemma 8.50

$$\Delta = v\Delta(m) = \sum_{\mu=e}^{m} v_{(\mu)}\Delta(\mu), \tag{8.74}$$

thus the claim follows.

Since a Bermudan swaption is an interest rate derivative on $L(m)$, we could apply the considerations of Subsection 8.4.3 directly to calculate its Δ. But the specific structure of the payoff function allows us to express the Δ as we described earlier in this chapter. Using the Bermudan structure of the payoff of a Bermudan swaption we thus obtain the algorithm presented in Chapter 12, Figure 12.46.

Gamma

We use the notation from Subsection 8.4.4 (Bermudan Delta) and Subsection 8.4.3 (Adjoint Gamma). In addition to the statements listed in Subsection 8.4.3, the following hold:

1. For any $1 \le j \le m$

$$w_{(j)} = vG^{(j)}(m) = \sum_{\mu=e}^{m} v_{(\mu)}G^{(j)}(\mu) = \overline{W}^{(j)}(1)^{\top},$$

where $\overline{W}^{(j)}(n)$ is the sequence from the Bermudan setting with respect to recursion (8.67). In particular, the $w_{(j)}$ are result vectors of Bermudan ARPs.

Denote by $w, \overline{W}(n) \in \mathbb{R}^{m \times m}$ the matrices whose columns are given by the $w_{(j)}, \overline{W}^{(j)}$, $j = 1, \dots, m$.

2. The matrices $E^i(n)$ are given by

$$E^i_{jk}(n) = \begin{cases} D_{ij}(n)\left(\dfrac{1}{L_i(n)} + \dfrac{\sigma_i^2 \tau_i \tau_n}{(1+\tau_i L_i(n))^2}\right) - L_i(n+1)\delta_{ij}\left(\dfrac{1}{L_i(n)^2} + \dfrac{\sigma_i^3 \tau_i \tau_n}{(1+\tau_i L_i(n))^3}\right), & i = k \ge n+1, \\[3mm] D_{ij}(n)\dfrac{\sigma_i \sigma_k \tau_k \tau_n}{(1+\tau_k L_k(n))^2} - L_i(n+1)\delta_{jk}\dfrac{\sigma_i \sigma_k \tau_k^2 \tau_n}{(1+\tau_k L_k(n))^3}, & i > k \ge n+1, \\[3mm] 0, & \text{otherwise.} \end{cases}$$

3. For any $e \le \mu \le m$ let $h^{(\mu)} := \text{Hess}(g_\mu)(L(\mu)) \in \mathbb{R}^{m \times m}$. For any $1 \le i, j \le m$

$$h^{(\mu)}_{ij} = \alpha_\mu \cdot \begin{cases} \dfrac{-\tau_i}{1+\tau_i L_i(i)}, & 1 \le j, i \le \mu - 1, \\[3mm] \dfrac{-\tau_j(1+\tau_\mu K)}{(1+\tau_j L_j(j))(1+\tau_\mu L_\mu(\mu))^2}, & 1 \le j \le \mu - 1, i = \mu, \\[3mm] \left(1 - \tau_\mu \dfrac{L_\mu(\mu) - K}{1+\tau_\mu L_\mu(\mu)}\right)\dfrac{-\tau_i}{1+\tau_i L_i(i)}, & j = \mu, 1 \le i \le \mu - 1, \\[3mm] \tau_\mu^2(L_\mu(\mu) - K)\dfrac{2+\tau_\mu L_\mu(\mu)}{(1+\tau_\mu L_\mu(\mu))^2}, & j = \mu = i, \\[3mm] 0, & \text{otherwise.} \end{cases}$$

We obtain

$$H = \text{Hess}(g)(L(m)) = \sum_{\mu=e}^{m} h^{(\mu)}.$$

Finally,

$$\Gamma = w + Y.$$

1. We use the same strategy as in the previous Subsection 8.4.3: the only condition which has not been checked so far is (8.58) on $G^{(j)}$. But for any $r \le \mu \le m, 1 \le j, k \le m, 1 \le i \le \mu$

the definition of L implies

$$G_{ik}^{(j)}(m) = \frac{\partial L_i(m)}{\partial L_j(1)\partial L_k(1)} = \frac{\partial L_i(\mu)}{\partial L_j(1)\partial L_k(1)} = G_{ik}^{(j)}(\mu). \qquad (8.75)$$

Since $G^{(j)}(1) = 0$, the rest of the claim follows from (8.53).

2. We have already calculated $v_{(\mu)} = \partial_j(g_\mu)(L(\mu))$ in (8.72). Deriving this equation again one obtains the result.

This leads to the implementation of the Γ in Chapter 12, Figure 12.47.

Vega

We use the notation from Subsection 8.4.4 and the results from Subsection 8.4.3. The following hold for a Bermudan swaption exercised at T_e.

1. The matrices $B(n)$ are given by

$$B_{ij}(n) = L_i(n+1)\begin{cases} \dfrac{\sigma_i \tau_j L_j(n)}{1 + \tau_j L_j(n)}, & n+1 \le i \le m, n+1 \le j \le i-1, \\[2mm] \mu_i(n) + \dfrac{\sigma_j \tau_j L_j(n)}{1 + \tau_j L_j(n)}, & n+1 \le i \le m, j = i, \\[2mm] 0, & \text{otherwise.} \end{cases}$$

2. The ARP

$$\text{Vega}(n+1) = D(n)\text{Vega}(n) + B(n), \qquad \text{Vega}(1) = 0$$

is Bermudan with start vector

$$v = \sum_{\mu=e}^{m} v_{(\mu)}.$$

Consequently,

$$\text{Vega} = v\text{Vega}(m) = \sum_{n=1}^{m-1} V(n+1)^\top B(n) = \overline{V}(1)^\top = \overline{W}(1)^\top,$$

where $\overline{V}(n)$ is the total adjoint sequence and $\overline{W}(n)$ is the total Bermudan sequence of this ARP.

This follows by explicitly deriving the evolution F_n.

8.5   APPLICATION TO TRIGGER SWAP

In this section we describe the application of adjoint techniques to another interest rate derivative, the *Trigger swap*. The Trigger swap is described in Schoenmakers, J. (2005). We first discuss the mathematical description and then we show how to derive the calculation of the sensitivities and the implementation.

8.5.1   Mathematical Modelling

A Trigger swap is a tuple $TS = (T, e, K, s, \kappa, \mathcal{N}, \phi)$ consisting of

1. a *tenor structure*

$$0 = T_1 < T_2 < \ldots < T_m < T_{m+1}$$

   with *tenor distances*

$$\tau_i := T_{i+1} - T_i, \ i = 1, \ldots, m,$$

   the *last observation date/maturity* T_m, a *first observation date* T_e, $1 \le e \le m$,
2. a *trigger level* $K \in [0.1]$,
3. a *spread rate* $s \in [0.1]$,
4. a *fixed rate* $\kappa \in [0.1]$
5. a *nominal value* $\mathcal{N} \in \mathbb{R}_{>0}$.

As for Bermudan swaptions we denote by

$$PV_{n+1} := PV_{n+1}(L(n)) := \prod_{i=1}^{n} \frac{1}{1 + \tau_i L_i(i)}$$

the discount factor. For any $e \le \tau \le m$ the function

$$g^{(\tau)}(L(m)) = \mathcal{N} \sum_{j=e}^{\tau-1} PV_{j+1} s \tau_j + \mathcal{N} \sum_{j=\tau}^{m} PV_{j+1} \tau_j (L_j(j) - \kappa)$$

is the *payoff function of a Trigger swap triggered at τ*. We consider a decomposition of the payoff of a Trigger swap.

1. The function $g^{(\tau)}$ can be decomposed by

$$g^{(\tau)}(L(m)) = \sum_{\mu=e}^{\tau-1} f_\mu^{(\tau)}(L(\mu)) + \sum_{j=\tau}^{m} g_\mu^{(\tau)}(L(\mu)),$$

   where

$$f_\mu^{(\tau)}(L(\mu)) = \mathcal{N} PV_{\mu+1} \tau_\mu, \qquad g_\mu^{(\tau)}(L(\mu)) = \mathcal{N} PV_{\mu+1} \tau_\mu \left(L_\mu(\mu) - \kappa \right).$$

2. Consequently, we obtain

$$\nabla g^{(\tau)}(L(m)) = \sum_{\mu=e}^{\tau-1} \nabla (f_\mu^{(\tau)})(L(\mu)) + \sum_{j=\tau}^{m} \nabla (g_\mu^{(\tau)})(L(\mu)). \tag{8.76}$$

Similarly to Bermudan swaptions, we derive conclusions concerning the Greeks of Trigger swaps from the general theorems on ARPs and general Greeks.

In addition, to calculate the derivations presented in Subsection 8.4.3, the following hold for a Trigger swap triggered at τ (we surpress the index τ in notation here):

1. The start vectors

$$v := \nabla(g)(L(m)),$$
$$\forall e \le \mu \le \tau - 1 : v_{(\mu)} := \nabla(f_\mu)(L(\mu)),$$
$$\forall \tau \le \mu \le m : v_{(\mu)} := \nabla(g_\mu)(L(\mu)),$$

satisfy

$$v = \sum_{\mu=e}^{m} v_{(\mu)}, \qquad (8.77)$$

$$v_{(\mu)}^{j} = \alpha_{\mu} \begin{cases} \dfrac{-\tau_j}{1 + \tau_j L_j(j)}, & e \le \mu \le \tau - 1, 1 \le j \le \mu, \\[3mm] \dfrac{\tau_j(\kappa - L_\mu(\mu))}{1 + \tau_j L_j(j)}, & \tau \le \mu \le m, 1 \le j \le \mu - 1, \\[3mm] 1 - \tau_\mu \dfrac{L_\mu(\mu) - \kappa}{1 + \tau_\mu L_\mu(\mu)}, & \tau \le \mu \le m, j = \mu, \\[3mm] 0, & \text{otherwise,} \end{cases} \qquad (8.78)$$

where

$$\alpha_\mu = \mathcal{N} \tau_\mu P V_{\mu+1}.$$

2. The Hessian

$$H := \mathrm{Hess}(g)(L(m)) = \sum_{\mu=e}^{m} \mathrm{Hess}(g_\mu)(L(\mu)) =: \sum_{\mu=e}^{m} h_{(\mu)}^{ij}$$

satisfy

$$h_{(\mu)}^{ij} = \alpha_\mu \begin{cases} \dfrac{\tau_j \tau_i}{(1 + \tau_j L_j(j))(1 + \tau_i L_i(i))}, & e \le \mu \le \tau - 1 : 1 \le j \le \mu : 1 \le i \le \mu : i \ne j, \\[3mm] \dfrac{2\tau_j^2}{(1 + \tau_j L_j(j))^2}, & e \le \mu \le \tau - 1 : 1 \le j \le \mu : 1 \le i \le \mu : i = j, \\[3mm] \dfrac{-\tau_i}{1 + \tau_i L_i(i)}, & \tau \le \mu \le m : 1 \le j, i \le \mu - 1, \\[3mm] \dfrac{-\tau_j(1 + \tau_\mu \kappa)}{(1 + \tau_j L_j(j))(1 + \tau_\mu L_\mu(\mu))^2}, & \tau \le \mu \le m, 1 \le j \le \mu - 1, i = \mu \\[3mm] \left(1 - \tau_\mu \dfrac{L_\mu(\mu) - \kappa}{1 + \tau_\mu L_\mu(\mu)}\right) \dfrac{-\tau_i}{1 + \tau_i L_i(i)}, & \tau \le \mu \le m, j = \mu, 1 \le i \le \mu - 1 \\[3mm] \tau_\mu^2(L_\mu(\mu) - \kappa) \dfrac{2 + \tau_\mu L_\mu(\mu)}{(1 + \tau_\mu L_\mu(\mu))^2}, & \tau \le \mu \le m, j = \mu = i, \\[3mm] 0, & \text{otherwise.} \end{cases}$$

3. The Δ of the Trigger swap is the result vector of a Bermudan ARP with respect to the decomposition (8.77). Consequently,

$$\Delta = v\Delta(m) = W(1)^{\mathsf{T}},$$

where $W(n)$ is the Bermudan sequence of the recursion

$$\forall 1 \le n \le m - 1 : \Delta(n + 1) = D(n)\Delta(n), \qquad \Delta(1) = I.$$

Here the matrices $D(n)$ are defined as in Subsection 8.4.4.

4. Using the notation from Subsection 8.4.4, the Γ can be expressed by $\Gamma = w + Y$. The rows $w_{(j)}$ of w are again result vectors

$$w_{(j)} = vG^{(j)}(m) = \overline{W}^{(j)}(1)^{\top},$$

of Bermudan ARPs with respect to the decomposition (8.77). Here $\overline{W}(n)$ is the total Bermudan sequence with respect to the recursion

$$\forall 1 \leq n \leq m - 1 : G^{(j)}(n+1) = D(n)G^{(j)}(n) + C^{(j)}(n), \qquad G^{(j)}(1) = 0.$$

5. The Vega of the Trigger swap is the result vector of a Bermudan ARP with respect to the decomposition (8.77). Consequently,

$$\text{Vega} = v\text{Vega}(m) = \overline{W}(1)^{\top},$$

where $\overline{W}(n)$ is the total Bermudan sequence with respect to the recursion

$$\text{Vega}(n + 1) = D(n)\text{Vega}(n) + B(n), \qquad \text{Vega}(1) = 0.$$

1. Follows directly from the definitions.
2. Follows from (8.78) and a direct calculation.
3. To verify that the ARP is Bermudan, we again verify the three conditions of the Bermudan criterion. It is clear that the start vectors (8.78) satisfy the first two conditions (8.56), (8.57). The third condition (8.58) has already been verified. Thus the ARP is Bermudan and the claim follows.
4. Follows from Subsections 8.4.3 and 8.4.4.
5. Follows from the considerations in Subsections 8.4.3 and 8.4.4.

8.5.2 Numerical Results

Using the implementation described in the previous section, we calculate the price and the Greeks for a typical Bermuda swaption and a typical Trigger swap. Moreover, we benchmark the various methods using the Bermuda swaption setting.

Bermudan Swaption   To specify a test scenario for a Bermudan swaption, we have to define the various parameters to be able to implement a Bermudan swaption into our software, so we set

1. the maturity to $m := 10$,
2. the first exercise time index to $e := 5$,
3. the tenor distances (in years) to

$$\tau_i := 0.5, \ i = 1, \ldots, m,$$

4. the nominal value to $\mathcal{N} := 10000$,
5. the payer-or-receiver-factor to $\phi := +1$ (that is, we consider a payer swap),
6. the initial values $L_i(1)$ of the Libors for the LMM simulation to

$$L_i(1) := 0.035, \ i = 1, \ldots, m,$$

7. the volatilities for these Libors to

$$\sigma_i := 0.2, \ i = 1, \ldots, m,$$

8. and the number of paths for the Monte Carlo simulation to 1000.

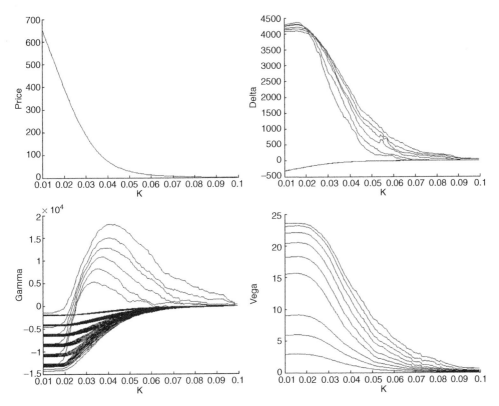

Figure 8.25   The price (top left), Δ (top right), Γ (bottom left) and Vega (bottom right) of a Bermudan swaption with respect to the strike

These parameters are fixed. In the following plots the strike rate K ranges from $K = 0.01$ to $K = 0.095$ in steps of 0.0005. For each of these strike rates we calculate the price $P \in \mathbb{R}$, the vector $\Delta \in \mathbb{R}^{1 \times 10}$, the matrix $\Gamma \in \mathbb{R}^{10 \times 10}$ and the vector Vega $\in \mathbb{R}^{10 \times 1}$. The results are illustrated in Figure 8.25.

Notice that the Δ consists of two groups of curves. Since the first possible exercise time index is $e = 5$, the curves for $\Delta_1, \ldots, \Delta_4$ are just discount curves, where $\Delta_5, \ldots, \Delta_{10}$ are the sensitivities to those initial values of Libor that determine the values at times, where one has to make an exercise decision. Consequently, these two types of curves behave rather differently. The same phenomenon also occurs for Γ.

Trigger Swap   To specify a test scenario for a Trigger swap, we have to define the various parameters. We set

1. the maturity to $m := 10$,
2. the first observation date to $e := 5$,
3. the tenor distances (in years) to

$$\tau_i := 0.5, \ i = 1, \ldots, m,$$

4. the nominal value to $\mathcal{N} := 10000$,

5. the trigger levels to a constant $K := 0.05$,
6. the spread rate to 0.2,
7. the fixed rate to $\kappa := 0.1$,
8. the initial values $L_i(1)$ of the Libors for the LMM simulation to

$$L_i(1) := 0.035, \; i = 1, \ldots, m,$$

9. the volatilities for these Libors to

$$\sigma_i := 0.2, \; i = 1, \ldots, m,$$

10. and the number of paths for the Monte Carlo simulation to 1000.

At first all these parameters are fixed. In the following plots the trigger level K varies from $K = 0.01$ to $K = 0.095$ in steps of 0.0005. For each of these levels we calculate the price $P \in \mathbb{R}$, the vector $\Delta \in \mathbb{R}^{1 \times 10}$, the matrix $\Gamma \in \mathbb{R}^{10 \times 10}$ and the vector Vega $\in \mathbb{R}^{10 \times 1}$. The results are displayed in Figure 8.26.

Notice that the Δ consists of two groups of curves. Since the first possible exercise time index is $e = 5$, the curves for $\Delta_1, \ldots, \Delta_4$ are just discount curves, where $\Delta_5, \ldots, \Delta_{10}$ are the sensitivities to those initial values of Libor that determine the values at times, where one has to

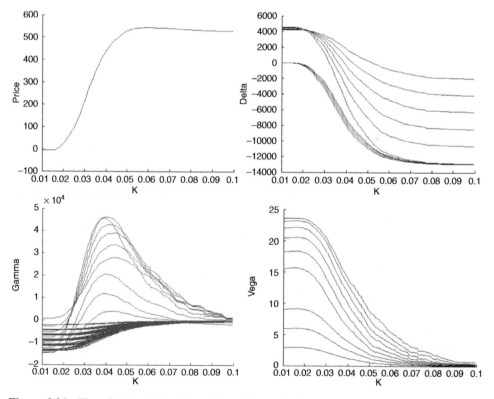

Figure 8.26 The price (top left), Δ (top right), Γ (bottom left) and Vega (bottom right) of a Trigger swap with respect to the strike

make an exercise decision. Consequently, these two types of curves behave rather differently. The same phenomenon occurs for Γ as well.

Benchmarks   We introduced three methods to calculate the Greeks, namely the forward method, the general adjoint method and the Bermudan adjoint method. Since they all yield the same result, it is interesting to see how they perform. To that end we run simulations using the Matlab scripts described in the previous section. More precisely we calculate all three Greeks of a Bermudan with all three methods. The parameters of the Bermudan swaption are as follows:

1. maturities from $m := 10$ to $m := 100$ in steps of 10,
2. first exercise time indices $e := \frac{m}{2}$,
3. tenor distances

$$\tau_i := 0.5, \ i = 1, \ldots, m,$$

4. nominal value $\mathcal{N} := 10000$,
5. payer-or-receiver-factor $\phi := +1$,
6. initial values $L_i(1)$ of the Libors

$$L_i(1) := 0.035, \ i = 1, \ldots, m,$$

7. and volatilities

$$\sigma_i := 0.2, \ i = 1, \ldots, m.$$

We set the number of paths for Monte Carlo simulation to 10.000 for Δ and Vega and to 1.000 for Γ. For each method and each Greek we stop the time the algorithm needs to run. On our test system[1] we obtained the results given in Figure 8.27. In each of these figures the maturity is plotted versus the runtime in seconds. The curve that connects the various data points is drawn using polynomial regression. The degree of the polynomial is chosen such that it equals the degree of the theoretical complexity class of the algorithm (see Figure 8.28). In every case we obtain that the theoretical complexities match the practical results of the benchmarks. The forward method performs worse than the others and becomes slower and slower with increasing maturity. The adjoint method and the Bermudan adjoint method exhibit nearly the same performance. As expected, the advantage of using the adjoint method is smallest when calculating the $\Gamma = w + Y$, because only the w can be calculated with adjoint methods, but the Y has to be calculated using the forward method.

8.5.3   The Likelihood Ratio Method (LRM)

The *likelihood ratio method* or LRM for short is based on *score functions* for a given model. The score function is a function which is multiplied with the payoff of the option such that the Greek can be represented by

$$\text{Greek}_\phi^{LR} := \mathbb{E}[h(S(\phi))\omega(\phi, S(\phi))], \tag{8.79}$$

---

[1] Intel Core 2 Duo CPU T5800@2.00Ghz, 4GB RAM, Windows 7, Matlab R2011a.

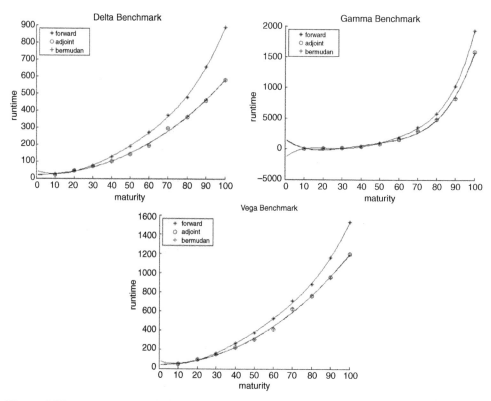

Figure 8.27   Benchmark for Δ (top left), Γ (top right) and Vega (bottom) in a Libor Market Model

$\omega(\cdot, \cdot)$ is the score function. The corresponding Monte Carlo estimator is given by

$$\widehat{\text{Greek}}_{\phi}^{LR} := \frac{1}{N} \sum_{i=1}^{N} h(S(\phi)^i)\omega(\phi, S(\phi)^i). \qquad (8.80)$$

To apply LRM we need additional information about the model, namely we must have an expression for the score function. The LRM (8.80) is an unbiased estimator for the Greek and can be used to compute Greeks for options with discontinuous payoff functions because the derivative of the payoff function is not needed. To see why discontinuous payoffs are unproblematic, we show how the *integration by parts formula* is applied. The basic idea is to shift the derivative operator from the payoff function to the density of the probability measure, which in most cases is sufficiently smooth. Several authors have studied the LRM

	forward	adjoint	bermudan
Δ	$\mathcal{O}(m^4)$	$\mathcal{O}(m^3)$	$\mathcal{O}(m^3)$
Γ	$\mathcal{O}(m^5)$	$\mathcal{O}(m^4)$	$\mathcal{O}(m^4)$
$Vega$	$\mathcal{O}(m^4)$	$\mathcal{O}(m^3)$	$\mathcal{O}(m^3)$

Figure 8.28   Theoretical complexity classes of the algorithms

in a very general setting. It can be seen as an application of the *calculus of variation on path space* or *Malliavin calculus*. The key observation is that using this calculus an analogue to the integration by parts formula can be derived and the score function is a *Skorohod integral*, which can be approximated by simulation. In this book we do not cover the theory of Malliavin calculus. We give an introduction to LRMs and a finite difference implementation of it. An introduction to Malliavin calculus and the Skorohod integral is given in Nualart, D. (1995).

To introduce the underlying mathematics we provide a basic example which only uses the integration by parts formula from ordinary calculus. We work within the Black–Scholes model. Then, the measure of logarithmic returns is normally distributed and the calculations can be carried out explicitly.

We start with the integration by parts. For differentiable functions $f, g : \mathbb{R} \to \mathbb{R}$ the integration by parts formula has the following relationship:

$$f(b)g(b) - f(a)g(a) = \int_a^b f'(s)g(s)ds + \int_a^b f(s)g'(s)ds. \tag{8.81}$$

Writing the expectation $\mathbb{E}[h(S(T))]$ as an integral and denoting the density by φ, the expectation can be derived by

$$\mathbb{E}\,[h(S_T)] = \int h(s)\varphi(s)ds. \tag{8.82}$$

Since we assume some model dynamic for the underlying S, the payoff function h evaluated for a given path of S and the density φ depend on model parameters. To this end we use the notation h_ϕ and φ_ϕ to express this dependence. Let us fix the parameter ϕ (for example the spot price $\phi = S(0)$). Now, to evaluate the Greek with respect to ϕ we consider

$$\mathbb{E}\left[\frac{\partial}{\partial\phi}h_\phi(S_T)\right] = \int \underbrace{\frac{\partial}{\partial\phi}h_\phi(s)}_{f'}\, \underbrace{\varphi_\phi(s)}_{g}\,ds.$$

With the notation above we apply the integration by parts rule, which leads to

$$\int h_\phi(s)\frac{\partial}{\partial\phi}\varphi_\phi(s)ds = \int h_\phi(s)\underbrace{\frac{\frac{\partial}{\partial\phi}\varphi_\phi(s)}{\varphi_\phi(s)}}_{=:\omega_\phi(s)}\varphi_\phi(s)ds.$$

The calculation can be seen as an option pricing problem with a new payoff function which is the initial one multiplied by the *score*, $\omega(\phi)$.

Having carried out the calculation of the weights the calculation of the Greek, for instance with respect to the spot price $S(0)$, is straightforward:

$$\text{Greek}_{S(0)}^{LR} = \frac{1}{N}\sum_{i=1}^N h_{S(0)}(S^i)\omega_{S(0)}(S^i).$$

Let us now give the explicit calculation for the Black–Scholes model. By denoting the logarithmic asset value $X(t) := \log(S(t))$, the explicit form for the density is given by

$$\varphi_{S(0)}(s) = \frac{1}{\sigma\sqrt{2\pi}S(0)}\exp\left(-\frac{1}{2}\left(\frac{\log(s) - X(0)}{\sigma}\right)\right).$$

Thus,

$$\frac{\partial_{S(0)}\varphi_{S(0)}}{\varphi_{S(0)}} = \frac{s - X(0)}{\sigma\sqrt{T}} \cdot \partial_{S(0)}X(0) = \frac{s - X(0)}{S(0)\sigma\sqrt{T}}$$

and the score function is

$$\omega_{S(0)}(s) = \frac{s}{S(0)\sigma\sqrt{T}}. \tag{8.83}$$

Another property of the LRM is that the score function does not depend on the payoff but on the underlying model. Therefore, we compute the Greek with respect to the spot value for any payoff using the derived score function.

Let us assume the option has maturity T and the model is the standard Black–Scholes one. To compute the Greeks we multiply the payoff under consideration by the following score functions:

$$\omega_{S(0)}^{\Delta}(s) = \frac{s}{S(0)\sigma\sqrt{T}} \tag{8.84}$$

$$\omega_{S(0)}^{\Gamma}(s) = \frac{s^2 - s\sigma\sqrt{T} - 1}{S(0)^2\sigma^2 T} \tag{8.85}$$

$$\omega_{\sigma}^{\nu}(s) = \frac{s^2 - 1}{\sigma} - s\sqrt{T}. \tag{8.86}$$

The score functions are evaluated at $s = Z_N$ with Z_N being the Gaussian variate used to generate the final value $S(T) = S(t_N)$.

8.5.4   Likelihood Ratio for Finite Differences – Proxy Simulation

The *proxy simulation scheme* was introduced by Fries, C. and Kampen, J. (2006) and further developed in Fries, C. and Joshi, M. (2008) and Fu, M. (2007). It is a purely numerical version of LRM. Initially used for diffusion processes it was extended to other processes in Kienitz, J. (2010). We consider two discretizations of the stochastic processes S. The first process, called the *target scheme denoted by X* is a discretization of the dynamics under consideration and the second one, called the *proxy scheme denoted by Y*, is a discretization which is easy to compute, for instance the Euler scheme.

We consider the expected value for different numeraires determined by two probability densities φ_X and φ_X. Applying an importance sampling argument given a payoff function h we have the following relation for the expected values with respect to the different densities:

$$\mathbb{E}_{\varphi_S}[h(S)] = \int h(s)\varphi_S(s)ds = \int h(s)\underbrace{\frac{\varphi_S(s)}{\varphi_X(s)}}_{=:\omega}\varphi_X(s) = \mathbb{E}_{\varphi_X}[h(X)\omega].$$

We wish to use the transition density. For the corresponding densities φ_X and φ_S used to compute expectations we require for almost all y that $\varphi_X(y) = 0 \Rightarrow \varphi_S(y) = 0$. Suppose we wish to compute some sensitivity with respect to a model-parameter ϕ. We simulate the proxy process Y. The sensitivity is then determined by multiplying the payoff function with a weight. This weight is not computed analytically as in the LRM but by using the schemes X and Y and the transition density. Thus, this is purely numerical. We consider the Monte Carlo estimator

$$\frac{1}{\text{NSim}} \sum_{i=1}^{\text{NSim}} h(X) \frac{\omega^i(\phi+\varepsilon) - \omega^i(\phi-\varepsilon)}{2\varepsilon} \tag{8.87}$$

with weight function

$$\omega^{n+1} = \prod_{j=1}^{n} \frac{\pi^X(t_j, Y_j; t_{j+1}, Y_j)}{\pi^Y(t_j, Y_j; t_{j+1}, Y_j)}. \tag{8.88}$$

Here π denotes the transition kernel for either the target or the proxy.

To derive approximations to the Greeks given the payoff h of an option we have to approximate

$$\frac{\partial}{\partial \Phi} \mathbb{E}\left[h(S^\Phi)\right] = \frac{\partial}{\partial \Phi} \int_{\mathbb{D}} h(x) \pi^\Phi(x) dx. \tag{8.89}$$

We briefly review the proxy method to obtain stable Greeks for discontinuous path-dependent payoff functions.

We take a stochastic process

$$S : t \longmapsto S(t) \tag{8.90}$$

and consider a discretization, $\tau = \{0 = t_0, t_1, \ldots, t_{NTime} = T\}$, of the stochastic process $S(t)$ in the interval $[0, T]$ and take the time discrete processes, $S_*(t)$, $t \in \tau$ as an approximation to S.

$$S_* : t \longmapsto S_*(t). \tag{8.91}$$

If an exact solution is available we use the time discrete process $S_*(t) = S(t)$, $t \in \tau$, directly. Furthermore, we take another approximation given by

$$S_0 : t \longmapsto S_0(t). \tag{8.92}$$

The latter can be an easy-to-implement scheme like an Euler scheme, for example. We call (8.91) the target scheme and (8.92) the proxy scheme. For the sequel we need the transition kernel of (8.91) and (8.92). In practice, however, there are models where the transition kernel for the process (8.90) is only available through its characteristic function.

The domain on which the density is defined is denoted by $\mathbb{D}$; often we have $\mathbb{D} = \mathbb{R}$ or $\mathbb{R}^+$. Now, we use simulated values S_i, $i = 1, \ldots, N$ and we apply the integration by parts formula and get

$$\frac{\partial}{\partial \Phi} \mathbb{E}[h_\Phi(S)] \approx \frac{1}{2\varepsilon} \left(\mathbb{E}[h_{\Phi+\varepsilon}(S_*)] - \mathbb{E}[h_{\Phi-\varepsilon}(S_*)]\right) \tag{8.93}$$

$$= \int_{\mathbb{D}} h(y) \frac{1}{2\varepsilon} \left(f^*_{\Phi+\varepsilon}(y) - f^*_{\Phi-\varepsilon}(y)\right) dy \tag{8.94}$$

$$= \int_{\mathbb{D}} h(y) \frac{\frac{1}{2\varepsilon} \left(f^*_{\Phi+\varepsilon}(y) - f^*_{\Phi-\varepsilon}(y)\right)}{f^0(y)} f^0(y) dy \tag{8.95}$$

$$\overset{MC}{\approx} \frac{1}{N} \sum_{i=1}^{N} h_\Phi(S_i) \frac{\left(\omega^i_{\Phi+\varepsilon}(S_i) - \omega^i_{\Phi-\varepsilon}\right)}{2\varepsilon}. \tag{8.96}$$

In the last step we used the notation

$$\omega_\psi(y) = \frac{f_\psi^*(y)}{f^0(y)}. \tag{8.97}$$

Full Proxy Scheme   First, we give an algorithm which implements the idea of using a proxy simulation. To this end we denote the number of simulations by *NSim* and the number of time steps per simulation by *NTime*. The algorithm to compute the value of the Greek with respect to the disturbed initial parameter $\Phi \pm \varepsilon$ is given by

---

Algorithm 8.1: Proxy method for computing Greeks

---

1 **for** $i = 1$ *to NSim* **do**
  for $j = 1$ *to Nt* **do**
   Simulate $\hat{S}_j^i$
   Compute the weights $\omega_{i,j}^{path}$
   Compute the weights $\omega^i = \prod_{j=1}^{NTime} \omega_{i,j}^{path}$
2 Compute the payoff

$$\hat{V} = \frac{1}{NSim} \sum_{i=1}^{NSim} h(\hat{S}_i)\omega^i(\hat{S}_i). \tag{8.98}$$

We used the fact that by Equation (8.97) we can compute the weights $\omega_i, i = 1, \ldots, NSim$ for the $i-$th path by

$$\omega_i(y) = \prod_{j=1}^{NTime} \frac{f_{\Phi+\varepsilon}(y) - f_{\Phi-\varepsilon}(y)}{f_\Phi(y)} = \prod_{j=1}^{NTime} \omega_{\Phi+\varepsilon} - \omega_{\Phi-\varepsilon}. \tag{8.99}$$

Mixed FD/Proxy Scheme   A straightforward generalization is the mixed proxy scheme. This is a method to combine the effectiveness for finite difference or pathwise estimators in case of continuous payoffs with that of the proxy method applied to discontinuous payoffs. Let K be the point of discontinuity of the given payoff function h, for instance the strike of a digital option. We decompose the payoff into two parts h_1 and h_2 by

$$h_1(x) = \Psi(x)h(x) \tag{8.100}$$
$$h_2(x) = (1 - \Psi(x))h(x) \tag{8.101}$$

with Ψ being a function fulfilling

$$\begin{cases} \Psi(x) \to 1 & \text{if} \quad \max(|x - K|) \to 0 \\ \Psi(x) \ll 1 & \text{if} \quad \max(|x - K|) > \varepsilon \end{cases}. \tag{8.102}$$

For instance the function Ψ can be chosen to be

$$\Psi(x; \alpha, \beta) = \exp\left(-\frac{1}{2}\frac{\max(|x - K| - \beta, 0)}{\alpha}\right), \quad \alpha, \beta \in \mathbb{R}^+. \tag{8.103}$$

The algorithm implementing this approach is given by

Algorithm 8.2: Mixed FD/Proxy Method for Computing Greeks

---

1 **for** $i = 1$ *to NSim* **do**
    for $j = 1$ *to Nt* **do**
        Simulate $\hat{S}^i_j$
        Simulate $\hat{S}^i_{j,\Phi\pm\varepsilon}$ at $t_j \in \{t_1, \ldots, t_{\text{NTime}} = T\}$
        Compute the weights $\omega^{\text{path}}_{i,j}$
        Compute the weights $\omega^i = \prod_{j=1}^{\text{NTime}} \omega^{\text{path}}_{i,j}$
2 Compute the payoffs

$$\hat{V}_1 = \frac{1}{\text{NSim}} \sum_{i=1}^{\text{NSim}} h_1(\hat{S}_i)\omega^i(\hat{S}_i) \tag{8.104}$$

$$\hat{V}_2 = \frac{1}{2\varepsilon\text{NSim}} \sum_{i=1}^{\text{NSim}} \left(h_2(\hat{S}^{\Phi+\varepsilon}_i) - h_2(\hat{S}^{\Phi-\varepsilon}_i) \right) \tag{8.105}$$

$$\hat{V} = \hat{V}_1 + \hat{V}_2 \tag{8.106}$$

We used Equation (8.97) to determine the weights.

Localized Proxy Scheme   Another method to combine finite difference and pathwise estimators for Greeks with proxy schemes is to implement a modified proxy scheme. We start with two schemes S_0 and S_Φ together with the function Ψ used in the mixed scheme. At each time step $t \in \tau$ we choose the modified scheme to be

$$S_+(t) = (1 - \Psi_t)S^\Phi(t) + \Psi_t S_0(t). \tag{8.107}$$

We use the scheme given by Equation (8.107) to compute the proxy estimator. This is interesting if the discontinuities occur along the path. This is, for instance, the case for Barrier options. This modified scheme is called the Localised Proxy Scheme.

8.5.5   Numerical Results

In this section we consider the Merton model, the Variance Gamma model and the Variance Gamma model with Gamma Ornstein–Uhlenbeck stochastic clock. The options we consider are:

- Digital option. For a given strike K the payoff is given by

$$h(S(T)) = 1_{\{S(T)>K\}}. \tag{8.108}$$

- Lookback option. For two strikes K_1 and K_2 and denoting the maximum on a path by $S^M(T) := \max_{0 \le t \le T} (S(t))$ we consider the following version of a Lookback option:

$$h(S) = \frac{S^M(T)}{K_1} 1_{\{K_2 > S^M(T) > K_1\}}. \tag{8.109}$$

```
% Proxy Simulation and weight calculation
for i=2:nsteps+1
    rvariate = (r + omega)*deltaT + mu*Yvec(i-1,:) ...
        + sigma*sqrt(Yvec(i-1,:)).*Zvec(i-1,:);
    lnS(i,:)= lnS(i-1,:) + rvariate;
    lnSupFD(i,:) = lnSupFD(i-1,:) + rvariate;
    lnSdownFD(i,:) = lnSdownFD(i-1,:) + rvariate;
    lnSsigup(i,:) = lnSsigup(i-1,:) + (r + omegau) * deltaT ...
        + mu*Yvec(i-1,:) + sigmau*sqrt(Yvec(i-1,:)).*Zvec(i-1,:);
    lnSsigdown(i,:) = lnSsigdown(i-1,:) + (r + omegad) * deltaT ...
        + mu*Yvec(i-1,:) + sigmad*sqrt(Yvec(i-1,:)).*Zvec(i-1,:);
    lnSrup(i,:) = lnSrup(i-1,:) + (ru-r)*deltaT + rvariate;
    lnSrdown(i,:) = lnSrdown(i-1,:) + (rd - r)*deltaT + rvariate;

    w(i-1,:) = prob(lnS(i,:), lnS(i-1,:));
    wsigup(i-1,:) = probs(lnS(i,:), lnS(i-1,:), sigmau);
    wsigdown(i-1,:) = probs(lnS(i,:), lnS(i-1,:), sigmad);
    wrup(i-1,:) = probr(lnS(i,:), lnS(i-1,:), ru);
    wrdown(i-1,:) = probr(lnS(i,:), lnS(i-1,:), rd);

    if i-1 == 1
        wup(1,:) = prob(lnS(2,:), lnSupFD(1,:));
        wdown(1,:) = prob(lnS(2,:), lnSdownFD(1,:));
    else
        wup(i-1,:) = w(i-1,:);
        wdown(i-1,:) = w(i-1,:);
    end
end
```

Figure 8.29 Calculation of the weights for applying the proxy method. `prob`, `probs` and `probr` are function handles for the transition probability for the standard parameters, the shifted parameters corresponding to volatility and to the rate r. For the Variance Gamma model we use `pvg2` from the source code examples

- Barrier option (Knock-Out option). The payoff is specified by two vectors, L and U, representing the lower barrier and the upper barrier level. The final payoff is given by

$$h(S) = \max(S(T) - K, 0) 1_{\{L(t) < S(t) < U(t)\}}. \qquad (8.110)$$

The Matlab implementation we provide is illustrated using no specific model.

The only things we need to modify in Figure 8.29 when using another model are the simulation scheme and the probability density calculation. For instance, Figure 8.30 shows the set up for the Merton model explicitly using the function `pmerton`. The difference becomes clear immediately and the approach using function handles makes the code much more readable and extendable.

The computed figures w, `wup`, `wdown`, ..., `wrdown` have to be applied to the payoff under consideration.

Once we have specified the payoff function, for instance one of the payoffs displayed in Figure 8.31, we can then apply the piece of code given in Figure 8.32.

In what follows we apply this piece of code to several pricing problems and to different models.

```
for i=2:nsteps+1
    Jump(i-1,:) = mu_J * Yvec(i-1,:) + sqrt(Yvec(i-1,:)) .* sig_J ...
    .* YNvec(i-1,:) - lambda * deltaT * (martcorrection-1);
    rvariate = (r-sigma^2/2)*deltaT + sigma * sqrt(deltaT) ...
    .*Zvec(i-1,:) + Jump(i-1,:);

    lnS(i,:)=lnS(i-1,:) + rvariate;
    lnSupFD(i,:)=lnSupFD(i-1,:) + rvariate;
    lnSdownFD(i,:)=lnSdownFD(i-1,:) + rvariate;
    lnSsigup(i,:)= lnSsigup(i-1,:) + (r-sigmau^2/2)*deltaT ...
    + sigmau * sqrt(deltaT) .*Zvec(i-1,:) + Jump(i-1,:);
    lnSsigdown(i,:) = lnSsigdown(i-1,:) + (r-sigmad^2/2)*deltaT ...
    + sigmad * sqrt(deltaT) .*Zvec(i-1,:) + Jump(i-1,:);
    lnSrup(i,:)= lnSrup(i-1,:) + (ru - r) * deltaT + rvariate;
    lnSrdown(i,:) = lnSrdown(i-1,:) + (rd-r)*deltaT + rvariate;

    w(i-1,:) = pmerton(lnS(i,:),lnS(i-1,:),deltaT,sigma, ...
        r,0,mu_J,sig_J,lambda);
    wsigup(i-1,:) = pmerton(lnS(i,:),lnS(i-1,:),deltaT,sigmau, ...
        r,0,mu_J,sig_J,lambda);
    wsigdown(i-1,:) = pmerton(lnS(i,:),lnS(i-1,:),deltaT,sigmad, ...
        r,0,mu_J,sig_J,lambda);
    wrup(i-1,:)= pmerton(lnS(i,:),lnS(i-1,:),deltaT,sigma, ...
        ru,0,mu_J,sig_J,lambda);
    wrdown(i-1,:) = pmerton(lnS(i,:),lnS(i-1,:),deltaT,sigma, ...
        rd,0,mu_J,sig_J,lambda);

    if i-1 == 1
        wup(1,:) = pmerton(lnS(2,:), lnSup(1,:),deltaT,sigma, ...
            r,0,mu_J,sig_J,lambda);
        wdown(1,:) = pmerton(lnS(2,:),lnSdown(1,:),deltaT,sigma, ...
            r,0,mu_J,sig_J,lambda);
    else
        wup(i-1,:) = pmerton(lnS(i,:), lnS(i-1,:),deltaT,sigma, ...
            r,0,mu_J,sig_J,lambda);
        wdown(i-1,:) = pmerton(lnS(i,:),lnS(i-1,:),deltaT,sigma, ...
            r,0,mu_J,sig_J,lambda);
    end
end
```

Figure 8.30 Assignment of the weights using the transition probability in the Merton model. For illustration we have replaced the function handle displayed in Figure 8.29 with the function encoding the transition probability for the Merton model, but the general code can be used just defining the appropriate handles

```
% Payoff Digital
pf = @(x,y) Digital(x,y);
% Payoff KnockOut
Lvec = [log(90) log(85) log(80)]; Uvec = [log(110) log(115) log(120)];
Tvec = [0 0.5 0.75 1.0];
pf = @(x,y) KnockOutPayoff(x,y,deltaT, Lvec, Uvec, Tvec);
% Payoff Lookback
H1 = log(105); H2 = log(125);
pf = @(x,y) Lookback(x,H1,H2);
```

Figure 8.31 Matlab implementation for several payoff functions

```
%Computation of weights
Wd = (prod(wup./w,1) - prod(wdown./w,1))/(2*eps(1));
% delta
Wg = (prod(wup./w,1) - 2 + prod(wdown./w,1))/eps(1)^2;
% gamma
Wsig = (prod(wsigup ./ w,1) - prod(wsigdown ./w,1))/(2*eps(2));  % vega
Wr = (prod(wrup ./ w,1) - prod(wrdown ./ w,1))/(2*eps(3));       % rho


payoffvec = pf(lnS,log(K));
payoffvecu = pf(lnSupFD,log(K));        % for delta/gamma
payoffvecd = pf(lnSdownFD,log(K));      % for delta/gamma
payoffvecsigu = pf(lnSsigup,log(K));    % for vega
payoffvecsigd = pf(lnSsigdown,log(K));  % for vega
payoffvecru = pf(lnSrup,log(K));        % for rho
payoffvecrd = pf(lnSrdown,log(K));      % for rho


payoffvec1 = payoffvec .* Wd;
payoffvec2 = payoffvec .* Wg;
payoffvec3 = payoffvec .* Wsig;
payoffvec4 = payoffvec .* Wr;
```

Figure 8.32   Assignment of the payoff vectors to be evaluated for the proxy estimator

The Merton Model

First, we consider the Merton model to price an option with digital payoff. We use the parameters $S(0) = 100$, $K = 100$, $T = 1.0$, $r = 0.07$, $d = 0.0$, $\sigma = 0.2$, $\lambda = 0.5$, $\mu_J = 0.05$ and $\sigma_J = 0.15$.

Digital Option   We have considered a disturbance of the initial parameters by 1% and the discretization $\tau = \{0, T\}$. Our results are summarized in Table 8.5.

We further illustrate the numbers from Table 8.5 by showing the full convergence diagrams (see Figure 8.33).

Let us examine a connection to other simulation approaches. Joshi, M. and Leung, T. (2007) suggest simulating jump times. Then, between jump times the process is a diffusion. We have two possibilities here. First, we may simulate jump times or, second, if we have fixed a time grid, we can simulate the jumps occurring in between grid points. Then, we use a simple scheme to simulate the diffusion component and apply the proxy using Gaussian densities.

Table 8.5   Comparison of Greeks for digitals using analytic, proxy and FD methods

Method	PV (SE)	Δ (SE)	Γ (SE)	v (SE)
Analytic	0.531270	0.016610	−2.800324e-004	−0.560070
MC Proxy	0.531576 (0.001460)	0.016641 (7.195974e − 005)	−2.844054e − 004 (4.769032e − 006)	−0.569254 (0.009541)
MC FD	0.531576 (0.001460)	0.016485 (2.722766e − 004)	−0.0428901 (0.018318)	−0.0022114 (0.12765)

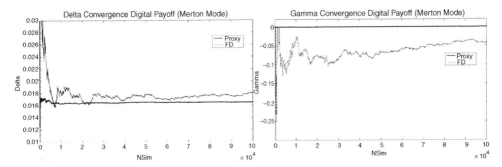

Figure 8.33 Proxy simulation to derive Δ (left) and Γ (right) for a Digital option in the Merton model

The Lookback Option   We choose the strikes for the Lookback option to be $K_1 = 105$ and $K_2 = 125$.

We have assessed a disturbance of the initial parameters by 1%. Our results are summarized in Table 8.6. Figure 8.34 further illustrates the results.

The Knock-Out Option   For the Knock-Out option we consider a time-dependent barrier structure given by the lower barrier denoted by $L(t)$ and the upper barrier denoted by $U(t)$. We consider

$$L(t) = \begin{cases} 90 & \text{if} \quad t \in (0, 0.5] \\ 85 & \text{if} \quad t \in (0.5, 0.75] \\ 80 & \text{if} \quad t \in (0.75, 1] \end{cases} \tag{8.111}$$

$$U(t) = \begin{cases} 110 & \text{if} \quad t \in (0, 0.5] \\ 115 & \text{if} \quad t \in (0.5, 0.75] \\ 120 & \text{if} \quad t \in (0.75, 1] \end{cases} \tag{8.112}$$

The numerical results are given in Table 8.7.

We show the running average Monte Carlo estimator in Figure 8.35.

Pure Jump Models – Variance Gamma

Second, we consider the Variance Gamma model. The parameters are chosen as follows: $S(0) = 100$, $K = 100$, $T = 1.0$, $r = 0.1$, $\sigma = 0.12136$, $\mu = -0.1436$ and $v = 0.1686$. The

Table 8.6 Comparison of Greeks for Lookbacks using proxy and FD methods

Method	PV (SE)	Δ (SE)	Γ (SE)	v (SE)
MC Proxy	0.442255 (0.0015907)	0.010877 (3.343906e − 004)	−0.001303 (7.155397e − 005)	−1.014196 (0.045195)
MC FD	0.442255 (0.0015907)	0.010304 (0.004983)	0.914718 (0.9967143)	−0.003827 (0.70262)

Table 8.7   Comparison of Greeks for Knock-Out options using FD and proxy methods

Method	PV (SE)	Δ (SE)	Γ (SE)	v (SE)
MC Proxy	0.564746 (0.0075695)	−0.0066871 ($0.9910932e − 004$)	−0.0072713 ($1.8442553e − 004$)	−8.6071757 (0.1745823)
MC FD	0.564746 (0.0075695)	−0.054896 (0.001825)	−2.167931 (6.893258)	−0.0174076 (4.8101873)

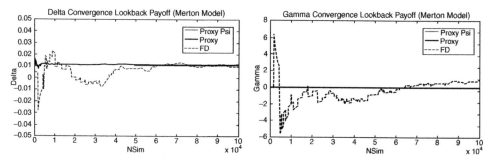

Figure 8.34   Proxy simulation to derive the Δ (left) and the Γ (right) for a Lookback option in the Merton model

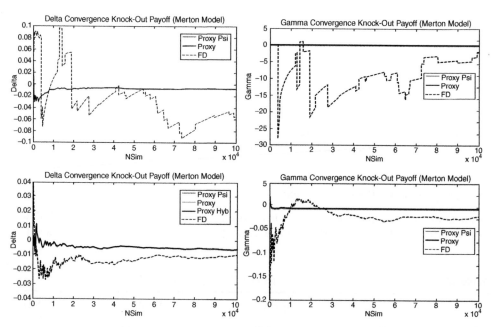

Figure 8.35   Proxy simulation for Δ (top and bottom left) and Γ (top and bottom right) for a Knock-Out barrier option in the Merton model. The difference between the top and the bottom results is that we have chosen different disturbance parameters. We used 0.1%(top) and 1%(bottom) of the initial spot price

Table 8.8 Comparison of Greeks obtained from proxy and FD methods in the Variance Gamma model

Method	PV (SE)	Δ (SE)	Γ (SE)	v (SE)
Analytic	0.697421	0.01844	−0.00136	−1.137605
MC Proxy	0.69721 (8.5077e − 002)	0.01841 (1.2547e − 004)	−0.00134 (3.707097)	−1.371968 (0.01568)
MC FD	0.69721 (8.5077e − 002)	0.0189337 (2.6670e − 004)	−4.52421e − 004 (0.083867)	−1.658869 (0.35365)

parameters have been chosen according to Madan, D.B., Carr P.P. and Chang E.C. (1998) or Ribeiro, C. and Webber, N. (2007a).

The Digital Option   The analytical price can be obtained using results from Madan, D.B., Carr P.P. and Chang E.C. (1998).

Table 8.8 shows the superiority of the proxy method to the finite difference approximation, in particular, if we want to estimate second order derivatives where the finite difference method is not suitable for obvious reasons. Figure 8.36 illustrates the results.

We have no significant difference between the proxy method and the mixture method in our setting. What we observe is that if we use the finite difference method and then add the proxy component we improve the results by adding more weight to the proxy scheme using the function Ψ.

If we are interested in the parameters not describing the subordinator process we should simulate the subordinator first. Let G_t be the value of the subordinator. This value represents the new time coordinate of the Brownian motion. To sample the value of Y at time $t + \Delta$ we use the value $Y(G(t))$. Then, we obtain values for the consecutive time step $t + \Delta$ in the scheme; we have for the logarithm of the underlying

$$Y(t + \Delta) = Y(t) + (r + \omega)\Delta + \mu \cdot G_t + \sigma \sqrt{G_t} Z_t. \tag{8.113}$$

Thus, for each step the transition density is Gaussian and so we can use the proxy method employing Gaussian transition densities instead of the Variance Gamma transition density.

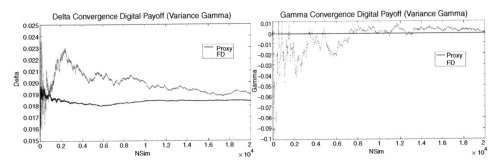

Figure 8.36 Proxy simulation for the Variance Gamma model of the Δ (left) and Γ (right) of a Digital option payoff. The disturbance parameter has been set to $\varepsilon = 0.001\%$ of the initial spot price

Table 8.9   Numerical results for computing Greeks in the Variance Gamma model

Method	PV (SE)	Δ (SE)	Γ (SE)	v (SE)
MC	0.6972542	0.0185616	−0.00134	−1.14317
	$(8.50774e - 004)$	$(1.44826e - 004)$	$(2.1025e - 005)$	(0.01813)

Proceeding this way in models like the Heston model, we can derive Greeks for all parameters not governing the behaviour of the stochastic volatility using, for example, the QE discretization and Gaussian transition densities for a fixed volatility. The interested reader can easily work out the details.

For the above model the (Gaussian) transition density is given by

$$\frac{1}{\sqrt{2\pi}\tilde{\sigma}} \exp\left(-\frac{x^2}{2\tilde{\sigma}^2}\right), \tag{8.114}$$

denoting $x = Y(t + \Delta) - Y(t) - (r + \omega)\Delta - \mu \cdot G_t$ and $\tilde{\sigma} = \sigma \sqrt{G_t}$.

In Table 8.9 we list the numbers we found using this approach. Further, we show this approach together with the finite difference approach in Figure 8.37.

The Lookback Option   We have applied the above algorithms to the Variance Gamma model and an option with a Lookback payoff. The results are displayed in Table 8.10 and Figure 8.38.

The Knock-Out Option   This last section considers option pricing in the Variance Gamma model and a Knock-Out payoff with time-dependent barrier level. The results are displayed in Table 8.11 and Figure 8.39.

The Variance Gamma Model Using Characteristic Functions

The Variance Gamma model can be taken as a benchmark. We apply the proxy method to derive sensitivities in Kienitz, J. (2010) and obtain stable results for this model. We will now compare the results using the approximation to the density and the characteristic function.

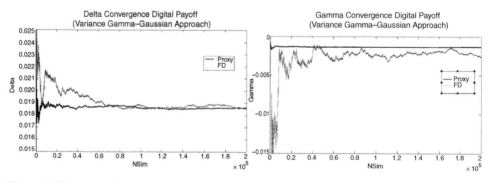

Figure 8.37   Proxy simulation for the Variance Gamma model and the Δ (left) and Γ (right) of a Digital option payoff. The disturbance parameter has been set to $\varepsilon = 0.001\%$ of the initial spot price

Table 8.10 Greeks computed for Lookbacks in the Variance Gamma model using proxy and FD methods

Method	PV (SE)	Δ (SE)	Γ (SE)
MC Proxy	0.6420 (6.6931e − 004)	0.0026 (3.5859e − 004)	0.5992 (6.4187e − 004)
MC FD	0.6420 (6.6931e − 004)	0.0032 (2.4314e − 004)	−0.0041 (5.4172e − 0043)

Table 8.11 Comparison of Greeks computed using proxy, proxy Psi and FD methods for Knock-Out option and the Variance Gamma model

Method	PV (SE)	Δ (SE)	Γ (SE)
MC Proxy	1.3647 (0.0099)	−0.1587 (0.0133)	−5.9908e − 004 (0.0256)
MC Proxy Psi	1.3647 (0.0099)	−0.12758 (0.0038)	−0.0323 (0.0098)
MC FD	1.3647 (0.0099)	−0.1428 (0.0044)	−0.0202 (0.0103)

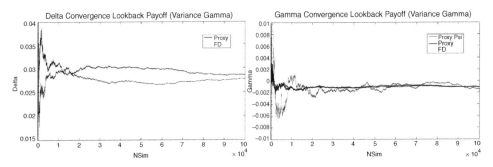

Figure 8.38 Proxy simulation to derive Δ for a Lookback option in the Variance Gamma model

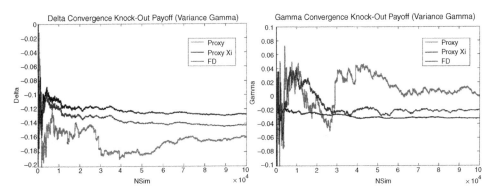

Figure 8.39 Proxy simulation to derive Δ (left) and Γ (right) for a Knock-Out barrier option in the Variance Gamma model

Table 8.12   Greeks for digitals using FD, proxy and proxy char method for the Variance Gamma model

Parameter	Proxy	Proxy Char
Δ_A	0.02862	
Δ	0.02824 (5.116e-004)	0.02824 (5.116e-004)
Γ_A	−0.001128	
Γ	−0.001150(7.368e-005)	−0.001150(7.368e-005)
$Vega_A$	−0.900909100578273	
$Vega$	−0.9031(0.0710)	−0.9031(0.0710)

Digital Option   The standard proxy methods have been shown to produce reliable and stable results when the payoff is discontinuous. We have chosen the case of a Digital option as one representative because closed form solutions exist to benchmark the Monte Carlo simulation method for the Variance Gamma model. We consider a Digital option with strike price $K = 101$. The corresponding Greeks are shown in Table 8.12.

The Vega is the change in the parameter σ and not with respect to implied volatility. We observe that there is virtually no difference between the method using the closed form expression and the estimator using the characteristic function. This is illustrated in Figure 8.40, which gives the running average of the estimators using the transition density in closed form and the density obtained from inverting the characteristic function. The latter samples are indicated by circles.

Knock-Out Options   For path-dependent options with discontinuous payoffs the proxy method produces reliable results. We consider Knock-Out options and show that the accuracy depends heavily on the choice of parameters for A and M used to numerically invert the characteristic function.

For the Knock-Out option we consider the example given in (8.110). We find the following results (Table 8.13):

Table 8.13   Greeks of a Knock-Out option using FD, proxy and proxy char methods in the Variance Gamma model

Parameter	Proxy	Proxy Char
Δ_{FD}	−0.2408	
Δ	−0.1464 (0.0279)	−0.1456 (0.0280)
Γ_{FD}	−1.0578	
Γ	0.1619(0.1891)	0.2328(0.1351)
$Vega_{FD}$		
$Vega$	35.2263(0.7343)	35.2263 (0.7343)

Figure 8.41 illustrates the proxy simulation using on the one hand the closed form transition kernel and on the other hand the transition density obtained using the characteristic function. We show how the estimates vary choosing the parameters A and M for indirectly computing the transition density.

The VG GOU Model

We consider the VG GOU model as introduced in Chapter 3, Subsection 3.4.2. In this case we take the same parameters as before but $r = 0.02$.

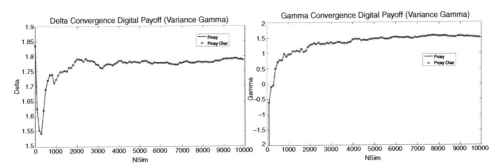

Figure 8.40 Proxy simulation for a Digital option using closed form and characteristic function version of the transition density for simulated Δ (left) and Γ (right)

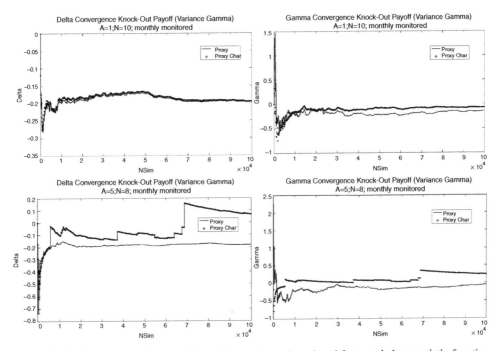

Figure 8.41 Proxy simulation for a Knock-Out option using closed form and characteristic function version of the transition density for simulating Δ (upper left) and Γ (upper right) with $A = 1$ and $M = 10$ as well as the Δ (bottom left) and Γ (bottom right) for $A = 5$ and $M = 8$

Table 8.14 Comparison of Monte Carlo and analytical prices for the Digital option and the proxy and proxy char method

Parameter	Proxy	Proxy Char
Δ_A	0.0275	
Δ	0.0283 (2.4050e-004)	0.0250 (0.0490)
Γ_A	−0.0017	
Γ	−0.0018(4.8989e-005)	−0.0012980(0.06930)

Table 8.15 Comparison of Greeks for a Knock-Out option using the FD and the proxy method in the VG GOU model

Parameter	5 steps per month	10 steps per month
Δ_{FD}	0.1084	0.1417
Δ	−0.0734(0.0041)	−0.0688 (0.0041)
Γ_{FD}	−3.6413	2.6507
Γ	0.2100(0.0092)	0.2055(0.0098)

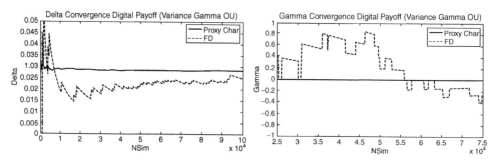

Figure 8.42 Proxy simulation for a Digital option for the Δ (left) and the Γ (right) for the VG GOU model

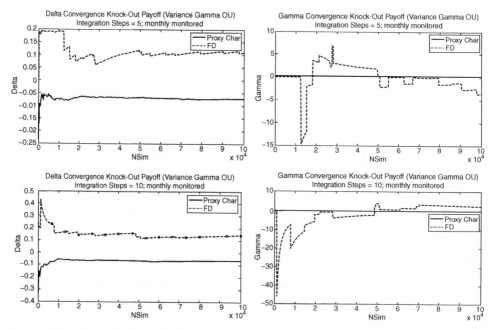

Figure 8.43 Proxy simulation for the Δ (top and bottom left) and the Γ (top and bottom right) of a Knock-Out option using 5 steps (upper left and right) and 10 steps (bottom left and right) to determine the stochastic clock of the VG GOU model

Digital Option   We again choose the case of a digital option as one representative and we use the VG GOU model.

We again consider a Digital option with strike price $K = 101$. The corresponding Greeks are shown in Table 8.14.

This is furthermore illustrated by Figure 8.42 and shows the running averages of the estimator using the proxy method with transition kernels obtained by inverting the characteristic function and the estimator using the finite difference method.

Knock-Out Option   We again consider the Knock-Out option from the previous section. The Greeks are shown in Table 8.15.

Figure 8.43 shows the running average of the estimators using the numerical inversion to calculate the transition density and the finite difference estimators. We considered 5 and 10 integration steps between the monitored times.

```
function y = BinTree_CP(S0, K, r, T, sigma, n, type)

% S0: Spot value
% K: Strike
% r: riskless rate
% T: Maturity
% sigma: volatility
% n: periods for tree
% type: 0 put, 1 call

dt = T / n;                             % length of one period
u = exp(sigma * sqrt(dt));              % up move
d = 1 / u;                              % down move
D = exp(-r * dt);                       % discount
p = (1/D - d) / (u - d);                % probability

S{n} = S0 * u^n * d.^(0:2:2*n);

if type == 0
    cp = 1;
else
    cp = -1;
end

v{n} = max(cp*(K - S{n}), 0);           % payoff at t_N

for i = n-1:-1:1

    S{i} = S0 * u.^i * d.^(0:2:2*i);
    v{i} = max(cp*(K - S{i}), 0);

    expected_val = p * v{i+1}(1:end-1) * D ...
        + (1-p) * v{i+1}(2:end) * D;    % expected value of price
    index = v{i} < expected_val;        % early exercise or not
    v{i}(index) = expected_val(index);  % value at t_i

end

y = p * v{1}(1) * D + (1-p) * v{1}(2) * D;  % option value t_0

end
```

Figure 8.44   Implementation of a binomial tree for pricing American Call and Put options

```
function [S, u, d, df, p] = createbintree(S0, T, n, r, sigma)
    dt = T / n;                         % length of one period
    u = exp(sigma * sqrt(dt));          % up move
    d = 1 / u;                          % down move
    df = exp(-r * dt);                  % discount
    p = (1/df - d) / (u - d);           % probability up

    S = zeros(2^n, n+1);
    S(:,1) = S0*ones(2^n,1);

    for i=1:1:n
        a = [u * ones(2^(n-i),1); d * ones(2^(n-i),1)];
        S(:,i+1) = S(:,i).*repmat(a, 2^(i-1),1);
    end

end
```

Figure 8.45   Implementation of a binomial tree

```
function y = asian_bintree(S, df, p, K, type)
n = size(S,2)-1;
v = cell(1, n+1);                       % option value

tmp = repmat(1:n, length(S), 1);
average_val = cumsum(S(:,2:end), 2) ./ tmp; % average value

if type == 0
    cp = 1;
else
    cp = -1;
end

v{n+1} = max(cp*(average_val(:,end)-K), 0); % payoff at t_N

iVec = 1:length(S);

for i = n:-1:2
    Jset = 1:2:2^i;
    expected_val = p * v{i+1}(Jset) * df ...
        + (1-p) * v{i+1}(1+Jset) * df;

    iVec = iVec(1:length(iVec)/2) * 2;

    v{i} = max(cp*(average_val(iVec,i-1)-K),0);  % payoff at t_i
    v{i}=max(v{i}, expected_val);                % option value t_i
end

y = p * v{2}(1) * df + (1-p) * v{2}(2) * df;     % option value t_0
```

Figure 8.46   Implementation of a binomial tree for pricing American Arithmetic Asian options

8.6 SUMMARY AND CONCLUSIONS

In this chapter we reviewed methods for pricing early exercise opportunities for options using simulation. The three main methods – Regression, Policy Iteration and Upper Bounds – were considered. For all methods and models we provided Matlab code as well as numerical examples. We studied the relative advantages of the methods as well as their restrictions in terms of their use for financial engineering.

In the second part of this chapter we showed how to compute Greeks by simulation. Again, we provided Matlab code and numerical results for the reader's convenience. To this end we reviewed three methods to compute Greeks using Monte Carlo simulation.

We considered a finite difference estimator, a path-wise estimation method and the likelihood ratio method. The path-wise method is robust and efficient especially when combined with adjoint methods. However, it cannot easily be applied to options with discontinuous payoffs. To this end we motivated the likelihood ratio method and a numerical clone called the proxy

```
function y = barrier_bintree(S, df, p, K, Barrier, type)
n = size(S,2)-1;
v = cell(1, n+1);                            % option value

if type == 0
    index = @(mval,x) mval > Barrier * ones(2^x,1);
    payoff = @(x) max(x- K,0);
    m_val = max(S,[],2);
else
    index = @(mval,x) mval < Barrier * ones(2^x,1);
    payoff = @(x) max(K-x,0);
    m_val = min(S,[],2);
end

v{n+1} = index(m_val,n) .* payoff(S(:,end));

iVec = 1:length(S);
for i = n:-1:2
    iVec = iVec(1:length(iVec)/2) * 2;

    if type == 0
        m_val = max(S(iVec,1:i),[], 2);
    else
        m_val = min(S(iVec,1:i),[], 2);
    end
    Jset = 1:2:2^i;
    expected_val = p * v{i+1}(Jset) ...
        + (1-p) * v{i+1}(1+Jset) * df;       % cont value

    v{i} = index(m_val,i-1) .* payoff(S(iVec,i));% current opt value
    v{i}=max(v{i}, expected_val);            % option value at t_i

end

y = p * v{2}(1) * df + (1-p) * v{2}(2) * df;   % option value at t_0
end
```

Figure 8.47 Implementation of a binomial tree for pricing American Barrier options

technique. We pointed out strengths and weaknesses and provided numerical results. Again, the code is included in the supporting material for this book.

8.7 APPENDIX – TREES

We have used a binomial tree as the benchmark for testing the simulation methods for American and Bermudan options. In this appendix we provide the code for the trees pricing an American Call/Put option, an Arithmetic Asian option and a Barrier option. The code is given in Figures 8.44 and 8.45–8.47.

For the exotic options we provide a construction method for a binomial tree, Figure 8.45 and corresponding payoff functions, Figures 8.46 and 8.47.

9

Calibration and Optimization

9.1 INTRODUCTION AND OBJECTIVES

In this chapter we consider the task of deriving model parameters by matching quoted option prices. This procedure is known as *calibration*. It relies on the assumption that there are sufficiently many liquidly traded options and that these can be valued efficiently and fast.

We give examples for the calibration of option pricing models specified in Chapters 2 and 3 using the algorithms outlined in Chapters 5 and 6. The standard calibration approach minimizes a distance between model prices, P^{model}, and market prices, P^{market}. The distance can be seen as an error measure. Common error measures are:

1. *AAE* (average absolute error)

$$AAE(x) = \frac{1}{N} \sum_{i=1}^{N} |P_i^{market} - P_i^{model}(x)|$$

2. *APE* (average percentage error)

$$APE(x) = \frac{1}{N} \sum_{i=1}^{N} \frac{|P_i^{market} - P_i^{model}(x)|}{\widehat{P}^{market}}, \quad \text{with} \quad \widehat{P}^{market} := \frac{1}{N} \sum_{k=1}^{N} P_k^{market}$$

3. *ARPE* (average relative percentage error)

$$ARPE(x) = \frac{1}{N} \sum_{i=1}^{N} \frac{|P_i^{market} - P_i^{model}(x)|}{P_i^{market}}$$

4. *RMSE* (root-mean-square error)

$$RMSE(x) = \frac{1}{\sqrt{N}} \sqrt{\sum_{i=1}^{N} (P_i^{market} - P_i^{model}(x))^2},$$

where N is equal to the number of quoted option prices and $x = (x_1, \ldots, x_n)^\top$ denoting the vector of model parameters. Each error measure is a real-valued function $f : \mathbb{R}^n \to \mathbb{R}$ of x. Since we are looking for a parameter vector x^* that best fits the model to available market prices, the calibration procedure can be interpreted as an optimization problem of the form

$$\min_{x \in \mathcal{X}} f(x), \quad \mathcal{X} \subseteq \mathbb{R}^n. \tag{9.1}$$

$\mathcal{X}$ is the admissible domain of the model parameters $x_1, \ldots, x_n$. In what follows we describe some well-known methods for optimization. We consider:

- Downhill Simplex method (*Nelder–Mead*).
- Damped Gauss-Newton method (*Levenberg–Marquardt*).
- L-BFGS Quasi-Newton method.

- Sequential Quadratic Programming.
- Differential Evolution.
- Simulated Annealing.

Starting from a given initial guess x^0 all presented methods iteratively compute solutions x^k for $k = 1, 2, \ldots$ resulting in a series of decreasing function values $f(x^k)$. The methods are different since they apply different methodologies such as *direct search*, *gradient based* or *probabilistic* approaches for suggesting a new approximation x^{k+1} to the solution x^* with $f(x^k) > f(x^{k+1})$. The methods can also be distinguished according to their convergence properties. Here, we distinguish between *locally* and *globally convergent* methods. Finally, there are methods leading to a *local* or a *global minimum*. Thus, the corresponding optimization algorithms are called a *local* or *global optimizer*.

Due to restrictions on the model parameters, for instance $\sigma \geq 0$ in the Black–Scholes model or $2\kappa\theta > \omega^2$ representing the Feller-condition for a square root process, the admissible domain $\mathcal{X}$ of model parameters typically forms a subset of $\mathbb{R}^n$. Thus, to guarantee an admissible solution $x^* \in \mathcal{X}$ we have to add constraints to the basic optimization problem, Equation (9.1). We distinguish between simple bound constraints represented by inequalities $lb \leq x \leq ub$, inequality constraints $g(x) \leq 0$ and equality constraints $h(x) = 0$ where the functions $g : \mathbb{R}^n \to \mathbb{R}^m$ and $h : \mathbb{R}^n \to \mathbb{R}^p$ are in general non-linear. The resulting optimization problem takes the form

$$
\begin{aligned}
\min_x \quad & f(x) \\
\text{subject to} \quad & g_i(x) \leq 0 && \text{for } i = 1, \ldots, m \\
& h_j(x) = 0 && \text{for } j = 1, \ldots, p \\
& lb_k \leq x_k \leq ub_k && \text{for } k = 1, \ldots, n.
\end{aligned}
\tag{9.2}
$$

All the methods except *Sequential Quadratic Programming* were invented to determine a minimizer of an unconstrained optimization problem, (9.1). Typically, this problem is much easier to solve than the constraint one, (9.2).

Thus, we start our calculations with the basic algorithms applicable for unconstrained optimization. Then, we solve the constraint optimization problem by extending the methods applied to the unconstraint problem.

The derivatives based Levenberg–Marquardt and L-BFGS methods can be modified to handle simple bound constraints by a method called *gradient projection*. Such derivatives based methods are also called *Newton methods* in the literature. The Sequential Quadratic Programming is also a Newton method based optimization approach which is especially designed to handle simple bounds as well as functional constraints. Levenberg–Marquardt, L-BFGS and Sequential Quadratic Programming need to apply derivatives of the function to be minimized. This function is called *objective function*. In the sequel the differentiability of the functions f but also of the functions g and h determining the constraints is an essential requirement for these methods. Since analytical formulae are rarely applicable and numerical differentiation is computationally very costly, it is sometimes preferable to use an algorithm which does not rely on derivatives at all. Direct search methods and stochastic optimization are examples of derivative-free optimizers. We consider *Downhill Simplex, Differential Evolution* and *Simulated Annealing* in this chapter. In contrast to the Newton method based optimizers the direct search optimizers are designed to find the global minimum in the presence of many local minima.

9.2 THE NELDER–MEAD METHOD

The *Nelder–Mead* or *Downhill Simplex method* is widely applied for non-linear and uncon-strained optimization. It is a direct search method and attempts to solve the optimization problem given some real-valued objective function $f : \mathbb{R}^n \to \mathbb{R}$, but it does not rely on the calculation of derivatives. As outlined in the article by Nelder, J.A. and Mead, R. (1965) the method starts from a given simplex S_0 and for each iteration step indexed by k identifies a vertex v^k_{max} determined by

$$v^k_{max} := \operatorname{argmax}_{x \in [v^k_0, \ldots, v^k_n]} f(x). \tag{9.3}$$

It is the vertex where the function takes its largest value. The vertex v^k_{max} of the simplex S_k is then replaced by a new point $\hat{v}$ such that $f(\hat{v}) < f(v^k_{max})$. The new simplex is called S_{k+1}. To construct the new vertex $\hat{v}$ of this simplex the method uses three operations called *reflection*, *expansion* and *contraction*.

Geometrically, a simplex S of non-zero volume in n dimensions is defined as the convex hull of $n + 1$ affine independent points $x_0, \ldots, x_n \in \mathbb{R}^n$.

Let $x_j - x_0$ be linear independent, $j = 1, \ldots, n$ and set

$$S := \left\{ \sum_{j=0}^{n} \lambda_j x_j \;\middle|\; \lambda_j \geq 0, j = 0, \ldots, n, \; \sum_{j=0}^{n} \lambda_j = 1 \right\}.$$

S defines a n-dimensional simplex with vertices $x_0, \ldots, x_n$.

For the unconstrained optimization problem we use the Nelder–Mead algorithm introduced in Woods, D.J. (1985). The vertices $v_0, \ldots, v_n$ are ordered subject to their function values, meaning that $f(v_0) \leq \ldots \leq f(v_n)$.

In contrast to optimization algorithms using derivatives there exist very few convergence results for the Downhill Simplex method (see Lagarias, J.C., Reeds, J.A., Wright, M.H. and Wright, P.E. (1998) and McKinnon, K.I.M. (1998)). Empirical studies applying Algorithm 9.1 have shown that choosing $\alpha = 1, 0.4 \leq \beta \leq 0.6$ and $2 \leq \gamma \leq 3$ leads to acceptable results for a collection of test cases.

Since the Downhill Simplex algorithm works for a wide range of objective functions it is not straightforward to define an adequate stopping criterion. To prevent Algorithm 9.1 from getting trapped in an endless loop we terminate the process when a predefined number of iterations k_{max} is reached. This standard rule should be extended by additional stopping criteria taking into account the change in the values of the objective function values or the size of the current simplex. Nelder, J.A. and Mead, R. (1965) propose using the standard deviation

$$\sigma_f := \left(\frac{1}{n+1} \sum_{i=1}^{n} (f(v_i) - \overline{f}_k)^2 \right)^{\frac{1}{2}} \quad \text{with} \quad \overline{f}_k = \frac{1}{n+1} \sum_{j=1}^{n} f(v_j)$$

of the objective function evaluated on the vertices of the simplex S_k as a stopping rule. If σ_f is below a sufficiently small chosen tolerance level $\varepsilon > 0$, the algorithm stops. The optimal solution is then given by vertex v_0.

An alternative choice might be the diameter of the simplex S_k, measuring the maximum distance between any two vertices of the simplex, that is

$$\operatorname{diam}(S) = \max_{i \neq j} \{ \|v_i - v_j\|_\infty \} \quad \text{for} \quad i, j = 0, \ldots, n.$$

Algorithm 9.1: Downhill Simplex method

(S.1) Initialize $0 < \alpha \leq 1, 0 < \beta < 1, \gamma > 1$ and the ordered vertices v_j for $j = 0, \ldots, n$ of simplex S_0. Choose a maximum number of iterations $k_{\max}$ and set $k := 0$

(S.2) **if** $k > k_{\max}$ **then**
| **stop**

(S.3) Calculate the centroid $\hat{v} := \frac{1}{n} \sum\limits_{i=0}^{n-1} v_i$

(S.4) *Reflection:* Calculate $x_r = (1 + \alpha)\hat{v} - \alpha v_n$ and set $v^k = x_r$.
if $f(x_r) < f(v_{n-1})$ **then**

(S.5) | **if** $f(x_r) < f(v_0)$ **then** *Expansion:*
| | Compute $x_e = (1 - \gamma)v_n + \gamma x_r$
| | **if** $f(x_e) < f(x_r)$ **then**
| | | set $v^k = x_e$

(S.6) **else** *Contraction:*
| **if** $f(v_{n-1}) \leq f(x_r) < f(v_n)$ **then** *Partial Outside:*
| | Set $x_c = (1 - \beta)\hat{v} + \beta x_r$
| **else** $f(x_r) \geq f(v_n)$ *Partial Inside:*
| | Set $x_c = (1 - \beta)\hat{v} + \beta v_n$
| **if** $f(x_c) < f(v_n)$ **then**
| | Set $v^k = x_c$
| **else** *Total Contraction:*
| | **for** $j = 1$ **to** n **do**
| | | $v_j = \frac{v_0 + v_j}{2}$
| | and set $v^k = v_n$

(S.7) Update simplex S_{k+1} by sorting $\{v_0, v_1, \ldots, v_{n-1}, v^k\}$. Set k:=k+1 and goto (S.2)

The Matlab built-in Downhill Simplex function `fminsearch` terminates if both the maximum absolute difference in function values $|f(v_0) - f(v_i)|$ is less than a predefined tolerance and the maximum distance of any vertex subject to the best vertex v_0 is sufficiently small. The distance, denoted by $\|\cdot\|_\infty$, is measured by the infinity norm, that is

$$\|v_0 - v_i\|_\infty := \max_{j=1,\ldots,n} |v_0(j) - v_i(j)| \quad \text{for} \quad i = 1, \ldots, n.$$

The initial simplex S_0 is constructed as follows. Choose a starting point $x_0 \in \mathbb{R}^n$ and calculate the points $x_1, \ldots, x_n$ using the equation

$$x_j = x_0 + e_j, \quad j = 1, \ldots, n, \tag{9.4}$$

with $e_j \in \mathbb{R}^n$ being the j-th unit vector. The ordered vertices v_j for $j = 0, \ldots, n$ of the simplex S_0 are then given by

$$v_j = \operatorname{argmin}_{x \in [x_0, \ldots, x_n] \backslash \Omega_j} f(x) \tag{9.5}$$

denoting $\Omega_j := \{v_0, \ldots, v_{j-1}\}$.

For $n = 2$ the individual steps of Algorithm 9.1 can be visualized. Figure 9.1 shows the reflection of vertex v_n at the centroid $\hat{v}$.

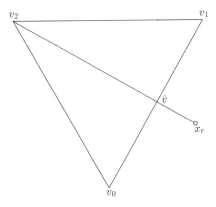

Figure 9.1 Reflection of v_n at the centroid $\hat{v}$

If the reflection point $x_r = (1 + \alpha)\hat{v} - \alpha v_n$ has a smaller objective function value $f(x_r)$ than the second worst vertex v_{n-1}, the worst vertex v_n is replaced by x_r. If, in addition, $f(x_r)$ is less than the objective function value $f(v_0)$ of the current best vertex v_0, the algorithm determines the expansion point $x_e = (1 - \gamma)v_n + \gamma x_r$, for a possible further enhancement and replaces v_n by x_e if $f(x_e) < f(x_r)$ (Figure 9.2).

On the other hand, the case $f(x_r) \geq f(v_{n-1})$ leads to a contraction step. Figure 9.3 displays a partial outside contraction, which is applied if $f(x_r) < f(v_n)$. In this case, the contraction point $x_c = (1 - \beta)\hat{v} + \beta x_r$ lies outside the simplex S_k. It is located on the line joining $\hat{v}$ and x_r.

A partial inside contraction (Figure 9.4) is applied if the reflection point x_r has a greater objective function value than the current worst vertex v_n and leads to the contraction point $x_c = (1 - \beta)\hat{v} + \beta v_n$ on the same axis as before, but now it is located inside the simplex S_k.

The generated contraction point x_c replaces v_n in the simplex S_k if it fulfils $f(x_c) < f(v_n)$; otherwise, the total contraction (Figure 9.5) shrinks any edge of simplex S_k by one half seen from the perspective of the best vertex v_0 and starts the new iteration using the shrunken vertex.

So far, the Nelder–Mead method is only applicable for unconstrained optimization problems. A common approach to extend it to handle both inequality and equality constraints is to specify

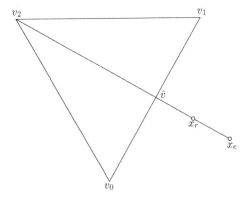

Figure 9.2 Expansion of the reflection point x_r

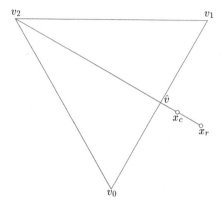

Figure 9.3   Partial outside contraction

penalty functions, assigning very large positive values to non-admissible vertices. The vertex leading to the worst value in the current iteration step is then reflected to the one which led to the worst result in the previous iteration. Box, M.J. (1965) show that this approach leads to the so-called *simplex flattening*. The diameter of the simplex quickly tends to zero near constraints and terminates, but with a wrong solution. How to overcome this issue when applying penalty functions is addressed in Subrahmanyam, M.B. (1989). It is proposed to use *delayed reflection*. If a vertex becomes non-admissible in the k-th iteration, then the order of this vertex is not changed until the next iteration step, which is $k + 1$, has been completed. Thus, the $k + 1$-th iteration is performed using the current value of the function at the non-admissible points. Although this can cause problems if the function is not well defined, outside the admissible domain the algorithm is known to produce reliable results in practice.

Consider the following minimization problem with constraints:

$$\min \quad f(x)$$
$$\text{subject to} \quad g(x) \leq 0.$$

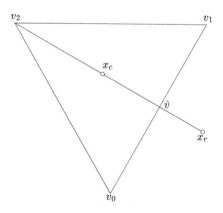

Figure 9.4   Partial inside contraction

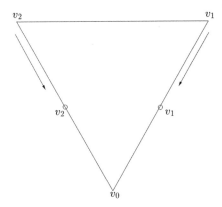

Figure 9.5 Total contraction/shrinkage

The inequality constraints are modelled using a non-linear function $g : \mathbb{R}^n \to \mathbb{R}^m$. The algorithm starts at a point $\tilde{x} \in \mathcal{X}$ from the admissible domain $\mathcal{X} = \{x \in \mathbb{R}^n : g(x) \le 0\}$. An admissible initial simplex S_0 that is contained in the domain $\mathcal{X}$ is constructed using the following procedure:

Set $\delta = 0.5$ and set

$$x_0(i) = \begin{cases} (1 - \delta)\tilde{x}(i) & \tilde{x}(i) \ne 0 \\ -\delta & \text{otherwise} \end{cases}, \quad i = 1, \dots, n.$$

If x_0 is not admissible, set $\delta \to \delta/2$ and repeat the step until the vertex becomes admissible. The unsorted vertices x_j for $j = 1, \dots, n$ are chosen according to

$$x_j = \begin{cases} \tilde{x} + \delta \tilde{x}(j - 1)e_{j-1} & \tilde{x}(j - 1) \ne 0 \\ \tilde{x} - \delta e_{j-1} & \text{otherwise} \end{cases}.$$

If any vertex becomes not admissible, set $\delta \to \delta/2$ and repeat the steps until all vertices fulfil the constraints and are therefore admissible. Then, the simplex S_0 equals the ordered list of vertices $\{v_0, \dots, v_n\}$ subject to their function values $f(v_0) \le \dots \le f(v_n)$ such as for the unconstrained case.

The first iteration of the Nelder–Mead algorithm with delayed reflection is a slightly modified version of the unconstrained case. Given the admissible simplex S_0 we calculate the centroid $\hat{v}$ and the reflection point x_r and set $v^k = x_r$. If v^k is not admissible, we replace v_n by v^k, and sort the vertices $\{v_0, v_1, \dots, v_{n-1}, v^k\}$ with respect to their function values and, finally, we set the simplex S_{k+1} corresponding to the ordered list of vertices.

If the reflection point x_r is an admissible point we distinguish two cases:

1. If $f(x_r) < f(v_{n-1})$ and $f(x_r) < f(v_0)$,
   we compute the expansion point x_e and set $v^k = x_e$ if x_e is admissible.
2. If $f(x_r) \ge f(v_{n-1})$,
   we compute the contraction point

$$x_c = \begin{cases} (1 - \beta)\hat{v} + \beta x_r & \text{if } f(x_r) < f(v_n) \\ (1 - \beta)\hat{v} + \beta v_n & \text{otherwise} \end{cases}.$$

If $f(x_c) < f(v_n)$ we set $v^k = x_c$ and otherwise we apply a total contraction step for S_k.

Table 9.1   Rosen–Suzuki problem solved by the Nelder–Mead method with delayed reflection

α	Iterations	$||x^* - \texttt{xMin}||_\infty$	fmin
0.98	11039	0.000001029626061	−43.99999999
0.95	3218	0.000000168552033	−43.99999999
0.90	1181	0.000000032541332	−43.99999999
0.85	914	0.000000089568320	−43.99999999
0.80	12621	0.007654478083445	−43.99953855
0.75	1733	0.080610646277009	−43.83886787
0.70	818	0.825380641779130	−41.27814787

For $k = 1, 2, \ldots$ the algorithm works as follows:

If v^{k-1} becomes non-admissible in the $k - 1$-th iteration we assign a large positive value to the vertex $v_i = v^{k-1}$, for instance $f(v_i) = 1E + 100$. The simplex S_k is not changed although the function values may no longer be sorted in ascending order any more. This step suggests the non-admissible point v_i for reflection during the next iteration; the procedure is denoted by *delayed reflection*.

The centroid $\hat{v}$ as well as the reflection and expansion points x_r, x_e are computed. The difference in this version of the algorithm is that $\hat{v}$ is not the centroid with respect to the n best points any longer since S_k is not adjusted for the new function value $f(v_i)$.

The main difference for the k-th iteration, $k > 0$, is the continuation in case $f(x_r) \geq f(x_{n-1})$. If additionally x_r is non-admissible or $f(v_n)$ is penalized, for instance $f(v_n) > 1E + 100$ set $v^k = x_r$. If both points lie within the admissible domain we apply the contraction step as in Algorithm 9.1.

The last step consists of updating the simplex S_k, but we have to take into account that a large positive value is assigned to the vertex $v_i = v^{k-1}$. Thus, it may become the worst vertex v_n of the simplex S_{k+1}.

Far from the boundary of the admissible domain $\mathcal{X}$ the delayed reflection algorithm works almost in the same way as the unconstrained Nelder–Mead method. If the current simplex is close to non-admissibility the algorithm primarily consists of reflection and expansion steps. This is due to the fact that close to the boundary of the constraint region either the reflection point x_r or the point v_n is usually a non-admissible point and therefore it is assigned to be a candidate for applying reflection in the next iteration. We observe that the optimal choice of the reflection parameter α highly depends on the considered problem as we show later (see Table 9.1). Subrahmanyam, M.B. (1989) proposes using $\alpha = 0.95$. Convergence is guaranteed as long as the reflection parameter $\alpha < 1$.

It is possible to assign equality constraints of the form $h(x) = 0$ with $h : \mathbb{R}^n \to \mathbb{R}^p$ by considering the two inequality constraints $-h(x) \leq 0$ and $h(x) \leq 0$.

9.2.1   Implementation

The unconstrained algorithm, Algorithm 9.1, can be applied by calling the function

```
function [xMin, fMin] = NelderMead(objF,x0,alpha,...
                                    beta,gamma,varargin)
```

The implementation of the delayed reflection method of Subrahmanyam, M.B. (1989) for constrained problems is applied by calling

```
function [xMin, fMin] = conNelderMead(objF,conF,x0,...
                                  alpha,beta,gamma,varargin)
```

The input parameters for both functions are the same except for the constraints function handle conF of function conNelderMead. While the function handles objF and conF as well as the initial guess x0 are required inputs, the remaining parameters are optional and they are set to default values if not specified by the user. The user-defined objective function should be designed to use the vector matrix functionality of Matlab and thus be able to evaluate matrix inputs without using loops. For instance, the *Beale function* which we consider in this chapter is given by the following piece of code

```
function y = beale(xMat)
% This function implements the 2D-Beale function
y = (1.5 - xMat(1,:)+ xMat(1,:).*xMat(2,:)).^2 ...
        + (2.25 - xMat(1,:) + xMat(1,:).*xMat(2,:).^2).^2 ...
        + (2.625 - xMat(1,:)+ xMat(1,:).*xMat(2,:).^3).^2;
```

The input parameter xMat is assumed to be a matrix with two rows and columns. The function for modelling constraints is assumed to be of the form

```
function gval = conF(x,varargin)
```

The output argument gval is a vector of length M. For $j = 1, \ldots, M$ the j-th coefficient is given by the function value $g_j(x)$ of the constraints function $g_j : \mathbb{R}^n \to \mathbb{R}$. We assume that any constraint is defined such that the inequality $g_j(x) \leq 0$ has to be fulfilled. For instance, the constraints of the *Rosen–Suzuki example* are implemented as follows

```
function y = myconEx2(x)
% inequality constraints Rosen-Suzuki-problem
%-----------------------------------------------------------
% g1(x)  = x1^2+x2^2+x3^2+x4^2+x1-x2+x3-x4-8 <= 0
% g2(x)  = x1^2+2*x2^2+x3^2+2*x4^2-x1-x4-10 <= 0
% g3(x)  = 2*x1^2+x2^2+x3^2+2*x1-x2-x4-5 <= 0
%-----------------------------------------------------------
y = zeros(3,1);
y(1)  = x(1)^2+x(2)^2+x(3)^2+x(4)^2+x(1)-x(2)+x(3)-x(4)-8.0;
y(2)  = x(1)^2+2*x(2)^2+x(3)^2+2*x(4)^2-x(1)-x(4)-10;
y(3)  = 2*x(1)^2+x(2)^2+x(3)^2+2*x(1)-x(2)-x(4)-5;
```

Lower and upper bounds $lb \leq x \leq ub$ are handled, letting $g_{lb}(x) = -x + lb$ and $g_{ub}(x) = x - ub$. Equality constraints $h(x) = 0$ can be incorporated, setting $g(x) = |h(x)| - \varepsilon$ with $\varepsilon > 0$ small.

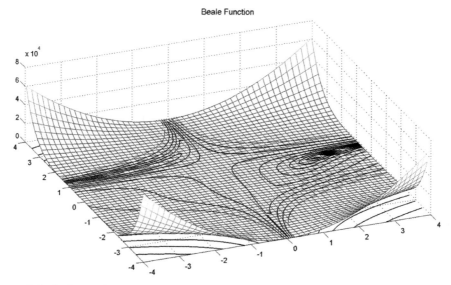

Figure 9.6 Surface and contour plot of the Beale function

9.2.2 Calibration Examples

First, we look at examples without constraints. The test functions under consideration and their minima are taken from Moré, J., Garbow, B. and Hillstrom, K. (1981). Figure 9.6 illustrates the Beale function as a surface and as a contour. The Beale function is defined by

$$f : \mathbb{R}^2 \to \mathbb{R}$$
$$f(x) = (1.5 - x_1 + x_1 x_2)^2 + (2.25 - x_1 + x_1 x_2^2)^2 + (2.625 - x_1 + x_1 x_2^3)^2. \quad (9.6)$$

The function takes its global minimum $f(x^*) = 0$ at $x^* = (3, 0.5)^\mathsf{T}$. We start the unconstrained downhill simplex optimization using the commands

```
% objective function
objF = @(x)beale(x)
% initial guess
x0 = [1;1];
% init Nelder Mead parameter
alpha = 1; % reflection coefficient
beta = 0.5; % contraction coefficient
gamma = 2.0; % expansion coefficient
% start optimization procedure
[xMin,fMin] = NelderMead(objF,x0,alpha,beta,gamma)
```

The algorithm stops after 118 iterations. The maximum absolute difference between the global minimizer x^* and the estimated solution xMin is less than $1e - 13$. The returned objective function value fmin is of the order $1e - 30$.

The second example is the *extended Rosenbrock function*

$$f : \mathbb{R}^n \to \mathbb{R}$$

$$f(x) = \sum_{i=1}^{n/2} 100(x_{2i} - x_{2i-1}^2)^2 + (1 - x_{2i-1})^2, \qquad (9.7)$$

with n being variable but an even number. The global optimum is $f(x^*) = 0$ at $x^* = (1, \ldots, 1)^\top$. Since none of the option pricing models specified in Chapters 2 and 3 has more than eight parameters, we consider $n = 10$. The objective function is defined using the function handle

```
objF = @(x) sum(100*(x(2:2:end,:) - x(1:2:end-1,:).^2).^2 ...
          + (1 - x(1:2:end-1,:)).^2);
```

To set up the initial guess $x^0 = (-1.2, 1, -1.2, 1, \ldots, -1.2, 1)^\top$ and to start the optimization procedure with default parameters, the following piece of code is used:

```
N = 10;
% initial guess
x0 = repmat([-1.2;1],N/2,1);
% start optimization procedure with default parameters
[xMin,fMin] = NelderMead(objF,x0)
```

At first, we follow the proposal of Nelder and Mead to terminate the algorithm when the standard deviation of the objective function values for all vertices is below a predefined tolerance. For a tolerance level $\varepsilon = 1e - 14$ the algorithm stops after 7017 iterations with an objective function value fMin $= 0.4630$ and a maximum distance $||x^* - \text{xMin}||_\infty = 0.8147$. This is far away from the global minimum. Thus, we decide to terminate the algorithm if both the standard deviation of the objective function values and the maximum distance of any vertex subject to v_0 are smaller than ε. Considering this alternative termination criterion, the algorithm stops after 13004 iterations. The norm $||x^* - \text{xMin}||_\infty$ of the difference between solution xMin and x^* is of the order $1e - 14$. For the above setup of the extended Rosenbrock function with $n = 10$ parameters the implemented Nelder–Mead algorithm needs an average computational time of about 10 seconds.

Let us now look at examples with constraints. We consider the minimization of the function

$$f : \mathbb{R}^4 \to \mathbb{R}$$
$$f(x) = x_1^2 + x_2^2 + 2x_3^2 + x_4^2 - 5x_1 - 5x_2 - 21x_3 + 7x_4, \qquad (9.8)$$

subject to the system of inequality constraints $g_i(x) \le 0$, $i = 1, 2, 3$ given by

$$g_1(x) = x_1^2 + x_2^2 + x_3^2 + x_4^2 + x_1 - x_2 + x_3 - x_4 - 8$$
$$g_2(x) = x_1^2 + 2x_2^2 + x_3^2 + 2x_4^2 - x_1 - x_4 - 10$$
$$g_3(x) = 2x_1^2 + x_2^2 + x_3^2 + 2x_1 - x_2 - x_4 - 5.$$

This minimization problem is known as a *convex Rosen–Suzuki problem*. The optimal solution is $x^* = (0, 1, 2, -1)$. Its objective function value is $f(x^*) = -44$. For different choices of the reflection parameter α and an initial guess of $x^0 = (0, 0, 0, 0)^\top$ Table 9.1 displays the results produced by calling the function

```
[xMin,fMin] = conNelderMead(objF,conF,x0,alfa(i),beta,gamma);
```

The contraction parameter β and the expansion parameter γ were set to the default values $\beta = 0.5$ and $\gamma = 2.0$.

The second constrained example minimizes the function

$$f : \mathbb{R}^2 \to \mathbb{R}$$
$$f(x) = \exp(x_1)\left(4x_1^2 + 2x_2^2 + 4x_1x_2 + 2x_2 + 1\right), \tag{9.9}$$

subject to the inequality constraints

$$g_1(x) = -x_1x_2 - 10$$
$$g_2(x) = x_1x_2 - x_1 - x_2 + 1.5$$

and the bound constraints $-10 \le x_i \le 10$ for $i = 1, 2$. The contour of the objective function values and the admissible domain $\mathcal{X}$ is visualized in Figure 9.7. Ignoring the inequality constraints $g_i(x) \le 0$, $i = 1, 2$, the minimum $f(x^*) = 0$ is reached for $x^* = (0.5, -1)^\top$.

Figure 9.7 shows that the constraints split $\mathcal{X}$ into two separated regions. Thus, the admissible domain $\mathcal{X}$ is non-convex. For such cases the outcome of the optimization procedure highly depends on the initial guess x^0. For instance, an initial guess of $x^0 = (2, -4)^\top$ being an element of the lower right domain, the function conNelderMead returns the solution $x^* = (1.1825, -1.7398)^\top$ with $f(x^*) = 3.0608$. On the other hand, if $x^0 = (0, 2)^\top$ lies inside the upper left part of the admissible domain, the optimization procedure stops with the result

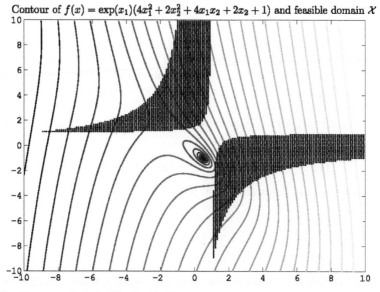

Contour of $f(x) = \exp(x_1)(4x_1^2 + 2x_2^2 + 4x_1x_2 + 2x_2 + 1)$ and feasible domain $\mathcal{X}$

Figure 9.7   Contour and admissible domain $\mathcal{X}$

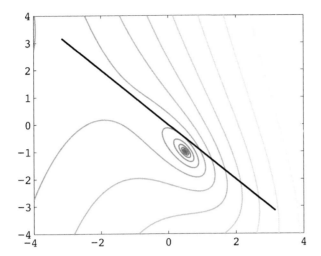

Figure 9.8 Contour and admissible domain $\mathcal{X}$

$x^* = (-9.5474, 1.0474)^\top$ and objective function value $f(x^*) = 0.0236$. This example illustrates that the algorithm results in sub-optimal solutions dependent on the initial guess if the admissible domain is non-convex.

If we replace g_2 by the equality constraint $h(x) = x_1 + x_2 = 0$, the admissible domain reduces to a straight convex line (Figure 9.8).

The constraints function now looks as follows:

```
function y = conF(x)
% constraints
%-------------------------
% -10 <= xi <= 10,  i=1,2
% g(x) = -x1*x2 - 10 <= 0
% h(x) = x1 + x2 == 0
%-------------------------
y = zeros(6,1);
y(1) = -x(1) - 10.0;
y(2) = x(1) - 10;
y(3) = -x(2) - 10.0;
y(4) = x(2) - 10;
y(5) = -x(1)*x(2) - 10.0;
y(6) = abs(x(1) + x(2))-sqrt(eps);
```

Starting with an initial guess of $x^0 = (1, -1)^\top$ function conNelderMead stops after 1113 iterations. The optimal solution derived is $x^* = (0.3660, -0.3660)^\top$ with $f(x^*) = 0.7728$.

As a direct search method the Nelder–Mead algorithm only requires the evaluation of the function values $f(x)$ to identify a minimizer x^*. Thus, direct search methods are applicable when the objective function is not differentiable. Later, we discuss algorithms such as *Differential Evolution* and *Simulated Annealing* which belong to the class of stochastic optimization.

Furthermore, such methods do not need a derivative to evaluate derivatives to find minima. An additional benefit of randomized search methods is their ability to escape from a local minimum and eventually converge to a value giving better results or even to a global minimum.

For now, we focus on classical optimization algorithms based on Newton's method for non-linear equations. The methods rely on the fact that a minimizer x^* of the function f is a stationary point of the function and therefore the non-linear equation $\nabla f(x^*) = 0$ has to be fulfilled. Assuming a twice-differentiable objective function f the Newton search direction can be found from the second-order Taylor approximation

$$f(x + h) \approx f(x) + \nabla f(x)^\top h + \frac{1}{2} h^\top \nabla^2 f(x) h.$$

Minimizing for each iteration k the quadratic function on the right-hand side the Newton search direction d_k is computed as the solution to the linear system

$$\nabla^2 f(x^k) d_k = -\nabla f(x^k). \tag{9.10}$$

To guarantee that the solution d_k is unique and a descending direction for f, we require a positive definite Hessian matrix $\nabla^2 f(x)$. If the Hessian matrix remains positive definite in each iteration step, k, and x^k is close to x^*, Newton's method converges quadratically to the minimum x^*. Unfortunately, Newton's method does not converge to the solution x^* in general if the initial guess x^0 is chosen too far away from x^*. Another difficulty is the solvability of the linear system for d_k. The problem is ill-conditioned or even not solvable, if the Hessian matrix is close to singular or even is singular. Although, these disadvantages render the standard Newton method inapplicable for general optimization problems. In the following paragraphs we review three versions of the standard Newton algorithm widely applied for non-linear optimization in practice.

The first method is a damped Gauss–Newton method common for least-squares curve fitting problems. The so-called Levenberg–Marquardt method combines the robustness of the gradient descent method and the locally quadratic convergence property of the Gauss–Newton method.

The second method is a limited memory quasi-Newton method called the L-BFGS method, shown in Figure 9.30. It successively creates search directions using a positive definite *Broyden–Fletcher–Goldfarb–Shanno* (BFGS) approximation to the exact Hessian matrix of the objective function. The *limited memory* approach (L) handles the storage of this matrix. Instead of n gradients it uses a smaller number $m < n$ to compute the Hessian approximation. This reduces the amount of memory required to store the Hessian matrix from n^2 to $n \cdot m$ and leads to a better performance when the dimension of the problem is high.

For both methods several extensions exist. We consider simple bound constraints based on gradient projection methods (see Conn, A., Gould, N. and Toint, P. (1988), Moré, J. and Toraldo, G. (1989), Byrd, R., Lu, P., Nocedal, J. and Zhu, C. (1994), Kanzow, C., Yamashita, N. and Fukushima, M. (2004), Shidong, S. (2006) and Hager, W. and Zhang, H. (2006)).

$$lb_i \leq x_i \leq ub_i \quad \text{for} \quad i = 1, \dots, n$$

Gradient projection methods apply the function

$$P(x; lb, ub)_i := \max\{\min\{x_i, ub_i\} lb_i\} \tag{9.11}$$

to project points along the direction of steepest descent

$$x(t) = P(x_k - t \nabla f(x_k); lb, ub) \tag{9.12}$$

onto the admissible domain $\mathcal{X}$.

For further insights into bound-constrained Levenberg–Marquardt and L-BFGS methods we refer readers to the abovecited literature. Finally, we focus on a Newton based method called *Sequential Quadratic Programming(SQP)* specifically designed to solve constrained optimization problem (9.2). To generate a new search direction d_k this method iteratively solves a subordinated optimization problem with quadratic objective function. We present a globally convergent (SQP)-algorithm using a modified BFGS update of the Hessian matrix.

9.3 THE LEVENBERG–MARQUARDT METHOD

Among practitioners the Levenberg–Marquardt method is a widely used technique to identify a solution for a non-linear least squares curve fitting problem. We consider N observations y_i, $i = 1, \ldots, N$ and a model function $g : \mathbb{R}^n \to \mathbb{R}$ of n model parameters $x_1, \ldots, x_n$. We assume that $N \geq n$. The N observable values, y_i, can for instance be market quotes corresponding to different setups p_i, $i = 1, \ldots, N$. We calculate the model values $g(x; p_i) = \widehat{y}_i$ and consider the residuals $r_i(x) := \widehat{y}_i - y_i$. Let $R = (r_1, \ldots, r_N)^\top$ be the N dimensional vector of residuals. Then, we wish to solve the following optimization problem:

$$\min_x \; f(x) := \frac{1}{2} \sum_{i=1}^{N} r_i(x)^2 = \frac{1}{2} R(x)^\top R(x), \tag{9.13}$$

Levenberg, K. (1944) and Marquardt, D. (1963) propose solving the curve fitting problem (9.13) using an iterative algorithm which combines the robustness of the method of steepest descent with the locally quadratic convergence property of the Gauss–Newton method.

Steepest Descent Method Far away from a local minimum the algorithm behaves like the method of steepest descent or gradient descent method. For the k-th iteration the search direction d_k of the steepest descent method is given by the gradient $\nabla f(x^k)$ of the objective function multiplied by -1, thus,

$$d_k := -\nabla f(x^k) = -R'(x^k)^\top R(x^k), \tag{9.14}$$

with

$$R'(x) = \left| \frac{\partial r_i}{\partial x_j} \right|_{\substack{i=1,\ldots,N \\ j=1,\ldots,n}} .$$

Starting from some initial guess x^0 the gradient descent method successively approximates the solution x^{k+1} by considering the equation

$$x^{k+1} = x^k + \lambda_k d_k, \quad \lambda_k \in (0, 1].$$

A common practice to guarantee a sufficient decrease in the function values $f(x^{k+1})$ for each iteration step $k = 0, 1, 2, \ldots$ is to estimate the parameter λ_k using an Armijo backtracking line search. To this end we estimate the smallest integer value $m \in \mathbb{N} \cup \{0\}$ such that λ_k defined by

$$\lambda_k := \beta^m, \quad \text{with } \beta \in (0, 1) \text{ fix}$$

fulfils the *Armijo condition* for a given parameter $\alpha > 0$

$$f(x^k - \lambda_k \nabla f(x^k)) - f(x^k) < -\alpha \lambda_k \|\nabla f(x^k)\|. \tag{9.15}$$

A common choice is $\alpha = 10^{-4}$. Thus, the Armijo line search maximizes the step size subject to (9.15).

Gauss–Newton Method   The search direction of Newton's method is given by the solution of the linear system (9.10). For the non-linear least squares problem (9.13) the Hessian matrix $\nabla^2 f(x)$ is given by

$$\nabla^2 f(x) = R'(x)^\top R'(x) + \sum_{i=1}^{N} r_i(x) \nabla^2 r_i(x).$$

Instead of using this formula to compute a new search direction the Gauss–Newton method applies an approximation of first order and has hence no second order terms $\sum_{i=1}^{N} r_i(x) \nabla^2 r_i(x)$. Then, the Hessian matrix is approximated by

$$\nabla^2 f(x) \approx R'(x)^\top R'(x). \tag{9.16}$$

The approximation (9.16) has several advantages compared to some standard Newton method. First, when the Jacobian matrix $R'(x)$ is determined the Gauss–Newton Hessian matrix can be derived by a simple matrix multiplication. Furthermore, if the current solution x^k is close to the minimizer x^*, the residuals $r_i(x)$ tend to be small and $R'(x)^\top R'(x)$ nearly coincides with the exact Hessian $\nabla^2 f(x)$.

   In this case the Gauss–Newton method converges much faster than the gradient descent method and its convergency rate is of the same order as that of Newton's method. Combining the Hessian approximation and Equation (9.10) the search direction d_k of the Gauss–Newton method in step k is defined by

$$d_k = -(R'(x^k)^\top R'(x^k))^{-1} R'(x^k)^\top R(x^k).$$

Whenever the Jabobian $R'(x^k)$ has full rank and the gradient $R'(x^k)^\top R(x^k)$ is non-zero, the search direction d_k is chosen such that following this direction leads to smaller values of the objective function. Since the relation (9.17) holds we have

$$d_k^\top \nabla f(x_k) = d_k^\top R'(x^k)^\top R(x^k) = -d_k^\top R'(x^k)^\top R'(x^k) d_k = -||R'(x^k)d_k||_2^2 < 0. \tag{9.17}$$

The Levenberg–Marquardt method represents a combination of the steepest descent and the Gauss–Newton method. In Levenberg, K. (1944) it is proposed to calculate a search direction d_k as the solution to the following modified Gauss–Newton equation:

$$(R'(x^k)^\top R'(x^k) + \lambda_k I) d_k = -R'(x^k)^\top R(x^k), \tag{9.18}$$

Here, I is the unit matrix and $\lambda_k > 0$ is a damping parameter. The matrix on the left-hand side of (9.18) is positive definite. Thus, the solution d_k is ensured to be a descent direction for the objective function f for all positive damping parameters. For small values of λ_k Levenberg's method behaves like the Gauss–Newton iteration and shows an almost quadratic convergence rate prevailing x^k that is close to x^*. For iterates far from the optimum, the damping parameter λ_k is usually very large and the search direction is approximately given by

$$d_k \approx -\frac{1}{\lambda_k} R'(x^k)^\top R(x^k).$$

The latter is nothing but a short step of the steepest descent method. In this case the Hessian matrix is not used and therefore it need not be calculated. In Marquardt, D. (1963) this issue is considered and one attributes information from the Hessian matrix by replacing the identity matrix I in Equation (9.18) with the matrix

$$D_k = \text{diag}\left(R'(x^k)^\top R'(x^k)\right).$$

D_k represents the diagonal of the Hessian matrix.

The considerations show that the choice of the damping parameter λ_k affects the search direction d_k as well as the length of each Levenberg–Marquardt step. Since this directly impacts the convergence rate and the stability of the method it is crucial how the damping parameter λ_k is determined and how it is updated in each iteration.

A common choice is to use

$$\lambda_0 := \tau \cdot \max_i \{D_0(i, i)\}_{i=1,\dots,n}. \tag{9.19}$$

This relates the initial damping in (9.18) to the magnitude of the eigenvalues of the initial Hessian matrix. The parameter $\tau \in (0, 1)$ depends on the specific problem and the quality of the initial guess x^0. A rule of thumb is to choose small values $\tau \in [10^{-8}, 10^{-5}]$ if we think that the initial guess is close to x^*. Otherwise, we choose larger values, for instance of size $\tau = 10^{-3}$ or even $\tau = 1$.

Several updating rules exist (see for instance Marquardt, D. (1963) or Fan, J. (2003)). The rules rely on the fact that the search direction d_k solves the *trust region problem*

$$\min_{d \in \mathbb{R}^n} \|R(x^k) + R'(x^k)d\|_2^2 \tag{9.20}$$

$$\text{subject to} \qquad \|d\|_2 \leq \Delta_k. \tag{9.21}$$

Thus, the Levenberg–Marquardt method is a trust region algorithm for non-linear least squares that implicitly modifies the trust region radius Δ_k via updating λ_k in each iteration. In a trust region method the size of Δ_k is adjusted with respect to the *gain ratio*, ρ_k, defined by

$$\rho_k = \frac{f(x^k) - f(x^k + d_k)}{m_k(0) - m_k(d_k)}. \tag{9.22}$$

This is the measure for the decrease of the objective function for step d_k and the predicted reduction by the quadratic model function m_k, defined by

$$m_k(d_k) := f(x^k) + d_k^\top \nabla f(x^k) + \frac{1}{2} d_k^\top \nabla^2 f(x^k) d_k$$

$$= f(x^k) + d_k^\top R'(x^k)^\top R(x^k) + \frac{1}{2} d_k^\top R'(x^k)^\top R'(x^k) d_k. \tag{9.23}$$

The denumerator in (9.22) is equal to

$$m_k(0) - m_k(d_k) = -d_k^\top R'(x^k)^\top R(x^k) - \frac{1}{2} d_k^\top R'(x^k)^\top R'(x^k) d_k$$

$$= -\frac{1}{2} d_k^\top \left(2R'(x^k)^\top R(x^k) + [R'(x^k)^\top R'(x^k) + \lambda_k I - \lambda_k I] d_k\right)$$

$$= \frac{1}{2} d_k^\top \left(\lambda_k d_k - R'(x^k)^\top R(x^k)\right).$$

Since the denominator is positive by construction the sign of ρ_k indicates whether the current step d_k is accepted or not. If ρ_k is less than zero the current step increases the objective function value and is rejected. In this case the damping parameter λ_k is increased to reduce the step length and to guarantee steps closer to the steepest descent direction. If ρ_k is close to one the quadratic model function $m_k(d_k)$ reasonably resembles the function value $f(x^k + d_k)$ and the damping λ_k is decreased to get closer to the Gauss–Newton method.

It is common in trust region based update strategies to use

$$\lambda_{k+1} = \begin{cases} \beta\lambda_k & \text{if } \rho_k < \rho_1 \\ \lambda_k & \text{if } \rho_k \in [\rho_1, \rho_2] \\ \dfrac{1}{\gamma}\lambda_k & \text{if } \rho_k > \rho_2 \end{cases}, \quad 0 < \rho_1 < \rho_2, \beta, \gamma > 1. \tag{9.24}$$

Empirical tests verify that the choice $\rho_1 = 0.25$, $\rho_2 = 0.75$, $\beta = 2$ and $\gamma = 3$ gives good results. The updating strategy increases the damping for small positive values ρ_k and at the same time slows down the performance of the quadratic model approximation of $f(x^k + d_k)$ in that case.

The main drawback of the trust region update rule is the existence of jumps in λ_{k+1}/λ_k across the thresholds of ρ_1 and ρ_2. Nielsen, H. (1999) avoids this by using the rule

$$\lambda_{k+1} = \begin{cases} \lambda_k \max\left\{\dfrac{1}{\gamma}, 1 - (\beta - 1)(2\rho_k - 1)^p\right\} & \text{if } \rho_k > 0 \\ \lambda_k \cdot \nu_k & \text{otherwise} \end{cases}, \tag{9.25}$$

with p being some odd integer and ν_k satisfying

$$\nu_{k+1} = \begin{cases} \nu_k = \beta & \text{if } \rho_k > 0 \\ 2\nu_k & \text{otherwise} \end{cases}, \quad \nu_0 = \beta, \tag{9.26}$$

Yamashita, N. and Fukushima, M. (2001) propose iterating the damping parameter subject to the rule

$$\lambda_k = ||R(x_k)||^2.$$

For this choice of the damping parameter the Levenberg–Marquardt method is quadratically convergent if the initial point x^0 is sufficiently close to x^* and $||R(x)||$ provides a local error bound near the solution. Unfortunately, when the initial point is chosen too far away from the solution x^* the term $||R(x_k)||$ may become very large. This leads to very small steps d_k and very slow convergence. The impact of the damping parameter totally vanishes when x^k is close to the solution and $||R(x_k)||$ is eventually very small. To improve upon this outcome Dan, H., Yamashita, N. and Fukushima, M. (2002) propose to use

$$\lambda_k = ||R(x_k)||^\nu, \nu \in (0, 2).$$

Considering only values for ν in the interval $(0, 2)$, it can be shown that the Levenberg-Marquardt method converges *superlinearly*. A further adjustment was introduced in Fan, J. and Pan, J. (2006) which incorporates some iteratively changed scaling parameter $\alpha_k > 0$ and they propose to use

$$\lambda_k = \alpha_k ||R(x_k)||^\nu,$$

where α_k is updated similarly to Nielsen's approach. For this update strategy superlinear convergence to a solution x^* for values $\nu \in (0, 1)$ and quadratic convergence for $\nu \in [1, 2]$ are proven.

The algorithm summarizes the steps of the Levenberg–Marquardt method with Nielsen's damping update strategy for $\beta = 2$, $\gamma = 3$ and $p = 3$, as in Madsen, K., Nielsen, H. and Tingleff, O. (2004).

Algorithm 9.2: Levenberg–Marquardt method with Nielsen damping

---

(S.1) Initialize x^0 and $v_0 = 2$, choose $\tau > 0$, a maximum number of iterations $k_{\max}$, tolerances
   $\varepsilon_1, \varepsilon_2 > 0$ small and set $k = 0$

(S.2) Calculate $\nabla^2 f_k := R'(x^k)^\top R'(x^k), \nabla f_k := R'(x^k)^\top R(x^k)$ and
   set $\lambda_k = \tau \max\{\nabla^2 f_k(i, i)\}_{i=1,\ldots,n}$

(S.3) **if** $||\nabla f_k||_\infty < \varepsilon_1$ **or** $k > k_{\max}$ **then**
   | **stop**

(S.4) Solve $(\nabla^2 f_k + \lambda_k I)d_k = -\nabla f_k$
   if $||d_k|| \leq \varepsilon_2(||x^k|| + \varepsilon_2)$ **then**
   | **stop**

(S.5) Evaluate $\rho_k = \dfrac{f(x^k) - f(x^k + d_k)}{m_k(0) - m_k(d_k)}$

   if $\rho_k > 0$ **then**
   | Set $x^{k+1} = x^k + d_k$, compute $\nabla^2 f_{k+1}, \nabla f_{k+1}$
   | update $v_{k+1} = 2$ and $\lambda_{k+1} = \lambda_k \max\left\{\frac{1}{3}, 1 - (2\rho_k - 1)^3\right\}$
   else
   | Set $x^{k+1} = x^k$, $\nabla^2 f_{k+1} = \nabla^2 f_k$, $\nabla f_{k+1} = \nabla f_k$
   | update $v_{k+1} = 2v_k$ and $\lambda_{k+1} = v_k \lambda_k$

(S.6) Set $k := k+1$ and go to step (S.3)

The algorithm always stops since three termination criteria are given and at least one of them is fulfilled. The maximum number of iterations $k_{\max}$ prevents the algorithm from becoming trapped in an infinite loop. The second criterion $||d_k|| \leq \varepsilon_2(||x_k|| + \varepsilon_2)$ terminates the algorithm if the gradual change from x^k to x^{k+1} becomes too small. The last termination criterion $||\nabla f_k||_\infty < \varepsilon_1$ reflects the fact that a minimizer x^* is a stationary point of f.

9.3.1 Implementation

The **immoptibox**-toolbox available from Nielsen, H. (2010) provides an open source Matlab implementation of Algorithm 9.2. The function

```
function [X,info,perf] = marquardt(fun,x0,opts,p1,p2,...)
```

implements the Levenberg–Marquardt method for the least squares problem (9.13) assuming that a user-defined analytic expression of the Jacobian matrix $R'(x^k)$ is given. The function requires an initial guess x0 and a function handle argument fun pointing to the objective function with header structure

```
function [R,JacJ] = objfun(xk,p1,p2,...)
```

The output arguments R and JacR are similar to the vector of residuals $R(x)$ and the Jacobian matrix $R'(x)$ evaluated at the current iterate xk. The objective function allows to specify additional parameters p1,p2, . . . which are not altered while the algorithm is running. This can for instance be observed market data $y \in \mathbb{R}^N$ which we wish to match.

The optional input argument opts of function marquardt(...) can be a struct with fields tau, tolg, tolx and maxeval changing the default options of the algorithm. tau is used in step (S.2) and controls the size of the initial damping parameter λ_0. The other constants determine the termination criteria of Algorithm 9.2. tolg and tolx present the tolerances ε_1, ε_2 and maxeval the maximum number of iterations k_{max} allowed. The default values are tau = 1e-3, tolg = 1e-4, tolx = 1e-8 and maxeval = 100.

The output argument X holds the solution vector x^*. In addition, if the argument perf is set, then X is a matrix holding the computed iterates x^k columnwise. The fields f, ng and mu of the struct perf retain a history of the function values $f(x^k)$, the gradient norm $||\nabla f(x^k)||_\infty$ and the damping parameter λ_k over all iterations $k = 0, 1, \ldots$. The output argument info holds information about the performance of the method such as the number of iterations used, the reason for termination or the final objective function value.

In a situation where the Jacobian matrix $R'(x)$ is not known explicitly, the **immoptibox**-toolbox offers the function

```
function [X,info,perf,B] = smarquardt(fun,x0,opts,B0,p1,p2,...)
```

Function smarquardt(...) implements a secant version of Algorithm 9.2 using a successively updated approximation B_k of the Jacobian matrix $R'(x)$.

Algorithm 9.3: Secant version of the Levenberg–Marquardt method

---

(S.1) Initialize x^0 and B_0, choose $\tau > 0$, a maximum number of iterations k_{max}, tolerances $\varepsilon_1, \varepsilon_2 > 0$ small, a relative step $\delta > 0$ and set $j = k = 0$

(S.2) Calculate $\nabla^2 f_k := B_k{}^\top B_k$, $\nabla f_k := B_k{}^\top R(x^k)$ and set $\lambda_k = \tau \max\{\nabla^2 f_k(i, i)\}_{i=1,\ldots,n}$

(S.3) **if** $||\nabla f_k||_\infty < \varepsilon_1$ **or** $k > k_{max}$ **then**
  | stop

(S.4) Solve $(\nabla^2 f_k + \lambda_k I)d_k = -\nabla f_k$
  if $||d_k|| \le \varepsilon_2(||x^k|| + \varepsilon_2)$ **then**
  | stop

(S.5) Set $j = \mod(j, n) + 1$
  if $|d_k(j)| < 0.8||d_k||_2$ **then**

$$\text{Set } h = \eta e_j \quad \text{for} \quad \eta := \begin{cases} \delta^2 & \text{if } x^k(j) = 0 \\ \delta|x^k(j)| & \text{otherwise} \end{cases}$$

  else
  | Set $h = d_k$

$$\text{Set } B_{k+1} = B_k + \frac{\left(R(x^k + h) - R(x^k) - B_k h\right) h^\top}{h^\top h}$$

(S.6) **if** $f(x^k + d_k) < f(x^k)$ **then**
  | Set $x^{k+1} = x^k + d_k$
  else
  | Set $x^{k+1} = x^k$

(S.7) Compute $\nabla^2 f_{k+1}$, ∇f_{k+1} and update λ_{k+1} as in Algorithm 9.2

(S.8) Set k := k+1 and go to step (S.3)

The update of the Jacobian matrix approximation B_k in step (S.5) depends on the size of the pseudo angle between d_k and the j-th unit vector e_j. If $|d_k(j)| < 0.8||d_k||_2$ this angle is "large" and the j-th column of B_k is updated using a forward finite difference approximation. Otherwise, the algorithm updates B_k performing the rank one update proposed in Broyden, C.G. (1965). In contrast to Algorithm 9.2 the secant version of the Levenberg–Marquardt method updates the Jacobian approximation B_k in each iteration, although the iterate x^k itself is kept unchanged if the descending condition $f(x^k + d_k) < f(x^k)$ is not satisfied. Therefore the gradient approximation $\nabla f_k := B_k^{\mathsf{T}} R(x^k)$ also changes when $R(x^k)$ is unchanged.

An approximation B_0 of the Jacobian matrix at the initial guess x_0 is passed to function smarquardt(...) using the optional input argument B0. If B0 is not given or is empty, the matrix is approximated using forward differences. The finite difference perturbation η is defined in (S.5). It is determined by the parameter δ which equals the field relstep of struct opts. By default relstep is set to 10^{-6}. In addition, the default maximum number of iterations maxeval is increased from 100 to maxeval$= 100 + 10n$ to compensate the worse convergence because of the absence of an analytical Jacobian matrix expression. Apart from B the output arguments X, info and perf coincide with function marquardt. The optional argument B of function smarquardt is the Jacobian approximation at the solution x^*.

9.3.2 Calibration Examples

Let consider the minimization of the Beale function, (9.6). If we define the residual vector $R(x)$ by

$$R(x) := \sqrt{2} \begin{pmatrix} 1.5 - x_1 + x_1 x_2 \\ 2.25 - x_1 + x_1 x_2^2 \\ 2.625 - x_1 + x_1 x_2^3 \end{pmatrix}. \tag{9.27}$$

Equation (9.6) is equal to the product $\frac{1}{2} R(x)^{\mathsf{T}} R(x)$. The Jacobian matrix $R'(x)$ is given by

$$R'(x) = \sqrt{2} \begin{pmatrix} -1 + x_2 & x_1 \\ -1 + x_2^2 & 2x_1 x_2 \\ -1 + x_2^3 & 3x_1 x_2^2 \end{pmatrix}. \tag{9.28}$$

We interpret the minimization as a non-linear least squares curve fitting problem which can be solved by the Levenberg–Marquardt method. Figure 9.9 shows the progress of marquardt (LM) and smarquardt (secant LM) for the Beale function example.

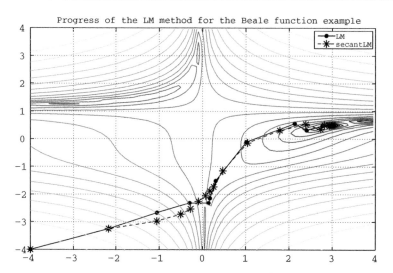

Figure 9.9   Comparison of LM methods using exact and approximated Jacobian matrices

We have implemented the residual function called `residualBeale`:

```
function [R,JacR] = residualBeale(x,sqr2)
% residual vector
R = sqr2*[1.5+x(1)*(x(2)-1);2.25+x(1)*(x(2)^2-
1);2.625+x(1)*(x(2)^3-1)];
% jacobian matrix
JacR = sqr2*[
              x(2)-1,   x(1);
              x(2)^2-1,  2*x(1)*x(2);
              x(2)^3-1,  3*x(1)*x(2)^2
            ];
```

We use the following piece of code to initiate the optimization processes:

```
% initial guess
x0 = [-4 -14]';
% objective function
fun = @residualBeale;
% additional parameter
p1 = sqrt(2);

% algorithmic parameters
opts.tolg = 1e-9; % tolerance gradient norm
opts.tolx = 1e-12; % tolerance step size
```

```
% start LM-method
[X,info,perf] = marquardt(fun,x0,opts,p1)
% start secant version of LM-method
[sX,sinfo,sperf] = smarquardt(fun,x0,opts,[],p1)
```

Starting from an initial guess $x^0 = (-4, 4)^\top$ both algorithms converge to the global minimum $x^* = (3, 0.5)^\top$. Both methods terminate since the gradient norm $||\nabla f_k||_\infty$ falls below the tolerance level tolg. The Levenberg–Marquardt method marquardt with analytical Jacobian matrix requires 16 iterations and 19 function evaluations until the termination criterion $||\nabla f_k||_\infty < \varepsilon_1$ is satisfied. The secant version of the Levenberg–Marquardt method marquardt is terminated after 21 iterations and 37 function evaluations. The number of function evaluations is larger and the convergence rate is slightly worse due to the fact that the method approximates the Jacobian matrix applying finite differences or Broyden's rank one update. But from Figure 9.10 we see that in the final phase both methods converge superlinear to the solution x^*.

As a second example we consider the calibration of the Variance Gamma model. We are looking for the set of model parameters σ, v and θ that minimizes the residuals $P_i^{market} - P_i^{model}$, $i = 1, \ldots, N$ between European Call option market prices P_i^{market} and calculated model prices P_i^{model}. To simplify matters, we generate a range of artificial market prices by using the function LewisCallPricingFFT. We consider the setup:

- Option parameters:

$$S = 100, \; K = (80, 85, \ldots, 115, 120)', \; T = (1, 3, 5)', \; r = 0.02, \; d = 0.01$$

- FFT parameters: $N = 2^{12}, \eta = 0.05$
- Model parameters Variance Gamma: $\sigma = 0.125, v = 0.375, \theta = 0.2$

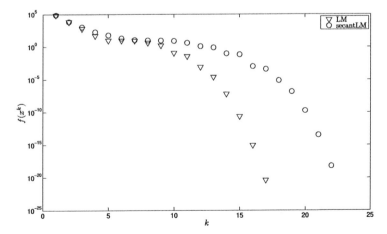

Figure 9.10   Superlinear convergence of the LM method using exact/approximated Jacobian matrices

The Call option prices are calculated using the function:

```
function cp = fftpricer(model,fftStruct,option)
% Function fftpricer calculates European call option prices
% by use of the Fast Fourier Transformation technique
%-----------------------------------------------------------------
% Input:     fftStruct: struct of FFT parameters
%                   fields: pricer -> function handle to fft pricing
%                                     routine
%                           N > 0(multiple of 2, e.g. N = 2^14),
%                           eta > 0(small real number,e.g. eta = 0.1)
%               option: struct of option parameters
%                   fields: S -> Spot price (size: 1 x 1)
%                           K -> Strike (size: M x 1)
%                           r -> risk free interest rate (size: 1 x 1)
%                           d -> dividend yield (size: 1 x 1)
%                           T -> maturity in years (size: P x 1)
%               model: struct of model parameters
%                   fields: modelID -> model name
%                           params -> vector of model parameters
%
% Output: cp: vector of option prices (M*P x 1)
%-----------------------------------------------------------------
pricerFFT = fftStruct.pricer;

lenT = length(option.T);
lenK = length(option.K);
cp = zeros(lenT*lenK,1);
for i = 1:lenT
    cp((i-1)*lenK+1:i*lenK,1) = pricerFFT(fftStruct,model,...
                 option.S,option.K,option.T(i),option.r,option.d);
end
```

The computed Call option prices corresponding to the above setup are displayed in Table 9.2.

Table 9.2   European Call option prices calculated with the Lewis method using FFT

Strike	Maturity		
K	1y	3y	5y
80.00	20.7779	24.2391	27.1953
85.00	16.4279	20.9687	24.3217
90.00	12.7318	18.0752	21.7263
95.00	9.7528	15.5409	19.3932
100.00	7.4158	13.3340	17.3005
105.00	5.6629	11.4476	15.4441
110.00	4.3100	9.8151	13.7830
115.00	3.3058	8.4290	12.3142
120.00	2.5326	7.2339	11.0018

The residual function passed to smarquardt is:

```
function R = residualPriceFFT(x,PM,fftStruct,option,modelID)
% Function residualPriceFFT calculates residual vector R(x) - PM -
P(x)
% between European call option prices observed on the market PM and
% model prices P(x) calculated for the model parameters x
%-----------------------------------------------------------------
% Input:   x: vector model parameters of length n
%          PM: vector of market prices of length M >= n
%
%          ...
%          modelID: model name string
%
% Output: R: vector of residuals PM_i - P_i(x), i = 1,...,M
%-----------------------------------------------------------------

% model struct
model.ID = modelID;
model.params = x;

% return residual vector PM - P(x)
R = PM - fftpricer(model,fftStruct,option);
```

We initiate the calibration procedure using the Matlab code:

```
% fft Struct
fftStruct.pricer = @LewisCallPricingFFT;
fftStruct.N = 2^12;
fftStruct.eta = 0.05;
% option struct
option.S = 100;
option.K = (80:5:120)';
option.r = 0.02;
option.d = 0.01;
option.T = [1; 3; 5];
% model struct
model.ID = 'VarianceGamma';
model.params = [0.125;0.375;0.2]; %sigma,nu,theta
% market prices
PM = fftpricer(model,fftStruct,option)

% initialize optimization procedure
%-----------------------------------------------------------------
% objective function
```

```
fun = @residualPriceFFT;
% initial guess
x0 = [0.3 0.6 0.4]';
% additional options
opts.tolx = 1e-12;
% start calibration
[X,info,perf] = smarquardt(fun,x0,opts,[],PM,fftStruct,option,
                                                    model.ID)
```

Figure 9.11 illustrates the progress of function smarquardt assuming an initial guess $x^0 = (0.3, 0.6, 0.4)$. The iterated outcomes x^k converge to the solution x^*. The Levenberg–Marquardt method stops after 25 iterations since the step size $||d_k||$ becomes too small. We consider a minimum step size of tolerance $\varepsilon_2 = 10^{-12}$.

9.4 THE L-BFGS METHOD

In this section we consider a limited memory quasi-Newton method for large-scale optimization. For standard Newton methods the computational costs to evaluate and store the Hessian matrix $\nabla^2 f(x)$ for a function $f : \mathbb{R}^n \to \mathbb{R}$ or an approximation $H \approx \nabla^2 f(x)$ grow proportional to n^2. Thus, standard Newton methods are not directly applicable to large optimization problems. Limited memory quasi-Newton methods approximate the Hessian matrix by a smaller number m, $m \ll n$, of vectors and reduce the required storage memory to be of proportion $m \cdot n$. Although quasi-Newton methods only obey linear convergence properties, such algorithms are applied in practice since they are robust and easy to implement. We focus on the L-BFGS method first described in Nocedal, J. (1980). The L-BFGS method is based on the BFGS approximation to the Hessian matrix. The main difference between the two methods is the amount of curvature information used to construct the Hessian approximation in the k-th

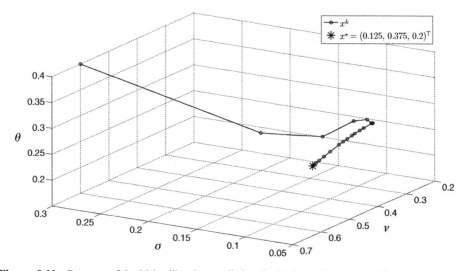

Figure 9.11 Progress of the LM calibration applied to the Variance Gamma model

step, H_k, and its inverse respectively. Starting from a sparse symmetric and positive definite matrix H_0 the BFGS updating formula for the k-th Hessian matrix approximation is given by

$$H_{k+1} = H_k - \frac{H_k s_k s_k^T H_k}{s_k^T H_k s_k} + \frac{y_k y_k^T}{y_k^T s_k}, \quad k = 0, 1, 2, \ldots, \tag{9.29}$$

with s_k and y_k defined by

$$s_k := x^{k+1} - x^k, \quad y_k := \nabla f(x^{k+1}) - \nabla f(x^k)$$

and the updated iterate $x^{k+1} = x^k + \lambda_k d_k$.

Considering (9.10), the search direction d_k is the solution of the linear system $H_k d_k = -\nabla f(x^k)$ which is $d_k = -H_k^{-1} \nabla f(x^k)$.

In general, inverse matrix calculations are ill-conditioned problems but in the special case of the BFGS update (9.29) a rank-two modification of matrix H_k is performed and the inverse is explicitly known, using the *Sherman–Morrison–Woodbury formula* (see Hager, W. (1989) for details). Applying the Sherman–Morrison–Woodbury formula the following iteration rule for H_k^{-1} can be derived:

$$H_{k+1}^{-1} = V_k^T H_k^{-1} V_k + \rho_k s_k s_k^T, \tag{9.30}$$

with

$$\rho_k = \frac{1}{y_k^T s_k}, \quad V_k = (I - \rho_k y_k s_k^T).$$

The search direction d_{k+1} is determined from the matrix-vector multiplication of the inverse BFGS approximation H_{k+1}^{-1} and the gradient $\nabla f(x^{k+1})$ multiplied by -1. Below we provide an efficient recursive calculation procedure for this matrix-vector multiplication during one L-BFGS iteration.

During the first m iterations the L-BFGS method and the BFGS method work almost in the same way, although the L-BFGS algorithm does not keep the matrices H_k^{-1} in memory for $k = 1, \ldots, m$. To save memory the L-BFGS method instead only stores the vector pairs $\{s^i, y^i\}$ for $i = k - m, \ldots, k - 1$ of BFGS corrections over the previous m iterations. For $k > m$ the curvature information $\{s^{k-m}, y^{k-m}\}$ is replaced by the most recent one $\{s^k, y^k\}$. The inverse Hessian approximation is then estimated by applying m times (9.30) to the initial matrix $H_{0_k}^{-1}$ of the k-th iteration. In contrast to the standard BFGS iteration, the L-BFGS method allows for a varying initial matrix from iteration to iteration. Considering only the last m BFGS updates for $k > m$, the matrix H_k^{-1} satisfies the equation

$$\begin{aligned}
H_k^{-1} = {}& (V_{k-1}^T \cdots V_{k-m}^T) H_{0_k}^{-1} (V_{k-m} \cdots V_{k-1}) \\
& + \rho_{k-m} (V_{k-1}^T \cdots V_{k-m+1}^T) s_{k-m} s_{k-m}^T (V_{k-m+1} \cdots V_{k-1}) \\
& + \rho_{k-m+1} (V_{k-1}^T \cdots V_{k-m+2}^T) s_{k-m+1} s_{k-m+1}^T (V_{k-m+2} \cdots V_{k-1}) \\
& \cdots \\
& + \rho_{k-1} s_{k-1} s_{k-1}^T.
\end{aligned} \tag{9.31}$$

This special structure of the inverse L-BFGS matrix allows us to compute the search direction d_k recursively from the following algorithm:

Algorithm 9.4: L-BFGS two loop-recursion

(S.1) Set $\hat{m} = \min\{m, k\}$ and $q = \nabla f(x^k)$

(S.2) **for** $i = 1$ **to** $\hat{m}$ **do**

$\quad\left|\quad\begin{aligned}\alpha_i &= \rho_{k-i}s_{k-i}^\top q\\ q &= q - \alpha_i y_{k-i}\end{aligned}\right.$

(S.3) Compute the matrix-vector product $r = H_{0_k}^{-1}q$

(S.4) **for** $i = \hat{m}, \hat{m} - 1, \ldots, 1$ **do**

$\quad\left|\quad\begin{aligned}\beta &= \rho_{k-i}y_{k-i}^\top r\\ r &= r - s_{k-i}(\alpha_i - \beta)\end{aligned}\right.$

(S.4) **return** r equal to $H_k^{-1}\nabla f(x^k)$

Assuming a diagonal matrix $H_{0_k}^{-1}$, the algorithm requires $4mn + n$ multiplications to calculate the matrix-vector product $H_k^{-1}\nabla f(x^k)$. Considering the complexity $\mathcal{O}(n^2)$ of a standard matrix-vector multiplication this recursion is not computationaly expensive. Furthermore, since the multiplication by the initial matrix $H_{0_k}^{-1}$ is not linked to the remaining steps, this matrix can be chosen independently and may vary while iterating. Liu, D. and Nocedal, J. (1989) propose to iterate $H_{0_k}^{-1}$ subject to

$$H_{0_k}^{-1} = \gamma_k H_0^{-1}, \quad \gamma_k = \begin{cases} 1 & k = 0 \\ \dfrac{s_{k-1}^\top y_{k-1}}{y_{k-1}^\top y_{k-1}} & \text{for } k = 1, 2, \ldots \end{cases}, \tag{9.32}$$

where the scaling factor γ_k reflects the size of the Hessian matrix along the most recent search direction. This is to ensure a well-scaled search direction d_k. As a positive spillover effect the full step length $\lambda_k = 1$ is accepted in many iterations of the L-BFGS method. To incorporate as much curvature information as possible a convenient choice for the sparse matrix H_0^{-1} would be to use the diagonal elements of the inverse Hessian $\nabla^2 f(x_0)^{-1}$ if the diagonal elements of the Hessian itself were positive. But the simplest choice, that is taking $H_{0_k}^{-1} = \gamma_k I$, leads to a considerable reduction of iterations when compared to the case of using a constant initial matrix.

The L-BFGS algorithm summarized below combines the methods from Liu, D. and Nocedal, J. (1989) and the initial matrix $H_{0_k}^{-1}$ adjustment according to (9.32). To ensure that the BFGS updating is stable, the step length λ_k is chosen to satisfy the *strong Wolfe conditions*: for $0 < c_1 < c_2 < 1$

$$f(x^k + \lambda_k d_k) \leq f(x^k) + c_1 \lambda_k \nabla f(x^k)^\top d_k \tag{9.33}$$

$$\nabla |f(x^k + \lambda_k d_k)^\top d_k| \leq c_2 |\nabla f(x^k)^\top d_k|. \tag{9.34}$$

Inequality (9.33) is the generalization of the Armijo condition, (9.15), applicable to any quasi-Newton method. It is designed to obtain a sufficient decrease in the objective function values. Although this condition is satisfied for all sufficiently small values λ_k, the step size may be too small to guarantee convergence. Those arbitrarily small choices of λ_k are ruled out by the curvature condition (9.34). Moreover, the curvature condition guarantees that a positive definite quasi-Newton update exists.

Algorithm 9.5: L-BFGS method

(S.1) Initialize x^0, matrix H_0^{-1}, choose integer $m < n$, constants $0 < c_1 < \frac{1}{2}$ and $c_1 < c_2 < 1$, tolerances $\varepsilon_1, \varepsilon_2 > 0$ small and a maximum number of iterations $k_{\max}$. Set $k = 0$

(S.2) **if** $||\nabla f(x^k)||_\infty < \varepsilon_1$ **or** $k > k_{\max}$ **then**
  | **stop**

(S.3) Calculate $H_{0_k}^{-1}$ from Equation (9.32) and compute $d_k = -H_k^{-1}\nabla f(x^k)$ using Algorithm 9.4

(S.4) Estimate step size $0 < \lambda_k \leq 1$ subject to (9.33) and (9.34). Update the iterate $x^{k+1} = x^k + \lambda_k d_k$
  if $||x^{k+1} - x^k||_\infty < \varepsilon_2$ **then**
  | **stop**

(S.5) Compute and store $s_k = x^{k+1} - x^k$ and $y^k = \nabla f(x^{k+1}) - \nabla f(x^k)$.
  if $k > m$ **then**
  | Delete the vector pair $\{s_{k-m}, y_{k-m}\}$

(S.6) Set $k := k+1$ and go to step (S.2)

As mentioned above, the L-BFGS algorithm coincides with the BFGS method for the first m iterations if $H_{0_k}^{-1} = H_0^{-1}$ is kept constant. For $k > m$ the L-BFGS algorithm approximates the inverse Hessian H_k^{-1} from the previous m vector pairs $\{s_i, y_i\}$ for $i = k - m, \ldots, k - 1$. Using the above algorithm to calculate the search direction d_k, the matrices H_k^{-1} are not determined explicitly and the overall required storage memory can therefore be reduced to an $m \cdot n$.

9.4.1 Implementation

A fast and accurate implementation of the L-BFGS algorithm, Algorithm 9.5, and the recursive algorithm, Algorithm 9.4, to calculate the matrix vector product $H_k^{-1}\nabla f(x^k)$ is available from the Matlab File Exchange (see Kroon, D.-J. (2008)). The implemented function called `fminlbfgs` supports the BFGS, L-BFGS and steepest descent quasi-Newton optimization methods. The function header is given by

```
function [x,fval,exitflag,info,grad] = fminlbfgs(fun,x0,opts)
```

The input `fun` is a function handle pointing to the objective function and variable `x0` holds the initial guess. The objective function is assumed to return the function value $f(x^k)$ at the current iterate x^k. If necessary, it can also return the gradient $\nabla f(x^k)$. By default the method assumes that the gradient is not set and it is approximated by finite differences. If the gradient can be computed analytically it should be used and, then, the field `GradObj` of option struct `opts` needs to be set. This can be done by setting it to `'on'`. In addition to the standard variables `TolX`, `TolFun`, `MaxIter` there are further options which are relevant when considering the L-BFGS method.

The field `HessUpdate` specifies the optimization procedure used and allows for the values `'bfgs'`, `'lbfgs'` and `'steepdesc'`. By default `fminlbfgs` applies the BFGS method and switches to L-BFGS when the number of parameters is larger than 3000. The number m of vector pairs $\{s_i, y_i\}$ for $i = k - m, \dots, k - 1$ kept in memory to approximate the Hessian in the L-BFGS algorithm, 9.5, determines the field StoreN. The default value is set to 20.

In step (S.4) of Algorithm 9.5 a step size λ_k that satisfies the strong Wolfe conditions (9.33) and (9.34) is required. Function fminlbfgs determines this step size by use of a line search procedure (see Nocedal, J. and Wright, S. (2006) or Madsen, K. and Nielsen, H. (2010)). The coefficients c_1 and c_2 are determined by the fields rho and sigma. The values are set to $c_1 = 0.01$ and $c_2 = 0.9$ by default.

The output arguments x, fval and grad are the solution x^*, its objective function value $f(x^*)$ and gradient $\nabla f(x^*)$. The integer exitflag identifies the termination criterion and the output struct info stores additional algorithmic information such as the step size λ_k or the overall number of iterations used.

Another version of a limited memory BFGS algorithm called minFunc has been implemented by Schmidt, M. (2009). In addition to the unconstrained optimization function min-Func, Schmidt's function package minConf handles simple constraints where the projection onto the admissible domain can be computed efficiently, for example this is the case when considering lower/upper bounds.

9.4.2 Calibration Examples

To illustrate the performance of the limited memory BFGS method when the number of parameters is large, we apply the function fminlbfgs to the extended Rosenbrock function (9.7). This is done for different values N and we compare the results of the L-BFGS and the BFGS methods. Tables 9.3 and 9.4 display the outcome for both methods and for values $N \le 1000$. The L-BFGS method approximates the inverse Hessian matrices H_k^{-1} implicitly using the vector pairs $\{s_i, y_i\}$ over the previous m iterations. We decide to set $m = \min\{N/2, 20\}$. Both methods assume an initial inverse Hessian matrix H_0^{-1} set to the identity matrix.

Table 9.3   Results of the L-BFGS method applied to Rosenbrock's function for different numbers of N

	L-BFGS			
N	$\|\|x^* - x^k\|\|_\infty$	$f(x^k)$	Time in sec.	Iterations
2	4.7347e-008	9.4098e-016	0.034126	36
10	4.4127e-009	5.7715e-016	0.030651	37
20	2.3244e-009	3.0666e-017	0.045375	37
40	1.2439e-010	4.6222e-017	0.047512	37
60	1.2354e-010	6.9596e-017	0.047757	37
80	1.2293e-010	9.3097e-017	0.049083	37
100	1.2132e-010	1.1783e-016	0.048750	37
200	1.2077e-010	2.4860e-016	0.050127	37
400	1.2217e-010	4.6780e-016	0.053732	37
600	2.0616e-010	6.6619e-016	0.056855	37
800	1.5369e-010	8.9574e-016	0.059734	37
1000	1.2020e-010	1.2091e-015	0.063233	37

Table 9.4 Results of the BFGS method applied to Rosenbrock's function for different numbers of N

		BFGS		
N	$\|x^* - x^k\|_\infty$	$f(x^k)$	Time in sec.	Iterations
2	5.7297e-009	1.2318e-017	0.02264	32
10	1.3454e-007	8.1872e-015	0.06946	93
20	1.3209e-006	1.6525e-012	0.10980	140
40	1.5694e-005	2.2119e-010	0.19985	194
60	3.7636e-005	7.8551e-010	0.27827	272
80	1.5149e-005	3.5047e-010	0.40289	347
100	1.8148e-005	4.8521e-010	0.52080	382
200	7.4264e-006	1.5175e-010	2.01536	592
400	8.3068e-006	1.9636e-010	20.07703	806
600	2.7497e-005	6.8335e-010	68.04037	925
800	1.1913e-005	3.9346e-010	162.12532	1021
1000	2.7062e-005	8.5665e-010	356.74054	1215

The objective function is given by Equation (9.7). For even $n \geq 2$ its gradient vector $\nabla f \in \mathbb{R}^n$ looks as follows:

$$\nabla f(x)_{2i-1} = 400x_{2i-1}(x_{2i-1}^2 - x_{2i}) + 2(x_{2i-1} - 1)$$
$$\nabla f(x)_{2i} = 200(x_{2i} - x_{2i-1}^2)$$
$$i = 1, \ldots, \frac{n}{2}.$$

In Matlab the gradient is calculated using:

```
% number of parameters: N >= 2 even
N = length(x);
% gradient vector
g = zeros(N,1);
g(1:2:N-1) = 400*x(1:2:N-1).*(x(1:2:N-1).^2 - x(2:2:N)) ...
             + 2*(x(1:2:N-1) - 1);
g(2:2:N) = 200*(x(2:2:N) - x(1:2:N-1).^2);
```

The extended Rosenbrock function and its gradient are implemented in the function objfunExtendedRosenbrock.

Both methods terminate since the difference of the solutions x^k or in the objective function values $f(x^k)$ from iteration k to $k+1$ becomes smaller than TolX or TolFun. A comparison of the results shows that the BFGS method with initial inverse Hessian matrix H_0^{-1} set to the identity matrix is only competitive to the L-BFGS method when the problem dimension is small. While the BFGS method for the Rosenbrock example requires over 1 minute of computational time on our machine[1] with $N = 600$, the L-BFGS method in the same time handles 1 million parameters. When we set H_0^{-1} equal to the inverse of the explicit Hessian matrix $\nabla^2 f(x^0)$ at the initial guess x^0 the BFGS method performs much better and is competitive for values $N \leq 100$.

[1] Intel Core 2 Duo, CPU T9400, 2.53GHz, 4GB RAM, Windows 7 Prof. 64bit

Table 9.5 Results of the BFGS method with explicit initial inverse Hessian applied to Rosenbrock's function for different numbers of N

N	$||x^* - x^k||_\infty$	$f(x^k)$	Time in sec.	Iterations
		BFGS		
2	1.2855e-008	6.8066e-017	0.02262	34
10	5.5579e-007	1.5106e-013	0.03255	48
20	3.1385e-004	4.6435e-008	0.03077	39
40	2.6881e-006	4.8056e-012	0.04619	58
60	1.7455e-003	2.1049e-006	0.03629	41
80	4.6484e-004	4.2229e-007	0.04160	41
100	3.1391e-006	6.4766e-011	0.06195	51
200	5.5106e-004	2.3150e-006	0.13665	40
400	4.5798e-006	8.3012e-010	1.31748	52
600	3.2867e-006	5.8667e-011	4.02341	57
800	2.9510e-006	7.9650e-011	8.18698	53
1000	1.9770e-006	6.3207e-011	14.93322	52

Tables 9.3 to 9.5 can be reproduced by calling the script file `lbfgsScriptRosenbrock`. The extracted code snippet below generates Table 9.3.

```
% number of parameters
N = [2, 10, 20:20:100,200:200:1000];
% initial guess
x0 = repmat([-1.2;1],N(end)/2,1);
% global minimizer
xstar = ones(N(end),1);

% L-BFGS
%--------------------------------------------------------------------
% option struct
opts = struct('GradObj','on','Display','off','HessUpdate',...
              'lbfgs','GoalsExactAchieve',1,'MaxIter',100*N(iend));
disp('                          L-BFGS ');
disp('   N      ||xstar-xk||      f(xk)     TotalTime     Iteration');
disp('--------------------------------------------------------------');
for i = 1:length(N)
    opts.StoreN = min(N(i)/2,20);
    % start L-BFGS method
    [xMin,fMin,exitflag,output] = ...
                fminlbfgs(@objfunExtendedRosenbrock,x0(1:N(i)),opts);
    errX = norm(xMin - xstar(1:N(i)),inf);
    s = sprintf('%4d %1.4e %0.4e %10.5f %5d ', ...
        N(i),errX,fMin,output.timeTotal,output.iteration); disp(s);
end
```

We set the initial guess to $x^0 = (-1.2, 1, \ldots, -1.2, 1)^\top$. The struct `opts` which carries the parameters of function `fminlbfgs` is generated by calling Matlab's built-in function `struct('Name', value, ...)`. The argument `'Name'` defines the name of the field in the struct and `value` sets the corresponding value. The function `sprintf` writes formatted data to a Matlab string and `disp` displays this string in the workspace.

As another example we consider the extended Powell singular function. For n being a multiple of 4 is given by

$$f : \mathbb{R}^n \to \mathbb{R}$$

$$f(x) := \sum_{i=1}^{n/4} (x_{4i-3} + 10x_{4i-2})^2 + 5(x_{4i-1} - x_{4i})^2$$

$$+ (x_{4i-2} - 2x_{4i-1})^4 + 10(x_{4i-3} - x_{4i})^4. \qquad (9.35)$$

Its gradient is given by

$$\nabla f(x)_{4i-3} = 2(x_{4i-3} + 10x_{4i-2}) + 40(x_{4i-3} - x_{4i})^3$$
$$\nabla f(x)_{4i-2} = 20(x_{4i-3} + 10x_{4i-2}) + 4(x_{4i-2} - 2x_{4i-1})^3$$
$$\nabla f(x)_{4i-1} = 10(x_{4i-1} - x_{4i}) - 8(x_{4i-2} - 2x_{4i-1})^3$$
$$\nabla f(x)_{4i} = -10(x_{4i-1} - x_{4i}) - 40(x_{4i-3} - x_{4i})^3, i = 1, \ldots, \frac{n}{4}.$$

Function (9.35) takes its minimum $f(x^*) = 0$ at the origin. The objective function and its gradient are implemented in the function `objfunExtendedPowell` given by

```
function [f,g] = objfunExtendedPowell(x)

N = length(x);
% auxiliary variables
aux1 = x(1:4:N-3) + 10*x(2:4:N-2);
aux2 = x(3:4:N-1) - x(4:4:N);
aux3 = x(2:4:N-2)-2*x(3:4:N-1);
aux4 = x(1:4:N-3) - x(4:4:N);

% objective function
f = sum(aux1.^2 + 5*aux2.^2 + aux3.^4 + 10*aux4.^4);

% gradient
if(nargout > 1)
    g = zeros(N,1);
    g(1:4:N-3) = 2*aux1 + 40*aux4.^3;
    g(2:4:N-2) = 20*aux1 + 4*aux3.^3;
    g(3:4:N-1) = 10*aux2 - 8*aux3.^3;
    g(4:4:N) = -10*aux2 - 40*aux4.^3;
end
```

Table 9.6 presents the results of the L-BFGS minimization, calling function `fminlbfgs` using the initial guess $x^0 = (3, -1, 0, 1, \ldots, 3, -1, 0, 1)^\top$. For any number of parameters N in

Table 9.6 Results of the L-BFGS method applied to the Powell singular function for different numbers of parameters N

	L-BFGS			
N	$\|x^* - x^k\|_2$	$f(x^k)$	Time in sec.	Iterations
200	2.3620e-003	5.2773e-012	0.07991	45
400	3.3403e-003	1.0555e-011	0.07624	45
600	4.0910e-003	1.5832e-011	0.08127	45
800	4.7239e-003	2.1109e-011	0.09153	45
1000	5.2815e-003	2.6387e-011	0.09940	45
2000	7.4692e-003	5.2773e-011	0.14399	45
4000	1.0563e-002	1.0555e-010	0.26329	45
6000	1.2937e-002	1.5832e-010	0.35439	45
8000	1.4938e-002	2.1109e-010	0.55993	45
10000	1.6702e-002	2.6387e-010	0.68188	45
100000	5.2816e-002	2.6387e-009	8.14852	45

In Table 9.6 the method terminates since the change in the objective function values $f(x^k)$ from iteration k to $k + 1$ was less than `TolFun` 10^{-8}. The results show that the L-BFGS method performs well for Powell's singular function when the number of parameters is large.

9.5 THE SQP METHOD

The most popular Newton method based algorithm for non-linear constrained optimization problems is the method *sequential quadratic programming* (SQP). The algorithm presented here is designed in line with the considerations in Geiger, C. and Kanzow, C. (2002). For the k-th iteration it solves an embedded optimization problem with quadratic objective function to find a search direction d_k for the main optimization problem. The authors illustrate that the solution of the proposed quadratic subproblem d_k forms a descent direction for the objective function f if the assumptions, $f, g_i, h_j \in C^2, i = 1, \ldots, m$ and $j = 1, \ldots, p$, as well as the Hessian matrix H_k being positive definite hold true. Starting from a locally convergent SQP algorithm we propose to use a penalty term in addition to an Armijo based step size control to globalize the convergence of the algorithm. This does not mean convergence to the global minimum but it does mean that choosing some starting point the algorithm converges. This globally convergent SQP algorithm is then modified to guarantee a nonempty set of admissible solutions for the quadratic subproblem.

Before introducing the SQP algorithm we need to point out two things. First, we need to define the necessary conditions a local minimizer x^* of the optimization problem, (9.2), has to fulfil. Second, we consider the *Lagrange–Newton iteration* for equality-constrained optimization problems, which is closely related to the original problem.

The Karush–Kuhn–Tucker Conditions A local minimizer x^* of an unconstrained optimization problem necessarily fulfils the stationary point condition, $\nabla f(x^*) = 0$. An equivalent criterion exists for a local minimizer of the constrained problem, (9.2), and is given by the *Karush–Kuhn–Tucker* (KKT) conditions.

If we define the *Lagrange function* $L : \mathbb{R}^{n+m+p} \to \mathbb{R}$ corresponding to the constrained optimization problem, (9.2), by

$$L(x, \lambda, \mu) := f(x) + \sum_{i=1}^{m} \lambda_i g_i(x) + \sum_{j=1}^{p} \mu_j h_j(x), \qquad (9.36)$$

with continuously differentiable functions f, g, h, the gradient subject to the variable x is

$$\nabla_x L(x, \lambda, \mu) = \nabla f(x) + \sum_{i=1}^{m} \lambda_i \nabla g_i(x) + \sum_{j=1}^{p} \mu_j \nabla h_j(x).$$

Then, the KKT conditions are

$$\nabla_x L(x, \lambda, \mu) = 0$$
$$h(x) = 0$$
$$\lambda \geq 0, \; g(x) \leq 0, \; \lambda^T g(x) = 0.$$

The parameters λ_i, $i = 1, \ldots, m$ and μ_j, $j = 1, \ldots, p$ are called *Lagrange multipliers*.

The Lagrange–Newton Iteration for Equality Constraints Let us consider the following problem:

$$\min_x \quad f(x) \quad \text{subject to} \quad h(x) = 0.$$

We assume twice continuously differentiable functions $f : \mathbb{R}^n \to \mathbb{R}$ and $h : \mathbb{R}^n \to \mathbb{R}^p$. If we define the function $\Phi : \mathbb{R}^{n+p} \to \mathbb{R}^{n+p}$ by

$$\Phi(x, \mu) := \begin{pmatrix} \nabla_x L(x, \mu) \\ h(x) \end{pmatrix},$$

we observe that $\Phi(x, \mu) = 0$ represents the KKT conditions of the problem. Thus, a minimizer of the equality constrained problem is given by a solution of the system of non-linear equations.

A common method to solve such equations is the Newton iteration. In the k-th step the Newton iteration linearizes the function Φ at the current point (x^k, μ^k), that is

$$\Phi_k(x, \mu) := \Phi(x^k, \mu^k) + \Phi'(x^k, \mu^k)(x - x^k, \mu - \mu^k) \qquad (9.37)$$

and then a solution (x^{k+1}, μ^{k+1}) of the approximated system, (9.37), is calculated thus,

$$\Phi_k(x, \mu) = 0.$$

Theoretically, the new solution (x^{k+1}, μ^{k+1}) is given by

$$(x^{k+1}, \mu^{k+1}) = (x^k, \mu^k) - \Phi'(x^k, \mu^k)^{-1} \Phi(x^k, \mu^k). \qquad (9.38)$$

Since the calculation of the inverse of the Jacobian matrix $\Phi'(x^k, \mu^k)$ is numerically inefficient, we do not explicitly solve (9.38) but we determine the residuum $(\Delta x^k, \Delta \mu^k)$ solving the linear system

$$\Phi'(x^k, \mu^k) \begin{pmatrix} \Delta x^k \\ \Delta \mu^k \end{pmatrix} = -\Phi(x^k, \mu^k). \qquad (9.39)$$

Then, the new iterative solution (x^{k+1}, μ^{k+1}) is defined by

$$x^{k+1} := x^k + \Delta x^k, \quad \mu^{k+1} := \mu^k + \Delta \mu^k.$$

It can be shown that if the Jacobian matrix $\Phi'(x^*, \mu^*)$ is invertible this method, called *Lagrange–Newton iteration*, has a local superlinear/quadratic order of convergence to a KKT point (x^*, μ^*).

In principle the Lagrange–Newton iteration could be extended to inequality constrained problems by using *NCP functions*. An NCP function is a function $\rho : \mathbb{R}^2 \to \mathbb{R}$ such that

$$\rho(a, b) = 0 \quad \Leftrightarrow \quad a \geq 0, b \geq 0 \quad \text{and} \quad ab = 0 \quad a, b \in \mathbb{R}.$$

Thus, NCP functions transform the inequality constraints of the KKT conditions into equality constraints. Unfortunately, most NCP functions are not everywhere differentiable, which eventually causes instabilities when evaluating the Jacobian matrix $\Phi'(x, \mu, \lambda)$.

The SQP method, on the other hand, is able to handle equality constraints as well as inequality constraints for the Newton iteration by solving subordinated quadratic problems. We start with the description of a locally convergent version and explain the solution of the subordinated quadratic problem in detail. We show how the basic algorithm can be extended to achieve global convergence and the existence of a solution by applying some modifications.

A local convergent SQP method

The system of linear Equations (9.39) can be written as

$$\begin{pmatrix} \nabla^2_{xx} L(x^k, \mu^k) & h'(x^k)^\top \\ h'(x^k)^\top & 0 \end{pmatrix} \begin{pmatrix} \Delta x^k \\ \Delta \mu^k \end{pmatrix} = - \begin{pmatrix} \nabla_x L(x^k, \mu^k) \\ h(x^k) \end{pmatrix}. \tag{9.40}$$

Defining $H_k := \nabla^2_{xx} L(x^k, \mu^k)$ leads to

$$H_k \Delta x^k + h'(x^k)\Delta \mu^k = -\nabla_x L(x^k, \mu^k),$$
$$\nabla h_j(x^k)^\top \Delta x^k = -h_j(x^k), \quad j = 1, \ldots, p. \tag{9.41}$$

With $\mu^+ := \mu^k + \Delta \mu^k$ the system (9.41) can be transformed to

$$H_k \Delta x^k + h'(x^k)\mu^+ = -\nabla_x f(x^k),$$
$$\nabla h_j(x^k)^\top \Delta x^k = -h_j(x^k), \quad j = 1, \ldots, p. \tag{9.42}$$

The linear system (9.42) can be interpreted as the KKT condition of the following optimization problem:

$$\min_{\Delta x^k} \nabla f(x^k)^\top \Delta x^k + \frac{1}{2}\Delta x^{k\top} H_k \Delta x^k$$

subject to

$$h_j(x^k) + \nabla h_j(x^k)^\top \Delta x^k = 0, \quad j = 1, \ldots, p$$

with a quadratic objective function.

Considering the optimization problem, (9.2), this implies determining the descending direction Δx^k for the k-th iteration step by solving the quadratic problem

$$\min_{\Delta x^k} \nabla f(x^k)^\top \Delta x^k + \frac{1}{2}\Delta x^{k\top} H_k \Delta x^k$$

subject to

$$g_i(x^k) + \nabla g_i(x^k)^\top \Delta x^k \leq 0, \quad i = 1\ldots, m$$
$$h_j(x^k) + \nabla h_j(x^k)^\top \Delta x^k = 0, \quad j = 1, \ldots, p$$

(9.43)

and setting $x^{k+1} := x^k + \Delta x^k$. In contrast to the original problem (9.2) the constraints of the problem, (9.43), are linearized. The objective function of the subordinated quadratic problem is a quadratic approximation to f in x^k and instead of $\nabla^2 f(x^k)$ we use the Hessian matrix of the Lagrangian function H_k or an adequate approximation to it.

By solving the quadratic optimization problem, (9.43), in each iteration step, it is now clear why the process is called sequential quadratic programming.

The locally convergent SQP-method can be summarized in the following algorithm:

Algorithm 9.6: Local SQP algorithm

(S.1) Choose $(x^0, \lambda^0, \mu^0) \in \mathbb{R}^{n+m+p}$, $H_0 \in \mathbb{R}^{n \times n}$ symmetric. Set $k = 0$

(S.2) **if** (x^k, λ^k, μ^k) *is a KKT point of* (9.2) **then**
| stop

(S.3) Calculate a solution $\Delta x^k \in \mathbb{R}^n$ of the quadratic problem (9.43) with Lagrangian multipliers λ^{k+1} and μ^{k+1}

(S.4) Update $x^{k+1} = x^k + \Delta x^k$ and $H_{k+1} \in \mathbb{R}^{n \times n}$

(S.5) Set $k := k + 1$ and go to step (S.2)

It is proven in Geiger, C. and Kanzow, C. (2002) that the local SQP method has an convergence behaviour equivalent to the Lagrange–Newton iteration if we use the Hessian matrix $H_k = \nabla_{xx}^2 L(x^k, \lambda^k, \mu^k)$ for all iteration steps $k \in \mathbb{N}$.

But applying the Hessian matrix H_k of the Lagrangian function can cause instabilities. If the matrix is not everywhere positive definite it is not possible to guarantee a solution $\Delta x \in \mathbb{R}$ of the quadratic problem, (9.43), for each iteration step. An appropriate choice for a positive definite Hessian matrix H_k was introduced in Powell, M.J.D. (1978). A modified BFGS quasi-Newton approximation of the Hessian matrix is proposed which guarantees that all matrices are positive definite as long as the initial matrix H_0 is definite.

Powell's modified BFGS formula

Powell's modified BFGS formula starts with a symmetric and positive definite matrix H_0. The matrices H_k are iteratively constructed by

$$H_{k+1} := H_k + \frac{\eta^k (\eta^k)^\top}{(s^k)^\top \eta^k} - \frac{H_k s^k (s^k)^\top H_k}{(s^k)^\top H_k s^k}.$$

(9.44)

The variables s^k and η^k are defined by

$$s^k := x^{k+1} - x^k \quad \text{and} \quad \eta^k := \theta_k y^k + (1 - \theta_k) H_k s^k,$$

with

$$y^k := \nabla_x L(x^{k+1}, \lambda^{k+1}, \mu^{k+1}) - \nabla_x L(x^k, \lambda^k, \mu^k),$$

$$\theta_k := \begin{cases} \dfrac{0.8(s^k)^\top H_k s^k}{(s^k)^\top H_k s^k - (s^k)^\top y^k}, & \text{if } (s^k)^\top y^k < 0.2(s^k)^\top H_k s^k. \\ 1, & \text{otherwise} \end{cases}$$

Geiger, C. and Kanzow, C. (2002) show that the iteration matrices H_{k+1} constructed by applying Powell's modified BFGS formula are positive definite if the vector $s^k = x^{k+1} - x^k \neq 0$ and the matrix H_k are symmetric and positive definite.

Quadratic Optimization – The core of the SQP iteration

The crucial point when applying the SQP algorithm above is the iterative solution of the subordinated quadratic problem, (9.43). We answer the question of how such a quadratic problem can in general be solved. Therefore, let us consider a quadratic minimization problem of the form

$$\min_y f(y) = \frac{1}{2} y^\top Q y + c^\top y + \omega$$

subject to

$$\begin{aligned} b_j^\top y &= \beta_j & j = 1, \dots, p \\ a_i^\top y &\le \alpha_i & i = 1, \dots, m, \end{aligned} \qquad (9.45)$$

with $Q \in \mathbb{R}^{n \times n}$ being a symmetric matrix, $c \in \mathbb{R}^n$, $\omega \in \mathbb{R}$, $a_i, b_j \in \mathbb{R}^n$ and $\alpha_i, \beta_j \in \mathbb{R}'$, $i = 1, \dots, m$, $j = 1, \dots, p$.

To identify a KKT point of (9.45) we solve a series of equality-constrained optimization problems. To this end we consider the set of indices

$$\mathcal{A}_k := \{i : a_i^\top y^k = \alpha_i, i = 1, \dots, m\}.$$

The set $\mathcal{A}_k$ determines the *active set* of inequality constraints for the current iteration point y^k. To solve the equality-constrained optimization problem we use the *active set strategy* for quadratic problems which we describe in the sequel. We define

$$A_k := \begin{pmatrix} \vdots \\ a_i^\top (i \in \mathcal{A}_k) \\ \vdots \end{pmatrix} \in \mathbb{R}^{|\mathcal{A}_k| \times n}, \quad B := \begin{pmatrix} \vdots \\ b_j^\top (j = 1, \dots, p) \\ \vdots \end{pmatrix} \in \mathbb{R}^{p \times n}$$

The algorithm can be summarized as follows:

Algorithm 9.7: Active set strategy for quadratic problems

(S.1) Choose $(y^0, \lambda^0, \mu^0) \in \mathbb{R}^{n+m+p}$ admissible for (9.45) and estimate
$\mathcal{A}_0 := \{i : a_i^\top y^0 \approx \alpha_i, \ i = 1, \ldots, m\}$. Set $k := 0$

(S.2) **if** (y^k, λ^k, μ^k) *is a KKT point of* (9.45) **then**
| **stop**

(S.3) Set $\lambda_i := 0$ for $i \neq \mathcal{A}_k$, calculate the solution $(\Delta y^k, \lambda_{\mathcal{A}_k}^{k+1}, \mu^{k+1})$ of

$$\begin{pmatrix} Q & A_k^\top & B^\top \\ A_k & 0 & 0 \\ B & 0 & 0 \end{pmatrix} \begin{pmatrix} \Delta y \\ \lambda_{\mathcal{A}_k} \\ \mu \end{pmatrix} = \begin{pmatrix} -\nabla f(y^k) \\ 0 \\ 0 \end{pmatrix}$$

(S.4) **if** $\Delta y^k = 0$ **then**
| **if** $\lambda_i^{k+1} \geq 0 \, \forall i \in \mathcal{A}_k$ **then**
| | **stop**
| **else**
| | Estimate index q with $\lambda_q^{k+1} = \min\{\lambda_i^{k+1} | i \in \mathcal{A}_k\}$,
| | set $y^{k+1} := y^k$, $\mathcal{A}_{k+1} := \mathcal{A}_k \setminus \{q\}$ and go to step (S.5)
else
| **if** $y^k + \Delta y^k$ admissible for (9.45) **then**
| | Set $y^{k+1} := y^k + \Delta y^k$, $\mathcal{A}_{k+1} := \mathcal{A}_k$ and go to step (S.5)
| **else**
| | Identify index r with
|
$$\frac{\alpha_r - a_r^\top y^k}{a_r^\top \Delta y^k} = \min\left\{\frac{\alpha_i - a_i^\top y^k}{a_i^\top \Delta y^k} \Big| i \notin \mathcal{A}_k \text{ with } a_i^\top \Delta y^k > 0\right\},$$
|
| | set $y^{k+1} := y^k + t_k \Delta y^k$ with $t_k := \frac{\alpha_r - a_r^\top y^k}{a_r^\top \Delta y^k}$, update $\mathcal{A}_{k+1} := \mathcal{A}_k \cup \{r\}$ and go to
| | (S.5)

(S.5) Set $k := k + 1$ and go to (S.2)

The algorithm stops within finite time and results in a unique solution for a symmetric and positive definite matrix Q and linear independent vectors a_i, $i \in \mathcal{A}_0$ and b_j, $j = 1, \ldots, p$. For details we refer readers to Geiger, C. and Kanzow, C. (2002).

Up to now our version of the SQP algorithm only converges if the initial guess (x^0, λ^0, μ^0) lies in a neighbourhood of a KKT point of the optimization problem, (9.2). To globalize the SQP method we restrict the step size of the increment Δx^k using an Armijo-based line search. Unfortunately, the step size restriction leads to problems. For an admissible vector x^k of the original problem, (9.2), there does not necessarily exist a valid increment Δx^k for the inner quadratic optimization problem. To overcome this, we modify the objective function f of the quadratic problem and relax the constraints. Then, we end up with a modified and globally convergent SQP method which is the algorithm we implemented in Matlab.

9.5.1 The Modified and Globally Convergent SQP Iteration

We introduce a globally convergent version of the SQP algorithm which guarantees that the quadratic problem is well defined as long as the Hessian matrix H_k of the Lagrangian function is positive definite. The globalization of the SQP method is achieved by an Armijo step size restriction for the exact L_1-penalty-function, P_1, given by

$$P_1(x; \alpha) := f(x) + \alpha \sum_{i=1}^{m} \max\{0, g_i(x)\} + \alpha \sum_{j=1}^{p} |h_j(x)|. \tag{9.46}$$

The penalty parameter $\alpha > 0$ can be chosen such that the solution Δx^k is always a descending direction for $P_1(\cdot; \alpha)$. The modified and globally convergent SQP algorithm can now be summarized as follows:

Algorithm 9.8: Modified and globally convergent SQP method

(S.1) Choose $(x^0, \lambda^0, \mu^0) \in \mathbb{R}^{n+m+p}$, $H_0 \in \mathbb{R}^{n \times n}$ symmetric, $\alpha_0 > 0$, $\beta \in (0, 1)$ and $\sigma \in (0, 1)$. Set $k = 0$

(S.2) **if** (x^k, λ^k, μ^k) *is a KKT point for* (9.2) **then**
   | **stop**

(S.3) Calculate a solution $(\Delta x^k, \xi^k, (\eta^+)^k, (\eta^-)^k)$ of the quadratic problem

$$\min \quad \nabla f(x^k)^\top \Delta x + \frac{1}{2} \Delta x^\top H_k \Delta x + \alpha_k \left(\sum_{i=1}^{m} \xi_i + \sum_{j=1}^{p} \eta_j^+ + \sum_{j=1}^{p} \eta_j^- \right).$$

$$\begin{aligned}
\text{s.t.} \quad & g_i(x^k) + \nabla g_i(x^k)^\top \Delta x \le \xi_i, && \xi_i \ge 0 \\
& h_j(x^k) + \nabla h_j(x^k)^\top \Delta x = \eta_j^+ - \eta_j^-, && \eta_j^+ \ge 0, \ \eta_j^- \ge 0 \\
& (i = 1, \dots, m) \quad (j = 1, \dots, p).
\end{aligned}$$

   with Lagrangian multipliers λ^{k+1}, $(\lambda^+)^{k+1}$, μ^{k+1}, $(\mu^+)^{k+1}$ and $(\mu^-)^{k+1}$

(S.4) **if** $\Delta x^k = 0$ **then**
   | **stop**
   else
   | Estimate the smallest value $l \in \mathbb{N} \cup \{0\}$ such that the inequality

$$P_1(x^k + t_k \Delta x^k; \alpha_k) \le P_1(x^k; \alpha_k) - \sigma t_k (\Delta x^k)^\top H_k \Delta x^k,$$

   | is fulfilled for the coefficient $t_k = \beta^l$

(S.5) Set $x^{k+1} = x^k + t_k \Delta x^k$, choose $H_{k+1} \in \mathbb{R}^{n \times n}$ symmetric and update

$$\alpha_{k+1} = \max\{\alpha_k, \max\{\lambda_1^{k+1}, \dots, \lambda_m^{k+1}, |\mu_1^{k+1}|, \dots, |\mu_p^{k+1}|\} + \alpha_0\}.$$

(S.6) Set $k := k + 1$, and go to step (S.2)

If we compare Algorithm 9.8 with its local convergent counterpart, we can identify three significant differences.

First, there is the Armijo based backtracking line search in step (S.4), which in combination with step (S.5) for α_k ensures that algorithm is globally convergent. The step size restriction is only a kind of Armijo rule since we disregard the calculation of the derivative $P_1'(x^k; \Delta x^k; \alpha)$ of the exact l_1-penalty-function (9.46). Geiger and Kanzow prove for the solution $(\Delta x^k, \xi^k, (\eta^+)^k, (\eta^-)^k)$ of the quadratic problem of step (S.3) that

$$P_1'(x^k; \Delta x^k; \alpha) \le -(\Delta x^k) H_k \Delta x^k < 0, \tag{9.47}$$

if $\alpha \geq \max\{\lambda_1^{k+1}, \ldots, \lambda_m^{k+1}, |\mu_1^{k+1}|, \ldots, |\mu_p^{k+1}|\}$. Thus, the vector Δx^k forms a descending direction for the exact L_1-penalty-function subject to the above assumptions. The algorithm stops if the solution Δx^k is equal to zero. In this case x^k presents a stationary point of the penalty-function $P_1(\cdot; \alpha)$, so that $P_1'(x^k; d; \alpha) \geq 0$ for all directions $d \in \mathbb{R}$. If, in particular, $(\Delta x^k, \xi^k, (\eta^+)^k, (\eta^-)^k) = (0, 0, 0, 0)$, then additional $(x^k, \lambda^{k+1}, \mu^{k+1})$ forms a KKT point of the constrained optimization problem, (9.2).

Third, for the modification of the quadratic problem of step (S.3) admissible points do always exist subject to the constraints. Furthermore, the problem is solvable if the matrix H_k is symmetric and positive definite for all iterations. To achieve this positive definiteness the constraints of the original quadratic problem, (9.43), have been relaxed using the variables ξ^k, $(\eta^+)^k$ and $(\eta^-)^k$. The additional factor of the modified objective function guarantees that the relaxation is as small as possible.

9.5.2 Implementation

Algorithm 9.8 is implemented in the function modSQP. The current declaration of the function is given by

```
function [xMin, fMin, perf] = modSQP(fobj,x0,fconst,...
                              lb,ub,H0,maxIter,varargin)
```

The output arguments xMin and fMin are the solution at termination and its objective function value. The variable perf is a struct with fields iter, itertotal, fk, xk and totaltime. iter stores the number of iterations neglecting the quadratic problem in each iteration. itertotal is the overall number of iterations also considering the inner quadratic problem. fk and xk keep a history of the objective function values and the iterates during the progress of the SQP method. totaltime returns the time in seconds required from the beginning to the end.

The input argument fobj is a function handle pointing to the objective function. x0 is the initial guess vector of the parameters to calibrate. The function handle argument fconst refers to the constraints function defining $g(x) \leq 0$ and $h(x) = 0$ and their Jacobian matrices. The algorithm expects a constraints function which is implemented by

```
function [G, JacG, H, JacH] = constraints(params,varargin)
```

Here G and H are the constraint function values $g(x) \leq 0$ and $h(x)$ evaluated at the parameter vector params. The output arguments JacG and JacH are the corresponding Jacobian matrices. Additional parameters necessary to evaluate g or h are assigned to the function through the variable parameter list varargin{:}. If any of the output arguments G or H equals an empty array [], the algorithm ignores this type of constraint. If only lower bounds, lb, or upper bounds, ub, exist, this function handle is omitted and will then automatically be set. If lb or ub are missing, the algorithm initializes the lower and upper bounds subject to:

```
% trivial bounds
lowerBounds = -Inf*ones(n,1); upperBounds = Inf*ones(n,1);
```

The remaining arguments H0 and maxIter define the initial Hessian matrix and the maximum number of iterations. In the absence of one or both inputs the default values are

```
H0 = eye(n); maxIter = n*100;
```

The function eye(n) generates the identity matrix of size $n \times n$. The variable parameter list varargin{:} can once again be used to pass additional arguments to the algorithm that are not modified within the optimization process. In each iteration the quadratic optimization problem of step (S.3) is solved by calling the function

```
function [xmin, lambda, mu] = quadOpt(x0,lam0,mue0,Q,c,gam, ...
                                      A,alfa,B,beta,lb,ub)
```

It implements the active set strategy for quadratic problems by Algorithm 9.7. Powell's modified BFGS-updating rule of the Hessian matrix (9.44) is implemented by the function

```
function newH = HessApprox(oldGradF,oldX,newGradF,newX,oldHessian)
% Implements Powell's modified BFGS Hessian update
%---------------------------------------------------
% Input:
% oldX/newX: current/new iterate
% oldGradF/newGradF: gradient of the considered function oldX/neX
% oldHessian: Hessian approximation at the current iterate
%
% Output:
% newH: Hessian approx at new iterate via Powell's modified BFGS-
updating
% residuum xk+1-xk
s = newX - oldX;
y = newGradF-oldGradF;

%auxiliary variables
Hs = oldHessian*s; sHs = s'*Hs; sy = s'*y;

if(sy >= .2*sHs)
    theta = 1.0;
else
    theta = .8*sHs / (sHs - sy);
end
eta = theta*y + (1-theta)*Hs;
newH = oldHessian + eta*eta' / (s'*eta) - Hs*s'*oldHessian / sHs;
end
```

The gradient of the Lagrangian function in Powell's updating rule, (9.44), requires the calculation of the gradient of the objective function f. The current version of the function modSQP(...) supports gradient estimation by implementing the function

```
function gradf = GradientEval(fobj,xk,fval,varargin)
```

It approximates the first derivatives via finite differences. To keep the computational effort manageable we decided to use one-sided forward differences

$$\nabla f(x^k)_i \approx \frac{f(x^k + he_i) - f(x^k)}{h}, \quad e_i(j) = \begin{cases} 1 & i = j \\ 0 & \text{otherwise} \end{cases} \in \mathbb{R}^n$$

for $i = 1, \ldots, n$ and small value $h > 0$ small. In our implementation we use $h = \sqrt{2^{-53}}||x^k||$ if $x^k \neq 0$. This is proposed in Madsen, K., Nielsen, H. and Sondergaard, J. (2002) minimizing the effects of truncation and rounding errors, otherwise $h = 2^{-53}$. Since the argument $fval$ assigns the current function value $f(x^k)$ to the function, this procedure only requires n additional function evaluations of the objective function $fobj$.

A direct implementation of Algorithm 9.8 with initial matrix H_0 equal to the $n \times n$ identity matrix showed that the generated solutions Δx^k of the quadratic problem can lead to non-admissible variables $x^{k+1} = x^k + \Delta x^k$ despite the mathematical fact that this could not happen. However, in practice, numerical issues such as rounding or error propagation can lead to this problem. As long as the function f can be evaluated outside the admissible range, the Armijo based update rule $x^k + t_k \Delta x^k$ in combination with the penalty-function $P_1(\cdot; \alpha)$ ensure that x^{k+1} is automatically projected to the admissible range. But if the admissible range of the minimization problem (9.2) coincides with the domain of definition of function f, an evaluation of the penalty-function $P_1(\cdot; \alpha)$ at x^{k+1} is often impossible. To ensure the admissibility of the variable x^{k+1} we modified step (S.4) in our implementation as follows:

(S.4)   Estimate the minimum entry level $l \in \{0, 1, 2, \ldots\}$, with:

$$g\left(x^k + \beta^l \Delta x^k\right) \leq 0.$$

Identify the smallest value $q \in \{l, l+1, l+2, \ldots\}$ such that the coefficient $\widehat{t_k} = \beta^q$ fulfils the inequality

$$P_1(x^k + \widehat{t_k} \Delta x^k; \alpha_k) \leq P_1(x^k; \alpha_k) - \sigma \widehat{t_k} (\Delta x^k)^\top H_k \Delta x^k.$$

This version of step (S.4) ensures that the evaluation of the penalty-function $P_1(\cdot; \alpha)$ is admissible at $x^k + \widehat{t_k} \Delta x^k$. The algorithm stops when the sequence $\{t^k\}_{k \in \mathbb{N}_0}$ falls below a predefined tolerance level.

Algorithm 9.8 terminates when the iterate (x^k, λ^k, μ^k) is a KKT point of the optimization problem or the estimated step size Δx^k equals zero. Both termination criteria are implemented using the predefined tolerance level $\varepsilon_1 = n \cdot \sqrt{2^{-52}}$ and the infinity norm $|| \cdot ||_\infty$. The implemented method also stops if the difference in the function values $||f(x^{k+1}) - f(x^k)||$ is less than the tolerance level ε_1. In addition, the method is terminated if the maximum number of iterations is reached or the value of the globalization parameter $\widehat{t_k}$ falls below a second tolerance level ε_2. This prevents the method from becoming stuck in an infinite loop.

9.5.3   Calibration Examples

Let us consider the following example:

$$\min_{x_1, x_2} \quad f(x_1, x_2) := -5x_1 + x_1^2 - 5x_2 + x_2^2 \tag{9.48}$$

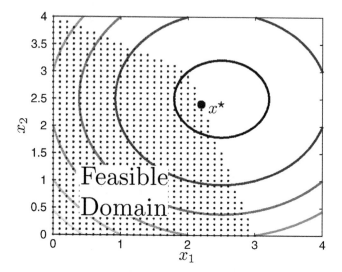

Figure 9.12   Contour and admissible domain of the optimization problem (9.48)

subject to

$$g_1(x_1, x_2) = x_1 + 2x_2 - 8 \leq 0$$
$$g_2(x_1, x_2) = 3x_1 + x_2 - 9 \leq 0$$
$$x_1, x_2 \geq 0.$$

Figure 9.12 plots the contour of the objective function and a part of the admissible domain $\mathcal{X}$ in the neighbourhood of the optimal solution. From this, we see that the unconstrained global optimizer would be reached for $x = (2.5, 2.5)^\top$. The optimal constrained solution instead is given by $x^* = (2.2, 2.4)^\top$ with objective function value $f(x^*) = -12.4$. The solution vector lies on the edge of the admissible domain, thus the inequality constraints are called active for x^*.

To calculate the optimal solution x^* we define the objective function:

```
function y = objectiveFunction(xvec)
% This function defines the objective function f
% min f(x1,x2) = -5x1 + x1^2 -5x2 + x2^2
%
y = xvec(1)*(xvec(1)-5)+xvec(2)*(+xvec(2)-5);
```

and the constraints:

```
function [g,Jacg,h,Jach] = constraintsFunction(xvec)
% This function defines the constraints
% g(x)<=0, h(x)=0 and their Jacobian matrices
%
g = [xvec(1)+2*xvec(2)-8; 3*xvec(1)+xvec(2)-9];
```

```
Jacg = [1 2; 3 1];

h = [];
Jach = [];
```

We start the modified SQP optimization by calling the function modifiedSQP(...) with initial guess $x^0 = (0.0, 4.0)^\top$ and the vector of lower bounds $lb = (0, 0)^\top$ for the minimization problem (9.48).

```
% feasible initial guess
x0 = [0.0;4.0];
% objective function
objF = @objectiveFunction;
% constraints function
constF = @constraintsFunction;
% lower bounds
lb = [0.0;0.0];

% start optimization
[xMin,fMin,perf] = modifiedSQP(objF,x0,constF,lb);
```

Without considering the inner quadratic problem the function modifiedSQP stops after 7 iterations with a maximum difference of residuum $||x^{k+1} - x^k||_\infty$ less than $n \cdot \sqrt{2^{-52}} \approx 3.0 \cdot 10^{-8}$ for $n = 2$. Figure 9.13 illustrates the progress of the SQP algorithm for the above example.

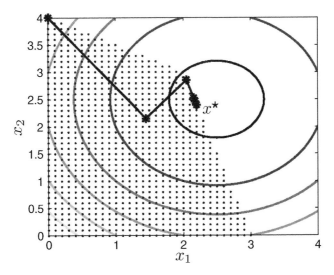

Figure 9.13 Progress of the SQP algorithm of optimization problem (9.48) with initial guess $x^0 = (0.0, 4.0)^\top$

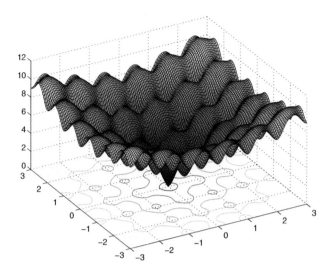

Figure 9.14 Ackley's function for $n = 2$

Figure 9.13 shows that the algorithm successively generates solutions along a descent direction of the objective function f. For iterates with active constraints the algorithm moves along the boundary of the admissible domain to achieve further enhancement.

As a second example we consider Ackley's function (Figure 9.14) given by

$$f : \mathbb{R}^n \to \mathbb{R}$$

$$f(x) = \exp(1) + 20\left(1 - \exp\left(-\frac{1}{5}\sqrt{\frac{1}{n}\sum_{i=1}^{n} x_i^2}\right) - \exp\left(-\frac{1}{n}\sum_{i=1}^{n} \cos(2\pi x_i)\right)\right). \quad (9.49)$$

For $n = 2$ the objective function exhibits many local minima. The global minimum $f(x^*) = 0$ is reached at $x^* = 0$.

Starting the SQP method with an initial guess $x^0 = (-2.5, 2.5)^\top$ and a parameter restriction of $-3 \le x^k(i) \le 3$ for $i = 1, 2$ generates the solution displayed in Figure 9.15.

An initial guess $x^0 = (2.4803, 0.7942)^\top$ instead results in Figure 9.16.

Figures 9.15 and 9.16 show that in the presence of many local minima the SQP algorithm converges but not necessarily to the global optimum. From Figure 9.16 we observe that the algorithm generates steps in a direction pointing in another direction and not to the global minimum of the objective function. On the other hand, from Figure 9.15 we see that although the direction might be optimal the step size can be too large and may overshoot the global minimum. In both cases the algorithm stops with a solution only locally optimal.

The minimization of Ackley's function should clarify that even if all convergence conditions of the objective function and its derivatives are fulfilled, the SQP algorithm as well as any other method described so far can only guarantee convergence to a local minimum $f(\tilde{x})$ of the optimization problem (9.2) with $f(\tilde{x}) \le f(x)$ for all x in a neighbourhood $U(\tilde{x})$. To identify the global minimizer x^* with $f(x^*) \le f(x)$ for all x in the admissible domain $\mathcal{X}$ it is necessary to switch to global optimization methods. To this end we introduce two widely used heuristic

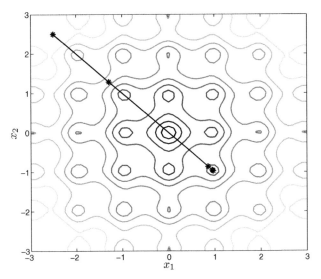

Figure 9.15 Progress of the SQP algorithm for Ackley's function and initial guess $x^0 = (-2.5, 2.5)^\top$

search methods that converge to a global minimum:

- Differential Evolution.
- Simulated Annealing.

Both methods belong to the class of stochastic optimizers. Just like direct search methods, stochastic optimizers do not require the calculation of values of any derivative of the objective function to identify a minimum solution. Furthermore, the acceptance of possible uphill steps and the simultaneous search in many different directions avoid these methods of stagnation

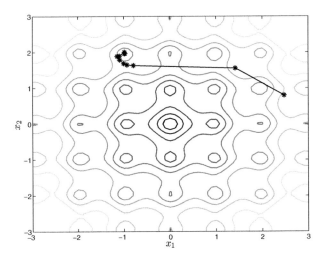

Figure 9.16 Progress of the SQP algorithm for Ackley's function and initial guess $x^0 = (2.4803, 0.7942)^\top$

or entrapment in a local minimum and, thus, enable them to find the global minimum in the presence of many local minima.

9.6 DIFFERENTIAL EVOLUTION

Differential Evolution, which was introduced in Storn, R. and Price, K. (1995), is a population-based search algorithm and belongs to the class of evolutionary or genetic algorithms. As a genetic algorithm it mimics the process of Darwinian evolution using techniques such as *inheritance, mutation, recombination, selection* and *crossover*. The algorithm is designed to converge to the global optimum.

The classic Differential Evolution algorithm for n parameters (see Price, K., Storn, R. and Lampinen, J. (2005), Chapter 2) starts with $M > 3$ candidate solutions given by $x_1^0 \ldots, x_M^0$. The starting points are randomly generated and taken from some subset $D \subset \mathbb{R}^n$ defined by

$$D := \left\{ x \in \mathbb{R}^n : lb(j) \le x(j) \le ub(j) \quad \text{for } j = 1, \ldots, n \right\}.$$

Figure 9.17 illustrates this using the Ackley function. We have applied lower and upper bounds denoted by $lb, ub \in \mathbb{R}^n$. Often it is assumed that the starting values are uniformly distributed in D and thus can be generated using a matrix $U \in \mathbb{R}^{n \times M}$ and setting

$$x_i^0(j) := U(j,i)[ub(j) - lb(j)] + lb(j).$$

For the entries of U we assume $U(j,i) \sim \mathcal{U}(0,1)$, $j = 1, \ldots, n$ and $i = 1, \ldots, M$. The starting points are interpreted as individuals of an initial population

$$P_0 = (x_i^0(j))_{\substack{j=1,\ldots,n \\ i=1,\ldots,M}} \in \mathbb{R}^{n \times M}$$

The Differential Evolution algorithm iteratively mutates the members of the population and selects the optimal mutations by specifying some fitness function. The fitness level of each individual is measured by an objective function. New trial solutions are generated applying mutation and crossover. The mutation vector v_i for $i = 1, \ldots, M$ is a weighted sum. We

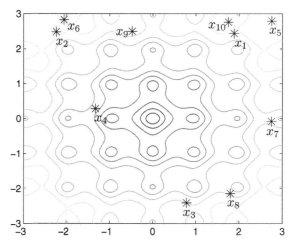

Figure 9.17 Contour plot of Ackley's function and an initial population P_0 with $n = 2$, $M = 10$ and $-3 \le x_i^0(j) \le 3$ for $i = 1, \ldots, M$ and $j = 1, \ldots, n$

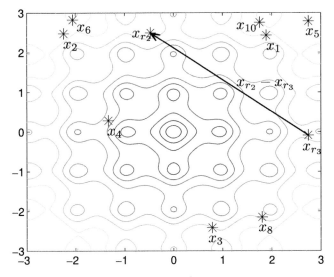

Figure 9.18   Difference vector $x_{r_2} - x_{r_3}$ for $r_2 = 9$ and $r_3 = 7$

randomly choose the individuals x_{r_1}, x_{r_2} and x_{r_3} with indices distinct from i and also pairwise distinct from each other. Then, the i-th candidate is constructed by

$$v_i := x_{r_1} + \beta \cdot (x_{r_2} - x_{r_3}), \quad \rho > 0. \tag{9.50}$$

Figure 9.18 plots the difference vector $x_{r_2} - x_{r_3}$ of the mutation step for the two *difference indices* $r_2 = 9$ and $r_3 = 7$.

The scaling factor $\beta > 0$ is chosen to control the rate of mutation. Usually β is chosen such that $\beta \in (0, 1)$. Figure 9.19 illustrates the mutation vector v_1 and the weighted sum $\beta(x_{r_2} - x_{r_3})$ assuming a scaling factor $\beta = 0.5$ and *base vector index* $r_1 = 3$.

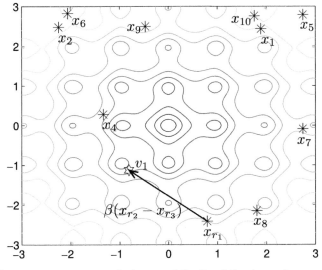

Figure 9.19   Mutant vector $v_1 = x_{r_1} + \beta \cdot (x_{r_2} - x_{r_3})$ for $\beta = 0.5$ and $r_1 = 3$

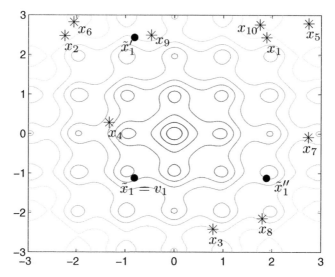

Figure 9.20   Possible outcomes $\tilde{x}_1$, $\tilde{x}_1'$ and $\tilde{x}_1''$ of the uniform crossover step

The crossover step recombines the mutation vector v_i with the current individual x_i to create a new trial vector $\tilde{x}_i$. Using uniform crossover we randomly determine an index $j_{rand} \in \{1, \ldots, n\}$, a vector $U \in \mathbb{R}^n$ of uniform random numbers $U(j) \sim \mathcal{U}(0,1)$ for $j = 1, \ldots, n$ and define

$$\tilde{x}_i(j) := \begin{cases} v_i(j) & \text{if} \quad U(j) \leq cp \text{ or } j = j_{rand} \\ x_i(j) & \text{otherwise} \end{cases}.$$

This uniform crossover guarantees that the trial vector $\tilde{x}_i$ at least differs from x_i for $j = j_{rand}$-th component. Figure 9.20 shows the $2^n - 1$ possible trial vector results $\tilde{x}_1$, $\tilde{x}_1'$ and $\tilde{x}_1''$ from the uniform crossover of mutant v_1 and target vector x_1 for dimension $n = 2$. The population for $M = 10$ individuals has been applied to Ackley's function.

Finally, the step called *selection* determines whether a trial solution $\tilde{x}_i$ replaces some individual of the current population and appears in the updated population P_{k+1}. The decision depends on the individual's fitness level measured by the objective function. A function value for $\tilde{x}_i$ such that $f(\tilde{x}_i) \leq f(x_i)$ of a trial solution compared to the individual x_i implies a higher probability of surviving and therefore it replaces the current one, that is replacing x_i with $\tilde{x}_i$. Since the selection allows for updates of the current population with candidate solutions that are only as fit as the target individual, the Differential Evolution algorithm avoids becoming trapped in flat regions or local optima of the objective function.

Similar to direct search methods the determination of a universally applicable termination criterion for the Differential Evolution algorithm is not unique. If the global minimum is known the stopping rule is easy to determine. For calibration problems in finance this value is usually around 0. But the setting that a model cannot fit all market prices is standard. Thus, only for test cases is a stopping rule incorporating the global maximum meaningful.

We consider other termination criteria. A widely applied rule limits the number of generations k by an upper bound k_{max}. This is equivalent to bounding the number of iterations for Newton method based optimizers. One difficulty of this approach is to set k_{max} large enough to allow enough iteration steps to converge to the optimum. Test cases show that a badly chosen k_{max} results in proposed solutions too far away from the global minimum. Choosing too large values of k_{max} unnecessarily increases the computational time of the algorithm. Instead of bounding the overall number of generations we define a limit for the number of consecutive trial vectors not being accepted. The algorithm can also be terminated subject to a predetermined statistical value such as the difference between the population's worst and best objective function value or the standard deviation of population vectors. However, none of these methods guarantees convergence to the global minimum.

The individual steps of the classic Differential Evolution algorithm can be summarized as follows:

Algorithm 9.9: Classic Differential Evolution method

(S.1) Initialize the population $P_0 \in \mathbb{R}^{n \times M}$ with $M > 3$ individuals $x_i^0 \in \mathbb{R}^n$
for $i = 1, \ldots, M$, define a crossover probability $cp \in [0, 1]$, a scaling factor $\beta \geq 0$, a maximum number of iterations k_{max}, a satisfactory fitness level TOL and set $k = 0$

(S.2) *Mutation:* **for** $i = 1$ **to** M **do**
randomly select three candidates $x_{r_j}^k$, $j = 1, 2, 3$ from the current population P_k with $r_1 \neq r_2 \neq r_3 \neq i$ and compute mutation vector

$$v_i^k := x_{r_1}^k + \beta \cdot \left(x_{r_2}^k - x_{r_3}^k \right)$$

(S.3) *Crossover:* **for** $i = 1$ **to** M **do**
calculate a random index $j_{rand} \in \{1, \ldots, n\}$ and draw a uniform random vector $U_k \in \mathbb{R}^n$. Define new individuals $\tilde{x}_i^k \in \mathbb{R}^n$ according to the "uniform crossover"

$$\tilde{x}_i^k(j) := \begin{cases} v_i^k(j) & \text{if } U_k(j) \leq cp \text{ or } j = j_{rand} \\ x_i^k(j) & \text{otherwise} \end{cases}$$

(S.4) *Selection:* **for** $i = 1$ **to** M **do**
Choose the solution candidate for the new population P_{k+1} subject to

$$x_i^{k+1} = \begin{cases} \tilde{x}_i^k & \text{if } f(\tilde{x}_i^k) \leq f(x_i^k) \\ x_i^k & \text{otherwise} \end{cases}$$

(S.5) **if** $k = k_{max}$ **or** $\exists$ i *with* $f(x_i^{k+1}) \leq$ TOL **then**
| stop
else
| Set $k := k + 1$ and go to (S.2)

Algorithm 9.9 is implemented by the free software *DeMat* for Matlab. In addition, DeMat contains several adjustments of the mutation, crossover and selection steps for increasing the efficiency of the basic algorithm. A short overview of DeMat's functionality can be found below. For a more detailed description we refer readers to Price, K., Storn, R. and Lampinen, J. (2005). Before we cover the functionality we briefly describe how Differential Evolution can be extended to handle constraints.

Constraints   The Differential Evolution algorithm can be extended to incorporate boundary constraints, $lb(j) \leq x(j) \leq ub(j)$, $j = 1, \ldots, n$. To ensure that any individual x_i^{k+1} of the updated population P_{k+1} is within the admissible range we replace the values $\tilde{x}_i^{k+1}(j)$ that violate the j-th boundary constraint after the crossover step (S.3) with randomly generated values within the admissible domain $\mathcal{X}$ by setting

$$\tilde{x}_i^k(j) := \begin{cases} U_j[ub(j) - lb(j)] + lb(j) & \text{if} \quad \tilde{x}_i^k(j) < lb(j) \text{ or } \tilde{x}_i^k(j) > ub(j) \\ \tilde{x}_i^k(j) & \text{otherwise} \end{cases}.$$

$U_j \sim \mathcal{U}(0, 1)$ is a uniform random number. This modified decision rule allows the domain D used to generate the initial population P_0 to differ from the admissible domain $\mathcal{X}$ when bound constraints exist.

For the more general case of a non-linear constraint function $g : \mathbb{R}^n \to \mathbb{R}^m$ the DeMat-Toolbox applies Lampinen's direct constraint handling method (see Lampinen, J. (2002)). The function g has to fulfil the inequality $g(x) \leq 0$. We then substitute the selection step (S.4) by the following rule:

$$x_i^{k+1} = \begin{cases} \tilde{x}_i^k & \text{if} \quad \begin{cases} \begin{cases} \forall j \in \{1, \ldots, m\} : g_j(\tilde{x}_i^k) \leq 0 \wedge g_j(x_i^k) \leq 0 \\ \text{and} \\ f(\tilde{x}_i^k) \leq f(x_i^k) \end{cases} \\ \text{or} \\ \begin{cases} \forall j \in \{1, \ldots, m\} : g_j(\tilde{x}_i^k) \leq 0 \\ \text{and} \\ \exists j \in \{1, \ldots, m\} : g_j(x_i^k) > 0 \end{cases} \\ \text{or} \\ \begin{cases} \exists j \in \{1, \ldots, m\} : g_j(\tilde{x}_i^k) > 0 \\ \text{and} \\ \forall j \in \{1, \ldots, m\} : \max\{g_j(\tilde{x}_i^k), 0\} \leq \max\{g_j(x_i^k), 0\} \end{cases} \end{cases} \\ x_i^k & \text{otherwise} \end{cases} \qquad (9.51)$$

Thus, the trial vector $\tilde{x}_i^k$ replaces the current population member x_i^k

- if both vectors are admissible, but the trial vector leads to a value being smaller or equal to the current one, or
- if the trial vector is admissible while the current individual is not admissible, or
- if both vectors are not admissible, but the trial vector violates the constraints being smaller or equal.

Without constraints, Lampinen's rule reduces to the original selection step of Differential Evolution. When constraints are included Lampinen's method compares the size of constraint violation for non-admissible solutions instead of comparing objective function values. Selecting non-admissible solutions with constraint violation which are smaller generally leads to faster convergence rates. Theoretically, this allows us to start with a population of non-admissible individuals. Lampinen's approach also reduces the overall amount of function evaluations in comparison with standard penalty function methods that evaluate all functions involved and for every trial solution. Objective function values are only computed if both the trial solution and the current iteration step are admissible. In the case of two non-admissible solutions the evaluation of the constraints is stopped immediately if the trial solution violates any constraint other than the current solution. A second advantage of this approach compared to standard penalty function methods is that it does not need any extra penalty parameters which have to be specified by the user. Lampinen also handles the problem of being locally trapped in the case when constraints exist. The current population is updated with candidates that are only as appropriate as the target individual compared to both their objective function values and their constraint violation.

9.6.1 Implementation

The main part of the DeMat-Toolbox is the file **deopt.m**. It provides strategies for mutation and crossover and methods to guarantee the validity of all parameters in the presence of bound constraints. The function `deopt` initializes the search algorithm, monitors the optimization progress and determines when to terminate the algorithm. In addition, it controls the output of results.

The file **left_win.m** contains the implementation of Lampinen's adjusted selection step. It defines if a trial vector survives the target vector, that is if we compare the objective function values or the amount of constraint violation.

These files are independent of the specific optimization problem under consideration and can be used without modification. The files **objfun.m**, **Rundeopt.m** and **PlotIt.m** instead depend on the actual optimization problem and, therefore, need to be specified by the user.

The file **objfun.m** is used to evaluate the objective function and possible constraints. The declaration of the function is as follows:

```
function S_MSE= objfun(FVr_temp, S_struct)
```

The input argument `FVr_temp` is the vector of parameters we wish to optimize. The second argument is a Matlab variable of type `struct`. It is defined in the file **Rundeopt.m** and stores a variety of problem dependent but constant parameters. The output of the function is kept in the variable `S_MSE`, which is also of type `struct` and contains the number of objective functions applied, `S_MSE.I_no`, their costs `S_MSE.FVr_oa`, the number of constraints `S_MSE.I_nc` and the amount of constraints violations `S_MSE.FVr_ca`. Since DeMat is designed for multi-objective minimization, we output the number of applied objective functions. Multi-objective minimization attempts to simultaneously minimize several individual objective functions.

The script file **Rundeopt.m** configures all necessary input parameters to specify the Differential Evolution strategies, population sizes, crossover probabilities and other parameters using `S_struct`. It also initializes the optimization procedure by calling the function

```
[FVr_x,S_y,I_nf] = deopt('objfun',S_struct)
```

For visualization purposes a user-defined file **PlotIt.m** can be passed to the DeMat-Toolbox. The plotting can be enabled and disabled respectively by setting the parameter `I_plotting` in Rundeopt.m equal to `1` or `0`.

The differential mutation step (S.2) requires the random selection of the base vector $x_{r_1}^k$ and the difference vectors $x_{r_2}^k$ and $x_{r_3}^k$ distinct from the target vector x_i^k and from one another. The simplest way to ensure that the base, the target and the difference indices are distinct from each other is realized by a series of `while` statements of the form presented in Figure 9.21.

Despite the fact that the procedure works well the possibility exists that some vectors are picked more than once per iteration step while others are omitted. Since both phenomena negatively affect the performance of Differential Evolution we have to guarantee that this does not happen. Each vector serves as a base vector just once per iteration step. The *random*

```
r1 = floor(rand*M);
while(r1 == i)
    r1 = floor(rand*M);
end
r2 = floor(rand*M);
while(r2 == i || r2 == r1)
    r2 = floor(rand*M);
end
r3 = floor(rand*M);
while(r3 == i || r3 == r2 || r3 == r1)
    r3 = floor(rand*M);
end
```

Figure 9.21   `while` statements to guarantee that base, target and difference indices are distinct

offset method provides an easy way to achieve that each target index i is assigned to a unique base index r_0. At the start of each iteration an offset σ_k is randomly chosen out of the range $\{0, \ldots, M\}$. Then, the base index r_0 is set to $r0 = mod(i + sigma\_k, M)$. This is an additive shift of the target index i by σ_k modulo M.

9.6.2   Calibration Examples

Let us demonstrate the workflow necessary to apply the DeMat-Toolbox. We are again considering Ackley's function (9.49) for $n = 2$. Figure 9.14 illustrates that in the neighbourhood of the global minimizer $x^* = 0$ many local minima exist. The implementation of the function `objfun()` is given in Figure 9.22.

The function `ackley` is defined in Figure 9.23.

The script file **Rundeopt.m** is displayed in Figure 9.24.

The number of population members is given by the constant `I_NP` and the length of each individual by `I_D`. We restrict the parameter values for the initial and the iterated populations to $-3 \leq x(j) \leq 3, j = 1, \ldots, n$. Setting the bound vectors `FVr_minbound` and `FVr_maxbound` as well as the constant `I_bnd_constr`. The algorithm terminates if the maximum number of function evaluations `I_itermax` is reached or the optimal value of the objective function of the current generation is below the threshold level `F_VTR`. We decide to use the classical algorithm with uniform crossover by setting `I_strategy = 1`, choosing a crossover probability of `F_CR = 0.8` and scaling by `F_weight = 0.85`. The remaining parameters control the graphical output and, thus, we do not explain their meaning.

```
function S_MSE= objfun(FVr_temp, S_struct)
%----evaluate Ackley's function----
F_cost = ackley(FVr_temp(1),FVr_temp(2))

%----Setup struct S_MSE----
S_MSE.I_nc       = 0;%number of constraints
S_MSE.FVr_ca     = 0;%no constraint violation
S_MSE.I_no       = 1;%number of objective functions
S_MSE.FVr_oa(1)  = F_cost;
```

Figure 9.22   Matlab implementation of the objective function applied for optimization

```
function res = ackley(X,Y)
% Ackley's function for two input arguments X,Y of same size
res = exp(1)+20*(1-exp(-0.2*sqrt(0.5*(X.^2+Y.^2))))...
        -exp(0.5*(cos(2*pi*X)+cos(2*pi*Y)));
```

Figure 9.23   Matlab implementation of Ackley function

Figures 9.25 to 9.28 illustrate the progress of the Differential Evolution algorithm for Ackley's function. In addition, Table 9.7 gives the coordinates and the objective function values of the fittest individuals corresponding to every 5-th population.

From Table 9.7 and Figures 9.25–9.28 we observe that in contrast to the SQP method the Differential Evolution algorithm converges to the global minimum of Ackley's function.

The second example considers the function

$$f : \mathbb{R}^7 \to \mathbb{R}$$
$$f(x) = (x_1 - 10)^2 + 5(x_2 - 12)^2 + x_3{}^4 + 3(x_4 - 11)^2 + 10x_5{}^6 + 7x_6{}^2 + x_7{}^4 - 4x_6x_7.$$

```
%-------------------------------------------------------------
% script file Rundeopt.m initializes and starts the optimization
%-------------------------------------------------------------
% population constants
    S_struct.I_D = 2;  % number of parameters being optimized
    S_struct.I_NP = 15; % number of population members
    S_struct.FVr_minbound = -3*ones(1,S_struct.I_D); % lower bounds
    S_struct.FVr_maxbound = 3*ones(1,S_struct.I_D); % upper bounds
% use/don't use as bound constraints if set to 1/0
    S_struct.I_bnd_constr = 1;
% termination criteria
    S_struct.F_VTR = 1e-12;  % value to reach
    S_struct.I_itermax = 50;  % maximum number of iterations
% define DE strategy
    S_struct.I_strategy = 1;  % classical DE
    S_struct.F_weight = 0.85; % mutation scaling factor
    S_struct.F_CR = 0.8;      % crossover probabilility
%---------Plotting---------
% use/skip plotting if set to 1/0
    S_struct.I_plotting = 1;
% after "I_refresh" iterations plot/print values
    S_struct.I_refresh = 5;
if (S_struct.I_plotting == 1)
    S_struct.FVc_xx = -3:0.05:3;
    S_struct.FVc_yy = S_struct.FVc_xx;

    [FVr_x,FM_y]=meshgrid(S_struct.FVc_xx,S_struct.FVc_yy) ;
    S_struct.FM_meshd = ackley(FVr_x,FM_y);

end

%-----------Start optimization-----------
[FVr_x,S_y,I_nf] = deopt('objfun',S_struct)
```

Figure 9.24   Matlab script for optimizing the Ackley function using Differential Evolution

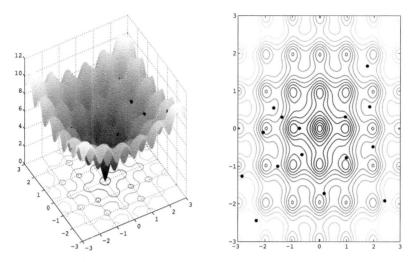

Figure 9.25 Progress of the Differential Evolution optimization: initial population P_0

We consider the inequality constraints $g_i(x) \leq 0$, $i = 1, \ldots, 4$ with

$$g_1(x) = 2x_1^2 + 3x_2^4 + x_3 + 4x_4^2 + 5x_5 - 127$$
$$g_2(x) = 7x_1 + 3x_2 + 10x_3^2 + x_4 - x_5 - 282$$
$$g_3(x) = 23x_1 + x_2^2 + 6x_6^2 - 8x_7 - 196$$
$$g_4(x) = 4x_1^2 + x_2^2 - 3x_1x_2 + 2x_3^2 + 5x_6 - 11x_7$$

and the bound constraints $-10 \leq x_i \leq 10$, $i = 1, \ldots, 7$. The best-known solution in the literature is given by $f(x^*) = 680.6300573$ with

$$x^* = (2.330499, 1.951372, -0.4775414, 4.365726, -0.6244870, 1.038181, 1.594227)^\top$$

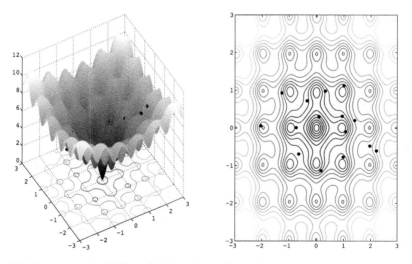

Figure 9.26 Progress of the Differential Evolution optimization: 5-th population evolution

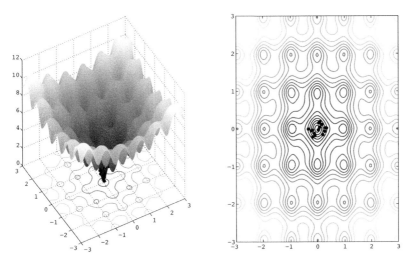

Figure 9.27   Progress of the Differential Evolution optimization: 15-th population evolution

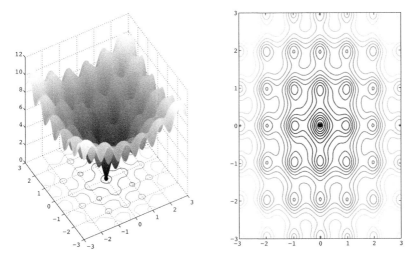

Figure 9.28   Progress of the Differential Evolution optimization: 30-th population evolution

Table 9.7   Coordinates and objective function values of the fittest individual during the Differential Evolution for Ackley's function

Population	Coordinates		Objective Function Value
P_k	$x^k(1)$	$x^k(2)$	$f(x^k(1), x^k(2))$
0	0.09258150	0.30322400	2.306483
5	0.08171200	0.04481400	0.481255
10	0.08171200	0.04481400	0.481255
15	0.03498590	−0.02566490	0.172226
20	0.01443240	0.03016920	0.124135
25	−0.01333270	−0.00403775	0.044562
30	0.000672868	0.00275017	0.008222

In Matlab the objective function can be implemented as follows:

```
function S_MSE = objfun(FVr_temp, S_struct)
%---evaluate cost function-------------------------------------
F_cost = myfun(FVr_temp);


%----Setup struct S_MSE----------------------------------------
S_MSE.I_nc       = 4; % number of constraints
S_MSE.FVr_ca     = mycon(FVr_temp); % constraint violation
S_MSE.I_no       = 1;% number of objective functions
S_MSE.FVr_oa(1)  = F_cost;
```

The functions myfun and mycon are given by

```
function y = myfun(x)
% Costs
y = (x(1)-10)^2 + 5*(x(2)-12)^2 + x(3)^4 + 3*(x(4)-11)^2 +...
    10*x(5)^6 + 7*x(6)^2 + x(7)^4 - 4*x(6)*x(7) - 10*x(6) - 8*x(7);
```

and

```
function y = mycon(x)
% auxiliary variables
v1 = 2*x(1)^2;
v2 = x(2)^2;
% Constraints
y = zeros(1,4);
y(1,1) = v1 + 3*v2^2 + x(3) + 4*x(4)^2 + 5*x(5) - 127;
y(1,2) = 7*x(1) + 3*x(2) + 10*x(3)^2 + x(4) - x(5) - 282;
y(1,3) = 23*x(1) + v2 + 6*x(6)^2 - 8*x(7) - 196;
y(1,4) = 2*v1 + v2 - 3*x(1)*x(2) + 2*x(3)^2 + 5*x(6) - 11*x(7);
```

The bound constraints $-10 \leq x_i \leq 10$ for $i = 1, \ldots, 7$ are considered by setting S_struct.I_bnd_constr = 1 and

```
S_struct.I_D = 7; % number of parameters
S_struct.FVr_minbound = -10*ones(1,S_struct.I_D); % lower bounds
S_struct.FVr_maxbound = 10*ones(1,S_struct.I_D); % upper bounds
```

We run the modified script file **Rundeopt.m**. Figure 9.29 plots the intermediate best objective function values during the classical Differential Evolution for a series of random

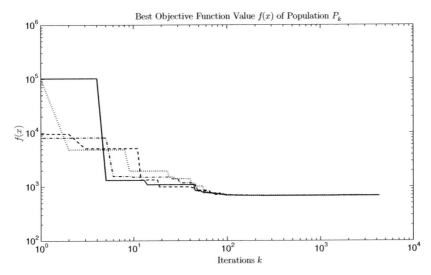

Figure 9.29   Best objective function values of the Differential Evolution optimization with constraints for different initial populations P_k

initial populations. We set the parameters $cp = 0.6$, $\beta = 0.7$ and the value to reach is set to S_struct.F_VTR = 680.631. The size of each population P_k is set to S_struct.I_NP = 5*S_struct.I_D and the maximum number of iterations is set, S_struct.I_itermax = 10000.

Figure 9.29 shows that the Differential Evolution method with Lampinen's direct constraint handling method (see Lampinen, J. (2002)) works well when the value to reach is known in advance.

9.7   SIMULATED ANNEALING

The basic idea for implementing Simulated Annealing is described in Metropolis, N., Rosenbluth, A.W., Rosenbluth, M.N., Teller, A.H. and Teller, E. (1953). The authors propose an algorithm that simulates the way in which a liquid metal slowly anneals and freezes into a minimum energy crystalline structure. The algorithm is based on the laws of thermodynamics which testify that for each temperature T the chance of achieving a thermal equilibrium state S^* with energy level E_* during the process of physical annealing is given by the probability (or *Boltzmann factor*)

$$P(S^*) = \frac{1}{Z(T)} \exp\left(-\frac{E_*}{k_B \cdot T}\right). \tag{9.52}$$

The constant $k_B = 1.3806488(13) \cdot 10^{-23} J/K$ is called the *Boltzmann constant* and $Z(T)$ is the partition function of all possible states. Assuming that the number of possible states is $N \in \mathbb{N}$, the partition function at temperature T is given by

$$Z(T) = \sum_{j=1}^{N} \exp\left(-\frac{E_j}{k_B \cdot T}\right). \tag{9.53}$$

In the k-th iteration step the Metropolis algorithm alters the current state S^k by a small random displacement to attain a trial state S^{k+1}. The size of the disturbance and its direction depend on the current temperature T and some random number generated from the *state-space density*. Then, we compute the energy difference $\Delta E = E_{k+1} - E_k$ and the quotient q, which is

$$q = \frac{P(S^{k+1})}{P(S^k)} = \frac{\exp\left(-\dfrac{E_{k+1}}{k_B \cdot T}\right)}{\exp\left(-\dfrac{E_k}{k_B \cdot T}\right)} = \exp\left(-\frac{\Delta E}{k_B \cdot T}\right). \tag{9.54}$$

Depending on the value of q we decide if the new state S^{k+1} is accepted or rejected. For $q > 1$ the energy level E_{k+1} of the candidate state is lower than the current one and the transition to S^{k+1} is accepted. If $q \leq 1$ the energy difference ΔE is positive and the transition to the higher energy state S^{k+1} is accepted with probability q. Therefore, we draw a uniform random number $u \sim \mathcal{U}(0, 1)$ and accept an uphill step if $u \leq q$ and reject it if $u > q$. For high values of the temperature T the quotient $\exp(-\Delta E / k_B T)$ is close to 1 and the algorithm allows several uphill moves. With decreasing temperature the proportion of steps increasing the energy level becomes smaller. The time spent at temperature T and its decrease is handled subject to a user specified annealing schedule. The standard Boltzmann annealing schedule is defined by

$$T(\kappa) = \frac{T_0}{\log(\kappa)}. \tag{9.55}$$

Here, T_0 denotes the user-defined initial temperature and κ is the annealing parameter. The annealing parameter typically is a function of the iteration step k and determines the time spent at each temperature level. Additional to Boltzmann's temperature annealing schedule, (9.55), the implementation of Matlab offers the following temperature schedules:

- Exponential: $T(\kappa) = T_0 \cdot 0.95^\kappa$ (default).
- Fast: $T(\kappa) = \frac{T_0}{\kappa}$.

In Matlab the annealing parameter κ is similar to the number of iterations until re-annealing. Re-annealing starts the search process again at a higher temperature level after the algorithm has accepted a certain number of new states. The function for optimizing using Simulated Annealing is `simulannealbnd`.

In Kirkpatrick, S., Gerlatt, C.D. Jr. and Vecchi, M.P. (1983) the Metropolis algorithm is adopted to solve mathematical optimization problems. Identifying analogies between the physical annealing and an optimization problem the authors construct a random search method, called Simulated Annealing. In this approach the space of possible states S consisting of a specific configuration of atoms corresponding to the domain $\mathcal{X}$ of admissible parameter vectors $x = (x_1, \ldots, x_n)^\top \in \mathcal{X}$. The energy level E of the individual states is an analogue to the objective function value $f(x)$ and the thermal equilibrium state is equivalent to a minimum solution x^*. For the product of the Boltzmann constant k_B and temperature T there is no analogy but Simulated Annealing replaces this product by an artificial control parameter also denoted as temperature T. In addition, standard Boltzmann Simulated Annealing adjusts the acceptance probability, (9.54), for $\Delta f = f(x^{k+1}) - f(x^k) > 0$ by replacing q with $\bar{q}$ given by

$$\bar{q} = \frac{1}{1 + \exp\left(\dfrac{\Delta f}{T}\right)} = \frac{\exp\left(-\dfrac{f(x^{k+1})}{T}\right)}{\exp\left(-\dfrac{f(x^{k+1})}{T}\right) + \exp\left(-\dfrac{f(x^k)}{T}\right)}. \qquad (9.56)$$

Under the assumption of only two possible states S^k and S^{k+1} it is equivalent to the probability that the process is in the state S^{k+1}. Since Δf and T are positive, the probability of accepted uphill steps is less than 1/2.

Transferring the ideas underlying the Metropolis algorithm to Simulated Annealing avoids the algorithm becoming trapped in a local minimum, because it allows for candidate solutions x^{k+1} that increase the value of the objective function, that is $f(x^{k+1}) > f(x^k)$. This enables us to find the global minimum in the presence of many local minima. Assume random displacements $\Delta x \in \mathbb{R}^n$ are being generated subject to the n-dimensional Boltzmann density:

$$g(x) = \frac{1}{\sqrt{(2\pi T)^n}} \exp\left(-\frac{x^\top x}{2T}\right) \qquad (9.57)$$

$$= \frac{1}{(2\pi)^{\frac{n}{2}} |\Sigma|^{\frac{1}{2}}} \exp\left(-\frac{1}{2}(x - \mu)^\top \Sigma^{-1}(x - \mu)\right),$$

with

$$\mu = \begin{pmatrix} 0 \\ \vdots \\ 0 \end{pmatrix} \in \mathbb{R}^n \quad \text{and} \quad \Sigma = \mathrm{diag}\begin{pmatrix} T \\ \vdots \\ T \end{pmatrix} \in \mathbb{R}^{n \times n}$$

Then, it is proven in Geman, S. and Geman, D. (1995) that Simulated Annealing converges to the global minimum of an optimization problem if the temperature T decreases subject to Boltzmann's temperature annealing schedule, (9.55), and T_0 chosen large enough. A similar result can be found for the fast annealing schedule, $T(\kappa) = T_0/\kappa$, when the perturbation is generated from the Cauchy distribution having the density

$$g(x) = \frac{T}{(x^\top x + T^2)^{\frac{n+1}{2}}}. \qquad (9.58)$$

Since the Cauchy distribution is equivalent to a Student-t distribution with one degree of freedom, a random sample distributed with respect to (9.58) can be obtained by sampling from the Student-t distribution with one degree of freedom and the outcome is then multiplied with the current temperature T_k.

Given Boltzmann's density, (9.57), we recognize that each component of the perturbation $\Delta x(j)$, $j = 1, \ldots, n$ is an independent and identically distributed Gaussian with mean $\mu = 0$ and standard deviation $\sigma = \sqrt{T}$. Thus, a trial solution x^{k+1} can be generated from n independent samples $z_j \sim \mathcal{N}(0, 1)$. Setting

$$x^{k+1}(j) = x^k(j) + \sqrt{T_k} z_j, \quad i = 1, \ldots, n \qquad (9.59)$$

to achieve a disturbance of length $\sqrt{T_k}$ the Matlab built-in functionality `simulannealbnd` divides the vector $\sqrt{T_k} z$ by the norm $||z||_2$.

A simplified version of Boltzmann's Simulated Annealing algorithm can be summarized as follows:

Algorithm 9.10: Boltzmann Simulated Annealing

(S.1) Initialize state $x^0 \in \mathbb{R}^n$ and temperature T_0. Define a maximum number of iterations k_{max}, a limit of iterations N until the next temperature annealing, a minimum allowed temperature T_{min} and set the annealing parameter $\kappa = 1$, $x^* = x^0$ (best solution so far) and $k = 0$

(S.2) **if** $k \geq \kappa \cdot N$ **then**

Estimate the current temperature from the Boltzmann annealing schedule (9.55)

$$T_\kappa = \frac{T_0}{\log(\kappa)}$$

and set $\kappa = \kappa + 1$

(S.3) Generate the random perturbation $\Delta x = \sqrt{T_k} z$ subject to (9.59), set $\tilde{x}^{k+1} = x^k + \Delta x$ and calculate the difference $\Delta f = f(\tilde{x}^{k+1}) - f(x^k)$

(S.4) **if** $\Delta f < 0$ **then**

Set $x^{k+1} = \tilde{x}^{k+1}$

if $f(x^{k+1}) < f(x^*)$ **then**

Set $x^* = x^{k+1}$

else

Draw a uniform random number $u \sim \mathcal{U}(0, 1)$, compute the acceptance probability (9.56)

$$q = \frac{1}{1 + \exp\left(\frac{\Delta f}{T_k}\right)}$$

and set

$$x^{k+1} = \begin{cases} \tilde{x}^{k+1} & \text{if } u \leq q \\ x^k & \text{otherwise} \end{cases}$$

(S.5) **if** $k = k_{max}$ **or** $T_k < T_{min}$ **then**

stop

else

set $k := k + 1$ and go to (S.2)

Just as with Differential Evolution, we choose to terminate the Simulated Annealing algorithm when a predefined maximum number of iterations k_{max} is reached. In addition, we propose to stop the random search if the current temperature T_k falls below a minimum temperature T_{min}, which is typically close to zero. Matlab's built-in function simulannealbnd allows termination criteria which consider the average difference of function values Δf over a number of iterations, a maximum number of function evaluations, a time limit or, if available, a known objective function value to reach.

Constraints For the numerical examples below we consider the built-in Simulated Annealing function simulannealbnd of Matlab's global optimization toolbox. This implementation of Simulated Annealing has the ability to handle simple bound constraints for the parameters. Starting from an admissible point x^k the algorithm ensures that the trial solution $\tilde{x}^{k+1}$ stays

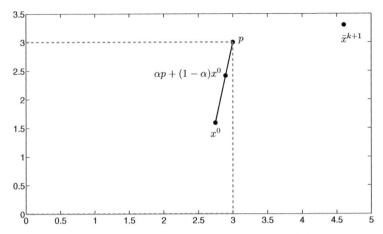

Figure 9.30 Projection $\alpha p + (1-\alpha)x^k$ of the non-admissible point $\tilde{x}^{k+1}$ to the admissible domain $\mathcal{X} = \{x \in \mathbb{R}^2 : 0 \leq x(j) \leq (3), j = 1, 2\}$

admissible by applying a linear projection. If any component $\tilde{x}^{k+1}(j)$, $j = 1, \ldots, n$ of the candidate solution $\tilde{x}^{k+1}$ is below some lower bound, lb, or above some upper bound, ub the algorithm defines a projection point $p \in \mathbb{R}^n$ by

$$p(j) := \begin{cases} lb(j) & \text{if } \tilde{x}^{k+1}(j) < lb(j) \\ \tilde{x}^{k+1}(j) & \text{if } lb(j) \leq \tilde{x}^{k+1}(j) \leq ub(j) \\ ub(j) & \text{otherwise.} \end{cases} \qquad (9.60)$$

Thus, p is located within $[lb, ub]$ and taking a uniform random number $\alpha \sim \mathcal{U}(0, 1)$ the new admissible point is generated taking the convex combination

$$\tilde{x}^{k+1} = \alpha p + (1-\alpha)x^k. \qquad (9.61)$$

This approach is similar to the gradient projection method for handling bound-constraints for the Levenberg–Marquardt and L-BFGS methods.

9.7.1 Implementation

Table 9.8 displays the progress of Simulated Annealing using `simulannealbnd` applied to the minimization of Ackley's function (9.49). The results have been obtained by calling the script `scriptAckleySA` (see Figure 9.31).

The function `saoptimset(@simulannealbnd)` returns all available options of the function `simulannealbnd`. A typical output is shown in Figure 9.32.

By default the algorithm uses the exponential temperature, $T(\kappa) = T_0 \cdot 0.95^\kappa$, annealing schedule (`@temperatureexp`) and random perturbation subject to the Cauchy density, (9.58), via the option parameter `@annealingfast`. Changing to the Boltzmann setup can be achieved by setting the following options:

```
options.AnnealingFcn = @annealingboltz
options.TemperatureFcn = @temperatureboltz
```

Table 9.8 Intermediate best results plus and the objective function values of Simulated Annealing process for finding the minimum of the Ackley function

Iteration	Coordinates of Best Points		Objective Function Values	
k	$x^*(1)$	$x^*(2)$	$f(x^*(1), x^*(2))$	$f(x^k(1), x^k(2))$
0	−3	−3	9.02377	9.02377
60	−0.1201	−0.495099	3.23528	6.00436
120	−0.0198613	0.0527215	0.241879	0.302903
180	−0.00135078	−0.00213586	0.00731792	0.00868362
240	6.34437e-005	−0.000109833	0.000359186	0.00111373
300	3.66071e-007	4.64017e-006	1.31657e-005	1.31657e-005
360	−5.50414e-008	−1.01464e-007	3.26491e-007	5.74563e-007
420	2.36876e-009	1.14468e-009	7.44113e-009	8.64484e-008
480	−8.31128e-011	−6.12618e-010	1.74862e-009	2.58626e-009
494	2.32054e-011	2.01331e-011	8.68949e-011	8.68949e-011

The acceptance probability `acceptancesa` coincides with the Boltzmann acceptance probability, (9.56), by default but also allows for user-defined temperature schedules, acceptance probability and annealing functions.

Finally, custom output and plot functions are supported. For instance, to generate Figure 9.34 we implemented the function displayed in Figure 9.33.

```
%─────────────────────────────────
% scriptAckleySA.m
%─────────────────────────────────

% lower/upper bounds
lb = [−3;−3]; ub = [3;3];
% objective function
fun = @ackley;
% initial guess
x0 = lb;

% Load/Set state of the random number generator.
load rngState
set(RandStream.getDefaultStream,'State',rngState.state);

% Set options of the Simulated Annealing algorithm
options = saoptimset(@simulannealbnd);
options.ObjectiveLimit = 1e−10; % objective function value to reach
options.TolFun = 1e−12; % average change in function values
options.MaxIter = 500; % maximum number of iterations
options.Display = 'diagnose'; % display intermediate results
options.DisplayInterval = 60; % display interval
options.InitialTemperature = 50; % initial temperature
options.ReannealInterval = 200; % iterations till reannealing

% start optimization
[x,fval,exitflag,output] = simulannealbnd(fun,x0,lb,ub,options)
```

Figure 9.31 Matlab script for applying Simulated Annealing to numerically determine the minimum of Ackley function

```
options =

              AnnealingFcn: @annealingfast
            TemperatureFcn: @temperatureexp
             AcceptanceFcn: @acceptancesa
                    TolFun: 1.000000000000000e-006
            StallIterLimit: '500*numberofvariables'
               MaxFunEvals: '3000*numberofvariables'
                 TimeLimit: Inf
                   MaxIter: Inf
            ObjectiveLimit: -Inf
                   Display: 'final'
           DisplayInterval: 10
                 HybridFcn: []
            HybridInterval: 'end'
                  PlotFcns: []
              PlotInterval: 1
                OutputFcns: []
        InitialTemperature: 100
          ReannealInterval: 100
                  DataType: 'double'
```

Figure 9.32 Default parameters of the structure variable options used in Matlab's Simulated Annealing implementation

```
function stop = PlotItBest(options,optimvalues, flag,structF)

stop = false;
switch flag
    % first iteration
    case 'init'
        set(gcf,'Color',[1 1 1])
        set(gca,'FontSize',16,'FontName','Helvecia')

        colormap('gray')
        % plot best solutions
        plotBest = plot(optimvalues.bestx(1),optimvalues.bestx(2),...
                        'Marker', '.','MarkerSize',20,...
                           'Color', [0 0 0],'LineWidth',2);
        set(plotBest,'Tag','PlotItBest');
        xlim([-3 3]);
        ylim([-3 3]);
        box('on');
        hold('all');
        % plot contour lines
        contour(structF.x,structF.y,structF.z,20,'LineWidth',1.5);
    % all other iterations
    case 'iter'
        plotBest = findobj(get(gca,'Children'),'Tag','PlotItBest');
        newX = [get(plotBest,'Xdata') optimvalues.bestx(1)];
        newY = [get(plotBest,'Ydata') optimvalues.bestx(2)];
        set(plotBest,'Xdata',newX, 'Ydata',newY);

end
```

Figure 9.33 Matlab code for visualization of the optimization procedure and its solution

Considering the variable `options` we see that by default termination is determined by the average change of function values `TolFun` over the last `StallIterLimit` number of iterations and the total number of function evaluations `MaxFunEvals`. In the script file `scriptAck-leySA` we extend the termination criteria adding the maximum number of iterations allowed, denoted by `MaxIter`. Since the global minimum of Ackley's function is known we also include a parameter `ObjectiveLimit` for comparison, to check whether the current proposed solution is close to the minimum.

The main difference in Matlab's Simulated Annealing functionality compared to the standard algorithm presented here is that Matlab uses a re-annealing procedure. While in the Simulated Annealing algorithm, 9.10, the temperature is decreased after N iterations, Matlab's built-in algorithm decreases the temperature in each iteration. In general, this procedure does not lead to a thermal equilibrium since annealing takes place too fast. Therefore, Matlab's algorithm starts the random search again at a level higher than the current temperature after a number of `ReannealInterval` points have been accepted.

Since the algorithm of Matlab is adapted from Ingber, L. (1995), the interested reader should consult that reference.

9.7.2 Calibration Examples

To present a comparable example to the Differential Evolution we set $n = 2$ and consider Ackley's function, (9.49), with simple bound constraints $-3 \leq x(j) \leq 3$, $j = 1, 2$. Figure 9.34 plots the progress of the Simulated Annealing algorithm as a path of the current best solutions x^* for every 5th iteration. The algorithm starts at an initial guess $x^0 = (-3, 3)^\top$ which is the lower left corner of the admissible domain. The algorithm terminates after 494 iterations because the best estimated function value $f(x^*(1), x^*(2))$ is below the user-defined threshold. In this case we set `options.ObjectiveLimit < 1e-10`. Analogously to Differential Evolution, Simulated Annealing proves its ability to find the global minimum of Ackley's function and, thus, converges to the global minimizer $x^* = (0, 0)^\top$. Several empirical tests verify this result even if the initial guess is randomly chosen within the admissible domain. In addition, the test shows that the overall number of iterations needed can be very large and dependent

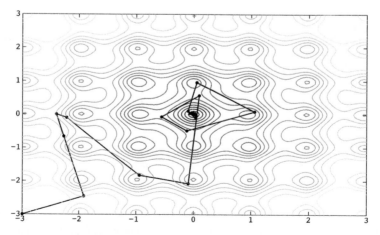

Figure 9.34 Progress of Simulated Annealing

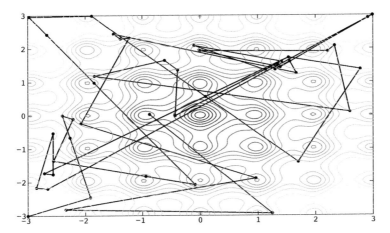

Figure 9.35 All steps of the Simulated Annealing for Ackley's function

on the initial guess and the generated random sequence during the annealing process. For a set of 100 batches, for instance, the number of iterations used by function simulannealbnd to achieve a value smaller or equal to $1e - 06$ of the objective function varies from about 300 to 28000. The maximum of the total time elapsed over all cases omitting intermediate outputs was less than 12.5 seconds.

Table 9.8 displays the intermediate results for every 60th iteration and the final solution after termination of the Simulated Annealing process. For iteration k it shows the best solution of all iterations so far, its objective function value and the objective function value of the current iteration.

Looking at Figure 9.34 it seems that outputs of the algorithm converge relatively straight-forward to the global minimum. But this is not the case since we have only plotted the best outcomes. The overall progress of Simulated Annealing over the first 60 iterations displayed in Figure 9.35 looks very different and shows a somewhat chaotic behaviour.

For the final example we consider the calibration of the Heston stochastic volatility model introduced in Chapter 2. The artificial market observables are generated using the function LewisCallPricingFFT applied to the parameter set

$$V_0 = \Theta = 0.04, \quad \kappa = 2.5, \quad \nu = 0.5, \quad \rho = -0.8$$

The objective function is given by the root-mean-square error between the market observables and the model prices.

```
function y = rmsefun(p,varargin)
% Function rmsefun calculates the root-mean-square error
% between European call option prices observed on the market
% and model prices.
% Input: p -> vector of model parameters
%        varargin -> PM, fftStruct, option, modelID

% residual vector
```

```
R = residualPriceFFT(p,varargin{:});
% root-mean-square error
y = sqrt(R'*R/length(R));
```

We compare the results of the SQP method with the results obtained by applying Differential Evolution and Simulated Annealing. The intermediate objective function values are displayed in Figure 9.36. To obtain the results we applied the SQP method using the syntax

```
% objective function
fun = @(x)rmsefun(x,PM,fftStruct,option,model.ID);

% Algorithmic Parameters
maxeval = 200*length(x0);    % maximum number of iterations
tol     = 1e-8; % convergence tolerance

%initial guess
x0 = [0.02 0.02 1 0.2 -0.3]';
% lower bounds
lb = [0 0 0 0  1]';
% upper bounds
ub = [1 1 5 2 1]';

% start calibration
[xMin,fMin,perfSQP] = modSQP(fun,x0,[],lb,ub,[],maxeval,tol)
```

The algorithm stops since the change in the objective function $f(k)$ from step k to $k+1$ is smaller than the tolerance level tol. The estimated minimum function value is

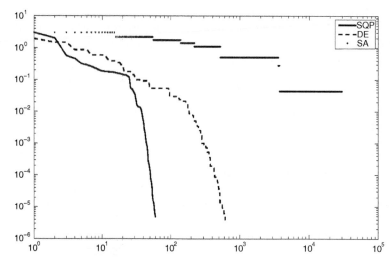

Figure 9.36 Convergence of SQP, Differential Evolution and Simulated Annealing method applied to calibration of the Heston model

fMin $= 4.7249 \cdot 10^{-6}$ and the infinity norm $||xMin - x^*||$ is equal to $8.8463 \cdot 10^{-5}$. Figure 9.36 shows that the SQP method converges most quickly compared to Differential Evolution and Simulated Annealing. The method requires approximately 8.5 seconds and 199 iterations until termination.

We describe how to set up Differential Evolution and Simulated Annealing. The value to reach is given by the outcome fMin of the SQP method. We apply the classical Differential Evolution with mutation scaling factor $\beta = 0.85$, crossover probability $cp = 0.8$ and a population number of $M = 50$. We use the following piece of code:

```
S_struct.FVr_minbound = lb'; % lower bounds
S_struct.FVr_maxbound = ub'; % upper bounds
S_struct.I_bnd_constr = 1;
```

The lower and upper bound vectors are set to be strict bound constraints for the population members during the optimization. To start the calibration procedure we define the struct field

```
S_struct.objfun = fun;
```

Then, we call the function deopt('objfun',S_struct). The objective function of the Differential Evolution is defined by

```
function S_MSE= objfun(FVr_temp, S_struct)
 F_cost = S_struct.objfun(FVr_temp); % evaluate rmse function
 %----Setup struct S_MSE--------------------------------------
 % I_nc-> number of constraints; FVr_ca-> value of constraint
          violation
 % I_no-> number of objective functions; FVr_oa-> objective
          function costs
 S_MSE = struct('I_nc',0, 'FVr_ca',0, 'I_no',1, 'FVr_oa',F_cost);
```

Since Differential Evolution and Simulated Annealing are stochastic search methods, the results can differ from one call to the other. Thus, we consider the average results for a series of 100 evaluations. The positive message is that independent of the initial population Differential Evolution converges to the global minimum and terminates with a smaller objective function value than fMin. However, the classic Differential Evolution method applied to the Heston model generates on average 30000 population members and requires an average time to termination of about 8.5 minutes. Further tests using different mutation and crossover strategies suggest that a slight speedup of the convergence is possible. The use of derivative based optimizers in the neighbourhood of local minima can increase the efficiency. Such combinations of different optimizers are known as *hybrid optimization methods*. For Simulated Annealing we consider the hybrid optimization technique when the maximum number of iterations k_{max} is reached.

The convergence of Simulated Annealing highly depends on the appropriate choice of the initial temperature T_0, the re-annealing interval and the annealing schedule. Although we applied many different combinations for the Heston model we were not able to generate adequate solutions using Matlab's Simulated Annealing implementation. Figure 9.36 shows that the objective function values of Simulated Annealing are far from the optimum, although the maximum number of iterations k_{max} is set to 30000. The corresponding average number of population members when we applied Differential Evolution was smaller. Thus, we decided to switch to a hybrid Simulated Annealing. For this approach the function `simulannealbnd` provides the options `HybridFcn` and `HybridInterval`. We consider the code

```
hybridopts = optimset('MaxIter',maxeval,'OutputFcn',
                                    @myOutputSAHybrid);
options.HybridFcn = {@fmincon,hybridopts};
options.HybridInterval = 'end';
```

We apply Matlab's non-linear constrained optimization function `fmincon` when Simulated Annealing is terminated. The value of the field `OutputFcn` points to the user-defined function given by

```
function stop = myOutputSAHybrid(x,optimvalues,state)
global structSA; % global struct variable
stop = false;

if strcmp(state,'iter') % intermediate solutions
    structSA.xk = [structSA.xk, x];
    structSA.fk = [structSA.fk, optimvalues.fval];
    structSA.iter = structSA.iter + 1;
end
```

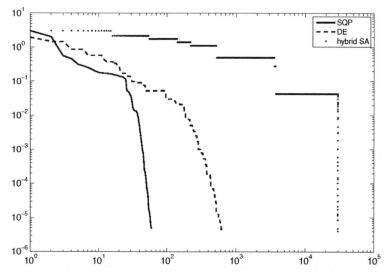

Figure 9.37 Convergence of SQP, Differential Evolution and hybrid Simulated Annealing method applied to calibration of the Heston model

Keeping a history of the intermediate values k, x^k and $f(x^k)$ generated by the function `fmincon`. Figure 9.37 shows that the hybrid Simulated Annealing method finds an adequate solution within a few iterations when switching to `fmincon` near the global minimum. By implementing the hybrid Simulated Annealing method we are able to reduce both the average number of iterations and the time to termination.

9.8 SUMMARY AND CONCLUSIONS

In this chapter we have reviewed several optimization methods which can be applied to calibrate parameters of financial models to market observable options. We have presented direct search methods (Nelder–Mead), Newton based optimizers (*Levenberg–Marquardt, L-BFGS, SQP*) and stochastic optimization methods (Differential Evolution, Simulated Annealing) and we have illustrated possible extensions of optimizers to handle constraints. We have provided several Matlab examples and have shown that the choice of the optimizer highly depends on the problem under consideration. While stochastic optimizers are designed to converge to global minima, the Newton based methods perform much better when the problem dimension is high. In those cases hybrid optimizers that combine properties of different classes of optimizers are preferable.

10

Model Risk – Calibration, Pricing and Hedging

in collaboration with Manuel Wittke

10.1 INTRODUCTION AND OBJECTIVES

This chapter is devoted to model risk. In this context model risk is the risk arising from applying a certain financial model for pricing and risk management. The model might be inappropriate in a context, the calibration might be wrong or the numerical methods unstable. Furthermore, another critical risk factor is that there is no reasonable hedge strategy for the model which we use for pricing. If there were different reasonable hedge strategies, we might choose the wrong one.

The risks we wish to focus on are the risks involved in the calibration, the pricing of exotic options and in hedging derivatives. All the risks are examined and we explain each risk thoroughly before we apply some financial model for valuation and hedging.

Calibration is the method of determining model parameters by minimizing a distance measure between market and model prices. Market prices can, for instance, be quoted option prices or time series data. The calibration leads to a best guess of the model parameters. This set of parameters are the model parameters which best fit the observed prices in terms of an error measure at a given time. Yet the parameter changes whenever we start the calibration. Models might be more or less suitable to minimize the error measure. Often we observe that models having many parameters are more flexible to fit market prices. But is such a model preferable to a model with fewer parameters? We argue that it is natural that different models lead to different errors when fitting to market data, but the error of the fit is not the only point we have to take into account when we work with models. If the hedges in a model are robust and stable and the model parameters can well be interpreted in terms of market observable variables such a model might be preferable. Another issue is the parameter stability when calibrating a model to daily data. Here the model parameters fluctuate and have different standard deviations.

Exotic options are derivatives where market quotes are rare or even unavailable. It is market practice to use models calibrated to plain Vanilla option prices to value exotic options. This can be seen as an extrapolation procedure. Often exotic options are path-dependent, but the calibration is to European style options, which means that the parameters are only calibrated to the terminal distributions. This generally leads to very different values, something that is even observed for standard exotic options such as Asian options or Barrier options when different models calibrated to European options are applied. We cover this issue in this chapter. Hedging plays a fundamental role in the financial industry, but applying hedges in a model risk context and its application to real market data are often left out in books on financial modelling.

We have already covered advanced models from a theoretical and numerical perspective, and now we consider such models applied to real market data. In doing so we face the problem of an *incomplete market*. In such markets a contingent claim cannot be perfectly hedged by choosing a unique self-financing trading strategy, as for instance in the Black–Scholes model. Therefore, it is the case that a model that fits market data perfectly by calibration may perform badly in terms of hedge effectiveness.

We introduce the calibration of models to market data in Section 10.2. Then, we discuss the performance of fully calibrated models to price exotic options in Section 10.3. We apply different hedge strategies in Section 10.4, giving numerical examples in using market data.

Throughout this chapter we explain how to use the numerical methods discussed in this book so that they are applicable for analysing dynamic hedging and the performance of the models and numerical methods.

10.2 CALIBRATION

As discussed in Chapter 9, *calibration* is a method that minimizes a distance measure between model and observed market prices of derivatives by determining the model parameters. In the end you can price derivatives with all moneyness and maturity combinations within one model. And this is exactly the desired effect when using Lévy or stochastic volatility models instead of a Black–Scholes model with an implied volatility surface. It is also market practice to use calibrated models for pricing exotic products where no quotes are available. One drawback of calibration is that model prices are not fitted exactly to the quoted market prices but, on the plus side, non quoted moneyness and maturity combinations can be priced by a structural model and not by an interpolation algorithm. Another issue with calibration is the parameter stability when a model is calibrated daily to market data, which includes the stability of the calibration error and the parameters themselves. In this section we wish to consider parameter stability on real market data. In the following we use the calibrated parameters for different models on DAX option data for the time period between 11 January 2007 and 9 January 2008, that is the interval [11/01/2007, 09/01/2008].

10.2.1 Similarities – Heston and Bates Models

First, we consider the Heston and Bates models. The Bates model is an extension of the Heston model. It allows for log-normal jumps in the underlying. The models were introduced in Chapters 2 and 3 respectively.

We have calibrated both models to time series data for DAX options from 11/01/2007 to 09/01/2008. The root-mean-square error for this period is displayed in Figure 10.1.

The Bates model has three additional parameters. The parameters can be used to better fit the short end of the implied volatility surface.

By extending models with a jump component we can ask ourselves what happens to the parameters which the models have in common. For the Heston and Bates models the common parameters are the instantaneous variance, the long term variance, the mean reversion speed, the volatility of variance and the correlation between the driving Brownian motions. Thus, we consider $V(0)$, θ, κ, ν and ρ and consider just one month in the history above, namely the time period from 11/01/2007 to 09/01/2008.

First, we consider a plain calibration without posing any restrictions. The results are plotted in Figure 10.2.

Now, let us consider the actual differences between the parameters. We wish to discover whether there are any empirical regularities for the calibrated parameters. This might give us

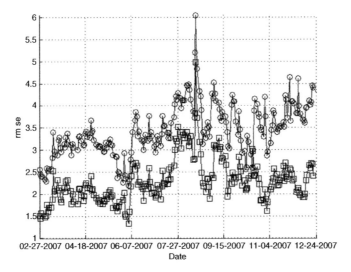

Figure 10.1   Root-mean-square errors for calibrating the Heston and Bates models to DAX option data from 11/01/2007 up to 09/01/2008. The Heston model is marked by circles and the Bates model by squares

a hint as to how we can align some of them. Figure 10.3 shows the absolute differences of the calibrated parameters.

We observe that the spot variance is nearly identical. The absolute difference is constant and nearly equal to 0.01. This phenomenon is also observed for the volatility of variance ν and the correlation ρ.

Thus, the mean reversion speed κ and the long term variance θ seem to be parameters which change in an irregular way for the Bates model. However, the time period does not allow for any statistical analysis. To achieve any statistical significance we have to consider much longer time intervals and carry out statistical testing of any assumption.

The difference in the parameters may correspond to model risk. To this end we wish to find some method to use a calibrated Heston model for the calibration of the Bates model. First, we restrict the parameters and set $V(0)$ equal to the square of ATM implied volatility, we set the long term variance $\theta = V(0)$, fix ν and κ and finally calibrate only the correlation ρ. Second, we can try to find regularities for the model parameters. For instance, Figure 10.3 suggests that the differences between certain model parameters are nearly constant. For this reason it might be an idea to use adjusted Heston parameters for calibrating the Bates model.

These are only two ideas which can be investigated further using our framework. As a last experiment we might think of using the additional parameters for the jump part in the Bates model as a kind of fine tuning tool. To this end we first calibrate a Heston model and use the calibrated parameters as fixed parameters for the Bates model. Thus, we only calibrate the parameters determining the jumps. The results are shown in Figure 10.4.

We observe that by applying this method we do not increase the overall fit to the option prices and that the volatility of the jump part σ_J is nearly identical to 0. This means the jump height is deterministic. Furthermore, the jump intensity λ is very small. It seems that the calibration suggests deterministic jumps appearing at a given level. Thus, we do not recommend applying this calibration method. Instead, if we wish to keep some of the calibrated Heston model

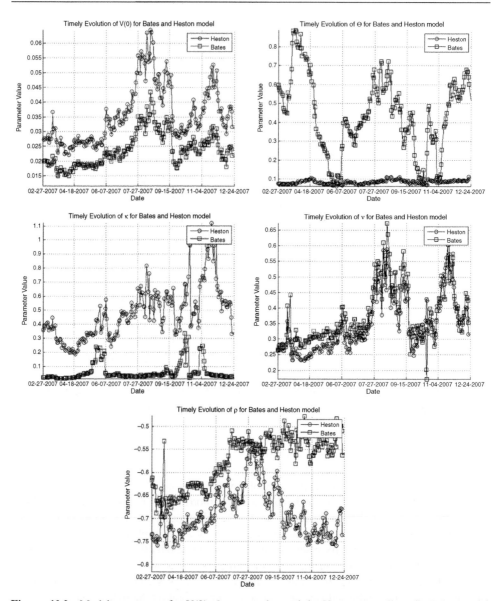

Figure 10.2 Model parameters for $V(0)$, θ, κ, v and ρ and the Heston as well as the Bates model inferred from option prices for the German DAX index using market data from 11/01/2007 up to 09/01/2008

parameters we look at Figure 10.3 again. This suggests that there is a deterministic transform between $V(0)$, v and ρ for the Heston model and the corresponding parameters for the Bates model with the mean reversion κ and the long term variance θ needing re-calibration. Thus, we could consider calibrating κ, θ, λ, μ_J and σ_J.

We have only given two ideas for examining the calibration of a class of models; there are many other methods that can be investigated.

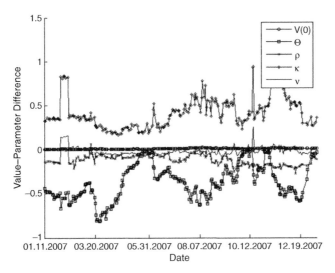

Figure 10.3 Absolute differences for the model parameters $V(0)$, θ, κ, ν and ρ and the Heston as well as the Bates model inferred from option prices for the German DAX index using market data form 11/01/2007 up to 09/01/2008

10.2.2 Parameter Stability

Suppose we calibrate a given model to a history of data at times $\{t_1, t_2, \ldots, t_N\}$. Let θ_i denote some model parameter calibrated at time t_i. Furthermore, denote by M_θ and V_θ the empirical mean and variance. We consider the measures

$$M_N := \frac{M_\theta^{-1}}{(N-1)} \sum_{i=2}^{N} \theta_{t_i} - \theta_{t_{i-1}}, \qquad \text{normed mean} \tag{10.1}$$

$$M_R := \frac{1}{(N-1)} \sum_{i=2}^{N} \frac{\theta_{t_i} - \theta_{t_{i-1}}}{\theta_{t_{i-1}}}, \qquad \text{relative mean} \tag{10.2}$$

$$V_N := \frac{V_\theta^{-1}}{(N-1)} \sum_{i=2}^{N} \left(\theta_{t_i} - \theta_{t_{i-1}} - M_N\right)^2, \qquad \text{normed std deviation} \tag{10.3}$$

$$V_R := \frac{1}{N-1} \sum_{i=2}^{N} \left(\theta_{t_i} - \theta_{t_{i-1}} - M_R\right)^2, \qquad \text{relative std deviation.} \tag{10.4}$$

We apply these measures to all calibrated models. The Matlab implementation for all functions is given in Figure 10.5.

From a theoretical and practical viewpoint we wish to allow changes of model parameters. This change should take place gradually or may be triggered by events such as crashes. If we observe frequent changes of the parameter regimes and jumps despite the fact that the observable market parameters' behaviour is relatively stable we have to reconsider the calibration procedure and pose additional constraints to the optimization problem. Or we may even have to think about abandoning the model we currently apply. It may happen, especially

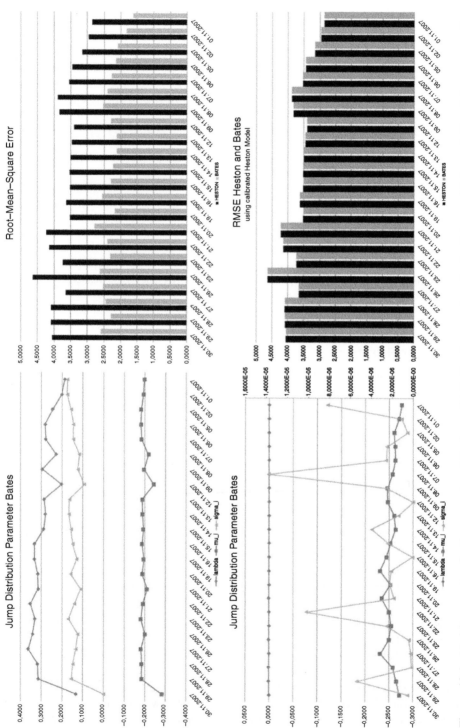

Figure 10.4 Model parameters for the parameter of the jump distribution λ, μ_J and σ_J for the Bates model (upper left) and the corresponding root-mean-square error in comparison to the Heston model (upper right). The same parameters are plotted for a calibrated Bates model but using a pre-calibrated Heston model (lower left). The other parameters are determined using a calibrated Heston model. For comparison we plotted the root-mean-square error to the Heston model (lower right). For the calibration we used data for the German DAX index from 11/01/2007 to 09/01/2008

```
function y = normmean(x)
    m = mean(x);
    diff = x(2:end) - x(1:end-1);
    y = mean(diff)/m;
end

function y = relmean(x)
    diff = (x(2:end) - x(1:end-1))./x(1:end-1);
    y = mean(diff);
end

function y = normvar(x)
    v = (std(x))^2;
    diff = (x(2:end) - x(1:end-1) - normmean(x)).^2;
    y = mean(diff)/v;
end

function y = relvar(x)
    diff = (x(2:end) - x(1:end-1) - relmean(x)).^2;
    y = mean(diff);
end
```

Figure 10.5   Matlab implementation of the measures (10.1) to (10.4)

after crashes, that we can observe changes in the regime of the model parameter. This is related to jumpy behaviour of the market parameters, for instance of the spot price or the implied volatilities. We have considered daily data for the DAX index and Call option prices from 11/01/2007 to 09/01/2008 and calibrated the following models to the corresponding market data:

- Black–Scholes.
- Heston.
- Merton Jump Diffusion.
- Bates.
- Variance Gamma (VG).
- Normal Inverse Gaussian (NIG).
- VG GOU.
- VG CIR.
- NIG GOU.
- NIG CIR.

We used weights that make sure that options around the ATM strike have more impact on the chosen error measure than for ITM or OTM options. As the optimizer we have chosen a fast Newton solver called the *Sequential Quadratic Programming (SQP) method*. This optimizer finds local minima but converges globally (see Chapter 9 for details and the code). As a starting value we have chosen to calibrate a model using the parameters calculated for the last day.

Let us consider the results obtained by calibration using our calibration framework. If further constraints are imposed on the calibration we can stabilize the calibrated parameters but we have to make sure that we allow enough degrees of freedom for reflecting different market conditions in the calibrated parameters, something which is not always an easy task.

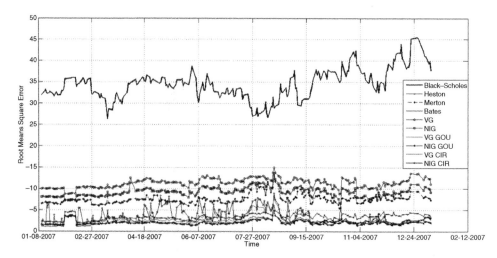

Figure 10.6 The root-mean-square error for all considered models for DAX option data from 01/08/2007 up to 02/12/2007

For each parameter we consider the calibrated time series, a histogram of the parameter realizations and, finally, a histogram of the daily parameter changes. This last is extremely useful when we analyse the model or even try to infer statistical information for parameter changes in a given model. Let us first consider the root-mean-square error for calibrating all models to DAX option data for 01/08/2007 up to 02/12/2007. Figure 10.6 shows the findings.

We observe that there is a huge difference in the model's ability to fit marked data and that the calibration error differs with respect to time. The models having a large number of parameters such as the Bates model or the VG GOU, VG CIR, NIG GOU or NIG CIR do fit the option prices best.

Diffusion Models

First, we consider the diffusion models which are the Black–Scholes model and the Heston model. The resulting values for (10.1) to (10.4) are given in Table 10.1 and Table 10.2. The parameter values are plotted in Figure 10.7 and Figure 10.8. We can see that the standard deviations of the stochastic volatility parameters are larger than the standard deviations of a global volatility parameter.

Table 10.1 The calibration measures (10.1)–(10.4) for the Black–Scholes model and DAX data from 11/01/2007 to 09/01/2008

	σ
M_N	−0.0007
M_R	−0.0006
V_N	0.0247
V_R	0.0

Table 10.2 The calibration measures (10.1)–(10.4) for the Heston model and DAX data from 01/08/2007 to 09/01/2008

	Vinst	Vlong	ρ	κ	ν
M_N	−0.0017	−0.0008	0.0006	−0.0022	−0.0023
M_R	0.0006	0.0006	0.0010	0.0129	0.0019
V_N	0.1057	0.1788	0.1219	0.2498	0.1545
V_R	0.0000	0.0000	0.0005	0.0089	0.0013

Black–Scholes   For the Black–Scholes model we use one parameter to fit all option prices.

Heston   We consider the Heston model. We show the value of the measures for calibration in Table 10.2.

Jump-Diffusion Models

Merton   In this paragraph we consider the Merton jump model. First, we consider the measures on the fluctuation of the model parameters. We observe that the variance of the parameters governing the jumps is higher than the variance of the diffusion parameter σ.

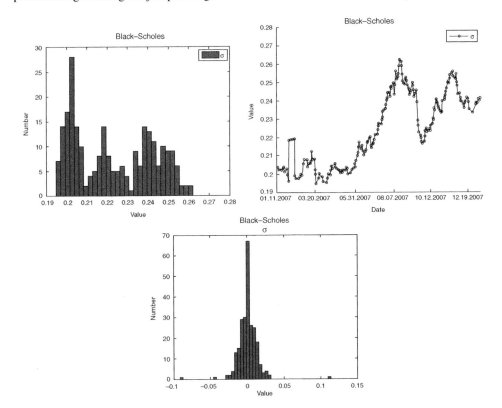

Figure 10.7 Parameter distribution and the timely evolution for the Black–Scholes model. We have plotted the frequencies on the top left and the timely evolution on the top right as well as the daily changes on the bottom. For the calibration we used data for the DAX index from 11/01/2007 up to 09/01/2008

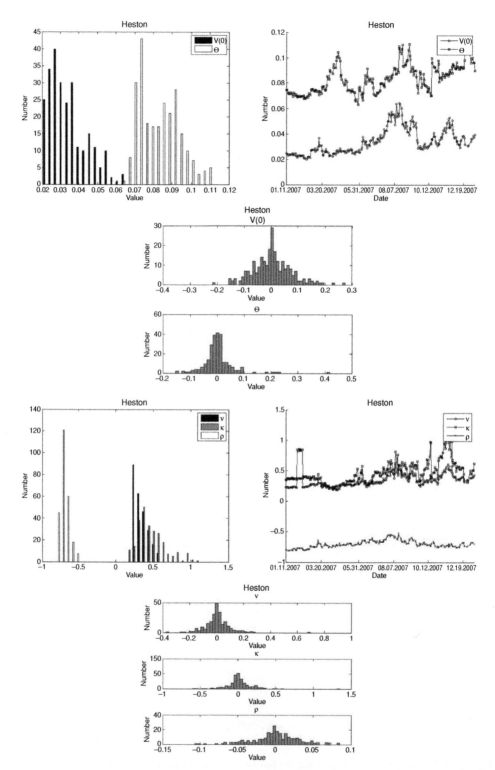

Figure 10.8 Parameter distribution and the timely evolution for the Heston model. We have plotted the frequencies on the left and the timely evolution on the right. In this figure the daily parameter changes are displayed in the centre. For the calibration we used data for the DAX index from 11/01/2007 up to 09/01/2008

Table 10.3 The calibration measures (10.1)–(10.4) for the Merton model and DAX data from 11/01/2007 to 09/01/2008

	σ	σ_J	μ_J	λ
M_N	−0.0007	0.0008	−0.0003	−0.0006
M_R	−0.0002	2.3595	0.0079	0.0097
V_N	0.0656	1.1100	0.4879	0.2946
V_R	0.0000	5.5766	0.0100	0.0002

Table 10.4 The calibration measures (10.1)–(10.4) for the Bates model and DAX data from 01/08/2007 to 09/01/2008

	Vinst	Vlong	ρ	κ	ν	σ_J	μ_J	λ
M_N	−0.0022	0.0034	0.0006	−0.0166	−0.0025	0.0007	−0.0012	0.0004
M_R	0.0006	0.0217	0.0015	0.0359	0.0033	0.0445	0.0067	0.0183
V_N	0.2186	0.0734	0.1581	0.3236	0.1695	0.2958	0.4254	0.3067
V_R	0.0000	0.0033	0.0007	0.0024	0.0017	0.0026	0.0006	0.0030

To get a better overview of the situation we have plotted the timely evolution of the parameters, the distributions and the distribution of the daily changes in Figure 10.9. Especially the results showing the histograms of the daily differences reflect the calibration measures of Table 10.3. The parameter distributions are displayed in Figures 10.10 and 10.11.

Bates   The Bates model has eight model parameters. We see that the fluctuation of the three jump parameters is smaller than for the Merton model. This is due to the fact that market changes can be compensated for by the other five parameters. Despite the fact that the Bates model has the most parameters they are relatively stable. The corresponding measures we introduced for measuring the goodness of the calibration are given in Table 10.4.

Lévy Process based Models

Now we come to another model class. The Variance Gamma and the Normal Inverse Gaussian model are pure jump models.

Variance Gamma   We consider the Variance Gamma model first. The fluctuation measures for the calibrated model are presented in Table 10.5.

Table 10.5 The calibration measures (10.1)–(10.4) for the VG model and DAX data from 11/01/2007 to 09/01/2008

	C	G	M
M_N	−0.0011	−0.0003	−0.0002
M_R	0.0061	0.0016	0.0045
V_N	0.1478	0.1806	0.2244
V_R	0.0032	0.0250	0.4367

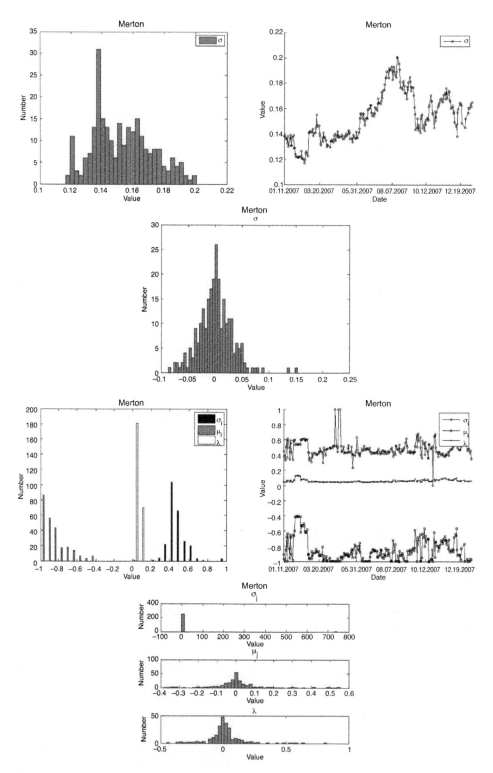

Figure 10.9 Parameter distribution and the timely evolution for the Merton model. We have plotted the frequencies on the left and the timely evolution on the right. The distribution of the daily parameter changes are presented in the center. For the calibration we used data for the DAX index from 11/01/2007 up to 09/01/2008

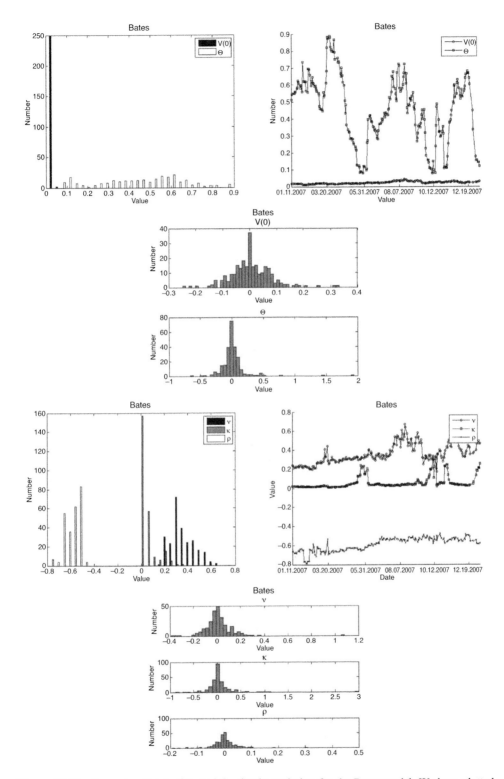

Figure 10.10 Parameter distribution and the timely evolution for the Bates model. We have plotted the frequencies on the left and the timely evolution on the right. For the calibration we used data for the DAX index from 11/01/2007 up to 09/01/2008

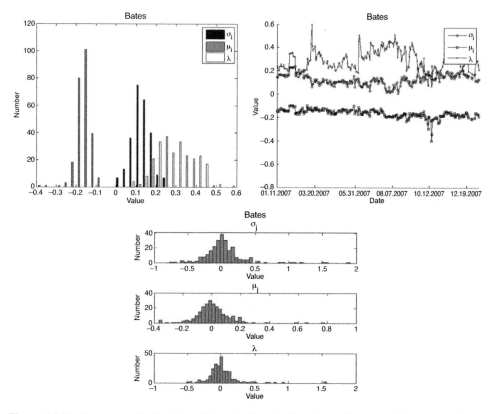

Figure 10.11 Parameter distribution and the timely evolution for the Bates model. We have plotted the frequencies on the left and the timely evolution on the right. For the calibration we used data for the DAX index from 11/01/2007 up to 09/01/2007 (continued)

We observe that the parameters are distributed on a wide range. Taking into account only the timely evolution displayed in Figure 10.12 might thus lead to a wrong conclusion on the stability of this model.

Normal Inverse Gaussian   The second model based on Lévy processes is the Normal Inverse Gaussian model. For this model we observe a slightly better fit to the market data than for the Variance Gamma model. The parameter stability is also slightly better, see Table 10.6.

Table 10.6 The calibration measures (10.1)–(10.4) for the NIG model and DAX data from 11/01/2007 to 09/01/2008

	α	β	δ
M_N	−0.0007	−0.0009	−0.0012
M_R	0.0138	0.0171	0.0017
V_N	0.3431	0.3957	0.0982
V_R	0.5941	0.4057	0.0001

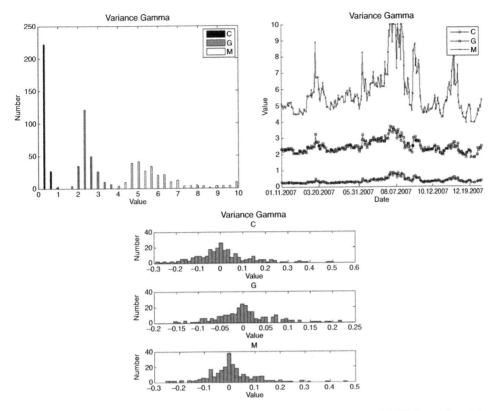

Figure 10.12   Parameter distribution and the timely evolution for the VG model. We have plotted the frequencies on the left and the timely evolution on the right. For the calibration we used data for the DAX index from 11/01/2007 up to 09/01/2008

Furthermore, the results shown in Figure 10.13 indicate that the stability is in fact somewhat better than for the Variance Gamma model. The only parameter which is distributed over a wide range of values is δ.

Lévy Process Based Models with Stochastic Volatility

Finally, we consider another class of models. These models are based on the Variance Gamma and the Normal Inverse Gaussian processes. The processes are modified such that a stochastic clock is added to model the information flow in the market leading to high and low market activity. In particular, we consider the VG GOU, NIG GOU, VG CIR and NIG CIR models.

We do not analyse each model in depth. The reader can assess the fluctuation of the parameters by considering Table 10.7. The parameter distributions are displayed in Figures 10.14, 10.15, 10.16 and 10.17.

10.3   PRICING EXOTIC OPTIONS

In this section we analyse the effect of different pricing models on exotic options. To this end we consider the Black–Scholes, Heston, Bates, VG and the VG CIR models which have

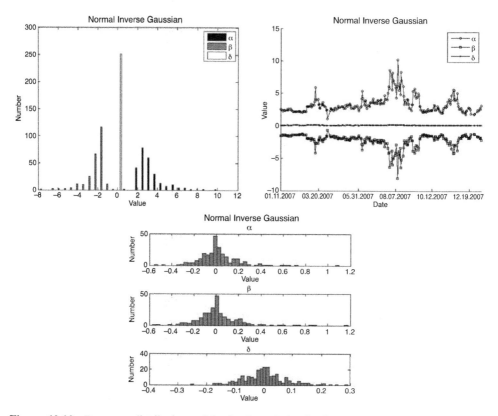

Figure 10.13   Parameter distribution and the timely evolution for the NIG model. We have plotted the frequencies on the left and the timely evolution on the right. For the calibration we used data for the DAX index from 11/01/2007 up to 09/01/2008

been calibrated to option prices using time series data starting from 11/01/2007 and ending on 09/01/2008 for DAX options.

First, we simply consider the timely evolution of the prices for several exotic options. This approach may help to gain intuition about the way a certain model or class of models acts on a given exotic options payoff and how a timely evolution in the model parameters changes the prices.

Second, to study the model dependence we have chosen to take the ATM strike. This is because ATM options are the most liquid and the calibration is set up to recover the ATM option prices exactly applying suitable weights. To remove other model aspects reflecting the changing market environment in terms of volatility we use the standard European Call and Put options from the corresponding model as normalizing constants. Thus, we divide by the value of the price of the corresponding European Call or Put option. The corresponding time evolution of the exotic options then resembles the differences stemming from the model used for pricing the exotic option.

The observed differences in model prices are very high, which suggests that we face a huge model risk. Further analysis shows that the price differences correspond to model classes and

Table 10.7 The calibration measures (10.1) – (10.4) for the VG GOU and the NIG GOU and DAX option data from 11/01/2007 to 09/01/2008

VG GOU	C	G	M	a	b	λ
M_N	−0.0019	−0.0001	−0.0016	0.0014	−0.0004	−0.0025
M_R	0.0080	0.0021	0.0055	0.0097	0.0015	0.0109
V_N	0.1695	0.1607	0.2454	0.1986	0.2102	0.4655
V_R	0.0739	0.1568	6.5143	0.0137	0.0053	0.0102

VG CIR	C	G	M	η	κ	λ
M_N	−0.0004	−0.0001	−0.0001	0.0036	0.0001	0.0006
M_R	0.0045	0.0021	0.0029	2.2868	0.0373	0.0061
V_N	0.2447	0.1607	0.4961	0.1822	0.5306	0.4731
V_R	0.0165	0.1568	1.3289	5.2473	0.0046	0.0055

NIG GOU	α	β	δ	a	b	λ
M_N	−0.0017	−0.0020	−0.0012	0.0017	−0.0003	−0.0026
M_R	0.0548	0.0749	0.0025	0.0135	0.0038	0.0138
V_N	0.6450	0.6671	0.2087	0.2032	0.3433	0.5015
V_R	91.1945	86.8714	0.0004	0.0231	0.0242	0.0105

NIG CIR	α	β	δ	η	κ	λ
M_N	−0.0002	−0.0006	−0.0007	0.0016	0.0000	0.0005
M_R	0.0123	0.0198	0.0052	3.4449	0.0943	0.0096
V_N	0.6670	0.5332	0.3804	0.5049	1.2005	0.5197
V_R	1.9331	1.2403	0.0006	11.9029	0.0175	0.0048

that the model risk is correlated to the market environment. Thus, it may either grow or decay if the risk factors, such as spot prices, volatilities or rates, move.

We address the question of measuring the model risk for pricing exotic options. To this end let us consider N models which we wish to apply for pricing an exotic option with payoff h. Two possible choices we might apply are

$$MD_{abs} = (a_{i,j})_{i,j}; \quad a_{i,j} = \left| P_i(h) - P_j(h) \right| \tag{10.5}$$

$$MD_{rel} = (r_{i,j})_{i,j}; \quad r_{i,j} = \frac{P_i(h) - P_j(h)}{P_i(h) + P_j(h)}. \tag{10.6}$$

The values of an option with payoff h in the model i are denoted by P_i. The measures use absolute and relative measures for quantifying the model difference. The numerical methods in this book can be used to analyse the measures from Equations (10.5) and (10.6).

To this end we first calibrate the models to market data using the optimization algorithms described in Chapter 9. Then, we simulate paths and apply the Monte Carlo method using the algorithms presented in Chapter 7.

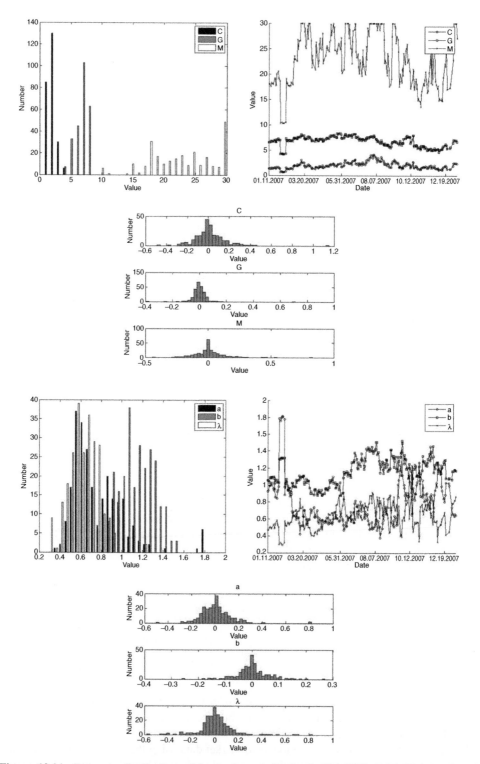

Figure 10.14 Parameter distribution and the timely evolution for the VG GOU model. We have plotted the frequencies on the left and the timely evolution on the right. For the calibration we used data for the DAX index from 11/01/2007 up to 09/01/2008

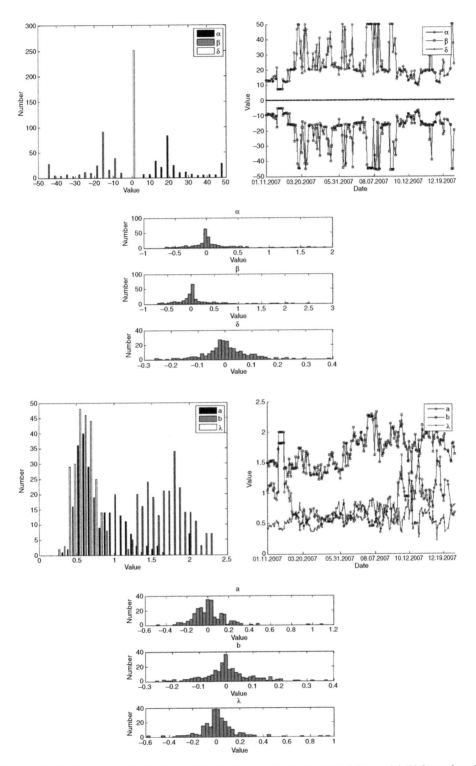

Figure 10.15 Parameter distribution and the timely evolution for the NIG GOU model. We have plotted the frequencies on the left and the timely evolution on the right. For the calibration we used data for the DAX index from 11/01/2007 up to 09/01/2008

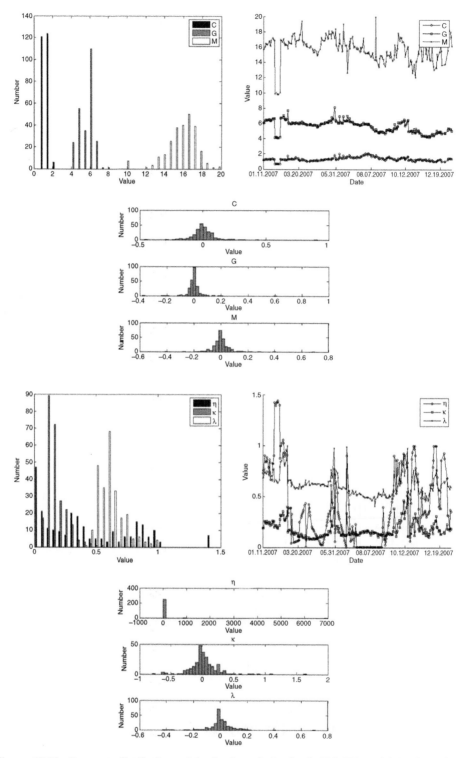

Figure 10.16 Parameter distribution and the timely evolution for the VG CIR model. We have plotted the frequencies on the left and the timely evolution on the right. For the calibration we used data for the DAX index from 11/01/2007 up to 09/01/2008

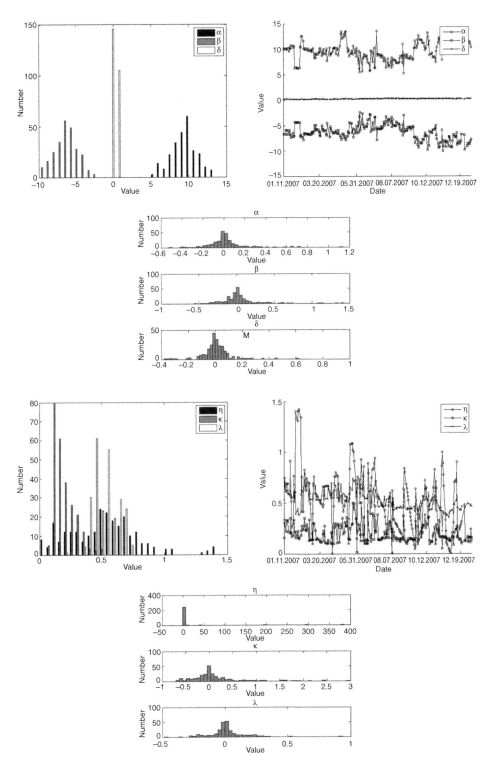

Figure 10.17 Parameter distribution and the timely evolution for the NIG CIR model. We have plotted the frequencies on the left and the timely evolution on the right. For the calibration we used data for the DAX index from 11/01/2007 up to 09/01/2008

10.3.1 Exotic Options and Different Models

Here we show the numerical results for the setup of the last section. We apply our tests to the following payoffs:

- Arithmetic Asian Option

$$h_{\text{Call}}(K, T) = \max\left(\frac{1}{N}\sum_{k=1}^{N} S(t_k) - K, 0\right)$$

$$h_{\text{Put}}(K, T) = \max\left(K - \frac{1}{N}\sum_{k=1}^{N} S(t_k), 0\right).$$

- Knock-Out Barrier Option

$$h_{\text{Call}}(K, T) = \max(S(t) - K, 0)1_{\{S(t) < B; t \in \{t_1, \dots, t_N\}\}}$$

$$h_{\text{Put}}(K, T) = \max(K - S(t), 0)1_{\{S(t) > B; t \in \{t_1, \dots, t_N\}\}}.$$

- Fixed Strike Lookback Options

$$h_{\text{Call}}(K, T) = \max\left(\max(S(t); t \in \{t_1, \dots, t_N\}) - K, 0\right)$$

$$h_{\text{Put}}(K, T) = \max\left(K - \min(S(t); t \in \{t_1, \dots, t_N\}), 0\right).$$

- Floating Strike Lookback Options

$$h_{\text{Call}}(S(T), T) = \max\left(\max(S(t); t \in \{t_1, \dots, t_N\}) - S(T), 0\right)$$

$$h_{\text{Put}}(S(T), T) = \max\left(S(T) - \min(S(t); t \in \{t_1, \dots, t_N\}), 0\right).$$

In addition to the exotic option prices we consider the normalized prices as suggested in the last section. We apply the following normalization using ATM options:

$$\text{NPrice}_{\text{exotic}} = \frac{\text{Price}_{\text{exotic}}}{\text{Price}_{\text{vailla}}}. \tag{10.7}$$

Applying this normalization we wish to remove the effects of the volatility level and extract the model risk. Figures 10.19 to 10.22 show the differences in model prices calibrated to the same set of market data. This confirms the results obtained by Schoutens, W., Simons, E. and Tistaert, J. (2004). But the new result is that the difference can be seen along the whole time scale. Furthermore, the payoffs seem to differentiate the prices with respect to a model class. Thus, stochastic volatility models, for instance, seem to perform in a similar way on exotic options. Before we give our results note that, except for the Black–Scholes model, the models show a very good fit to the Vanilla Call and Put prices (see Figure 10.18). The reason why the Black–Scholes model does not fit the prices is that we use only one single parameter to fit the option prices for all strikes and maturities.

10.4 HEDGING

In general there are three methods for hedging. First, we consider *static hedging*. A static hedge of a complex claim is a portfolio of basic financial products. This portfolio is chosen such that it reasonably replicates the payoff of the complex claim. If there exists a perfect static hedge the complex claim is replicated perfectly. In theory to set up a perfect static hedge it is

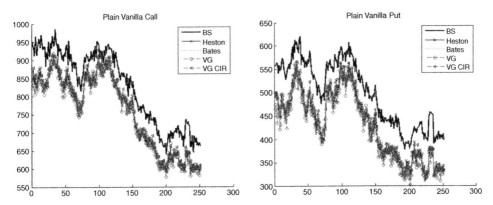

Figure 10.18   We consider the pricing of plain Vanilla European Call and Put options. Option prices are calculated each day in the period from 11/01/2007 up to 09/01/2008. The model parameters were calibrated to Vanilla Calls. The figure illustrates that the models are calibrated reasonably well to the market data

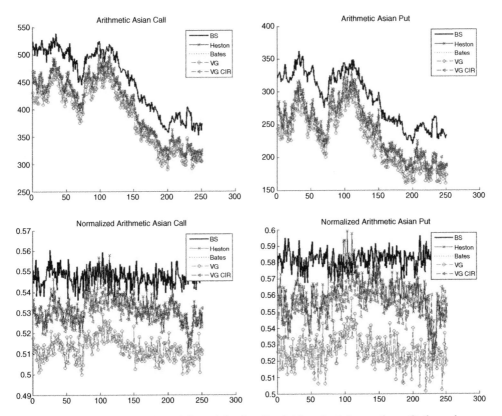

Figure 10.19   We consider the pricing of fixed strike Arithmetic Asian options. Option prices are calculated each day in the period from 11/01/2007 up to 09/01/2008. The model parameters were calibrated to Vanilla Calls. The figure shows the Call and Put option prices (upper left and right) and the normalized versions (bottom left and right)

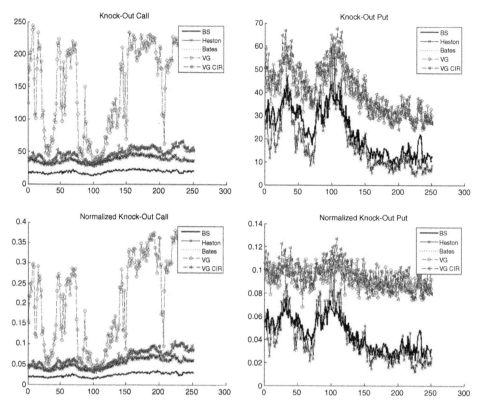

Figure 10.20   We consider the pricing of Knock-Out Barrier options. Option prices are calculated each day in the period from 11/01/2007 up to 09/01/2008. The model parameters were calibrated to Vanilla Calls. The figure shows the Call and Put option prices (upper left and right) and the normalized versions (bottom left and right) for barrier level set at $0.9 \cdot S(0)$ for Puts and $1.1 \cdot S(0)$ for Calls

necessary to buy or sell a continuum of options which, of course, is not possible in practice. Therefore, we also speak of a perfect static hedge if we can replicate it nearly perfectly (see for instance the example on CMS in Chapter 1, Subsection 1.4.2).

Not every exotic claim can be decomposed into basic options and can be exactly replicated. In such cases, static hedges can be constructed by either applying super-hedging or sub-hedging. To this end we hedge more or less risk by imposing an upper or lower bound on the complex claims's payoff. Thus, the prices of the complex claim and the prices of the hedge portfolio representing a super-hedge/sub-hedge can differ significantly.

Second, we choose to dynamically hedge the complex claim leading to the *dynamic hedging*. This corresponds to setting up an initial portfolio of hedge instruments having the same price as the complex claim which is then periodically adjusted. This is done to offset the movement of the driving risk factors and thus compensates for the price movements of the complex claim. For setting up the portfolio we should choose financial instruments which reflect the nature of the risk factors involved in the complex claim; otherwise, the dynamic hedge does not qualify as a hedge. We face several difficulties here. Dynamic hedging involves transaction costs which can be significant and hedging is only possible at discrete time points. This leads to a discretization bias. Furthermore, situations may arise where hedging activities cause prices of

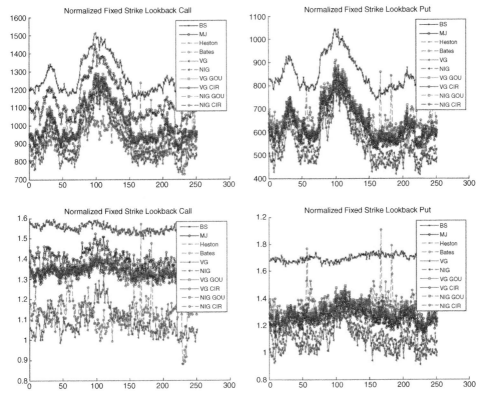

Figure 10.21 We consider the pricing of fixed strike Lookback options. Option prices are calculated each day in the period from 11/01/2007 up to 09/01/2008. The parameters we use are the calibrated parameters for the models. The figure shows the Call and Put option prices (upper left and right) and the normalized version (bottom left and right)

the hedged items to move leading to further hedging. This effect is observed, for instance, for CMS spread trading and is known as the *gamma trap*.

Finally, in practice traders combine both types of hedges. A static hedge involves infinitely more simple products and can thus only partially be set up or is only set up for the most probable market scenarios. This is called a *semi-static hedge*. Thus, situations arise in which the semi-static hedge has to be adjusted, which explains the qualifying word *semi*.

In this section we consider the problem of dynamically hedging a given payoff or claim using different models and payoffs.

10.4.1   Hedging – The Basics

For an introduction to hedging we refer readers to Fries, C. (2006). Let us consider a market consisting of $d \in \mathbb{N}$ securities or underlyings. $\underline{S}(t) = (S_0(t), S_1(t), \ldots, S_d(t))^T$. The vector $\underline{S}(t), t \in [0, T]$ represents the timely evolution of the market. Furthermore, let us assume that there is a filtration $(\mathcal{F}_t)_t$ which mathematically models the information flow in the market. A filtration can be seen as the mathematical model of the revelation of information to the market. $\underline{S}$ is adapted to the filtration $(\mathcal{F}_t)_t$ meaning that $\underline{S}(t)$ is $\mathcal{F}_t$-measurable. Let us also assume that

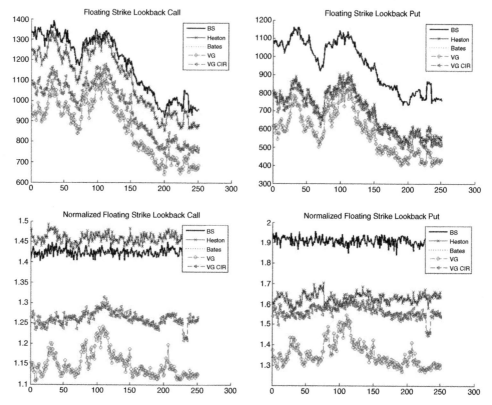

Figure 10.22 We consider the pricing of floating strike Lookback options. Option prices are calculated each day in the period from 11/01/2007 up to 09/01/2008. The model parameters were calibrated to Vanilla Calls. The figure shows the Call and Put option prices (upper left and right) and the normalized versions (bottom left and right)

there is at least one strictly positive asset which serves as a measure or numeraire; in many situations it is the so-called bank account. The bank account $S_0(t)$ is a stochastic process such that $S_0(0) = 1$ and

$$dS_0(t)/S_0(t) = r(t)dt,$$

with $r(t)$ being a positive function. This numeraire corresponds to the risk neutral measure. Without loss of generality we assume that S_0 is chosen to be the numeraire. We call $\underline{S}^* := \underline{S}/S_0$ the discounted prices.

An option is characterized by its payoff function h. Mathematically, this payoff function maps a path ω to a real number $h(\omega)$ which is the option value along the path ω. We denote the discounted payoff by h^*.

Assume we have some option with payoff h which we wish to approximate using a portfolio of assets $\underline{S}$. To this end we introduce a hedging strategy. We consider a vector of functions $\underline{\phi} = (\phi_0, \phi_1, \ldots, \phi_d)^T$ and assume that $\phi_1, \ldots, \phi_d$ are *previsible*. This means that the hedging strategy only takes into account the information which is available in the market up to the current time. Especially in relation to jump processes, the strategy does not anticipate jumps.

In terms of the filtration this means that a previsible process is adapted to $\mathcal{F}_{t-}$ and thus it is not able to anticipate jumps or events which are not measurable with respect to $\mathcal{F}_{t-}$. Each ϕ_i is the quantity of the asset S_i in this portfolio. Thus, $\underline{\phi}(t)\underline{S}(t) - h(t)$ or $\underline{\phi}(t)\underline{S}^*(t) - h^*(t)$ is the profit-and-loss resulting from the hedge strategy at time t and its discounted value respectively. The cumulated profit-and-loss up to time T is given by the difference between the initial value of the hedge portfolio with its timely evolution and the value of the claim at time T:

$$PL(\underline{\phi}(T)) = \underline{\phi}(0)\underline{S}(0) + \int_0^T \underline{\phi}(t)d\underline{S}(t) - h(T). \qquad (10.8)$$

Here $\underline{\phi}(0)\underline{S}(0)$ is the initial value of the hedge portfolio and the value is equal to the arbitrage free value of the claim $E[h^*(T)]$ if the hedge strategy is perfect and self-financing, as in the Black–Scholes model. We further assume that the stochastic integral in Equation (10.8) is well defined.

A hedging strategy ϕ is called *self-financing* if there is no withdrawal or investment of money. This is defined by $dPF(t) = \underline{\phi}(t)d\underline{S}(t)$. We can conclude that the profit-and-loss of a perfect and self-financing hedge is zero and we end up with

$$h(T) = \underline{\phi}(0)\underline{S}(0) + \int_0^T \underline{\phi}(t)d\underline{S}(t). \qquad (10.9)$$

The initial value of the hedge is equal to the value of the claim and the payoff at time T is replicated perfectly. Thus, the payoff of the option can be perfectly matched by re-balancing a portfolio consisting of assets from $\underline{S}$ without withdrawing money or investing fresh money in the portfolio. But this is only guaranteed if the martingale measure is unique, which is the case for the Black–Scholes model. The hedge strategy is then given by $\underline{\phi}(t) = \frac{\partial V(t)}{\partial \underline{S}(t)}$. The price of a European Call or Put option is determined by the Black–Scholes pricing formula but can be determined equally well by dynamically hedging the option.

If the risk neutral measure is not unique we face an incomplete market as it is the case for Lévy models. In incomplete markets hedging costs may arise because we can only set up a hedge that replicates the final payoff on average. Thus, generally the variance of a hedged portfolio is not zero. As an example we consider a Lévy model such as Variance Gamma for which we observe infinitely many jumps that cannot be hedged in practice. For another example we take the Heston model. The variance is stochastic and it is not a tradeable security. We can still consider the models under a martingale measure and obtain arbitrage free prices, but the martingale measure is no longer unique. Another source of incompleteness is discrete time hedging. We approximate the integral in Equation (10.8) with a sum to conduct the hedge strategy in a real market environment.

One method of dealing with market incompleteness is to enlarge the market. For instance, we can consider the variance of some asset being a tradeable asset. This can then be used to force completeness in a stochastic volatility model.

Another method is to consider different hedge strategies such as variance optimal hedging to account for the incompleteness.

10.4.2 Hedging in Incomplete Markets

In this section we consider the issue of dynamically hedging a derivatives contract in an incomplete market. The hedging strategy cannot be separated from the model which we apply for pricing. Therefore, we consider hedging strategies for financial models based on diffusions, jump diffusions, pure jump processes or stochastic volatility models. Using the methods described in this book it is possible to simulate the profit-and-loss of a hedging strategy. Therefore it is possible to determine the hedge errors for a strategy leading to zero on average, which we call the *hedge effectiveness*. This helps to determine if a hedging strategy is reliable or it may turn out that balancing has to be done too frequently meaning the transaction costs set off the hedging effect. It is useful to compare different hedging strategies or to analyse the hedge performance for certain time periods using historical option price data.

For the dynamic hedging we need measures which suggest how to adjust the hedging portfolio to keep track of the movement of risk factors. To this end we have considered the calculation of sensitivities of option prices with respect to model parameters. We used semi-analytic methods from Chapter 6 and simulation based methods from Chapter 7.

In this section we consider the dynamic hedging in a model which constitutes an incomplete market. We derive a hedging strategy which does not perfectly offset the risk, thus there is a positive probability for realizing a profit or a loss.

Variance Optimal Hedging

One approach is to consider the payoff at maturity and find a trading strategy which is not adjusted to minimize the variance locally at some time point but choose it in a way that the global variance is minimized. This approach is considered in Duffie, D. and Richardson, H. (1991) and in Hubalek, F., Kallsen, J. and Krawczyk, L. (2005). The authors call it *Variance Optimal Hedging*. Let us briefly summarize some results for Variance Optimal Hedging.

In this approach we consider the statistical (or real world) measure $\mathbb{P}$ and the value of a discounted payoff h (which corresponds to some martingale measure) denoted by $\tilde{h}$. We wish to find a trading strategy ϕ^* in collaboration with an initial instalment V_0^* such that

$$(V_0^*, \phi^*(t)) = \inf_{V_0, \phi(t)} \mathbb{E}^{\mathbb{P}}\left[\left(\tilde{h} - V_0 - \int_0^T \phi(s)dS(s)\right)^2\right]. \tag{10.10}$$

We have to stress the fact that the profit-and-loss due to hedging is measured in the statistical measure (real world measure). Since this is the actual cost of hedging, the choice of this measure seems natural and reasonable. But at second glance we observe that not only the strategy but also the initial investment is determined. This, however, again depends on the chosen martingale measure and therefore refers to the risk neutral pricing approach. We do not go into the details of implementing full-blown Variance Optimal Hedging and its applications since it is outside the scope of this book. Further discussions of and references to this issue can be found in Cont, R. and Tankov, P. (2004), Hubalek, F., Kallsen, J. and Krawczyk, L. (2005) and Heath, D., Platen, E. and Schweizer, M. (2001) and in the references therein. The practical application of this approach is analysed in Cont, R., Tankov, P. and Voltchkova, E. (2005).

The considerations in the cited literature lead to a modification of the Variance Optimal Hedging approach, which is called *Minimum Variance Hedging*. First, the expectation for Equation (10.10) is replaced by some risk neutral expectation keeping in mind

- that the measure and therefore the expectation are not unique, for instance for Lévy or stochastic volatility models;
- that it depends on the calibration procedure since the parameters of the model and therefore of the chosen risk neutral measure are derived from quoted liquid option prices.

We wish to outline the implementation. To this end we choose some martingale measure $\mathbb{Q}$. This measure is determined by choosing a martingale dynamics and the parameters by calibrating the model to given market data. Then, we have to find a trading strategy ϕ^* such that it is self-financing and

$$(V_0, \phi^*(t)) := \inf_{V_0, \phi(t)} \mathbb{E}^{\mathbb{Q}} \left[\left(h^*(T) - V_0 - \int_0^T \phi(s) dS(s) \right)^2 \right].$$

The solution to this problem can be found by considering Kunita, H. and Watanabe, S. (1967). The result is an orthogonal decomposition with respect to some stochastic integral of a square integrable martingale S^* and some stochastic variable R. It is thus an orthogonal decomposition into a hedgeable and some unhedgeable risk component. We have

$$h^*(T) = V_0^* + \int_0^T \phi^*(s) dS^*(s) + R(T). \tag{10.11}$$

The strategy suggested by Equation (10.11) is optimal in a global and a local sense. Thus, if we consider the variance of the difference of the discounted payoff $h^*(t)$ and subtract the hedgeable risk given by the integral with respect to S^*, the strategy ϕ^* can be derived and is given by

$$\phi^* = \frac{\langle dV^*, dS^* \rangle}{\langle dS^*, dS^* \rangle},$$

where $\langle \cdot, \cdot \rangle$ is a short-hand notation for quadratic variation.

Using this approach we find for

- Geometric Brownian motion (Δ-hedge)

$$\phi^* = \frac{\partial V(t)}{\partial S(t)}. \tag{10.12}$$

- Jump models (as outlined)

$$\phi^* = \frac{\sigma^2 \frac{\partial V(t)}{\partial S(t)} + \frac{1}{S(t)} \int_{-\infty}^{\infty} (e^z - 1) \left(V_t(S(t)e^z) - V(S(t)) \right) v_X(dz)}{\sigma^2 + \int_{-\infty}^{\infty} (e^z - 1) v_X(dz)}. \tag{10.13}$$

- Stochastic volatility models (leverage between underlying and volatility)

$$\phi^* = \frac{\partial V(t)}{\partial S(t)} + \frac{\partial V(t)}{\partial y(t)} \frac{\rho v}{\sigma S(t)}. \tag{10.14}$$

- Stochastic volatility models with jumps (leverage and jumps)

$$\phi^* = \frac{1}{\sigma^2 + \int_{-\infty}^{\infty} (e^z - 1) v_X(dz)} \left(\left(\sigma^2 \frac{\partial V(t)}{\partial S(t)} + \frac{\partial V(t)}{\partial y(t)} \frac{\rho v}{\sigma S(t)} \right) \right.$$

$$\left. + \frac{1}{S(t)} \int_{-\infty}^{\infty} (e^z - 1) \left(V_t(S(t)e^z) - V(S(t)) \right) v_X(dz) \right). \tag{10.15}$$

Table 10.8 Models and model parameters for the numerical comparison of Δ-hedging and Minimum Variance Hedging. For the Merton model we take $\sigma = 0.25$

Model	Parameters		
Merton	$\mu_J = 0.05$	$\sigma_J = 0.15$	$\lambda = 0.1$
Variance Gamma	$\sigma = 0.12$	$\nu = 0.2$	$\theta = -0.14$
NIG	$\alpha = 18.42141$	$\beta = -15.08623$	$\delta = 0.31694$

We apply the option pricing algorithms based on Fourier transform to calculate Minimum Variance Hedge strategies. We observe that for some $\lambda \in \mathbb{R}\backslash\{0\}$

$$\max(\lambda S - K, 0) = \begin{cases} \lambda \max(S - K/\lambda, 0), & \lambda > 0 \\ \lambda \min(S - K/\lambda, 0), & \lambda < 0 \end{cases}$$

and thus, for the Call option price we find for $\lambda > 0$ that

$$C(t, \lambda S(t), K) = \lambda C(t, S(t), K/\lambda).$$

To this end we need a range of option prices corresponding to different strikes and this is exactly what the methods based on fast Fourier transform (FFT) provide to compute the integrals given in Equations (10.13) and (10.15).

Furthermore, we must emphasize that with these methods we can also compute the corresponding hedge strategies for Bermudan and even American options. We only have to combine results from Chapters 5 and 6 and the representations for the minimum variance hedge strategies. Using prices for exotic options is difficult since often such prices are only available by using Monte Carlo simulation techniques.

Numerical Examples For a numerical example of the Minimum Variance Hedge we use the models presented in Table 10.8. For our considerations we only take into account the integral part of Equation (10.13). Thus, we plotted

$$\phi^* = \frac{\frac{1}{S(t)}\int_{-\infty}^{\infty}(e^z - 1)(V_t(S(t)e^z) - V(S(t)))\,\nu_X(dz)}{\sigma^2 + \int_{-\infty}^{\infty}(e^z - 1)\,\nu_X(dz)}.$$

For the full mean variance ratio we have to add the Δ and the Vega part using, for instance, one of the methods described in Chapter 6. The results are plotted in Figure 10.23.

Quadratic Hedging

Since we have seen that it is in general impossible to derive a hedging strategy with vanishing variance for complex models, the idea is to make the variance (and higher moments) as small as possible. To this end we apply the theory described in Foellmer, H. and Schweizer, M. (1989) and Schweizer, M. (1991), which suggests measuring a localized hedging error and minimizing it in terms of the variance. The authors call this approach *Quadratic Hedging*. This strategy is designed to exactly match the final payoff. But a drawback of the approach is that it leads to non-self-financing trading strategies. Let us briefly illustrate the approach and consider the *cost process* C_t with respect to a trading strategy ϕ, that is

$$C_t(\phi) := V_t(\phi) - G_t(\phi),$$

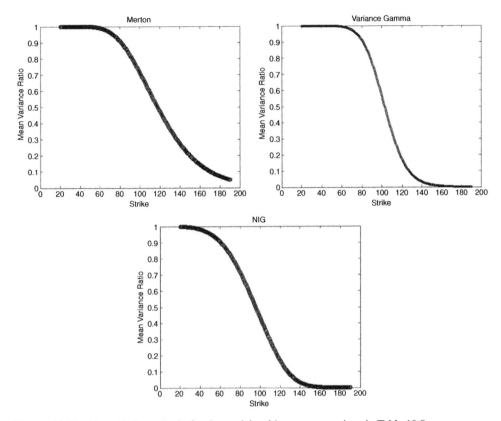

Figure 10.23 Mean Variance Ratio for the models with parameters given in Table 10.8

where

$$V_t(\phi) = \phi S, \quad G_t(\phi) = \int_0^t \phi(s) dS(s).$$

This correspond to the current value of the hedge portfolio following the trading strategy ϕ and the gain from changes in the risk factors S. Discounting and for some random variable X, denoting the discounted variable by $\tilde{X}$, leads us to consider

$$\tilde{C}_t(\phi) = \phi(0) + \phi(t)\tilde{S}(t) - \int_0^t \phi(s) d\tilde{S}(s).$$

Choosing some measure $\mathbb{Q}$ the original idea is to minimize

$$\mathbb{E}^{\mathbb{Q}}[(C_T - C_t)^2 | \mathcal{F}_t].$$

This is intended for all trading strategies, which is technically challenging and leads, as mentioned, to non-self-financing strategies.

A Worked Out Example

In this subsection we wish to outline the dynamic hedging for the Merton model (see Chapter 3, Subsection 3.2.2). Thus, the considered dynamic hedge is one example for hedging in an incomplete market since the Merton model allows for jumps in the underlying.

Let us assume that the forward stock price is given by $S_f(t) := S(t) \exp((r-d)(T-t))$ and thus

$$\frac{dS_f(t)}{S_f(t-)} = \underbrace{-\int_{-\infty}^{\infty} \left(e^z - 1\right) v_X(dz)\, dt + \sigma dW(t) + (\exp(J) - 1)dN(t).}_{=:\mu}$$

Denoting by C_f the forward option price, we have for the profit-and-loss after applying a certain hedging strategy ϕ:

$$PL(\phi_t) = C_f(T) - C_f(t) - \int_t^T \phi_u dS_f(u).$$

Since the Itô integral and the Itô formula can be generalized to jump-diffusion processes we can apply it to derive a pricing equation analogous to the Black–Scholes pricing equation. Thus, we have

$$0 = \frac{\partial C_f}{\partial t}(t, S_f) - \mu \frac{\partial C_f}{S_f}(t, S_f) + \frac{\sigma^2}{2} \frac{\partial^2 C_f}{S_f^2}(t, S_f) S_f^2 + \int_{-\infty}^{\infty} \left(C_f(t, S_f e^z) - C_f(t, S_f)\right) v(dz).$$

We are interested in deriving a self-finance trading strategy ϕ describing the units of underlying and the units of the bank account. The self-financing strategy ϕ is non-anticipating since it is caglad and not cadlag. Thus, the profit-and-loss for a self-financing trading strategy is given by

$$PL(\phi(t)) = \int_t^T \left[\frac{\partial C_f}{\partial u}(u, S_f(u^-)) - \frac{\partial C_f}{\partial S_f}(u, S_f(u^-))\mu S_f(u^-)\right] du$$

$$+ \int_t^T \frac{1}{2} \frac{\partial^2 C_f}{\partial S_f^2}(u, S(u^-))\sigma^2 S_f(u^-)^2 du + \int_t^T \frac{\partial C_f}{\partial S_f}(u, S_f(u^-))\sigma S_f(u^-)dW(u)$$

$$+ \sum_{n=1, t<T(n)<T}^{N(T)} \left(C_f(T(n), S_f(T(n)^-) + \Delta S_f(t)) - C_f(T(n), S(T(n)^-))\right)$$

$$+ \int_t^T \phi(u)\mu S_f(u^-)du - \int_t^T \phi(u)\sigma S_f(u^-)dW(u)$$

$$- \sum_{n=1, t<T(n)<T}^{N(T)} \phi(T_n)(\exp(J) - 1) S_f(T(n)^-).$$

Since the value of the strategy ϕ satisfies the pricing equation at time t, we find

$$PL(\phi(t)) = \int_t^T \left(\frac{\partial C_f}{\partial S_f}(u, S_f(u^-)) - \phi_u \right) \sigma S_f(u^-) dW(u)$$

$$+ \sum_{n=1, t<T(n)<T}^{N(T)} \left(C_f(T(n), S_f(T(n)^-) + \Delta S_f(t)) - C_f(T(n), S_f(T(n)^-)) \right)$$

$$- \int_t^T \int_{-\infty}^{\infty} \left(C_f(u, S_f(u^-) \exp(x)) - C_f(u, S_f(u^-)) \right) v(dx) du$$

$$+ \int_t^T \phi(u) \mu S_f(u-) du - \sum_{n=1, t<T(n)<T}^{N(T)} \phi(T(n)) (\exp(J) - 1) S_f(T(n)^-).$$

The first, the second together with the third and fourth lines are martingales and therefore the sum is a martingale. From the martingale property we find that the expected value of the strategy is 0 and choosing $\phi(t) = \frac{\partial C_f}{\partial S_f}$ does not guarantee a realized value of 0 for the hedging portfolio at maturity T. This hedge does not offset the risk from the jump component. Therefore, we have to adjust the hedging portfolio. We do this by considering a strategy ϕ which minimizes the variance of $PL(\phi(t))$. To this end we calculate the variance of the profit-and-loss with respect to the trading strategy ϕ:

$$\mathbb{V}[PL(\phi_t)] = \mathbb{E}\left[\int_t^T \left| \left(\frac{\partial C_f}{\partial S_f}(u, S_f(u^-)) - \phi(u) \right) \sigma S_f(u^-) \right|^2 du \right]$$

$$+ \mathbb{E}\left[\int_t^T \int_{-\infty}^{\infty} \left| C_f(u, S_f(u^-) \exp(z)) - C_f(u, S_f(u^-)) \right. \right.$$

$$\left. \left. - \phi(u)(\exp(z) - 1) S_f(u^-) \right|^2 v(dz) du \right].$$

To find the actual minimizer we differentiate $PL(\phi(t))$ with respect to $\phi(t)$ and solve for the strategy for which the derivative vanishes. Using the Itô isometry for jump-diffusion processes we find

$$0 = \left(\frac{\partial C_f}{\partial S_f}(t, S_f(t^-)) - \phi(t) \right) \sigma^2 S_f(t^-)^2$$

$$+ \int_{-\infty}^{\infty} (C_f(t, S_f(t^-) \exp(x)) - C_f(t, S_f(t^-)) - \phi(t)$$

$$(\exp(z) - 1) S_f(t^-))(\exp(z) - 1) S_f(t^-) v(dz)$$

and, therefore, for the minimal variance hedge strategy

$$\phi(t) = \frac{\sigma^2 \frac{\partial C_f}{\partial S_f}}{\sigma^2 + \int_{-\infty}^{\infty} (\exp(z) - 1)^2 v(dz)}$$

$$+ \frac{\frac{1}{S_f(t^-)} \left(\int_{-\infty}^{\infty} (C_f(t, S_f(t^-) \exp(z)) - C_f(t, S_f(t^-)))(\exp(z) - 1) v(dz) \right)}{\sigma^2 + \int_{-\infty}^{\infty} (\exp(z) - 1)^2 v(dz)}.$$

This strategy is the optimal hedge and is valid for all t up to maturity T. Only for special choices for the payoff or the model parameters is a realized value of 0 possible and therefore leads to a perfect hedge. All linear payoffs, for instance the forward, can be perfectly hedged. For $\sigma = 0$ and a Lévy measure given by $v(dz) = \lambda\delta(z_0)$ such a strategy is feasible and in this case we take

$$\phi(t) = \frac{C_f(t, S(t^-)\exp(z_0)) - C(t, S(t^-))}{(\exp(z_0) - 1)S(t^-)}.$$

The arguments can be put into a more general framework. This is done using the *Hamilton–Jacobi–Bellmann equation* from stochastic control theory. We refer readers to Bergomi, L. (2004), Ahn, H. and Wilmott, P. (2003) and Ahn, H. and Wilmott, P. (2007) for details. In this case the general idea is to consider the mean and the variance of the optimal hedging strategy $\phi(t)$. Then, a value function J is specified which includes the strategy $\phi(t)$ as a parameter. The function J fulfils a certain differential equation, the Hamilton–Jacobi–Bellmann equation. This equation has to be solved for certain models and option pricing problems.

We consider the Heston model and keep the notation we have used throughout the book. Then, with ϕ denoting the hedging strategy, it is possible to find equations for a particular model. In the case of the Heston model the equations are given by

$$\frac{\partial m}{\partial t} + Lm - rm = -(\mu - r + d)S\phi$$

$$\frac{\partial v}{\partial t} + Lv - 2rv = -VS^2\left(\phi + \frac{\partial m}{\partial t} + \frac{\rho\epsilon}{S}\frac{\partial m}{\partial V}\right)^2 - (1 - \rho^2)\sigma^2 V\left(\frac{\partial m}{\partial V}\right)^2,$$

with the differential operator L

$$L = \mu S\frac{\partial}{\partial t} + \kappa(\Theta - V)\frac{\partial}{\partial V} + \frac{1}{2}VS^2\frac{\partial^2}{\partial S^2} + \frac{1}{2}\epsilon^2 V\frac{\partial^2}{\partial V^2} + \rho\epsilon SV\frac{\partial^2}{\partial S\partial V}$$

and boundary conditions given by $m(T, S, V) = -f(S)$ and $v(T, S, V) = 0$.

We find for the optimal strategy $\phi(t)$

$$\phi(t) = -\frac{\partial m}{\partial S} - \frac{\rho\epsilon}{S}\frac{\partial m}{\partial V}$$

or in terms of the price $P = -m$:

$$\phi = -\frac{\partial P}{\partial S} + \frac{\rho\epsilon}{S}\frac{\partial P}{\partial V}.$$

For a jump-diffusion model also considered in Ahn, H. and Wilmott, P. (2007), we find

$$\phi(t) = -\frac{\sigma^2\frac{\partial m}{\partial S} + \lambda\mathbb{E}[J^2]\frac{m(t,S(1+J))-m(t,S)}{S\mathbb{E}[J^2]}}{\sigma^2 + \lambda\mathbb{E}[J^2]}.$$

This gives for the optimal strategy $\phi(t)$ and the price P

$$\phi \approx \frac{\partial P}{\partial S} + \frac{1}{2}\frac{\lambda\mathbb{E}[J^3]}{\sigma^2 + \lambda\mathbb{E}[J^2]}S\frac{\partial^2 P}{\partial S^2}.$$

For the Merton model we could replace $\mathbb{E}[J^2]$ by σ_j^2.

Therefore, we recover the results we already derived by the detailed calculation at the beginning of this section.

For Lévy models with the diffusive part modelled by some volatility σ, the optimal strategy ϕ for Vanilla options does not depend on the model. Suppose we have an expression of the implied volatility denoted by $\hat{\sigma}_K$. Then, the strategy corresponding to the strike K is given by

$$\phi_K = \Delta_K^{BS} - \frac{1}{S} \text{Vega}_K^{BS} \frac{d\hat{\sigma}_K}{d\log(K)}.$$

10.4.3   Discrete Time Hedging

In general the hedging strategies are set up in continuous time. Since in practice the portfolio can only be re-balanced at discrete time points t_i, $i = 1, \ldots, N$, we have to account for the discretization bias. Proceeding this way a transaction is required for re-balancing and therefore we have to take into account the corresponding transaction costs. To this end it may be the case that it is economically reasonable to apply longer time periods for hedging and thus keep the transaction costs low but face a higher market risk.

In addressing such questions when setting up hedging strategies for advanced models the numerical methods proposed in this book can be applied.

For instance, we can sample paths using the discretization schemes presented in Chapters 7 and 8 as well as the efficient pricing and calibration routines from Chapters 5, 6 and 9.

If we do not wish to consider transaction costs we face the discretization bias arising from approximating a continuous model to a discrete one. Thus, when deriving hedging strategies we have to analyse their discretization bias either by using analytic error estimates or by performing numerical analysis.

Another approach is suggested in Mahayni, A. (2003). Here the author considers starting from a hedge being only possible in discrete time and suggests using a discrete model for pricing.

All in all, the discrete hedging not only introduces a discretization bias but comes with a trade off because each adjustment involves hedging costs. We have outlined some hedging strategies for advanced financial models. Now, we wish to summarize the approaches of hedging in stochastic volatility models with jumps and models based on (stochastic volatility) Lévy models.

Δ-Hedging

The simplest dynamic hedge corresponds to a hedging strategy taking into account only the underlying asset and the bank account. For this approach, called Δ-*hedging*, we have to compute the quantity of the underlying $S(t)$ in the hedging portfolio. We therefore need to be able to calculate

$$\Delta(t) = \frac{\partial V(t)}{\partial S(t)}. \tag{10.16}$$

The hedge parameters of the Δ-hedge are $\phi(t_i)$ units of the asset and $N(t_i)$ units of the bank account given as

$$N(t_i) = V(t_i) - \phi(t_i) \cdot S(t_i), \tag{10.17}$$

$$\phi(t_i) = \Delta(t_i). \tag{10.18}$$

If we consider that re-balancing is only possible at times $t_0, \ldots, t_N$ and we wish to re-balance the hedging portfolio at time $t_{i+1} > t_i$, we end up at time t_{i+1} with a gain of

$$G(t_{i+1}) = \Delta(t_i)(S(t_{i+1}) - S(t_i)) + N(t_i)(B(t_{i+1})^{-1} - 1).$$

The loss of the hedge strategy at time t_i is given by a discrete version of Equation (10.8), given by

$$L(t_i) = V(t_i) - (\phi(t_0) \cdot S(t_0) + N(t_0)) - \sum_{j=1}^{i} G(t_j).$$

We switched the signs to have positive values for the losses. Using the numerical methods presented in Chapters 5 to 8 we are able to compute this quantity for a variety of models. A simulation of the Δ-hedge can also be carried out by using a simulation routine such as the one provided in Figure 10.24.

We used the functions bankaccount and hedgecosts which are given in Figure 10.25.

```
function pf = simulatehedge(data,strategy,pricer)
% initialize variables
pf.delta = zcros(strategy.n,1,strategy.m);
pf.bank = zeros(strategy.n,1,strategy.m);
pf.gain = zeros(strategy.n,1,strategy.m);
pf.value = zeros(strategy.n,1,strategy.m);
pf.loss = zeros(1,strategy.m);
pf.cumgains = zeros(strategy.n,1,strategy.m);
% simulate asset paths
stockPath = data.path(data.S0,data.t,strategy.n,strategy.m,data.r);
% ——— hedge procedure
for j=1:strategy.m  % m hedges
        i = 1;
        %——— Start Parameter
        dt = data.t/strategy.n;      % time steps
        df = exp(-data.r*data.t);    % discount factor
        strikePrice = stockPath(1,j);
        %——— Option Value and Hedge Parameters
        [pf.value(i,1,j),pf.delta(i,1,j),~]= pricer.greeks1(data.t, ...
            0, stockPath(i,j), 0, df, data.params, strikePrice, 1);
        pf.bank(i,1,j) = bankaccount(pf,stockPath(:,j),i,j);
    for i = 2:strategy.n      % Loop within one hedge
            %——— Option Value and Hedge Parameters
            ttm = data.t-(i-1)*dt;    % time to maturity
            df = exp(-data.r*ttm);
            [pf.value(i,1,j),pf.delta(i,1,j),~]= pricer.greeks1(ttm, ...
                0, stockPath(i,j), 0, df, data.params, strikePrice, 1);
            %——— Hedgeparameter Portfoliohedge
            pf.bank(i,1,j) = bankaccount(pf,stockPath(:,j),i,j);
            %——— Gain and Loss—Process Portfoliohedge
            [pf.gain(i,1,j), pf.cumgains(i,1,j), pf.loss(1,j)] = ...
                hedgecosts(stockPath(:,j),data.r,dt,i,j);
    end
    end
end
end
```

Figure 10.24 Matlab code to simulate a Δ-hedge for any given model

```
% the bank account
function bank = bankaccount(pf,stockPath,i,j)
    bank = (pf.value(i,1,j) - stockPath(i,1) * pf.delta(i,1,j));
end
% hedgecosts
function [gain,cumgain,loss] = hedgecosts(pf,stockPath,spotRate,dt,i,j)
    gain = pf.delta(i-1,1,j)*(stockPath(i,1) ...
        -stockPath(i-1,1)) + pf.bank(i-1,1,j)*(exp(spotRate*dt)-1);

    cumgains = pf.cumgains(i-1,1,j) + pf.gain(i,1,j);

    loss = pf.value(i,1,j) - pf.value(1,1,j)- pf.cumgains(i,1,j);
end
```

Figure 10.25   Matlab code for the bank account and the hedging costs used by the function `simulatehedge`

Here m asset paths with n time steps are simulated by a function path, and the values as well as the sensitivities are computed by the function `greeks1`. With the simulated asset paths m Δ-hedges are simulated and the results are stored in a struct variable called `pf`. Using this setup every model can be compared by its hedging performance by plotting the loss distribution of the simulated hedge as a histogram. With slight modifications even historical data can be used to simulate the hedge performance, as we show in Subsection 10.4.4. There we use market data for the German DAX index and we apply different models for hedging options.

Higher Order Hedging

We have introduced the Δ-hedge. This method only takes into account for first order changes of the underlying asset due to the fact that it applies the first derivative of the price with respect to the underlying. We now include higher order effect and take into account changes of additional parameters such as the volatility. This leads to a consideration higher order or mixed derivatives. If we consider further risk factors other than the underlying it means that we have to include other assets for hedging. For instance, it becomes necessary to offset the risk of changes in volatility taking a European option as another hedging instrument.

To determine the quantity of an instrument in the hedging portfolio we consider the model sensitivities with respect to market movements. This corresponds to calculating the Greeks.

- Δ, see Equation (10.16)
- Γ, given by

$$\Gamma(t) := \frac{\partial^2 V(t)}{\partial S(t)^2}.$$

- Vega, given by

$$\text{Vega}(t) := \frac{\partial V(t)}{\partial \sigma(t)}.$$

In order to apply a second order hedge we consider the option to be hedged with a value of $V_1(t)$ and the bank account $N_1(t)$. We consider another option, possibly with another payoff, strike or maturity. We denote its value by $V_2(t)$. To compose the hedging portfolio we determine the number of units of both options and the bank account in the portfolio. To this end we consider the case of a Δ/Γ-hedge and the following system of equations:

$$V_1(t_i) = \phi_1(t_i) \cdot S(t_i) + \phi_2(t_i) \cdot V_2(t_i) + N_1(t_i),$$ (10.19)

$$\Delta_1(t_i) = \phi_1(t_i) + \phi_2(t_i) \cdot \Delta_2(t_i),$$ (10.20)

$$\Gamma_1(t_i) = \phi_2(t_i) \cdot \Gamma_2(t_i).$$ (10.21)

This means we have to calculate the sensitivity and adjust the quantity of the corresponding hedge instrument accordingly.

If the volatility $\sigma(t)$ is not a constant but given as a parametric representation we can adjust the Δ-hedge by considering the Vega instead of the Gamma in our hedging portfolio. We replace Equation (10.21) by

$$\text{Vega}_1(t_i) = \phi_2(t_i) \cdot \text{Vega}_2(t_i).$$

For stochastic volatility models such as the Heston model we apply for instance the COS method. For calculating the Vega we use with the COS method

$$\text{Vega} = \frac{1}{2} \mathcal{R}\left(\frac{\partial\varphi(0)}{\partial V(0)} \frac{x-a}{b-a} \right) V_0 + \sum_{k=1}^{N} \mathcal{R}\left(\frac{\partial\varphi\left(\frac{k\pi}{b-a}\right)}{\partial V(0)} \exp(ik\pi)\frac{x-a}{b-a} \right) V_k.$$

A simulation of the hedge is performed by utilizing the simulation routine given in Figure 10.26.

The following functions are used for setting up the simulation by `simulatehedge`, as shown in Figure 10.27.

Here, the second option used for the hedge portfolio differs from the first option. The option has a different maturity and strike price. Precisely, it uses the maturity date `t2` and the strike price of the option to be hedged multiplied by a constant `s2`.

Mean Variance Hedging

The Mean Variance hedge uses the same hedge procedures as the Δ-hedge and can be incorporated into our framework. We change Equation (10.21) and use

$$\phi(t_i) = \phi^*(t_i).$$

10.4.4 Numerical Examples

For this numerical test we determine the hedge performance of different models. In our first example we simulate trajectories using an NIG model. These trajectories represent the market. In our second example we use real market data for the German DAX index.

Given the simulated NIG trajectories, we consider the NIG, the VG and the Heston model as our pricing model and apply a Δ- as well as a Δ/Γ-hedge strategy.

We fix some maturity T and simulate daily spot values for the underlying. We wish to hedge a European Call option of maturity T_1 with the strike set to the simulated spot price. This means that we only consider ATM options. We repeat the simulation and the hedging `NSim` times and collect the final hedge costs. This leads to the distribution of the hedge costs.

For the NIG model we consider the parameters $\alpha = 5.5222$, $\beta = -3.3131$ and $\delta = 0.1291$. The VG is parametrized by $\sigma = 0.8986$, $\nu = 5.2242$ and $\theta = 12.0033$ and finally the

```
function pf = simulatehedge(data,strategy,pricer)
% initialize parameters
n = strategy.n;
m = strategy.m;
pf.delta = zeros(n,2,m);
pf.gamma = zeros(n,2,m);
pf.weights = zeros(n,2,m);
pf.bank = zeros(n,1,m);
pf.gain = zeros(n,1,m);
pf.value = zeros(n,1,m);
pf.loss = zeros(1,m);
pf.cumgains = zeros(n,1,m);
% simulate asset paths
stockPath = data.path(data.S0,data.t,n,m,data.r);
% ----- hedge procedure
for j=1:m        % m hedges
        i = 1;
        %---- Start Parameter
        dt = data.t/n;               % time steps
        df = exp(-data.r*data.t);     % discount factor 1
        df2 = exp(-data.r*data.t2);   % discount factor 2
        strikePrice = stockPath(1,j);
        strikePrice2 = stockPath(1,j)*strategy.s2;
        %---- Option Value and Hedge Parameters
        [pf.value(i,1,j),pf.delta(i,1,j),pf.gamma(i,1,j)] = ...
            pricer.greeks1(data.t, 0, stockPath(i,j), 0, df, ...
            data.params, strikePrice, 1);
        %---- 2nd Option Value and Hedge Parameters
        [pf.value(i,2,j),pf.delta(i,2,j),pf.gamma(i,2,j)] = ...
            pricer.greeks1(data.t2, 0, stockPath(i,j), 0, df2, ...
            data.params2, strikePrice2, 1);
        %---- Hedgeparameter Portfoliohedge
        [pf.weights(i,2,j), pf.weights(i,1,j)] = weights(pf,i,j);
        pf.bank(i,1,j) = bankaccount(pf,stockPath(:,j),i,j);
    for i = 2:n       % Loop within one hedge
        %---- Option Value and Hedge Parameters
        ttm = data.t-(i-1)*dt;       % time to maturity
        ttm2 = data.t2-(i-1)*dt;     % time to maturity2
        df = exp(-data.r*ttm);
        df2 = exp(-data.r*ttm2);
        [pf.value(i,1,j),pf.delta(i,1,j),~] = pricer.greeks1(ttm, ..
            0, stockPath(i,j), 0, df, data.params, strikePrice, 1);
        %---- 2nd Option Value and Hedge Parameters
        [pf.value(i,2,j),pf.delta(i,2,j),pf.gamma(i,2,j)] = ...
            pricer.greeks1(ttm2, 0, stockPath(i,j), 0, df2, ...
            data.params2, strikePrice2, 1);
        %---- Hedgeparameter Portfoliohedge
        [pf.weights(i,2,j), pf.weights(i,1,j)] = ...
            weights(pf,i,j);
        pf.bank(i,1,j) = bankaccount(pf,stockPath(:,j),i,j);
        %---- Gain and Loss-Process Portfoliohedge
        [pf.gain(i,1,j), pf.cumgains(i,1,j), pf.loss(1,j)] = ...
            hedgecosts(pf,stockPath(:,j),data.r,dt,i,j);
    end
end
end
```

Figure 10.26 Matlab code to simulate a Δ / Γ-hedge for any given model

```
% weights
function [w1, w2] = weights(pf,i,j)
    w1 = pf.gamma(i,1,j)/pf.gamma(i,2,j);
    w2 = pf.delta(i,1,j) - pf.delta(i,2,j)...
                              * pf.weights(i,2,j);
end

% bank account
function bank = bankaccount(pf,stockPath,i,j)
    bank = pf.value(i,1,j) - stockPath(i,1)...
        * pf.weights(i,1,j) - pf.weights(i,2,j) * pf.value(i,2,j);
end
% hedge cost
function [gain,cumgain,loss] = hedgecosts(pf,stockPath,spotRate,dt,i,j)
    gain = pf.weights(i-1,1,j)*(stockPath(i,1)...
        - stockPath(i-1,1)) + pf.weights(i-1,2,j)*(pf.value(i,2,j)...
        -pf.value(i-1,2,j))+ pf.bank(i-1,1,j)*(exp(spotRate*dt)-1);

    cumgain = pf.cumgains(i-1,1,j) + pf.gain(i,1,j);

    loss = pf.value(i,1,j) - pf.value(1,1,j)- pf.cumgains(i,1,j);
end
```

Figure 10.27 Matlab code necessary for calculating weights, bank account value and hedge costs

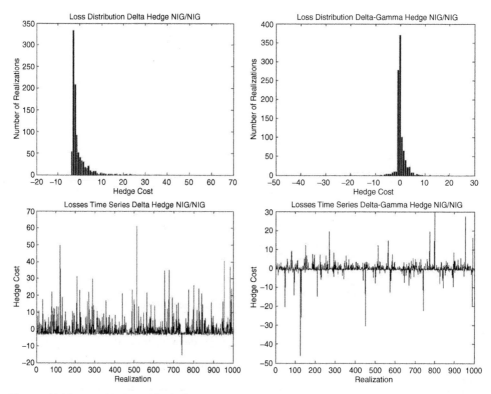

Figure 10.28 Distribution of the hedge costs for a Δ- and a Δ/Γ-hedge where the market is assumed to follow an NIG process and the model is also an NIG model. The top row shows the histograms of the Δ-hedge (top left) and the Δ/Γ-hedge (top right). The corresponding time series data are presented in the bottom line, the Δ-hedge (bottom left) and the Δ/Γ-hedge (bottom right)

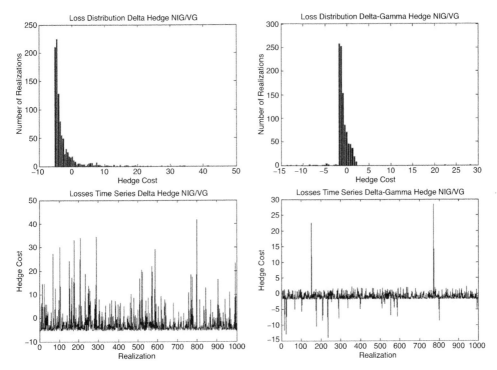

Figure 10.29 Distribution of the hedge costs for a Δ- and a Δ/Γ-hedge where the market is assumed to follow an NIG process and the model is a VG model. The top row shows the histograms of the Δ-hedge (top left) and the Δ/Γ-hedge (top right). The corresponding time series data are presented in the bottom line, the Δ-hedge (bottom left) and the Δ/Γ-hedge (bottom right)

Heston model $V(0) = 0.0150$, $\Theta = 0.0415$, $\kappa = 2.1813$, $\nu = 0.3161$ and $\rho = -0.9351$. In Figures 10.28 to 10.30 the hedge costs are presented as histograms and as a time series. The most striking fact is the bad performance when hedging jumps using a diffusion model, as illustrated in Figure 10.30.

Considering several issues for real market data we present some of the results of Kienitz, J., Wetterau, D. and Wittke, M. (2011). We have taken the time series data, interest rate data and option data for the DAX index starting on 02/01/2006 up to 22/08/2011. Figure 10.31 shows the performance of several hedge strategies.

The hedging performance on real market data shows that the hedging performance of the Black–Scholes model, taking into account the quoted options prices and thus the implied volatility surface, is better than the advanced models for the considered index and time period. Figure 10.32 illustrates the Mean Variance Hedging approach for the NIG and the VG model. This shows that the hedging performance does not increase for these models.

All of these considerations, whether purely model based ones or the real data based ones, show that model risk cannot be neglected when we price and hedge options. The model risk is very relevant for options other than Vanilla options. Since we usually calibrate models to Vanillas the prices are similar but the hedging determines how we risk manage exotic options and determines the profit-and-loss. We observed large differences for pricing and hedging also using different models.

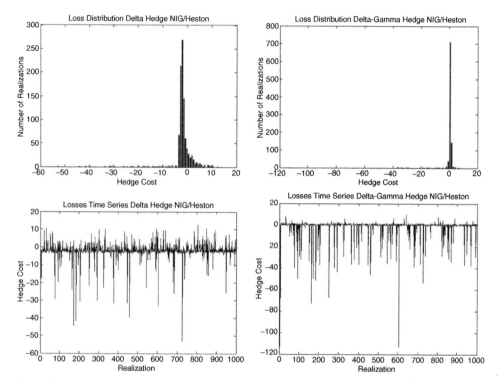

Figure 10.30 Distribution of the hedge costs for a Δ- and a Δ/Γ-hedge where the market is assumed to follow an NIG process and the model is a Heston model. The top row shows the histograms of the Δ-hedge (top left) and the Δ/Γ-hedge (top right). The corresponding time series data are presented in the bottom line, the Δ-hedge (bottom left) and the Δ/Γ-hedge (bottom right)

We consider two different notions of quantifying model risk, discussed in Cont, R. (2006). To this end let us look at different models $\mathcal{M}_i$, $i = 1, \ldots, N$. For the first approach we take $p_1, \ldots, p_N$ for the probability that the model is the correct one. Then, we take as a measure for model risk the weighted squared difference of the option prices $V_{\mathcal{M}_i}$ from the models and the market V_M

$$\sqrt{\sum_{i=1}^{N} p_i (V_{\mathcal{M}_i} - V_M)^2}. \tag{10.22}$$

This approach is called the *Bayesian Model Risk Measure*. Here we face the problem of quantifying p_i, $i = 1, \ldots, N$. If we take $p_i = \frac{1}{2}$, Equation (10.22) is the standard deviation of the option price V within the possible model range.

Another approach that does not need to determine p_i is the *Worst-Case Model Risk Measure*. To this end we take

$$V_{\mathcal{M}_j} - V_{\mathcal{M}_k}, \tag{10.23}$$

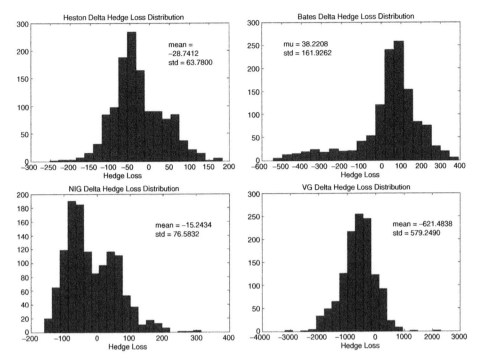

Figure 10.31 Performance of several Δ-hedging strategies on market data for the DAX index (02/01/2006 to 22/08/2011) using the Heston model (top left), the Bates model (top right), the NIG model (bottom left) and the VG model (bottom right)

with

$$\{j \mid i = 1, \ldots, N, V_{\mathcal{M}_j} \geq V_{\mathcal{M}_i}\}$$

$$\{k \mid i = 1, \ldots, N, V_{\mathcal{M}_k} \leq V_{\mathcal{M}_i}\}.$$

This is simply the difference of the highest option price and the lowest of all the models under consideration. This might be an indicator of model risk. We can determine the risk measures using the methods presented in this book.

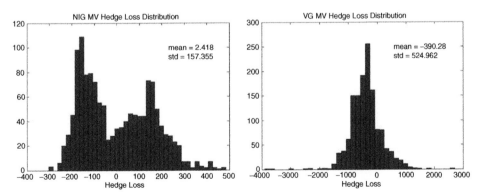

Figure 10.32 Performance of a Mean Variance Hedging strategy on market data for the DAX index 02/01/2006 to 22/08/2011 using the NIG model (left) and the VG model (right)

10.5 SUMMARY AND CONCLUSIONS

In this chapter we considered the issue of model risk. We analysed the model risk involved in calibration, exotic option pricing and hedging. To this end we considered the models we introduced in the first chapters of this book. We applied our numerical methods to derive model parameters from quoted market data. We used option prices for the DAX index.

First, we observed the well-known fact that the calibration error is different for all models, but in a model class the error is comparable. Furthermore, the price of exotic options is significantly different across the model classes.

Then, we considered different hedge strategies. Models incorporating jumps or stochastic volatility do not lead to complete markets, and therefore there is unhedgeable risk. In this case a perfect dynamic hedge cannot be specified in general. We considered different dynamic hedge strategies. The well-known Δ and Δ / Γ strategies were outlined and compared to Mean Variance Hedging. To do this we calculated the profit-and-loss distribution corresponding to the hedge strategy. Finally, we considered discrete time hedging strategies and gave numerical illustration of their performance on real world data.

The methodology developed here was illustrated using Matlab code and can thus be applied to further research into the topics of model risk and calibration. It can serve as the base for other hedge strategies and proprietary methods for hedges and research in this area.

We observed that dynamic hedging is the second-best solution since it involves not only the pricing of the derivative but also the variance of the claim to be hedged. Thus, the final variance of the claim together with the hedge has to be analysed. The realized hedging costs are highly path-dependent and there is a trade-off between re-balancing the hedge and the transaction costs. If possible, we prefer a static hedge, something that is also recommended by Ahn, H. and Wilmott, P. (2008).

Part III

IMPLEMENTATION, SOFTWARE DESIGN AND MATHEMATICS

Matlab – Basics

11.1 INTRODUCTION AND OBJECTIVES

This chapter discusses the basic operations and the syntax of Matlab. To keep the book self-contained we focus on the methods and issues we have applied for our implementations in this book. This chapter consists of eight sections. After some general remarks in Section 11.2 the next section covers matrices and vectors. We use such data structures in all our methods. Both data structures are not only basic building blocks but are also necessary to develop stable and efficient programs.

Another very important aspect is the use of functions and function handles. We elaborate on the usage within Matlab in Section 11.4. We cover the basic usage of functions and conclude with advanced applications of function handles. Mastering functions and function handles is important for advanced coding using Matlab.

Matlab already provides functionality for solving some problems that arise in financial modelling. The additional functionality is put into packages known as toolboxes. The functionality from a toolbox can be used if the user owns a corresponding licence. In Section 11.5 we cover Financial, Financial Derivatives, Portfolio Optimization, Fixed Income, Statistics, Optimization and Global Optimization toolboxes. The first four toolboxes are directly linked to financial modelling and the other three toolboxes can be used to solve calibration problems without programming proprietary optimizers.

Finally, in Sections 11.6 and 11.7 we consider some Matlab built-in functions which we apply in our applications and for plotting. The choice is motivated by what the authors think is mostly convenient for coding financial models and developing pricing applications.

11.2 GENERAL REMARKS

Let us begin with variable names. Variables in Matlab consist of any combination of characters and numbers. The name of the variable has to start with a character. Thus,

```
NPV, NetPresentValue, CGM2SGM, z1 or Z1
```

are allowed whereas

```
@NPV, $NetPresentValue, 2cgm, 1z or 1Z
```

are not allowed. We strongly recommend using names that reflect the value which is represented. Thus, npv should represent the net present value, for instance. Let us give an overview of different types of Matlab data.

Numbers   An integer in Matlab can be represented in different ways. Table 11.1 summarizes the possibilities.

In addition to integers Matlab uses floating point numbers for numerical computations. The double-precision or more simply termed *double numbers* require 64 bits for their

Table 11.1   Types, values and the range in Matlab

Type	Values	Matlab
Signed 8-bit integer	-2^7 to 2^7-1	`int8`
Signed 16-bit integer	-2^{15} to $2^{15}-1$	`int16`
Signed 32-bit integer	-2^{31} to $2^{31}-1$	`int32`
Signed 64-bit integer	-2^{63} to $2^{63}-16$	`int64`
Unsigned 8-bit integer	0 to 2^8-1	`uint8`
Unsigned 16-bit integer	0 to $2^{16}-1$	`uint16`
Unsigned 32-bit integer	0 to $2^{32}-1$	`uint32`
Unsigned 64-bit integer	0 to $2^{64}-1$	`uint64`

representation. Single-precision numbers only need 32 bits for their representation. Complex numbers can be represented by two doubles. We consider complex numbers in a separate section of this chapter.

Two special types are `Inf` and `NaN`. The first represents infinity while the second indicates that the expression is not a number.

The logical data type or Boolean type is either true or false.

Characters and Strings   Often it is necessary to process text. For instance, this is the case when naming columns, specifying labels in a diagram or creating formatted output to illustrate numerical results. Matlab handles text using the type `character`. A character array is called `string`. For instance,

```
>> char1 = 'a';
```

assigns the single character 'a' to the variable `char1` which is of type 1×1 character array. This information can be displayed by using the command

```
>> whos char1
```

We can define another variable `char2` and gather `char1` and `char2` into a new variable `char3` by

```
>> char2 = 'bcde'; char3 = [char1, char2];
```

We transform `int` or other numerical types into strings by using the `int2str` or `num2str`. This is sometimes necessary to include numbers in a string. But it is also possible that a number is input to Matlab as a string. To convert it into the corresponding number we use the function `str2num`. For instance, we find

```
>> num = str2num('900');
```

results in `num` being equal to 900 and `num` is of type `double`.

```
mystruct = struct('field1', values1, 'field2', values2, ...)
mystruct = struct('field1', {}, 'field2', {}, ...)
mystruct = struct
mystruct = struct([])
mystruct = struct(myobj)
```

Figure 11.1 Matlab code for implementing different methods for creating a structure array, `struct`, as displayed by the Matlab documentation

Struct   Let us now consider `struct` data types. A `struct` is a structure array which can be created using the syntax displayed in Figure 11.1.

We use a sequence of entries encoding the name *fieldN* to act as a codifier and map a *valueN* to this codifier. The second method corresponds to creating an empty struct called `mystruct` but all the fields have names corresponding to the codifier *fieldN*. If we wish to create a variable which is of type `struct` but does not hold any other information, we simply use the third or forth command.

Finally, the last variable `mystruct` is a structure array that is identical to the input structure array `myobj`. If the input is not a structure array Matlab does not convert the input but creates a 1 × 1 `struct` with `myobj`. If `myobj` is a class, all class information is lost.

Elements of a `struct` can be accessed in two ways. The most simple and most common way is to access the data by specifying the name of the field. This corresponds to `fieldN` in our example. Another but more complex method is to apply dynamic field names. Such field names are used when creating a structure array or adding data at run-time. Thus, the field is not some predefined name but a name which is generated at run-time, for instance by the counter within a loop or the current date/time. We consider `mystruct=struct` and we wish to dynamically add data to `mystruct`. We have chosen to run a calibration using historical data. We suppose that the date is encoded using a variable called `optdata`. Then, we dynamically specify the corresponding fields by using `mystruct.(DExpression)` = `value`; where `DExpression` is determined at run-time. For the dynamic expression we choose `datestr(optdata, 'mmmddyy')` and then we store the calculated prices at each date into `mystruct` by `mystruct.(datestr(optdata, 'mmmddyy'))` = `price`;. A struct data type is often applied when storing data. For instance, we apply it when we gather information necessary for calibration or optimization. For such financial applications several initial data pieces such as the starting point for the optimization, the objective function we wish to apply or the number of iterations for the optimization algorithm have to be stored.

Matlab Functions and Programming   It is possible to enter Matlab commands directly using the front end of Matlab. This is very convenient for ad hoc calculations or for plotting functions, but more complex issues need to be programmed. To this end Matlab offers the possibility to create user-defined functions and place them into m-files. Furthermore, such files can be used as scripts. Thus, it is possible to execute several commands one after the other or call functions and use the output as input to other functions. The user can also write programs using standard coding methods such as `if...then...else...end`, `for()...end` or `while...loop` methods.

Finally, it is possible to extend the Matlab objects with user-defined objects. The latter is known as *object-oriented programming* and is discussed in the next chapter.

11.3 MATRICES, VECTORS AND CELL ARRAYS

In this section we consider the basic data structures: matrices, vectors and cell arrays.

11.3.1 Matrices and Vectors

Matlab was developed for manipulating and computing with matrices. Thus, Matlab is a shortcut for *matrix laboratory*. The software has been continually upgraded ever since and now offers a wide range of built-in functions, methods and programming facilities. Instead of working with numbers sequentially, Matlab is designed to work with matrices. Since Matlab is a high-performance programming language for matrix computation, it is best to think of arguments and data in terms of a matrix. A matrix in Matlab is a rectangular array of numbers and can, for example, be defined as follows:

```
A = [1 3 -1 4; 2 3 5 0; 0 4 1 7]
```

The matrix A is a 3×4-matrix. By pressing the return button the matrix A will be stored in the Matlab workspace.

```
A =

     1     3    -1     4
     2     3     5     0
     0     4     1     7
```

The same result would be obtained if we entered

```
A = [
        1, 3, -1, 4
        2, 3,  5, 0
        0, 4,  1, 7
    ];
```

In this case the output is suppressed since we used the semicolon at the end of the input.
    The basic conventions of how to define matrices in Matlab can be summed up by

- square brackets [ ] define the start/end of the matrix
- blanks or commas separate row elements
- the end of a row is indicated by a semicolon ''' or a new line.

We call matrices of size $N \times 1$ *vectors*.

Matlab offers functions to assign or retrieve entries of a matrix A. A single value of the matrix of size $N \times M$ is assigned by setting $A(j, k)$ for $j = 1, \ldots, N$ and $k = 1, \ldots, M$. Using, for instance, $j = 3$ and $k = 1$

```
A(3,1) = 0.5*A(1,4)
```

This leads to the matrix A with entries

```
A =
        1        3       -1        4
        2        3        5        0
        2        4        1        7
```

It is also possible to assign more than one entry at once by using the colon operator "`:`".

```
A(1,:)
```

for example returns the first row of A, that is

```
ans =
        1        3       -1        4
```

Whereas by the command

```
A(:,2:end-1)
```

a submatrix is returned. For this example we get

```
ans =
        3       -1
        3        5
        4        1
```

The above example illustrates another feature of matrix assignment in Matlab. A reference to the last element of a row or column is given by the keyword end. Thus, elements can be assigned without having information about the size of the matrix under consideration. Of course, Matlab also offers the possibility to return the size of a matrix A. Let us take an example.

```
[N,M]  = size(A)
N = size(A,1)
M = size(A,2)
```

The first call of function `size()` returns both the number of rows N as well as the number of columns M. If we are interested in the size of a special dimension of matrix A we call `size(A,dim)`. To determine the size of a one-dimensional array we use the function `length()`.

Another option for assigning entries of a matrix are logical operators such as '==', '~=', '>' or '<'. If we wish to divide all elements of matrix A with $A(j, k) > 2$ by 3 the following piece of code can be used:

```
I = A > 2;
A(I) = A(I)/3;
```

The first command returns a binary matrix I which is of the same size as A. The entries of matrix I are: $I(j, k) = 0$ for $A(j, k) \leq 2$ and $I(j, k) = 1$ otherwise.

```
I =
        0       1       0       1
        0       1       1       0
        0       1       0       1
```

This matrix is then used as a special kind of indexation for the matrix A.

Since Matlab is designed for matrix computations almost every operator and function is designed to handle matrices and vectors. In many cases this offers the opportunity to work efficiently without using for-loops or if-statements. To understand this it is necessary to recall some basic facts from linear algebra. It should be clear that the elementary operators '+', '−', '/' and '∗' do not work for matrices if the dimensionality does not coincide. The code

```
A = [1 3 -1 4; 2 3 5 0; 0 4 1 7];
B = [1 3; 5 1; 2 -1; 4 7];
A + B
```

produces the following error message:

```
??? Error using ==> plus
Matrix dimensions must agree.
```

This is the case since A is a 3×4-matrix while B is a 4×2-matrix. The multiplication, given by

```
A * B
```

works well and the result is

```
ans =
        30      35
        27       4
        50      52
```

This is a new matrix of size 3×2. The above example shows that Matlab obeys the standard matrix manipulation rules. For the exponent operator '∧' this has the direct consequence that

```
A^2
```

fails if the matrix A is not an $N \times N$-matrix.

If we wish to add a vector $x \in \mathbb{R}^{N \times 1}$ to each column of a matrix $A \in \mathbb{R}^{N \times M}$ or need to multiply the elements of two matrices A and B componentwise, if they are of the same size Matlab offers an efficient way to program that. In most programming languages the method of choice would be loops. This solution could be performed in Matlab but there exist more sophisticated and efficient ways. The first one is the dot operator '.' which defines componentwise operations and is typically used in combination with the operators '∗', '/' and '∧'. For two matrices A and B of the same size the code

```
A ./ B
```

is used to divide the elements $A(j, k)$ by $B(j, k)$ componentwise for all $j = 1, \ldots, N$ and $k = 1, \ldots, M$. The componentwise square of all entries of matrix A is given by

```
A.^2
```

A second solution for componentwise operations is to use the function `repmat()`, which replicates and tiles arrays. For a given matrix A the function call `B = repmat(A,M,N)` creates a new matrix B consisting of $M \times N$ tiles of copies of A.

Thus, to calculate the sum of vector $x \in \mathbb{R}^{N \times 1}$ and each column of matrix $A \in \mathbb{R}^{N \times M}$ we replicate the vector x M-times. For $x = (0, -2, 5)^\top$ the command

```
xMat = repmat(x,1,4)
```

results in a matrix xMat given by

```
xMat =
     0      0      0      0
    -2     -2     -2     -2
     5      5      5      5
```

The matrix xMat is of the same size as matrix $A \in \mathbb{R}^{3 \times 4}$ and each column is a copy of the vector x. The command

```
xMat + A
```

produces the desired sum without using loops. Since we have defined vectors as matrices of size $N \times 1$ the function `repmat` cannot be directly applied if we wish to add a vector

$y \in \mathbb{R}^{M \times 1}$ to the rows of matrix A. A simple solution to overcome this problem is to work with the transposed matrix $A^{\top}$ and add the vector y to its columns. Here, the transposed matrix $A^{\top}$ is calculated with

```
B = A'
```

This results in the matrix B of size 4×3

```
B =
      1      2      2
      3      3      4
     -1      5      1
      4      0      7
```

So far we have only considered real valued matrices. Now, we also consider matrices with complex entries and we consider the transposition operator. Thus, we need to look at complex numbers in Matlab. A complex number is defined by $x := a + ib$ with $a, b \in \mathbb{R}$ and the imaginary unit $i := \sqrt{-1}$. To display the imaginary unit in Matlab we enter

```
1I
```

which results in

```
ans =
        0 + 1.0000i
```

Other complex numbers can easily be entered in Matlab. For $a, b \in \mathbb{R}$ we set

```
x = a + 1I*b
```

Let us define a complex valued matrix B_c. To this end we multiply a complex scalar with the identity matrix eye(4,3) of the same size as B and add the outcome to the original matrix B by setting

```
complexMat = (1 + 1I*2)*eye(size(B))
Bc = B + complexMat
```

Now, the matrix B_c is a complex valued matrix. The final output looks as follows:

```
complexMat =
   1.0000 + 2.0000i           0                    0
        0             1.0000 + 2.0000i             0
        0                     0            1.0000 + 2.0000i
        0                     0                    0
```

```
Bc =
    2.0000 + 2.0000i    2.0000               2.0000
    3.0000              4.0000 + 2.0000i     4.0000
   -1.0000              5.0000               2.0000 + 2.0000i
    4.0000                   0               7.0000
```

As mentioned above, the transposition operator has to be handled with care in this case. The operation $B_c^\top$ returns

```
ans =
    2.0000 - 2.0000i    3.0000              -1.0000              4.0000
    2.0000              4.0000 - 2.0000i     5.0000                   0
    2.0000              4.0000               2.0000 - 2.0000i     7.0000
```

which is the transposed matrix of B_c. Thus, the complex conjugate of the entries is applied. If we had wanted to obtain the following result:

```
ans =
    2.0000 + 2.0000i    3.0000              -1.0000              4.0000
    2.0000              4.0000 + 2.0000i     5.0000                   0
    2.0000              4.0000               2.0000 + 2.0000i     7.0000
```

we should have used the command

```
conj(Bc')
```

In the previous example we saw that Matlab features a built-in function to create identity matrices. We generated the identity matrix of size $N \times M$ by calling the function eye(N,M). But Matlab offers more functions for special matrices, for instance.

```
zeros(10,3)
ones(4,5)
```

The functions zeros(N,M) and ones(N,M) return matrices of size $N \times M$ with value 0 and 1 respectively for all entries. These functions can, for example, be meaningful in terms of pre-allocating data.

We see below that the function diag() works differently according to its inputs.

```
diag(A)
diag([2; -3; 1; 4])
```

For matrices A the command `diag(A)` returns the vector of diagonal elements of A.

```
ans =
     1
     3
     1
```

For a vector x the command `A = diag(x)` leads to a diagonal matrix A with $A(j,k) = x(j)$ for $j = k$ and $A(j,k) = 0$ otherwise.

```
A =
     2     0     0     0
     0    -3     0     0
     0     0     1     0
     0     0     0     4
```

11.3.2 Cell Arrays

A cell array is a collection of containers called *cells* in which you can store different types of data. We can consider a cell array as a general purpose matrix. Each of the cells in that array can contain data of a different type, size and dimension. Cell arrays have the same restrictions as standard arrays. In particular, they have to be rectangular in shape. This means that all rows must be of the same length. All columns also have to be of the same length and so on for higher dimensions.

We use curly brackets { and } for creating a cell array. Thus, the initialization

```
Array = [1, 2];
CArray = {1,2}
```

creates an array `Array` and a cell array `CArray`. Let us consider another cell array also denoted by `CArray`:

```
CArray = {{Array, 1,2}, {'TestName', '28.05.2011'}};
cellplot(CArray)
```

The command `cellplot(CArray)` displays the structure of `CArray`. The result is displayed in Figure 11.2.

Another function to display the content of a cell array is `celldisp`. This function gives the fine structure of the cell array by displaying every element and not a high-level information.

We can assign values to a cell array by defining it directly, as we have shown. This was carried out when we set up `CArray`. But there is the possibility to assign each element. To this end we set up `CArray` by using

```
CArray{1} = {Array, 1,1};
CArray{2} = {'TestName', '28.05.2011'};
```

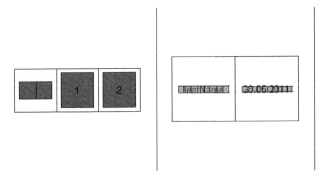

Figure 11.2   Display of the function `cellplot` for the cell array `CArray`

This is also the syntax for accessing the values of a cell array. Suppose we wish to access the cell $(n_1, \ldots, n_d)$ in a cell array `CArray`. We use the syntax `CArrayn{1,2,...,nd}`. If we use non-curly brackets instead we only see the overall structure but we cannot access the elements.

We can pre-allocate empty cell arrays by using the keyword `cell` and the size of the cell array. The command is

```
CArray = cell(2,3,5,3);
```

This creates a four-dimensional cell array of size 2, 3, 5, 3. It is also the most efficient way of pre-allocating a cell array.

A very important cell array is `varargin`. We can use `varargin` to keep the arguments supplied to a function flexible. It is also used to pass values of different types, for instance, a number, a string and a struct. To use a function with flexible arguments we have to define it using the syntax

```
function out = func(x,y,varargin)
...
end
```

Now, we have to account for multiple arguments. Thus, we have to check how many and of which type are the input arguments. To this end we can use something like

```
for i = 1:2:length(varargin)
    switch varargin{i}
        ...
    end
end
```

Another cell array which can be applied to your daily coding is `varargout`. Suppose we wish to plot a graph which can, for instance, be some volatility or yield curve. Usually, we use

```
function plotvol(f,xl,xr,xstep)
    x = xl:xstep:xr;
    y = f(x);
    plot(x,y);
end
```

Sometimes we wish to display the x range and the values y. To do so we can use `varargout`. We use

```
function varargout = plotvol(f,xl,xr,xstep)
    x = xl:xstep:xr;
    y = f(x);
    plot(x,y);
    if (nargout == 2)
        varargout = {x,y}
    elseif (nargout == 1)
        vararggout = {y}
    end
end
```

The latter function allows us to specify which output we wish. Thus, there are three possibilities of calling the function `plotvol`:

```
[x,y] = plotvol(f,xl,xr,xstep);
y = plotvol(f,xl,xr,xstep);
plotvol(f,xl,xr,xstep);
```

11.4   FUNCTIONS AND FUNCTION HANDLES

In this section we consider functions and function handles. Functions are either built-in functions or user-defined functions. A function handle is a pointer to some specific function. Using function handles it is possible to fix certain input parameters. This method can be used for binding functions at run-time.

11.4.1   Functions

This subsection provides a short summary of built-in functions in Matlab. All standard functions such as trigonometric functions or exponentials are available. Furthermore, there are

Table 11.2   Built-in elementary trigonometric functions

Trigonometric	Description
acos	Inverse cosine; result in radians
acosd	Inverse cosine; result in degrees
acosh	Inverse hyperbolic cosine
acot	Inverse cotangent; result in radians
acotd	Inverse cotangent; result in degrees
acoth	Inverse hyperbolic cotangent
acsc	Inverse cosecant; result in radians
acscd	Inverse cosecant; result in degrees
acsch	Inverse hyperbolic cosecant
asec	Inverse secant; result in radians
asecd	Inverse secant; result in degrees
asech	Inverse hyperbolic secant
asin	Inverse sine; result in radians
asind	Inverse sine; result in degrees
asinh	Inverse hyperbolic sine
atan	Inverse tangent; result in radians
atan2	Four-quadrant inverse tangent
atand	Inverse tangent; result in degrees
atanh	Inverse hyperbolic tangent
cos	Cosine of argument in radians
cosd	Cosine of argument in degrees
cosh	Hyperbolic cosine
cot	Cotangent of argument in radians
cotd	Cotangent of argument in degrees
coth	Hyperbolic cotangent
csc	Cosecant of argument in radians
cscd	Cosecant of argument in degrees
csch	Hyperbolic cosecant
hypot	Square root of sum of squares
sec	Secant of argument in radians
secd	Secant of argument in degrees
sech	Hyperbolic secant
sin	Sine of argument in radians
sind	Sine of argument in degrees
sinh	Hyperbolic sine of argument in radians
tan	Tangent of argument in radians
tand	Tangent of argument in degrees
tanh	Hyperbolic tangent

several functions for manipulating complex numbers, special functions or numerical integration, for instance.

Elementary Functions   Matlab has many built-in elementary functions. We list elementary trigonometrix, exponential functions for computing with complex numbers and other elementary functions in Tables 11.2 to 11.5.

Special Functions   We employed built-in special functions in Matlab when considering the SABR model, for instance. These functions are summarized in Table 11.6.

Table 11.3   Built-in elementary exponential functions

Exponential	Description
exp	Exponential
expm1	Compute exp(x)-1 accurately for small values of x
log	Natural logarithm
log10	Common (base 10) logarithm
log1p	Compute log(1+x) accurately for small values of x
log2	Base 2 logarithm and dissect floating-point numbers into exponent and mantissa
nextpow2	Next higher power of 2
nthroot	Real nth root of real numbers
pow2	Base 2 power and scale floating-point numbers
power	Array power
reallog	Natural logarithm for nonnegative real arrays
realpow	Array power for real-only output
realsqrt	Square root for nonnegative real arrays
sqrt	Square root

Table 11.4   Built-in functions for handling complex numbers in Matlab

Complex	Description
abs	Absolute value and complex magnitude
angle	Phase
anglecomplex	Construct complex data from real and imaginary components
conj	Complex conjugate
cplxpair	Sort complex numbers into complex conjugate pairs
i	Imaginary unit
imag	Imaginary part of complex number
isreal	Check if input is real array
j	Imaginary unit
real	Real part of complex number
sign	Signum function
unwrap	Correct phase angles to produce smoother phase plots

Table 11.5   Built-in elementary functions for rounding and remainder calculation

Rounding and Remainder	Description
ceil	Round towards positive infinity
fix	Round towards zero
floor	Round towards negative infinity
idivide	Integer division with rounding option
mod	Modulus after division
rem	Remainder after division
round	Round to nearest integer

Table 11.6 A list of special functions in Matlab. This list is the same as the output in the Matlab documentation

Special Function	Description
airy	Airy functions
besselh	Bessel function of third kind (Hankel function)
besseli	Modified Bessel function of first kind
besselj	Bessel function of first kind
besselk	Modified Bessel function of second kind
bessely	Bessel function of second kind
beta	Beta function
betainc	Incomplete beta function
betaincinv	Beta inverse cumulative distribution function
betaln	Logarithm of beta function
ellipj	Jacobi elliptic functions
ellipke	Complete elliptic integrals of first and second kind
erf	Error function
erfc	Complementary error function
erfcinv	Inverse complementary error function
erfcx	Scaled complementary error function
erfinv	Inverse error function
expint	Exponential integral
gamma	Gamma function
gammainc	Incomplete gamma function
gammaincinv	Inverse incomplete gamma function
gammaln	Logarithm of gamma function
legendre	Associated Legendre functions

11.4.2   Function Handles

Apart from classes Matlab typically distinguishes between two types of M-files. A *script m-file* is a collection of commands which Matlab simply executes one after another when we call the script. No input arguments are passed to the script, nor are outputs returned. Scripts can access existing workspace data or create new variables which are valid in the current workspace until they are deleted. Functions, called *function m-files*, specify the name of a function which can take input arguments and return output arguments. Variables defined within a function are *local* and invisible for access from outside the function. Function m-files start with the keyword `function`. Furthermore, the first line defines both the name of the function and the number of input and output arguments. By way of illustration let us define the function myAdd.

```
function y = myAdd(A,B)
%    myAdd(A,B) componentwise sum of matrices A and B
%- - - - - - - - - - - - - - - - - - - - - - - - - - -
%    Input: matrices A,B of size N x M
%    Output: A + B
%- - - - - - - - - - - - - - - - - - - - - - - - - - -
```

```
[N,M]  =  size(A);
if N == size(B,1) && M == size(B,2)
    y = A + B;
else
    error('Matrix dimensions must agree')
end
```

The function's name is myAdd and should coincide with the name of the m-file called myAdd. The function expects two input arguments *A* and *B*. It returns one output argument *y*. The first five lines are comments and contain information about the function. These comments are displayed if we enter

```
help myAdd
```

The rest of the file defines the algorithm and thus executable code. The function myAdd can easily be executed by entering

```
myAdd(A,B)
```

Another possibility to invoke functions is the feval() statement. feval(f,x_1,...,x_n) evaluates the specified function, f, for the given arguments, $x_1, \ldots, x_n$. Therefore, the function, myAdd, can also be executed by using

```
feval('myAdd',A,B)
```

A function is specified by its name, which is a string. Instead of working with a string it is also possible to use function handles. A function handle in Matlab is constructed by using the @ sign in front of the function's name. We create a function handle for myAdd by using the syntax

```
fhandle = @myAdd;
```

The function handle fhandle can be seen as a reference to the function myAdd. Therefore, the function myAdd can now be called by means of its handle. The syntax is

```
fhandle(A,B)
```

As already mentioned, the function handle fhandle can also be passed to the function feval() to evaluate myAdd by using

```
feval(fhandle,A,B)
```

Function handles can reference any user-defined function as well as Matlab built-in functions. This allows us to use functions as input arguments to other functions. For illustration purposes let us define the following function:

```
function y = evalFhandle(fhandle,varargin)
y = fhandle(varargin{:})
```

The function `evalFhandle` has two input arguments. The first one is a function handle `fhandle` which is a reference to another function. For the second input argument we use the Matlab keyword `varargin` since it is not known in advance how many input arguments the referenced function needs. The Matlab keyword `varargin` allows for an input argument list of variable length. For instance, let us assume the function handle `fhandle` is given by

```
fhandle = @max;
```

Then, the variable argument list could be of length one, two or three dependent on the programmer's needs. While the command

```
evalFhandle(fhandle,A)
```

returns a row array containing the maximum elements taken from each column of matrix A, the maximum row elements are given by

```
evalFhandle(fhandle,A,[],2)
```

The function call

```
evalFhandle(fhandle,A,B)
```

instead returns an array of the same size as A and B with the componentwise largest elements taken from A or B. This shows that `evalFhandle` is nothing other than a user-defined version of `feval()`.

Function Handles and Cell Arrays   In Chapter 8 we solved the problem of passing basis functions used for regression into a function. We did not wish to specify directly how many basis functions we supplied. To this end we needed some object which could not only store function handles but also had some functionality to get the number of elements of data. To this end we used the code in Figures 11.3 and 11.4 which is for the functions 1, x and x^2.

```
B = @(x) {{ones(length(x),1) x x.^2}};
```

Figure 11.3   Matlab implementation of the basis functions applied for calculating the Monte Carlo value of a Bermudan option using the Longstaff–Schwarz method

```
Acell = B(s);                 % eval basis function in cell array B
A = cell2mat(Acell{:,:});     % convert to matrix
```

Figure 11.4   Matlab implementation of the evaluation of basis functions and conversion of a cell array to a matrix

The type B is now a cell array and each element stores a function handle to the specific function $1, x$ or x^2. Furthermore, we used the fact that for some index s it is possible to evaluate all the functions in B. The outcome is again a cell array. To work with a cell array as a matrix the function cell2mat transforms the cell array to a matrix.

11.5   TOOLBOXES

The functionality of Matlab can be extended by toolboxes. We consider some of these extensions in this section.

11.5.1   Financial

The Financial Toolbox provides many useful functions to be applied by a financial engineer, in particular the mathematical and statistical analysis of financial data. For instance, we compute prices and yields of securities. For derivatives, we perform sensitivity analysis and create hedging strategies. Matlab already provides the common market conventions for accounting and is able to adjust business days. For portfolios we can apply the toolbox functionality to measure covariances, control risk and identify optimal allocations under the Markowitz mean-variance approach. The results from the optimization can be illustrated in terms of mean-variance efficient frontier plots or surfaces of portfolio weights under different levels of risk aversion. To visualize and analyse financial time series data the toolbox offers a variety of charting functions, including *Bollinger bands*, *candlestick charts* and *moving-average plots*. The toolbox also provides a wide range of functions to analyse the term-structure of interest rates and model fixed-income securities.

Since a discussion of the full functionality is beyond the scope of this book, we restrict ourselves to some helpful functions when dealing with financial derivatives. For further applications we refer readers to the documentation.

Market prices of European Call and Put options can be quoted in terms of the implied Black–Scholes volatility σ_{BS}. To transform the volatilities into prices we use the Matlab built-in implementation of the Black–Scholes formula, blsprice. For a given spot price S, strike K, interest rate r, time to maturity T, volatility v and dividend yield d the function is called by the command

```
[c,p] = blsprice(S,K,r,T,v,d)
```

It is also possible to compute the implied volatility given the other parameters and the price of the option. For a given vector/matrix of option values V with known input parameters $S, K,$

r, d and T the implied Black–Scholes volatility surface can be calculated by

```
vol = blsimpv(S,K,r,T,V,d)
```

We did not set the input after V since it is used to determine the accuracy of the zero search procedure. If we do not specify a value Matlab takes the standard value. Additional to the prices and implied volatilities of European Call and Put options are built-in functions for calculating the hedge sensitivities:

```
% Delta: sensitivity of option value with respect to S
[cD,pD] = blsdelta(S,K,r,T,v,d)
% Gamma: sensitivity of Delta with respect to S
cpG = blsgamma(S,K,r,T,v,d)
% Rho: sensitivity of option value with respect to r
[cR,pR] = blsrho(S,K,r,T,v,d)
% Theta: sensitivity of option value with respect to T
[cT,pT] = blstheta(S,K,r,T,v,d)
% Vega: sensitivity of option value with respect to v
cpV = blsvega(S,K,r,T,v,d)
```

11.5.2 Financial Derivatives

The Financial Derivatives Toolbox provides functionality to analyse derivative securities and portfolios containing several types of fixed-income and equity-based financial instruments. The toolbox supports the following interest-rate derivatives: bonds, bond options (Puts and Calls), caps, fixed-rate notes, floating-rate notes, floors, swaps, swaptions and callable and puttable bonds. For equity, Asian, Barrier, Compound, Lookback and Vanilla stock options (Put and Call options) can be priced and analysed. The toolbox also implements algorithms to calculate prices and sensitivities for these instruments using trees and interest-rate tree based implementations of pricing models.

11.5.3 Fixed-Income

The Fixed-Income Toolbox provides functions to model and analyse the term structure of fixed-income securities. The fitting of yield curves to market data can be achieved using parametric fitting models or bootstrapping. Prices, rates and sensitivities of many different fixed-income securities, including swaps, credit default swaps, bond futures and convertible bonds, can be calculated. Furthermore, tools to determine prices, yields and cash flows for mortgage-backed securities, corporate bonds, treasury bonds, municipal bonds, certificates of deposit and treasury bills are included.

In Chapter 2, Subsection 2.2.2 we introduced the Hull–White dynamic to model the *short rate*. The corresponding SDE is Equation (2.13). The model replaces the constant risk free rate r by a mean reverting Ornstein–Uhlenbeck process. The model parameters are chosen to match the initial term structure of market interest rates. Considering the characteristic function `cf_hullwhite` given in Figure 2.5, the initial term structure is represented by the input argument `ircurve`. The variable is an object of the class `@IRDataCurve`. The class is used

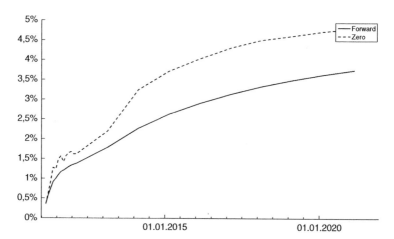

Figure 11.5   Bootstrapped zero and forward interest rates from the implemented function bootstrap

to construct an interest-rate curve object from dates and data. For instance, we generate a discount curve irdc by the following syntax:

```
data = [1.0000 0.9759 0.9535 0.9325 0.9129 0.8944 0.8771 ...
                  0.8607 0.8452 0.8305 0.8165 0.8032 0.7906]';
dates = daysadd(today,[0 30:30:360],5);
irdc = IRDataCurve('Discount',today,dates,data)
```

The corresponding output is as follows:

```
irdc =
 IRDataCurve
  Type: Discount
    Settle: 734888 (20-Jan-2012)
   Compounding: 2
 Basis: 0 (actual/actual)
  InterpMethod: linear
 Dates: [13x1 double]
  Data: [13x1 double]
```

The first property, Type, of IRDataCurve is the type of the interest-rate curve under consideration. The curve object supports these types: Forward, Zero and Discount. The property, Settle, specifies the settlement date of the securities corresponding to the given interest rate data and dates. The scalar values Compounding and Basis determine the compounding frequency per year and the day-count basis for IRDataCurve. The default values are for semi-annual compounding and 'actual/actual day-counting'. The property InterpMethod specifies how intermediate values are interpolated.

From an existing `IRDataCurve` curve object we determine the forward rates, zero rates and discount factors for different input dates by using the functions `getForwardRates`, `getZeroRates` and `getDiscountFactors`.

To construct an interest-rate curve object from market data the class `@IRDataCurve` offers the function `bootstrap`. For instance, the zero rate curve and forward rate curve given in Figure 11.5 is bootstrapped from par rates of deposit and par swap rates using the following piece of code:

```
dates = [datenum(2011,02,21) datenum(2011,03,18) datenum(2011,04,18) ...
         datenum(2011,05,18) datenum(2011,06,20) datenum(2011,07,18) ...
         datenum(2011,08,18) datenum(2011,09,19) datenum(2011,10,18) ...
         datenum(2011,11,18) datenum(2011,12,19) datenum(2012,01,18) ...
         datenum(2012,02,20) datenum(2013,02,18) datenum(2014,02,18) ...
         datenum(2015,02,18) datenum(2016,02,18) datenum(2017,02,20) ...
         datenum(2018,02,19) datenum(2019,02,18) datenum(2020,02,18) ...
         datenum(2021,02,18)]';
rates = [0.349 0.542 0.729 0.903 0.987 1.072 1.153 1.190 1.233 1.278 ...
         1.317 1.343 1.367 1.791 2.263 2.609 2.874 3.094 3.272 3.416 ...
         3.538 3.642]'/100;
InstrumentTypes = {'Deposit';'Deposit';'Deposit';'Deposit';...
                   'Deposit';'Deposit';'Deposit';'Deposit';...
                   'Deposit';'Deposit';'Deposit';'Deposit';...
                   'Deposit';'Swap';'Swap';'Swap';'Swap';...
                   'Swap';'Swap';'Swap';'Swap';'Swap'};
settle = datenum(2011,02,16);
Instruments = [repmat(settle,length(dates),1),dates,rates];
bootcurve = IRDataCurve.bootstrap('Zero', settle, ...
    InstrumentTypes, Instruments,'InterpMethod','pchip');
zeroRates = bootcurve.getZeroRates(dates);
fwdRates = bootcurve.getForwardRates(dates);
```

For further information on the Fixed-Income Toolbox, its classes and object oriented programming we refer readers to the documentation and to Chapter 12.

11.5.4   Optimization

The Optimization Toolbox provides implementations of common algorithms for standard and large-scale optimization problems. The toolbox is capable of solving continuous and discrete problems with and without constraints. Methods for linear and quadratic programming, binary integer programming, non-linear optimization, non-linear least squares curve fitting, systems of non-linear equations and multiobjective optimization are included.

Apart from problem and optimizer specific arguments the Matlab optimization functions can be called by the following general syntax:

```
[x,fval,exitflag,output] = functionName(fun,x0,options)
```

The input argument x0 is an initial guess of the parameters and fun is a function handle to the objective function we wish to minimize. The argument options is a struct. The entries of the struct variable are used to manipulate default parameters of the algorithm, for instance MaxIter is used to set the maximum number of iterations. The output argument x is the estimated solution and fval its objective function value at x. The output parameter exitflag is an integer value identifying the termination criterion. The struct output contains several pieces of algorithmic information. For example, the number of iterations taken or the number of function evaluations. We do not try to provide a list of all possible settings. The Matlab documentation should be considered for all options.

Unconstrained Optimization

Let f be a function given by

$$f : \mathbb{R}^n \to \mathbb{R}. \tag{11.1}$$

Optimizers for unconstrained minimization problems attempt to solve

$$\min_{x \in \mathbb{R}^n} f(x).$$

For these kinds of problems the optimization toolbox provides the functions fminunc and fminsearch.

FMINUNC The function fminunc is a gradient-based optimizer. The large-scale mode implements a subspace trust-region method based on the interior-reflective Newton method proposed in Coleman, T. and Li, Y. (1996). If the Hessian matrix is not supplied by the user it is approximated using sparse finite differences. The medium-scale mode implements a quasi-Newton method with cubic line search procedure. The user can choose between the BFGS update of the Hessian matrix (for example in Shanno, D.F. (1970)), the DFP update on its inverse (for example in Fletcher, R. (1980)) or the method of steepest descent. We call the additional function fminunc by

```
[x,fval,exitflag,output,grad,hessian] = fminunc(fun,x0,options)
```

Additional output arguments grad and hessian represent the gradient and the Hessian matrix at the solution x.

FMINSEARCH This function aims to find a minimum of the unconstrained optimization problem above using the Nelder–Mead simplex search method of Lagarias, J.C., Reeds, J.A., Wright, M.H. and Wright, P.E. (1998). The method belongs to the class of direct search methods. Such methods do not require any numerical or analytic gradient information to identify a minimum solution.

Constrained Optimization

Let f be given by Equation (11.1). Solvers for constrained optimization problems attempt to find a solution to

$$\min_{x \in \mathcal{X}} f(x).$$

The set $\mathcal{X}$ presents the admissible domain of parameters x and is a subset of $\mathbb{R}^n$. The constraints defining the admissible domain are separated by considering

- Bound constraints: $lb_i \leq x_i \leq ub_i$ for $i = 1, \ldots, n$
- Linear constraints: $Ax \leq b$ and $A_{eq}x = b_{eq}$ with matrices $A \in \mathbb{R}^{q \times n}$, $A_{eq} \in \mathbb{R}^{p \times n}$ and vectors $b \in \mathbb{R}^q$, $b_{eq} \in \mathbb{R}^p$
- Non-linear constraints: $g_i(x) \leq 0$ and $h_j(x) = 0$ with $g_i, h_j : \mathbb{R}^n \to \mathbb{R}$ for $i = 1, \ldots, r$ and $j = 1, \ldots, s$.

FMINBND   The function `fminbnd` is designed to find a minimum of a continuous one-dimensional function $f : \mathbb{R} \to \mathbb{R}$ on a fixed interval $I := \{x \in \mathbb{R} | lb \leq x \leq ub\}$. The method is based on the golden section search, considered, for instance, in Brent, R.P. (1973), and on parabolic interpolation. In contrast to an initial guess `x0`, the user has to define the lower and upper bounds `lb` and `ub` of the considered interval. The function `fminbnd` is evaluated using the command

```
x = fminbnd(fun,lb,ub,options)
```

LSQNONLIN   This function solves nonlinear least-squares curve fitting problems by applying the Levenberg–Marquardt method or by a trust-region-reflective algorithm based on Coleman, T. and Li, Y. (1996). Considering the trust-region-reflective algorithm the function `lsqnonlin` can handle simple bound constraints on the parameters. The syntax to call the function `lsqnonlin` considering any input and output argument is given by

```
[x,resnorm,residual,exitflag,output,lambda,jacobian] = ...
                              lsqnonlin(fun,x0,lb,ub,options)
```

The output arguments `residual`, `jacobian` and `resnorm` store the vector of function values `fun(x)`, the Jacobian matrix and the squared norm `sum(fun(x).^2)` evaluated at x. The output argument `lambda` holds the Lagrange multipliers at x. This is subject to the bound constraints `lb` and `ub`. The bound constraints are vectors of length n defining the lower and the upper bounds $lb_i \leq x_i \leq ub_i$ for $i = 1, \ldots, n$.

LSQLIN   This function solves the linear least-squares problem

$$\min_{x \in \mathcal{X}} \frac{1}{2}\|B \cdot x - d\|_2^2 \qquad B \in \mathbb{R}^{m \times n}, d \in \mathbb{R}^m.$$

The method handles linear constraints and bound constraints on the parameters. The large-scale model once again uses a subspace trust-region method in combination with preconditioned conjugate gradients. The large-scale method can only be considered when the matrix C has at least as many rows as columns and only bound constraints are defined. In the presence of linear constraints the solution is based on an active set method similar to the one given in Gill, P., Murray, W. and Wright, M. (1981) applying function `quadprog`.

```
x = lsqlin(B,d,A,b,Aeq,beq,lb,ub,x0,options)
```

Instead of a function handle `fun` pointing to the function $f(x) = Bx - d$ the input arguments `B` and `d` define f implicitly. The input arguments `A`, `b`, `Aeq` and `beq` present the matrices and vectors defining the linear constraints $Ax \leq b$ and $A_{eq}x = b_{eq}$. The lower and upper bounds are given by `lb` and `ub`. A value `lb(i) = -Inf` or `ub(i) = Inf` determines that the i-th component is unbounded from below or from above. If any type of constraint does not exist the argument is replaced by an empty array `[]`. The list of output arguments of function `lsqlin` is equal to that of `lsqnonlin`.

FMINCON   The function `fmincon` is applied to solve constrained optimization problems for bound, linear and non-linear constraints. It is applicable when the objective f and the constraints g and h are twice differentiable. Function `fmincon` can only be applied if constraints are specified. Using the command `fmincon(fun,x0,A,b)` only linear inequality constraints are considered. If bounds and non-linear constraints are specified we use the syntax `fmincon(fun,x0,[],[],[],[],lb,ub,nonlcon)`. An optimization problem with any kind of constraint can be solved by using the command

```
x = fmincon(fun,x0,A,b,Aeq,beq,lb,ub,nonlcon,options,p1,p2,...)
```

The input arguments `A`, `b`, `Aeq` and `beq` are the linear constraints. The arrays `lb` and `ub` are the lower and upper bounds respectively. The function handle argument `nonlcon` points to the non-linear constraints function. This function is required to be of the structure given by

```
function [g,h] = nonlcon(x,p1,p2,...)
% g_i(x) <= 0, i = 1,...,m
g = ...;
% h_j(x) = 0, j = 1,...,p
h = ...;
```

If either g or h of the output arguments is set to `[]` the function `fmincon` does not take into account the corresponding type of constraints. By default the constrained problem is solved by applying a trust-region-reflective algorithm applied to the Lagrange function. Thus, the function `fmincon` provides a specific list of output arguments.

```
[x,fval,exitflag,output,lambda,grad,hessian] = fmincon(...)
```

The output arguments `lambda`, `grad` and `hessian` contain the Lagrange multipliers, the gradient and the approximation to the Hessian matrix at the proposed solution. Alternatively, applying the trust-region-reflective method one of the following algorithms can be used:

- Interior-point method.
- SQP-algorithm.
- Active-set method.

The algorithm is selected by using the command `optimset`. For instance, to use the SQP algorithm we set

```
options = optimset('Algorithm','sqp')
```

and then pass `options` to the function `fmincon`.

11.5.5 Global Optimization

The Global Optimization Toolbox provides algorithms for finding the global minimum of a function in the presence of multiple local minima. Multistart methods, global and pattern search, genetic algorithm and simulated annealing solvers are implemented. The genetic algorithm and pattern search solvers can be customized by the user, for instance by modifying fitness scaling options or by defining polling functions. The global optimizers can be applied to unconstrained as well as constrained optimization problems. The objective or constraints function can be continuous, discontinuous or stochastic.

Genetic Algorithm   The Global Optimization Toolbox provides the functions `ga` and `gamultiobj` to identify the minimum of a single and multi-component objective function by using genetic algorithms. In Section 9.6 we described a special genetic algorithm called Differential Evolution. In general, a genetic algorithm is a random search method that is built on Darwin's evolutionary theory. The fitness level of the individuals in a population over several generations is improved by inheritance, mutation, selection and crossover. The genetic algorithms implemented in Matlab are based on Goldberg, D. (1989), Conn, A., Gould, N. and Toint, P. (1991), Conn, A., Gould, N. and Toint, P. (1997) and Deb, K. (2001). To solve an unconstrained problem the function `ga` is called by using the command `x = ga(fitnessfcn,nvars)`. The input arguments `fitnessfcn` and `nvars` define the fitness function and the problem dimension. The function `ga` can handle constraints of any kind. A constrained problem with bound, linear and non-linear constraints can be solved by the command

```
x = ga(fitnessfcn,nvars,A,b,Aeq,beq,LB,UB,nonlcon,options)
```

The struct `options` allows us to manipulate any algorithmic parameter. A complete list of available parameters is generated by calling `gaoptimset`. The complete output list of function `ga` is given by

```
[x,fval,exitflag,output,population,score] = ga(...)
```

The struct `output` returns information such as the number of generations and a message describing the state of the optimizer. This message, for instance, gives the user an indication of which termination criterion is fulfilled. To be able to reproduce the results, the state of the random generator , just before the algorithms is started, is stored in the field `output.rngstate`. The output arguments `population` and `score` hold the final population and its value at termination. Function `gamultiobj` supports the same functionalities and optional parameters as `ga` but for a multi-component fitness function.

Simulated Annealing   The function `simlannealbnd` attempts to find the global minimum of an unconstrained or bound constrained objective function of several variables using a Simulated Annealing algorithm. Matlab's implementation of the simulated annealing algorithm is adapted from Ingber, L. (1995). In Section 9.7 we described a general Simulated Annealing algorithm and gave examples of how to apply the function `simlannealbnd` to a bound-constrained optimization problem.

11.5.6   Statistics

We do not cover all functions and methods provided by the Statistics Toolbox; for our purposes it is sufficient to consider the basics for handling probability distributions and random number generation.

Probability Distributions

When working with probability distributions we are interested in calculating values from the probability density, the cumulative distribution and we wish to determine quantiles. The general way of dealing with that issue in Matlab is by calling a function which is constructed as follows.

The first part of the function's name refers to the distribution while the second part refers to the quantity in which we are interested. Let *probdistname* represent the name of the distribution and *probdistmethod* refer to the value we wish to calculate. Then, the general name would be

```
probdistnameprobdistmethod(.)
```

Possible values for *probdistname* are given in Table 11.7.

The possible applications of *probdistmethod* are summarized in Table 11.8.

Table 11.7   Some distributions which are supported by the Statistics Toolbox of Matlab. All distributions can be found in Matlab's documentation

probdistname	Description
norm	normal distribution
logn	log-normal distribution
chi2	central χ^2-distibution
ncx2	non-central χ^2-distribution
gam	gamma distribution
poiss	Poisson distribution
beta	beta distribution
exp	exponential distribution
t	student *t*-distribution
nct	non-central *t*-distribution

Table 11.8 Methods for handling distributions provided by the Statistics Toolbox of Matlab

probdistmethod	Description
pdf	Probability density functions
cdf	Cumulative distribution functions
inv	Inverse cumulative distribution functions
stat	Distribution statistics functions
fit	Distribution fitting functions
like	Negative log-likelihood functions
rnd	Random number generators

For instance, for the normal distribution we have *probdistname*=norm and if we are interested in obtaining a value from the density we would use

```
normpdf(x)
```

The latter syntax highlights another aspect. We have to provide information about the distribution. For the example we can call the function normpdf in different ways:

```
normpdf(x)
normpdf(x,m)
normpdf(x,m,s)
```

The first call simply gives the function value of the density of the standard normal distribution at x. The second leads to a value from the normal density with mean m and standard deviation 1. The final call gives the value of a normal distribution with mean m and standard deviation s at x.

Thus, if we do not wish to use the standard parameterization from Matlab we have to specify the distributional parameters. For the possible parameters and the distributions we refer readers to Matlab's documentation.

Random Number Generation

Another important point is the generation of variates due to a given distribution. Here, we wish to illustrate how to use Matlab functionality to generate pseudo as well as quasi random numbers.

Pseudo Random Numbers   If we wish to generate uniform random numbers we can generate a stream. We have the possibility to choose several parameters that determine this stream. The general syntax is

```
[s1,s2,...,sn]=RandStream.create('gentype','NumStreams',n,'Seed', s)
```

Table 11.9   List of uniform random number generators that Matlab provides

'gentype'	Name	Streams > 1	Period
mt19937ar	Mersenne twister (default)	No	$2^{19936} - 1$
mcg16807	Multiplicative congruential	No	$2^{30} - 1$
mlfg6331_64	Multiplicative lagged Fibonacci	Yes	2^{124}
mrg32k3a	Combined multiple recursive	Yes	2^{127}
shr3	congShift-register + with linear cong.	No	2^{64}
swb2712	Modified subtract with borrow	No	2^{1492}

The string 'gentype' determines which method Matlab applies for generating uniform random numbers. Table 11.9 summarizes all possibilities. Moreover, we can sometimes generate several streams s1, ..., sn. The number of streams is determined by the integer n for the property 'NumStreams'.

A very useful setting especially for testing numerical schemes in Monte Carlo simulation is the property 'Seed'. The integer value determines where the random sequence starts and thus setting the seed to a predefined value guarantees that we use the same random numbers. Another useful property is 'CellOutputLogical'. We have to specify if this property is true or false. When true the output is a cell array but the default setting is to false.

The output, uniform random numbers, is transformed into variates from a given distribution. However, Matlab provides functionality to generate random numbers due to a given distribution by using the standard random stream called *GlobalStream*. We have already outlined the syntax for using such methods in Chapter 9.

Quasi Random Numbers   For quasi random numbers the syntax is similar. We generate a stream using the function

```
qstr = qrandstream(qrsequence, d, 'Skip', s, 'Leap', l, 'Scram-
bling', sc)
```

This is the general syntax for setting up a quasi random number stream. We have to specify values for qrsequence, N, s, l and sc. The first variable refers to the quasi random sequence we wish to apply. We have three choices: we can choose either 'halton' (Halton), 'lhs-design' (Latin Hypercube) or 'sobol' (Sobol) here. The variable d is an integer value and specifies the dimensionality of the stream. The property 'Scrambling' refers to the possibility to assign a shuffling or scrambling method to the original quasi random number sequence. Finally, the integer values s and l for the properties 'Skip' and 'Leap' specify that we start the stream at the s-th number of the sequence and then we take only every l-th element from the original sequence.

Having initialized a quasi random number stream using

```
mystream = qrandstream('sobol',4,'Skip',46,'Leap',23);
```

for instance, we use the function qrand(q,N) with the created stream q and the number of points N we wish to generate. Thus, applying the function to the stream mystream and creating 100 points we can use

```
myqrn = qrand(mystream,100);
```

We could also use quasi random numbers by creating quasi random number sets using the functions `haltonset` and `sobolset`. With these functions it is possible to directly initialize a set of quasi random numbers. The initialization is similar to `qrandstream` and we provide it for Sobol numbers here.

```
mysobolset = sobolset(d,'Skip',s,'Leap', 1, 'Scramble', sc);
```

Now, to generate N Sobol numbers we have to use the function `net(q,N)`. The syntax for generating 100 numbers from the set `mysobolset` is

```
mysobol = net(mysobolset,100);
```

11.5.7 Portfolio Optimization

In addition to general optimization problems we need to examine a special class of optimization problems which arises in portfolio selection and portfolio optimization.

QUADPROG The function `quadprog` is designed to solve quadratic programming problems of the form

$$\min_{x} \ f(x) := \tfrac{1}{2}x^\top Hx + c^\top x$$
$$\text{subject to} \quad Ax \le b$$
$$A_{eq}x = b_{eq}$$
$$lb \le x \le ub$$

H is an $n \times n$ symmetric matrix, $c \in \mathbb{R}^n$ is a vector and A, A_{eq}, b, b_{eq}, lb and ub define the linear constraints and bounds. In Chapter 9, Section 9.5 we have already solved a quadratic problem which was the key part of the SQP algorithm for non-linear constrained optimization. There, we pointed out that function f is strict convex if the matrix H is positive definite. In this case any admissible solution x of the quadratic problem is already a unique global minimizer of f. If the matrix H equals zero, the quadratic programming problem reduces to a linear one. Despite the fact that `quadprog` also works for such problems, Matlab offers the specific function `linprog` for linear programming.

To familiarize readers with the usage of `quadprog` let us examine a quadratic programming problem. This arises when considering Markowitz mean-variance portfolio selection theory (see Markowitz, H. (1952)). A portfolio P consisting of N risky assets is given and we denote by $R_P(t)$ rate of return at time t. The rate of return is given by

$$R_P(t) := \sum_{i=1}^{N} w_i R_i(t), \quad \sum_{i=1}^{N} w_i = 1,$$

with $w = (w_1, \ldots, w_N)^\top$ being a vector of portfolio weights and the linear rate of return

$$R_i(t) := \frac{A_i(t) - A_i(t-1)}{A_i(t-1)}, \quad \text{for} \quad i = 1, \ldots, N \tag{11.2}$$

of asset A_i from time $t-1$ to t. Since the investment horizon is a date in the future, the rates of return $R_i(t+1)$ are random variables. The future outcome of the portfolio is measured by means of the expected rate of return

$$\mu_P = E[R_P] = \sum_{i=1}^{N} w_i E[R_i]$$

and its uncertainty by means of the expected variance of the portfolio given by

$$\sigma_P^2 := E[(R_P - \mu_P)^2] = \sum_{i=1}^{N}\sum_{j=1}^{N} w_i w_j Cov[R_i, R_j] = \sum_{i=1}^{N} \cdot \sum_{j=1}^{N} w_i w_j \sigma_i \sigma_j \rho_{ij}.$$

In the latter equation ρ_{ij} are the correlation coefficients between the rates of return R_i and R_j and σ_i is the standard deviation of R_i. This can equivalently be written in matrix/vector notation:

$$\mu_P = w^{\top}\mu \qquad \sigma_P^2 = w^{\top}\Sigma w,$$

where μ is the vector of expected returns and Σ denotes the positive definite covariance matrix with $\Sigma(i, j) = \sigma_i \sigma_j \rho_{ij}$ for $i, j = 1, \ldots, N$.

The main ideas of modern portfolio theory are the concepts of *risk aversion* and *diversification*. Diversification simply describes the meaning of 'Don't put your eggs in one basket' in terms of investment strategies. It is assumed that spreading out the investment budget among different asset classes reduces the overall risk.

On the other hand risk aversion refers to the investment decision itself. If two or more investment strategies produce the same amount of expected return, the risk averse investor prefers the strategy with the lowest expected amount of risk. This is also termed as being *efficient*.

Thus, the mean-variance portfolio optimization problem can be summarized by searching for the combination of portfolio weights w that for a certain amount of expected return R^* lead to the minimum expected portfolio risk/variance. In mathematical terms this is equivalent to solving the quadratic programming problem

$$\min \ w^{\top}\Sigma w$$
$$\text{subject to} \quad -w^{\top}\mu \le -R^*$$
$$(1, \ldots, 1)w = 1$$
$$(0, \ldots, 0)^{\top} \le w.$$

Starting from a collection of historical data we approximate the expected returns $E[R_i]$ and covariances $Cov[R_i, R_j]$ for $R_i \in \mathbb{R}^M$ and $i, j = 1, \ldots, N$ using the sample mean $\widehat{\mu}$ and the sample covariance matrix $\widehat{\Sigma}$ given by

$$\widehat{\mu}_i = \frac{1}{M}\sum_{k=1}^{M} R_i(k)$$

$$\widehat{\Sigma}_{i,j} = \frac{1}{M-1}\sum_{k=1}^{M}(R_i(k) - \widehat{\mu}_i)(R_j(k) - \widehat{\mu}_j).$$

In Matlab this can be achieved by using the following piece of code:

```
% M: number of samples
% N: number of assets
[M,N] = size(data)
% sample mean
mu = mean(data)';
% sample covariance
Sigma = cov(data);
```

The variable data is a matrix of linear returns. For $i = 1, \ldots, M$ and $j = 1, \ldots, N$ the data data(i,j) is the linear return $R(t_i)$ of asset j. We retrieve the matrix from a Matlab formatted binary file (MAT-file) called **LinRetMat.mat** by using the command

```
load 'LinRetMat'
```

The equality constraint $\sum_{i=1}^{N} w_i = 1$ and the short sales constraints $w_i \geq 0$ for $i = 1, \ldots, N$ are given by

```
% weights sum to one
Aeq = ones(1,N);
beq = 1.0;
% no short-sales
A = -eye(N);
b = zeros(N,1);
```

We call the function quadprog using

```
H = 2.0*Sigma;
c = zeros(N,1);
[weightsP,sigmaP2] = quadprog(H,c,A,b,Aeq,beq);
```

The resulting vector weighstP represents the weights w of the minimum variance portfolio. The value sigmaP2 is equal to the expected variance σ_P^2 of this portfolio and its expected return is given by

```
muP = weightsP'*mu;
```

Figure 11.6 gives plots of the efficient frontier and of the weights of the efficient portfolios starting from the minimum variance portfolio up to the maximum return portfolio. The maximum return portfolio is given by a full investment in the asset with the highest expected return.

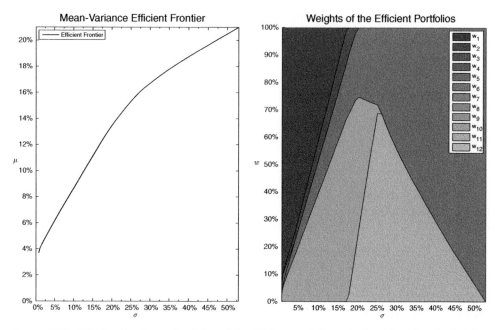

Figure 11.6   Efficient frontier and weights of the efficient portfolios calculated by using the function quadprog

We calculate the set of efficient portfolios by applying the function quadprog iteratively. The Matlab code is given by

```
% maximum return
muMax = max(mu);
% number portfolios
M = 25;
% stepsize of returns
delta = (muMax - muP)/(M-1);

% preallocate cache
weightsMat = zeros(N,M);      % matrix of portfolio weights
sigmaVec = zeros(M,1);        % expected volatility of portfolios
muVec = zeros(M,1);           % expected return of portfolios

% add minimum variance portfolio
weightsMat(:,1) = weightsP;
sigmaVec(1) = sqrt(sigmaP2);
muVec(1) = muP;

% compute efficient portfolios
for i = 2:M
    % set equality constraints w1 + w2 +...+ wN = 1 and w'*mu = R
    Aeq = [ones(1,N); mu'];
```

```
      beq = [1.0; muP + (i-1)*delta];
      % start optimization
      [weightsMat(:,i),sig2] = quadprog(H,c,A,b,Aeq,beq);
      sigmaVec(i) = sqrt(sig2);
      muVec(i) = weightsMat(:,i)'*mu;
  end
```

For further insights to quantitative asset allocation, addressing general markets and investment horizons distinct from the estimation interval, we refer readers to Meucci, A. (2007).

LINPROG   A general linear programming problem is of the form

$$\min \ f(x) := c^{\top} x$$
$$\text{subject to} \quad Ax \leq b$$
$$A_{eq} x = b_{eq}$$
$$lb \leq x \leq ub.$$

The function linprog provides two algorithms to solve the problem. The first one is based on LIPSOL and identifies a solution to the linear problem by use of a primal-dual interior-point method. The second algorithm is a variation on the well-known simplex method for linear programming.

The code

```
[x,fval] = linprog(f,A,b,Aeq,beq,lb,ub,x0)
```

solves a linear programming problem defined by the objective function f subject to linear equality and inequality constraints given in terms of the matrices A, A_{eq} and the vectors b, b_{eq}. We also provide lower and upper bounds, lb and ub. The user is able to set an initial guess x_0 but this is not a necessary input parameter. If x_0 is missing, linprog first solves another linear problem identifying an admissible solution for the initial problem. If there are no equality constraints, we set Aeq = [] and beq = [].

linprog offers additional input and output arguments. For a detailed description of all possibilities enter the command doc linprog into the Matlab workspace.

For a better understanding of how to use the function linprog let us consider Markowitz's portfolio selection problem. Markowitz solves a quadratic programming problem to identify the efficient portfolio. For a given amount of return R^* carries the minimum amount of risk.

A different approach that minimizes the Conditional Value at Risk (CVaR) of portfolio losses has already be described in Chapter 4, Subsection 4.6.8 and is proposed in Rockafellar, R.T. and Uryasev, S. (2000) and Uryasev, S. (2000). Their approach results in solving a linear programming problem instead. This is solved by using the Matlab built-in function linprog. Let us briefly summarize their approach.

For each vector of portfolio weights w the rate of return R_P of the portfolio is a random variable. If we denote the joint density of the underlying asset returns $R = (R_1, \ldots, R_N)^{\top}$ by $p(R)$, the probability of R_P exceeding a certain amount R^* is given by

$$\int_{R_p > R^*} p(R) dR.$$

Denoting the loss associated with vector w by $f(w, R) = -R_P = -w^\top R$ and $\alpha = -R^*$, this is equivalent to

$$\int_{f(w,R)\le\alpha} p(R)dR =: \Psi(w, \alpha).$$

This is the probability of $f(w, R)$ not exceeding a threshold α. Seen as a function of α for w fixed, $\Psi(w, \alpha)$ represents the cumulative distribution function for the loss associated with w. Assuming that $\Psi(w, \alpha)$ is continuous with respect to α, the β-VaR and β-CVaR for the loss $f(w, R)$ associated with w and any probability level $\beta \in (0, 1)$ can be defined by

$$\beta\text{-VaR}(w) := \min\{\alpha \in \mathbb{R} : \Psi(w, \alpha) \ge \beta\}$$

$$\beta\text{-CVaR}(w) := \frac{1}{1-\beta} \int_{f(w,R)\ge\beta\text{-VaR}(w)} f(w, R)p(R)dR.$$

The β-VaR is the smallest value α such that the probability $P[f(w, R) > \alpha]$ of a loss exceeding α is not larger than $1 - \beta$. Therefore, β-VaR presents the $(1 - \beta)$-quantile of the loss distribution $\Psi(w, \alpha)$. The β-CVaR, also known as *expected shortfall*, is the conditional expected loss associated with w if the β-VaR is exceeded.

Rockafellar, R.T. and Uryasev, S. (2000) determine the β-CVaR of the loss associated with any feasible $w \in \mathcal{X}$ from the equation

$$\beta\text{-CVaR} = \min_{\alpha\in\mathbb{R}} F_\beta(w, \alpha),$$

with

$$F_\beta(w, \alpha) := \alpha + \frac{1}{1-\beta} \int_{R\in\mathbb{R}^N} \max\{f(w, R) - \alpha, 0\}p(R)dR.$$

The β-CVaR of the loss is given by the left endpoint of the nonempty, closed and bounded interval

$$A_\beta(w) = \arg\min_{\alpha\in\mathbb{R}} F_\beta(w, \alpha).$$

It is proposed to solve the following optimization problem:

$$\min_{w\in\mathcal{X}} \beta\text{-CVaR}(w) = \min_{(w,\alpha)\in\mathcal{X}\times\mathbb{R}} F_\beta(w, \alpha),$$

where the admissible set $\mathcal{X}$ is defined by

$$\mathcal{X} := \left\{ w \in \mathbb{R}^N : w_i \ge 0\, i = 1, \ldots, N \wedge \sum_{i=1}^{N} w_i = 1 \wedge -w^\top \mu_P \le -R^* \right\}.$$

Given a collection of sample vectors $R^1, \ldots, R^q$ distributed according to the density $p(.)$, the function $F_\beta(w, \alpha)$ is approximated by

$$F_\beta(w, \alpha) \approx \tilde{F}_\beta(w, \alpha) := \alpha + \frac{1}{q(1-\beta)} \sum_{k=1}^{q} \max\{f(w, R^k) - \alpha, 0\}.$$

With respect to α the approximation $\tilde{F}_\beta(w, \alpha)$ is convex and piecewise linear. In terms of the auxiliary variables u_k with

$$u_k \ge 0 \quad \text{and} \quad -f(w, R^k) + \alpha + u_k \ge 0 \quad \text{for } k = 1, \ldots, q$$

the minimization of $\tilde{F}_\beta(w, \alpha)$ over $\mathcal{X} \times \mathbb{R}$ is equivalent to solving a linear programming problem for the vector of variables $x = (\alpha, w_1, \ldots, w_N, u_1, \ldots, u_q)^\top \in \mathbb{R}^{1+N+q}$. The vector c in the objective function $c^\top x$ is given by

$$c^\top = \left(1, 0, \ldots, 0, \tfrac{1}{q(1-\beta)}, \ldots, \tfrac{1}{q(1-\beta)}\right)^\top.$$

In Matlab the objective function takes the form

```
function y = objfCVaR(beta, q, N)
y = [1, zeros(1,N), 1/(1-beta)*1/q*ones(1,q)];
```

The linear equality and inequality constraints are given by

$$A = (-1) \cdot \begin{pmatrix} 1 & R_1^1 & \cdots & R_N^1 & 1 & 0 & \cdots & \cdots & 0 \\ 1 & R_1^2 & \cdots & R_N^2 & 0 & 1 & 0 & \cdots & 0 \\ \vdots & \vdots & & \vdots & \vdots & \ddots & \ddots & \ddots & \vdots \\ 1 & R_1^{q-1} & \cdots & R_N^{q-1} & 0 & \cdots & 0 & 1 & 0 \\ 1 & R_1^q & \cdots & R_N^q & 0 & \cdots & \cdots & 0 & 1 \end{pmatrix}, \quad b = \begin{pmatrix} 0 \\ \vdots \\ 0 \end{pmatrix}$$

$$A_{eq} = \begin{pmatrix} 0 & -\mu_1 & \cdots & -\mu_N & 0 & \cdots & 0 \\ 0 & 1 & \cdots & 1 & 0 & \cdots & 0 \end{pmatrix}, \quad b_{eq} = \begin{pmatrix} -R^* \\ 1 \end{pmatrix}.$$

The implemented function in Matlab is as follows:

```
function [A,b,Aeq,beq,lb,ub] = constCVaR(Sample,mu,Rstar)
% q: number samples
% N: number assets
[q,N] = size(Sample);

% inequality constraints
A = zeros(q,1+N+q);
A(1:end,1) = -1;
A(1:end,2:N+1) = -Sample;
A(1:end,N+2:end) = -eye(q);

b = zeros(q,1);

% equality constraints
Aeq = zeros(2,1+N+q);
Aeq(1,2:N+1) = -mu';
Aeq(2,2:N+1) = 1;

beq = zeros(2,1);
beq(1) = -Rstar;
beq(2) = 1;
```

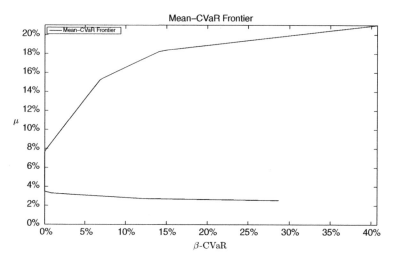

Figure 11.7   Mean-CVaR-frontier of portfolios calculated by using the function `linprog`

```
% lower/upper bounds
lb = zeros(1+N+q,1);
ub=[Inf;ones(N,1);Inf*ones(q,1)];
```

If we consider the linear returns, (11.2), the sample vectors R^k for $k = 1, \ldots, q$ are given by

$$R^k := (R_1(t_k), \ldots, R_N(t_k))^\top. \tag{11.3}$$

We approximate the expected loss α by the corresponding sample mean $\widehat{\alpha} = -w^\top \widehat{\mu}$. Considering the same linear returns as above, Figure 11.7 displays plots of the CVaR-frontier after applying the function `linprog`. The results are generated by using the following piece of code:

```
% confidence level
beta = 0.99;

% number portfolios
NumPorts = 50;
% target returns
Rstar = min(mu):(max(mu)-min(mu))/(NumPorts-1):max(mu);
% objective function vector
f = objfCVaR(beta, M, N);
% constraints matrices
[A, b, Aeq, beq, lb, ub] = constCVaR(data, mu, Rstar(1));

CVaR    = zeros(NumPorts,1);
weights = zeros(N,NumPorts);

for i = 1:NumPorts
    beq(1) = -Rstar(i);
```

```
    [optimvar, CVaR(i)] = linprog(f, A, b, Aeq, beq, lb, ub);
    weights(:,i) = optimvar(1:N);
end
```

11.6 USEFUL FUNCTIONS AND METHODS

11.6.1 FFT

In Chapter 5 we introduced fast and accurate semi-analytical numerical methods based on Fourier transform techniques to calculate prices of European Call and Put options for the models reviewed in Chapters 2 and 3. In Chapter 6 some of these methods were extended to price options with early exercise features as well as discretely monitored Barrier options. In our proposed implementation we make use of the Matlab built-in functions `fft` and `ifft`. For a vector x of size n the commands

```
y = fft(x);
x = ifft(y);
```

are used to calculate the discrete Fourier transform of x and its inverse

$$\text{fft:} \qquad y(k) = \sum_{j=1}^{n} x(j)\omega_n^{(j-1)(k-1)} \qquad\qquad k = 1, \ldots, n$$

$$\text{ifft:} \qquad x(j) = \frac{1}{n}\sum_{k=1}^{n} y(k)\omega_n^{-(j-1)(k-1)} \qquad j = 1, \ldots, n.$$

The number $\omega_n = e^{(2\pi i)/n}$ is the n-th root of unity.

The functions `fft` and `ifft` are based on the FFTW library. For $n = n_1 \cdot n_2$ the n-point discrete Fourier transform is computed using the Cooley–Tukey algorithm (Cooley, J. W. and Tukey, J.W. (1967)). This algorithm recursively decomposes the problem into smaller Fourier transform problems of size n_1 and n_2. While a direct implementation of the above sums requires n^2 numerical operations, the Cooley–Tukey algorithm reduces the overall computational effort to $\mathcal{O}(n \log(n))$.

11.6.2 Solving Equations and ODE

ODE   In mathematical finance the problem of solving ordinary differential equations (ODE) is omnipresent. For instance, we encountered ODE when deriving characteristic functions for affine linear models in Chapters 2, 5 and 6 and when we determined the value of CMS spread options in Chapter 4.

Using Matlab we can choose between several built-in ODE solvers. We have summarized the methods in sequence. In practice *stiff* differential equations are hard to solve. This refers to the fact that certain ODE are numerically hard to solve applying standard numerical methods since they are unstable unless the step size applied is very small. We do not give a definition of *stiffness* here but we summarize the built-in algorithms. For more information we refer readers to Moler, C. (2008).

- ode45

  Implementation of an explicit Runge–Kutta (4, 5) formula, the *Dormand–Prince pair* (see Dormand, J.R. and Prince, P.J. (1980)). It is a one-step solver. For computing the next step at t_{n+1} it only applies the current values at time step t_n. The algorithm is designed to handle non-stiff problems of medium accuracy. It should be the first try for solving an ODE in Matlab.

- ode23

  Implementation of an explicit Runge–Kutta (2, 3) pair described in Bogacki, P. and Shampine, L.F. (1989). The algorithm implemented is a one-step solver. For non-stiff problems it exhibits a low accuracy. It is most efficient when applied for large error tolerances or moderately stiff problems.

- ode113

  Implementation of a variable-order predictor–corrector method known as the *Adams–Bashforth–Moulton predictor–corrector* algorithm. It often performs more efficiently than ode45 at stringent tolerances and in cases where the function supplied to the ODE is numerically very expensive to calculate. In contrast to ode45 and ode23 it is a multi-step solver and applies the solutions at several preceding time points to determine the current solution. It is designed to solve non-stiff systems of any accuracy. Use for stringent error tolerances or computationally intensive ordinary differential equation functions.

- ode15s

  Implementation of a variable-order solver based on the *numerical differentiation formulas* (NDFs). Optionally, it uses the *backward differentiation formulas* (BDFs, also known as *Gear's method*), which are usually less efficient. The solver applies a multi-step method. A practical tip from Moler, C. (2008) is to try it if ode45 fails or is not very efficient, if it is suspected that the problem under consideration is a stiff one or if we wish to solve a differential-algebraic problem.

- ode23s

  The implementation is based on a modified Rosenbrock formula of order two. Because it is a one-step solver, it is often more efficient than ode15s at crude tolerances. It can solve some kinds of stiff problems for which ode15s is not effective. We use it for large error tolerances with stiff systems or with a constant mass matrix.

- ode23t

  The implementation is based on the trapezoidal rule using a free interpolant. Use this solver if the problem is only moderately stiff and you need a solution without numerical damping. The function ode23t can solve differential-algebraic equations. For moderately stiff problems it provides only low accuracy. We use it for moderately stiff problems where you need a solution without numerical damping.

- ode23tb

  The implementation of TR-BDF2 is based on an implicit Runge–Kutta formula. This formula uses a trapezoidal rule and a BDF of order two. By construction, the same iteration matrix is used in evaluating both stages. Like ode23s, this solver is often more efficient than ode15s at crude tolerances. For stiff problems it gives only low accuracy. We use it for large error tolerances with stiff systems or if there is a mass matrix.

To apply any of the methods summarized above we provide the syntax here. First, we need to define a function handle, which we call odefunchandle, a starting value which is called

```
% kappa, xi, zeta, betaQuer,T, q1, a, b, c, d and V are arrays/numbers
tmp2 = @(t,y) odefkt(y,kappa,xi,1/(2*zeta)+betaQuer1^2/4, ...
    sigmaSRQuadrat(t,fix,end1,T,q1,a,b,c,d),V);
lsg = ode23(tmp2,[0,T(fix)],[0 0]);
```

Figure 11.8 Applying the ODE solver ode23 to the problem of parameter averaging

s0 and a time-grid called tgrid. Now, we can apply the following syntax to solve the ODE defined by odefunchandle:

```
[T,Y]  = odesolver(odefunchandle,tgrid,s0)
```

The odesolver is any of the methods for solving an ODE.

We applied the ODE solver ode23 to calculate the average parameters for a Libor Market Model with stochastic volatility and time-dependent parameters in Chapter 4, Subsection 4.2.2.

To this end we considered the piece of code given in Figure 11.8.

Figure 11.9 gives the function supplied to the solver ode23.

11.6.3 Useful Functions

Finally, we look at some useful functions which we have not considered so far.

- sum, cumsum

  The functions sum and cumsum are used to sum up numbers. Let myArray be an $n_1 \times n_2 \times, \ldots, \times n_N$ dimensional array. First, we consider

```
mysum = sum(myArray);
mysumd = sum(myArray,d);
```

The first command assigns the sum along different dimensions. If we consider vectors, that is myArray is $1 \times n$ or $n \times 1$, then sum assigns the sum of all elements to mysum and is thus a scalar. For a matrix, that is myArray is $n_1 \times n_2$, the assignment leads to a vector of length n_2. If A is a vector, sum(A) returns the sum of the elements. Thus, the columns of myArray are treated as vectors and the output vector holds the sum of elements per column.

The second statement is used to specify the dimension for which the sum is applied.

```
mycumsum = cumsum(myArray);
mycumsum = cumsum(myArray,d);
```

```
function dy = odefkt(y,kappa,xi,mu,sigma,V)
dy = zeros(2,1);     % a column vector
dy(1) = - kappa * V * y(2);
dy(2) = -kappa*y(2) -xi^2/2 * y(2)^2 + mu *sigma;
end
```

Figure 11.9 The Matlab implementation supplied to the ODE solver ode23 for pricing CMS spread options

The first statement returns the cumulative sum along different dimensions of the array myArray. Let us consider two special cases. First, if myArray is a vector, cumsum(myArray) returns a vector containing the cumulative sum of the elements and if myArray is a matrix it returns a matrix of the same size as myArray containing the cumulative sums for each column. The second statement can be used to specify the dimension for taking the sums.

- prod, mprod
  The application of the functions prod and mprod is the same as for the statements sum and cumsum, but instead of taking the sum we consider multiplication.
- interp1, interp2, interp3
  The statements are used for one-, two- or three-dimensional interpolation, respectively. If we consider

```
ZI = interpN(X,Y,Z,XI,YI); % N=1,2,3
```

ZI contains elements corresponding to the elements of XI and YI and determined by interpolation within the two-dimensional function specified by matrices X, Y and Z. Both arrays of the same format need to be monotonic. Matrices X and Y specify the points at which the data Z is given. Out of range values are returned as NaN.

XI and YI can be matrices, in which case interp2 returns the values of Z corresponding to the points (XI(i,j),YI(i,j)). Alternatively, we can provide the row and column vectors xi and yi, respectively. In this case, interp2 interprets these vectors as if you issued the command meshgrid(xi,yi).

```
% assumes X = 1:n; Y = 1:m; [m,n] = size(Z);
ZI = interpN(Z,XI,YI);
ZI = interpN(Z,ntimes);
```

The first statement assumes that X=1:n; Y=1:m with [m,n]=size(Z). The second statement creates interleaving interpolates between every element working recursively for ntimes. By specifying a string method we can choose the type of interpolation performed.

The interpolation method can be set to nearest, linear, spline or cubic which corresponds to nearest neighbour interpolation, linear interpolation (default), cubic spline interpolation or cubic interpolation, as long as data are uniformlyspaced. Otherwise, the interpolation is done applying the spline option.

For one-dimensional interpolation the options pchip and v5cubic are available. This corresponds to piecewise cubic Hermite and an interpolation algorithm used in an early version of Matlab. This method does not extrapolate. If x is not equally spaced, spline is used.

While the two- and three-dimensional interpolation methods do not allow for extrapolation except for using constant values, we specify an option for non-constant extrapolation for the one-dimensional case. We consider

```
yi = interp1(x,Y,xi,method,'extrap')
yi = interp1(x,Y,xi,method,extrapval)
```

The extrapolation is done by applying the specified method or by using the value extrap-val.

- quad, quadl, quadv
  These are methods for numerically evaluating an integral using adaptive Simpson quadrature (quad), vectorized quadrature (quadv) or adaptive Lobatto quadrature (quadl)

```
q = quadN(fun,a,b);      N = "",v,l
q = quadN(fun,a,b,tol;   N = "",v,l
```

11.7 PLOTTING

In this last section we briefly review methods for creating output as plots. For financial applications it is often very convenient to visualize data, for instance if we consider the performance of a trading strategy, a hedge or the outcome of a calibration. To this end we consider

- Two-dimensional plots (graphs, histograms).
- Three-dimensional plots (surfaces).

11.7.1 Two-Dimensional Plots

Our aim is to plot the graph of the function

$$f : \mathbb{R} \to \mathbb{R}$$
$$x \mapsto \sin\left(\cos\left(x^3 \pi\right)\right)$$

with $A \subset \mathbb{R}$. The graph for f is the set $(x, f(x))$. For simplicity we assume that $A = [x_1, x_2]$. First, we discretize the interval by using 100 points equally spaced in A.

```
x1 = 0; x2 = 1; N = 100; h = (x2-x1)/N;
% method 1
>> x = linspace(0,1,N)
% method 2
>> x = 0:h:1;
```

We have set up the discretization A_d of the interval using the set $A_d := \{0, h, 2h, \ldots, 1\}$. Now, we calculate the values of the function f for each member of A_d and plot the values using the function plot.

```
>> f = @(x) sin(cos(x.^3*pi));
>> y = f(x);
>> plot(x,y);
```

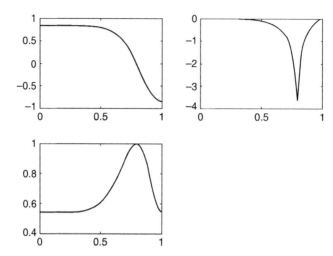

Figure 11.10   Using subplot to split the graphics window and placing plots in each sub-window

We add a title and labels by using the plot editor or using

```
>> title('Some Function');
>> xlabel('x');
>> ylabel('y');
```

A very convenient feature of Matlab is that the string for assigning a title or a label can also be any TEX command. For further options and tricks for illustration and plotting see the documentation of Matlab.

To conclude this subsection we wish to outline methods for combining plots. We can plot several graphs at once. Suppose we have assigned the values for x and three function handles f1, f2 and f3. Then,

```
>> plot(x,f1(x),x,f2(x),x,f3(x));
```

leads to a plot with three graphs.

This result can be obtained by calling the function plot three times. Since calling the function plot implicitly clears the graphics output, we have to use the function hold. Thus,

```
>> plot(x,f1(x); hold on;
>> plot(x,f2(x)); plot(x,f3(x)); hold off;
```

leads to the same result.

Finally, the graphics window can be split into an $n_1 \times n_2$ array of smaller graphics windows. We can then place a plot into one of the sub-windows. The counting convention is 1 to $n_1 \cdot n_2$ row-wise and window 1 being the top-left window. The commands lead to the graphs plotted in Figure 11.10 where we used the function handles f1, f2 and f3.

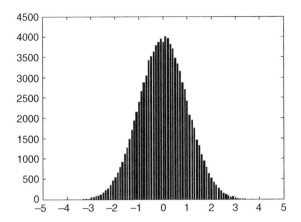

Figure 11.11   Using hist to create and display histograms

```
>> subplot(221), plot(x,f1(x));
>> subplot(222), plot(x,f2(x));
>> subplot(223), plot(x,f3(x));
```

The fourth sub-window corresponding to subplot(224) is empty.

Let us now consider the task of illustrating the performance of a hedging strategy either using some model or using historical data. We measure the performance of the strategy by storing the hedging error with respect to the *n*th sample. A histogram is a practical way to show the performance. To do this we consider the function hist. We apply it in the following way:

```
>> x = -4:0.1:4;
>> y = randn(100000,1);
>> hist(y,x)
```

To this end we provide the buckets, denoted by *x*, and where we place the samples, denoted by *y*. The function hist implements this method. The outcome is displayed in Figure 11.11.

11.7.2   Three-Dimensional Plots – Surfaces

A *surface* is a function.

$$f : A \times B \to \mathbb{R}$$
$$(x, y) \mapsto f(x, y),$$

with $A, B \subset \mathbb{R}^2$. The surface is the set $(x, y, f(x, y))$. In order to be able to plot the function we need to specify the range $A \times B$ and discretize this range. To this end we first create the discretization using meshgrid and then we calculate the function values and store them using the variable z. We have chosen to use the function $\sin(x^2 + y^2)$.

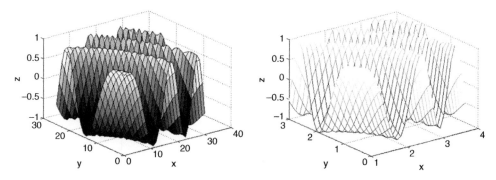

Figure 11.12   Using the functions `surf` (left) and `mesh` (right) to plot a surface

```
>> [x,y] = meshgrid(1:.1:4, 0.5:.1:3);
>> z = sin(x.^2+y.^2);
```

The plotting can be done using either `surf` (method 1) or `mesh` (method 2).

```
% method 1
>> surf(z)
% method 2
>> mesh(x,y,z)
```

Figure 11.12 shows the differences between applying `surf` and `mesh`.

We can think of $z(i, j)$ being the value of the function at $(x(i), y(j))$. There is yet another possibility to visualize the surface. This can be done by using the function `contour`. This is illustrated in Figure 11.13.

All the above methods have been applied to create the figures and illustrations in this book.

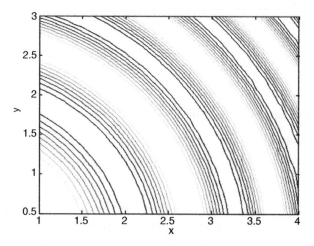

Figure 11.13   Using the function `contour` to plot a surface

11.8 SUMMARY AND CONCLUSIONS

In this chapter we have summarized the basic functionality of Matlab necessary to understand the basics of the code provided in the supporting material for this book. Our choice of topics was motivated by what we think a quant has to know when applying Matlab. We have focused on the use of vectors, matrices and functions and considered some very useful built-in algorithms.

After some general remarks on variables and on Matlab we covered two of the most important topics for programming financial applications: using matrices and functions. To this end we considered both topics in some detail. We illustrated how to apply matrices to improve upon the speed and the efficiency of a Matlab program and we explained which Matlab functions are necessary to manipulate matrices. This was also the guiding idea for describing functions. We showed how to define and call a user-defined function. Furthermore, we introduced function handles, which allow you to widen the scope and enhance your Matlab programs significantly.

Toolboxes extend the functionality of Matlab covering a particular area of mathematics. For instance, we covered the following toolboxes: Financial, Financial Derivatives, Fixed-Income, Optimization, Global Optimization, Statistics and Portfolio Optimization. Of course, it was beyond our remit to cover every single aspect of the functionality a toolbox has. Therefore, we only covered functions which we think are interesting and particularly useful for solving quantitative finance problems.

We gave a brief overview of special functions for Fourier transform and for solving ODEs. We also included a short section on plotting and displaying data. This only covered the basics and was meant to help readers understand the source code.

We have had to leave out other useful, but for our purposes not vital, information. We did not cover the programming of Graphical User Interfaces, nor did we comment on important issues such as the Matlab compiler or using the Excel-link interface. For such issues we refer readers to the documentation of Matlab or books on applying Matlab in general (see, for example, Brandimarte, P. (2006), Yang, W.Y., Cao, W., Chung, T.S. and Morris, J. (2005), Moler, C. (2008) or Günther, M. and Jüngel, A. (2010)).

12
Matlab – Object Oriented Development

12.1 INTRODUCTION AND OBJECTIVES

In this chapter we review the object oriented programming approach in Matlab. First, we give a brief introduction to the Matlab OO model in the first section, Section 12.2. To this end we introduce classes and class methods. We show how to encapsulate data and functionality using classes. We apply classes to design hierarchies for financial models, pricers and optimizers in Sections 12.3 to 12.5. In Section 12.6 we consider Design Patterns. Such programming paradigms are proposed to write reusable and robust code in a generic fashion. We briefly outline how to apply Design Patterns for financial modelling and especially in combination with Matlab. For general discussions and the application to C++ see Duffy, D. (2004), Duffy, D. (2006) or Duffy, D. and Kienitz, J. (2009).

In the final sections, 12.7 and 12.8, we cover the implementation of a calibration framework for options based on Fourier transform methods and the implementation of the Libor Market Model. For the Libor Market Model we implement the adjoint method in a very general way. We use the implementation to apply it to the calculation of Greeks for Bermudan swaptions and Trigger swaps.

12.2 THE MATLAB OO MODEL

In this section we wish to outline the basic principles of Matlab's object oriented programming model and how to use it for financial engineering applications.

We consider

- Abstraction and Separation.
- Designing Class Hierarchies.
- Interactions.

12.2.1 Classes

A user-defined class is an object that encapsulates data, methods and events. The Matlab programming model distinguishes between two kinds of classes. For *handle classes* a reference to data contained in the class is used, whereas *value classes* make copies of the data when instances of such classes are copied or passed to some function.

A *class* is a definition that specifies certain characteristics which all instances of the class share. The characteristics are determined by the properties, methods and events that define the class and the values of attributes that modify the behaviour of each of those class components. Class definitions describe how objects of the class are created and destroyed, what data the object contains and how we manipulate this data.

```
classdef myclass
   properties
      myprivateproperty1;            % no value set
      myprivateproperty2 = 512;      % set to some value
   end

   methods
      ....                           % some methods
   end

   methods
      ...                            % some methods
   end
end
```

Figure 12.1   Matlab implementation of a class using properties and methods

The building blocks of a class are used to specify the class, the methods and the events. The keywords are

1. `classdef`
2. `properties`
3. `methods`
4. `events`.

The key syntax to define a class is the `classdef` statement, (1). This statement is followed by the class name and, as we shall see later on, information concerning inheritance. The statement is closed with the keyword `end`. Within a `classdef` statement we specify `properties`, (2), `methods`, (3) and `events`, (4). A class can have several such statements. For instance, we have given a class definition in Figure 12.1. In this class definition there is one properties block and two methods blocks. Thus, we observe that it is possible to use many statements and that the statements can be of the same type. Often we use different methods statements to specify different access properties.

Class Properties

Let us start with the `properties` statement. This statement is used to declare the private and public member data of the class. *Public data* means that these data can be accessed from outside of the class. *Private data*, on the other hand, can only be accessed by a member function of the same class. The variables defined in the `properties` statement can be set to static, using a constructor or some `set/get` functions.

Let us comment briefly on the essential access attributes for properties. First, we distinguish between `SetAccess` and `GetAccess`. Both properties can be specified independently from each other. If we wish to set both attributes at once we can simply use `Access`. In Figure 12.2 we specified the variable `myprivateproperty1` by specifying both access properties. The same result is achieved for declaring `myprivateproperty2` by specifying only the overall access properties.

If we do not specify any access property, then it is `public` by default, as shown in Figure 12.3.

```
classdef myclass
   properties
      myprivateproperty1;        % no value set
      myprivateproperty2 = 512;  % set to some value
   end

   properties (SetAccess = private, GetAccess = private)
      myprivateproperty1;        % accessible by member functions only
   end

   properties (Access = private)
      myprivateproperty2;        % accessible by member functions only
   end
end
```

Figure 12.2   Matlab implementation of a class using properties. We apply private properties here

The Matlab command `properties` takes as an input an existing class name and displays the names of its public properties. According to which public properties are displayed, the user can see how the interface can be used and how data can be accessed.

Properties can be declared to be static properties. The Matlab keyword for declaring a static property is a `Constant=true` statement. In this case subclasses inherit the constant properties but the property cannot be changed. Furthermore, set methods are ignored when applied to a constant property.

Another very important property attribute is `Abstract`. The default setting is a `Abstract=false`. This property is extremely useful for setting up class hierarchies, which we discuss later in this chapter.

For a subclass to force the programmer to implement a certain property we define a so-called *base class* and declare the properties to be abstract. This means that a subclass has to implement these properties as non-abstract properties. Otherwise, the code would not work. Using an abstract property we have to keep in mind that it is not possible to use a static or a default value and that it is not possible to implement `set/get` methods for abstract properties.

All property attributes can be found in the Matlab documentation by entering `doc` in the Matlab frontend and choosing the part on object oriented programming.

```
classdef myclass
   properties
      myproperty1;        % no value set
      myproperty2;        % no value set
   end

   properties (SetAccess = public, GetAccess = public)
      myproperty2;
   end
end
```

Figure 12.3   Matlab implementation of a class using properties. We apply public properties here

Let us consider possible attributes and their usage.

- `AbortSet` which is of Boolean type and can therefore be either `true` or `false`. The setting `false` is the default setting.
  If this property is set to `true` and this property belongs to a handle class, then the property value is not set if the new value coincides with the current value. This is useful since handle classes often act as triggers for events. Therefore this behaviour prevents the triggering of property `PreSet` and `PostSet` events.
- `Abstract` is a Boolean value and is set to `false` by default.
  If the property is set to `true` it has no implementation but a subclass must redefine this property without setting `Abstract=true`. Furthermore, we have to provide an implementation of the method. Abstract properties cannot define `set`/`get` methods and cannot set initial values. All subclasses must specify the same values as the superclass for the properties `SetAccess` and `GetAccess`.
- `Access` is a string and set to `public` by default.
  The keyword `public` allows unrestricted access. The other keywords restrict the access. We use `protected` to assign access from other classes or derived classes and `private` to assign access by methods of the class only.
  We use `Access` to set `SetAccess` and `GetAccess` at the same time and to the same value. To find out about the access properties we have to access the values of `SetAccess` and `GetAccess`.
- `Constant` is a Boolean value and set to `false` by default.
  We set this property to `true` if we wish to have only one single value for this property across all instances of the class. We have to keep in mind that subclasses inherit constant properties but cannot change them and properties being `Constant` properties cannot be dependent (see the property `Dependent` below). Since setting values is not possible, Matlab ignores any properties specified by setting the `SetAccess` property.
- `Dependent` is also a Boolean value and set to `false` by default.
  If for some property we declare `Dependent=false`, the property value is stored in the object's data which is the usual behaviour. If we use `Dependent=true`, the property value is not stored in the object's data. The `set`/`get` functions cannot access the property and perform actions on the property. This is a desired behaviour since dependent properties depend on other properties and therefore we wish to prevent users from setting such properties. Matlab does not display the names and values of dependent properties for which the programmer did not define a `get` method.
- `GetAccess` is a string and the default setting value is `public`.
  The possible values are the same as for `Access`.
- `GetObservable` is a Boolean value and set to `false` by default.
  If `GetObservable=true` and the class is a handle class, we are able to create listeners which are able to access this property. The listeners are called whenever the property value is called. This can be a very useful property for financial engineering since, for instance, a yield curve should be updated if a rates update has occurred.
- `Hidden` is a Boolean value and is set to `false` by default.
  This property determines whether the property should be shown in a property list or not.
- `SetAccess` is a string and by default the value is `public`.
  The possible values are the same as for `Access`. Furthermore, it can be set to `immutable`, meaning that the property can only be set when calling the constructor.

- `SetObservable` is a Boolean variable and by default set to `false`.
  If we apply `SetObservable=true` and the class is a handle class, then we are able to create listeners that are able to access this property. This is the same as for `GetObservable`.
- `Transient` is a Boolean value and set to `false` by default.
  If we use `Transient=true`, the property value is not saved when the object is saved to a file.

Class Methods

Member functions of a class are called *methods* in Matlab. Such functions encapsulate special functionality and behaviour of the class. We use methods to act on member data or properties of the class to calculate output or modified class values which can be used by standard Matlab functions or other user-defined classes.

Some methods are functions that access class properties as well as use input data to produce a function value and return it. Other methods are used to set up or destroy a specific class instance. Such methods are called *constructors* and *destructors* respectively. Finally `set/get` methods are used to set property values or get the corresponding values.

The following paragraphs provide an overview of the methods and their usage.

Ordinary Methods or Member Functions   *Ordinary methods* are also called *member functions*. Such functions act on other objects and return objects. The input objects can be any standard Matlab data type but can also be some user-defined class. This also holds true for the returned values. Member functions cannot modify input arguments. This means that if we take as an input some variable `invar` a member function can assign some other value to this variable but we cannot return the modified value of `invar`. We use member functions to implement algorithms which enable the class to act on objects. The member functions can only be called if an instance of the classes has already been created. We have two possibilities to define member functions. On the one hand, we can put the implementation into the `classdef` block of the class. On the other hand, we can separate the implementation into an m-file placed into the class directory.

- The most simple method is to define the member function in the `classdef` block. In the block we would define the function as if we were writing a standard Matlab function. We use the keyword `function` then, specifying the output, the function name and the input arguments. The code implementing the function is followed by an `end` statement.
  We have to give some additional information. Taking the code presented in Figure 12.4 we observe that the first argument of `myfunction` is `obj`. This refers to the current class. Thus, each member function has to provide this argument and we can call the method either by `myclass.myfunction(v)` or by `myfunction(myclass,v)`. Note that constructors as well as `set/get` functions have to be placed into the `classdef` block and cannot be implemented in a separate file.
- It is possible to place methods into separate files of the class folder. To this end the function has to be created like a standard Matlab function. In particular, a `classdef` statement must not be used. If it is needed to specify certain attributes we have to declare the method's signature within a methods block in the `classdef` block. In Figure 12.5 we have given the implementation of `myfunction2` only, declaring the function but placing the implementation in a separate file.

```
classdef myclass                          % a class
    properties
        a = [];
    end
    methods (AttributeName = value, ...)
        function y = myfunction1(obj,v)   % a method / function
            y = obj.a + v;
        end                               % end function
...
    end                                   % end method
...
end                                       % end class
```

Figure 12.4   A Matlab class with a method statement implementing `myfunction`

The function is implemented in a separate file. The implementation is placed into the Matlab file **myfunction2.m**. This file is placed into the same directory.

Applying the second method we have to keep track of the declaration in the class file and the implementation of the member function in a separate file. This is necessary since attributes for a method defined in a separate file must declare this method in a method's block within the `classdef` statement and, of course, the syntax declared in the method's block must match the method's in the function's implementation which is possibly in another m-file.

The member function can be called in two different ways. These are termed the *dot notation* and the *function notation*. Let us denote an instance of a class by `obj`. We suppose furthermore that `obj` has a member function `memfunction1` taking one variable as input. We can then call the function using the function calls

- `obj.memfunction1(var)`
- `memfunction1(obj,var)`.

We specify the access using the keywords `public`, `protected` and `private`. Using `public` access allows any piece of software to access the method of the class. By using the `protected` keyword we restrict the access to the class as well as to derived classes. Using `private` access means that the data can only be accessed by members of the class. Applying inheritance it is important to keep in mind that private methods are not inherited but protected

```
classdef myclass                          % a class
    methods (AttributeName = value, ...)  % a method
        y = myfunction2(obj,v1,v2);       % a function
        ...
    end                                   % end methods
...
end                                       % end class
```

Figure 12.5   A Matlab class with a `methods` keyword. The function `myfunction2` is defined but not implemented within the `classdef` statement

methods are.

- `Abstract` is a Boolean value and by default set to `false`.
  An abstract method has no implementation. It serves as an interface and such a method has to be implemented by subclasses. We must emphasise that subclasses – in difference to C++ for instance – are not required to define the same number of input and output arguments. We recommend using the same format as in the abstract method when implementing the specialized version in the subclass. An abstract method does not have the typical Matlab syntax for a function. We do not need the keywords `function` and `end`.
- `Access` is a string and can take the values `public`, `protected` or `private`.
  This keyword determines which code can call this method:
  - `Access=public` means unrestricted access.
  - `Access=protected` means that methods in a class or subclasses have unrestricted access.
  - `Access=private` means that class methods only and not from subclasses have unrestricted access.
- `Hidden` is a Boolean value and is by default set to `false`.
  Any information using `methods` or `methodsview` is suppressed if we set `Hidden=true`. The information appears if we set `Hidden=false`.
- `Sealed` is a Boolean value and by default set to `false`.
  If a method is sealed, `Sealed=true`, it cannot be redefined in a subclass. Trying to redefine it would lead to an error.
- `Static` is a Boolean value and by default set to `false`.
  A static method does not depend on the instance of an object. The user can call it simply by writing `class.staticmethodname`. We advise against using static methods in this way. A method should always depend on the class which it implements.

Constructors   Special methods are *constructor methods*. A constructor creates instances of the class which it implements. To this end this function can create a bare class. But this function can also use input arguments to initialize member data. Further, it can use algorithms to produce values which are assigned to member data. It can also use the input data to create other user-defined structures which are member data of the class they create. To underpin the importance of this member function a constructor has to have the same name as the class and the type of the output argument is always the class itself. The constructor cannot have more than one output argument. The only task it has to fulfil is to instantiate a specific object.

Using multiple constructors is possible in Matlab. (This issue is discussed when we consider *overloading*.) The constructor method must be defined within the `classdef` block and, therefore, cannot be placed in a separate file like other member functions. It is not always necessary to define a constructor. If no constructor has been implemented, Matlab uses some standard constructor which returns a scalar object.

- Destructor methods: such methods are called either explicitly or the Matlab application calls them automatically when the object is destroyed. For instance, this is the case if we delete an object, `obj`, using `delete obj` or if there are no references left to the object.
- Property methods: such methods encapsulate the data of the class. We can provide methods to access the properties. Such methods include `set` and `get` methods. The type of a property that can be accessed has to be defined within the `classdef` block and cannot be placed in separate files.

- Static methods: such methods are functions that are associated with a class. Static methods do not have to operate on class objects. Furthermore, static methods do not require an instance of the class to be referenced during calling the method. The programmer uses static methods in a class when this method behaves in a class specific way.
- Overloading a constructor: conversion methods are overloaded constructor methods from other classes that enable your class to convert its own objects to the class of the overloaded constructor. For example, if your class implements a double method, then this method is called instead of the double class constructor to convert your class object to a Matlab object of type double.
- Abstract methods, Virtual methods: such methods serve to define methods of a class that cannot be instantiated. This is usually a base class in a class hierarchy. The way abstract methods are used is to define a common interface used by subclasses. Programmers often term base classes *interfaces*, which refers to the fact that abstract methods are applied.

12.2.2   Handling Classes in Matlab

We have to keep some technical aspects in mind when developing object oriented applications in Matlab. Classes are placed into folders on the Matlab path or on the current path in the working directory. Matlab supports two types of folders, namely @-folders and ordinary path folders. The name of the first type of folders begin with @. Such folders are not on the Matlab path but its parent folder is. This type of folder has to be applied if our class definition is separated into several files. The folder has to have the same name as the class and due to this restriction it is only possible to place the definition of one class into one folder. Thus, summarizing a @-folder is contained in a path folder. The actual file implementing the class has the same name as the @-folder and the files which implement the class are all in the folder.

We can place our code for user-defined class definitions in folders that are on the Matlab path. These classes are visible on the path like any ordinary function and they also behave like any ordinary function.

We consider a folder that has the name of the file to match the name of the class. Using a path folder eliminates the need to create a separate @-folder for each class. In this case the entire class definition must be contained within a single file.

We encourage the programmer to use class names which describe the class behaviour in its context. To this end consider a collection of model classes. If a class is called *Heston* it should implement the Heston model. If you keep this rule in mind, you will not get confused with your classes. The following example is taken from the Matlab documentation. However, we do not advocate using such class structures. We take a folder with the following files:

- `fldr1/myclasss.m` (defines class myclass)
- `fldr2/myclass.m` (defines function myclass)
- `fldr3/@myclass/myclass.m` (defines class myclass)
- `fldr4/@myclass/bar.m` (defines method bar)
- `fldr5/myclass.m` (defines class myclass).

Despite the fact that this example is a long way from good programming practice, Matlab determines the usage of `myclass` by the following decision rule. Class `fldr1/myclass.m` takes precedence over the class `fldr3/@myclass` since it is before `fldr3/@myclass` on the path.

Class `fldr3/@myclass` takes precedence over function `fldr2/myclass.m` since it is a class in an @-folder and `fldr2/myclass.m` is not a class (@-folder classes take precedence over functions).

Function *fldr2/myclass.m* takes precedence over class *fldr5/myclass.m* because it comes before class *fldr5/myclass.m* on the path and because class *fldr5/myclass.m* is not in an @-folder. Classes not defined in @-folder abide by path order with respect to functions.

Class *fldr3/@myclass* takes precedence over class *fldr4/@myclass*; therefore, the method bar is not recognized as part of `myclass` (which is defined only by *fldr3/@myclass*).

If *fldr3/@myclass/myclass.m* does not contain a `classdef` keyword, then *fldr4/@myclass/bar.m* becomes a method of `myclass` defined in *fldr3/@myclass*. See the Matlab documentation for further explanations.

12.2.3 Inheritance, Base Classes and Superclasses

In this subsection we consider the method of *inheritance*. The idea is to use the method of abstraction to organize classes into hierarchies. This allows the programmer to reuse as much code as possible and helps to keep the maintainability of a software application. We call each level of the hierarchy a *layer*. For a given layer the top layer is called *base class* or *superclass* in Matlab. The other classes in the hierarchy are called *subclasses* or *derived classes*. From layer to layer the implementation becomes increasingly specific. Often the class at the top of a hierarchy has basic data or even only defines member functions which are abstract and thus only provide interfaces to interact with other user-defined and Matlab built-in objects and functions.

We see classes as conceptions of existing objects. Thus, in financial engineering we wish to encapsulate certain behaviour, data and functionality into the class. An option, for instance, has a price. Thus, when designing a financial instrument hierarchy and implementing options we should implement the function *price* as an interface. We wish to find characteristics of the objects and use abstraction to implement corresponding classes. Furthermore, abstraction also means to tear off some facts of the financial instruments. This means information necessary to describe the financial instrument which is not necessary for calling the methods of the current class need not be member data of the class. For pricing options we do not have to know who actually traded the option or if it is already back-office confirmed or not.

For financial applications we design several hierarchies to specialize the application of models, pricers and other methods. The guiding idea is to be more specialized at each layer of the hierarchy. To this end we wish to design a software system using hierarchies such that common data and member functions are put into the base class. Then, whenever inheritance is applied these data and the common functions are passed to the subclass. In the subclass we add certain functionality which is necessary for further specialization to fulfil particular purposes. This has several advantages over sequential programming only based on functions and simple data structures. Since we use this approach to avoid reproducing code, the member functions common to all classes can be implemented in the base class. This approach enhances the software development since it adds flexibility. A subclass can be deleted, changed or added to the hierarchy without changing the software programming model. Interfaces stay the same since the base class is not altered. Where this is the case, the software application does not need to be redesigned. If we decide to change the base class, for instance by adding member data common to all classes, this change is automatically adopted by all classes in the hierarchy.

Let us look into a specific issue of inheritance. We wish to consider the *interface inheritance*. Matlab supports this method of inheritance. This is done by defining abstract member functions, abstract methods, in the base class. Each subclass that inherits from the base class has to provide an implementation of the abstract method. This is related to the concept of *virtual*

```
classdef mysubclass < mybaseclass1 & mybaseclass2 & ... & mybaseclassN
```

Figure 12.6 The class mysubclass is defined using inheritance from a set of base classes. It inherits from mybaseclass1,..., mybaseclassN

functions in other object oriented programming languages. To this end we provide a common interface which could be a function which is called but the executed algorithm depends on the instantiated class of the hierarchy. Take, for instance, an optimizer. The function *optimize* is common to all optimizers. But the applied optimization method called by this function depends on the particular class that is instantiated. Thus, it can call an optimization method based on heuristic search or some gradient based optimization method. For implementation we have to choose the attribute *abstract*.

The issue of code reusability is partially solved by the inheritance mechanism. This means that subclasses not only inherit the member functions from the base class but also extend the methods of the base class by providing new methods. This can be achieved in such a way that common aspects do not have to be implemented again. Only functions and algorithms that are special to the subclasses have to be considered.

Before we consider further issues of inheritance we consider the definition of a subclass. To this end suppose we have already implemented some classes called mybaseclass1, mybase-class2,..., mybaseclassN. To define a subclass mysubclass we consider Figure 12.6.

It is of course possible to use only one base class but we have given the general syntax in Figure 12.6. This shows that we have to use '&' for inheritance from several classes. At this stage we must point out that subclasses do not inherit the attributes of the base class.

The behaviour of subclasses is that of the base class. The main thing to remember is that these special classes having additional functionality or data but they belong to some context. Thus, the context is specified by the base class. This is also reflected in the behaviour of subclass and base class methods. It is possible for a subclass to operate on base class methods but not vice versa. This would contradict the abstraction principle.

Let us come back to the construction of a subclass in Figure 12.6. If we consider the case where we inherit from mybaseclass1 and mybaseclass2, we instantiate the class mysubclass by calling its constructor. If we are deriving a class from a superclass that is contained in a package and we wish to initialize the object for the superclass we have to include the package name.

```
classdef mysubclass < mybaseclass1 & mybaseclass2
   methods
      function s = mysubclass(args,...)
         if nargin == 0            % Matlab calls constructors
            ...
         end
         s = s@mybaseclass1(args);  % mybaseclass1 constructor
         s = s@mybaseclass2(args);  % mybaseclass2 constructor
      end
   end
end
```

Figure 12.7 The class mysubclass is defined using inheritance from mybaseclass1 and my-baseclass2. It specifies an alternative way of constructing it

This syntax allows us to control the order in which the base class constructors are called, or whether they are called at all. In the latter case, Matlab calls the base class constructors without any argument. It is therefore important that in a base class the constructor can be called without arguments. This is referred to as the *standard constructor*. The order in which Matlab calls the standard constructors is not specific and it seems there is none. Furthermore, the user can control which arguments are passed to the base class constructors. Sometimes not all input arguments are necessary to call the base class constructor.

If the programmer creates class hierarchies with more than two layers it is only possible to call base class constructors from the next level. To explain this, let us suppose we derive `mysubclass2` from `mysubclass1`, which is derived from `mybaseclass1`. Then, `mysub-class1` can call the constructor from `mybaseclass` but `mysubclass2` cannot. But it can call the constructor of `mysubclass1`.

One final remark relates to the Matlab function `isa`. This function acts on Matlab objects but also on user-defined objects. In a given class hierarchy this function returns the most specific type of the current object. For the classes considered above, `mysubclass1` would return that the object is of type `mysubclass` and not `mybaseclass1` or `mybaseclass2`.

12.2.4 Handle and Value Classes

We have already pointed out that there are two kinds of classes which can be implemented. Now, we consider the difference between these two classes and their corresponding scope for creating applications.

An instantiated value class is associated with its assigned variable. For value classes a copy of the original object is made when reassigned or passed to a function. If a variable to which an instance of a value class is assigned is passed as an argument into a function it must return the modified object; otherwise, the modification is only valid in the functions scope.

In difference to a value class a constructor of a handle class returns a handle object. As is the case for function handles, this is a reference to the created object. If the handle is assigned to different variables, all these variables are only references to a single object. Furthermore, passing handle classes into a function causes no copying of the object. In certain circumstances this is very convenient but it may also cause difficulties. If a handle class is passed into some function it may be altered.

Using Classes   Having introduced the basic properties of handle and value classes we now suggest when to use the corresponding classes. In general, we use handle classes when we wish to create references to data contained in an instance of a class. A handle class is useful when we wish to create a single object with many other objects referencing to this data. In financial modelling this could be a volatility surface and other classes, for instance classes representing deal specific data.

In contrast, value classes do not have to be unique. For instance, consider creating European Call option objects. In this case each instance would represent an object with different maturity or strike or possibly with the same strike and maturity. Option classes can be copied and then the data can be modified without changing the original object.

Which kind of class to use depends on the application we wish to create. For instance, we have chosen to implement models as value classes but pricers as handle classes.

The standard Matlab documentation gives further applications not specific to financial engineering.

12.2.5 Overloading

In this section we consider a very convenient method for programming termed *overloading*. Two different notions of overloading are considered. It is possible to overload a function as well as an operator.

Overloading a function or an operator means that the function or operator behaves differently depending on the context in which it is used. For instance, if we take a class hierarchy it is possible to redefine a function which is on a lower level of the hierarchy. Here is an example for the application. Take a model class hierarchy. Suppose the base class is defined such that it takes a characteristic function and applies fast Fourier transform (FFT) methods for pricing simple Call options. On the lowest level in the hierarchy we have implemented the Black–Scholes model. Of course, we do not wish to use the general pricing method but the known analytic solution. Thus, we can apply overloading the pricing function and simply use the Black–Scholes formula.

Function Overloading   When working with base classes and inheritance the implementation of a member function might work only for a given instance of a class. Thus, this set up can be used to implement what is termed *function overloading*. Readers should note that in the Matlab object oriented programming model it is possible to identify to which class a certain member function belongs. Suppose we have a certain subclass that implements a function called `memberfunction1`. This function is also defined in the corresponding base class or as a global function using an m-file. If an instance of a class then has a member function implemented in the class definition, `classdef` block, which is also called `memberfunction1` then this implementation is used. We use `class1`, displayed in Figure 12.8, and implement two methods, called `memberfunction1` and `memberfunction2`.

We consider the class `class2` which inherits from `class1`. The code is given in Figure 12.9.

If we instantiate two objects `c1=class1()` and `c2=class2()`and call the methods `memberfunction1` and `memberfunction2` for each class, we observe that the output is 1 and 2 for c1 and 3 and 2 for c2. Thus, the function `memberfunction1` has been overloaded in `class2`.

```
classdef class1
    properties
    end

    methods
        function y = class1()
        end

        function y = memberfunction1(obj)
            y = 1;
        end

        function y = memberfunction2(obj)
            y = 2;
        end
    end
end
```

Figure 12.8   A class implemented as a Matlab object having two member functions

```
classdef class2 < class1
    properties
    end

    methods
        function y = class2()
        end

        function y = memberfunction1(obj)
            y = 3;
        end
    end
end
```

Figure 12.9   A class implemented as a Matlab object which overloads `memberfunction1`

Operator Overloading   We are able to create new proprietary data structures using Matlab classes. In most applications we need operators such as $+$, $-$, $*$ or $/$ to act on the new data structures. We wish to use the symbols belonging to the standard operators to denote corresponding functionalities for new classes. To this end we wish to assign a new meaning to the standard operators if used in the context of the new data. Let us take a class representing some financial instrument, for instance a swap. We assume that it has a member function for displaying the cash flow of the instrument. If we consider a portfolio of two or more such instruments we might be interested in adding the corresponding cash flows. To this end it is convenient to overload the operator $+$. Figure 12.10 displays a possible implementation where class1 and class2 represent the financial instruments.

A complete list of the operators that can be overloaded can be found in the Matlab documentation. This includes the operators shown in Table 12.1.

12.3   A MODEL CLASS HIERARCHY

We have implemented a simple model class hierarchy. To do so we implemented a base class *model* from which all other model classes inherit. Then, we implemented all the models in the second layer of the hierarchy. Thus, there is no further classing or separation of the single models.

We could have introduced further distinction levels, for instance between local volatility, stochastic volatility or Lévy models. But from our point of view further splitting is not reasonable since some models consist of two parts which can belong to two categories, which,

```
function y = plus(class1,class2)
    % Plus Implement class1 + class2 for CashFlow
    class1 = CashFlow(class1);
    class2 = CashFlow(class2);
    k = length(class2.coef) - length(class1.coef);
    y = CashFlow([zeros(1,k) class1.coef]+[zeros(1,-k) class2.coef]);
end
```

Figure 12.10   Implementation of overloading the operator + for adding cash flows

Table 12.1 Some operators that can be overloaded in Matlab

Operation	Method to define	Description
a + b	plus(a,b)	Binary addition
a - b	minus(a,b)	Binary subtraction
-a	uminus(a)	Unary minus
+a	uplus(a)	Unary plus
a.*b	times(a,b)	Element-wise multiplication
a*b	mtimes(a,b)	Matrix multiplication
a./b	rdivide(a,b)	Right element-wise division
a.\b	ldivide(a,b)	Left element-wise division
ab	mrdivide(a,b)	Matrix right division
ab	mldivide(a,b)	Matrix left division
a.^b	power(a,b)	Element-wise power
a^b	mpower(a,b)	Matrix power
a < b	lt(a,b)	Less than
a > b	gt(a,b)	Greater than
a <= b	le(a,b)	Less than or equal to
a >= b	ge(a,b)	Greater than or equal to
a ~= b	ne(a,b)	Not equal to
a == b	eq(a,b)	Equality
a & b	and(a,b)	Logical AND
a | b	or(a,b)	Logical OR
~a	not(a)	Logical NOT

for instance, is the case for the Bates model. This model has a stochastic volatility model component as well as a jump component. There are many more ways of specifying the model class hierarchy. For example, think about separating the models by the markets they model. But this is also not reasonable since some models such as the Heston model are used for different markets. The Heston model is used to price equity as well as foreign exchange options and is also used for volatility modelling for interest rate derivatives. Figure 12.11 shows the implemented model class hierarchy.

The base class model is very simple and is displayed in Figure 12.12.

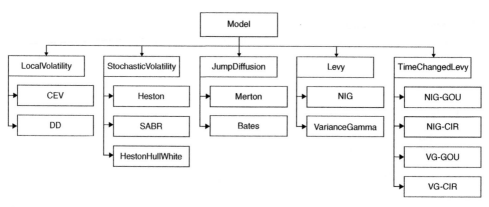

Figure 12.11 UML diagram for representing a model class hierarchy

```
classdef model < handle
% This is the base class for all financial models
    properties (Abstract)
        pnparams;              % number of modelparameters
        pparams;               % modelparameters
        pmarket;               % The markets where model is appropriate
        c1;
        c2;
        c4;
    end

    methods
        function y = model(m)
            m.pnparams = [];
            m.pparams = [];
            m.pmarket = [];
        end
    end

    methods
        function initcumulants(m,T,r,d)
            m.c1 =1;
            m.c2 = 2;
            m.c4 = 4;
        end
    end
end
```

Figure 12.12   Base class `model` for implementing models in Matlab

Example   We use the class hierarchy when we consider the builder pattern in Subsection 12.6.1 and, therefore, we do not detail the use of models here. We consider the Heston model as being one subclass inheriting from the base class `model`. The implementation is displayed in Figures 12.13 and 12.14. First, we add further properties which we think are useful for financial engineering applications.

We furthermore specify the constructor which is used to create an instance of the Heston model. This model can then be used by other pieces of software. Finally, we provide the implementation of the cumulants and the characteristic function of the model. We use the characteristic function for calculating prices of European options by the FFT method, as discussed in Chapters 5 and 6.

Having implemented the Heston model it is easy to add further models to the class hierarchy. Included as source code are many more models, including the Bates model, models based on (time-changed) Lévy processes or the Heston–Hull–White model.

12.4   A PRICER CLASS HIERARCHY

We considered several methods of pricing in Chapters 5 to 8. The different methodologies for pricing options have to be mapped to a class hierarchy. To do this we start by implementing a base class *pricer*. From this class the more specific classes inherit. In this book we only consider the FFT pricing but the hierarchy can be extended by adding classes for Monte Carlo Simulation, Finite Difference pricing or analytic formulae. The corresponding hierarchy is given in Figure 12.15.

```
classdef hestonmodel < model
    % Implementation of the Heston Stochastic Volatility model
    % dS(t) = (r-d) S(t) dt + sqrt(V(t)) S(t) dW_2(t)
    % dV(t) = kappa (theta - V(t)) dt + nu sqrt(V(t)) dW_2(t)
    % S(0) = s0
    % V(0) = v0
    %
    % kappa is the mean reversion
    % theta is the long term variance
    % nu is the volatility of variance
    % rho is the correlation between W_1 and W_2
    % v0 is the spot variance
    % S0 is the spot underlying

    properties %(SetAccess = 'public', GetAccess = 'public')
        pnparams = [];
        pparams = [];        % this is a struct
        pmarket = '';
        c1 = [];
        c2 = [];
        c4 = [];
        cal = [];
        caltime = [];
    end

    properties (Constant = true)    % constants
        pname = 'Heston';
    end
```

Figure 12.13   Matlab class for implementing the Heston model. Part I – properties

The base class is as usual a very basic implementation since it only determines the top level of the class hierarchy. We only specify the interfaces in the base class. The actual implementation is given in the subclasses. The Matlab implementation of the base class is displayed in Figure 12.16.

It is important to implement the whole hierarchy since there are financial instruments which cannot be priced using FFT methods or analytical formulae. Sometimes applying Monte Carlo Simulation is the only way to approximate the price.

The classes from this class hierarchy can be supplied as handles to option classes, for instance if the option class implements a function pv. The pricer can then be applied within this function.

Example   We take the Carr–Madan method as an example of a subclass in the pricer class hierarchy. To this end the class fftcm implementing the Carr–Madan method inherits from the base class displayed in Figure 12.16. The implementation is given in Figures 12.17 and 12.18.

We used two different functions for deriving the price. The functions are called price1 and price2. The difference is that by using price1 it is only possible to consider either Call options or Put options. When we call the second function for a given range of quoted strikes and spot prices, price2 calculates prices of Call and Put options at once. To this end it calculates the price of out-of-the-money options. The spot price is used to determine whether an option is an out-of-the-money Call or Put option.

```
    methods
        function m = hestonmodel(params)
            m.pparams.kappa = params.kappa;      % the mean reversion
            m.pparams.theta = params.theta;      % the long term variance
            m.pparams.nu = params.nu;
% the volatility of variance
            m.pparams.rho = params.rho;
% the correlation to underlying
            m.pparams.v0 = params.v0;            % the initial variance
            m.pparams.S0 = params.S0;
% spot value of underlying
            m.pnparams = 5;
        end
    end
    methods
        function initcumulants(m,T,r,d)
            % compute cumulants
            vInst = m.pparams.v0; vLong = m.pparams.theta; ...
            kappa = m.pparams.kappa;
            omega = m.pparams.nu; rho = m.pparams.rho;
            m.c1 = (r-d).*T + 0.5*((1-exp(-kappa*T))*(vLong-vInst)...
                /kappa - vLong*T);
            m.c2 = 1/8/kappa^2*(omega*T.*exp(-kappa*T)*(vInst-vLong)...
                *(8*kappa*rho-4*omega)...
                +8*rho*omega*(1-exp(-kappa*T))*(2*vLong-vInst)...
                +2*vLong*T*(-4*kappa*rho*omega + omega^2 + 4*kappa^2)...
                +omega^2/kappa*((vLong-2*vInst)*exp(-2*kappa*T)...
                +vLong*(6*exp(-kappa*T)-7)+2*vInst)...
                +8*kappa*(vInst-vLong)*(1-exp(-kappa*T)));
            m.c4 = 0.0;
        end

    end


    methods (Static)
        function phi = cf(u,T,t_star,r,d, params)
            vInst = params(1); vLong = params(2); kappa = params(3);
            omega = params(4); rho = params(5);

            lenT = length(T);

            alfa = repmat((-1.0/2.0)*(u.*u+u*1i),1,lenT);
            beta = repmat(kappa - rho*omega*u*1i,1,lenT);
            omega2 = omega*omega;
            gamma = (1.0/2.0) * omega2;
            D = sqrt(beta.*beta - 4.0*alfa*gamma);

            bD = beta-D;
            eDt = exp(-D * diag(T-t_star));
            G = bD ./ (beta+D);
            B = (bD ./ omega2) .* ((1.0-eDt) ./ (1.0-G.*eDt));
            psi = (G .* eDt -1.0) ./ (G -1.0);
            A = (kappa*vLong / omega2)*(bD*diag(T-t_star)-2.0*log(psi));

            phi = exp(A+B*vInst+repmat(1i*u,1,lenT)...
                *diag((r-d).*(T-t_star)));
        end

    end
    end
    % ... get/set methods omitted
end
```

Figure 12.14 Matlab class for implementing method for the Heston model. Part II – methods

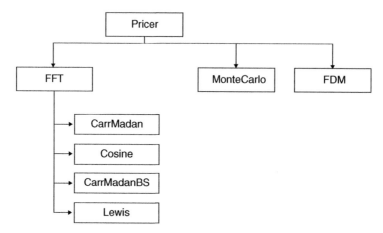

Figure 12.15   UML diagram for representing a class hierarchy implementing pricers for options. We separate FFT based methods, Monte Carlo methods and Finite Difference methods. Each class inherits from the base class pricer

```
classdef fftbase
    % the base class for all fft based pricers
    properties (Abstract)
        pN;
        peta;
        lambda;
        b;
        ku;
        jvec;
        vj;
    end

    methods (Abstract)
        currentN = getCurrentN(OBJ)
        currentfunc = getCurrentFunc(OBJ)
        currentVj = getCurrentVj(OBJ)
        currentEta = getCurrentEta(OBJ)
        currentjvec = getCurrentJvec(OBJ)
        currentku = getCurrentKu(OBJ)
        curentB = getCurrentB(OBJ)
        y = price1()    % price1 computes the price for Calls or Puts
        y = price2()    % price2 computes the price for Calls and Puts
    end
end
```

Figure 12.16   Matlab implementation of the base class for all methods based on Fourier transform

```matlab
classdef fftcm < fftbase
    % classtype: derived class
    %
    % Description: This class uses the characteristic function to
    %              compute the prices of calls, puts at once
    %
    %

    properties
        pN = [];
        peta = [];
        lambda = [];
        b = [];
        ku = [];
        jvec = [];
        vj = [];
        % The member functions (additionally to base class)
        pcharfunc = [];        % characteristic function
        valfunc1 = [];         % valfunction for calls or puts
        valfunc2 = [];         % valfunction used for simultaneous pricing
        palpha = [];
    end

    methods (Access = 'public')
        % Constructor
        function ocm = fftcm(N,eta,charfunc,alpha)
            ocm.pN = 2^N;                               % from base
            ocm.peta = eta;
            ocm.pcharfunc = charfunc;
            % set characteristic function
            ocm.palpha = alpha;
            ocm.lambda = (2 * pi) / (ocm.pN * ocm.peta);% spacing
            ocm.b = (ocm.pN * ocm.lambda) / 2;
            uvec = (1:ocm.pN)';
            ocm.ku = - ocm.b + ocm.lambda * (uvec - 1);
            ocm.jvec = (1:ocm.pN)';
            ocm.vj = (ocm.jvec-1) * ocm.peta;

            % Version without Black-Scholes adjustment, see ref1
            ocm.valfunc1 = ...
                @(T, t, r, d, params) ...
                    feval(ocm.pcharfunc,ocm.vj - (ocm.palpha + 1) ...
                    * 1i, T,t,r,d, params)./ repmat( ...
                    ocm.palpha^2 + ocm.palpha - ocm.vj.^2 + 1i ...
                    *(2*ocm.palpha + 1) * ocm.vj,1,length(T));

            ocm.valfunc2 = ...
                @(T, t, r, d, params) ...
                (repmat(1./(1+1i*ocm.vj),1,length(T)) ...
                 - feval(ocm.pcharfunc, ocm.vj -1i, T, t,r,d, params) ...
                 ./ repmat(ocm.vj.^2 - 1i*ocm.vj,1,length(T))) ...
                 *diag(exp(-r.*T))- repmat(1./(1i*ocm.vj),1,length(T));
        end
```

Figure 12.17 Implementation of the class fftcm for the Carr–Madan method to compute option prices using Fourier transforms. Part I, continued in Figure 12.18

```
function y = price1(ocm, T, t, S0, d, df, params,dataK,cp)
    % computes a range of option prices (calls / puts); cp = 1
    % (Call), cp = 0 (Put)
    ret = ocm.valfunc1(T,t,-log(df)./T,d,params);
    tmp = (ret.*exp(1i * repmat(ocm.vj,1,length(T))* ocm.b))...
        *diag(df) * ocm.peta;
    tmp(isnan(tmp)) = max(max(tmp));

    tmp = (tmp / 3) .* repmat((3 + (-1).^ocm.jvec ...
        - ((ocm.jvec - 1) == 0) ),1,length(T));

    cpvec = real(repmat(exp(-ocm.palpha * ocm.ku),1,length(T)) ...
        .* fft(tmp) / pi);

    if(cp == 1)
    % call
        y = S0 * (exp(t) * real(interp1(ocm.ku,cpvec,log(dataK))));
    else
    % put via put call parity
        y = S0*((exp(t)*real(interp1(ocm.ku,cpvec,log(dataK))))...
            - ones(size(dataK),1) + dataK);
    end
end

function y = price2(ocm, T, t, S0, d, df, params, dataK)
% computes a range of option of calls and put simultaneously
    ret = ocm.valfunc2(T,t,-log(df)/T,d,params);
    tmp = (ret.*exp(1i * repmat(ocm.vj,1,length(T))* ocm.b)) ...
        *diag(df) * ocm.peta;
    tmp(isnan(tmp)) = max(max(tmp));

    tmp = (tmp / 3) .* repmat((3 + (-1).^ocm.jvec ...
        - ((ocm.jvec - 1) == 0) ),1,length(T));

    cpvec = real(repmat(exp(-ocm.palpha * ocm.ku),1,length(T)) ...
        .* fft(tmp) / pi);

    y = S0 * (exp(t) * real(interp1(ocm.ku,cpvec,log(dataK))));
    end
end % end methods
    % set / get methods not listed
end % class definition
```

Figure 12.18 Implementation of the class fftcm for the Carr–Madan method to compute option prices using Fourier transforms. Part II, continued from Figure 12.17

The main methods are the constructor fftcm and the pricing functions price1 and price2.

12.5   AN OPTIMIZER CLASS HIERARCHY

To arrive at the optimization class hierarchy we decided to implement the base class *Optimizer* and two classes inheriting from this base class. On the one hand we consider Newton based optimizers and hence the base class *Newton*. On the other hand we consider heuristics based optimizers such as Differential Evolution or Simulated Annealing. To this end we consider the base class *Heuristic*. For implementing such methods a gradient or a Hessian matrix is

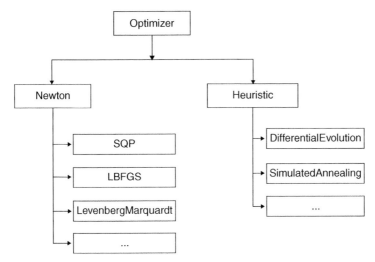

Figure 12.19 UML diagram for a class hierarchy representing optimizer. The base class is optimizer and all other members of the hierarchy inherit from this class. We have chosen to separate two types of optimizers, namely Heuristic and Newton based optimizers. The latter use gradients and/or Hessian matrices and are thus based on calculating derivatives. Implementations of such pricers are SQP or Levenberg–Marquardt. Heuristic optimizers include Differential Evolution or Simulated Annealing

unnecessary. The optimization methods are based on observed physical processes or biological mechanisms.

The class hierarchy is given in Figure 12.19. We have three layers in the hierarchy. The third layer is the actual class which implements the optimization method. The optimization methods we use for calibrating option pricing models are illustrated in Chapter 9.

Example Let us consider the optimization methods Differential Evolution and Simulated Annealing. The classes diffevo and optsimanneal are instantiated using two struct types, P_struct and S_struct, and a pricer. Then, the function optimize is called which is common to all optimizers. Figures 12.20 and 12.21 display the application of the optimize functions implemented in the corresponding class files. Our goal is to show that the code is very similar. Thus, we can use the same type of code for different optimization methods. Had

```
function [FVr_x, S_y, I_nf] = TestOptClasses_DE(P_struct, ...
                                               S_struct, ...
                                               pricer)

diffevo = optdiffevo(P_struct, S_struct, pricer); % call constructor

[FVr_x,S_y,I_nf] = diffevo.optimize();                % call optimize

clear diffevo;
end
```

Figure 12.20 Using the optdiffevo class by calling the constructor with two struct types and a pricer class

```
function [FVr_x, S_y, I_nf] = TestOptClasses_SA(P_struct, ...
                                               S_struct, ...
                                               pricer)

annealer = optsimanneal(P_struct, S_struct, pricer);
% call constructor

[FVr_x,S_y,I_nf] = annealer.optimize();                    % call optimize

clear annealer;

end
```

Figure 12.21   Using the `annealer` class by calling the constructor with two `struct` types and a `pricer` class

we designed the optimization function such that the optimizer is passed to the function as an argument, we would just have to write one single function. This is different to sequential programming, where we have to implement one particular function for one optimizer or use *if...else* statements to differentiate between the algorithms. Such a software application quickly becomes very hard to maintain.

First, consider the code for applying Differential Evolution as the optimizing algorithm.

We compare the implementation of differential evolution with that for Simulated Annealing. By comparing the corresponding code snippets we observe the similarity and recognize that object oriented programming can be used to clearly structure a software application and reuse existing code.

The code looks much more condensed and we can use this type of function for any optimizer we add to the class hierarchy (Figure 12.22).

12.6   DESIGN PATTERNS

The object oriented approach can be further extended. To this end we consider *design patterns*. Design patterns are an essential part of generic programming and enhancing the reusability of code (see Gamma, E., Helm, R., Johnson, R. and Vlissides, J. (1995), Duffy, D. (2004), Duffy, D. (2006) or Duffy, D. and Kienitz, J. (2009))

We distinguish three main classes of design patterns:

- Creational (factory, abstract factory, builder, singleton, prototype).
- Behavioural (visitor, observer, template, strategy).
- Structural (flyweight, composite, decorator, bridge, facade).

```
function [FVr_x, S_y, I_nf] = TestOptClasses(optimizer, ...
                                             pricer)

[FVr_x,S_y,I_nf] = optimizer.optimize();   % call optimize
end
```

Figure 12.22   Using the `optimizer` class by calling the constructor with two `struct` types and a `pricer` class

Design patterns are approved solutions to software development problems that appear in different contexts and situations. They have been developed to help the programmer to structure software applications and make the development more flexible by improving the maintainability of the software. Often several patterns can be applied to achieve an efficient and practical solution. The developer has to decide which pattern is the most effective one in the particular context. Design patterns are part of the generic programming paradigm.

Design patterns are also an essential part of programming when developing applications in Java, C++ or C#. Below we consider some patterns and their implementation in Matlab. As far as we know, this field has not been studied in any textbook before and we will show that using design patterns can improve applications and even prototyping using Matlab. We consider three specific design pattern and give examples of their application for financial modelling. We have chosen to take the Builder, the Visitor and the Strategy patterns.

12.6.1 The Builder Pattern

The *builder pattern* belongs to the family of creational patterns. We wish to separate the creation of objects from the representation of the objects. We have many different objects which are instantiated in the same way. For instance, take our model class hierarchy. The main inputs to a model constructor are the model parameters. Thus, a particular model is built by calling the constructor with these parameters.

For managing the creation of objects we need a class or script which takes the input, creates the concrete builder and initiates the process of building an object. This instance is called the *director*.

Using this design pattern we have achieved the creation of a (complex) that object is separated from its representation in the software architecture and we can add concrete builder classes to the system.

Application of Builder   We consider the model builder, Figure 12.23. It shows the corresponding UML diagram. We start with our model class hierarchy and we wish to apply the builder design pattern.

Let us consider the implementation of the mechanism displayed in Figure 12.23. In what follows we present the necessary Matlab classes and an example of using the classes to build models. First, we need the director, which we call `modelbuilderdirector`. This is implemented as a handle class in Figure 12.24. Of course, using the builder pattern is not restricted to a certain class hierarchy but any hierarchy should have its own builder. This is particularly interesting when setting up complex models. For example, a Libor Market Model builder can build a model by linking input arguments such as correlation, local volatility, stochastic volatility or other information about the particular Libor Market Model.

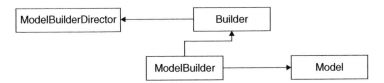

Figure 12.23   UML diagram for a model builder implementation

```
classdef modelbuilderdirector < handle
    % modelbuilderdirector
    %    Detailed explanation goes here

    properties
        pmodelbuilder;
    end

    methods
        function m = modelbuilderdirector()
            m.pmodelbuilder = [];
        end
        function y = setmodelbuilder(m,mb)
            m.pmodelbuilder = mb;
            y = true;
        end
        function y = getmodel(m)
            y = m.pmodel;
        end
        function y = buildmodel(m,params,market)
            m.pmodelbuilder.buildparam(params);  % set the parameter
            m.pmodelbuilder.buildmarket(market); % set the market
            y = m.pmodelbuilder.pmodel;          % return the model
        end
    end
end
```

Figure 12.24   The class modelbuilderdirector

Applying our implementation the main functionality is the method buildmodel. Here, all the information necessary to work with a model is used to pass it to the pmodelbuilder, which is able to instantiate a particular model.

In order to actually apply the class modelbuilderdirector we need to pass a class of type builder to the director, which is then able to build a particular model. To this end we coded the class modelbuilder which is shown in Figure 12.25. The class modelbuilder inherits from the base class builder. The latter is the base class for all builder functionality. We also use the mechanism to create pricers or optimizers.

Let us consider the implementation for building a Heston model displayed in Figure 12.26. The hestonmodelbuilder inherits from the class modelbuilder and implements the function hestonmodelbuilder. This function calls the constructor of pmodel, which is a particular model. In our case this is a Heston model. Finally, the methods buildparam(m,params) and buildmarket(m,market) are called.

In the implementation given in Figure 12.26 the builder is able to create a standard model if no input arguments are specified. The usual way of using the builder is to call it with input arguments which represent the model parameters.

However, sometimes we only wish to create a standard model where we set the model parameters later, for instance after a successful calibration of the model.

Example   We consider the building blocks of a model builder and show how we set up a Heston model. The Matlab script is presented in Figure 12.27.

```
classdef modelbuilder < builder
    % This is the base class for building models
    %    To create a certain model ...

    properties (Abstract)
        pmodel;
    end

    methods
        function y = getmodel(m)
            y = m.pmodel;
        end
    end

    methods (Abstract)
        buildparam()
        buildmarket()
    end

end
```

Figure 12.25   The class modelbuilder which inherits from the base class builder

```
classdef hestonmodelbuilder < modelbuilder
    % hestonmodelbuilder initializes a hestonmodel
    %    first a heston model is initialized
    %    second the parameters are initialized wrt input data

    properties
        pmodel; % this is a Heston model
    end

    methods
        function m = hestonmodelbuilder()
            default.kappa = 1;
            default.theta = 1;
            default.omega = 1;
            default.rho = 1;
            default.v0 = 1;
            %default.S0 = 1;
            m.pmodel = hestonmodel(default);
        end
        function buildparam(m,params)
            m.pmodel.pparams.v0 = params(1);
            m.pmodel.pparams.theta = params(2);
            m.pmodel.pparams.kappa = params(3);
            m.pmodel.pparams.omega =  params(4);
            m.pmodel.pparams.rho = params(5);
        end

        function buildmarket(m,market)
            m.pmodel.pmarket = market;
        end
    end

end
```

Figure 12.26   Class definition of a hestonmodelbuilder

```
% define the struct for the stochastic volatility models
sv_struct.kappa = 0.5;           % mean reversion
sv_struct.nu = 0.15;             % vol of variance
sv_struct.theta = 0.2;           % long term variance
sv_struct.rho = -0.7;            % correlation
sv_struct.v0 = 0.2;              % initial variance
sv_struct.S0 = 100.0;            % spot price

mbd = modelbuilderdirector();    % init modelbuilderdirector
hmb = hestonmodelbuilder();      % init builder (heston)
mbd.setmodelbuilder(hmb);        % pass builder to director
hm = mbd.buildmodel(sv_struct,'eq');% call the buildmodel method

hm.print()                       % call a method

clear hm;                        % clear model
clear hmb;                       % clear heston model builder
clear mbd;                       % clear modelbuilderdirector
clear sv_struct;                 % clear struct
```

Figure 12.27 Matlab script for using the model class hierarchy together with the design pattern builder

We build a variable sv_struct to store the model parameters. Then, we invoke the modelbuilderdirector and the hestonmodelbuilder by calling the corresponding constructors. We pass an instance of a Heston model builder, hmb, to the director by calling the function mbd.setmodelbuilder(hmb) with the instance hmb as the argument. The director is then able to build a Heston model. We instantiate a model hm by assigning the output of the member function mbd.buildmodel(sv_struct,'eq'). The arguments are necessary since the interface for building models is implemented taking two arguments of type struct and string. After calling the hm.print() to make clear that a Heston model has been created, we delete all the classes created.

12.6.2 The Visitor Pattern

Suppose we have a class hierarchy and classes dedicated to performing operations on class data or on other objects. Now, it happens that we wish to extend the functionality of the class. This may be necessary to include other algorithms for pricing or changing the numerical scheme for an existing model in a Monte Carlo simulation application. One way to achieve this goal is to add certain functionality to the class under consideration. This makes it necessary to change the implementation of the whole class hierarchy, in particular by editing the base class every time we add new functionality. Another non-intrusive way is to apply the *visitor pattern*.

The visitor pattern allows the programmer to add new functionality or add new methods to an object structure without changing the actual classes of the hierarchy. We achieve our goal by implementing a new class hierarchy. This visitor class hierarchy has to be set up once and then the programmer can add new methods. All classes have to implement a function called visit which operates on the given class hierarchy by specifying the input argument to be the base class. On the other hand each class of the hierarchy which is extended by functionality has to implement an accept function taking the corresponding visitor base class as an argument.

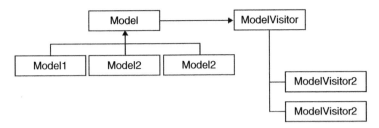

Figure 12.28   UML diagram for the design pattern visitor

We have set up the `modelvisitor` base class as a handle class with just one method, which is the `visit` method (see Figure 12.28 and the corresponding code in Figure 12.29).

Before we can apply the visitor design pattern we have to extend the base class `model` to handle visitors. This is done by adding the code given in Figure 12.30 to the class `model`. This is equivalent to adding one further method to the standard ones.

This defines the interface for the `modelvisitor`. In Figure 12.31 we give a simple implementation of a `modelvisitor`. Now, we have created an interface which can be applied to add new functionality to the classes of the model hierarchy. We do not have to change the base class when we add new functionality.

We consider the class `modelvisitor1` in Figure 12.31; it only implements very basic functionality. In fact, we take some model value using the function `model.getval()` and multiply the corresponding number with 5.0. But more complex applications such as implementing schemes for the discretization of SDE are also possible (see Duffy, D. and Kienitz, J. (2009) for details; there, the authors consider a fully functional software design for handling SDEs and provide a full description together with UML diagrams and C++ code; this setup can be ported to Matlab using the visitor pattern discussed here.

Example   We wish to outline the use of a visitor. To this end we give a simple Matlab script which applies the visitor design pattern to models. Figure 12.32 shows the implementation.

```
classdef modelvisitor < handle
    % Since no virtual functions we only state one function
    % and use if statement in the inherited classes for modelvisitor
    % each call in if statement would correspond to a classes in real
    % oo programming
    methods (Abstract)
        y = visit(m,model)
    end

    %usually:
    % methods (Abstract)
    %    y = visit(m,model1)
    %    y = visit(m,model2)
    %
    %    ...
    %
    %    y = visit(m,modelx)

    % inherited class has to implement one of the above function
end
```

Figure 12.29   Implementation of `modelvisitor` as a Matlab class

```
% Possibility to use a visitor
    methods (Abstract)
        y=accept(model, modelvisitor) % interface for extending a model
    end
```

Figure 12.30   Extension of the functionality of the base class model for adding visitors

The output of the script is '*I am a Heston model*', '*I am a Heston model visitor, the value is 8*'. Thus, the visitor acts on an instance of a Heston model and sets some value to 8. Then, another visitor is applied and the output is '*Visiting Heston*' and '*I am a Heston model visitor, the value is 450*'. This visitor now sets the value to 450.

This is only to demonstrate the usage of the pattern and illustrate the basic set up for including this idea for further use in advanced applications.

12.6.3   The Strategy Pattern

We often face the problem that the behaviour of an object is determined by the context or the state of another object. For instance, we might obtain a variable *option* which can take the values $1, \ldots, 5$. With respect to the value of option a certain algorithm is executed. We wish that the corresponding algorithms might change in the future. Furthermore, we wish to add further algorithms since another value for option might be added in the future.

The solution to this problem is the *strategy pattern*. To achieve this we implement a base class strategyclass that has an abstract member function, called the *interface*. All subclasses implement the interface. Due to the context, which in our case is the value of the variable

```
classdef modelvisitor1 < modelvisitor

    properties (SetAccess = 'public', GetAccess = 'public')
        a;
    end

    methods
        function obj = modelvisitor1(value)
            obj.a = value;
        end

        function print(m)
            sprintf('I am a Heston model visitor, the value is %d',m.a)
        end

        function y = visit(modelvisitor,model)
            %if strcmp(model.Modelname,'Heston')
                fprintf('Visiting Heston');
                modelvisitor.a = model.getval() * 5.0;
                y = true;
            %   end
        end
    end

end
```

Figure 12.31   Implementation of modelvisitor1, which inherits from modelvisitor

```
% Test the model visitor

% create the struct to build a heston model
sv_struct.kappa = 0.5;          % mean reversion
sv_struct.nu = 0.15;            % volatility of variance
sv_struct.theta = 0.2;          % long term variance
sv_struct.rho = -0.7;           % correlation
sv_struct.v0 = 0.2;             % initial variance
sv_struct.S0 = 100.0;           % spot price

mbd = modelbuilderdirector();   % init modelbuilderdirector
hmb = hestonmodelbuilder();     % init particular builder (heston)
mbd.setmodelbuilder(hmb);       % pass the builder to director
hm = mbd.buildmodel(sv_struct,'eq');% build the model

hm.print()                      % print

hmv = modelvisitor1(8);         % init modelvisitor
hmv.print()                     % print
hm.accept(hmv);                 % call visitor

hmv.print()                     % print

% delete all classes
clear hm;
clear hmb;
clear mbd;
clear hmv;
```

Figure 12.32   Script applying the visitor design pattern to models

option, we instantiate an object. This is a subclass derived from `strategyclass` and therefore provides an implementation of the interface. Using this approach the specific implementation can be modified to fit the necessary functions. It is easy to add new functionality or modify existing implementations without having to change the other parts of the software.

The UML description of the strategy pattern is given in Figure 12.33. This is the blueprint which we wish to set up using Matlab.

Application Strategy   We implement the general design pattern in Matlab. To this end we create a handle class `strategy`, as shown in Figure 12.34. It has a constructor and two methods: `setstrategy` and `runstrategy`. The methods are used to set a new strategy and to run it.

We use the class `strategytype`, displayed in Figure 12.35, to implement different strategies. We have chosen this set up for considering different optimizers. This is extremely

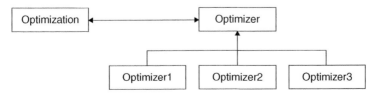

Figure 12.33   UML diagram of the strategy design pattern

```
classdef strategy < handle
% This is the base class for all financial models
    properties
        psttype = {};
    end

    methods
        function m = strategy(v)
            m.setstrategy(v);
        end
        function setstrategy(m,v)
            m.psttype = strategytype.newtype(v);
        end

        function y = runstrategy(m)
            y = m.psttype.runstrategy();
        end

    end
end
```

Figure 12.34   Implementation of the design pattern strategy in Matlab

```
classdef strategytype

    properties

    end

    methods (Abstract)
        runstrategy(t)
    end

    methods (Static)
        function y = newtype(v)
            switch lower(v)
                case 'de'              % differential evolution
                    y = strategytype1;
                case 'sqp'             % sequential quadratic
                    y = strategytype2;
                case 'neldermead'      % nelder mead
                    y = strategytype3;
                case 'fmincon'         % matlab fmincon
                    y = strategytype4;
                case 'sa'              % simulated annealing
                    y = strategytype5;
                otherwise
                    y = errorstrategy;
            end
        end
    end

end
```

Figure 12.35   Implementation of different strategies for an optimizer

```
classdef strategytype1 < strategytype

    properties
    end

    methods
        function y = runstrategy(m)
            fprintf('StragegyType1');
            y = 1;
        end
    end
end
```

Figure 12.36   Simple implementation of a certain strategy with a simple method `runstrategy`

convenient when we wish to test several optimizers on historical market data. For instance, we often need to know if we can apply a local search algorithm which is fast or if we have to rely on a slow global search procedure. Furthermore, we wish to test the performance of guessing the starting point determination for several local optimizers. To this end we have to be flexible when choosing the applied algorithm.

Each strategy has to implement the function `runstrategy`. This method actually executes the strategy. Using optimizers, this means applying a particular optimization algorithm to some objective function. For a pedagogical example let us take Figure 12.36. In this simple case the strategy just prints a string. But for real applications this can be any Matlab function or user-defined function.

Finally, in Figure 12.37 we show how we can apply the strategy by considering a simple example.

Using this Matlab script we initialize a strategy using a string as input. The output is simply *1* and *2* showing that the corresponding strategy is called. This mechanism can be applied whenever we have to choose between different possibilities.

12.7   EXAMPLE – CALIBRATION ENGINE

In this section we describe the development of a calibration engine for equity models. Upon this implementation the reader can build a proprietary calibration methodology. We wish to

```
clear; clc;

s = strategy('de');
dummy = s.runstrategy();
dummy

s.setstrategy('sqp');
dummy = s.runstrategy();
dummy
clear s;
```

Figure 12.37   Matlab script using the strategy

use quoted option prices and a model which is able to price the options. To this end we apply

1. Market data and weighting.
2. Model choice and parameters.
3. Choosing a pricing algorithm.
4. Choosing an optimizer.
5. Choosing an objective function.
6. Start the calibration and store the calibrated parameters.

Starting with (1) we have to choose the market data. To do this we rely on a realtime data provider and store quotes on a spreadsheet or in a database. The spot values of the underlying, the term structure of zero coupon rates and possibly the dividend yields also have to be stored. Further, with respect to trading volume and liquidity issues we wish to assign a weight to the option which we later use for calibration. By doing so we can ensure that the most liquid options have a higher weight than illiquid options.

In step (2) we choose a model which we wish to calibrate. The model has a number of model parameters. We wish to be able to specify which model parameters we calibrate and which we keep fixed. In Chapters 2 and 3 we saw that different parameters affect certain structures such as the shape of the implied volatility surface in the same way or in an opposite way. To accomodate this it is possible to fix certain parameters to achieve more stability.

In step (3) we choose the pricing algorithm using, for instance, one of the methods presented in Chapters 5 and 6.

Step (4) is the choice of the optimizer. When we need the results immediately and may also guess reasonable start parameters, a Newton based optimizer such as SQP (see Chapter 9, Section 9.5) is a good choice. In cases where we do not know very much about good initial parameters, a global optimizer such as Differential Evolution or Simulated Annealing (see Chapter 9, Sections 9.6 and 9.7) is the best choice.

Another crucial step is the choice of the objective function in step (5). We provide four different objective functions:

- Root-mean-square error (rmse):

$$\frac{1}{\sqrt{N}}\sqrt{\sum_{k=1}^{N}\omega_k(P_{\text{Model}}^{\Theta} - P_{\text{Market}})^2}$$

- Average absolute error (aae):

$$\frac{1}{N}\sum_{k=1}^{N}\omega_k|P_{\text{Model}}^{\Theta} - P_{\text{Market}}|$$

- Absolute absolute error as percentage of the mean price (apem):

$$\frac{N}{\sum_{k=1}^{N}\omega_k P_{\text{Market}}}\sum_{k=1}^{N}\frac{|P_{\text{Model}}^{\Theta} - P_{\text{Market}}|}{N}$$

- Average relative percentage error (arpe):

$$\frac{1}{N}\sum_{k=1}^{N}\omega_k\frac{|P_{\text{Model}}^{\Theta} - P_{\text{Market}}|}{P_{\text{Market}}}.$$

The weights $\omega_i, i = 1, \ldots, N$ have been specified in step (1) when we considered the market data.

Finally, we start the calibration and store the parameters for further usage in step (6). The parameters can be used to price complex path-dependent options using Monte Carlo simulation, for instance. Finally, we give some examples for calibrating a model to market data. We use the model class, the pricing methods and the optimization class hierarchies given in Sections 12.3 to 12.5. The entire pricing code is available as source code.

To manage the whole system we implement a script called the director. This script takes four parameters as input. We need to specify the model we wish to calibrate, the method we wish to apply for calculating the model prices, the optimizer which is used for finding the minimum of the objective function and which parameters we wish to calibrate. To this end we describe the main functionality of the director and the builder since we have already considered the other classes and their functionality.

12.7.1   Calibrating a Data Set or a History

For calibrating a model we suppose that the relevant data are stored in a spreadsheet. Of course storage in some other type of database system is also possible but not discussed here. In order to apply the Matlab application to calibration we have to retrieve the relevant data from the spreadsheet and then create the necessary instances of Matlab classes. On the spreadsheet we specify:

- Model for calibration (for example VG, NIG, VG CIR).
- Pricing method (for example COS, Carr–Madan, Lewis).
- Objective function (function and weights).
- Optimizer (for example Differential Evolution, SQP).
- Market data (for example spot prices, volatilities, rates).

Then, we have to implement some interface to retrieve the data from the spreadsheet. This can be done by using standard Matlab functionality for communicating with Excel. The script presented in Figure 12.38 takes account of this issue.

Having opened the file, we use the function statement

```
xlsread1(File,'SheetName','CellRange');
```

to retrieve the data from *File*, sheet *SheetName* and range *CellRange*.

To create an instance of the model we consider the `modelbuilderdirector`. This class takes as an input some model from the model class hierarchy and by calling the member function `buildmodel` we create an instance of the corresponding model class. This class is then used by the calibration application. Let us look at the code for setting up a model. This piece of code is given in Figure 12.39. This can be integrated into the script, which takes care of managing the interaction of the classes and prepares all the data necessary for calling the constructors for the relevant classes.

```
Excel = actxserver ('Excel.Application');
File = 'LOCATION, e.g. C:\Users\Matlab\TestCases.xlsm';
Excel.Workbooks.Open(File);
```

Figure 12.38   Matlab code for opening an Excel sheet and keeping it open to read stored data

```
mbd = modelbuilderdirector();    % modelbuilder

params = xlsread1(File,'Params','E8:I8');
mbd.setmodelbuilder(hestonmodelbuilder());
```

Figure 12.39 Code for setting up a model by passing a `modelbuilder` to the `modelbuilderdi`-`rector` class together with the necessary parameters

Furthermore, we use a struct to gather the relevant data for calibration. This is all done by calling the function `readparamsneu` with a filename *File*. It is possible to specify the format in which the data are stored even if they are read from a database or some text file. This function then returns the struct for optimization, the optimizer, the pricer, the number of parameters and the model we wish to calibrate to market data.

We see that the pricer is completely decoupled from the optimization routine. Thus, it is possible to implement a pricing model for some interest rate model or some credit-equity hybrid model and supply it to the optimization algorithm. The only thing we have to take into account is that we provide some objective function as a function handle to the optimizer.

Often we wish to backtest a model or study the calibration performance of a model using historical data. To this end we design the code to be applicable for calibrating a history of data.

Finally, we have to close the connection to the data storage system which in our case is a spreadsheet. This is done by the code presented in Figure 12.40.

We have now explained all the necessary steps for applying the calibration engine to calibrate a given model to market data. For researching the timely evolution of model data and the testing of hedge strategies it is necessary to calibrate one or more models to historical option data. To this end we consider the test case of the German DAX index. We have created a Matlab script which we apply to calibrate a history of data from 07/01/2007 to 09/01/2008. Within the script we use all the object oriented machinery we have considered in this chapter. The corresponding code is given in Figure 12.41.

First of all we have to choose which source we use to retrieve the data and specify the output file. Then, we proceed by gathering the basic data. We transform the data into data structures, which we use for the calibration algorithms. This is done by applying the function `DAXCalibParams`. Then, for each dataset in the history we use the prepared data within Matlab. The data are passed to an instance of an optimizer class which has a pricing algorithm and some objective function which we wish to minimize. The information which pricer and which objective function we use is given as external input and we have linked it to the spreadsheet. It is the same spreadsheet we use for storing the market data. We have chosen Excel since it is the most convenient way to illustrate the general mechanism but the user can apply other database applications using the Access, Sybase or Oracle databases. For many sets of market data and long histories it might become necessary to retrieve the market data for each set separately. This reduces the execution speed of the calibration since we have to start some SQL query or open some Excel sheet for all calibrations.

```
Excel.Quit;                      % Quit Excel
Excel.delete;                    % Sign out
clear Excel;                     % clear variable
```

Figure 12.40 Matlab code for closing the connection to a spreadsheet where data are stored

```
clear; clc;
%-----------File Information-----------
File = 'DAX_Vols';

%-------Get Data from Excel or Database-----------
[data_struct] = DAXDataBloomi(File);                    % Read data
[calib_struct,P_struct,S_struct, pricer] = ...
    DAXCalibParams(File);                              % Prepare data

% Prepare the output arrays
nParas = length(P_struct.usevec(P_struct.usevec==true));
results = zeros( ...
    length(calib_struct.data_start:calib_struct.data_end),nParas);
funcvalue = zeros( ...
    length(calib_struct.data_start:calib_struct.data_end),1);

%---------------Calibration----------------
k=1;                                                   % index variable
optFunction = FactoryOptimizer(S_struct, pricer);% create opt instance
for i=calib_struct.data_start:calib_struct.data_end
    if(k>1)
        P_struct.params = results(k-1,:);% previously calib data
        P_struct.params
    end
    P_struct = DAXStructSlicer(P_struct, data_struct, i);
    [tmpResults,tmpValue]= optFunction(P_struct);
    funcvalue(k) = tmpValue;                   % add value of obj func
    results(k,:) = tmpResults;                 % add calib params
    k=k+1;                                     % increase index
end
if(strcmp(calib_struct.plotvar,'ja'))                  % plot results or not
        DAXPlot(P_struct,pricer,results, ...
            data_struct.stockDates,k-1,i);
end

%-----------------Output the results-----------
%-----------------Open Excel or Database-----------
Excel = actxserver ('Excel.Application');              % Use Excel
outputfile = '.../DAXresults';
invoke(Excel.Workbooks,'Open',outputfile);

%---------------Write to Excel or Database-----------
xlswrite1(outputfile, ...
    results, [P_struct.modelname,'_',S_struct.optmethod], 'B2');
xlswrite1(outputfile, ...
    data_struct.stockDates,[P_struct.modelname,'_', ...
    S_struct.optmethod],'A2');
xlswrite1(outputfile, ...
    funcvalue, [P_struct.modelname,'_',S_struct.optmethod],'J2');

%---------------Close Excel or Database-----------
invoke(Excel.ActiveWorkbook,'Save');                   % Save the results
Excel.Quit;                                            % Quit Excel
Excel.delete;                                          % Sign out
clear Excel;                                           % clear variable
```

Figure 12.41 Matlab code for calibrating a model to a history of market data and for storing the model parameters for each point in the history

In the script shown in Figure 12.41 we have chosen to use the previously calibrated data as the starting point for the current optimization. For genetic algorithms such a starting point is not necessary. For some models there exists an educated guess for the best parameter set, but this is currently not implemented and may differ according to the particular application to which the calibration is applied.

12.8   EXAMPLE – THE LIBOR MARKET MODEL AND GREEKS

In Chapter 8 we considered the calculation of hedge sensitivities in the Libor Market Model (LMM). After introducing the object oriented programming paradigm and the corresponding Matlab functionality we give a detailed explanation of our implementation. We wish to present an implementation that is easy to use. Furthermore, we would like the implementation to reflect the versatility of the adjoint method.

It is useful to implement an abstract class LMMDer which contains all properties and methods required by a general interest rate derivative that is represented by an LMM simulation. Then, we implement two concrete subclasses, BSwap and TrigSwap, derived from the superclass LMMDer. The advantage of this approach is that the subclasses inherit all the properties and methods from the superclass. We do not have to implement the same piece of code twice. Of course, we could also derive a third or fourth subclass from LMMDer if we wish to analyse other interest rate derivatives.

We only discuss in detail the important algorithms of these classes.

12.8.1   An Abstract Class for LMM Derivatives

In Figure 12.42 we give the key part of the definition of the class LMMDer. We focus on the necessary aspects of mapping a Libor based derivative to Matlab code and use the implementation to apply the adjoint method for calculating Greeks.

The method LMM_Simulation outputs the Libors for all paths and stores the result in the variable LIBORs. The functions BuildFactorMatricesD, BuildMatricesC, BuildMatricesE and BuildTranslationMatricesB calculate auxiliary data required by the algorithms that actually calculate the value of the Greek. The matrices $D(n)$ and $E(n)$ are determined by the general theory presented in Chapter 8, Subsection 8.4.3. The matrices $C(n)$ and $B(n)$ are given in Chapter 8, Subsection 8.4.4. The corresponding algorithms just fill these matrices with data and are not presented here.

The most important methods are forward_method, adjoint_method and finally bermudan_method, all of which we show here.

The forward method given in Figure 12.43 implements the general forward recursion. It is useful to separate the cases where all matrices $C(n)$ are zero and where the start vector v is also zero since the outcome of the algorithm is then zero. In fact such cases occur when calculating Greeks. The algorithm returns the result vector w in variable w and all the matrices $A(n)$ are stored in A. This is useful since all $A(n)$ are required, for example for calculating the Gamma.

Analogously, the adjoint method given in Figure 12.44 directly implements the backward recursion described in Chapter 8, Subsection 8.3.3. This implementation is optimized in a similar fashion to the forward method when some input parameters are zero.

Finally, the Bermudan adjoint method, displayed in Figure 12.45, implements the necessary modifications to apply the method to Bermudan ARPs such as those considered in Chapter 8.

```
classdef LMMDer
    %An abstract superclass for handling LMM Derivatives

    %Input Parameters
    properties (GetAccess='public', SetAccess = 'public')
        m=10              %maturity
        tau = []          %vector of tenor distances
        L=[]              %LIBOR initial values
        sigma=[]          %volatilities for LIBORs
        paths=100         %number of paths in Monte Carlo Simulation
    end

    %Output
    properties (GetAccess='public', SetAccess = 'protected')
        LIBORs=[]         %LIBORs of LMM Simulation
        Price=[]          %Price
        Delta=[]          %Delta
        Gamma=[]          %Gamma
        Vega=[]           %Vega
    end

    methods
        %constructor
        function LD = LMMDer()
        end
    end

    %Abstract (=virtual) Methods to be overloaded in subclasses
    methods (Abstract =true, Access = 'protected')
        H = BuildMatrixH(LD, DMat, V, omega)
        V = BuildStartVectorsV(LD, omega)
        Delta = DeltaPath(LD, D, V, method, omega)
        w = GammaPath(LD, D, C, V, method, omega)
        Vega = VegaPath(LD, D, BMat, V, method, omega)
        LD = CalcPrice(LD)
    end

    methods

        LD = LMM_Simulation(LD)

        D = BuildFactorMatricesD(LD,omega)
        C = BuildMatricesC(LD, Delta, E)
        E = BuildMatricesE(LD, D, omega)
        BMat = BuildTranslationMatricesB(LD, omega)

        [w A] = forward_method(LD, A1, B, C, v)
        w = adjoint_method(LD, A1, D, C, v)
        w = bermudan_method(LD, A1, D, C, V, r)

        Delta = CalcDelta(LD, method)
        Gamma = CalcGamma(LD, method)
        Vega = CalcVega(LD, method)
    end

end
```

Figure 12.42   An abstract class for a general LMM derivative

```
function [w A] = forward_method(LD, A1, D, C, v)
%Forward method
    if(~isempty(C))
        [m, q, N] = size(C);            %calculate dimensions
        N = N+1;
        A = zeros(m,q,N);               %initialize A
        A(:,:,1)=A1;
        for n = 1:N-1                   %run forward recursion
            A(:,:,n+1) = D(:,:,n)*A(:,:,n) + C(:,:,n);
        end
    else                                %assumes that all C(n)=0
        m = size(D,1);                  %calculate dimensions
        N = size(D,3)+1;
        A = zeros(m,m,N);               %initialize A
        A(:,:,1)=A1;
        for n = 1:N-1                   %run forward recursion
            A(:,:,n+1) = D(:,:,n)*A(:,:,n);
        end
    end
    if(~isempty(v))                     %calculate result
        w = v * A(:,:,N);
    end
end
```

Figure 12.43   General forward method

```
function w = adjoint_method(LD, A1, D, C, v)
    if(~isempty(C))                     %General case
        [m, q, N] = size(C);            %calculate dimensions
        N = N+1;
        V=v.';                          %initialize V
        Vbar = zeros(q,1);              %initialize Vbar
        for n = N-1:-1:1                %run backward recursion
            Vbar = Vbar + C(:,:,n).' * V;
            V = D(:,:,n).' * V;
        end
        w = Vbar.';
    else                                %assumes that all C(n)=0
        m = size(D,1);                  %calculate dimensions
        N = size(D,3)+1;
        V=v.';                          %initialize V
        for n = N-1:-1:1                %run backward recursion
            V = D(:,:,n).' * V;
        end
        w = zeros(1,m);
    end

    if(~isempty(A1))                    %assumes A(1)=0 otherwise
        w = w + V.' * A1;               %calculate result
    end
end
```

Figure 12.44   General adjoint method

```
function w = bermudan_method(LD, A1, D, C, V, r)
    if(~isempty(C))
        [m, q, N] = size(C);         %calculate dimensions
        N = N+1;
        W = V(N,:).';                %initialize W
        Wbar = zeros(q,1);           %initialize Wbar
        for n = N-1:-1:r             %run backward recursion
            Wbar = Wbar + C(:,:,n).' * W;
            W = D(:,:,n).' * W + V(n,:).';
        end
        for n = r-1:-1:1
            Wbar = Wbar + C(:,:,n).' * W;
            W = D(:,:,n).' * W;
        end
        w = Wbar.';
    else                             %runs optimized version, if all C(n)=0
        m = size(D,1);               %calculate dimensions
        N = size(D,3)+1;
        W = V(N,:).';                %initialize W
        for n = N-1:-1:r             %run backward recursion
            W = D(:,:,n).' * W + V(n,:).';
        end
        for n = r-1:-1:1
            W = D(:,:,n).' * W;
        end
        w = zeros(1,m);
    end
    if(~isempty(A1))                 %assumes A(1)=0 otherwise
        w = w + W.' * A1;            %calculate result
    end
end
```

Figure 12.45   Adjoint Bermudan method

The methods `CalcDelta`, `CalcGamma` and `CalcVega` calculate Greeks using a Monte Carlo estimator. For each path the Greek is calculated by one of the methods described above and the average over all paths is returned. The calculation of the Greeks in a single path is realized by application of the virtual methods `DeltaPath`, `GammaPath` and `VegaPath`. We used virtual methods here since their implementation depends on the derivative under consideration. The implementation of the Delta is shown in Figure 12.46 and is a rather direct implementation of the general results (see Chapter 8, Subsection 8.4.3). The Gamma, shown in Figure 12.47, is more involved since we have to calculate both components of $\Gamma = w + Y$ (see Chapter 8, Subsection 8.4.3). The implementation of the Vega, see Figure 12.48, on the other hand is again a direct implementation of the general results (see Chapter 8, Subsection 8.4.3).

12.8.2   A Class for Bermudan Swaptions

We now take the specialized case of a Bermudan swaption. Figure 12.49 shows the implementation of the class.

The properties e, K, phi and nom store the additional data required for modelling a Bermudan swaption.

```
function Delta = CalcDelta(LD, method)
    Delta = zeros(1,LD.m);                  %Initialize
    for omega = 1:LD.paths                  %Calculate Delta in all paths
        D = BuildFactorMatricesD(LD, omega);
        V = BuildStartVectorsV(LD, omega);
        Delta = Delta + DeltaPath(LD,D,V,method,omega);
    end
    Delta = Delta / LD.paths;               %Calculate average
end
```

Figure 12.46   Calculating the Delta for LMM

```
function Gamma = CalcGamma(LD, method)
    Gamma = zeros(LD.m,LD.m);                    % Initialize
    for omega = 1:LD.paths                       % Calc Gamma in all paths
        V = LD.BuildStartVectorsV(omega);% Calc auxiliary parameters
        v = sum(V);
        D = LD.BuildFactorMatricesD(omega);
        E = LD.BuildMatricesE(D, omega);
        [w Delta ] = LD.forward_method(eye(LD.m), D, [], v);
        C = LD.BuildMatricesC(Delta, E);
        H = LD.BuildMatrixH(Delta, V, omega);
        Y = zeros(LD.m,LD.m);                    % Calc Y component
        Y = Delta(:,:,LD.m).' * H * Delta(:,:,LD.m);
        Gamma = Gamma + Y;
        w = GammaPath(LD,D,C,V,method,omega);% Calc w component
        Gamma = Gamma + w;                       % finally obtain Gamma
    end
    Gamma = Gamma / LD.paths;                    % Calc average
end
```

Figure 12.47   Calculating the Gamma for LMM

```
function Vega = CalcVega(LD, method)
    Vega = zeros(1,LD.m);
    for omega = 1:LD.paths        % Calc Vega in all paths
        D = BuildFactorMatricesD(LD, omega);
        BMat = BuildTranslationMatricesB(LD, omega);
        V = BuildStartVectorsV(LD, omega);
        Vega = Vega + VegaPath(LD, D, BMat, V, method, omega);
    end
    Vega = Vega / LD.paths;       % Calc average
end
```

Figure 12.48   Calculating the Vega for LMM

```
classdef BSwap < IRD.LMMDer

    properties           % Input Parameters
        e=5              % first exercise time index, 1 <= e <= m
        K=0.3            % strike rate
        phi=1            % payer (=+1) or receiver (=-1) swaption?
        nom=10000        % nominal value
    end

    properties (GetAccess='private', SetAccess ='private')
        optimal=[]       %optimal exercise indices
    end

    methods
        function B = BSwap()    % constructor
            B = B@IRD.LMMDer;
        end

        B = LSM_Simulation(B)   % Least Squares Monte Carlo
    end

    % Making abstract methods from superclass concrete
    methods (Access='protected')
        H = BuildMatrixH(B, DMat, V, omega)
        V = BuildStartVectorsV(B, omega)
        Delta = DeltaPath(LD, D, V, method, omega)
        w = GammaPath(LD, D, C, V, method, omega)
        Vega = VegaPath(LD, D, BMat, V, method, omega)
        B = CalcPrice(B)
    end

end
```

Figure 12.49 A subclass for Bermudan swaptions

Since a Bermudan swaption gives the holder the right to exercise at predefined discrete times we have to find the optimal exercise strategy. The method LSM_Simulation solves this task by applying regression to this problem. The result, which is the optimal exercise time index for each path, is stored in the property optimal.

The method BuildMatrixH calculates the Hessian of the payoff function; analogously BuildStartVectorsV calculates the start vectors for the recursions. The algorithms output arrays with data according to the general formulae.

The calculations of the various Greeks for one path omega are carried out in the routines DeltaPath, GammaPath and VegaPath, but with all the earlier preparations these routines call the general forward or adjoint methods with the correct parameters. As an instructive example, the code for DeltaPath is shown in Figure 12.50. Here method is a string that controls which method is called.

12.8.3 A Class for Trigger Swaps

We now specialize and consider the case of a Trigger swap; the main functionality of the implementation is shown in Figure 12.51.

```
function Delta = DeltaPath(B,D,V,method,omega)
   Delta = zeros(1,B.m);
   r = B.optimal(omega);
   if(r)   % otherwise the delta in this path is zero
       if(strcmp(method,'for'))
           v = sum(V);
           Delta = B.forward_method(eye(B.m),D,[],v);
       elseif(strcmp(method,'adj'))
           v = sum(V);
           Delta = B.adjoint_method(eye(B.m), D, [] , v);
       elseif(strcmp(method,'ads'))
           Delta = B.bermudan_method(eye(B.m), D, [], V, r);
       end
   end
end
```

Figure 12.50 Calculating the Delta on one path

```
classdef TrigSwap < IRD.LMMDer

    properties        % Input Parameters
        e=5           % first observation date
        K=[]          % Trigger Levels
        s=0.2         % Spread Rate
        kappa=0.1;    % fixed rate
        N=10000;      % nominal value
        Triggered;    % Time index where triggered
    end

    methods
        function TS = TrigSwap
            TS = TS@IRD.LMMDer;
        end
    end

    methods
        TS = Initialize(TS)
        TS = CalcTriggered(TS);
        TS = MCPayoff(TS);
    end

    % Making abstract methods from superclass concrete
    methods (Access='protected')
        H = BuildMatrixH(TS, DMat, V, omega)
        V = BuildStartVectorsV(TS, omega)
        Delta = DeltaPath(TS, D, V, method, omega)
        w = GammaPath(TS, D, C, V, method, omega)
        Vega = VegaPath(TS, D, BMat, V, method, omega)
        TS = CalcPrice(TS)
    end

end
```

Figure 12.51 A subclass for Trigger swaps

```
function TS = CalcTriggered(TS)
    TS.Triggered = ones(TS.paths,1) * (TS.m+1);
    for omega = 1:TS.paths
        for n = TS.e:TS.m
            if(TS.LIBORs(n,n,omega)>TS.K(n))
                TS.Triggered(omega) = n;
                break
            end
        end
    end
end
```

Figure 12.52   Calculating the triggers of a Trigger swap

The main conceptual difference between the Trigger swap and the Bermudan swaption is the fact that a Trigger swap does not grant an option to exercise but it is *triggered* automatically. Because of this we have to adapt the data such as the functions `BuildMatrixH` and `BuildStartVectorsV` according to the considerations in Chapter 8, Section 8.5. Thus, we have to implement a method which calculates the time indices at which the Trigger swap is actually triggered. This parameter is necessary for all the other routines and plays the same role as the optimal exercise index for the Bermudan swaption. In contrast to the optimal exercise index, the trigger index can be calculated in a deterministic fashion, as shown in Figure 12.52.

This concludes the examples of applying the object oriented programming paradigm using Matlab.

12.9 SUMMARY AND CONCLUSIONS

We have reviewed the object oriented programming approach in Matlab. We described the basic building blocks and explained how the approach can be used for practical applications. Then, we showed how to implement basic design patterns in Matlab and how they can be applied to financial modelling applications. Finally, we described an object oriented framework for calibrating financial models together with the corresponding UML diagrams describing the overall structure of the implementation and the design as well as the source code. The second example for applying object oriented programming was the implementation of a Libor Market Model together with the adjoint method for efficiently computing Greeks.

13

Math Fundamentals

13.1 INTRODUCTION AND OBJECTIVES

We wish to keep this book as self-contained as possible. To this end we have decided to give all the relevant mathematical concepts, fix the notation and review the main results which we have applied throughout. We cover the following topics:

- Random Variables and Probability Theory.
- The Characteristic Function, its properties and the Fourier Transform.
- Fundamentals of Diffusion Processes and jump-diffusion Processes.
- Fundamentals of Lévy Processes.

Since this book focuses on financial models and the numerical implementation of advanced models we do not aim to treat the mathematical theory fully and rigorously. Therefore, uniqueness and existence results as well as proofs for theorems such as the Lévy–Itô decomposition are not even outlined. The interested reader is referred to Di Nuno, R.B., Oksendahl, E. and Proske, F. (2008), Schoutens, W. (2003), Cont, R. and Tankov, P. (2004), Kyprianou, A. (2006), Feller, W. (1968) and Feller, W. (1971), to name a few.

Let us fix some notation

$\mathbb{N}$	natural numbers	$\mathbb{Z}$	negative and positive integers
$\mathbb{R}$	real numbers	$\mathbb{R}^+$	$\{x \in \mathbb{R} \mid x \geq 0\}$
$\mathbb{R}^*$	$\{x \in \mathbb{R} \mid x \neq 0\}$	$\mathbb{C}$	complex numbers
$\mathbb{C}^*$	$\{z \in \mathbb{C} \mid z \neq 0\}$		

We often apply the O/o notation. Let us consider two functions

$$g : \mathbb{R} \to \mathbb{R}$$

$$f : \mathbb{R} \to \mathbb{R}.$$

We write

$$f(x) \underset{x \to x_0}{=} O(g(x)) \leftrightarrow \lim_{x \to x_0} \frac{f(x)}{g(x)} = K \in \mathbb{R} \tag{13.1}$$

$$f(x) \underset{x \to x_0}{=} o(g(x)) \leftrightarrow \lim_{x \to x_0} \frac{f(x)}{g(x)} = 0. \tag{13.2}$$

13.2 PROBABILITY THEORY AND STOCHASTIC PROCESSES

We now provide a brief introduction to probability theory and review important facts and theorems. This, of course, cannot be a complete introduction; we do not give proofs, nor do we point to important theoretical results. For further reading at both the advanced and the introductory levels, see Bauer, H. (1992), Bauer, H. (2002), Billingsley, P. (1999), Feller,

W. (1968) and Feller, W. (1971). For an introductory description see Kienitz, J. (2007a) and Kienitz, J. (2007b).

13.2.1 Probability Spaces

To define a probability space we need three building blocks, which we introduce in this subsection. First, we consider a set Ω. This is the set of all events.

Let $\mathcal{P}(A)$ denote the set of all subsets of a set A. For Ω we consider $\mathcal{F} \subset \mathcal{P}(\Omega)$ and call $\mathcal{F}$ a σ-*algebra* if

- $\Omega \in \mathcal{F}$
- $F \in \mathcal{F}$ implies $F^C := \Omega \backslash F \in \mathcal{F}$
- $F_n \in \mathcal{F}$ implies $\cup_{n \in \mathbb{N}} F_n \in \mathcal{F}$.

Let $\mathcal{F}_0$ be a collection of sets all of which should be elements of a σ-algebra, then

$$\sigma(\mathcal{F}_0) := \bigcap_{\substack{\mathcal{B} \text{ is} \\ \sigma\text{-algebra}, \mathcal{F}_0 \subset \mathcal{B}}} \mathcal{B}$$

is the smallest σ-algebra containing $\mathcal{F}_0$. A σ-algebra is a collection of all observable events. In addition to the σ-algebra $\mathcal{F}$ we consider a function

$$\mathbb{P} : \mathcal{F} \to [0, \infty] \tag{13.3}$$

$$F \mapsto \mathbb{P}(F).$$

We call $\mathbb{P}$ a *probability measure* if it obeys the following properties:

1. $\mathbb{P}(\emptyset) = 0$
2. $F_n \subset \mathcal{F}, n \in \mathbb{N}$, with $F_i \cap F_j = \emptyset$ for all $i \neq j$ implies $\mathbb{P}(\cup_{n \in \mathbb{N}} F_n) = \sum_{n=1}^{\infty} \mathbb{P}(F_n)$
3. $\mathbb{P}(\Omega) = 1$.

If only (1) and (2) hold, $\mathbb{P}$ is called a *measure*.

We call

$$(\Omega, \mathcal{F}, \mathbb{P}) \tag{13.4}$$

a *probability space* and a *measure space* only if (3) is not fulfilled.

Examples

- Let $\Omega = \mathbb{R}$ and take $\mathcal{F} = \mathcal{B}(\mathbb{R})$, the *Borel σ-algebra*. As the measure we take the *Lebesgue measure*, denoted by dx. Then, $(\mathbb{R}, \mathcal{B}(\mathbb{R}), dx)$ is a measure space.
- Let $\Omega = \mathbb{R}$, $\mathcal{F} = \mathcal{B}(\mathbb{R})$ but now take the measure $\lambda(x) = 1/(2\pi)e^{-x^2/2}dx$. Then, $(\mathbb{R}, \mathcal{B}(\mathbb{R}), \lambda)$ is a probability space.

13.2.2 Random Variables

For our purposes we are only interested in real valued random variables. A real valued *random variable X* is a function

$$X : \Omega \to \mathbb{R} \tag{13.5}$$

$$\omega \mapsto X(\omega),$$

which is *measurable*. This ensures that sets of the Borel σ-algebra $\mathcal{B}(\mathbb{R})$ are mapped to sets contained in $\mathcal{F}$ and a measure can be assigned via the mapping $\mathbb{P}$, (13.3). The measurability condition is the condition that for each $U \in \mathcal{B}(\mathbb{R})$ we have

$$X^{-1}(U) := \{\omega \in \Omega | X(\omega) \in U\} \in \mathcal{F}. \tag{13.6}$$

For a (probability) measure $\mathbb{P}$, a number $p \geq 1$ and a random variable X we define

$$\mathbb{E}[X^p] := \int_\Omega X^p d\mathbb{P}. \tag{13.7}$$

The set of all p times $\mathbb{P}$-integrable functions is given by

$$\mathcal{L}^p := \mathcal{L}^p(\Omega, \mathcal{F}, \mathbb{P}) := \{X \mathbb{E}[|X|^p] < \infty\}. \tag{13.8}$$

If we take the set

$$\mathcal{N} := \{X|X = 0 \quad \mathbb{P} \text{ almost everywhere}\}.$$

The set

$$L^p := \mathcal{L}^p/\mathcal{N} \tag{13.9}$$

is a *Banach space* with norm $\mathbb{E}[|X|^p]^{1/p}$. In case $p = 2$, L^p is a *Hilbert space*. For $p = 1$ we call the quantity of Equation (13.7) the *expectation*. For a given square integrable random variable X we denote the *variance* by

$$\mathbb{V}[X] := \mathbb{E}\left[(X - \mathbb{E}[X])^2\right]. \tag{13.10}$$

Furthermore, we can define *higher moments*. If for some natural number k the random variable X is k-integrable, we call

$$\mathbb{E}[(X - \mathbb{E}[X])^k]$$

the *k-th moment*. Another definition we use when we deal with multi-dimensional models is the *covariance*. Let $X, Y \in L^2$ be two random variables. We denote the covariance of X and Y, COV, by

$$COV[X, Y] := \mathbb{E}[(X - \mathbb{E}[X])(Y - \mathbb{E}[Y])] = \mathbb{E}[XY] - \mathbb{E}[X]\mathbb{E}[Y]. \tag{13.11}$$

Closely related to the covariance is the *correlation* given by

$$CORR[X, Y] := \frac{COV[X, Y]}{\sqrt{\mathbb{V}[X]\mathbb{V}[Y]}}. \tag{13.12}$$

13.2.3 Important Results

In this section we consider important results on random variables which we apply for Monte Carlo simulation. To state the results let $(\Omega, \mathcal{F}, \mathbb{P})$ be a probability space. Let $X_i \in L^2, i \in \mathbb{N}$ random variables with $COV[X_i, X_j] = 0$ for all $i, j = 1, 2, \ldots$.
Furthermore, let $\sup_i \mathbb{V}[X_i] < \infty$ and $\mathbb{E}[X_i] = \mu$.
We consider the arithmetic average of the first n random variables X_i:

$$S(n) := \frac{1}{n}\sum_{k=1}^n X_k \tag{13.13}$$

Laws of large numbers   For all $\varepsilon > 0$ we have the *weak law of large numbers*:

$$\lim_{n \to \infty} \mathbb{P}\left[|S(n) - \mu| \geq \epsilon\right] = 0. \tag{13.14}$$

There is another version of the law of large numbers called the *strong law of large numbers*:

$$\lim_{n \to \infty} S(n)(\omega) - \mathbb{E}[S(n)] = 0 \quad \mathbb{P} \text{ almost everywhere.} \tag{13.15}$$

Finally, we give another law of large numbers. Take X_i, $i \in \mathbb{N}$, which are integrable, independent and identically distributed random variables. Define $\mu := \mathbb{E}[X_1]$. Then, we have by *Kolmogorov's law of large numbers*

$$\frac{1}{n} \sum_{k=1}^{n} X_k(\omega) \xrightarrow[n \to \infty]{} \mu \quad \mathbb{P} \text{ almost everywhere.} \tag{13.16}$$

The last result follows from *Etemadi's law of large numbers*. Now, let $X_1, X_2, \ldots$ be integrable, identically distributed random variables such that for each i, j, $i \neq j$ the random variables X_i and X_j are independent. Then,

$$\frac{1}{n} \sum_{k=1}^{n} X_k(\omega) \xrightarrow[n \to \infty]{} \mu \quad \mathbb{P} \text{ almost everywhere.} \tag{13.17}$$

The slight but important difference to the last result is that the random variables only need to be pairwise independent! If we wish to apply the Monte Carlo method we need some kind of criteria for when to abort the simulation. The law of large numbers does not yield any information on when to stop it.

To provide such criteria we take a sequence $(V_i)_{i \in \mathbb{N}}$ of independent, identically distributed random variables with $\mathbb{E}[V_i^2] = \sigma^2 < \infty$, $i \in \mathbb{N}$. For example, each of the random variables can be a payoff function h applied to a sample X. We denote by $\hat{S}_n$ the empirical estimator of the arithmetic average of the first n outcomes and by V_0 the expectation $\mathbb{E}[V_i]$ which is the same for all V_i, $\in \mathbb{N}$ just as it is the variance denoted by $\sigma^2 = \mathbb{V}[V_1]$. The convergence speed of the estimator $\hat{V}_n$ is determined by its variance $\sigma_{\hat{V}_n}$. We have

$$\hat{V}_n := \frac{\hat{S}_n - V_0}{\sigma/\sqrt{n}} \to \mathcal{N}(0, 1) \text{ as } n \to \infty. \tag{13.18}$$

This result is known as the *central limit theorem* in the Feller–Lévy version and it states that for re-scaled independent identically distributed random variables the limiting distribution is the standard normal distribution. We use

$$\hat{\sigma}_n := \sqrt{\frac{1}{n-1} \sum_{i=1}^{n} (V_i - \hat{V}_n)^2} \tag{13.19}$$

as the sample standard deviation. The quantity of Equation (13.19) will serve as a measure for accuracy of the statistical estimator.

Lindeberg–Feller Central Limit Theorem   The Feller–Lévy version of the central limit theorem is the basic form of the central limit theorem. This version has been extended in several ways. One result, the Lindeberg–Feller version of the central limit theorem, is widely applied in financial mathematics, hence we give this result here.

Let $(V_i)_{i \in \mathbb{N}}$ be independent random variables with $\mu_i := \mathbb{E}[V_i]$, $\sigma_i^2 := \mathbb{V}[V_i] \leq +\infty$ for $i \in \mathbb{N}$ and $s_N^2 = \sigma_1^2 + \ldots + \sigma_N^2$. For all $\varepsilon > 0$ the following relation holds:

$$\lim_{N \to \infty} \frac{1}{s_N^2} \sum_{n=1}^{N} \int_{\{|X_n - \mu_n| \leq s_N\}} (X_n - \mu_n)^2 \, d\mathbb{P} = 0, \tag{13.20}$$

then, we have

$$\frac{1}{s_N} \sum_{n=1}^{N} (V_n - \mu_n) \longrightarrow \mathcal{N}(0, 1). \tag{13.21}$$

Equation (13.20) is known as the *Lindeberg criterion*.

Explicit Calculations of the Confidence Intervals   We choose a confidence level α, $\alpha \in (0, 1)$, such that the true value of V_0 lies within the interval $[L(\alpha, S), R(\alpha, S)]$ with probability $1 - \alpha$. The latter notation indicates that the left and the right boundary depend on the chosen α and on the estimator of the average. This interval is called the *confidence interval*, and we denote it by I_α. It is a random interval characterized by

$$\mathbb{P}[I_\alpha] = 1 - \alpha.$$

Let h be some function and if we replace $h(X)$ by a realization x of X the interval $[L(h(x)), U(h(x))]$ is a real interval. From the Tchebychev inequality, which relates the probability to the variance, we guess that smaller values for the variance $\mathbb{V}[\cdot]$ improve the estimate of V_0. In our setting this inequality is

$$\mathbb{P}\left[|\hat{V}_n - V_0| \geq k\right] \leq \frac{\mathbb{V}[\hat{V}_n - V_0]}{k^2}$$

and therefore ensures that the width of the confidence interval is reduced as a function of the number of simulations. This inequality cannot be used in practice to construct confidence intervals and is of theoretical interest only. To construct confidence intervals we use the central limit theorem.

To state this theorem let $z_{1-\alpha/2}$ denote the α-quantile of the $\mathcal{N}(0, 1)$ distribution, that is for $Z \sim \mathcal{N}(0, 1)$,

$$\mathcal{N}(-z_{1-\alpha/2} \leq Z \leq z_{1-\alpha/2}) = 1 - \alpha.$$

The confidence interval is now determined as follows:

$$1 - \alpha \approx \mathbb{P}_{\mathcal{N}}\left[-z_{1-\alpha/2} \leq \frac{\sqrt{n}\,(\hat{V}_n - V_0)}{\sigma} \leq z_{1-\alpha/2}\right]$$

$$= \mathbb{P}_{\mathcal{N}}\left[-z_{1-\alpha/2}\frac{\sigma}{\sqrt{n}} \leq \hat{V}_n - V_0 \leq z_{1-\alpha/2}\frac{\sigma}{\sqrt{n}}\right]$$

$$= \mathbb{P}_{\mathcal{N}}\left[\hat{V}_n - z_{1-\alpha/2}\frac{\sigma}{\sqrt{n}} \leq V_0 \leq \hat{V}_n + z_{1-\alpha/2}\frac{\sigma}{\sqrt{n}}\right].$$

Thus, the confidence interval I_α is given by

$$I_\alpha = \left[\hat{V}_n - z_{1-\alpha/2}\frac{\sigma}{\sqrt{n}}, \hat{V}_n + z_{1-\alpha/2}\frac{\sigma}{\sqrt{n}}\right].$$

In general, we do not know the standard deviation σ used to construct I_α. To overcome this difficulty we use the sampled standard deviation given by Equation (13.19). Then, the confidence interval becomes

$$I_\alpha = \left[\hat{V}_n - z_{1-\alpha/2}\frac{\hat{\sigma}_n}{\sqrt{n}}, \hat{V}_n + z_{1-\alpha/2}\frac{\hat{\sigma}_n}{\sqrt{n}} \right].$$

In fact, when using the estimated standard deviation, we find that

$$\frac{\hat{V}_n - \mu}{\hat{\sigma}_n/\sqrt{n}} \sim t_{n-1}$$

has t-distribution with $n-1$ degrees of freedom. According to this we have to replace the quantile $z_{1-\alpha/2}$ by the quantile of the t-distribution, that is

$$I_\alpha = \left[\hat{V}_n - t_{n-1,\alpha/2}\frac{\hat{\sigma}_n}{\sqrt{n}}, \hat{V}_n + t_{n-1,\alpha/2}\frac{\hat{\sigma}_n}{\sqrt{n}} \right].$$

In the sequel we use the normal quantile as a good approximation. The real value V_0 lies within I_α with probability $1 - \frac{\alpha}{2}$.

Let us briefly discuss some properties of I_α. The total width of the interval is given by

$$\frac{2z_{1-\alpha/2}\hat{\sigma}_n}{\sqrt{n}}.$$

Therefore, the width does depend on α, n and $\hat{\sigma}_n$. For a fixed α by increasing the number of simulations we get smaller intervals and therefore more accurate estimates of V_0. Since length$(I_\alpha) \propto \frac{1}{\sqrt{n}}$, it follows that decreasing the length of I_α by $1/2$ the number of simulations has to be increased by a factor of 4. It can be shown that it is the symmetric interval which has the smallest width.

Note that it is possible to reduce the error for our simulation by reducing the variance of the problem. Such methods are called *variance reduction methods*. We will come back to such methods when discussing option pricing problems.

A Limit Theorem   We consider a sequence $(f_n)_n \in L^p$ with $1 \le p < \infty$ and assume that there exists $g \in L^p$, $g \ge 0$ such that

$$|f_n| \le g$$

for all $n \in \mathbb{N}$. Then there exists $f \in L^p$ such that

$$f : \quad \to \quad f \quad \text{(almost everywhere)}$$
$$f_n \to_{L^p} f.$$

This convergence result is known as the *Lebesgue convergence theorem*. This theorem is applied, for instance, when interchanging limits when calculating Greeks.

13.2.4 Distributions

In this section we look briefly at the distributions we apply in the main part of this book and fix the notation we use. We give the formula for the probability density and illustrate the effect of the parameters. We consider the following distributions:

- Normal/Gaussian distribution, $\mathcal{N}(\mu, \sigma)$
- Log-Normal distribution, $\mathcal{LN}(\mu, \sigma)$
- Gamma distribution, $\mathcal{G}$ (χ^2, χ_{NC}, Exponential distribution, $\mathcal{E}$)
- Beta distribution, $\mathcal{B}$
- Inverse Gaussian distribution, $\mathcal{IG}$
- Poisson distribution, $\mathcal{P}$
- Uniform distribution, $\mathcal{U}$.

In each case we denote by f the probability density and by F the cumulative distribution function.

Normal/Gaussian Distribution   We consider the function

$$f_{\mu,\sigma} : \mathbb{R} \to \mathbb{R}^+$$

$$x \mapsto \frac{1}{\sqrt{2\pi\sigma^2}} \exp\left(-\frac{(x-\mu)^2}{2\sigma^2}\right).$$

The cumulative distribution function is given by the *erf* function. We have:

$$F_{\mu,\sigma}(x) = \frac{1}{2}\left(1 + \operatorname{erf}\left(\frac{x-\mu}{\sigma\sqrt{2}}\right)\right).$$

Figure 13.1 shows $f_{\mu,\sigma}$ for different parameters μ and σ.
  If $F_X = F_{\mu,\sigma}$ we write $X \sim \mathcal{N}(\mu, \sigma)$, then

$$\mathbb{E}[X] = \mu$$

$$\mathbb{V}[X] = \sigma^2.$$

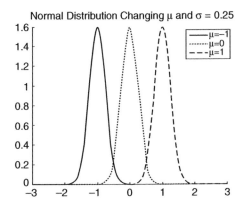
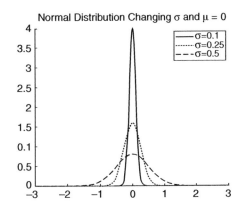

Figure 13.1   Normal distribution and changing the values for the mean μ (left) and standard deviation σ (right)

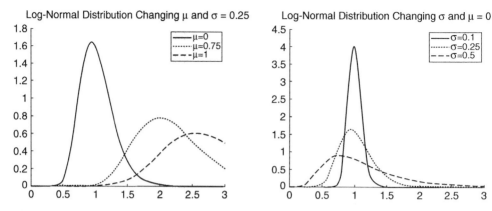

Figure 13.2 Log-Normal distribution and changing the values for mean μ (left) and standard deviation σ (right)

Log-Normal Distribution We consider the function

$$f_{\mu,\sigma} : \mathbb{R}^+ \to \mathbb{R}^+$$

$$x \mapsto \frac{1}{\sqrt{2\pi}\sigma x} \exp\left(-\frac{(\log(x)-\mu)^2}{2\sigma^2}\right).$$

The cumulative distribution function is given by

$$F_{\mu,\sigma}(x) = \frac{1}{2}\mathrm{erfc}\left(-\frac{\log(x)-\mu}{\sigma\sqrt{2}}\right),$$

with $\mathrm{erfc}(x) = 1 - \mathrm{erf}(x)$ being the complementary error function. The influence of the parameters μ and σ on the shape of the probability density function is illustrated in Figure 13.2.

If $F_X = F_{\mu,\sigma}$ we write $X \sim \mathcal{LN}(\mu,\sigma)$ and we have for the moments of X

$$\mathbb{E}[X] = \exp\left(\mu + \frac{\sigma^2}{2}\right)$$

$$\mathbb{V}[X] = \left(\exp(\sigma^2) - 1\right)\exp\left(2\mu + \sigma^2\right).$$

Gamma Distribution Let $a, b \in \mathbb{R}^+$ and consider the mapping

$$f_{a,b} : \mathbb{R}^+ \to \mathbb{R}^+$$

$$x \mapsto x^{a-1}\frac{\exp\left(-\frac{x}{b}\right)}{b^a \Gamma(a)},$$

where $\Gamma(x)$ is the *Gamma function*, that is

$$\Gamma(x) = \int_0^\infty t^{x-1}\exp(-z)dz.$$

Figure 13.3 illustrates possible shapes of the probability density with respect to the parameters.

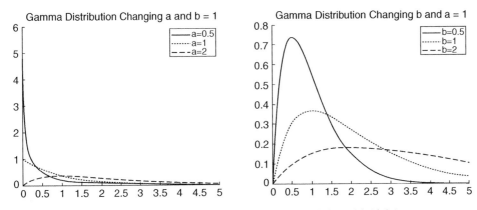

Figure 13.3   Gamma distribution and changing the parameters a (left) and b (right)

The cumulative distribution is given by

$$F_{a,b}(x) = \frac{\gamma(a, x/b)}{\Gamma(a)},$$

where $\gamma(a, b)$ is the *lower incomplete Gamma function*, that is

$$\gamma(a, x) = \int_0^x s^{a-1} \exp(-s)ds.$$

For a random variable X with $F_X = F_{a,b}$ we denote $X \sim \mathcal{G}(a, b)$.

Exponential and Chi-Square Distribution   Special cases of the Gamma distribution are the Exponential and χ^2 distribution.

- Let $v \in \mathbb{R}^+$. If $X \sim \mathcal{G}(v/2, 2)$ we write $X \sim \chi^2(v)$.
- Let $\lambda > 0$. If $X \sim \mathcal{G}(1, 1/\lambda)$ we write $X \sim \mathcal{E}(\lambda)$.

Beta Distribution   Let $a, b \in \mathbb{R}$. The probability density of the Beta distribution is given by

$$f : [0, 1] \rightarrow \mathbb{R}^+$$

$$x \mapsto \frac{1}{B(a, b)} x^{a-1}(1 - x)^{b-1},$$

where $B(a, b)$ is the *Beta function*, that is

$$B(a, b) = \int_0^1 x^{a-1}(1 - x)^{b-1}dx.$$

The cumulative distribution

$$F_{a,b}(x) = \frac{B_x(a, b)}{B(a, b)} = I_x(a, b),$$

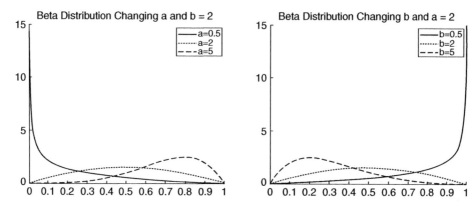

Figure 13.4   Beta distribution and changing the parameters a (left) and b (right)

with $B_x(a, b)$ being the *incomplete beta function*, that is

$$B_x(a, b) = \int_0^x s^{a-1}(1 - s)^{b-1} ds$$

and $I_x(a, b)$ the *regularized incomplete Beta function*.

For a random variable X with $F_X = F_{a,b}$ we denote the distribution by $X \sim \mathcal{B}(a, b)$. The expectation and the variance are given by

$$\mathbb{E}[X] = \frac{a}{a + b}$$

$$\mathbb{V}[X] = \frac{ab}{(a + b)^2(a + b + 1)}.$$

We illustrate the Beta distribution for different parameters in Figure 13.4.

Inverse Gaussian Distribution   We consider the function

$$f_{a,b} : \mathbb{R}^+ \to \mathbb{R}^+$$

$$x \mapsto \left(\frac{b}{2\pi x^3}\right)^{1/2} \exp\left(-\frac{b(x - a)^2}{2a^2 x}\right).$$

The cumulative distribution function for the Inverse Gaussian distribution is

$$F_{a,b}(x) = \mathcal{N}\left(\sqrt{\frac{b}{a}}\left(\frac{x}{a} - 1\right)\right) + \exp\left(\frac{2b}{a}\right)\mathcal{N}\left(-\sqrt{\frac{b}{x}}\left(\frac{x}{a} + 1\right)\right),$$

where $\mathcal{N}(x) = \frac{1}{2}\left(1 + \text{erf}\left(\frac{x}{\sqrt{2}}\right)\right)$.

Figure 13.5 illustrates possible shapes of the distribution for different parameters a and b.

A random variable X with $F_X = F_{a,b}$ we denote $X \sim \mathcal{IG}(a, b)$ and the expectation and the variance are given by

$$\mathbb{E}[X] = a$$

$$\mathbb{V}[X] = a^3/b.$$

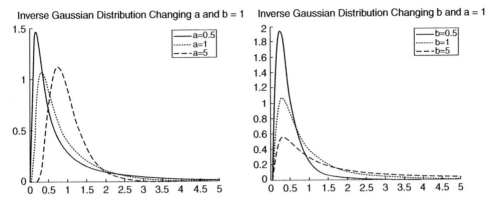

Figure 13.5   Inverse Gaussian distribution and changing the parameters a (left) and b (right)

Poisson Distribution   We consider the mapping

$$f_\lambda : \mathbb{N} \to \mathbb{R}^+$$

$$k \mapsto \exp(-\lambda)\frac{\lambda^k}{k!}.$$

This density corresponds to a Poisson distributed random variable. The cumulative distribution function is given by

$$F_\lambda(x) = \exp(-\lambda)\sum_{k=0}^{x}\frac{\lambda^k}{k!}.$$

The parameter $\lambda \in \mathbb{R}^+$ is called the *intensity*. Figure 13.6 illustrates different probability distribution densities for different values of λ.

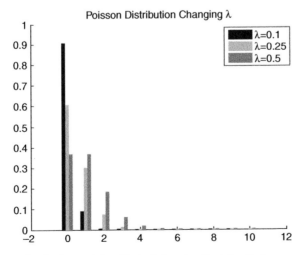

Figure 13.6   Poisson distribution and the effect of changing the intensity λ

For a random variable X with $F_X = F_{a,b}$ we denote the distribution by $X \sim \mathcal{P}(a, b)$. The expectation and the variance are

$$\mathbb{E}[X] = \lambda$$

$$\mathbb{V}[X] = \lambda.$$

Uniform Distribution   Finally, we consider the mapping

$$f_{a,b}(x) : [a, b] \to \mathbb{R}$$

$$x \mapsto \frac{1}{b-a}.$$

$f_{a,b}$ is the density of a uniformly in [a, b] distributed random variable. It has cumulative distribution

$$F_{a,b}(x) = \frac{x-a}{b-a}.$$

For a random variable X with $F_X = F_{a,b}$ we denote $X \sim \mathcal{U}[a, b]$. The expectation and variance are

$$\mathbb{E}[X] = \frac{a+b}{2}$$

$$\mathbb{V}[X] = \frac{(b-a)^2}{12}.$$

13.2.5 Stochastic Processes

Let us consider some probability space $(\Omega, \mathcal{F}, \mathbb{P})$ together with a filtration denoted by $(\mathcal{F}_t)_t$, $t \in [0, T)$. By *filtration* we mean an indexed set of σ-algebras $\mathcal{F}_t \subset \mathcal{F}$ such that $\mathcal{F}_s \subset \mathcal{F}_t$, for all $s \leq t$. The σ-algebra $\mathcal{F}_t$ can be seen as the information available up to time t.

A probability space having this property is called a *filtered probability space*. It can distinguish information currently available in the market from that which is still a possible scenario and therefore random. The class of processes we study fulfils this property. We study *non-anticipating* processes. For a given filtration $(\mathcal{F}_t)_t$ a process $(X_t)_t$ is called *adapted* to the filtration if X_t is $\mathcal{F}_t$-measurable.

Let $\{X_t : t \geq 0\}$ be a collection of random variables. For any fixed $\omega \in \Omega$,

$$X(\cdot, \omega) : \mathbb{R}^+ \to \mathbb{R}$$

$$t \mapsto X(t, \omega)$$

is called a *trajectory* or *path*. For fixed $t \in \mathbb{R}^+$, $X(t, \cdot)$, given by

$$X(t, \cdot) : \Omega \to \mathbb{R}$$

$$\omega \mapsto X(t, \omega)$$

is a random variable with a given distribution $F_{X(t)}(X(t) \leq x)$. Thus, to analyse a financial model it is necessary to consider the distributional properties as well as the path properties of the underlying stochastic process.

To define a martingale first we have to consider conditional expectations. Let us take a sub-σ-algebra $\mathcal{F}^* \subset \mathcal{F}$ and a $\mathbb{P}$-integrable random variable X. If for all sets $A \in \mathcal{F}^*$ a random variable X_o satisfies

$$\int_A X d\mathbb{P} = \int_A X_0 d\mathbb{P}.$$

We define the conditional expectation of X with respect to $\mathcal{F}^*$:

$$\mathbb{E}^{\mathcal{F}^*}[X] := \mathbb{E}[X|\mathcal{F}^*] := X_0.$$

We call a process a *martingale* if for all $0 \leq s \leq t$ we have

$$\mathbb{E}^{\mathcal{F}_s}[X_t] = X(s)$$

and a sub (super) martingale if

$$\mathbb{E}^{\mathcal{F}_s}[X_t] \geq X(s), \quad \text{resectively } \mathbb{E}^{\mathcal{F}_s}[X_t] \leq X(s).$$

13.2.6 Lévy Processes

In this section we consider Lévy processes. We define this class of stochastic processes and summarize the results applied in the main body of the book. Furthermore, we consider special Lévy processes such as *Diffusion processes*, *Poisson processes* and *jump-diffusion processes*.
   A stochastic process $(X(t))_{t \in [0,T]}$ is called a *Lévy process* if the following properties hold:

- The paths of X are $\mathbb{P}$-almost surely right continuous and all left limits exist (*cadlag* property)
- $\mathbb{P}[X_0 = 0] = 1$
- For $0 \leq s \leq t$, $X_t - X_s$ is equal in distribution to X_{t-s}
- For $0 \leq s \leq t$, $X_t - X_s$ is independent of $\{X_u : u \leq s\}$.

See Sepp, A. (2003), Cont, R. and Tankov, P. (2004) and Kyprianou, A. (2006) for further details.
   Let $(X(t))_t$ be a cadlag stochastic process. We consider the jumps of the process. To this end we take for $t \in [0, T]$

$$J(t) := X(t) - X(t^-),$$

with $X(t^-) := \lim_{s \to t, s < t} X(s)$. Then, for all $U \in \mathbb{B}([0, T])$ we define

$$N(t, U) := \sum_{0 \leq s \leq t} 1_U(J(s)). \tag{13.22}$$

The quantity N appearing in (13.22) is called the *number of jumps* of size $J(s) \in U$. Since $(X(t))_t$ is assumed to be cadlag we have $N(t, U) < \infty$ for all $U \in \mathcal{B}(\mathbb{R}^*)$. The function

$$N : \mathcal{B}(0, \infty) \times \mathcal{B}(\mathbb{R}^*) \to \mathbb{R}$$

$$(a, b] \times U \mapsto N(b, U) - N(a, U)$$

is called a *Poisson Random Measure* or a *Jump Measure*.

The Lévy Measure Let $(X(t))_t$ be a Lévy process on $\mathbb{R}^d$. The measure v on $\mathbb{R}^d$ defined by

$$v(A) = \mathbb{E}[\#\{t \in [0, 1]|J(t) \neq 0, \Delta X(t) \in A\}], \quad A \in \mathcal{B}(\mathbb{R}^d)$$

is called the *Lévy measure* of the process $(X(t))_t$. The Lévy measure encodes the jump structure of the process $(X(t))_t$ since it is the expected number per unit of time of jumps whose size belongs to A. The definition of the Lévy measure above is closely connected to Poisson random measures since we could have defined v by

$$v(U) := \mathbb{E}[N(1, U)], \quad U \in \mathcal{B}(\mathbb{R}^*).$$

There is a compensated version of the Poisson random measure. We call

$$\bar{N}(dt, dz) := N(dt, dz) - v(dz)dt$$

the *Compensated Poisson Random Measure* or *Compensated Jump Measure* associated to $X(t)$.

Subordination   The Lévy measure v_S is obtained by subordinating a Brownian motion W to some Lévy process L with Lévy measure v; that means $S(t) = W(L(t))$ is given by

$$v_S(x) = \int_0^\infty \exp\left(-\frac{(x - \mu t)^2}{2t}\right) \frac{v(dt)}{\sqrt{2\pi t}}.$$

Here, we assume that the subordinator has zero drift. The Variance Gamma model and the Normal Inverse Gaussian model can be represented as subordinated Brownian motions.

- The Gamma process has Lévy measure

$$v_\Gamma(x) = \frac{c \exp(-\lambda x)}{x} 1_{\{x>0\}}$$

and density

$$p(x, t; 0, 0) = \frac{\lambda^{ct}}{\Gamma(ct)} x^{ct-1} \exp(-\lambda x) 1_{\{x>0\}}.$$

- The Inverse Gaussian process has Lévy measure

$$v_{IG}(x) = \frac{c \exp(-\lambda x)}{x^{3/2}} 1_{\{x>0\}}$$

and density

$$p(x, t; 0, 0) = \frac{ct}{x^{3/2}} \exp(2ct\sqrt{\pi\lambda}) \exp(-\lambda x - \pi c^2 t^2/x) 1_{\{x>0\}}.$$

Properties of the Lévy Measure   A Lévy measure satisfies the following properties:

$$\int_{|x|\leq 1} x^2 v(dx) < \infty \text{ and } \int_{|x|\geq 1} v(dx) < \infty.$$

Any transformation of the Lévy measure which preserves the above conditions leads to a new Lévy measure. Suppose that there exists a real vector $\underline{a} \in \mathbb{R}^d$ such that the transformation

$$\tilde{v}(dx) := \exp(\langle \underline{a}, x\rangle)v(dx) \tag{13.23}$$

preserves the properties. Then this is called *exponential tilting*. Equation (13.23) is called the *Esscher transform*.

The Esscher Transform   We can transform the measure into an equivalent martingale measure $\mathbb{P}_{mart}$. Let f_t denote the density of the real world measure of $S(t)$, where S is a Lévy process. For some real number θ we consider

$$f_t^\theta(x) = \frac{\exp(\theta x) f_t(x)}{\int_{-\infty}^\infty \exp(\theta y) f_t(y) dy}.$$

Now, θ is chosen such that $S(0) := \exp(-(r-d)t) \cdot \mathbb{E}^\theta[S(t)]$ is a martingale. In the financial setting we denote the riskless rate by r and the dividend yield by d. Thus, the martingale we consider is $\exp(-(r-d)t)S(t)$ and is called the discounted asset price. To determine the variable θ we have to solve

$$\exp(r-d) = \frac{\varphi(-i(\theta+1))}{\varphi(-i\theta)}.$$

If φ is the characteristic function of $X(t)$, then the characteristic function for the Esscher transformed process is $\varphi_\theta = \varphi(u - i\theta)/\varphi(-i\theta)$.

For the Normal distribution we find that the parameter is $\theta = (r - d - \mu)/\sigma^2$ and therefore

$$f_1(x) = \frac{\exp(\theta x - (x - \mu + \sigma^2/2)^2)/(2\sigma^2)}{\int_{-\infty}^\infty \exp(\theta y - (y - \mu + \sigma^2/2)^2/(2\sigma^2)) dy}.$$

For the NIG distribution following $NIG(\alpha, \beta, \delta, m)$, we find that the Esscher transformed model is given by

$$NIG(\alpha, \theta + \beta, \delta, m).$$

Fact – Lévy–Itô Formula and Path Properties   The next result allows us to decompose a general Lévy process into three basic building blocks. Each of the blocks determines path properties. The result is called the *Lévy–Itô Formula*. We take again the function $\Psi(z)$. We write it as follows:

$$\Psi(z) = \underbrace{iaz + \frac{1}{2} z^T \sigma^2 z}_{(1)} \qquad (13.24)$$

$$+ \underbrace{\nu(\mathbb{R} \backslash (-1, 1)) \int_{|x| \geq 1} (1 - e^{izx}) \frac{\nu(dx)}{\nu(\mathbb{R} \backslash (-1, 1))}}_{(2)}$$

$$+ \underbrace{\int_{0 < |x| < 1} (1 - e^{izx} + izx) \nu(dx)}_{(3)}.$$

The above formula can be used to split any Lévy process into three components. We only consider the one-dimensional setting. The first component, the process corresponding to (1) from Equation (13.24), is a Brownian motion with volatility σ and some drift. We have

$$X_t^{(1)} = -at + \sigma W(t), \quad t \geq 0.$$

We note that the drift is only unique if the cut-off is specified. We take the standard cut-off function $x \wedge 1$.

The second component, the process corresponding to (2) from Equation (13.24) is a compound Poisson process. With the usual notation we can write this process as

$$X_t^{(2)} = \sum_{n=0}^{N(t)} Y_n, \quad t \geq 0.$$

The intensity of the Poisson counting process N is given by $v(\mathbb{R}\setminus(-1, 1))$ and the independent variables Y_n are distributed according to $\frac{v(dx)}{v(\mathbb{R}\setminus(-1,1))}$.

Finally, the last component, the process corresponding to (3) from Equation (13.24) is a *square integrable martingale* with almost surely countable number of jumps on each finite interval which is of magnitude less than 1. It is given by

$$X_t^{(3)} = \sum_{n \geq 0} \left\{ \lambda_n \int_{2^{-n+1} \leq |x| < 2^{-n}} (1 - e^{izx}) F_n(dx) \right.$$
$$\left. + iz\lambda_n \left(\int_{2^{-n+1} \leq |x| < 2^{-n}} x F_n(dx) \right) \right\},$$

where

$$\lambda_n := v \left(\{x : 2^{-(n+1)} \leq |x| < 2^{-n}\} \right)$$
$$F_n(dx) := v(dx)/\lambda_n.$$

Therefore, the process $X_t^{(3)}$ can be seen as a superposition of independent compound Poisson processes with different intensity and some additional drift. Thus, the class of Lévy processes extends the class of jump-diffusion processes.

The results show that a Lévy process is characterized by a vector a, a positive definite matrix σ and a positive measure v.

These three objects uniquely determine a Lévy process. The triple (σ, v, a) is called the *Lévy triplet* of the process $(X(t))_t$.

Stochastic and Ordinary Exponentials   Let $(X(t))_t$ be a Lévy process and let σ denote the diffusion component of the Lévy triplet. There exists a unique cadlag process $(Z(t))_t$ such that

$$dZ(t) = Z(t^-)dX(t), Z(0) = 1.$$

The stochastic process $Z(t)$ is called *stochastic exponential* or *Doléans-Dade* exponential of $X(t)$, sometimes denoted by $\mathcal{E}(X)$.

The ordinary exponential of $X(t)$ is the process $\exp(X(t))$.

The stochastic and the ordinary exponentials of a Lévy process are different notions and thus in general $Z(t) \neq \exp(X(t))$. For instance, the stochastic exponential need not be a strictly positive process. It is only non-negative if $v_X((-\infty, -1]) = 0$. But there is a theorem connecting both exponentials. It proves that both approaches are equivalent if $Z > 0$. The notion equivalent in this case means that the corresponding stochastic processes are of the same class. In fact, we have

1. Let $X(t)$ be a real valued Lévy process and $Z = \mathcal{E}(X)$. If $Z > 0$ almost surely then there exists some Lévy process $L(t)$ such that $Z(t) = \exp(L(t))$.
2. Let $L(t)$ be a real valued Lévy process and $S(t) = \exp(L(t))$. Then there exists some Lévy process $X(t)$ such that $S(t) = \mathcal{E}(X)$.

The process $L(t)$ in (1) can be specified in terms of $X(t)$ and also of the corresponding Lévy triplet. In case (2) the process $X(t)$ is specified in terms of $L(t)$ and also of the corresponding Lévy triplet of $X(t)$. See Cont, R. and Tankov, P. (2004) for details.

Fact – Lévy–Khintchine Formula   Let $(X_t)_t$ be a Lévy process. We consider the random variable X_1 and denote by $\mathbb{E}[e^{-izX_1}]$ the characteristic function. We can write the latter in the form $e^{-\Psi(z)}$. The *Lévy–Khintchine Formula* states that for any Lévy process the function $\Psi(z)$ is given by

$$\Psi(z) = iaz + \frac{1}{2}z^T\sigma^2 z + \int_{\mathbb{R}} (1 - e^{izx} + izx1_{\{|x|<1\}})v(dx), \tag{13.25}$$

with a being a vector, σ a positive definite matrix and v a positive measure.

Levy Processes and Infinitely Divisible Distributions   For a random variable X we consider its cumulative distribution F_X. The random variable X or equivalently the distribution F_X is *infinitely divisible* if for all $n \in \mathbb{N}$ there exist independent, identically distributed random variables $X_1 \ldots, X_n$ such that

$$X \sim \sum_{j=1}^{n} X_j \text{ or equivalently } F_X = F_{X_1} * \ldots * F_{X_n}, \tag{13.26}$$

where $*$ denotes the convolution product defined by

$$(f * g)(t) := \int_{-\infty}^{\infty} f(s)g(t - s)ds.$$

Infinite divisibility can be expressed using the characteristic function. To do so let φ_X be the characteristic function of X. The random variable X is infinitely divisible if and only if for each $n \in \mathbb{N}$ there exists a random variable Y with characteristic function φ_Y such that

$$\varphi_X(u) = (\varphi_Y(u))^n .$$

Lévy processes are connected to infinitely divisible distributions. We only consider the one-dimensional case. It is a fact that X is infinitely divisible if and only if there exists a triplet (σ, v, a), with σ a positive number, $a \in \mathbb{R}$ and v a positive measure with $v(0) = 0$ and $\int_{\mathbb{R}} (1 \wedge |x|^2)\, v(dx) < \infty$ such that

$$\mathbb{E}\left[e^{izX}\right] = \exp\left(iau - \frac{z^2\sigma}{2} + \int_{\mathbb{R}} \left(1 - e^{izx} + izx\right)1_{\{|x|<1\}}\right) v(dx)\right).$$

Thus, for every Lévy triplet there exists an infinitely divisible distribution and vice versa.

With the definition of the Lévy triplet at hand let $L(t)$ be a Lévy process on $\mathbb{R}^d$ with triplet (σ, v, a) and let M be an $n \times d$ matrix. Then

$$\tilde{L}(t) := ML(t)$$

is a Lévy process on $\mathbb{R}^n$ with triplet $(MAM^\top, \tilde{v}, \tilde{\gamma})$ and

$$\tilde{\sigma} = M\sigma M^\top$$

$$\tilde{v}(B) = v(\{x \mid Mx \in B\})$$

$$\tilde{a} = Ma + \int_{\mathbb{R}^n} y(1_{\{|y| \le 1\}}(y) - 1_{\{Mx \mid |Mx| \le 1\}}\tilde{v}(dy).$$

13.2.7   Stochastic Differential Equations

We use as reference for all the concepts discussed in this subsection von Weizsäcker, H. and Winkler, G. (1990), Jacod, J. and Shiryaev, A.N. (2002) and Oksendal, B. (2007). This list is of course not complete and there are many other useful and readable books on stochastic analysis, SDE and stochastic integrals.

Let X be a continuous function

$$X : [0, T) \to \mathbb{R}$$

$$t \mapsto X(t).$$

We consider the *quadratic variation*, denoted by $\langle X \rangle_t$. To define it we consider a sequence of discretizations T_i, $i \in \mathbb{N}$ with $T_i \subset T_{i+1}$ for each i with $\max_{t_i \in T_j, t_i \le t} |t_{i+1} - t_i| \to 0$ for all t. Then, we define – actually it is well defined! – the quadratic variation to be the limit

$$\sum_{t_i \in T, t_i \le t} (X(t_{i+1}) - X(t_i))^2 \xrightarrow[i \to \infty]{} \langle X \rangle_t. \tag{13.27}$$

If $\langle X \rangle_t$ is continuous we say X has a continuous quadratic variation process or is of continuous quadratic variation. For some given continuous function g we have

$$\sum_{t_i \in T_j, t_i \le t} g(t_i)(X(t_{i+1}) - X(t_i))^2 \xrightarrow[i \to \infty]{} \int_0^t g(s)\langle X \rangle_s$$

and if g is differentiable, we define $\int_0^t g(X_s)dX_s := \lim_{n \to \infty} \sum g'(X(t_i))(X(t_{i+1}) - X(t_i))$ for the limit we call it the (pathwise) Itô integral. For this notion of the integral and for g being continuously differentiable we can show

$$g(X(t)) - g(X(0)) = \int_0^t g'(X(s))dX_s + \frac{1}{2}\int_0^t g''(X(s))d\langle X \rangle_s.$$

Furthermore,

$$\langle g(X) \rangle_t = \int_0^t g(X_s)d\langle X \rangle_s.$$

By applying a convergence theorem based on completion we can extend the integral to more general functions. The reader is referred to the literature such as von Weizsäcker, H. and Winkler, G. (1990) or Di Nuno, R.B., Oksendahl, E. and Proske, F. (2008).

Let W be a Brownian motion. Since a typical path $W(\omega)$ is a continuous function with $\langle W \rangle_t = t$, it has bounded quadratic variation, which makes it possible to assign the integral. A *stochastic differential equation*, or SDE for short, is represented by

$$dX(t) = \mu(t, X(t))dt + \sigma(t, X(t))dW(t)$$

$$X(0) = x_0$$

can be justified as a shorthand notation for

$$X(t) - X(0) = \int_0^t \mu(s, X(s))ds + \int_0^t \sigma(s, X(s))dW(s).$$

For further information and mathematical results we refer readers to von Weizsäcker, H. and Winkler, G. (1990) or any other text on stochastic integration or stochastic differential equations.

Another useful notion is the quadratic covariation. To illustrate this notion let us consider two stochastic processes $X(t)$ and $Y(t)$. The quadratic covariation is defined by

$$\sum_{t_i \in T, t_i \le t} (X(t_{i+1}) - X(t_i))(Y(t_{i+1}) - Y(t_i)) \xrightarrow[i \to \infty]{} \langle X, Y \rangle_t.$$

A useful method to determine $\langle X, Y \rangle_t$ is to use *polarization*, that is

$$\langle X, Y \rangle_t = \frac{1}{2} (\langle X + Y \rangle_t - \langle X \rangle_t \langle Y \rangle_t).$$

This identity is applied in Chapter 10, Subsection 10.4.2 where we derive the mean variance hedging strategy.

The stochastic integral and therefore the Itô calculus can be generalized to other processes. In what follows we give the one- and multi-dimensional Itô formulae for Lévy processes. The standard Itô formula for diffusion processes is a special case.

The Itô Formula – 1 dim   Let $X(t)$ be a Lévy process and let $f : (0, \infty) \times \mathbb{R} \to \mathbb{R}$ be a twice continuously differentiable function and define

$$Y(t) := f(t, X(t)).$$

Then, the process $Y(t)$ is a Lévy process and its SDE is given by

$$dY(t) = \frac{\partial f}{\partial t}(t, X(t)) + \frac{\partial f}{\partial x}(t, X(t))\mu(t)dt + \frac{\partial f}{\partial x}(t, X(t))\sigma(t)dW(t)$$

$$+ \frac{1}{2}\frac{\partial^2 f}{\partial x^2}(t, X(t))\beta^2(t)dt + \int_{\mathcal{R}^*} \Big[f(t, X(t) + \gamma(t, z)) - Y(t)$$

$$- \frac{\partial f}{\partial x}(t, X(t))\gamma(t, z) \Big] v(dz)dt$$

$$+ \int_{\mathcal{R}^*} \Big[f(t, X(t^-) + \gamma(t, z)) - f(t, X(t^-)) \Big] N(dt, dz).$$

The Itô Formula – _d_ dim   We consider a d_1-dimensional Brownian motion $W(t) = (W_1(t), \ldots, W_{d_1}(t))$ and d_2 independent compensated Poisson random measures $N((dt, dz) = (N_1(dt, dz_1), \ldots, N_{d_2}(dt, dz_{d_2}))$. For $z = (z_1, \ldots, z_{d_2}) \in (\mathbb{E}^+)^{d_2}$ and d Lévy processes of the form

$$dX(t) = \mu(t)dt + \sigma(t)dW(t) + \int_{(\mathbb{R}^+)^d} \gamma(t, z)N(dt, dz).$$

We have the following d-dimensional Itô formula:

Let $X(t)$ be a d-dimensional Lévy process. Let $f : (0, \infty) \times \mathbb{R}^d \to \mathbb{R}$ be a twice continuously differentiable function and define

$$Y(t) := f(t, X(t)).$$

Then, the process $Y(t)$ is a Lévy process and its SDE is given by

$$dY(t) = \frac{\partial f}{\partial x_i}(t, X(t))dt + \sum_{i=1}^{d} \frac{\partial f}{\partial x_i}\mu_i(t)dt$$

$$+ \sum_{i=1}^{d} \sum_{j=1}^{d_1} \frac{\partial f}{\partial x_i}(t, X(t))\sigma_{i,j}(t)dW_j(t) + \frac{1}{2}\sum_{i=1}^{d} \sum_{j=1}^{d_1} \frac{\partial^2 f}{\partial x_i \partial x_j}(t, X(t))(\sigma\sigma^T)_{ij}(t)dt$$

$$+ \sum_{k=1}^{d_2} \int_{\mathbb{R}^*} \left[f(t, X(t) + \gamma^k(t, z)) - f(t, X(t)) - \sum_{i=1}^{d} \frac{\partial f}{\partial x_i}(t, X(t))\gamma_{ik}(t, z) \right] v_k(dz_k)dt$$

$$+ \sum_{k=1}^{d_2} \int_{\mathbb{R}^*} \left[f(t, X(t^-) + \gamma^{(k)}(t, z)) - f(t, X(t^-)) \right] N_k(dt, dz_k).$$

Geometric Brownian Motion and Beyond   We apply the Itô formula to define _Geometric Lévy processes_. To this end we consider the following SDE:

$$dY(t) = Y(t^-)\left[\mu(t)dt + \sigma(t)dW(t) + \int_{\mathbb{R}^*} \gamma(t, z)N(dt, dz) \right] \qquad (13.28)$$

$$Y(0) = y_0.$$

If $\mu(t)$, $\sigma(t)$ and $\gamma(t, z)$ are predictable processes with $\gamma(t, z) > -1$ for almost all $(t, z) \in [0, \infty) \times \mathbb{R}^*$ and almost surely

$$\int_0^t \left[|\mu(s)| + \sigma^2(s) + \int_{\mathbb{R}^*} \gamma^2(s, z)v(dz) \right] ds < \infty,$$

then, using the Itô formula, it can be shown that $Y(t)$ is the solution to the equation

$$Y(t) = Y_0 \exp(X(t)), \qquad (13.29)$$

with

$$X(t) = \int_0^t \left[\mu(s) - \frac{1}{2}\sigma^2(s) + \int_{\mathbb{R}^*} [\log(1 + \gamma(s, z)) - \gamma(s, z)] v(dz) \right] ds$$

$$+ \int_0^t \sigma(s) dW(s) + \int_0^t \int_{\mathbb{R}^*} \log(1 + \gamma(s, z)) N(ds, dz).$$

We call the process $Y(t)$ defined by (13.29) or in terms of the SDE by (13.28) a *geometric Lévy process*. If $N = 0$ we recover Geometric Brownian motion.

Diffusion Processes

In this subsection we consider special diffusion processes, namely the Ornstein–Uhlenbeck and Affine processes.

Ornstein–Uhlenbeck Processes Let us consider the solution to the stochastic differential equation

$$dX(t) = \lambda(\mu - X(t))dt + \sigma dW(t) \tag{13.30}$$

$$X(0) = x_0.$$

The solution to Equation (13.30) is given by

$$X(t) = X(0)e^{-\lambda t} + \mu(1 - e^{-\lambda t}) + \int_0^t \sigma e^{-\lambda(t-s)} dW(s),$$

with $\alpha(t) = \frac{\sigma^2}{2\lambda^2}(1 - e^{-\lambda(t-s)})$. The expectation and the covariance are

$$\mathbb{E}[X(t)] = X(0)e^{-\lambda t} + \mu \left(1 - e^{-\lambda t}\right) \text{ and } \mathbb{COV}[X(t), X(s)] = \frac{\sigma^2}{2\lambda}\left(e^{\lambda(t-s)} - e^{-\lambda(t+s)}\right).$$

The transition probability $\mathbb{P}(X(t) \le x | X(0) = x_0)$ is known in closed form. It is given by

$$\mathbb{P}(X(t) \le x) = \frac{1}{\sqrt{2\pi(1 - e^{-2t})}} \int_{-\infty}^x \exp\left(-\frac{(y - x_0 e^{-t})^2}{2(1 - e^{2t})}\right) dy.$$

For short rate modelling another version of the process (13.30) is considered, namely

$$dX(t) = -\lambda X(t)dt + \sigma dW(t).$$

In this case the solution is given by

$$X(t)X(s)e^{\lambda(t-s)} + \sigma \int_s^t e^{-a(t-u)} dW(u).$$

Affine Processes A stochastic process given by some SDE

$$dX(t) = \mu(X(t))dt + \sigma(X(t))dW(t)$$

is *affine* if

$$\mu(X(t)) = \mu_0 + \mu_1 X(t)$$

$$\sigma(X(t))\sigma(X(t))^\top = (\sigma_0) + (\sigma_1)^\top X(t)$$

$$r(X(t)) = r_0 + r_1^\top(X)(t)$$

for any $a_0 \in \mathbb{R}^n$, $a_1 \in \mathbb{R}^{n \times n}$, $\sigma_0 \in \mathbb{R}^{n \times n \times n}$, $\sigma_1 \in \mathbb{R}^{n \times n \times n}$, $r_0 \in \mathbb{R}$ and $r_1 \in \mathbb{R}^n$.

Jump-diffusion processes

The class of diffusion processes can be extended by adding a jump component based on a compensated Poisson process. The first jump-diffusion model applied to finance was the Merton model (Merton, R. (1976)).

The distributional assumption is that the jumps are logarithmic normally distributed with a certain jump height and jump volatility and a jump intensity parameter λ governing the jump frequency.

Itô Formula   We now give a version of the general Itô formula, (13.24), adapted to jump-diffusion processes. We consider the following jump-diffusion process:

$$X(t) = X(0) + \int_{t_0}^t \mu(u, X(u^-))du + \int_{t_0}^t \sigma(u, X(u^-))dW(u) + \sum_{n=1}^{N(t)} \Delta X(n), \qquad (13.31)$$

with $\mu()$ and $\sigma()$ being continuous non-anticipating processes with $\mathbb{E}[\int_{t_0}^t \sigma(u, X(u-))^2 du] < \infty$ and $\Delta X(n)$ is a shorthand notation for $\Delta X(n) = X(T(n)) - X(T(n-))$ with $T(n)$, $n = 1, \ldots, N(t)$ being the jump times of N.

Let $f : [t_0, \infty) \times \mathbb{R} \to \mathbb{R}$ two times differentiable, then

$$f(t, X(t)) = f(t_0, X(t_0)) + \int_{t_0}^t \left[\frac{\partial f}{\partial u}(u, X(u-)) \right.$$

$$\left. + \frac{\partial f}{\partial X}(u, X(u-))b(u, X(u-)) \right]du$$

$$+ \int_{t_0}^t \frac{1}{2}\frac{\partial^2 f}{\partial X^2}(u, X(u-))\sigma^2(u, X(u-))du \qquad (13.32)$$

$$+ \int_{t_0}^t \frac{\partial f}{\partial X}(u, X(u-))\sigma(u, X(u-))dW(u)$$

$$+ \sum_{n=1, T(n) \leq t}^{N(t)} (f(T(n), X(T(n-)) + \Delta X(n)) - f(T(n), X(T(n-)))). \qquad (13.33)$$

Suppose we have some Call option with maturity T paying $h(T)$. We let $C(t)$ denote the Call option price and $C_f(t) = \exp(r(T - t))C(t)$ the forward price of the option at time t. Since $\mathbb{E}[C_f(T)|\mathcal{F}(t)] = C_f(t)$ the price $C_f(t)$ is a martingale. Thus, the corresponding process has 0 drift.

By applying the Itô formula, (13.33), to $y(t) = \log(S_f(t))$ and denoting $k = \int_{-\infty}^{\infty} \exp(x - 1)\nu(dx)$

$$dC_f(t) = \frac{\partial C_f}{\partial t}dt + \left(r - d - \frac{\sigma^2}{2} - k\right)\frac{\partial C_f}{\partial y}dt + \frac{1}{2}\sigma^2\frac{\partial^2 C_f}{\partial y^2}dt$$

$$+ \sigma\frac{\partial C_f}{\partial y}dW(t) + \underbrace{\left(C_f(t, y(t-) + \Delta y(t)) - C_f(t, y(t-))\right)dN(t)}_{(1)}.$$

Then, taking expectation, (1) is simply $\int_{-\infty}^{\infty}\left(C_f(t, y(t-) + \Delta y(t)) - C_f(t, y(t-))\right)\nu(dx)dt$. Setting the expected value to 0 leads to

$$0 = \frac{\partial C_f}{\partial t} + \left(r - d - \frac{\sigma^2}{2} - k\right)\frac{\partial C_f}{\partial y} + \frac{1}{2}\frac{\partial^2 C_f}{\partial y^2}$$

$$+ \int_{-\infty}^{\infty}\left(C_f(t, y + x) - C_f(t, y)\right)\nu(dx).$$

Now, switching back to $C(t) = \exp(r(T - t))C_f(t)$ leads to

$$rC(t) = \frac{\partial C}{\partial t} + \left(r - d - \frac{\sigma^2}{2}\right)\frac{\partial C}{\partial y} + \frac{1}{2}\sigma\frac{\partial^2 C}{\partial y^2}$$

$$+ \int_{-\infty}^{\infty}\left(C(t, y + x) - C(t, y) - (\exp(x) - 1)\frac{\partial C}{\partial y}\right)\nu(dx).$$

Other Processes Used for Modelling   A stochastic process $\{X_t : t \geq 0\}$ defined on some probability space $(\Omega, \mathcal{F}, \mathbb{P})$ is said to be an *additive process* if it possesses the following properties:

- The paths of X are $\mathbb{P}$-almost surely right continuous with left limits.
- $\mathbb{P}[X_0 = 0] = 1$.
- For $0 \leq s \leq t$, $X_t - X_s$ is independent of $\{X_u : u \leq s\}$.

We refer readers to Cont, R. and Tankov, P. (2004) and Sato, K. (1999) for details and further information.

13.3 NUMERICAL METHODS FOR STOCHASTIC PROCESSES

In this section we consider some necessary machinery for applying numerical methods to stochastic processes.

13.3.1   Random Number Generation

The two main methods for generating uniform variates are *pseudo random number generation* and *quasi random number generation*. Using pseudo random numbers one aims to mimic randomness. This is not the case for quasi random numbers. The latter are determined numbers that fulfil certain irregularity criteria.

A reliable pseudo random number generator delivers numbers $U_i \in [0, 1]$, $i \in \mathbb{N}$ such that:

- $U_i, i \in \mathbb{N}$ are empirically uniformly distributed.
- $U_i, i \in \mathbb{N}$ are mutually independent.

An effective generator should have these properties but it also should be reliable in the sense that the results are reproducible, computationally efficient and portable.

For quasi random numbers the mutual independence is not valid. The numbers produced by such a generator do not try to mimic randomness and independence; instead, dependence is used to achieve low discrepancy.

Pseudo Random Number Generators   First, we consider the class of *congruential random number generators*. For positive integers a and m such a generator produces uniforms due to the algorithm

$$X_{i+1} = aX_i \bmod m$$

$$U_{i+1} = X_{i+1}/m.$$

The starting value X_0 is known as the *seed* of the generator. It can be shown that a congruential generator returns to its starting value. This means that outcomes of random experiments based on these random numbers will eventually be repeated if the number of samples is large. Such *cycles* or *periods* need to be very large in order to get reliable values. In the above setting we achieve a period with maximal length if a^{m-1} is a multiple of m and a^{j-1} is not a multiple of m for all $j = 1, \ldots, m-2$.

Furthermore, we might think of improving the algorithm by considering a modulus of $(aX_i + c$ with respect to m denoted by $(aX_i + c) \bmod m$ for some positive integer with $c < m$. It has been shown that this does not improve the properties of the generator very much.

It is advisable to choose the interval $[0, 1]$ since some of the transform methods map the points 0 and 1 to $-\infty$ and $+\infty$. This can cause errors at runtime due to the fact that the endpoints of the interval are mapped to infinity. The generator uses two congruential generators and implements a shuffling mechanism to increase its period of returning to the starting value. For further information the reader may consult Knuth, D. E. (1997) or Glasserman, P. (2004) and the references therein.

Shift Register Random Generators

The most important example of this class of generators is the *Mersenne Twister*. At the time of writing it is possible to find several updates and extensions of this generator. For example, a 64-bit implementation is available in Matlab.

The general idea is to produce a vector of concatenated bits from which we derive integer values and, based on these integers, real numbers in the unit interval $[0, 1]^d$.

Since the full-blown theory uses results from polynomial algebra over Galois fields we cannot review it here. We just present some ideas of the general mechanism applied in the Mersenne Twister algorithm.

The basic algorithm has grown from ideas originating in the *Generalized Feedback Shift Register* (GFSR) and *Twisted Generalized Feedback Register Generators* (TGFSR).

The name Mersenne Twister stems from the usage of certain positive integers known as *Mersenne primes*.

The main issue in the algorithm is the concept of a *Feedback Shift Register* (FSR). Such generators are of the form

$$b(n) = c(k-1)b(n-1) \oplus c(k-2)b(n-2) \oplus \ldots \oplus c(0)b(n-k), \qquad (13.34)$$

with $\oplus$ denoting the *xor* operation. This is adding two numbers and take the remainder after dividing by 2.

For $k \geq 1$ we introduce operators $H^k b(n) = H^{k-1}b(n+1)$ and rewrite Equation (13.34) and subtracting the right side we obtain

$$H^k - c(q-1)H^{k-1} - \ldots - c(0) = 0 \bmod 2.$$

This equation is related to primitive polynomials which we examine below when we introduce Sobol numbers.

These generators have been refined by introducing the idea of the GFSR. They are based on primitive polynomials of the form $x^p + x^q + 1$ and a recurrence relation $x(i) = x(i-p) \oplus x(i-q)$ where all the entries are equal to 0 or 1. It can be shown that the maximum period is achieved if the number n is a Mersenne prime. A Mersenne prime is a number that can be written as

$$2^n - 1, \text{ for some } n \in \mathbb{N}.$$

It has also been shown that the generators considered so far depend heavily on the initial seed and that they have small periods. The class of TGFSR is based on linear recurrence of the form $x(l+n) = x(l+m) \oplus x(l)M$ with M being a matrix with entries 0 or 1.

Finally, the Mersenne Twister is a variant of TGFSR which provides equidistribution in up to 623 dimensions and has a period of $2^{19937} - 1$. The algorithm generates vectors of *words* of length w representing uniform pseudo random integers between 0 and $2^w - 1$. Dividing by $2^w - 1$ or 2^w leads to a uniform variate. Choosing either $2^w - 1$ or 2^w depends upon whether the user wishes 1 to be a possible outcome or not. For fixed r the algorithm is based on the recurrence

$$x(k+n) = x(k+m) \oplus (x(k)^u|x(k+1)^l)M, \qquad (13.35)$$

with $x(k)^u$ denoting the u upper $w - r$ bits of $x(k)$ and $x(k)^l$ the r lower bits. The symbol '|' denotes concatenation. For more details and references and the theory behind all the generators, see Tausworthe, R. C. (1965), Lewis, T. G. and Payne, W. H. (1973), Matsumoto, M. and Kurita, Y. (1992) and Matsumoto, M. and Nishimura, T. (1998).

The Mersenne Twister generator is fast and gives reliable results. It is certainly worth implementing it and applying it for Monte Carlo simulation problems.

Quasi Random Number Generators   Quasi random numbers and quasi Monte Carlo simulation have been used by many researchers. References include the papers by Acworth, P., Broadie, M. and Glasserman, P. (1998), Berman, L. (1997) and Boyle, P., Broadie, M. and Glasserman, P. (1997). Many low discrepancy number sequences underlying such generators have been proposed. Well-known sequences are Halton, Sobol, Faure or Niederreiter sequences. See Halton, J.H. (1960), Halton, J.H. and Smith, G.B. (1964), Sobol, I. (1977), Sobol, I. and Levitan, Y.L. (1976), Faure, H. (1982) and Niederreiter, H. (1988).

Sobol Numbers

Sobol numbers are popular in the finance community. Therefore, we give a brief overview of their construction and describe our implementation in some detail. To understand the implementation we begin with the mathematical concepts and basic examples on how to code this kind of quasi random number generator.

Direction Numbers

At the heart of Sobol number generation lies the concept of so-called *direction numbers*.

Let *maxbit* denote the maximal number of bits allowed by the compiler. On a 32-bit machine, *maxbit* $= 32$. For each of the dimensions under consideration we consider *maxbit* numbers v_i, $i = 1, \ldots, maxbit$, one for each bit in its binary representation.

A direction number can be represented either as

$$v_i = 0.v_{i1}v_{i2} \ldots, \tag{13.36}$$

where v_{ij} is the *j*-th bit following the binary point in the expansion of v_i or as

$$v_i = \frac{m_i}{2^i}, \quad i = 1, 2, \ldots, maxbit. \tag{13.37}$$

We calculate the *n*-th Sobol number x_n for each dimension using the numbers v_i, $i = 1, \ldots, maxbit$. Since the construction is carried out in the interval $(0, 2^{maxbit} - 1)$, we consider

$$\frac{x_n}{2^{maxbit}} \tag{13.38}$$

to actually derive a Sobol number in the interval $(0, 1)$. The only constraints on the direction numbers are that only the *i* left-most bits can be non-zero and the *i*-th left-most bit must be set.

Primitive Polynomials

Continuing, we choose a *primitive polynomial* for each dimension. A primitive polynomial P modulo m of degree q is irreducible with respect to m and of order $m^q - 1$, that is it cannot be written as a product of polynomials of lower degree. For the number theoretic background the reader may consult Jäckel, P. (2002). We consider a primitive polynomial P of degree q of the form

$$P(x) = x^q + a_1 x^{q-1} + \ldots + a_{q-1} x + 1, \quad a \in \{0, 1\}. \tag{13.39}$$

The first q initial direction numbers v_i, $i = 1, \ldots, q$ can be chosen arbitrarily within the abovementioned constraints and the others are determined via a recurrence relation holding for primitive polynomials

$$v_i = a_1 v_{i-1} \oplus a_2 v_{i-2} \oplus \ldots \oplus a_{q-1} v_{i-q+1} \oplus v_{i-q} \oplus v_{i-q}/2^q, \quad i > q, \tag{13.40}$$

where we denoted the XOR operator for bitwise addition by $\oplus$. If two bits are equal, the bitwise XOR returns 0 and otherwise 1.

In terms of the m_i the recurrence relation reads

$$m_i = 2a_1 m_{i-1} \oplus 2^2 a_2 m_{i-2} \oplus \ldots \oplus 2^{q-1} a_{q-1} m_{i-q+1} \oplus 2^q m_{i-q} \oplus m_{i-q}, \quad i > q. \tag{13.41}$$

Completing the Construction

For each new draw we select a *generating integer* $\gamma(n)$ with γ being a bijective function $\gamma : \mathbb{N} \to \mathbb{N}$. In the simplest case we choose $\gamma = id$. Given the generating integer we are able to compute x_n by

$$x_n := \sum_{j=1}^{d} v_j 1_{\{j\text{-th bit counting from the right of } \gamma(n) \text{ is set}\}}. \tag{13.42}$$

The sum is meant to be in the sense of bitwise XOR, using the shorthand notation $\oplus$.

Thus, to generate the actual Sobol number we need to divide by 2^{maxbit}.

As mentioned above, the generating integer could simply be $\gamma(n) = n$, which was originally proposed by Sobol, but other choices are also possible. One popular choice is $\gamma(n) = G(n)$ with G being a *Gray Code* given by $G(n) := n \oplus [n/2]$.

Example

To illustrate the theory we give an example. To this end let us take the primitive polynomial

$$P(x) = x^3 + x^2 + 1. \tag{13.43}$$

We choose the initial direction numbers as follows:

i	1	2	3
m_i	1	1	5
v_i	0.1	0.01	0.101

where m_i and v_i are linked via $v_i = m_i/2^i$.

The next direction numbers are computed by the recurrence relation (13.40) or (13.41). This gives for m_4 and m_5

m_4	$=$	$10 \oplus 8 \oplus 1$
	$=$	$1010 \oplus 1000 \oplus 01$
	$=$	3

m_5	$=$	$6 \oplus 8 \oplus 1$
	$=$	$110 \oplus 1000 \oplus 01$
	$=$	15

Then, to obtain the first numbers of the Sobol sequence $x_{n+1} = x_n \oplus v_c$, we start with $x_0 = 0$. Here c denotes the right-most zero-bit in the binary representation of n. In the following we denote a number n in binary notation. For example, $n = 100$ means $n = 1 \times 2^2 + 0 \times 2^1 + 0^0 = 4$. Then, the first four Sobol numbers are

$$x_1 \underset{n=01 \to c=2}{=} x_0 \oplus v_1 = 0.0 \oplus 0.1 = 0.1(bin) = 0.5$$

$$x_2 \quad = \quad x_1 \oplus v_2 = 0.1 \oplus 0.01$$
$$n= 10 \rightarrow c = 1 \quad 0.11(\text{bin}) = 0.55$$
$$=$$
$$x_3 \quad = \quad x_2 \oplus v_1 = 0.11 \oplus 0.1$$
$$n= 011 \rightarrow c = 3 \quad 0.01(\text{bin}) = 0.25$$
$$=$$
$$x_4 \quad = \quad x_3 \oplus v_3 = 0.01 \oplus 0.0011$$
$$n= 110 \rightarrow c = 1 \quad 0.111(\text{bin}) = 0.875.$$
$$=$$

13.3.2 Methods for Computing Variates

Several methods have been suggested to transform uniform random numbers on the unit interval into random variates of a given distribution. We review two main concepts.

The Inverse Method

This is the method of choice if it is available. Suppose that we wish to generate variates of a random variable X having cumulative distribution function $F_X = P(X \leq x)$ with inverse

$$F_X^{-1}(u) := \inf\{x : F_X(x) \geq u\}. \tag{13.44}$$

Then, $F_X^{-1}(U) = X$, where $U \sim \mathcal{U}(0, 1)$. Thus, if we can compute the function F_X^{-1} and generate a uniform $u \in [0, 1]$, we set

$$x := F_X^{-1}(u) \tag{13.45}$$

to compute a sample from the distribution of X.

HINT: If we apply a quasi random number generation mechanism such as Sobol sequences the inverse transform should be the method of choice since it needs only one uniform random variate which is converted. Other methods may need several.

We verify that this method leads to random variates from the desired distribution

$$\mathbb{P}[X \leq x] = \mathbb{P}[F_X^{-1}(U) \leq x]$$
$$= \mathbb{P}[U \leq F_X(x)]$$
$$= F_X(x).$$

The input variable U can be seen as a random percentile. The inverse F_X^{-1} maps the random percentile to the corresponding percentile of the probability under consideration.

Acceptance/Rejection and Ratio of Uniforms

The *Acceptance/Rejection Method* was introduced by John von Neumann and can be applied to a wide range of distributions. Suppose that we wish to sample from a distribution with density f. Assuming there exists another probability density g such that

$$f(x) \leq cg(x) \quad \text{for all } x \text{ in the sample space and } c \in \mathbb{R}^+. \tag{13.46}$$

An assumption is that it should be easy and fast to sample from g. Then, we sample X from g and accept it as a variate with probability $\frac{f(X)}{cg(X)}$. Otherwise, it is rejected and the procedure is applied as long as the number is accepted.

To prove that this method leads to variates from the desired distribution, we denoted by Z a variate obtained from the acceptance-rejection procedure conditional on $U \leq f(X)/cg(X)$. For a given event A we consider

$$\mathbb{P}(Z \in A) = c\mathbb{P}(X \in A | U \leq f(X)/cg(X))$$

$$= \frac{\mathbb{P}(X \in A | U \leq f(X)/cg(X))}{\mathbb{P}(U \leq f(X)/cg(X))}$$

$$= c \int_A \frac{f(x)}{cg(x)} g(x) dx$$

$$= \int_A f(x) dx.$$

Since we accept with probability $1/c$, c should be near 1. Otherwise, too many uniforms are needed for one sample of the desired distribution.

A method that is related to the acceptance-rejection method is the *ratio of uniforms method*. To introduce the method let $f \geq 0$ be a density function. Consider a uniformly distributed vector (U_1, U_2) in the two-dimensional region

$$A := \{ u = (u_1, u_2) \in [0, 1]^2 : u_1 \leq \sqrt{f(u_2/u_1)} \}.$$

The density of U_2/U_1 is then proportional to f. Let A be contained in a rectangle R. We apply the following version of acceptance/rejection:

Generate $U = (U_1, U_2) \in R$ and accept it if $U_1 \leq \sqrt{f(U_2/U_1)}$; otherwise, reject it and repeat this procedure until $U_1 \leq \sqrt{f(U_2/U_1)}$.

13.4 BASICS ON COMPLEX ANALYSIS

In this section we review the basics on complex numbers and complex analysis. The reader can find the mathematical theory in Ahlfors, L.V. (1979) and Rudin, W. (1974) or any other text on complex analysis.

13.4.1 Complex Numbers

Quadratic equations with real coefficients do not necessarily have a real solution. For instance, consider the quadratic equation

$$x^2 + 1 = 0. \tag{13.47}$$

To assign a solution to such equations *complex numbers*, $\mathbb{C}$, have been introduced. Complex numbers are composed of a *real part* and an *imaginary part*. The basic imaginary unit is called i. It solves the Equation (13.47); that means $i^2 = -1$. It can be shown that complex numbers are well defined and that there is an addition as well as a multiplication. A complex number $z \in \mathbb{C}$ can be written as

$$z = a + ib,$$

with real numbers a and b. We call

$$\mathcal{R}(z) := a \tag{13.48}$$

$$\mathcal{I}(z) := b \tag{13.49}$$

the real part (13.48) and the imaginary part (13.49) of z. We add two complex numbers z_1 and z_2 by simply adding the real and the imaginary parts. Multiplying two complex numbers is not straightforward. We have

$$z_1 \cdot z_2 = (a_1 + ib_1) \cdot (a_2 + ib_2) = a_1 a_2 + i a_1 b_2 + i a_2 b_1 - i b_1 b_2$$
$$= a_1 a_2 - b_1 b_2 + i(a_1 b_2 + a_2 b_1).$$

We can think of another representation of a complex number and even get another interpretation of complex multiplication. We can write

$$z = |z|(\cos(\phi) + i \sin(\phi)), \text{ with } |z| := \sqrt{a^2 + b^2}$$

and ϕ is the angle between the real axis and the straight line connecting the origin and (a, b). The mapping $\arg : \mathbb{C} \to \mathbb{R}$ assigns to each z its argument $\arg(z)$. Note that this mapping is only specified up to multiplicatives of 2π and therefore is no function. To make arg into a function we can restrict it to take values in $(0, 2\pi)$ or $(-\pi, \pi)$ or extend the image of the mapping which leads to the concept of a Riemannian surface (see Fischer, W. and Lieb, I. (1981) or Freitag, E. (2010)).

The conjugate $\bar{z}$ of a complex number $z = a + ib$ is the function $conj$ given by

$$conj : \mathbb{C} \to \mathbb{C}$$

$$z \mapsto \bar{z} = \mathcal{R}(z) - i\mathcal{I}(z).$$

Furthermore, we have

$$\mathcal{R}(z) = \frac{z + \bar{z}}{2}, \quad \mathcal{I}(z) = \frac{z - \bar{z}}{2i}.$$

13.4.2 Complex Differentiation and Integration along Paths

For an open set $U \subset \mathbb{C}$ a function

$$f : U \to \mathbb{C}$$

$$z \mapsto f(z)$$

is called *complex differentiable* in $z_0 \in U$, if there exists a function $\Delta(z)$ which is continuous in z_0 such that

$$f(z) = f(z_0) + (z - z_0)\Delta(z). \tag{13.50}$$

Equation (13.50) is equivalent to

$$f'(z_0) := \lim_{z \to z_0} \frac{f(z_0) - f(z)}{z_0 - z}.$$

The limit is taken in U and the fraction is a complex division. If f is complex differentiable for all $z_0 \in U$ then f is *holomorphic* on U. The integral of the function f is defined by setting

$$\int_a^b f(x)dx = \int_a^b \mathcal{R}(f(x))dx + i \int_a^b \mathcal{I}(f(x))dx.$$

If we take a function $g : [c, d] \to [a, b]$ such that g is monotonic, continuous and piecewise differentiable, then

$$\int_c^d f(g(x))g'(x)dx = \int_a^b g(x)dx.$$

We call a piecewise continuously differentiable function $\gamma : [a, b] \to U \subset \mathbb{C}$ a *path* in U. Using the concept of a path it is possible to define integrals along the path. To this end let $\gamma : [a, b] \to \mathbb{C}$ be a path and $f : \gamma([a, b]) \to \mathbb{C}$ be a continuous function. We define

$$\int_\gamma f(z)dz := \int_a^b f(\gamma(x))\gamma'(x)dx.$$

The multiplication $f(\gamma(x))\gamma'(x)$ is a complex multiplication.

Let I and J be two compact real intervals. We call $\varphi : J \to I$ a transformation from J to I if φ is surjective and piecewise continuously differentiable. For an injective transformation it is possible to consider its inverse, the transformation φ^{-1}. Let $\gamma_1 : [a, b] \to \mathbb{C}$ and $\gamma_2 : [c, d] \to \mathbb{C}$ be two paths such that γ_2 can be obtained from γ_1 applying a transformation, that is $\gamma_2 = \varphi \circ \gamma_1$. Then, for a continuous function $f : \gamma_1([a, b]) \to \mathbb{C}$ we have

$$\int_{\gamma_1} f(z)dz = \int_{\gamma_2} f(z)dz.$$

Thus, the value of the integral does not depend on the parameterization of the integration path. Furthermore, for some path γ denoting by γ^{-1} the path traversed in the opposite direction, we have

$$\int_{\gamma_1} f(z)dz = -\int_{\gamma_1^{-1}} f(z)dz.$$

13.4.3 The Complex Exponential and Logarithm

Let us consider

$$\exp : \mathbb{C} \to \mathbb{C} \qquad (13.51)$$

$$\exp(z) \mapsto \sum_{n=0}^{\infty} \frac{z^n}{n!}$$

The function $\exp(\cdot)$ defined by (13.51) is called the *complex exponential function*. It can be shown that the function is well defined. Let us consider the complex sine, $\sin(\cdot)$, and cosine, $\cos(\cdot)$, functions

$$\sin(z) = \sum_{n=0}^{\infty} \frac{(-1)^n}{(2n+1)!} z^{2n+1}$$

$$\cos(z) = \sum_{n=0}^{\infty} \frac{(-1)^n}{(2n)!} z^{2n}.$$

The functions $\exp(\cdot)$, $\sin(\cdot)$ and $\cos(\cdot)$ are related by the following formulae:

$$\exp(iz) = \cos(z) + i\sin(z) \tag{13.52}$$

$$\cos(z) = \frac{1}{2}\left(e^{iz} + e^{-iz}\right)$$

$$\sin(z) = \frac{1}{2i}\left(e^{iz} - e^{-iz}\right). \tag{13.53}$$

Let us consider the complex number $z = a + ib$ and represent z in the plane by coordinates (a, b). This point can also be represented by a radius r and an angle ϕ such that $(a, b) = r(\cos\phi, \sin\phi)$. If this representation holds, it holds for any angle $\phi_k = \phi + 2\pi ik, k \in \mathbb{Z}$. We call the (r, ϕ)-representation *polar coordinates* and ϕ_k the argument, *arg*. If we restrict the values for ϕ to $(-\pi, \pi)$ or $(0, 2\pi)$ then the argument is unique. Let $z \in \mathbb{C}$ and (r, ϕ) be its polar coordinates, then we denote $|z| = r$ and $arg(z) = \phi \in (-\pi, \pi)$.

For any $z \in \mathbb{C}^*$ we can find $w \in \mathbb{C}$ such that $w = \exp(z)$. In that case $z_k := z + 2\pi k, k \in \mathbb{Z}$ also fulfils this equation. We call each z_k a *logarithm* of w. Any logarithm is of the form

$$w = \log(|z|) + i\arg(z).$$

The expression $\arg(z)$ is only uniquely determined up to multiples of 2π, any two logarithms w_1 and w_2 of a complex number z differ by a factor of $2\pi k, k \in \mathbb{Z}$.

For $U \subset \mathbb{C}^*$, $f : U \to \mathbb{C}$ such that $\exp(f(z)) = z$ for all $z \in U$ is called a *branch* of the logarithm.

Having defined the logarithm for two complex numbers z_1 and z_2 we can define

$$z_1^{z_2} := \exp(z_2 \log(z_1))$$

as the power function. The same problem we face for the logarithm or the *arg* function we can observe here, too. We say a branch of arg exists if there exists a continuous function $a : U \to \mathbb{R}$ such that $a(z)$ is an argument of z. For practical purposes and computer implementation it is often common to use $\arg : \mathbb{C}^* \to (-\pi, \pi]$, $z \mapsto \arccos(\mathcal{R}(z)/|z|)$, if $\mathcal{I}(z) \geq 0$ and $z \mapsto -\arccos(\mathcal{R}(z)/|z|)$, i $\mathcal{I}(z) < 0$. The map $\log : \mathbb{C}\backslash\mathbb{R}^- \to \mathbb{C}$, $z \mapsto \log(|z|) + i\arg(z)$ is the *main branch of the logarithm* or simply the *complex logarithm*. This function is holomorphic and satisfies $\log(z)'(z) = 1/z$.

13.4.4   The Residual Theorem

For a collection of paths γ_k, $k = 1, \ldots, N$ and multiplicities $n_k \in \mathbb{Z}$. First, we call $\Gamma = \sum_{k=1,\ldots,N} n_k \gamma_k$ a *cycle*. Let us denote by $A(\gamma)$ the starting point of γ and $E(\gamma)$ the endpoint of γ. We call a cycle Γ *closed* if for $z \in \mathbb{C}$

$$\sum_{\kappa_a \in A(\gamma_{\kappa_a})} n_{\kappa_a} = \sum_{\kappa_e \in E(\gamma_{\kappa_e})} n_{\kappa_e}.$$

We call

$$n(\Gamma, z_0) := \frac{1}{2\pi i}\int_\Gamma \frac{dz}{z - z_0} \tag{13.54}$$

the *rotation number* or *winding number*. Let $f : I \to \mathbb{C}$ a holomorphic function with only isolated singularities. Let $\kappa(r, z)$ denote a parameterization of a circle of radius r around $z \in U$. Then we call

$$\operatorname{res}_z(f) = \frac{1}{2\pi i} \int_{\kappa(r,z)} f(z)dz \tag{13.55}$$

the *residue* of f at $z \in U$. Complex integrals of holomorphic functions f having only isolated singularities and Γ being a cycle can be evaluated by using the residue

$$\int_\Gamma f(z)dz = 2\pi i \sum_{z \in U} n(\Gamma, z)\operatorname{res}_z(f). \tag{13.56}$$

If we consider the power function again, for any $U \subset \mathbb{C}^*$ there is a branch of arg if and only if

- there exists a branch of log on U.
- For a given cycle Γ in U we have $n(\Gamma, a) = 0, a \in U$.

13.5 THE CHARACTERISTIC FUNCTION AND FOURIER TRANSFORM

In this section we consider the *characteristic function* of a random variable X and we show the close connection to the *Fourier transform*. We summarize the results applied to option pricing in Chapters 5 and 6.

Let X be a random variable with distribution function $F(x)$. The characteristic function φ for the random variable X is given by

$$\varphi : \mathbb{R} \to \mathbb{C}$$

$$\varphi(u) \mapsto \mathbb{E}[\exp(iuX)] = \int_{-\infty}^{\infty} \exp(iux)dF(x). \tag{13.57}$$

The *characteristic exponent* is the logarithm of the characteristic function. It is given by

$$\psi(u) = \log(\varphi(u)). \tag{13.58}$$

Suppose that for the random variable X the n-th moment exists, that is $\mathbb{E}[|X|^n] < \infty$ then it is given by

$$\mathbb{E}[X^n] = i^{-n} \frac{d}{du^n}\varphi(u)\Big|_{u=0}. \tag{13.59}$$

The *cumulant function*, k, the *moment-generating function*, θ, and the *cumulant characteristic function*, φ, are given by

$$k(u) = \log(\varphi(iu)) \tag{13.60}$$

$$\theta(u) = \varphi(iu) \tag{13.61}$$

$$\varphi(u) = \log(\varphi(u)). \tag{13.62}$$

- Uniqueness: Let F_1 and F_2 be cumulative distribution functions. F_1 and F_2 are identical if and only if their characteristic functions φ_1 and φ_2 are identical. Thus, the distribution and the probability density are completely characterized by their characteristic function.

- Inversion: If φ is the characteristic function of the cumulative distribution function F, then

$$F(x) = \frac{1}{2} - \frac{1}{\pi} \int_0^\infty \frac{\mathcal{R}(e^{-iux}\varphi(u))}{u} du. \tag{13.63}$$

- Density and Cumulative Density: Let F be the cumulative distribution with density f. Suppose φ is the corresponding characteristic function, then

$$F(x) = \frac{1}{2} + \frac{1}{2\pi} \int_{-\infty}^\infty \frac{e^{iux}\varphi(-u) - e^{-iux}\varphi(u)}{iu} du$$

$$f(x) = \frac{1}{2\pi} \int_{-\infty}^\infty e^{-iux}\varphi(u)du = \frac{1}{\pi} \int_0^\infty e^{iux}\varphi_X(u)du.$$

The Plancharel/Parseval Theorem

The space of square integrable functions $f : \mathbb{R} \to \mathbb{C}$ on $\mathbb{R}$ with respect to the Lebesgue measure dx is denoted by $L^2(\mathbb{R}, dx)$. It is a complex Hilbert space if we take the inner product for all $f, g \in L^2(\mathbb{R}, dx)$

$$\langle f, g \rangle := \int_{-\infty}^\infty f(x)\bar{g}(x)dx.$$

For the Fourier transforms $\mathcal{F}(f)$ and $\mathcal{F}(g)$ of f and g we have

$$\langle \mathcal{F}(f), \mathcal{F}(g) \rangle = \int_{-\infty}^\infty \mathcal{F}(f)(x)\bar{\mathcal{F}}(g)(x)dx.$$

Thus, using the definition of the operator $\mathcal{F}$ we state the *Plancharel/Parseval theorem*:

$$\int_{-\infty}^\infty f(x)\bar{g}(x)dx = \frac{1}{2\pi} \int_{-\infty}^\infty \mathcal{F}(f)\overline{\mathcal{F}(g)}(x)dx. \tag{13.64}$$

A direct consequence is the fact that Fourier transforms preserve the norm $\|f\| := \sqrt{\langle f, f \rangle}$.

Generalized Fourier transform Let φ denote the Fourier transform of a given function f and suppose the φ is analytic in the strip $I(z) := \{z \in \mathbb{C} : a \leq \mathcal{I}(z) \leq b\}$ for real numbers a and b such that $a < b$. For $z = \mathcal{R}(z) + i\mathcal{I}(z)$ the inverse of the generalized Fourier transform of φ is given by

$$f(x) = \frac{1}{2\pi} \int_{i\mathcal{I}(z)-\infty}^{i\mathcal{I}(z)+\infty} e^{izx}\varphi(z)dz. \tag{13.65}$$

The properties of the standard Fourier transform also hold for the generalized version of the transform. In particular, the Plancharel/Parseval identity holds true. For more information and facts about the theory of Fourier transforms, see Titchmarsh, E.C. (1975).

Let X be a random variable with cumulative distribution function F. We consider

$$\varphi_X(t) = \mathbb{E}[\exp(itX)] = \int_{-\infty}^{\infty} \exp(itx)dF(x). \qquad (13.66)$$

If the distribution function has a density with respect to the Lebesgue measure, $dF(x) = f(x)dx$, we have

$$\varphi_X(t) = \mathbb{E}[\exp(itX)] = \int_{-\infty}^{\infty} \exp(itx)f(x)dx. \qquad (13.67)$$

Let d be a natural number and $x, y \in \mathbb{R}^d$. If we define

$$\langle x, y \rangle := \sum_{j=1}^{d} x_j y_j.$$

The d-dimensional characteristic function, $\varphi_X : \mathbb{R}^d \to \mathbb{C}$, is given by

$$\varphi_X(u) = \mathbb{E}[\exp(i\langle u, X \rangle)] = \int_{-\infty}^{\infty} \exp(i\langle u, x \rangle)dF(x). \qquad (13.68)$$

Example: Normal Distribution   We calculate the characteristic function of a normal distributed random variable $X(t) = \mu t + \sigma W(t) \sim \mathcal{N}(\mu t, \sigma^2 t)$.

$$\mathbb{E}[e^{iu(X(t))}] = \int_{-\infty}^{\infty} \frac{\exp(iux)}{\sqrt{2\pi}\sigma t} \exp\left(-\frac{1}{2}\left(\frac{x-\mu t}{\sigma t}\right)^2\right) dx$$

$$= \int_{-\infty}^{\infty} \frac{1}{\sqrt{2\pi}\sigma t} \exp\left(-\frac{1}{2\sigma^2 t^2}(x^2 - 2x\mu t + \mu^2 t^2 - 2\sigma^2 ixut^2)\right) dx$$

$$= \int_{-\infty}^{\infty} \exp\left(\mu iut - \frac{\sigma^2 u^2 t}{2}\right) \frac{1}{\sqrt{2\pi}\sigma t} \exp\left(-\frac{1}{2\sigma^2 t}(x - (\mu + i\sigma^2 u))^2\right) dx$$

$$= \exp\left(\mu iut - \frac{\sigma^2 u^2 t^2}{2}\right).$$

Example: Jump Diffusions   First, we consider a Poisson process $(N(t))_t$.

$$\mathbb{E}[\exp(iuN(t))] = \sum_{j=0}^{\infty} \mathbb{E}[\exp(iuN(t))|N(t) = j]$$

$$= \sum_{j=0}^{\infty} \frac{\exp(-\lambda t)(\lambda t)^j}{j!} \exp(iuj)$$

$$= \exp(\lambda t(\exp(iu - 1))).$$

We combine the results to compute the characteristic function of a jump-diffusion process using independence by

$$\mathbb{E}[\exp(iuX(t))] = \mathbb{E}\left[\exp\left(iu\left(\mu t + \sigma W(t) + \sum_{j=0}^{N(t)} J\right)\right)\right]$$

$$= \exp\left(iu\mu t - \frac{\sigma^2 u^2 t}{2}\right)\mathbb{E}\left[\mathbb{E}\left[\exp\left(iu\sum_{j=0}^{N(t)} J\right) \Big| J = x, N(t) = n\right]\right]$$

$$= \exp\left(iu\mu t - \frac{\sigma^2 u^2 t}{2}\right)\sum_{n=0}^{\infty}\frac{\exp(-\lambda t)(\lambda t)^n}{n!}\prod_{k=1}^{n}\int_{-\infty}^{\infty}\exp(iux)v(dx)/\lambda$$

$$= \exp\left(iu\mu t - \frac{\sigma^2 u^2 t}{2}\right)\sum_{n=0}^{\infty}\frac{\exp(-\lambda t)\left(\lambda t\int_{-\infty}^{\infty}\exp(iux)v(dx)/\lambda\right)^n}{n!}$$

$$= \exp\left(iu\mu t - \frac{\sigma^2 u^2 t}{2}\right)\exp(-\lambda t)\exp\left(\lambda t\int_{-\infty}^{\infty}\exp(iux)v(dx)/\lambda\right)$$

$$= \exp\left(iu\mu t - \frac{\sigma^2 u^2 t}{2}\right)\exp\left(\lambda t\left(\int_{-\infty}^{\infty}\exp(iux)v(dx)/\lambda - 1\right)\right).$$

Finally, we can put it in a slightly different form:

$$\mathbb{E}[\exp(iuX(t))] = \exp\left(iu\mu t - \frac{\sigma^2 u^2 t}{2}\right)\exp\left(\lambda t\left(\int_{-\infty}^{\infty}\exp(iux)v(dx)/\lambda - 1\right)\right)$$

$$= \exp\left(iu\mu t - \frac{\sigma^2 u^2 t}{2}\right)\exp\left(t\int_{-\infty}^{\infty}(\exp(iux) - 1)\,v(dx)\right).$$

This holds since $\int_{-\infty}^{\infty} v(dx) = \lambda$. Let $m_J := \int_{-\infty}^{\infty} xv(dx)/\lambda$ and consider $M(t) = X(t) - \lambda m_J t$, then

$$\mathbb{E}[\exp(iuM(t))] = \exp\left(t\left(iu\mu - \frac{\sigma^2 u^2}{2} + \int_{-\infty}^{\infty}(\exp(iux) - 1 - iux)v(dx)\right)\right).$$

The characteristic function can also be expressed as

$$\exp(t\Phi(u)),$$

where

$$\Phi(u) = iu\mu - \frac{\sigma^2 u^2}{2} + \int_{-\infty}^{\infty}(\exp(iux) - 1 - iux)\,v(dx).$$

Thus, $\Phi(u)$ is the characteristic exponent.

The defining feature of a compound Poisson process is that there is a finite number of jumps in any finite interval. For an infinite number or infinite activity the measure v may not be a finite measure as is the case for some Lévy processes. If the process has an infinite number of jumps in any finite interval we need a mechanism for counting the jumps. This role is played by the Lévy measure.

The characteristic function of a compound Poisson process is given by

$$\mathbb{E}[\exp(i\langle u, X(t)\rangle)] = \exp\left(t\lambda \int_{\mathbb{R}^d} \left(e^{i\langle u,x\rangle} - 1\right) v(dx)\right).$$

If we set $v(A) = \lambda f(A)$ then we can write the characteristic function as

$$\mathbb{E}[\exp(i\langle u, X(t)\rangle)] = \exp\left(t \int_{\mathbb{R}^d} \left(e^{i\langle u,x\rangle} - 1\right) v(dx)\right).$$

Thus, v is the Lévy measure of a compound Poisson process. We say a Lévy process $L(t)$ hits a barrier $h \in \mathbb{R}$ if

$$P(h) := \mathbb{P}[L(t) = h \text{ for at least one } t > 0] > 0.$$

Consider the set of points a Lévy process can hit, that is

$$\{h \in \mathbb{R} | P(h) > 0\}.$$

For $x \in \mathbb{R}^+$ the *first passage time* is defined by

$$\tau_x^+ := \inf\{t > 0 | L(t) > x\}.$$

The process $L(t)$ is said to creep upwards if for all $x \geq 0$

$$\mathbb{P}[L(\tau_x^+) = x] > 0.$$

It creeps downwards if $-L(t)$ creeps upward.

A Lévy process creeps upwards if and only if L has one of the following properties:

1. L has bounded variation and $d > 0$ where d denotes the drift in the Lévy Khintchine exponent
2. L has a Gaussian component
3. L has unbounded variation, no Gaussian component and

$$\int_0^1 \frac{x v([x, \infty))}{\int_{-x}^0 \int_{-1}^y v((-\infty, u]) du dy} dx < \infty$$

(see Miller, P.W. (1973), Rogers, L.C.G. (1984) and Vigon, V. (2002)).

A Lévy process creeps upwards **and** downwards if and only if it has a Gaussian component.

13.6 SUMMARY AND CONCLUSIONS

We have given all the necessary definitions to keep this book as self-contained as possible and have reviewed the main mathematical concepts and theorems which we apply to option pricing problems and their implementation using numerical methods.

List of Figures

List of Tables

Bibliography

Acworth, P., Broadie, M. and Glasserman, P. A comparison of some Monte Carlo and quasi Monte Carlo methods for option pricing. In *Monte Carlo and Quasi-Monte Carlo Methods*, ed. P. Hellekalek, F. Larcher, H. Niederreiter and P. Zinterhof, Springer-Verlag, 1–18, 1998.

Ahlfors, L.V. *Complex Analysis*. McGraw-Hill, 1979.

Ahn, H. and Wilmott, P. Stochastic volatility and mean-variance analysis. *Wilmott Magazine*, 6:84–90, 2003.

Ahn, H. and Wilmott, P. Jump diffusion, mean and variance: How to dynamically hedge, statically hedge and to price. *Wilmott Magazine*, 3:96–109, 2007.

Ahn, H. and Wilmott, P. Dynamic hedging is dead! Long live static hedging! *Wilmott Magazine*, 1:80–87, 2008.

Andersen, L. Simple and Efficient Simulation of the Heston Stochastic Volatility Model. *Journal of Computational Finance*, 11:1–42, 2008.

Andersen, L. and Andreasen, J. Volatility skews and extensions of the Libor Market Model. *Applied Mathematical Finance*, 1:247–270, 2000.

Andersen, L. and Piterbarg, V. *Interest Rate Modeling – Volume I: Foundations and Vanilla Models*. Atlantic Financial Press, 2010a.

Andersen, L. and Piterbarg, V. *Interest Rate Modeling – Volume II: Term Structure Models*. Atlantic Financial Press, 2010b.

Andersen, L. and Piterbarg, V. *Interest Rate Modeling – Volume III: Products and Risk Management*. Atlantic Financial Press, 2010c.

Antonov, A., Arneguy, M. and Audet, N. Markovian Projection to a Displaced Volatility Heston model. Available at SSRN, 2008.

Antonov, A. and Misirpashaev, T. Markovian projection onto a displaced diffusion. *International Journal of Theoretical and Applied Finance*, 12(4):507–522, 2009.

Attari, M. Option pricing using Fourier transforms: A numerically efficient simplification. Working Paper, Charles River Associates, 2004.

Barndorff-Nielsen, O.E. Normal inverse Gaussian distributions and the modeling of stock returns. Research Report, Department of Theoretical Statistics, Aarhus University, 300, 1995.

Bauer, H. *Mass- und Integrationstheorie*. De Gruyter, 1992.

Bauer, H. *Wahrscheinlichkeitstheorie*. De Gruyter, 2002.

Benaim, S., Dodgson, M. and Kainth, D. An arbitrage free method for smile extrapolation. *Preprint*, 2010. URL http://www.quarchhome.org/RiskTailsPaper_v5.pdf.

Bender, D., Kolodko, A. and Schoenmakers, J. Enhanced policy iteration for American options via scenario selection. *Quantitative Finance*, 8(2):135–146, 2008.

Bergomi, L. Smile dynamics. *Risk*, 9:117–123, 2004.

Berman, L. Accelerating Monte Carlo: Quasirandom sequences and variance reduction. *Journal of Computational Finance*, 1:79–95, 1997.

Beyer, P. and Kienitz, J. Pricing forward start option in models based on Lévy processes. *The Icfai University Journal of Derivatives Markets*, 6(2):7–23, 2009.

Billingsley, P. *Convergence of Probability Measures*. Wiley, 1999.

Black, F. and Litterman, R. Global portfolio optimization. *Financial Analysis Journal*, 48:28–43, 1992.

Black, F. and Scholes, M. The pricing of options and corporate liabilities. *Journal of Political Economy*, 81:637–659, 1973.

Bogacki, P. and Shampine, L.F. A 3(2) pair of Runge–Kutta formulas. *Applied Mathematics Letters*, 2:1–9, 1989.

Box, M.J. A new method of constrained optimization and a comparision with other methods. *Computer Journal*, 8:42–52, 1965.

Boyarchenko, S.I. and Levendorskii, S.Z. *Non-Gaussian–Merton–Black–Scholes Theory*, World Scientific, 2002.

Boyle, P., Broadie, M. and Glasserman, P. Monte Carlo methods for security pricing. *Journal of Economic Dynamics and Control*, 21:241–250, 1997.

Brandimarte, P. *Numerical Methods in Finance and Economics: A MATLAB-Based Introduction*, Wiley, 2006.

Breeden, D. and Litzenberger, R. Prices of state-contingent claims implicit in option prices. *Journal of Business*, 51:621–65, 1978.

Brent, R.P. *Algorithms for Minimization without Derivatives*. Prentice-Hall, 1973.

Brigo, D. and Mercurio, F. *Interest Rate Models – Theory and Practice*, 2nd edn, Springer, 2006.

Broadie, M. and Cao, M. Improved lower and upper bound algorithms for pricing American options by simulation. *Quantitative Finance*, 8(8):845–861, 2008.

Broadie, M. and Kaya, O. Exact simulation of stochastic volatility and other affine jump diffusion processes. *Operations Research*, 542, 2006.

Broyden, C.G. A class of methods for solving nonlinear simultaneous equations. *Mathematics of Computation*, 19(92):577–593, 1965.

Brunick, G. A Weak Existence Result with Application to the Financial Engineer's Calibration Problem. PhD thesis, Carnegie Mellon University, 2008.

Byrd, R., Lu, P., Nocedal, J. and Zhu, C. A limited memory algorithm for bound constrained optimization. *SIAM Journal of Scientific Computing*, 16(5):1190–1208, 1994.

Carr, P. and Madan, D. Option valuation using the fast Fourier transform. *Journal of Computational Finance*, 24:61–73, 1999.

Carr, P. and Wu, L. Time-changed Lévy processes and option pricing. *Journal of Financial Economics*, 71:113, 2004.

Carr, P., Geman, H., Madan, D. and Yor, M. The fine structure of asset returns: An empirical investigation. *Journal of Business*, 75:305–332, 2002.

Carr, P., Geman, H., Madan, D. and Yor, M. Stochastic volatility for Levy processes. *Mathematical Finance*, 13:345, 2003.

Castanga, A. and Mercurio, F. Vanna–Volga methods applied to FX derivatives: From theory to market practice. *RISK*, 1, 2007.

Chang, C., Chung, S. and Stapelton, R.C. Richardson Extrapolation techniques for the pricing of American style options. *Journal of Futures Markets*, 27(8):791–817, 2007.

Chen, B., Oosterlee, C.W. and van der Weide, H. Efficient unbiased simulation scheme for the SABR stochastic volatility model. *Preprint*, 2010.

Chesney, M. and Scott, L. Pricing European currency options: A comparison of the modified Black–Scholes model and a random variance model. *Journal of Financial and Quantitative Analysis*, 24:267–284, 1989.

Coleman, T. and Li, Y. An interior, trust region approach for nonlinear minimization subject to bounds. *SIAM Journal on Optimization*, 6:418–445, 1996.

Conn, A., Gould, N. and Toint, P. Global convergence of a class of trust region algorithms for optimization with simple bounds. *SIAM Journal of Numerical Analysis*, 25:433–460, 1988.

Conn, A., Gould, N. and Toint, P. A globally convergent augmented lagrangian algorithm for optimization with general constraints and simple bounds. *SIAM Journal on Numerical Analysis*, 28(2):545–572, 1991.

Conn, A., Gould, N. and Toint, P. A globally convergent augmented lagrangian barrier algorithm for optimization with general inequality constraints and simple bounds. *Mathematics of Computation*, 66(217):261–288, 1997.

Cont, R. Model uncertainty and its impact on the pricing of derivative instruments. *Mathematical Finance*, 16:519, 2006.

Cont, R. and Tankov, P. *Financial Modelling with Jump Processes*. Chapman & Hall, 2004.

Cont, R., Tankov, P. and Voltchkova, E. Option pricing models with jumps: Integro differential equations and inverse problems. *ECCOMAS*, 2005.

Cooley, J.W., and Tukey, J.W. An algorithm for the machine calculation of complex Fourier series. *IEEE Trans. on Audio and Electroacoustics*, 15(2):297–301, 1967.

Dan, H., Yamashita, N. and Fukushima, M. Convergence properties of the inexact Levenberg–Marquardt method under local error bound. *Optimization Methods and Software*, 17:605–626, 2002.

Davison, M. and Surkov, V. Efficient construction of robust hedging strategies under jump models. Preprint – University of Western Ontario, 2010.

Deb, K. *Multi-Objective Optimization Using Evolutionary Algorithms*. John Wiley & Sons, 2001.

Derman, E. and Kani, I. Riding on a smile. *Risk*, 7:32–39, 1994.

Di, Nuno R.B., Oksendahl, E. and Proske, F. *Malliavin Calculus for Lévy Processes with Applications to Finance*, 2nd, edn, Springer, 2008.

Dormand, J.R. and Prince, P.J. A family of embedded Runge–Kutta formulae. *Journal of Computational and Applied Mathematics*, 6:19–26, 1980.

Duffie, D. and Richardson, H. Mean-Variance Hedging in Continuous Time. *Annals of Applied Probability*, 1:1, 1991.

Duffie, D., Pan, J. and Singleton, K. Transform analysis and asset pricing for affine jump diffusions. *Journal of Computational Finance*, 68:1343–1376, 2000.

Duffy, D. *Financial Instrument Pricing Using C++*. John Wiley & Sons Ltd, Chichester, 2004.

Duffy, D. *Introduction to C++ for Financial Engineers*. John Wiley & Sons Ltd, Chichester, 2006.

Duffy, D. and Kienitz, J. *Monte Carlo Frameworks – Building Customisable and High-performance C++ Applications*. John Wiley & Sons Ltd, Chichester, 2009.

Dupire, B. Pricing with a Smile. *Risk*, 7:18–20, 1994.

Fan, J. A modified Levenberg–Marquardt algorithm for singular system of nonlinear equations. *Journal of Computational Mathematics*, 21(5):625–636, 2003.

Fan, J. and Pan, J. Convergence properties of a self-adaptive Levenberg–Marquardt algorithm under local error bound condition. *Computational Optimization and Applications*, 34:47–62, 2006.

Fang, F. and Oosterlee, K. A novel pricing method for European option based on Fourier-Cosine series expansions. *SIAM Journal on Scientific Computing*, 31(2):826–848, 2008a.

Fang, F. and Osterlee, K. Pricing early-exercise and discrete Barrier Options by Fourier-Cosine series expansion. *Preprint*, 2008b.

Faure, H. Disrepance de suites associees a un systeme de numeration (en dimension s). *Acta Arithmetica*, pages 337–351, 1982.

Feller, W. *An Introduction to Probability Theory and Its Applications, vol. I*, 3rd edn. John Wiley & Sons Ltd, Hoboken, 1968.

Feller, W. *An Introduction to Probability Theory and Its Applications, vol. II*, 2nd edn. John Wiley & Sons Ltd, Hoboken, 1971.

Fischer, W. and Lieb, I. *Funktionentheorie*, Vieweg, 1981.

Fletcher, R. *Practical Methods of Optimization, vol. 1, Unconstrained Optimization*. John Wiley & Sons, Chichester, 1980.

Foellmer, H., and Schweizer, M. Hedging by Sequential Regression: An Introduction to the Mathematics of Option Trading. *ASTIN Bulletin*, 18:147, 1989.

Freitag, E. *Complex Analysis 2*. Springer, 2010.

Fries, C. *Financial Mathematics*. John Wiley & Sons Ltd, Chichester, 2006.

Fries, C. Localized proxy simulation schemes for generic and robust Monte-Carlo Greeks. *Preprint*, 2007. URL http://www.christian-fries.de.

Fries, C. and Joshi, M. Partial proxy simulation schemes for generic and robust Monte-Carlo Greeks. *Journal of Computational Finance*, 12(1), 2008. URL http://www.christian-fries.de.

Fries, C. and Kampen, J. Proxy simulation schemes for generic and robust Monte-Carlo sensitivities and high accuracy drift approximation (with applications to the Libor Market Model). *Journal of Computational Finance*. 10(2), 2006. URL http://www.christian-fries.de.

Fu, M. Variance-Gamma and Monte Carlo. In: *Applied and Numerical Harmonic Analysis: Advances in Mathematical Finance*, Springer, pages 21–34, 2007.

Gamma, E., Helm, R., Johnson, R. and Vlissides, J. *Design Patterns: Elements of Reusable Object-Oriented Software.* Addison-Wesley, 1995.

Gatheral, J. *The Volatility Surface.* John Wiley & Sons Ltd, Hoboken, 2006.

Geiger, C. and Kanzow, C. *Theorie und Numerik restringierter Optimierungsaufgaben.* Springer, 2002.

Geman, S. and Geman, D. Stochastic relaxation, Gibbs distribution and the Bayesian restoration in images. *IEEE Trans. on Patt. Anal. Mac. Int.,* 6(6):721–741, 1995.

Giles, M. and Glasserman, P. Smoking adjoints: Fast Monte Carlo Greeks. *Risk Magazine,* 1, 2006.

Gill, P., Murray, W. and Wright, M. *Practical Optimization.* Academic Press, 1981.

Glasserman, P. *Monte Carlo Methods in Financial Engineering.* Springer, 2004.

Glasserman, P. and Kim, K.-K. Gamma Expansion of the Heston Stochastic Volatility Model. *Preprint,* ssrn.com, 2008.

Goldberg, D. *Genetic Algorithms in Search, Optimization & Machine Learning.* Addison-Wesley, 1989.

Grzelak, L.A., Oosterlee, C.W. and van Weeren, S. Extension of stochastic volatility models with Hull-White interest rate process. *Reports of the Department of Applied Mathematical Analysis, Delft University of Technology,* 2008.

Grzelak, L., Oosterlee, C.W. and van Weeren, S. Efficient Option Pricing with multi-factor Equity-Interst Rate Hybrid Models. in *Quantitative Finance,* 2009.

Grzelak, L., Oosterlee, C.W. and van Weeren, S. On the Heston model with Stochastic Interest Rates. *SIAM J. Financial Math.,* 2(1):255–286, 2011.

Günther, M. and Jüngel, A. *Finanzderivate mit MATLAB: Mathematische Modellierung und numerische Simulation.* Vieweg, 2010.

Günther, M. and Kahl, C. Complete the Correlation Matrix. *SIAM Journal on Matrix Analysis and Applications,* 2004.

Gyoengy, I. Mimicking the one-dimensional marginal distributions of processes having an Ito differential. *Probability Theory and Related Fields,* 71:501–516, 1986.

Hagan, P., Lesniewski, A. and Woodward, D. Probability Distribution in the SABR Model of Stochastic Volatility. *Working Paper,* http://lesniewski.us/papers/ProbDistForSABR.pdf, 2005.

Hagan, P.S., Kumar, D., Lesniewski, A.S. and Woodward, D.E. Managing Smile Risk. *Wilmott Magazine,* 1:84–108, 2002.

Hager, W. Updating the Inverse of a Matrix. *SIAM Journal on Optimization,* 31(2):221–239, 1989.

Hager, W. and Zhang, H. A new active set algorithm for box constrained optimization. *SIAM Journal on Optimization,* 17(2):525–557, 2006.

Halton, J.H. On the efficiency of certain quasi-random sequences of points in evaluation multi-dimensional integrals. *Numerische Mathematik,* 2:84–90, 1960.

Halton, J.H. and Smith, G.B. Algorithm 247: Radical-Inverse Quasi-Random Point Sequence. *Communications of the ACM,* 7:701–702, 1964.

Haugh, M. and Kogan, L. Pricing American options: A duality approach. *Operations Research,* 2001.

Heath, D., Platen, E. and Schweizer, M. A comparison of two quadratic approaches to hedging in incomplete markets. *Mathematical Finance,* 11:385, 2001.

Henry-Labordere, P. A General Asymptotic Implied Volatility for Stochastic Volatility Models. SSRN, http//ssrn.com/abstract=698601, 2005.

Heston, S. A closed form solution for options with stochastic volatility with applications to bond and currency options. *Rev. Fin. Studies,* 6:327–343, 1993.

Hout, t' K., Bierkens, J., Ploeg Van der, A.P.C. and Panhuis t', J. A semi-closed form analytic pricing formula for call options in a hybrid Heston–Hull–White model. *Proceedings of the 58th Study Group Mathematics with Industry,* 2007.

Hubalek, F., Kallsen, J. and Krawczyk, L. Variance optimal hedging for processes with stationary independent increments. *Annals of Applied Probability,* 8:1, 2005.

Hughett, P. Error bounds for numerical inversion of a probability characteristic function. *SIAM Journal of Numerical Analysis,* 40(3):1368–1392, 1998.

Hull, J. *Options, Futures and Other Derivatives,* 8th edn, Prentice Hall, 2011.

Hull, J. and White, A. The Pricing of Options on Assets with Stochastic Volatilities. *Journal of Finance,* 42(29):281–300, 1987.

Ingber, L. Adaptive simulated annealing (ASA): Lessons learned. *Polish Journal Control and Cybernetics,* 1995.

Islah, O. Solving SABR in Exact Form and Unifying it with LIBOR Market Model. *SSRN eLibrary,* 2009.

Jäckel, P. *Monte Carlo Methods in Finance*. John Wiley & Sons Ltd, Chichester, 2002.

Jäckel, P. More Likely Than Not. *http://www.jaeckel.org*, 2005.

Jackson, K., Jaimungal, S. and Surkov, V. Fourier Space Time-stepping for Option Pricing with Levy Models. *Preprint* – University of Western Ontario, Toronto, 2007.

Jacod, J. and Shiryaev, A.N. *Limit theorems for stochastic processes*. Springer, 2002.

Jaimungal, S. and Surkov, V. Stepping Through Fourier Space. *Preprint* – University of Western Ontario, Toronto, 2008.

Jaimungal, S. and Surkov, V. Valuing Early Exercise Interest Rate Options with Multi-Factor Affine Models. *Preprint* – University of Western Ontario, Toronto, 2010.

Joshi, M. and Leung, T. Using Monte Carlo simulation and importance sampling to rapidly obtain jump-diffusion prices of continuous barrier options. *Journal of Computational Finance*, pages 93–105, 2007.

Joshi, M. and Rebonato, R. A stochastic volatility, displaced diffusion extension of the LIBOR market model. *Working Paper*, Quantitative Research Centre of the Royal Bank of Scotland, 2001.

Kammeyer, H. and Kienitz, J. The Heston Hull White Model I – Finance and Analytics. *Wilmott Journal*, January, 2012a.

Kammeyer, H. and Kienitz, J. The Heston Hull White Model II – Fourier Transform and Monte Carlo Simulation. *Wilmott Journal*, March, 2012b.

Kammeyer, H. and Kienitz, J. The Heston Hull White Model III – The Implementation. *Wilmott Journal*, May, 2012c.

Kanzow, C., Yamashita, N. and Fukushima, M. Levenberg–Marquardt methods for constrained non-linear equations with strong local convergence properties. *Journal of Computational and Applied Mathematics*, 172:375–397, 2004.

Kienitz, J. Stochastic Processes in Finance I. *Wilmott Magazine*, 2007a.

Kienitz, J. Stochastic Processes in Finance II. *Wilmott Magazine*, 6, 2007b.

Kienitz, J. A Note on Monte Carlo Greeks using the Characteristic Function. 2008. URL http://www.ssrn.com/sol3/papers.cfm?abstract_id=1307605.

Kienitz, J. The CGMY model. *The Encyclopedia of Quantitative Finance* (ed. Cont), John Wiley & Sons Ltd, 2009.

Kienitz, J. Monte Carlo Greeks for Advanced Financial Applications – Jump Diffusion and (Time-Changed) Lévy Processes based Models. *International Review of Applied Financial Issues and Economics*, 2(1), 2010.

Kienitz, J. Pricing CMS Spread Options. Talk on ICBI Global Derivatives, Paris, 2011.

Kienitz, J. and Wittke, M. Option Valuation in Multivariate SABR Models. *Working Paper*, University of Technology Sydney, 2010.

Kienitz, J., Wetterau, D. and Wittke, M. Hedge Analysis for Advanced Equity Models. Marcus Evans Conference, *Model Risk*, 9, 2011.

Kienitz, J., Wetterau, D. and Wittke, M. *Interest Rate Derivatives – From Theory to Market Practice by Implementation (including object oriented VBA code)*. In preparation, 2013.

Kiesel, R. and Lutz, M. Efficient Pricing of CMS Spread Options in a Stochastic Volatility LMM. *Working Paper, SSRN*, 2010.

Kirkpatrick, S., Gerlatt, C.D. Jr. and Vecchi, M.P. Optimization by Simulated Annealing. *Science*, 220:671–680, 1983.

Knuth, D.E. *The Art of Computer Programming, vol 2, Seminumerical Algorithms*, 3rd edn. Addison–Wesley, 1997.

Kroon, D.-J. fminlbfgs. 2008. URL http://www.mathworks.com/matlabcentral/fileexchange/23245-fminlbfgs-fast-limited-memory-optimizer.

Kunita, H. and Watanabe, S. On Square Integrable Martingales. *Nagoya Math. J.*, 30, 1967.

Kyprianou, A. *Introductory Lectures on Fluctuations of Lévy Processes with Applications*. Springer, 2006.

Lagarias, J.C., Reeds, J.A., Wright, M.H. and Wright, P.E. Convergence properties of the Nelder – Mead simplex method in low dimensions. *SIAM Journal Optimization*, 9(1):112–147, 1998.

Lampinen, J. A Constraint Handling Approach for the Differential Evolution Algorithm. *Proceedings of the 2002 Congress on Evolutionary Computation (CEC'02)*, 2:1468–1473, 2002.

Leclerc, M., Liang, Q. and Schneider, I. Fast Monte Carlo Bermudan Greeks. *Risk Magazine*, 1, 2009.

Lee, R. Implied Volatility: Statics, Dynamics, and Probablistic Interpretation. *In: Recent Advanced in Applied Probability*, Springer, 2002.

Leoni, P. and Schoutens, W. Multivariate Smiling. *Wilmott Magazine*, 1, 2008.

Lesniewski, A. Notes on the CEV model. *Preprint*, 2009.

Levenberg, K. A Method for the Solution of Certain Non-Linear Problems in Least Squares. *Quarterly of Applied Mathematics*, 2:164–168, 1944.

Lewis, A. *Option Valuation under Stochastic Volatility*. financepress, 2000.

Lewis, A. A simple option formula for general jump-diffusion and other exponential Lévy processes. *Preprint*, 2001. URL http://www.optioncity.net, Working Paper.

Lewis, T.G. and Payne, W.H. Generalized feedback shift register pseudorandom number algorithm. *Journal of the Association for Computing Machinery*, 20(3):456–468, 1973.

Liebscher, E. Construction of asymmetric multivariate copulas. *Journal of Multivariate Analysis*, 99(10):2234–2250, 2008.

Lipton, A. The vol smile problem. *Risk*, pages 61–65, 2002.

Liu, D. and Nocedal, J. On the limited memory BFGS method for large scale Optimization. *Mathematical Programming*, 45:503–528, 1989.

Lord, R. and Kahl, C. Optimal Fourier inversion in semi-analytical option pricing. *Preprint*, 2007.

Lord, R., Fang, F., Bervoets, G. and Oosterlee, C.W. A fast and accurate FFT-based method for pricing early-exercise options under Lévy processes. *SIAM J. Sci Comput. 2008*, 30(4):1678–1705, 2008.

Luciano, E. and Schoutens, W. Multivariate Variance Gamma Modelling with Applications in Equity and Credit Risk Derivatives Pricing. *Financial Modelling Workshop, ULM*, 2005.

Luciano, E. and Semerano, P. Generalized normal mean variance mixture and subordinated Brownian motion. *International Center for Economic Research*, 2007.

Luciano, E. and Semerano, P. *Multivariate Variance Gamma and Gaussian dependence: A study with copulas*. Carlo Alberto Notebooks 96, 2008.

Lutz, M. Extracting Correlations from the Market: New correlation parametrizations and the calibration of a Stochastic Volatility LMM to CMS Spread Options. *Preprint, SSRN*, 2010.

Lyness, J.N. and Moler, C.B. Numerical differentiation of analytic functions. *SIAM J. Numer. Anal.*, 4(2):202–210, 1967.

Madan, D. and Seneta, E. The V.G. model for share market returns. *J. Business*, 63:511–524, 1990.

Madan, D.B., Carr P.P. and Chang E.C. The Variance Gamma Process and Option Pricing. *European Finance Review*, 2:79–105, 1998.

Madsen, K. and Nielsen, H. Introduction to optimization and data fitting. *DTU Informatics*, 2010. URL http://www.imm.dtu.dk/pubdb/p.php?5938.

Madsen, K., Nielsen, H. and Sondergaard, J. Robust Subroutines for Non-Linear Optimization. *Technical Report IMM-REP-2002-02, IMM*, 2002.

Madsen, K., Nielsen, H. and Tingleff, O. Methods for Non-Linear Least Squares Problems, 2nd edn. Lecture Note, Technical University of Denmark, 2004.

Mahayni, A. How to Avoid a Hedging Bias. *Wilmott Magazine*, 6:64–69, 2003.

Markowitz, H. Portfolio Selection. *Journal of Finance*, 7:77–91, 1952.

Marquardt, D. An Algorithm for Least-Squares Estimation of Nonlinear Parameters. *Journal of Applied Mathematics*, 11:431–441, 1963.

Marris, D. *Financial option pricing and skewed volatility*. MPhil Thesis, University of Cambridge, 1999.

Matsumoto, M. and Kurita, Y. Twisted GFSR Generators. *Research Institute of Mathematical Sciences*, Kyoto University, 1992.

Matsumoto, M. and Nishimura, T. Mersenne Twister: A 623-dimensionally equidistributed uniform pseudo random number generator. *Transactions on Modelling and Computer Simulations: Special Issue on Uniform Random Number Generation*, 1998.

McKinnon, K.I.M. Convergence of the Nelder–Mead Simplex Method to a Nonstationary Point. *SIAM Journal on Optimization*, 9(1):148–158, 1998.

Merton, R. Option pricing when underlying stock returns are discontinuous. *Journal of Financial Economics*, 3:125–144, 1976.

Metropolis, N., Rosenbluth, A.W., Rosenbluth, M.N., Teller, A.H. and Teller, E. Equations of State Calculations by Fast Computing Machines. *Journal of Chem. Physics*, 21:1087–1092, 1953.

Meucci, A. Beyond Black–Litterman. *Risk*, 9:114–119, 2006.

Meucci, A. *Risk- and Asset Allocation*. Springer, 2007.

Miller, P.W. Exit properties of stochastic processes with stationary independent increments. *Transactions of the American Mathematical Society*, 178:459–479, 1973.

Moler, C. *Numerical Computing with Matlab*, MathWorks, 2008. URL http://www.mthworks.de/moler/chapters.html.

Moré, J., Garbow, B. and Hillstrom, K. Testing unconstrained Optimization Software. *ACM Transactions on Mathematical Software*, 7:17–41, 1981.

Moré, J. and Toraldo, G. Algorithms for bound constrained quadratic programming problems. *Numerische Mathematik*, 55:377–400, 1989.

Nelder, J.A. and Mead, R. A Simplex Method for Function Minimization. *Computer Journal*, 7(4), 1965.

Niederreiter, H. Low-discrepancy and low-dispersion sequences. *Journal of Number Theory*, 30:51–70, 1988.

Nielsen, H. immoptibox – A Matlab Toolbox for Optimization and Data Fitting. URL http://www2.imm.dtu.dk/~hbn/immoptibox/. v2.2, 2010.

Nielsen, H. Damping parameter in Marquardt's method. *Technical Report IMM-REP-1999-05, IMM*, 1999.

Nocedal, J. Updating quasi-Newton matrices with limited storage. *Mathematics of Computation*, 35:773–782, 1980.

Nocedal, J. and Wright, S. *Numerical Optimization*. Springer, 2006.

Nowakcyk, N. and Kienitz, J. Affine Recursion Problem and a General Framework for Adjoint Methods for Calculating Sensitivities for Financial Instruments. *SSRN*, 2011.

Nualart, D. *Malliavin Calculus and Related Topics*, Springer, 1995.

Obloj, J. Fine tune your smile. *Wilmott Magazine*, 3, 2007.

Oksendal, B. *Stochastic Differential Equations*. Springer, 2007.

Paulot, L. Asymptotic Implied Volatility at the Second Order with Applications to the SABR Model. *Preprint*. URL http://www.ssrn.com/sol3/papers.cfm?abtract_id=1413649, 2009.

Piterbarg, V. Markovian Projection Method for Volatility Calibration. *Available* at SSRN, 2006.

Powell, M.J.D. A fast algorithm for nonlinearly constrained optimization calculations. *Lecture Notes in Mathematics 630*, Springer Verlag, pages 144–157, 1978.

Price, K., Storn, R. and Lampinen, J. *Differential Evolution: A Practical Approach to Global Optimization*. Springer, 2005.

Rebonato, R. *Modern Pricing of Interest-Rate Derivatives*, John Wiley & Sons Ltd, Chichester, 2002.

Rebonato, R. *Volatility and Correlation,* 2nd edn., John Wiley & Sons Ltd, Chichester, 2004.

Reiner and Rubinstein. Exotic Options. *Working Paper*, 1992.

Ribeiro, C. and Webber, N. A Monte Carlo Method for the Normal Inverse Gaussian Option Valuation Model Using an Inverse Gaussian Bridge. *Preprint*. URL http://www2.warwick.ac.uk/fac/soc/wbs/research/wfri/rsrchcentres/forc/preprintseries/pp_04.133.ps, 2007a.

Ribeiro, C. and Webber, N. Correcting for simulation bias in Monte Carlo Methods to value exotic options in models driven by Lévy processes. *Stochastic Finance 2004, Autumn Scholl & International Conference*, 2007b.

Rockafellar, R.T. and Uryasev, S. Optimization of Conditional Value-at-Risk. *Journal of Risk*, 2(3):21–41, 2000.

Rogers, L.C.G. A new identity for real Lévy processes. *Annals of the Institute of Henry Poincaré*, 20:21–34, 1984.

Rosinski, J. Series representations of Lévy processes from the perspective of point processes. *In: Lévy Processes: Theory and Applications,* eds O.E. Barndorff-Nielsen, T. Mikosch and S.I. Resnick, Birkhäuser, pages 401–415, 2001.

Rubinstein, M. Displaced diffusion option pricing. *Journal of Finance*, 38(1):213–217, 1983.

Rudin, W. *Real and complex analysis,* 2nd edn. McGraw-Hill, 1974.

Rydberg, T.H. The normal inverse Gaussian Lévy process: Simulation and approximation. *Comm. Statist. Stochastic Models*, 13:342, 1997.

Sato, K. *Lévy Processes and Infinitely Divisible Distributions*. Cambridge University Press, 1999.

Schmidt, M. minFunc and minConf – Matlab software by Mark Schmidt. 2009. URL http://www.di.ens.fr/~mschmidt/Software/.

Schoebel, R. and Zhu, J. Stochastic Volatility with an Ornstein–Uhlenbeck Process: An Extension. *European Finance Review*, 3:23–46, 1999.

Schoenmakers, J. *Robust Libor Modelling and Pricing of Derivative Products*. Chapman Hall/CRC Financial Mathematics Series, 2005.

Schoutens, W. *Lévy process in Finance: Pricing Financial Derivatives*, Wiley Series in Probability and Stochastics, 2003.

Schoutens, W., Simons, E. and Tistaert, J. A Perfect Calibration! Now What? *Wilmott Magazine*, 2, 2004.

Schroder, M. Computing the constant elasticity of variance option pricing formula. *Journal of Finance*, 44(1):211–219, 1989.

Schweizer, M. Option Hedging for Semimartingales. *Stochastic Processes and their Applications*, 37:229, 1991.

Semerano, A multivariate variance gamma model for financial applications. *Journal of Theoretical and Applied Finance*, 11:1–18, 2009.

Sepp, A. Fourier transform for option pricing under affine jump diffusions: An overview. *Preprint*, Institute of Mathematical Science, University of Tartu, 2003.

Shanno, D.F. Conditioning of Quasi-Newton Methods for Function Minimization. *Mathematics of Computing*, 24:647–656, 1970.

Shaw, W.T. *Lecture on Risk Management*. AIMS Summer School, Cape Town, 2011.

Shidong, S. *A Levenberg–Marquardt Method for Large-Scale Bound-Constrained Nonlinear Least-Squares*. PhD thesis, Faculty of Graduate Studies, University of British Columbia, Vancouver, 2006.

Sobol, I. Uniformly Distributed Sequences with additional Uniform Properties. *USSR Computational Mathematics and Mathematical Physics*, 16:236–242, 1977.

Sobol, I. and Levitan, Y.L. The Production of Points Uniformly Distriuted in a Multidimensional Cube (in Russian). *Preprint IPM Akad. Nuak SSSR, Moscow*, 40, 1976.

Squire, W. and Trapp, G. Using complex variables to estimate derivatives or real functions. *SIAM Review*, 10(1):110–112, 1998.

Stein, E.M. and Stein, J.C. Stock Price Distribution with Stochastic Volatility: An Analytic Approach. *Review of Financial Studies*, 4:727–752, 1991.

Storn, R. and Price, K. Differential evolution: A simple and efficient adaptive scheme for global optimization over continuous spaces. *Technical Report TR-95012,ICSI*, 1995.

Subrahmanyam, M.B. An Extension of the Simplex Method to Constrained Nonlinear Optimization. *Journal of Optimization Theory and Applications*, 62(2):311–319, 1989.

Surkov, V. Option Pricing using Fourier Space Time-stepping Framework. PhD thesis, University of Western Ontario, Toronto, 2009.

Svoboda, S. On the similarity between displaced diffusion and CEV processes. *Preprint, OCIAM*, University of Oxford, 2006.

Talbot, A. The accurate numerical inversion of Laplace transforms. *Journal of the Institute of Mathematics and Its Applications*, 23, 1979.

Tankov, P. Simulation and option pricing in Lévy copula models. *Preprint*, 2006.

Tausworthe, R.C. Random numbers generated by linear recurrence modulo two. *Mathematics of Computation*, 19:201–209, 1965.

Titchmarsh, E.C. *Introduction to the Theory of Fourier Integrals*. Oxford University Press, 1975.

Uryasev, S. Conditional value-at-risk: Optimization algorithms and applications. *Financial Engineering News*, 2000.

van Haastrecht, A. and Pelsser, A. Efficient, almost exact simulation of the Heston stochastic volatility model. *Preprint, ssrn.com*, 2010.

Vigon, V. Votre Lévy rampe-t-il? *Journal of the London Mathematical Society*, 65(1):243–256, 2002.

von Weizsäcker, H. and Winkler, G. *Stochastic Integrals*. Vieweg, 1990.

West, G. Principle Component Analysis. *Lecture Notes*, 2005. URL http://www.finmod.co.za/pca.pdf.

Wilmott, P. *Paul Wilmott Introduces Quantitative Finance*, 2nd edn. John Wiley & Sons Ltd, Chichester, 2007.

Wittke, M. Convexity Correction by a Finite Replication Portfolio. *SSRN*, 2011.

Woods, D.J. *An Interactive Approach to Solving Multi-Objective Optimization Problems*. PhD thesis, Department of Mathematical Sciences, Rice University, 1985.

Wu, Q. Series expansion of the SABR joint density. *Mathematical Finance*, 11. URL http://www.ssrn.com/sol3/papers.cfm?abtract_id=1367966, 2010.

Wystup,   U.   Vanna-Volga   Pricing.   *Preprint.*   URL   http://www.mathfinance.de/wystup/papers/
    wystup_vannavolga_eqf.pdf, 2008.

Yamashita, N. and Fukushima, M. On the rate of convergence of the Levenberg–Marquardt method.
    Computing Supplement, 15:239–249, 2001.

Yang, W.Y., Cao, W., Chung, T.S. and Morris, J. *Applied Numerical Methods Using MATLAB*, John
    Wiley & Sons Ltd, 2005.

Index

Printed and bound by CPI Group (UK) Ltd, Croydon, CR0 4YY

23/04/2025

14660973-0001